# BIOFEEDBACK
## *and* SELF-CONTROL 1971

# EDITORS

# BIOFEEDBACK and *SELF*-CONTROL 1971

an *Aldine Annual on the regulation of bodily processes and consciousness*

ALDINE PUBLISHING COMPANY

Chicago

First published 1972 by
Aldine·Atherton, Inc.
Address all inquiries to
Aldine Publishing Company
529 South Wabash Avenue
Chicago, Illinois 60605

Library of Congress Catalog Card Number 74-151109
ISBN 0-202-25085-7
Printed in the United States of America

Second Printing, 1974

*591.188*
*B 615*

*7/11/75*

*Article 1*
Reprinted with permission of the authors. Paper presented at the Second International Invitation Conference on Humanistic Psychology, 1971; Wurzburg, Germany and at the 17th International Congress of Applied Psychology, 1971; Liege, Belgium.
*Article 2*
Reprinted with permission of the publisher and author from the *Archives of General Psychiatry*, Vol. 25, 1971, pp. 429-435. Copyright 1971, American Medical Association.
*Article 3*
Reprinted with permission of the publisher and author from the *Archives of General Psychiatry*, Vol. 25, 1971, pp. 436-441. Copyright 1971, American Medical Association.
*Article 4*
Reprinted with permission of the publisher and author from the *Archives of General Psychiatry*, Vol. 25, 1971, pp. 481-489. Copyright 1971, American Medical Association.
*Article 5*
From *On the Psychology of Meditation* by Claudio Naranjo and Robert Ornstein. Copyright © 1971 by Claudio Naranjo and Robert Ornstein. Reprinted by permission of The Viking Press, Inc.
*Article 6*
Reprinted with permission from *Science*, Vol. 174, 1971, pp. 897-904. Copyright 1971 by the American Association for the Advancement of Science.
*Article 7*
Reprinted with permission of The American Physiological Society from the *American Journal of Physiology*, Vol. 221, 1971, pp. 795-799.
*Article 8*
Reprinted with permission of the publisher and author from *Psychophysiology*, Vol. 7, 1971, pp. 451-464. Copyright © 1971, The Society for Psychophysiological Research.
*Article 9*
Reprinted with permission of the publisher and author from *Psychonomic Science*, Vol. 23, 1971, pp. 197-199.
*Article 10*
Reprinted with permission of the publisher and author from *Psychophysiology*, Vol. 8, No. 5, 1971, pp. 556-575. Copyright © 1971, The Society for Psychophysiological Research.
*Article 11*
Reprinted with permission of Springer-Verlag and the author from *Kybernetik*, Vol. 9, No. 4, 1971, pp. 156-158.
*Article 12*
From *The Journal of Nervous and Mental Disease*, Vol. 153, 1971, pp. 205-217. Copyright 1971, The Williams & Wilkins Co. Reproduced by permission.
*Article 13*
Reprinted with permission of the publisher and author from *American Scientist*, Vol. 59, 1971, pp. 236-245.
*Article 14*
Reprinted with permission of the publisher and author from *Science*, Vol. 174, 1971, pp. 431-435. Copyright 1971 by the American Association for the Advancement of Science.
*Article 15*
Reprinted with permission from Harper & Row, Publishers and the author from *Psychosomatic Medicine*, Vol. 33, No. 4, 1971, pp. 57-62.

An appealing feature of the biofeedback area lies in its vigorous mingling of ideas and issues. It abounds with questions. Among them: Can the processes of consciousness be modified? Can one voluntarily alter one's own physiology? And what is meant by *voluntary* control? How useful is the example of the mystics—the disciplines of Zen, Yoga, and Sufism—in accomplishing such control on a practical, everyday basis? Can the striking modification of autonomic responses, which has been achieved with animal preparations, also be attained at the human level? Are there ways of modifying the individual's reaction to stress? What are the prospects for applying such techniques to the gamut of psychosomatic or stress-related disorders? Will the biofeedback experiments evolve into a viable body of techniques with numerous practical applications, or are they fated, like the steam engine of the Alexandrian Greeks, to remain a laboratory toy?

Within the biofeedback area, one major concern has been whether the new technique might be used to produce alterations in consciousness, or at least in certain aspects of consciousness. Such an endeavor inevitably brings up the question as to whether the phenomena of consciousness are indeed a legitimate object of inquiry within a scientific psychology. The unwary layman would think the answer surely would be "yes." But such commonsense solutions are not always the way of psychology. Within the field, controversy has continued to flourish over whether the study of consciousness is a fit topic of inquiry for a scientific psychology. And in fact, for some decades the phenomena of consciousness were officially read out of psychology by Watson and others of kindred temperament. To be sure, there were cogent grounds for objecting to what had been the main investigative tool of 19th century psychology, the introspective method (in which the individual observes and then reports on his own mental processes). Chief among the objections was the difficulty of verifying statements made by the self-observer or introspector. Thus, when introspectors disagreed, as they often did, how could one prove who was right?

An intriguing feature of the biofeedback techniques is that they may offer some fresh ways of looking at introspective evidence, and may provide means for examining at least some of the events of consciousness in a scientifically acceptable fashion. As Kamiya pointed out (*Biofeedback and Self-Control, Reader,* Introduction) the new approach represents a confluence of elements from several disciplines, including electronics and feedback control systems, psychophysiology, the introspective (or self-report) tradition, and instrumental conditioning techniques. These instrumental conditioning techniques arose from what has formed a central emphasis of the 20th century experimental psychology in North America, the study of learning. In keeping with the behaviorist tradition, this work focused on the external and the verifiable — the visible behavior of the organism. Internal events, physiological as well as experimental, were generally excluded from this enterprise. Psychology was confined to events outside the skin.

During the 1950's and 1960's however, experimental psychology began to break away from the limitations of its self-imposed skin-bag boundary. For example, it was shown that autonomic activity — long-thought impervious to the assaults of instrumental (operant) conditioning, could in fact be dramatically modified in animal preparations if appropriate techniques were employed.

At the human level, Kamiya had begun experimenting with voluntary control of the EEG alpha rhythm. Basing his approach on the instrumental (operant) conditioning techniques so successfully employed with animals, Kamiya provided his subjects with continuous information through headphones as to whether they were producing alpha or not—a soft tone indicated alpha was present, no tone, its absence. For many subjects, alpha appeared to be associated with an experiential state generally characterized as tranquil, serene, a "letting go" attitude, and with an absence or dampening of visual imagery. This observation suggested that perhaps individuals could learn to modify their experiential state by using feedback techniques to alter their own physiology.

We believe these developments constitute a point of departure for a fresh approach in experimental psychology; namely, that psychology will return to an exploration of the internal environment. And the techniques of instrumental conditioning, which have proved so successful in modifying visible, external behavior, may prove similarly useful in changing internal events—not only physiological events, but perhaps also those of an experiential nature.

## INFERENCES ABOUT CONSCIOUSNESS

As already noted, a major objection to studying the events of consciousness had been that the conclusions of such study were deemed difficult or impossible to verify. It is our contention, however, that *some* events or aspects of consciousness can be verified and hence are admissible as scientific evidence. This statement hinges on the assumption that the core of scientific inquiry is the making of testable inferences—statements which can be proved or disproved by means of experimental observations. Since they are capable of disproof, such statements can aid us in the selection and elimination of alternative hypotheses.

Can we make any testable statements about the phenomena of consciousness? A few, although much remains to be learned. As a result of experimental work in recent years, we are able to specify with greater precision than before, the conditions under which certain types of mental activity are likely to occur.

A useful illustration of this point, showing how certain statements about the psychological experience we call dreaming can be verified, may be drawn from contemporary sleep research. (See *Biofeedback and Self-Control, Reader,* pp. 775-788.)

In recent years it has been amply demonstrated that vivid, visual dreaming occurs within rapid eye movement (REM) periods. This phase of sleep is characterized by bursts of rapid eye movements, low-voltage desynchronized cortical rhythms, and markedly heightened autonomic variability. Awakenings within REM periods produce a high incidence of dream recall—80 to 90 percent. This material is likely to be vivid, fanciful and emotion-charged. Awakenings at other times during the sleep cycle (nonREM) yield a far lower recall of mental activity (estimates average at approximately 30 percent). Physiologically, nonREM sleep shows an absence of REM bursts, EEG voltages are slow and of high amplitude, autonomic activity such as pulse rate is slow and regular. Mental activity is also quite different from that of REM sleep. Compared to REM recall, nonREM mental activity is prosaic and thought-like, lacks much evidence of emotion and the narrative element is generally missing.

Additional experiments have further supported the idea that vivid visual dreaming occurs in REM sleep. For example, there is a significant correlation between the physical duration of a REM period and the sleeper's estimate of how long he had been dreaming (if he is questioned after a REM awakening). There is a positive relationship between the degree of physical activity in a dream report and the density of REMs, and so forth. Of course, these observations do not mean that we are able to infer the particulars of dream content on the basis of watching rapid eye movement patterns. But they do allow us to destroy certain alternative interpretations of the data which have been proposed—for example, that REM recall may simply be material made up by the subject to satisfy the expectations of the experimenter; or that the reported REM dream is actually recall of a mental event which occurred earlier in the night (perhaps outside of any REM period).

As a result of this research, which has employed verbal reports of dreaming in combination with physiological measures such as REMs, we are now able to specify with much greater precision than before the conditions under which dreaming takes place. And our conception of dreaming has changed dramatically in the process. We know, for example, that dreaming is not a rare event, but occurs universally in humans. Nor does the dream last only a second or two, as many had thought. On the contrary, REM sleep and the associated dream experience occupy at least 20 percent of time asleep.

We believe that the same general approach may be applied in the exploration of certain mental activity other than dreaming. A possible outcome of this research is that we may be able to specify the conditions under which some types of mental activity are likely to occur. Further, with the addition of feedback techniques, we may be able to teach people to produce at will the physiological conditions favorable for the appearance of certain kinds of mental activity.

To be more specific, lest the patience of the critical reader is wearing thin, let us take the example of the EEG theta rhythm. Theta (4-7 Hz) is the dominant brainwave rhythm shown by the subject who is in the process of falling asleep.

Strong sensations of drowsiness are present, and the quality of thinking is quite different from ordinary waking thought. If the subject pays careful (and passive) attention he will become aware of a flow of images, often of hallucinatory intensity. Most of them are brief, though some may classify as "dreamlets." Associated affect is generally mildly pleasant or neutral. Formerly regarded as a rarity, such hypnagogic or sleep-onset imagery has been found to be an everyday occurrence (as is nocturnal dreaming).

Once we know with some confidence that hypnagogic imagery is associated with theta EEG frequencies, we can then go on to ask: What happens if a subject is given feedback training to control his theta rhythms? Will hypnagogic imagery occur? The evidence is that it does. For example, Green and his associates (*Biofeedback and Self-Control, 1970*, pp. 1-28) who have worked extensively with theta feedback techniques, describe the theta condition as a reverie state rich in imagery. In our Colorado laboratory, we have similarly noted that when subjects are successful in producing theta, they experience a flow of visual imagery.

Proceeding on the assumption that theta EEG is associated with hypnagogic imagery, we can ask further questions regarding the properties of this low arousal condition. What happens if we train a subject to remain in theta for some time, rather than just for a few seconds as occurs when he normally falls asleep? Perhaps his experience will become more dream-like in nature. What is the effect of presenting stimuli, in various sensory modalities, during theta? Is information processing different in character from that which occurs during normal wakefulness? Are there transformations similar to those sometimes occurring in dreams; e.g., the ring of the alarm clock becomes a fire alarm?

Further, the circumstances favorable for the production of theta may be of more general theoretical interest. Several writers have noted the existence of similarities between the conditions propitious for the appearance of theta imagery and the conditions under which certain hallucinatory experiences occur (phenomena such as dreams, some meditative experiences, the hallucinations of hypnosis and sensory isolation). For example, in each of the foregoing types of alteration in consciousness—in comparison with normal, alert wakefulness—there is a reduction in sensory input to the brain, both of external and internal (proprioceptive) input. Secondly, there is a shift in arousal level towards sleep; and sensations characteristic of parasympathetic activity, such as warmth and heaviness, frequently occur. Finally, there is a shift to a passive, "letting it happen" attitude in which the individual assumes the role of a quiet spectator before the stream of unfolding internal events.

Before concluding this section, we must again stress that this new approach—feedback psychophysiology in the study of mental events—does not mean the severing of all reality moorings in favor of an uninhibited "anything goes, any statement is valid" orientation. Rather, a central feature of the approach is that it focuses on testable inferences. As Hilgard (*Biofeedback and Self-Control, Reader,* pp. 763-774) has indicated, it falls squarely within the functionalist tradition in psychology; he refers to it as "contemporary functionalism." Of course, many questions pertaining to mental phenomena will not be answerable by this method. But the future may hold additional techniques in store.

## OVERVIEW OF 1971 SELECTIONS

We have found this year that we missed several good articles which should have been reprinted in the 1970 Annual and in the Reader, and we have included them with the 1971 selections. We will continue, in future annuals to pick up important articles that we might have neglected in previous years and to reprint them when space permits.

Unfortunately it is not possible in this preface to do full justice to the many fine papers included in this year's Annual. The editors have, in any case, chosen papers with an eye to presenting a variety of viewpoints. Some of the authors sound a cheerful, confident note. Others voice gloomier sentiments and emphasize that, at least on the human level, little is known for sure and that much caution is needed.

In the *Overview and Theory* section the Davidson and Krippner paper offers a very useful survey of the field as it now stands. Gaarder's paper is a theoretical one, linking feedback techniques with the cybernetic model.

The next section deals with the *Modification of Consciousness,* and discusses both feedback and non-feedback techniques for producing alterations in consciousness.

Of interest to the reader will be Gaarder's remarks on the historical background of the biofeedback technique. Here he makes the perceptive observation that the artificial closing of an external feedback loop has frequently occurred without any explicit recognition that a new principle has been discovered. Hence, some disagreement is likely to arise as to who originated the method. For example, with a little poetic license, the technique could be traced back to Narcissus, the mythological figure who became fatally enchanted with his own reflection in a pond.

Another fascinating paper in this section is the one by Ornstein in which meditative practices are analyzed in terms of contemporary psychology. Special attention is drawn to the selective nature of our sensory systems. Normally we think of these as gathering information, but actually they function as much to exclude it—probably to protect us from being overwhelmed by a great flood of irrelevant and useless sense data.

What enters awareness, therefore, is a highly filtered sensory input. The salient aspects of consciousness become those useful for survival on this planet. An early expression of this idea may be found in the works of the French philosopher, Henri Bergson, who wrote of "mind as a reducing valve." Such a view suggests the possibility that our ordinary, garden-variety consciousness leaves us with a restricted and even distorted perception of reality—a recurring theme in the meditative disciplines.

Incidentally, the book from which this chapter is taken may be recommended as an unusually lucid exposition of meditative practices, their practice and history. The volume will be particularly appreciated by the occidental who has tried to flounder through some of the mystifying prose of the oriental sources without Ornstein and Naranjo acting as a reducing (and clarifying) valve.

The following section, *Central Nervous System Activity: Human,* deals with feedback control of EEG activity. Mulholland and Peper link the EEG alpha rhythm to the oculomotor system—when oculomotor activity is present (as in visual tracking, for example) alpha is blocked; when the oculomotor system is quiescent, alpha is present. A complementary theory is presented by Lynch and Paskewitz, who view alpha generation as a disinhibition phenomenon. Also, they discuss the ticklish problem of determining baseline levels of alpha.

The next section includes two selections on the modification of *CNS Activity in Animals.* Black describes an elegant series of experiments on the conditioning of hippocampal theta in dogs. Also of interest are his remarks as to what we mean by the term "voluntary."

Autonomic conditioning continues to be a vigorous area of research, both at the human and animal levels. DiCara's paper provides a stimulating review of the conditioning of specific autonomic responses and suggests a number of potential applications. In two excellent contributions, Weiss—on the basis of previous work with avoidance-escape schedules and their effects on ulceration in rats—develops a model to account for and predict the probability of ulcer formation in animals. His model predicts that ulceration will increase as the number of coping attempts increases. Ulceration will also increase as the amount of relevant feedback decreases; the theory, which generated correct predictions, also accounts for the "Executive Monkey" work of Brady and his associates in the late 1950's.

This year's section on *Hypnosis* contains a number of intriguing papers. The first four of these focus on Barber's challenging reconceptualization of this controversial phenomenon. A particularly enjoyable paper is the one by Barber and Meeker which reveals the secrets of the stage hypnotist.

## COMMENTS ON APPLICATIONS

Perhaps the area of greatest potential importance for the biofeedback techniques lies in their therapeutic applications. Fortunately, our hopes in this direction are not solely based on what has been accomplished with the feedback techniques up to this point. Though many investigators are not particularly aware of it, there is a rich older tradition, pertaining to the clinical application of self-regulation practices, which can be drawn upon.

One important source is the work of Jacobson. Beginning his investigations many years ago while a psychology student of William James and Hugo Münsterberg at Harvard, Jacobson developed his technique of progressive muscle relaxation. For further details on the method, the reader is referred to Jacobson's classic work, *Progressive Relaxation* (1938), still in print and an excellent source of ideas for what might eventually be accomplished with feedback techniques. Over the years, Jacobson has treated a great variety of stress-related disorders with his technique; e.g., anxiety neuroses, insomnia, essential hypertension, asthma, ulcers. This work continues at Jacobson's clinic in downtown Chicago.

A related important source of ideas may be found in autogenic training, a therapeutic approach developed many years ago by the Berlin neurologist, J. H. Schultz. There is ample literature on the subject, mostly in German. An extensive English account may be found in Luthe's recent five-volume *Autogenic Therapy* (1969, 1970)—a series containing over 2400 references.

A brief description of the autogenic training technique can be found in the editorial note prefacing the excerpts from Luthe's recent volumes. Essentially, there are six basic or "standard" exercises which are designed to enable the trainee to shift readily into a low arousal (tropotropic) condition. The first exercise focuses on cultivating feelings of heaviness in the extremities. The second exercise focuses on the cultivation of warmth sensations in the extremities. Like progressive relaxation, autogenic training has been applied to a wide variety of disorders, particularly those which are thought to be stress-linked; e.g., insomnia, ulcers, essential hypertension, tachycardia, to name a few. (Reprinted in this year's Annual are excerpts pertaining to angina pectoris, essential hypertension, and hypercholesteremia.)

As with progressive relaxation a central characteristic of autogenic training is that it involves a shift to a low arousal condition—sympathetic activity is diminished, muscle tension is lowered and alpha and theta frequencies appear in the EEG. The trainee practices by himself several times a day, and the time for each exercise is short—about one minute. With frequent daily practice a highly overlearned response seems to develop and the individual becomes able to shift readily into a low arousal condition at will. After four to eight weeks of such regular training a change in the physiological reactivity of the trainee is said to occur, so that he less easily becomes hyperaroused in the face of a variety of stresses. Instead, he develops the ability to moderate his arousal level.

Some related observations may also be drawn from transcendental meditation, now becoming well-known in this country. As shown by Wallace, Benson and Wilson (pp. 134-137) this technique likewise involves a shift to a low arousal condition; e.g., heart rate and respiration are diminished. Metabolic rate, as indicated by lowered oxygen consumption and blood lactate levels, is also reduced.

In view of the striking similarities in the physiological consequences of progressive relaxation, autogenic training, and transcendental meditation, a central question becomes how best to achieve the low arousal condition which occurs with each of these techniques. Our working hypothesis is that a *combined* approach will be useful, one which integrates feedback training on several parameters with subsequent home practice in the absence of instruments—the individual must eventually learn to do it well on his own.

Over the past several years, Budzynski and I have noted that thorough muscle relaxation can be learned by means of EMG feedback training. But perhaps this approach—viewed as a means of quickly reaching a low arousal condition—can be strengthened through feedback training on other responses in addition to muscle. Thus, we are currently experimenting with a sequential training program. Subjects first learn muscular relaxation, a comparatively easy task. Then they are trained on the more difficult endeavor of increasing skin temperature (an autonomic response linked to increased peripheral bloodflow). Finally, they are given feedback training on the subtle task of increasing their theta levels. The approach essentially involves the shaping of a low arousal condition. Whether it will prove more valuable than just muscle relaxation by itself remains to be seen.

Such a combined approach may be useful in the conditioning of specific autonomic responses in humans. Subjects would train first in the more general response of muscle relaxation. Then they would be shifted to a more specific task such as decreasing heart rate or blood pressure. This approach could also be of theoretical interest in testing an idea suggested by Miller, 1969 (*Biofeedback and Self-Control, Reader,* pp. 3-25) that skeletal muscle responses may, in fact, interfere with learning to modify an autonomic variable. Perhaps muscle activity acts as "noise" and obscures the comparatively faint signal put out by the to-be-conditioned autonomic variable. Initial training in muscle relaxation would reduce such "noise" and might thereby aid in the conditioning of a particular autonomic response.

Training subjects to be able to readily shift into a low arousal condition might have considerable therapeutic value. An intriguing idea advanced in the autogenic training literature (see Luthe, *Autogenic Therapy* 1969, 1970) is that the regular cultivation of such a low arousal shift has effects which are opposite to those produced by the "defense-alarm" reaction. This powerful, sympathetico-adrenal response appears to be an integral part of a variety of stress disorders. Though adaptive under conditions of primitive living where strenuous physical exertions are necessary for survival, under conditions of civilized living, the sustained evocation of the defense-alarm reaction seems likely to lead to stress-related diseases. Methods of moderating this reaction, such as those suggested by the biofeedback techniques, might evolve into a practical treatment for some of the stress disorders which are so prevalent in our society.

This volume could not have been published without the cooperation of various organizations, journals, publishers, and authors who granted permission to reprint their individual articles. Each ariticle was photographed and printed exactly as it originally appeared in order to complete the Annual as soon as possible. A Reader containing papers published before 1971 and an Annual for the year 1970 were published last year. And in June of each coming year we plan to bring out a new Annual covering the major works published in the previous year.

JOHANN STOYVA<br>
For the Editors

# CONTENTS

# I

# THEORY AND OVERVIEW

# Biofeedback Research: 1
# The Data and Their Implications

## Richard Davidson and Stanley Krippner

Abstract: Biofeedback techniques are based on the principle that certain responses are made when informational feedback is received by the organism. These responses are adjusted, corrected, and modified as feedback is continually received until it is determined that a final goal has been achieved. This new field of research has important implications for the study of altered states of consciousness, creativity, parapsychology, psychosomatic medicine, medical diagnosis, therapy, and education. The data are reviewed concerning biofeedback with both animal and human subjects.

## Historical Background

Since the time of Plato a dichotomy has been maintained between "reason," on the one hand, and "emotions" on the other. Associated with "reason" are the voluntary responses of the skeletal muscles, while "emotions" are related to the presumably involuntary glandular and visceral responses. This invidious schism was described by Plato (1875) as involving the "superior rational soul" in the head and the "inferior souls" in the rest of the body. This tradition was passed on and further elucidated by the eminent French neuroanatomist Bichat (1969) who first made the distinction between the cerebrospinal nervous system (of the "great brain" and spinal cord) controlling skeletal responses, and the dual chain of ganglia ("little brains") running down on either side of the spinal cord in the body below and controlling emotional and visceral responses. He deemphasized the role of the ganglionic system by referring to it as "vegetative."

3

This conception of the nervous system has persisted, in one form or another, to the present time. Learning theory has maintained that there are two forms of conditioning, classical and instrumental, the former being inferior to the latter (Skinner, 1938). In classical or Pavlovian conditioning (which is thought to be involuntary) a conditioned stimulus (a signal of some kind) is presented along with an innate unconditioned stimulus (such as food) that normally elicits a certain innate unconditioned response (such as salivation). After a time, the conditioned stimulus elicits the same response as the unconditioned stimulus. In instrumental (or operant) conditioning a reinforcement, or reward, is given whenever the desired conditioned response is elicited by a conditioned stimulus (such as a certain signal). The possibilities of learning are limited in classical conditioning, as the stimulus and response must have a natural, direct relationship to begin with. In instrumental learning, on the other hand, the reinforcement strengthens any immediately preceding response. Therefore, a given response can be reinforced by a variety of rewards and a given reward can reinforce a variety of responses.

These assumptions have coalesced into the point of view that instrumental learning is possible only for skeletal responses mediated by the "superior" cerebrospinal (or central) nervous system. Conversely, classical conditioning is the only procedure available for the "inferior" visceral, emotional, and presumably involuntary responses mediated by the autonomic nervous system.

Recently, there has been an abundance of data (Barber, et al., 1971; Miller, 1969a; DiCara, 1970; Kimmel, 1967) pertinent to these assumptions, all of which demonstrate that the traditional view concerning the autonomic nervous system is fallacious. Kimmel (1967) in a review of recent research on this topic concluded, "At the present time it would appear that Skinner's assumption that autonomically mediated responses cannot be modified instrumentally was both premature and probably incorrect. Apparent instrumental conditioning effects have been reported in recent years using several different autonomically mediated responses and a variety of instrumental conditioning methods." (p. 344.)

## Further Evidence for Voluntary Control of Autonomic Functions

Western science in recent years has demonstrated what Yogis and other practitioners of meditation have known for centuries (Trungpa, 1970). Wenger and Bagchi (1961) conducted physiological studies of autonomic functions among yoga practitioners in India. They discovered one subject who could perspire from the forehead on command within one and one-half to ten minutes. The act was accompanied by a marked increase in systolic blood pressure of which he was unaware. The authors found no one with voluntary control over the internal anal or urethral sphincters, but they did find some individuals who employed a catheter or other form of tube and, with its help, were able to draw up water into the bladder or lower bowel. They discovered another subject who was able to defecate at will if any fecal matter was present.

Prominent among the many claims of unusual bodily control that emanate from practitioners of yoga is the ability to stop the heart and radial pulse. In another investigation, Wenger, Bagchi and Anand (1961) studied this claim in four subjects. The heart did not stop in any subject. However, for three subjects there were brief periods during which the authors could detect no heart sounds with a stethoscope and the palpable radial pulse disappeared; even so, electrocardiogram records showed the heart to be in continuous action. The fourth subject claimed only to slow his heart which he did on three different occasions. The authors explained this result in the following way. The subjects employed strong abdominal contraction and breath arrest with closed glottis during which an increase in intrathoracic pressure occurred to the point where venous return to the heart was markedly reduced. The heart continued to contract but it pumped little blood.

The above examples demonstrate some of the difficulties associated with the study of voluntary autonomic control. Miller (1969a, p. 435) summarizes these difficulties, stating that "responses that are the easiest to measure -- namely, heart rate, vasomotor responses, and the galvanic skin response -- are known to be affected by skeletal responses, such as exercise, breathing and even tensing of certain muscles, such as those in the diaphragm. Thus, it is hard to rule out the possibility that, instead of directly learning a visceral response, the subject has learned a skeletal response, the performance of which causes the visceral change being recorded." This problem, specifically with regard to heart rate, has been pointed out by others (e.g., Peper, 1971b).

Very much related to direct control of autonomic functions are those changes that accompany Zen meditation. In an electroencephalographic study of Zen meditation, Kasamatsu and Hirai (1966) observed the appearance of alpha waves (without regard to opened eyes) within 50 seconds after the initiation of meditation. The alpha waves (defined as 8-13 cps) continued to appear and their amplitudes increased. As the meditation progressed, the authors observed a decrease in the alpha frequency. In some subjects a rhythmical theta (defined as 5-7 cps) train was observed. In another EEG study, Anand, Chhina and Singh (1961) investigated four Yogis during meditation and during ordinary rest. All the Yogis demonstrated prominent alpha activity in their normal resting EEG records. During meditation the duration and amplitude of the alpha increased. This alpha activity could not be blocked by various sensory stimuli during meditation. Other studies of meditation (Bagchi and Wenger, 1957; Wallace, 1970) that employed a number of physiological measurements have demonstrated the meditative state to be more deeply quiescent -- in terms of physiological and metabolic activity -- than a state of ordinary restfulness.

The foregoing discussion demonstrates the capacity of the organism to exercise control over some of the bodily functions formerly held to be involuntary. These data refute the traditional beliefs concerning the "inferior" nature of the autonomic nervous system. In commenting about the research on yoga, Dalal and Barber (1969, p. 162) conclude, "There is evidence to indicate ...that the breathing and postural exercises, which are part of some but not all systems of yoga, may be accompanied by significant autonomic changes and may give rise to enduring changes in autonomic balance with possible beneficial effects on mental and physical health."

Since work with practitioners of Eastern disciplines reveals that it is possible for an organism to exercise control over various of its internal functions, how can others, particularly Westerners, be helped to attain this same kind of control? What are the implications of voluntary control of internal states with regard to psychosomatic illness, altered states of consciousness, and other related phenomena? These questions will be discussed in further sections of this paper. The next sections will review the recent research concerning the control of internal responses both in animals and in humans and its implications.

## The Biofeedback Paradigm

The concept of biofeedback involves an organism placed in a closed feedback-loop where information concerning one or more of his bodily processes is continually made known to him. This system is illustrated in a clock diagram in Figure 1 (Hart, 1967). When the organism possesses this type of information about a bodily process it can learn to control this function.

In the animal studies reported in this area, a direct form of reinforcement is usually employed to motivate the animal to learn, such as electrical stimulation of the pleasure center of the brain (the medial forebrain bundle in the posterior portion of the lateral hypothalamus) or escape from electrical shock. The human studies employ more subtle reinforcements, often social in nature -- such as pleasing the experimenter. The production of the specific criterion response in some human experiments may also be self-reinforcing as indicated by verbal reports from alpha subjects (Kamiya, 1969; Honorton, Davidson and Bindler, 1971).

Thus, biofeedback techniques are based on the principle that certain responses are made when informational feedback is received by an organism. These responses are adjusted, corrected, and modified, as feedback is continually received, until it is determined that a final goal has been achieved.

## Learning of Autonomic Responses in Animals

Because of some of the methodological problems involved in research in this area, it was advisable to employ animals as subjects in a variety of studies to clarify certain key issues and control for assorted confounding variables. (These problems will be further elucidated when the human research is discussed.) Another advantage that was derived from the animal work was that it opened the way for new avenues of study with humans.

Following Miller's early comments (1961, 1963, 1964) on the far-reaching implications of instrumental learning of autonomically mediated responses not only for theories of learning and its neurophysiological basis, but also for practical problems of psychosomatic symptoms and of individual differences in patterns of autonomic responses, he and his colleagues undertook a systematic investigation of this area. Before Miller began his studies in this area, Sluki, Adam, and Porter (1965) demonstrated that internal events could be discriminated in animals, a necessary condition for autonomic response learning. Sluki and his colleagues surgically implanted an intestinal loop in five Rhesus monkeys. The monkeys were trained to press a lever when the balloon connected to the loop was inflated and not to press the lever when there was no stimulation. The results indicated that the monkeys successfully discriminated between the presence and absence of the internal stimulus.

Miller began his series of studies with an attempt to instrumentally modify the classical response employed in

classical conditioning, namely, salivation (Miller and
Carmona, 1967). Ten thirsty dogs were rewarded with small
amounts of water for spontaneous bursts of salivation or
for pauses without salivation. After 40 days of training,
the results indicated that both groups' response rates
changed systematically in the direction expected with
instrumental conditioning. The changes made by each
individual dog were independently significant.

Next in the series of investigations from Miller's
laboratories was a study performed by Trowill (1967).
Trowill's procedure was the first to employ deep curarization (use of the drug curare to paralyze the skeletal-
muscular system) coupled with electrical stimulation of
the pleasure center as a reinforcer. He used rats as
subjects, half of them being rewarded for rates above the
average, and half for rates below average. In addition,
yoked control subjects were employed for some of the
experimental subjects in each group. It has been demonstrated (Church, 1964) that there is a systematic bias in
the yoked control design; however, the major criticism
of the use of such yoked controls is blunted by the fact
that heart rates were conditioned both to increase and
decrease. Trowill's results indicated that 15 of 19 subjects rewarded for fast heart rates increased their rates
and that 15 of 17 subjects rewarded for slow heart rates
decreased their rates. Both of these mean changes were
statistically significant although the amount of change
demonstrated was quite small.

In a subsequent study, Miller and DiCara (1967)
endeavored to see, "(a) whether larger changes in the
heart rates of curarized rats can be achieved by 'shaping'
the response, i.e., progressively shifting rats to a
more difficult criterion after they have learned to meet
an easier one, and (b) whether a visceral discrimination
can be learned so that the response will be more likely to
occur in the stimulus situation in which it is rewarded
than in the one in which it is not." (p. 12.) Miller
and DiCara replicated the Trowill experiment with one
major modification: after achieving the easy criterion of
a small change, the subjects were required to meet
progressively more difficult criteria for reward. The
results were quite dramatic; both groups showed changes
of approximately 100 beats per minute and the obtained
differences were statistically significant. The rats
also learned to respond discriminatively to the stimuli
signaling that cardiac changes would be rewarded.

Even though the subjects in the above studies were
deeply curarized, it is conceivable that they still might
show evidence of action potentials in electromyographic
(EMG) recordings. Black (1966) has suggested that this

might be the case, implying that although skeletal-muscular activity has been interrupted by curare, the activity of the motor cortex has not, and there may be conditioned motor cortex responses which mediate instrumental conditioning of the autonomic nervous system (ANS). It seems likely that if such impulses influenced the ANS, their effect would be general, influencing many autonomic structures. Thus, if it could be demonstrated that reinforcement of one response was independent of other closely related responses, Black's (1966) alternative explanation could be set aside.

Miller and Banuazizi (1968) performed such a study by comparing the effects of rewarding either heart-rate change or spontaneous intestinal contractions on the rate of response of both systems. The results indicated that deeply curarized rats rewarded for increased or decreased intestinal contraction showed progressive changes in the appropriate direction but heart rate did not change; conversely, rats rewarded for high or low rates of heartbeat, respectively, learned to change rates appropriately but showed no changes in intestinal contraction. Thus, Black's (1966) hypothesis was eliminated.

A remaining question concerned the possible effects of using electrical stimulation of the brain as a reinforcer. Could the results have been obtained using another kind of reinforcer? DiCara and Miller (1968a) sought to answer this question by employing an avoidance response design. They attempted to train curarized rats to increase or decrease their heart rates in order to escape and/or avoid electric shock applied to the base of the tail. The results supported the hypothesized effect. These effects have also been demonstrated in the non-curarized state (DiCara and Miller, 1969).

Other studies from Miller's laboratories have shown that animals can exert specific control over a variety of subtle responses. Miller and DiCara (1968) have demonstrated instrumental learning of urine formation, independent of other physiological responses. DiCara and Miller (1968b) have successfully trained rats to vasodilate in one ear and not the other. They conclude from their results that there is greater specificity of action in the sympathetic portion of the autonomic nervous system than is usually attributed to it.

Taken as a whole, the above studies indicate that with training an organism can learn to control any bodily function for which one can get a means of recognition. Additional work with animals has been reported by different independent investigators which further support and extend the work of Miller and his colleagues.

Plumlee (1969) employed an avoidance procedure in the instrumental learning of increases in blood pressure in the monkey. Four subjects were presented with ten second tones which terminated with shocks. The tones were immediately terminated without shock if the animal's diastolic blood pressure rose above a criterion level and remained high for one second. Trials began whenever the pressure dropped below the criterion level. The results indicated that all subjects learned the avoidance task. However, only one control subject was employed, using a yoked control design. Since blood pressure was only trained in one direction, Church's (1964) criticism of this type of control design stands. Another confounding variable was that "in all monkeys, contractions of the leg extensor and arm flexor muscles...accompanied the rise when the pressure requirement for avoidance was high." (Plumlee, 1969, p. 289.) This may indicate that the author did not find a genuine effect, but rather it seems as if this skeletal response was learned, which in turn, modified the visceral response.

In another study of instrumental conditioning of blood pressure, Benson, Herd, Morse and Kelleher (1969) employed a more sophisticated technique than Plumbee (1969). They instrumentally conditioned three squirrel monkeys on an avoidance schedule to increase their mean arterial blood pressure to hypertensive levels. They then reversed the schedule so that only decreases in blood pressure prevented the delivery of the aversive stimulus. When the animals were on this schedule, mean blood pressure consistently returned toward control values.

A recent study of operant conditioning of heart rate (Engel and Gottlieb, 1970) employed three Rhesus monkeys as subjects. The authors employed an avoidance design as the reinforcer. The three monkeys were trained to both slow and speed their heart rate. All animals learned the desired task.

A number of studies has recently appeared attempting to instrumentally condition electrocortical activity. In a study employing four cats as subjects, Wyrwicka and Sterman (1968) systematically reinforced the spontaneous occurrence of 12-20 cps slow-wave spindles. The cats were in the waking state and were food deprived when brought into the experimental chamber. This slow wave spindle has been termed the "sensorimotor rhythm" (SMR) by the authors. The rhythm essentially consists of a 12-20 cps burst of synchronized EEG activity over the motor cortex in an awake animal whose EEG from other cortical areas is clearly desynchronized. After several sessions, with 50 reinforcements per session, this sensorimotor rhythm appeared more frequently and demon-

strated a regular temporal pattern of occurrence. There
was a consistent behavioral correlate of this type of
electrophysiological activity: the animal appeared to
freeze, cease all activity and assume a definite stereotyped posture. Each animal developed its own specific
posture. When the parameters were reversed and reinforcement was made contingent upon the occurrence of a
desynchronized (low voltage, high frequency) electrical
pattern, the previously conditioned SMR response faded
and was replaced by a consistently desynchronized pattern.
The cats' behavior also changed accordingly. The authors
state that the cats "became constantly active, searching
the chamber, circling and performing frequent discrete
spontaneous movements. The previously-observed quiescent
postures were absent from their behavior." (Wyrwicka and
Sterman, 1968, p. 706.) It therefore appears, from the
results of this study, that training an organism in a
specific electrophysiological response can concurrently
effect a change in gross behavior patterns.

There is, however, one major shortcoming in the
execution of the Wyrwicka and Sterman (1968) study. The
observed EEG changes could have been mediated by the gross
behavior changes. In other words, the animals' gross
behavioral responses could have been conditioned, which in
turn affected their electrocortical activity. The authors
attempt to rule out this alternative hypothesis by stating
"the appearance of a given posture was necessary but not
sufficient for the occurrence of SMR activity. The
latter typically developed several seconds after the
stereotyped posture was assumed." (Wyrwicka and Sterman,
1969, p. 707.) The fact still remains, however, that the
authors should have provided for a more adequate control
of this confounding variable.

In an extension of the previous study, Sterman, Howe
and Macdonald (1970) found that SMR activity conditioned
in the waking state enhanced a similar electrocortical
pattern recorded during sleep, namely, the spindle-burst.
In addition to this modification of the EEG, the mean
duration of quiet-sleep epochs was also significantly increased immediately after SMR conditioning. The authors
concluded from this study that there is "a common neural
mechanism for these two EEG phenomenon, with functional
continuity across wakefulness and sleep." (p. 1148.)
This finding has direct bearing on the nature of state
dependent learning and communication across states
(Hastings, 1971).

In summarizing the research employing animals as subjects, a number of general conclusions may be drawn. First,
the research demonstrates that it is indeed possible to
instrumentally modify an autonomically mediated response.

It has been demonstrated that very specific, subtle responses are amenable to this type of modification. The operant conditioning of a specific response can be made independent of all other response systems. One of the most important findings is that any bodily function that can be monitored and fed back to the subject can be modified through instrumental procedures. Nowhere in the recent literature has it been reported that an autonomically mediated response is not amenable to instrumental learning. Aside from the implications this finding has for theories of learning, namely, that the autonomic nervous system is just as flexible in terms of what can be learned as those responses mediated by the central nervous system, the data compel present day scientists to re-examine the traditional assumptions about the origin of psychosomatic illnesses. This topic will be discussed in the final section of the paper.

<u>Learning</u> <u>of</u> <u>Autonomic</u> <u>Responses</u> <u>in</u> <u>Man</u>

There has been a controversy in the literature concerning the question of instrumental autonomic conditioning in humans. This phenomenon has been clearly demonstrated in animals under the influence of curare, but studies with man involve additionally complex variables. In a review of the literature, Katkin and Murray (1968) stated, "Although it seems safe to conclude that instrumental ANS conditioning has been demonstrated in curarized animals, it is not safe to conclude that it has been demonstrated definitely in humans." (p. 66.) The authors cite three basic minimal criteria for the acceptability of evidence for instrumental conditioning. The first is the demonstration that the response being reinforced shows an increase in frequency, or amplitude, or probability of occurrence over the level shown in a free-operant (baseline) period. The second criterion is that the design of the experiment should include the appropriate controls, and the third criterion is that the experiment should rule out alternative hypotheses such as peripheral or cognitive mediation.

In a reply to the Katkin and Murray (1968) paper, Crider, Schwartz and Shnidman (1969) point out a number of erroneous assumptions. Specifically, they convincingly demonstrate that the three criteria offered are either invalid, or that the evidence does not support the rejection of the experiments on the bases of the criteria. Crider, Schwartz and Shnidman (1969) conclude that "While the incontrovertible study of operant autonomic conditioning on the human has yet to be carried out, there exists nonetheless a sizable literature whose import is that human autonomic functions can be effectively controlled with operant procedures. Given the problematic status of the alternative explanations offered by Katkin and Murray, we would further conclude that this control has been effected through the direct instrumental strengthening of the autonomic response itself." (p. 460.)

Since the recent research on the instrumental conditioning of electrodermal responses, peripheral vascular activity and heart rate has been reviewed elsewhere (Kimmel, 1967; Katkin and Murray, 1968; Crider, Schwartz and Shnidman, 1969), this section will focus primarily on the learning of electrocortical and electromyographic responses -- two areas that have not been discussed in the previous reviews.

The most widely investigated of all the brain rhythms is alpha, a rhythm of 8-13 cps, usually averaging about 30 microvolts and occurring most frequently in the human during the state of relaxed wakefulness (Lindsley, 1960). In a comprehensive review of the literature on the physiological basis of the alpha rhythm (Anderson and Anderson, 1968), the thalamus was implicated as the structure exercising control over cortical alpha activity. There have been a number of early reports on the use of a biofeedback system in the suppression and habituation of the alpha rhythms (e.g., Mulholland and Runnals, 1962a, 1962b), as well as still earlier reports on the classical conditioning of EEG alpha (e.g., Jasper and Shagass, 1941; Knott and Henry, 1941). These reports did not assess subjective states associated with the concurrent electrocortical activity nor did any of the previous studies attempt to enhance EEG alpha through instrumental learning procedures.

The first investigator to attempt the study of operant control of EEG alpha and associated changes in mental activity was Kamiya (1962, 1967, 1968, and 1969). Kamiya (1962) was first interested in the question of whether human subjects could be trained to discriminate the presence and absence of alpha. The subject was told that from time to time he would hear a bell ring once and when he heard it, he was to make a guess as to whether he was producing or not producing alpha. As soon as he made his response, the experimenter told him if he was correct. The results indicated that after several sessions of training, most subjects had increased their discrimination accuracy well above the 50 per cent chance level.

Kamiya (1967, 1968, 1969) then turned his attention to the question of whether subjects can exercise control over their alpha activity and produce this brain wave pattern on command. He constructed an automated biofeedback system resembling the diagram in Figure 1. The system employed an electronic device which would turn on a sine-wave tone in the subject's room whenever the alpha rhythm was present. The tone would cease as soon as the alpha rhythm would disappear. Kamiya then conducted a number of experiments where he would tell the subject to turn the tone either on or off. In the first phase of this research he only trained people to suppress their alpha, finding that six of his seven subjects were able to perform this task (Kamiya, 1969). In another experiment employing three conditions (an alpha generation condition, alpha suppression and a basal level rest period) Kamiya (1969) found a marked difference between generation and suppression. The basal level, however, was higher than the generation condition. These data, however, do not refute the fact that autonomic learning has occurred, for it is quite likely that basal level alpha can change (Crider, Schwartz and Shnidman, 1969). It should also be noted that the alpha during the generation trials was of a higher amplitude than the alpha present in the baseline periods.

The verbal reports that Kamiya (1969) collected from his high alpha subjects are provocative. He indicates that besides the general feeling of pleasantness that all subjects described, there seems to be "some kind of general relaxation of the mental apparatus, not necessarily relaxation in the motor system, but a kind of a general calming-down of the mind." (p. 514.) He further reports that critical faculties seem to cease during alpha abundance. Kamiya (1969) also speculates on the personality characteristics associated with high and low alpha producers. He states that people with a history of introspection and those who employ such words as "images," "dreams," and "feelings" in their vocabulary, seem to be better at the alpha generation task than subjects who do not use these words.

The description of the subjective reports associated with the alpha rhythm has been criticized by some investigators (e.g., Mulholland, 1971) who feel that these descriptions are artifactual and easily explained by demand characteristics. However, in a recent well controlled experiment, Paskewitz, Lynch, Orne and Costello (1970) employed a yoked control design where some subjects were receiving non-contingent feedback. This group obtained learning curves quite similar to those recorded during correct, contingent feedback. However, the subjective experiences reported during the control of alpha activity appeared to be uniquely associated with contingent feedback. This fact demonstrates the validity of these subjective reports and it is important to make note of this point with respect to the subsequent discussion of other studies.

In an attempt to replicate and further elucidate Kamiya's findings, Hart (1967) performed an elaborate study which included a non-feedback control group, an important addition which was lacking in Kamiya's studies. The design of the experiment included two experimental groups, one in which the subjects received both in-session feedback training and post-session information about their scores. The subjects in the second experimental group did not receive post-session information but did receive in-session alpha feedback. The subjects in the control group received only post-session information about their trial-by-trial alpha levels and they too, were told to try to improve their alpha scores. The results indicated that 13 of 16 subjects in the experimental groups significantly increased their alpha indices within ten training sessions. The subjects in the first experimental group, with both in-session and post-session feedback, demonstrated greater alpha increases than subjects in the second experimental group, who received only in-session feedback. Three of the five control subjects also showed alpha increments. The two experimental groups and the control group did not significantly differ from each other.

The findings obtained by Hart and Kamiya have essentially been replicated by Green, Green and Walters (1969, 1970). Their experiment (Green, Green and Walters, 1970) consisted of training three different physiological functions concurrently in the same subject (EMG, temperature, and alpha) so that a comparison with the previous findings is somewhat tentative. Another major difference incorporated into the Green, Green and Walters (1970) study was that they were training alpha in the eyes-open condition using visual feedback, whereas the previous two investigators employed auditory feedback in the eyes-closed condition. The Green, Green and Walters (1970) study did not contain the important no-feedback control group; however, the results obtained are unlikely to be elicited from a no-feedback resting condition. In some subjects they obtained up to 100 per cent alpha in a ten second epoch while speaking with eyes open. The subjective reports of their subjects closely resemble those obtained by the two previous investigators (Hart, 1967; Kamiya, 1969).

In a study employing both an eyes-closed and eyes-open condition with auditory feedback, Nowlis and Kamiya (1970) replicated the previous findings including those concerning the subjective reports of the subjects. Sixteen subjects worked in the eyes-closed condition while ten were employed in the eyes-open condition. The basic procedure involved giving the subjects a 15 minute "insight" period where they were told to explore what made the tone

go on or off. After this period, the subject was given a
two minute trial where he was instructed to keep the
tone off and then another two minute trial for keeping
the tone on. The results indicated that every subject
succeeded in having more alpha in the final "on" trial as
compared with the final "off" trial. In addition, 21 of
the 26 subjects obtained more alpha in the "on" trial
than in the baseline trial, while for 19 of the 26 subjects the amount of alpha in the "off" trial was less
than the baseline. Both of these proportions were
statistically significant.

Brown (1970) obtained results similar to the
previously mentioned studies. Feedback was given by a
light signal and experimental trials were obtained with
subject's eyes open. Her data also suggest that those subjects who subjectively lost awareness of all environmental
factors except the light, or who felt "dissolved into the
environment" tended to have higher levels of alpha abundance, whereas subjects who remained aware of the environment obtained much lower levels of EEG alpha.

A study designed to assess subjective states during
the actual feedback experiment rather than through a post-
experimental interview was attempted by Honorton, Davidson,
and Bindler (1971). They employed a "state report scale"
consisting of five numbers on a continuum of external
attention through internal awareness. Each subject, with
eyes closed, completed ten two minute trials of alpha
generation and ten two minute trials of suppression
interspersed with ten two minute rest periods. The mean
percentage of alpha in the generation condition was
significantly higher than in the rest condition, while
the rest condition was significantly higher than suppression.'

The findings of this study appear to contradict some
of the conclusions reached by others (Kamiya, 1969;
Paskewitz, Lynch, Orne, and Costello, 1970). The differences may be attributed to the present authors'
procedure in that this study consisted of alternating
blocks of generation and suppression trials with rest
periods in-between. The present study also recorded EOG
and EMG activity. The results indicated that low state
reports (externally directed attention) were associated
with greater REM activity than high state reports (inward
directed attention). It was further discovered that EMG
activation was significantly less frequent on trials with
high state reports (inward attention). The alpha generation condition was associated with a significantly higher
state report than the alpha suppression group. These
findings taken together suggest that increments in alpha
are associated with a decrease in externally-directed

attentive activity and an increase in relaxation.

In an attempt to uncover the mechanisms involved in
the control of alpha, a series of studies were conducted
(Peper and Mulholland, 1970; Peper, 1970; Peper, 1971a)
which implicated ocular-motor activity as a major mediating
mechanism. In one study (Peper, 1970), the subjects were
instructed to track a small moving target whenever it was
visible. The visibility of the target was controlled
through the external EEG feedback path, so that the
presence of alpha made the target appear (the contingencies
were reversed for half the subjects). The results demonstrated that in "no case could a subject initiate or
continue to track without blocking his alpha EEG."
(p. 108.) Peper indicates that the task of tracking
involves efferent ocular-motor commands which desynchronize
occipital alpha. In another experiment (Peper, 1970) the
subject was instructed either to "pay attention" to a
light as it went on or "not to pay attention" as it went
on. He found a difference between these two conditions
which again relates to the ocular-motor command theory.
It should be noted that Peper's (1970) theory does not
speculate upon the origin of alpha activity being in the
ocular-motor system. In addition, it has been recently
demonstrated that a subject with both eyes removed showed
normal EEG alpha activity (Chapman, Cavonius, and Ernest,
1971). Peper (1971a) presents further data to support
and extend the ocular-motor command hypothesis.

It should be noted, on the other hand, that among
some alpha subjects, alpha activity is not significantly
related to eye position (Fenwick, 1966) and that some
subjects can demonstrate alpha control with their eyes
in either the up or down position (Kamiya, 1967).

In a detailed review and discussion of the mechanisms
of EEG alpha control, Lynch and Paskewitz (1971) put
forth a theory involving disinhibition. They state that
"Alpha activity occurs in the feedback situation when an
individual ceases to pay attention to any of a number of
stimuli which normally block this activity. These
stimuli may be cognitive, somatic, emotional or anything,
in fact, which will lead to alpha blocking." This theory
is quite consistent with the previous findings of Peper
(1970) and extends his theory beyond the ocular-motor
system.

We will presently discuss the research pertaining to
the voluntary control of specific muscle or motor units
(a motor unit is defined as a spinal anterior horn cell,
its axon, and all the muscle fibers on which the terminal
branches of the axon end). A motor unit fires when an
impulse reaches the muscle fibers, the response being a

brief twitch. Accompanying the twitch is an electrical potential which when recorded, is known as the electromyogram (EMG). Harrison and Mortensen (1962) were the first to demonstrate that individual motor units could be voluntarily controlled through the use of a biofeedback system. They observed that some of their subjects were able to isolate and contract as many as six motor units independently; they caution, however, that "success in this effort (voluntary control) varied with individual subjects and with the same subject at various times during the course of a particular experiment." (p. 113.)

Basmajian (1963) has extended the previous findings and has demonstrated that subjects can acquire quite subtle control over individual motor units. The author observed that subjects learned such fine control and were able to produce "various gallop rhythms, drum-beat rhythms and roll effects." (p. 441.)

In an attempt to induce deep relaxation in subjects, Green, Walters, Green and Murphy (1969), trained subjects to achieve zero firing (absence of tension) in large forearm muscle bundles. The results indicated that seven of 21 subjects were able to achieve the criterion of zero firing within 20 minutes and they were able to maintain it for 30 minutes or more. It is particularly interesting to note that five of the seven subjects who achieved the zero tension level reported body image changes. The authors state that the subjects made such comments as "my arm feels...as if it is moving away from me," and "I had to look at my hand to see if it was still in the same place." (p. 372.)

In a series of studies, a group at the University of Colorado Medical Center (Budzynski and Stoyva, 1969; Budzynski, Stoyva and Adler, 1970) demonstrated feedback control of the frontalis (forehead) muscles and showed that by relaxing this group of muscles, a person could alleviate tension headaches. Budzynski and Stoyva (1969) obtained results demonstrating that the feedback group evidenced much greater relaxation than the no-feedback and irrelevant feedback control groups. In an extension of these findings to five patients with tension headache, Budzynski, Stoyva and Adler (1970) found that biofeedback training reduced both the patients' subjective experience of headache, and the EMG potential recorded from the frontalis. It is important to note that the changes observed in the laboratory were transferred to everyday life. After completing the training program, the patients reported "(1) a heightened awareness of maladaptive rising tension; (2) an increasing ability to reduce such tension, and (3) a decreasing tendency to overreact to stress, e.g., 'Things don't seem to bother me as much as they used to.'" (p. 210.)

In concluding this section on biofeedback research
with man, it can be stated that a person can be trained
to exercise voluntary control over many bodily functions,
including a variety of discrete and subtle responses.  It
should further be noted that there often seems to be a
change in one's mental state concurrent with biofeedback
training.  Many authors (e.g., Kamiya, 1969; Green, Green
and Walters, 1970; Honorton, Davidson and Bindler, 1971)
have stated that some of their subjects enter into
altered states of consciousness during training of this
kind.  A discussion of the meaning and implications of
these new findings will be contained in the next section.

## The Implications of Biofeedback Training

The biofeedback paradigm has much to contribute to
the philosophy of psychology and more generally, to the
philosophy of science.  In the human biofeedback loop,
there is a closed system created which enables the individual to use "volition" and "will" to control his physiological processes.  Unlike the animal experiments where
there is a specified reinforcer (such as brain stimulation)
to motivate the organism, the human situation employs no
such external devices.  Green, Green and Walters (1970)
have stated that "It is not possible to define in an
operational way the meaning of the word 'voluntary,' but
all of us have a feeling of voluntary control, at least
part of the time...." (p. 3.)  This feeling of voluntary
control is particularly important in the training situation
because the subject experiences himself as the locus of
control.  He is the agent in the situation and through an
act of choice and an exercise of will, he is able to
demonstrate control over his own internal states.  The
feedback apparatus should be conceived of as a tool to
enable an individual to exercise finer control over many
aspects of himself.

This type of self-control has many important ramifications.  Maslow (1962) described one of the characteristics of the self-actualized person as being able to
resist "rubricization."  By this he meant that the
integrated person was capable of resisting certain cultural biases and forms of societal conditioning.  With
the application of biofeedback techniques, large numbers
of people can evolve into more integrated beings, who are
less subject to manipulation and more inner-directed.

Very much related to this concept of self-control is
the dictum, "Know Thyself," which Socrates (cited by
Murphy, 1970) held to be a central problem in philosophy.
Through the use of biofeedback techniques, Socrates'

maxim can be realized in many unprecedented ways. With the self-control of a variety of internal parameters, individuals may be able to function in new psychological states as yet unidentified, permitting them to explore latent and undeveloped aspects of their beings.

Murphy (1969) points out that there are "psychological states for which there are no good names, including feeling states, cognitive states and volitional states, upon which human destiny almost literally may depend, with resulting understanding of those profound alterations in states of consciousness, well known to the East, regarding which Western man usually has expressed doubt or scorn." (p. 523.) This view has been criticized by some writers (e.g., Johnson, 1970), but it should be noted that with the rapid development of sophisticated electronic instrumentation, much will be possible in the future that is considered unlikely today.

With the instrumentation now available, it is not only possible to evolve new states by controlling a variety of internal parameters, but one can also help people attain states that have been known to Zen and yoga practitioners for centuries. By studying these practitioners with physiological recording techniques, we can determine what aspects of their physiology they alter to attain these states. One can then begin to train people to control a number of specific functions that were found to be altered in, e.g., Zen meditation. It should be cautioned, however, that this is not "instant Zen" training and will never be. It should rather be conceived of as a crude attempt to enable Western man to place his physiology in a receptive state that will more easily allow his psychology to be altered. This is very much analogous to Maslow's need hierarchy (Maslow, 1954, 1962) applied to transpersonal states. At the base of the hierarchy are physiological needs, with the self-actualizing needs at the top. In other words, the physical organism must be integrated before full psychological actualization can take place. One way to achieve a well functioning and more integrated physiology is through the use of biofeedback systems.

The psychological states that we are discussing are normally considered to be "private events," unobservable and henceforth not amenable to scientific study. However, with the advent of biofeedback technology we are evolving a science of "subjective" experience. Through the use of converging operations (Stoyva and Kamiya, 1968; Stoyva, 1970) we can obtain objective evidence for the existence of hypothetically constructed psychological states. That is, if we ask a subject what is going through his mind and we simultaneously obtain a variety

of physiological measures, we can determine whether a
specific physiological indicator correlates with the subject's verbal report.  In this way we can objectively
identify mental states.  This strategy has been employed
in the study of dreaming (Aserinsky and Kleitman, 1953);
when the subject reported a dream, investigators generally
found that he was emitting rapid eye movements.  Thus,
the physiological indicator increases our confidence in
the verbal reports of subjects and enables us to demonstrate via inference, the presence of a variety of mental
states.  Through the combined use of verbal reports and
physiological measures, "subjective" states of consciousness can be studied with a scientific precision that was,
until recently, unavailable.

Another important implication for biofeedback techniques lies in the creative process.  There exists
anecdotal and clinical evidence suggesting that altered
states of consciousness may facilitate the creative act
(Krippner, 1969).  By enabling individuals to enter non-
ordinary states of consciousness, creative ability may be
enhanced.  Murphy (1958) delineates several stages of the
creative process, designating the first stage as
"immersion."  The individual sensitively contemplates the
surrounding environment in preparation for a synthesis and
consolidation of experiences which eventually leads to the
act itself.  It is particularly in the first stage, that
of immersion and contemplation, that biofeedback techniques might prove to be quite useful.  The alpha state
has often been described as a passive, contemplating type
of experience (Kamiya, 1969).  Sometimes the subject
might even experience a fusion of himself with the
surrounding environment.  If a person can be taught to
voluntarily attain this type of state, his creative
ability might possibly be facilitated.  Green, Green and
Walters (1970) are particularly interested in this area
as they state that the main goal of their research is to
develop "psychophysiological training for creativity."
They have initiated a project with theta brain wave
activity which appears to be associated with hypnagogic-
like reverie.  They note that the combination of reverie
and awareness appears to be an essential ingredient of
creativity and are attempting to train subjects to
voluntarily produce this rhythm.

An important but often neglected implication of biofeedback is in the study of paranormal phenomena.  Can biofeedback techniques be used to train such "psi" abilities
as "extra-sensory"perception (ESP)?  Parapsychological
data does not adequately answer this question, but we can
offer some tentative hypotheses.  It appears from several
studies (e.g., Ullman and Krippner, 1970; Krippner and
Davidson, 1970; Honorton, 1969; Cavanna, 1970) that ESP

appears to be facilitated in altered states of consciousness. Possibly, when an individual shifts into a different mental state, he becomes temporarily "suspended"
from cultural habits and societal conditioning and is
more amenable to subtle forms of communication such as
the "extra-sensory." Thus, by training a person to shift
voluntarily into different states, these "extra-sensory"
processes may be enhanced.

The findings to date demonstrate the complexity of
this area. There have been several studies on the relationship between the alpha rhythm and ESP; the findings
are often contradictory. For instance, Honorton (1969)
and Morris and Cohen (1969) have obtained results suggesting a positive relationship between ESP and alpha.
Negative relationships have been reported by Stanford and
Lovin (1970) and Honorton and Carbone (1971). No evidence
of any relationship has been reported by Stanford (1971)
and Stanford and Stanford (1969). A recent attempt has
been made to resolve this problem (Honorton, Davidson and
Bindler, 1971 ) and other researchers are currently
attempting to obtain more concrete data on the nature of
"psi favorable" states of consciousness.

Another method that might possibly be employed in the
application of biofeedback principles to parapsychology
is the study of a variety of physiological parameters in
gifted or "psychic" subjects. By utilizing extremely
sensitive electronic recording devices, investigators
might be able to identify certain physiological processes
that accompany "psi" transmission and reception. If
such parameters can be identified, they are potentially
amenable to change with the application of biofeedback.
However, parapsychology may well be at the stage where it
must wait for technology to develop sensitive instruments
for the detection of the subtle bodily changes which are
thought to accompany psi phenomena (Cavanna, 1970).

Since the subjective reports of subjects in a high
alpha state (e.g., Kamiya, 1969) resemble some of those
reports subjects offer while under the influence of
marijuana (Tart, 1970), a natural use of biofeedback is
to provide an alternative to drug use. Not only is it a
less hazardous means to alter one's consciousness, but
biofeedback places the person in direct control of his
experience rather than being dependent on a chemical.
The use of this technique with individuals who are using
the more dangerous drugs is particularly important.
Possibly, if scientists can provide a means for these
people to regulate their own states of consciousness at
will, the quantity of drugs they use might decline.

Some data already exist to support this contention.

One psychological team (Wolverton, Bokert, and Markowitz, 1971), working with heavy drug users, provided training for the group in a variety of techniques including yoga, meditation, and autogenic training as described by Schultz and Luthe (1959). The team of researchers report several marked preliminary changes in the group's drug taking habits. The use of a biofeedback system that provides immediate feedback of the results to the subject might add to and strengthen these results.

The medical application of biofeedback training has profound implications for a variety of disorders. It has been shown that heart rate learning observed in animals can also be demonstrated in the human being (e.g., Shearn, 1962; Hnatiow and Lang, 1965; Engel and Chism, 1967). Individuals with cardiac dysfunctions can often be taught to control their own heart systems to alleviate the disorder. This procedure has many advantages over such traditionally oriented practices as chemotherapy. Drug effects are usually quite general, often with serious effects. Biofeedback training, on the other hand, can be quite specific in its affects; this specificity has been demonstrated in humans ( Shapiro, Tursky and Schwartz, 1970 ; Engel and Hansen, 1966).

Biofeedback procedures also place the patient in a position of importance in the healing process; it is the patient who is responsible for his own recovery. These procedures have already been applied in a clinical setting to patients suffering from premature ventricular contractions -- a form of cardiac arrythmia. A group of investigators at the Harvard University Medical School (Weiss and Engel, 1971) have successfully trained some of their patients to control this type of arrythmia.

In speculating on the possible future employment of biofeedback techniques in medicine, a number of possibilities emerge. First, if a disorder has a specific physiological component, it is potentially amenable to self-control. This can be extended to quite subtle responses, such as the acidity (Ph) level of the stomach. In ulcer patients, with the aid of biofeedback procedures, control can be gained over the fluids in the stomach and thereby heal the ulcer. Biofeedback can also be extended to the area of preventitive medicine. If this type of training is integrated into school curricula at an early age, an individual may emerge who can exercise this control over many body functions in a variety of situations. For example, in an instance where the individual is bleeding from a minor wound, he could voluntarily retard the blood flow.

Another possible medical application is the diagnosis

of neurological dysfunctions. It has been reported (e.g., Bakan, 1971) that the two hemispheres of the brain differ in the quantity of alpha produced. It may be possible to determine the type, degree, and location of brain damage by the way an individual reacts to biofeedback training of alpha when each hemisphere is worked with separately as well as together.

Miller (1969b) has pointed out the connection between biofeedback training and psychosomatic medicine. Instrumental autonomic learning can be invoked as an explanation of many psychosomatic symptoms which, perhaps, could be reversed through biofeedback training. Miller (1969a) notes:

> Suppose a child is terror-stricken at the thought of going to school in the morning because he is completely unprepared for an important examination. The strong fear elicits a variety of fluctuating autonomic symptoms, such as a queasy stomach at one time and pallor and faintness at another; at this point his mother, who is particularly concerned about cardiovascular symptoms, says, "You are sick and must stay home." The child feels a great relief from fear, and this reward should reinforce the cardio-vascular responses producing pallor and faintness." (p. 444.)

It is in this manner that psychosomatic symptoms could arise. Since a given instrumental response can be strengthened by a variety of different rewards on different occasions, new theoretical possibilities are opened concerning the origin, reinforcement, and treatment of these symptoms.

The final, and possibly most important, implication of biofeedback training is for education (Mulholland, 1971). Many writers have urged that the scope of education should be broadened to encompass a more thorough understanding of one's bodily processes and how this knowledge enhances the self-concept (e.g., Krippner, 1970; Watts, 1966). The learning of a variety of bodily responses should begin at an early age. For example, alpha and theta training could be incorporated into the educational process so that individuals can shift easily into different mental states.

Eventually, a record could be kept of each pupil's brain wave patterns and overt responses. This record would be fed into instructional devices to provide an individually adapted program based on each person's learning curve, short term memory strength, changes in consciousness while learning, special skills and disabilities, and his perceptual and cognitive styles (Krippner, 1970).

Through these types of programs, individuals could be taught, in a relatively efficient manner, to cultivate aspects of their potential that are usually neglected and often wasted. Hopefully, with the current revolution in electronics, we can extend this promising technique to new areas of human life and help humanity evolve into a more integrated, creative and actualized species.

**Richard Davidson**

Research Assistant, Dream Laboratory, Maimonides Medical Center, Brooklyn, N.Y.; Member, Metropolitan Leadership Program, New York University, Bronx, N.Y.


**Stanley Krippner**

Director, Dream Laboratory, Maimonides Medical Center, Brooklyn, N.Y.; Adjunct Professor, Metropolitan Leadership Program, New York University, Bronx, N.Y.

This paper was presented at the Second International Invitation-Conference on Humanistic Psychology, July 21-24, University of Wurzburg, Wurzburg, Federal German Republic, and at the Seventeenth International Congress of Applied Psychology, July 25-30, 1971, Liege, Belgium. Preparation of the paper was supported by grants from the Mary Reynolds Babcock Foundation, the Irving F. Laucks Foundation, and the W. Clement and Jessie V. Stone Foundation.

References

Anand, B. K., Chhina, G. S., and Singh, B. Some aspects of electroencephalographic studies in Yogis. Electroencephalography and Clinical Neurophysiology, 1961, 13, 452-456.

Anderson, P., and Anderson, S. A. Physiological Basis of the Alpha Rhythm. New York: Appleton-Century Crofts, 1968.

Aserinsky, E., and Kleitman, N. Regularly occurring periods of eye motility and concomitant phenomena during sleep. Science, 1953, 118, 274-284.

Bagchi, B. K., and Wenger, M. A. Electrophysiological correlates of some Yogi exercises. In Electroencephalography, Clinical Neurophysiology and Epilepsy. First International Congress of Neurological Sciences, Brussels, 1957, Volume III. London: Pergamon Press, 1959.

Bakan, D. The eyes have it. Psychology Today, 1971, 4, 64-67.

Barber, T. X., et al. (eds.). Biofeedback and Self-Control. Chicago: Aldine, 1971.

Basmajian, J. V. Control and training of individual motor units. Science, 1963, 141, 440-441.

Benson, H., Kerd, A. J., Morse, W. H., and Kelleher, R. T. Behavioral induction of arterial hypertension and its reversal. American Journal of Physiology, 1969, 217, 30-34.

Bichet, X., cited in Miller, N. E. Learning of visceral and glandular responses. Science, 1969a, 163, 434-445.

Black, A. H. The operant conditioning of heart rate in curarized dogs: some problems of interpretation. Paper presented at the meeting of the Psychonomic Society, St. Louis, October, 1966.

Brown, B. B. Recognition of aspects of consciousness through association with EEG alpha activity represented by a light signal. Psychophysiology, 1970, 6, 442-452.

Budzynski, T. H., and Stoyva, J. M. An instrument for producing deep muscle relaxation by means of analog information feedback. Journal of Applied Behavior Analysis, 1969, 2, 231-237.

Budzynski, T. H., and Stoyva, J. M., and Adler, C.
Feedback-induced muscle relaxation: application to
tension headache. Journal of Behavior Therapy and
Experimental Psychiatry, 1970, 1, 205-211.

Cavanna, R. (Ed.). Psi Favorable States of Consciousness. New York: Garrett Publications, 1970.

Chapman, R. H., Cavonius, C. R., and Ernest, J. T. Alpha
and kappa electroencephalogram activity in eyeless
subjects. Science, 1971, 171, 1159-1161.

Church, R. M. Systematic effect of random error in the
yoked control design. Psychological Bulletin, 1964,
62, 122-131.

Crider, A., Schwartz, G. E., and Shnidman, S. On the criteria
for instrumental autonomic conditioning: a reply to
Katkin and Murray. Psychological Bulletin, 1969, 71,
455-461.

Dalal, A. S., and Barber, T. X. Yoga, "yogic feats," and
hypnosis in the light of empirical research.
American Journal of Clinical Hypnosis, 1969, 11,
155-166.

DiCara, L. Learning in the autonomic nervous system.
Scientific American, January, 1970.

DiCara, L., and Miller, N. E. Changes in heart rate
instrumentally learned by curarized rats as avoidance
responses. Journal of Comparative and Physiological
Psychology, 1968a, 65, 1-7.

DiCara, L., and Miller, N. E. Instrumental learning of
vasomotor responses by rats: learning to respond
differentially in the two ears. Science, 1968b, 159,
1485-1486.

DiCara, L., and Miller, N. E. Transfer of instrumentally
learned heart-rate changes from curarized to non-
curarized state: Implications for a mediational
hypothesis. Journal of Comparative and Physiological Psychology, 1969, 68, 159-162.

Engel, B. T., and Chism, R. A. Operant conditioning of
heart rate speeding. Psychophysiology, 1967, 3, 418-
426.

Engel, B. T., and Gottlieb, S. H. Differential operant
conditioning of heart rate in the restrained monkey.
Journal of Comparative and Physiological Psychology,
1970, 73, 217-225.

Engel, B. T., and Hansen, S. P.  Operant conditioning of
    heart rate slowing.  Psychophysiology, 1966, 3,
    176-187.

Fenwick, P. B.  The effects of eye movement on alpha
    rhythm.  Electroencephalography and Clinical Neuro-
    physiology, 1966, 21, 618.  (Abstract.)

Green, E. E., Green, A. M., and Walters, E. D.  Self
    regulation of internal states.  In Proceedings of
    the International Congress of Cybernetics, London,
    1969.

Green, E. E., Green, A. M., and Walters, E. D.  Voluntary
    control of internal states: psychological and
    physiological.  Journal of Transpersonal Psychology,
    1970, 2, 1-26.

Green, E. E., Walters, E. D., Green, A. M., and Murphy,
    G.  Feedback technique for deep relaxation.
    Psychophysiology, 1969, 6, 371-377.

Harrison, V. F., and Mortensen, O. A.  Identification and
    voluntary control of single motor unit activity in
    the tibialis anterior muscle.  Anatomical Record,
    1962, 144, 109-116.

Hart, J. T.  Autocontrol of EEG alpha.  Paper presented
    at the Seventh Annual Meeting of the Society for
    Psychophysiological Research, San Diego, October
    20-22, 1967.

Hastings, A.  State dependent learning and altered states
    of consciousness.  Paper presented at the Third
    Interdisciplinary Conference on the Voluntary
    Control of Internal States, Council Grove, Kansas,
    April, 1971.

Hnatior, M., and Lang, P. J.  Learned stabilization of
    cardiac rate.  Psychophysiology, 1965, 1, 330-336.

Honorton, C.  Relationship between EEG alpha activity and
    ESP card-guessing performance.  Journal of the
    American Society for Psychical Research, 1969, 63,
    365-374.

Honorton, C., and Carbone, M.  A preliminary study of
    feedback-augmented EEG alpha activity and ESP card-
    guessing performance.  Journal of the American
    Society for Psychical Research, 1971, 65, 66-74.

Honorton, C., Davidson, R. J., and Bindler, P.  Feedback-
    augmented EEG alpha, shifts in subjective state, and

ESP card-guessing performance. Journal of the American Society for Psychical Research, 1971, 65, 308-323.

Jasper, H., and Shagass, C. Conditioning occipital alpha rhythm in man. Journal of Experimental Psychology, 1941, 28, 373-388.

Johnson, L. C. A psychophysiology for all states. Psychophysiology, 1970, 6, 501-516.

Kamiya, J. Conditioned discrimination of the EEG alpha rhythm in humans. Paper presented at the meeting of the Western Psychological Association, San Francisco, April, 1962.

Kamiya, J. EEG operant conditioning and the study of states of consciousness. In D. X. Freedman (Chm.), Laboratory studies of altered psychological states. Symposium at the American Psychological Association, Washington, D.C., September 4, 1967.

Kamiya, J. Conscious control of brain waves. Psychology Today, 1968, 1, 57-60.

Kamiya, J. Operant control of the EEG alpha rhythm and some of its reported effects on consciousness. In C. T. Tart (Ed.), Altered States of Consciousness. New York: John Wiley and Sons, 1969.

Kasamatsu, A., and Hirai, T. An electroencephalographic study on the zen meditation (zazen). In C. T. Tart (Ed.), Altered States of Consciousness. New York: John Wiley and Sons, 1969.

Katkin, E. S., and Murray, E. N. Instrumental conditioning of autonomically mediated behavior: theoretical and methodological issues. Psychological Bulletin, 1968, 70, 52-60.

Kimmel, H. D. Instrumental conditioning of autonomically mediated behavior. Psychological Bulletin, 1967, 67, 337-345.

Knott, J. R., and Henry, C. E. The conditioning of the blocking of the alpha rhythm of the human EEG. Journal of Experimental Psychology, 1941, 28, 134-143.

Krippner, S. The psychedelic state, the hypnotic trance and the creative act. Journal of Humanistic Psychology, 1968, 8, 49-67.

Krippner, S.  What are boys and girls for?  Journal of Learning Disabilities, 1970, 3, 45-47.

Krippner, S., and Davidson, R. J.  Religious implications of paranormal events occurring during chemically-induced 'psychedelic' experiences.  Pastoral Psychology, 1970, 21, 27-34.

Lindsley, D. B.  Attention, consciousness, sleep and wakefulness.  In J. Field (Ed.) Handbook of Physiology, Section 1: Neurophysiology, Vol. III, Washington, D.C.  American Physiological Society, 1960.

Lynch, J. J., and Paskewitz, D. A.  On the mechanisms of the feedback control of human brain wave activity. Journal of Nervous and Mental Disease, 1971, in press.

Maslow, A. H.  Motivation and Personality.  New York: Harper and Row, 1954.

Maslow, A. H.  Towards a Psychology of Being.  Princeton: D. Van Nostrand, 1962.

Miller, N. E.  Integration of neurophysiological and behavioral research.  Annals of the New York Academy of Sciences, 1961, 92, 830-839.

Miller, N. E.  Some reflections on the law of effect produce a new alternative to drive reduction.  In M. E. Jones (Ed.), Nebraska Symposium on Motivation: 1963.  Lincoln: University of Nebraska Press, 1963, 89-91.

Miller, N. E.  Some implications of modern behavior theory for personality change and psychotherapy.  In D. Byrne and P. Worchel (Eds.), Personality Change. New York: John Wiley and Sons, 1964.

Miller, N. E.  Learning of visceral and glandular responses.  Science, 1969a, 163, 434-445.

Miller, N. E.  Psychosomatic effects of specific types of training.  Annals of the New York Academy of Sciences, 1969a, 159, 1025-1040.

Miller, N. E., and Banuazizi, A.  Instrumental learning by curarized rats of a specific visceral response, intestinal or cardiac.  Journal of Comparative and Physiological Psychology, 1968, 65, 1-7.

Miller, N. E., and Carmona, A.  Modification of a visceral response, salivation in thirsty dogs, by instrumental training with water reward.  Journal of Comparative and Physiological Psychology, 1967, 63, 1-6.

Miller, N. E., and DiCara, L.  Instrumental learning of heart rate changes in curarized rats: shaping and specificity to discriminative stimulus.  Journal of Comparative and Physiological Psychology, 1967, 63, 12-19.

Miller, N. E., and DiCara, L.  Instrumental learning of urine formation by rats: changes in ural blood flow.  American Journal of Physiology, 1968, 215, 677-683.

Morris, R. L., and Cohen, D.  A preliminary experiment on the relationships among ESP, alpha rhythms and calling patterns.  Journal of Parapsychology, 1969, 33, 341.  (Abstract.)

Mulholland, T. B.  Can you really turn on with alpha?  Paper presented at a meeting of the Massachusetts Psychological Association, Boston College, May 7, 1971.

Mulholland, T. B., and Runnals, S.  A stimulus-brain feedback system for evaluation of alertness.  Journal of Psychology, 1962a, 54, 69-83.

Mulholland, T. B., and Runnals, S.  Evaluation of attention and alertness with a stimulus-brain feedback loop.  Electroencephalography and Clinical Neurophysiology, 1962b, 14, 847-852.

Murphy, G.  Human Potentialities.  New York: Basic Books, 1958.

Murphy, G.  Psychology in the year 2000.  American Psychologist, 1969, 24, 523-530.

Murphy, G.  Experiments in overcoming self-deception.  Psychophysiology, 1970, 6, 790-799.

Nowlis, D. P., and Kamiya, J.  The control of electro-encephalographic alpha rhythms through auditory feedback and the associated mental activity.  Psychophysiology, 1970, 2, 1-26.

Paskewitz, D. A., Lynch, J. J., Orne, M. T., and Castello, J.  The feedback control of alpha activity: conditioning or disinhibition?  Psychophysiology, 1970, 6, 637-638.  (Abstract.)

Peper, E.  Feedback regulation of the alpha electroencephalograph activity through control of the
internal and external parameters. Kybernetik, 1970,
7, 107-112.

Peper, E.  Reduction of efferent motor commands during
alpha feedback as a facilitator of EEG alpha and a
precondition for changes in consciousness. Nature,
1971a, in press.

Peper, E.  Voluntary control of heart rate: problem in
feedback. Preprint, 1971b.

Peper, E., and Mulholland, T.  Methodological and
theoretical problems in the voluntary control of
electroencephalographic occipital alpha by the
subject. Kybernetik, 1970, 7, 10-13.

Plato, The Dialogues of Plato, B. Jowett, translator.
London: University of Oxford Press (second edition),

Plumlee, L. A.  Operant conditioning of increases in
blood pressure. Psychophysiology, 1969, 6, 283-290.

Schultz, J., and Luthe, W.  Autogenic Training. A
Psychophysiologic Approach in Psychotherapy. New
York: Grune and Stratton, 1959.

Shapiro, D., Tursky, B., and Schwartz, G. E.  Differentiation of heart rate and systolic blood pressure in
man by operant conditioning. Psychosomatic
Medicine, 1970, 32, 417-423.

Shearn, D. W.  Operant conditioning of heart rate.
Science, 1962, 137, 530-531.

Skinner, B. F.  The Behavior of Organisms: An Experimental Analysis. New York: Appleton-Century-Crofts,
1938.

Slucki, H., Adam, G., and Porter, R. W.  Operant discrimination of an interoceptive stimulus in Rhesus
monkeys. Journal of the Experimental Analysis of
Behavior, 1965, 8, 405-414.

Stanford, R. G.  EEG alpha activity and ESP performance:
a replicative study. Journal of the American
Society for Psychical Research, 1971, 65, 144-154.

Stanford, R. G., and Lovin, C.  EEG alpha activity and
ESP performance. Journal of the American Society for
Psychical Research, 1970, 64, 375-384.

Stanford, R. G., and Stanford, B. E. Shifts in EEG alpha rhythms as related to calling patterns in ESP run-score variance. Journal of Parapsychology, 1969, 33, 39-47.

Sterman, M. B., Howe, R. C., and Macdonald, L. R. Facilitation of spindle-burst sleep by conditioning of electroencephalographic activity while awake. Science, 1970, 167, 1146-1148.

Stoyva, J. M. The public (scientific) study of private events. International Psychiatry Clinic, 1970, 7, 355-368.

Stoyva, J. M., and Kamiya, J. Electrophysiological studies of dreaming as the prototype of a new strategy in the study of consciousness. Psychological Review, 1968, 75, 192-205.

Tart, C. T. Marijuana intoxication: common experiences. Nature, 1970, 226, 701-704.

Trowill, J. A. Instrumental conditioning of the heart rate in the curarized rat. Journal of Comparative and Physiological Psychology, 1967, 63, 7-11.

Trungpa, C. Meditation in Action. Berkeley: Shambala, 1970.

Ullman, M., and Krippner, S. Dream Studies and Telepathy: An Experimental Approach. New York: Parapsychological Foundation, 1970.

Wallace, R. K. Physiological effects of transcendental mediation. Science, 1970, 167, 1751-1754.

Watts, A. W. The Book on the Taboo Against Knowing Who You Are. New York: Macmillan, 1966.

Weiss, T., and Engel, B. T. Operant conditioning of heart rate in patients with premature ventricular contractions. Psychosomatic Medicine, 1971, in press.

Wenger, M. A., and Bagchi, B. K. Studies of autonomic functions in practitioners of yoga in India. Behavioral Science, 1961, 6, 312-323.

Wenger, M. A., Bagchi, B. K., and Anand, B. K. Experiments in India on "voluntary" control of the heart and pulse. Circulation, 1961, 24, 1319-1325.

Wolverton, C. T., Bokert, E., and Markowitz, I. From

alpha to zen: alternatives to drugs.  Preprint,
1971.  (Preliminary report.)

Wyrwicka, W., and Sterman, M. B.  Instrumental conditioning of sensorimotor cortex EEG spindles in the
waking cat.  Physiology and Behavior, 1968, 3,
703-707.

# Control of States of Consciousness: 2
## I. Attainment Through Control
## of Psychophysiological Variables

Kenneth Gaarder

*A model is made of psychological processes as a homeostatic adaptive control system describable by momentary states with transformations occurring between states. According to the model a major determinant of psychophysiological state and state of consciousness is the nature of the information transmitted between subsystems. Control of state is therefore achieved through control of the information transmitted between subsystems.*

T HE PURPOSES of this paper are to synthesize observations from a number of fields which lead to concepts of control of state of consciousness through control of psychophysiological variables and to provide an overview of these concepts of control. Some of the fields involved are cybernetics, feedback

Accepted for publication April 5, 1971.
From the Washington School of Psychiatry, Washington, DC.
Read before the Department of Psychiatry, Ohio State University, Columbus, Feb 20, 1970, and the Adult Psychiatry Branch, National Institute of Mental Health, Bethesda, Md, Feb 27, 1970.
Reprint requests to 4221 Oakridge Lane, Chevy Chase, Md 20015 (Dr. Gaarder).

and information theory, homeostatic physiology, physical (Hatha) yoga, sensory deprivation experiments, physiological therapies such as autogenic training and progressive relaxation, and psychoanalytic studies of character armor. While the ideas are not all particularly new, what may be new is current receptiveness to such ideas and, through the use of cybernetic analogies, the possibility of conceptualizing and stating them in lucid and concrete terms. Although the validity of the ideas is well established and may be elaborately justified, for the sake of simplicity the ideas are stated herein in a declarative manner without extensive proof or explanation.

### Homeostatic Adaptive Control Systems (HACS)

Since the time of Claude Bernard there has been gradually increasing awareness of the importance of homeostatic mechanisms.[1] The necessity of using feedback-mediated adaptive control mechanisms as a cornerstone of physiology is well recognized even though much work remains to be done on the specifics of such mechanisms. In the psychological realm, however, very little has been done beyond the farsighted, intuitive generalizations of a few early thinkers to make explicit use of homeostatic adaptive concepts.[2,3]

Taken broadly, the homeostatic adaptive control system (HACS) idea can be thought of as saying that one overriding purpose of all psychological and physiological mechanisms is to ensure the survival of the organism or of its own kind.[4] The major means used by the HACS is to have feedback control the value of essential psychophysiological variables to keep them within critical limits. Thus, from the viewpoint of cybernetics, any understanding of a psychological mechanism is incomplete if it does not explain how the mechanism is adaptive, how it uses feedback, and how it maintains essential internal variables within acceptable limits. (Perhaps one reason the HACS view has been so long in coming into psychological explanation is because of an apparent inadequacy with which we are not yet prepared to deal fully here. This is the failure of HACS ideas to make lucid why and how behavior in adapting to a new situation so often results in a drastic change from the previous state. Here we are confronted with the paradox of stasis versus kinesis—that in order to maintain some things the same inside, it is necessary to change others drastically. Thus, a naked man turned outside on a cold day must run very fast [kinesis] in order to maintain his body temperature [stasis.] This means we are dealing as much or more with a *dynamic* system [homeo*kinesis*[3]] as with a *static* [homeo*stasis*] system. Here, however, we will not pursue this question.)

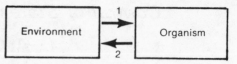

Fig 1.—*Flow diagram of the relationship between the organism and the environment. Channel 1 represents the flow of information from the environment to the organism and channel 2 represents the flow of information from the organism to the environment. This diagram is homomorphic with Fig 2.*

In order to translate the generalities dealt with above into more concrete terms, we may make use of diagrams which summarize the HACS functions of the organism in the form of information flow diagrams. Aside from oversimplification, these diagrams can be thought of as specifying the relationship between the organism and the environment (Fig 1) and between the designated components of the organism as well (Fig 2). (In cybernetic terminology this is saying that the diagrams are homomorphic with the organism and the environment.[4]) Each box in the diagrams represents a particular system, while each arrow represents the communication channels between two systems. Since all organs of the body may be put in one or another of the boxes as appropriate, the diagram is complete. The most important parts of the diagrams, from the view of the HACS, are the arrows, which represent channels which communicate information between the various components. At a gross level of analysis, it can be appreciated that any one channel— for example, the channel carrying information from the sensory systems to the central processor—may vary greatly in what it carries.

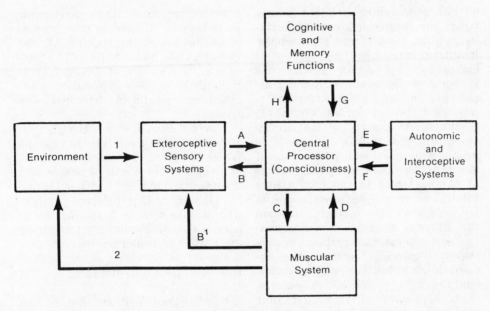

Fig 2.—*Flow diagram of the homeostatic adaptive control system. See text for description of channels labelled A through H.*

Thus, if one is sitting in a quiet room with the eyes shut, the channel from the sensory system is carrying relatively little visual and auditory information to the brain compared to its activity while watching television, in which a great deal of visual and auditory information must be transmitted.

While it has long been appreciated that purely physiological systems, such as the heart-lungs-blood-tissue system are in a state of dynamic equilibrium, it is a less familiar idea to impose upon ourselves the injunction that the same must also be true of the information processing system just described. This is, however, the demand placed upon us by our logic to this point. This requires that we imagine each box (with its component subsystems) to have particular rates of input and output of information with particular composi-

tions which must somehow or other result in the system as a whole being adaptive, being in homeostatic equilibrium, and being able to exert appropriate control. These unfamiliar strictures must await the further elaboration of ideas herein for their justification to emerge.

**State and Transformation**

Having stated the idea of a balance within the HACS diagrammed, it becomes possible to carry the analysis a bit further and posit two additional descriptors of the system —state and transformation. The first of these—state—is taken to be the momentary state of the system, with the moment being appropriately long enough to define a particular state but not so long as to encompass change of state. (Here again we simplify as we skip over the way in which hierarchically higher units of behavior which require longer times for completion can be designated as states occupying increasing lengths of time.[3,5]) This concept is elaborated by Ashby,[4] who has shown how the state of a determinate system can be defined by knowing the last value of each variable of the system, plus the last increment of input to the system. This means, at any moment, the *state* of our HACS is defined by the values of the variables in the boxes, plus the value of the information just received over the arrows. (Again simplifying, we assume the organism is a *determinate* system because there is enough truth in the assumption so that we may take advantage of it.) While recognizing that the power of this particular idealized situation is not matched by our knowledge of an organism at any moment, we may none the less hold on to the method of analysis because of what it will provide for us later.

Once knowing the state of the HACS and the value of the new input, we are able to identify what the new state will be. The process of reaching the new state is *transformation*—the going from one state to another. In a broad sense the history of the HACS is a chain of states—$S_1$ $S_2$ $S_3$ ... $S_n$ etc—with the change from one state to the next being the transformations— STSTSTSTST . . . etc. Merely noting that sometimes the transformation may be from a particular state to the same state allows for a flexible notational system covering enduring states as well as constantly changing ones.

We have now arrived at a basis for representing the behavior of an organism as a chain of psychophysiological states with the changes between states being represented by transformations. Any particular state may be defined by the process of designating the values of the variables of the systems in the boxes and the nature of the information in the arrows representing information channels between the boxes.

Having identified the HACS in a state of dynamic equilibrium as one frame of reference describing an organism and the chain of states and transformations as another frame of reference with a different perspective, we are now in a position to go back and examine the components of the HACS a bit more closely.

## Homeostatic Control Links

Our method will be that of defining the control links or information channels, as shown in Fig 1 and Fig 2 with the description of the subsystems joined by the channels being implied in the definitions.

**Environmental Influences (Channel 1).**—These involve things in the environment which impinge upon the organism, whether primarily as energy or as information. Seeing and hearing a fire truck drive by is primarily an informational issue even though the information is transmitted by the energy of light and sound. Although for the most part the environment impinges as information as diagrammed, there are, of course, also the impingements as energy per se. Thus, the jet airliner carrying a man from Chicago to New York or the brickbat knocking another man unconscious have energic properties which transcend their informational content. We will only concern ourselves with the impingement of the environment as energy carrying information, however, and it is, of course, the purpose of the exteroceptive sensory systems to convey this information.

*Sensory Input Channel (Channel A)*.—A major determinant of the content of the sensory input channels is the impinging environment. If nothing is "there," little is transmitted, and if too much is "there" it may be nearly impossible to turn it off. Since the sensory systems are interposed between the environment and the central nervous system, these channels convey only that from the external environment to which the sensors are capable of responding.

*Sensory Input Feedback Control (Channels B and B¹)*.—Feedback mechanisms to control sensory input exist which are now being studied at the neurophysiological level.[5] One manifestation of these mechanisms is the capacity to focus attention selectively from one sensory modality to another and to attend selectively within a particular modality to a particular part of the environment. Thus, a person fixating his gaze on a point is nevertheless able to attend selectively to one or another quadrant of his vision or centrally or peripherally, as he chooses.

*Muscular Control (Channel C)*. —The commands of the brain to the muscular system are carried over this channel. An example of differences in quantity of information transmitted over a channel is provided by comparing the activity of muscle nerves while relaxing versus the activity during motor tasks. An example of differences in quality of information transmitted over a channel is provided by the enormous difference in requirement for complex control between maintaining posture and tonus with the expenditure of considerable energy versus the expenditure of the same amount of energy in a highly complex motor task where the information must be contained in a more complex structure. For the sake of completeness, we also wish to recall that no muscle nerve firing at all is possible, contrary to old notions of constant tonic firing.[6]

**Feedback to the Environment and Effector of the Environment (Channel 2)**.—Once the commands to the muscular system are transformed by the muscles into muscular actions, they then impinge upon the environment as information (eg, in speech and gestures) or as energy (eg, in moving an object). Our diagrams show concretely the often unappreciated truth that almost the only output of the brain to the world is muscle movement, which is power amplified and therefore apt to be disjunctive. Certainly there is much to ponder and reflect upon in this and in the simple observation that the awake human rarely fails to make movements several times a minute.

*Muscle Feedback (Channel D)*.— Channels for the feedback of muscle performance exist in proprioceptive fibers in muscle, as well as in other interoceptive and exteroceptive receptors which reflect what the muscle has done. An example of how this operates is provided by the so-called stretch reflex. By passively flexing a joint so as to stretch a muscle, muscle firing can be elicited in the muscle. This means that a positive feedback has been established where increased tension on the muscle is signalled centrally to cause the return message of still further increase in the tension on the muscle by muscular contraction "ordered" from centrally. An example of change of state is provided by the decoupling of the muscle feedback so that during sleep or deep relaxation no such reflex contraction occurs.

*Autonomic Control (Channel E).—* —Central control of various autonomic functions is exerted through the autonomic control channels. Thus, heart rate, skin temperature, gut motility, tear secretion, pupillary response, and other autonomic functions are regulated. Of course, as the term indicates, there is also a great deal of autonomous or local control of these functions as well.

*Interoceptive and Autonomic Feedback (Channel F).—*These are the nervous channels which convey information about the state of visceral functions to the central nervous system. Although these channels are well known from experimental evidence, they are for the most part not considered to impinge upon consciousness. Evidence from autogenic training[7] and yogic training,[8] however, makes it appear this is because of a lack of discriminative learning and not because of an intrinsic impossibility of perceiving visceral function.

*Central Nervous System Information Flow (Channels G and H).—* In diagramming the HACS, certain arbitrary distinctions have been made. Thus, analogy to current computer technology has led to designating a "central processor" to carry out the major functions of the central nervous system. At the same time, the content of the stream of consciousness, as elaborated by James,[9] is highly reflective of a part of the functioning of a central processor. Because of the capacity of the stream of consciousness to vary in its cognitive and mnemonic contents and because of the alternation of these contents with sensory and motor contents in the shifting of attention, it was decided to place the cognitive and

mnemonic functions in a separate system with connecting links to the central processor. Thus, channel H represents the command of the central processor calling for cognitive and mnemonic activity and channel G represents the elicited cognitive or mnemonic material presented for central processing and is apt to be associated with consciousness of thought or memory.

## Control of State Through Control of Inputs

Having proceeded from the recognition of a HACS to the acknowledgment of momentary states of the HACS and transformations between those states, our next task is to show how the psychophysiological state and the state of consciousness is defined by and controlled by the information channels between the subsystems in the boxes of Fig 2. Ashby has shown in his "law of experience"[4] how a system can be brought to a desired state by controlling the input over a sequence of varying steps (ie, through several states and transformations). By simply using a chain of input steps (ie, controlling the information channel in a particular way) we can, therefore, bring any particular subsystem to the state we wish, and we may ignore concern for the particular state of the subsystem from which we start. Instead, we will concentrate on control of the information channels (input parameters) as the major mechanism in control of state. We will show how unique psychophysiological states can be created by the control of the input parameters of the subsystems.

Although Ashby has given proof of his law of experience, we will merely provide examples to illustrate the law without demonstrating proof. We will first give examples in which a single channel is altered and discuss the effect of this upon the state of the organism. Later, we will see that more than one channel is always affected, when examples of complex change of channels to achieve change of state are given. One reason all channels are always affected is because we are dealing with a homeostatic system where changing one variable has farreaching effects on most other variables.

**Control of Sensory Input (Channel 1 and Channel A).**—The extensive literature on sensory deprivation is concerned with methods which reduce the input to the exteroceptive sensory systems (channel 1) and thereby reduce the output of these systems (channel A) to the central nervous system. The profound effects of this upon the psychophysiological state and the state of consciousness have been well documented.[10]

A less-known method of reducing exteroceptive sensory input is through the use of a drug (phencyclidine [Sernyl] which has a specific blocking effect on the thalamic neuclei, where sensory input (channel A) is received by the central processor. Again, a profound alteration of the state of consciousness is produced.[11] Another method of controlling exteroceptive sensory input is by sensory overload, where all modalities are maximally stimulated. An example of this would be the so-called psychodelic environment where flashing colored lights and loud rock music bombard the senses. Ashby's law of experience is operative when trance-like states are produced with stereotyped rhythms which absorb the mind.

**Control of Sensory Feedback (Channel B).**—Thus far the examples have controlled sensory input by controlling the external environment to provide specific input or by controlling the input channel capacity by drug blockage. Another method of controlling sensory input is by controlling the feedback to the sensory system. One example is selecting the content of the visual world by means of the feedback of eye movements.[5] Thus, in order to avail oneself of the sensory input of a printed page, one must engage in a highly programmed feedback activity of scanning the page with eye jumps and fixations. Without the use of this feedback control, the structured input cannot exist. Further examples are provided by selectively attending to or excluding areas of the visual environment. Thus, shown a nude, some people look at, and others look away from, the genital areas. Feedback control is undoubtedly involved in the focusing of attention on sensory modalities or within sensory modalities, although the linkages have not yet been worked out. Thus, the capacity of the human to hear selectively one speaker at a cocktail party where there are others speaking more loudly is certainly mediated by feedback mechanisms. What is not generally recognized, however, is that by using sensory feedback in this particular way a person is altering the balance of information flow so as to produce a particular unique psychophysiological state.

**Control of Muscle Tension (Channel C).**—The range of issues in the control of muscle tension extends from the use of the muscular system for complex motor tasks, includes the use of muscle tension in the maintenance of character armor,[12,13] and reaches to the achievement of (nearly) total relaxation in Jacobson's[14] deep muscle relaxation therapy as practiced by himself and those modifying his efforts,[15,16] and to the total muscle relaxation universally achieved in sleep. Basmajian[6] has contributed the important findings that total muscle relaxation with no muscle bundle firing is indeed possible and does occur, and that single muscle units can be taught to fire selectively, thus showing ideals of no activity or of precise control of activity of anatomical units.

We wish again to point out that a specific behavioral state is a unique state of psychophysiological organization as we remind ourselves that the state of executing a highly complex motor task (such as a quarterback carrying out a football play or a tennis player returning a ball) is uniquely different from all of the other states to which we refer. In particular, we can describe the channel during complex motor tasks as having a large informational content and a low entropy (ie, a high degree of organization). In other words, a complex motor task is programmed from a large set of alternative possibilities in its own specific way.

Reich[13] and Braatoy[12] have shown how some individuals virtually live their lives within a particular state of muscle tension commonly involving specific rigidity of postural tone and facial expression. Murphy[27] also reviews how the muscle tension chronically inhibits the flood of painful memories which return if the individual relaxes. Thus, in these individuals we see two distinct states —"before" and "after." Before the relaxation the memories are not accessible to consciousness and after relaxing a psychological reorganization takes places.

Jacobson,[14] Whatmore and Kohli,[16] Wolpe,[18] Schultz and Luthe,[7] and Malmo[15] have from various frames of reference endorsed the beneficial effects of deep muscle relaxation and have arrived at an empirically valid finding which may someday be recognized as of the highest importance. This is the fact that anxiety cannot exist in the presence of deep muscle relaxation. Thus, at the present time it appears that minimal activity of channels C and D precludes the existence of anxiety and that one empirical treatment of anxiety consists of simply reducing muscle tension. This appears to be a stable cornerstone upon which important neurophysiological and therapeutic structures can be built.

Sleep is the other state in which complete muscle relaxation is achieved and is readily seen to be a unique psychophysiological state with its own unique organization. Many interesting transformations are regularly programmed—the change from waking to sleeping state and the changes from one state to another within sleep—ie, from one stage of sleep to another. It is well to remind ourselves that the adaptive function of sleep is not yet known.[19]

**Control of Muscle Feedback (Channel D).**—Although we have just dealt with the question of control of muscle tension, we have done so by the oversimplification of ignoring that one of the most potent methods of controlling muscle tension utilizes the monitoring of proprioceptive feedback from the muscular system. Self-observation and the findings of Jacobson and others imply that the reason we are not able to control muscle tension is that we are not able to recognize it. This is the "Great Truism of Information Theory"—that a variable cannot be controlled unless information about it is available to the controller. It means that one of the major functions of muscle relaxation training is the discriminative learning of the recognition of muscle tension level. Further, external feedback techniques[20] take advantage of this issue to provide another way of learning control more rapidly.

**Control of Autonomic Variables and Control of Interoceptive and Autonomic Feedback (Channels E and F).**—Because artificially considering a single autonomic channel in isolation does not provide as starkly simple examples as those given above, we will consider both channels of the autonomic loop together. By the very token of these functions being autonomic—ie, relatively automatic and involuntary—they tend to be outside of consciousness and, therefore, their feedback is not readily available to consciousness without discriminative training which most of us have forsworn. Likewise, because many of these automatic functions such as cardiac-respiratory-vascular regulation and digestive regulation must be carried on in one form or another regardless of other activity and because their activity does not usually set the stage for the state of the organism as a whole as vividly as do sensory and motor activity, clear examples of domination of the organism by autonomic functioning are not seen. Even the autonomic aspects of sexual and excretory activities are closely related to the function of the organism as a whole.

Yogic control[8] is a major instance of autonomic control which is being frequently verified by experimental observation, so that conscious voluntary control of heart rate, skin temperature, intestinal peristalsis, and so forth by trained adepts is now readily acknowledged.

Deranged control of autonomic variables as an operationally valid concept having etiological and therapeutic importance is also becoming evident in such diseases as essential hypertension, where a useful understanding can begin by thinking of the disease as primarily a regulating mechanism somehow set at the wrong level.

**Control of Cognitive and Mnemonic Variables and the Control of Their Feedback (Channels G and H).**—Because these variables are not yet available to direct observation through any other agency than introspective consciousness, not as much of a clearcut nature can be readily said of them as of the other systems. Also, as with the autonomic variables, we are now into the area in which the other systems can readily be made to dominate (for the moment, and in any single instance) this system by their activity. Thus, one may say with considerable confidence that no single line of poetry has ever been composed by a quarterback while getting a pass off to a receiver nor has any sprinter ever remembered anything outside the scope of his race while halfway down the track. These trite examples serve to illustrate the unappreciated truism that cognitive and mnemonic functions are highly dependent on the state of the sensory and muscular systems. Indeed, one can define as necessary for cognition and memory a certain lowering of sensory and motor activities below critical limits which would interfere too much.

**Control of State Through Complex Control of Information Channels.**—By now the point has been well estabished that the earlier examples of control of state through control of a single channel are oversimplified and that in every instance the true nature of the situation is better defined by a specification of the information on all of the channels. In addition, it can be seen that some physiological variables which reflect overall activity, such as arousal level, are appropriately considered as being made up of an "average" of the activity in all of the channels. Thus, in high arousal such as fleeing an attack, many channels have a great deal of activity, in contrast to low arousal, such as in quiet relaxation, where most channels have little activity. We will now look at some instances of states where consideration of several channels is essential.

**Yogic Asanas.**—In the typical yogic asana (posture) particular muscle groups are placed under tension. This elicits the stretch reflex, which consists of (1) the stretching of the muscle through assuming a particular posture; (2) the feedback proprioceptive signal of the stretch (channel D); (3) the central processing of this information; and (4) the "reflex" of muscle nerve firing in the same group, resulting in muscle activity in that group (channel C). Thus, the asana has an alerting effect through the effect of this cycle of activity on the reticular activating system.

**Yogic or Zen Meditation.**—Meditation not only has the effects of the meditative asana just discussed, but in addition the sensory system (channel A) is put into a state of relative deprivation and stereotypy by being in a quiet calm environment and by using sensory feedback control (channel B) to focus on a single potential input in a single way. Further, cognitive and mnemonic functions are consciously controlled by voluntarily limiting the content of thought, usually in a stereotyped way.

**Yogic   Autonomic   Control.**— Once all of the above preconditions are fulfilled, it appears possible to focus the attention consciously upon a specific autonomic function and thereby gain control of it.[21] The fact that our lack of training makes these things virtually impossible for most of us to achieve should not keep us from acknowledging their reality in others.

**Free Associative State.**—It is by now obvious that any mental state has a unique psychophysiological state accompanying it, which can be fairly well defined by defining the content of the information channels. This is true of the psychoanalytic free associative state. Thus, Braatoy's[12] work on muscle relaxation as a precondition for recall of painful memory defines the content of the channels to and from the muscular system (channels C and D) and the quiet, softly lit room (channel 1) helps to determine the sensory input (channel A). The defining characteristic of the free associative state would be the ready availability of free-floating thought and memory (channels G and H), but it is apparent that it cannot be achieved without first controlling the muscular and sensory systems.

**Control of State Through External Feedback.**—Consideration of our model to this point makes obvious another method of gaining further control of the state of the organism, which is to provide an external artificial feedback channel by measuring a particular psychophysiological variable and providing information about the variable to the organism. This is the powerful technique which is the major topic described in the following article.[20]

## Further Concepts Implied by the Model

Because of the limitations of space, and in order to deal with one topic at a time, we will not pursue further some concepts which we are on the verge of using, but which would have to carry us as far ahead as the ground over which we have already passed. These concepts have to do with: (1) the time duration of a state, with the definition chosen determining whether one is dealing with a time domain of the order of a "moment"[22] (25 to 50 msec) or of higher units of time; (2) the hierarchy of time-defined units becoming informational-behavioral units in a way analogous to the informational hierarchical structuring of language into *letters-words-sentences*[5,23]; (3) the programming of these units into chains with algorithmic structure; and (4) the structure of these informational-behavioral chains of units of states as a thing in itself. Insofar as we have developed a general frame of reference for viewing psychological phenomena, many implications for all areas of psychology follow which remain to be explored.

## References

1. Langley LL: *Homeostasis.* New York, Reinhold Publishing Corp, 1965.
2. Hartmann H: *Ego Psychology and the Problem of Adaptation.* New York, International Universities Press 1958.
3. Iberall AS, Cardon SZ: Hierarchical regulation in the complex biological organism. *Record of the IEEE Systems Science and Cybernetics Conference.* October 1969, pp 145-151.
4. Ashby WR: *An Introduction to Cybernetics.* New York, John Wiley & Sons Inc, 1963.
5. Gaarder K: Eye movements and perception, in Young FA, Lindsley DB (eds): *Early Experience and Visual Information Processing in Perceptual and Reading Disorders.* Washington, DC, National Academy of Sciences, 1970, pp 79-93.
6. Basmajian JV: *Muscles Alive.* Baltimore, Williams & Wilkins Co, 1967.
7. Schultz JH, Luthe W: *Autogenic Training.* New York, Grune & Stratton Inc, 1959.
8. Koestler A: *The Lotus and the Robot.* New York, Macmillan Co Publishers, 1961.
9. James W: *Principles of Psychology.* New York, Dover Publications Inc, 1960.
10. Ludwig AM: Altered states of consciousness. *Arch Gen Psychiat* 15:225-234, 1966.
11. Bakker CB, Amini FB: Observations on the psychotomimetic effects of Sernyl. *Compr Psychiat* 2:269-280, 1961.
12. Braatoy T: *Fundamentals of Psychoanalytic Technique.* New York, John Wiley & Sons Inc, 1954.
13. Reich W: *Character Analysis,* ed 3. New York, Orgone Institute Press, 1949, pp 39-113.
14. Jacobson E: *Progressive Relaxation.* Chicago, University of Chicago Press, 1938.
15. Malmo RB: Emotions and muscle tension. *Psychology Today* 3:64-83, 1970.
16. Whatmore GB, Kohli DR: Dysponesis: A neurophysiological factor in functional disorders. *Behav Sci* 13:102-124, 1968.
17. Murphy G: Experiments in overcoming self-deception. *Psychophysiology* 6:790-799, 1970.

18. Wolpe J: *The Practice of Behavior Therapy.* New York, Pergamon Press, 1969.

19. Gaarder K: A conceptual model of sleep. *Arch Gen Psychiat* 14:253-260, 1966.

20. Gaarder K: Control of States of Consciousness: II. Attainment through external feedback augmenting control of psychophysiological variables. *Arch Gen Psychiat* 25:436-441, 1971.

21. Tart CT (ed): *Altered States of Consciousness.* New York, John Wiley & Sons Inc, 1969.

22. Harter MR: Excitability cycles and cortical scanning: A review of two hypotheses of central intermittency in perception. *Psychol Bull* 68:47-58, 1967.

23. Polanyi M: Life's irreducible structure. *Science* 160:1308-1313, 1968.

# II

# MODIFICATION OF CONSCIOUSNESS

# Control of States of Consciousness: 3

## II. Attainment Through External Feedback

## Augmenting Control

## of Psychophysiological Variables

Kenneth Gaarder

*By electronically feeding back to a subject information about his psychophysiological variables of which he would ordinarily be unaware, it is possible for the subject to learn to control these variables. Thus, electroencephalographic alpha states can be produced at will, complete muscle relaxation can be achieved, and control of skin temperature can be exercised when the appropriately recorded variable is fed back to the subject. Implications of this for psychiatric treatment are discussed, especially in the treatment of specific psychosomatic diseases and in the treatment of anxiety states associated with muscle tension.*

THIS PAPER is entirely concerned with the use of external feedback as a means of controlling psychophysiological variables. The

Accepted for publication April 5, 1971.

From the Washington School of Psychiatry, Washington, DC.

Read before the Adult Psychiatry Branch, National Institute of Mental Health, Bethesda, Md, Feb 27, 1970, and the Washington Psychiatric Society, Washington, DC, March 23, 1970.

Reprint requests to 4221 Oakridge Lane, Chevy Chase, Md 20015 (Dr. Gaarder).

basic idea behind this technique is that by artifically (usually electronically) measuring some psychophysiological variable (thereby making it an "output") and then feeding it back to the subject producing it through a sensory channel (thereby making it an "input"), the subject has available the possibility of gaining control of the variable. For example, if the electroencephalogram (EEG) is measured in the usual way with skin surface electrodes and electronic amplifiers and if the EEG signal is then processed to cause a signal to be given whenever alpha rhythm is present, the subject learns to be able to cause alpha rhythm to be present or absent when he wishes. The principle of external feedback may be understood concretely by referring to the Figure. Here is shown the homeostatic adaptive control system[1] of the body with the crucial addition (designated by the heavy arrows) of feedback loops completed between an internal process and the sensory input system. Thus channel 1 completes the loop between the central nervous system and sensory input by means of EEG as just described,

**49**

while channels 2 and 3 complete feedback loops with the muscular and autonomic systems respectively as described later.

**The Great Truism of Information Theory.**—The essential principle upon which this technique rests can best be stated as *a variable cannot be controlled unless information about the variable is available to the controller*. This is a truism because it is a self-evident statement within the context of cybernetic principles. It is an important truism, however, because unrecognized the world has one shape and recognized another. When the variable to be controlled belongs to the controller and when information about the variable is presented to the controller, this completes a feedback loop. An elementary understanding of this truism can be gained by study of the error-controlled regulator in Ashby's *Introduction to Cybernetics*.[2] Although some beginnings have been made at providing a more rigorous analysis of psychophysiological feedback than the elementary one just given,[3] there is not yet a great deal more known about the matter.

**Early History of External Feedback.**—Such an easily achieved goal as the artificial closing of an external feedback loop has occurred many times without the formal logic of its occurrence being necessarily appreciated. One such early example is Narcissus seeing himself mirrored in the pond and becoming self-absorbed. The feedback provided by a mirror is used daily when men shave and women apply makeup and is used by a school of German physiotherapists to train self-awareness. Another hoary example of closing a feedback loop is provided by masturbation in which a motor output is used to stimulate a sensory input channel to achieve a sought-for psychophysiological state.

Completing an external feedback loop electronically has been practical for about 50 years and it is of interest that one of the first things Adrian did with the EEG was to observe his own alpha rhythm and how it was affected by eye movements.[3] Likewise, Jacobson[4] reports closing a feedback loop verbally by telling his subjects how they were doing while he observed their electromyograph (EMG).

Another example of early use of feedback was by Margolin and Kubie[5] who placed a microphone to pick up a patient's respiration and heart beat and used the amplified playback to induce a hypnoid state. In all of these instances the use of feedback was incidental to other concerns of the investigator.

**Current History of External Feedback Research.**—It is not easy in reporting the current use of external feedback to do justice to all the investigations involved. One reason is that most current knowledge of the field has not yet been published. Another is that new facets of the early work keep turning up. A third reason is because current feedback work has emerged from different scientific disciplines. Finally, most of us are now fully aware that history, as well as beauty, is in the eye of the beholder and it is necessary to acknowledge the limitations to the scope of one's vision of a scene in which one stands. In making a best effort, however, it seems valid to divide the current history of external feedback into two phases. In the first phase, several investigators used the principles of external feedback without an explicit recognition that a new principle has been discovered, while in the second phase it began to become

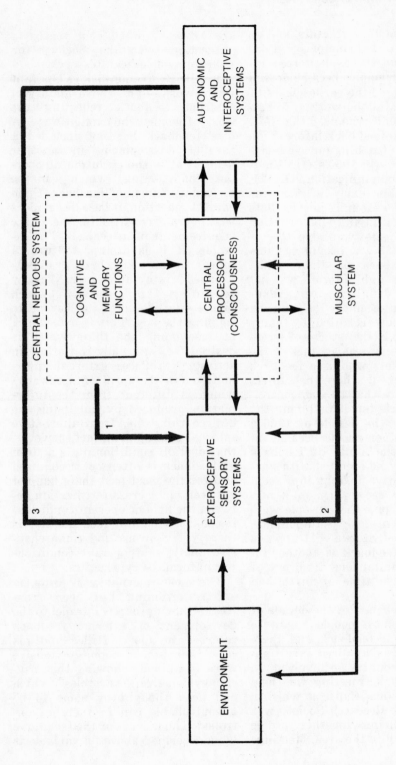

*Psychophysiological feedback. Three examples of closing feedback loops are shown by the heavy arrows superimposed upon the homeostatic adaptive control system diagram. In each instance it is assumed that the heavy arrow represents a unit consisting of physiological transducer, amplifier, signal-reducing element, and signal display. Channel 1, feedback of the EEG; channel 2, feedback of the EMG; channel 3, autonomic feedback, such as heart rate or skin temperature feedback.*

clear to these investigators and to others that new principles did indeed exist and the explicit recognition of the principles became an end in itself. One of the earliest uses of feedback was in the work of Whatmore and Kohli[6] who used the EMG as a means to feed back information to patients in teaching muscle relaxation in the early 1950's (G. Whatmore, oral communication, Oct 21, 1969). Another early worker was Kamiya[7] who found in the late 1950's while studying alpha rhythm that his subjects were able to control a signal he was providing them of the presence of their alpha rhythm. Although his work was not published in definitive form, Kamiya's findings became widely known and he is now credited by many with founding the study of feedback. Hefferline[8] was another of the earliest workers who used feedback in an experiment where the subject was not aware that he was controlling his muscle tension. During the early part of the decade of 1960 a number of other people became interested in the study of feedback and each may be credited with having had creative insight into feedback and the recognition of a new principle. Among these people were Brown,[9] Green et al,[10] Mulholland,[3] Murphy,[11] and Stoyva.[12] It appears valid to see feedback as another instance of simultaneous discovery of an idea whose time of birth had come.

In the latter part of the decade of 1960 many more people began to study external feedback and there are now over a hundred investigators in this country so involved. In 1969 a scientific meeting was held in Santa Monica, Calif, at which a Bio-Feedback Research Society was formed to bring together people doing research in the area. Meetings are expected to be held yearly in connection with the Society for Psychophysiological Research.

**Feedback Framework vs Operant Framework.**—The above history of external feedback reflecting the work of people who explicitly recognize feedback has not included a parallel development in another field. That is the evolution of operant conditioning, which can be viewed as a form of feedback. Upon careful reflection, it becomes evident that operant conditioning meets the requirements of a feedback. For example, if it is desired to train a pigeon to tap a key, he is gradually "shaped" into tapping the key by rewarding any activity which brings him closer to the key or to tapping the key. This is a feedback because doing the thing which is desired (ie, internally initiating an activity) produces external information (in the form of a reward) which is different from the information produced by not doing the desired thing (ie, from alternative internal states). The fact, however, that operant conditioning is a form of feedback is often not recognized and for the most part there has not yet been much cross-fertilization between the field of operant conditioning and the field of feedback nor is there yet rigorous and comprehensive analysis of operant conditioning in terms of cybernetics.

The most relevant work in operant conditioning has been from Neal Miller's group.[13] Parallel to the development of external feedback referred to above, Miller and his co-workers have done extensive work in animals showing that psychophysiological variables which had been thought by some to be uncontrollable can in fact be controlled. The essence of the technique is as described above: a variable is measured and if it moves in the desired direction reward is given and information is thereby fed back (naturally, punishment for the variable moving in the undesired direction may also be used). Using this technique Miller's group has found it possible to control many autonomic variables. Thus, heart rate, intestinal motility, blood pressure, and skin temperature of selected body regions have been controlled.

One major factor appears to differentiate the feedback of operant conditioning from other feedback. That factor is what might best be called the *valence* of the feedback. Whereas in other techniques (which are used mainly with humans) the information is usually fed back in "neutral" form on a dial or other display, in operant conditioning (which is usually with animals) the information is fed back in the form of a compelling reward or punishment and thereby given a motivating value to the subject. While it is true that the human subject in an ordinary feedback experiment is influenced by his own motivation to succeed at the task or by the social reinforcement of approval from the experimenter or therapist, these influences lack the compelling quality of food to a starved animal or electric shocks. At such point as we understand how to provide the kind of compelling valence to feedback information which is achieved in conditioning experiments without treating the subject in a demeaning manner, some important advances in the use of feedback might be expected.

## Method

**General.**—The method of external feedback can best be summarized by saying that it is deceptively simple and in that simplicity lies its success

or its failure. When a particular psychophysiological variable is continuously measured, usually the resultant measurement is a fairly complex signal containing a great deal of information. Most often simply presenting the raw signal to the subject as a feedback would overwhelm him with irrelevant information. Thus, in EEG feedback control, progress was begun by filtering the raw signal for alpha rhythm to feed back to the subject the information of whether alpha rhythm was present or not. Here again, however, the method is not as simple as it would appear since alpha rhythm is not just present or absent. Instead, one must have recourse to an elementary classification of signals to designate them as continuous (analog) or discontinuous (digital). Then, among the alternatives are feedback signals which (1) merely say whether an immediate criterion level of alpha is present or not; (2) show both the presence of alpha and its amplitude; (3) show the amount of alpha in a recent short epoch; or (4) show the percent of time a criterion level of alpha was present in a recent short epoch. When it is further recognized that the signal may be fed back in one of several sense modalities such as sight or hearing and that the signal may be scaled into one of several dimensions of that modality, such as pitch or volume, it can be seen that the problem of choosing a feedback is not simple at all. At the present time almost every investigator has chosen a slightly different method of feedback and comparative studies have only begun to be undertaken,[14] so that there is only a small basis for comparing one investigator's work with another.

Another problem has been mentioned above—for the most part the feedback information in human experiments has been relatively neutral or lacking in valence, so as to lack a compelling quality. Also, it is necessary to prescribe a context within which feedback is used—whether in timed sessions or ad lib; whether with other techniques or alone; whether alternating feedback trials with no feedback trials will accelerate learning, etc.

EEG Feedback.—The most extensively studied area of feedback is in the EEG. Here it is found that subjects are quite readily able to learn to produce large amounts of alpha in their occipitoparietal or occipitotemporal EEGs.[7,9] They quite uniformly associate alpha with a pleasant state of mind which is relaxed, quiet, slow, and tranquil as contrasted to the state with beta (low voltage fast) activity which is more alert, fast, aroused, and restless.

Among the fascinating problems raised which are beginning to be studied are those of (1) comparing feedback-induced high alpha states with those induced by yogic or zen meditative techniques[15]; (2) comparing occipital alpha with alpha from other parts of the brain which is more difficult to control (L. Fehmi, oral communication, Oct 21, 1969); (3) seeing how far alpha frequency can be slowed and speeded and the effect of so doing; (4) seeing the degree to which high alpha and high beta states are mutually antagonistic versus the degree to which they can coexist (B. Brown, oral communication, Oct 22, 1969); and (5) seeing if other brain activity such as theta or 40-Hz waves can be controlled (L. Fehmi and B. Brown). Finally, work has yet to be reported showing what effect learning to control alpha states might have upon long-term anxiety syndromes and what aspects of defensive states are compatible and incompatible with high alpha states.

EMG Feedback.—The predominant reason for pursuing the study of EMG feedback has been the finding that complete muscle relaxation is incompatible with anxiety.[4,6,16,17] The issue is to see whether deep muscle relaxation can be learned more readily with EMG feedback than without, and so far several studies have pointed in that direction.[6,14,18,19] The technique is simpler than in EEG feedback because so far only a single dimension of

muscle activity—the short-term averaged EMG—has been used. Even here, however, choices must be made between binary, digital, or continuous signal processing; between linear and logarithmic scales; and between auditory and visual displays. Likewise, electrode sites must be chosen from which to measure muscle activity, with alternatives of ranging widely over many muscle groups as done by Whatmore and Kohli[6] versus settling to a few sites as has been done by Cleaves,[14] Budzynski et al,[18] Jacobs and Fenton,[19] and myself. There is also the alternative of measuring postural muscles which reflect postural tone versus facial muscles which reflect a "psychosocial tone." Contrary to former belief, Basmajian[20] and others have shown it possible for muscles to have no nervous tone, so that there is no EMG activity to be recorded. Complete absence of activity is most readily achieved in postural muscles. On the other hand, facial muscles, such as the frontalis (forehead) muscle, do not go below $2\mu v$ of integrated muscle activity and most subjects do not reach less than about $4\mu v$ to $6\mu v$ of activity. It is not yet clear whether this is residual muscle activity or if the EMG is picking up other activities such as electro-oculogram and EEG.

Although it appears likely that almost anyone would learn to relax muscle tension better with EMG feedback than without and that everyone could learn to relax more than they presently do, it has not been shown that it would be so much easier to obtain the results Jacobson[4] and Whatmore and Kohli[6] claim because of feedback as to be worth the trouble, nor has it yet been shown unequivocally that muscle tension release is of great value. Rather limited work suggests that most people who achieve fairly deep relaxation do not enter a radically altered state of consciousness, but that a few subjects who have previously experienced altered states of consciousness from drugs or meditation may show facility for relaxing even more deeply and achieving an altered state similar to the alpha state from this still deeper relaxation (C.M. Cleaves, oral communication, March 13, 1970). It is not yet known whether alpha states and low EMG states are equivalent since EEG measurement has not been reported in subjects during deep relaxation.

**Autonomic Feedback.**—A large number of studies, mostly employing operant techniques, have shown that it is possible to use feedback to gain self-control over various aspects of the autonomic nervous system, especially the cardiovascular system. Heart rate has been studied extensively, with many studies showing that it is possible for subjects to raise and lower their rates.[13,21,22] Blood pressure has been lowered in other experiments.[23] Specific changes in the peripheral vascular system are also possible. Since local skin temperature is largely controlled by the state of the peripheral vasculature this is a convenient measure of the vascular system. Miller[13] has found rats can be conditioned to raise the temperature of one of their ears while Green et al[10] have found subjects readily learning to control skin temperature when feedback is available.

The galvanic skin response (GSR) is another autonomic variable which can be fed back to the subject, and has been found to add a useful dimension to psychotherapy[24] (see below).

## Comment

**Treatment of Specific Disease.**— From what has been said about feedback so far, it has some obvious potential uses in the treatment of disease. One simply considers a disease in which the pathological alteration of a physiological variable is an integral part of the condition and then uses feedback as a means of learning to return the variable to normal limits. Among the stark possibilities which immediately come to mind are the treatment of hypertension by feedback control of blood pressure, the treatment of vasoconstrictive peripheral vascular disease by the feedback learning of vasodilation, the treatment of anxiety by learning deep muscle relaxation through feedback EMG, and the treatment of epilepsy by feedback EEG teaching the suppression of spike activity. So far, the major therapeutic use of feedback has been in the treatment of muscle tension, with reports by Jacobs and Fenton,[19] Budzynski et al,[18] and Whatmore and Kohli[6] showing usefulness.

**Feedback in Psychotherapy.**— Where a patient's disease is not clearly related to a specific derangement of psychophysiological variables, there are several approaches which can be used. One would be to use feedback to teach the achievement of psychophysiological states which are considered desirable in themselves. This might be done either as a treatment per se or as an adjunct to another treatment procedure. According to the claims of Jacobson,[4] Shultz and Luthe,[25] Whatmore and Kohli[6] and the adherents of Yoga and Zen[15] there is an intrinsic hygienic value in being able to achieve deep muscle relaxation and altered states of consciousness associated with alpha rhythm. Feedback electromyography and feedback electroencephalography both show great promise as ready means of achieving these goals and no doubt investigators will pursue the question of these procedures having intrinsic merit by themselves. On the other hand, it appears likely that feedback techniques might supplement and facilitate other treatment techniques. One instance which readily comes to mind is the use of feedback to objectify and facilitate the deep muscle relaxation considered necessary for systematic desensitization in behavioral therapy.[16] In psychoanalytic psycho-therapies many patients are too anxious to be able to cooperate usefully in the necessary intellectual work who might perhaps be helped by relaxation with EEG and EMG feedback. Thus, feedback might help patients to achieve the psychophysiological state accompanying free association.[1]

Another use of feedback in psychotherapy is as a source of objective information about the body state which would otherwise go unnoticed. This is possible because most of us are generally unaware of our bodily reactions as we are involved in an interpersonal transaction. Ephron[24] found that the occurrence of GSR was related to rapidly passing mental states which occurred while defensive operations were put into effect and that the noticing of this by both the patient and the therapist had a useful role in the treatment.

**Limitations of Feedback Techniques.**—All of the suggested uses of feedback are based on the very promising research reported. It must be clearly recognized, however, that there are as yet no definite studies unequivocally proving the value of feedback and it is quite possible that feedback will be found to have no great usefulness in the treatment of disease. This must await further study and replication by different investigators.

When studies are done, it is clear the investigator must be aware of a number of issues in order to design useful experiments. One of these is the design of apparatus which optimally achieves the particular use of feedback desired. For example, if one wishes to use feedback to learn control of a particular variable, the best signal to extract from the data

is probably a fairly complex continuous one upon which the subject would concentrate. On the other hand, when feedback is used in psychotherapy to indicate a change of emotional state, it is desirable to have a very simple signal which will be obvious when it occurs but which will allow the patient to pay attention to other things such as the discourse between himself and the therapist.

From these simple instances of design of apparatus one progresses into the issues mentioned earlier of the specific property of the signal from which the subject can most easily achieve the desired result. This leaves the multiple choices of picking the desired variable, picking the specific property to be displayed, picking the sensory modality for the display, and picking the quality within the modality to express the the signal. In addition, there is the problem of whether one can combine simple feedback techniques with operant techniques so as to give a suitable valence to the information without at the same time introducing undesirable elements into the procedure.

A number of important issues in research strategy have been raised implicitly in the above discussion. One of these has to do with the questions which are asked. It is a good deal easier to pick a specific disease, such as Raynaud's disease, and ask whether the condition is helped by using feedback to increase peripheral circulation than it is to ask whether it is adaptive for Western man in an urban culture to be able to produce a tranquil alpha state at will. It seems highly desirable that both sorts of question should be studied. Another issue has to do with how one discovers the best way to use feedback. Here the choice is between designing controlled experiments versus casting about with pilot studies. Because of the large number of variables to be considered in experimenting, it seems desirable to use pilot studies to determine the most promising directions in which to proceed and then do controlled experiments to validate hints from pilot work.

Information about the Bio-Feedback Research Society may be obtained from its chairman, Thomas B. Mulholland, PhD, Perception Laboratory, Veterans Administration Hospital, 200 Springs Rd, Bedford, Mass 01730.

# References

1. Gaarder K: Control of states of consciousness: I. Attainment through control of psychophysiological variables. *Arch Gen Psychiat* **25**:429-435, 1971.

2. Ashby WR: *An Introduction to Cybernetics.* New York, John Wiley & Sons Inc, 1963.

3. Mulholland T: Feedback electroencephalography. *Activ Nerv Sup* **10**:410-438, 1968.

4. Jacobson E: *Progressive Relaxation.* Chicago, University of Chicago Press, 1938.

5. Margolin S, Kubie L: An apparatus for the use of breath sounds as a hypnogogic stimulus. *Amer J Psychiat* **100**:610, 1944.

6. Whatmore GB, Kohli DR: Dysponesis: A neurophysiological factor in functional disorders. *Behav Sci* **13**:102-124, 1968.

7. Kamiya J: Operant control of the EEG alpha rhythm and some of its reported effects on consciousness, in Tart CT (ed): *Altered States of Consciousness.* New York, John Wiley & Sons Inc, 1969.

8. Hefferline RF: The role of proprioception in the control of behavior. *Trans NY Acad Sci* **20**:739-764, 1958.

9. Brown B: Recognition of aspects of consciousness through association with EEG alpha activity represented by a light signal. *Psychophysiology* **6**:442-452, 1970.

17. Malmo RB: Emotions and muscle tension. *Psychology Today* **3**:64-83, 1970.

18. Budzynski T, Stoyva J, Adler C: Feedback-induced muscle relaxation: Application to tension headache. *J Behav Ther Exper Psychiat* **1**:205-211, 1970.

19. Jacobs A, Fenton GS: Visual feedback of myoelectric output to facilitate muscle relaxation in normal persons and patients with neck injuries. *Arch Phys Med* **50**:34-39, 1969.

20. Basmajian JV: *Muscles Alive.* Baltimore, Williams & Wilkins Co, 1967.

21. Frazier TW: Avoidance conditioning of heart rate in humans. *Psychophysiology* **3**:188-202, 1966.

22. Brener J, Hothersall D: Heart rate control under conditions of augmented sensory feedback. *Psychophysiology* **3**:23-28, 1966.

23. Shapiro D, Tursky B, Gershon E, et al: Effects of feedback and reinforcement on the control of human systolic blood pressure. *Science* **163**:588-590, 1969.

24. Ephron LR: *Physiological Feedback in Psychotherapy,* thesis. Harvard University, Cambridge, Mass, 1968.

25. Schultz JH, Luthe W: *Autogenic Training.* New York, Grune & Stratton Inc, 1959.

10. Green E, Green AM, Walters ED: Self regulation of internal states, in *Proceedings of the International Congress of Cybernetics, London, 1969.* To be published.

11. Murphy G: Psychology in the year 2000. *Amer Psychologist* **24**:523-530, 1969.

12. Stoyva J: The public (scientific) study of private events, in Hartman E (ed): *Sleep and Dreaming.* New York, Little Brown & Co, 1970, pp 355-368.

13. Miller N: Learning of visceral and glandular responses. *Science* **163**:434-445, 1969.

14. Cleaves CM: *The Control of Muscle Tension Through Psychophysiological Information Feedback,* thesis. George Washington University, Washington, DC, 1970.

15. Tart CT: *Altered States of Consciousness.* New York, John Wiley & Sons Inc, 1969.

16. Wolpe J: *The Practice of Behavior Therapy.* New York, Pergamon Press, 1969.

# Bimodal Consciousness 4

## Arthur J. Deikman

*The human organism has two basic modes of function: (1) the receptive mode oriented toward the intake of the environment, and (2) the action mode oriented toward manipulation of the environment. Both physiological and psychological dimensions are integrated in these modes. By utilizing this model we can understand a number of puzzling phenomena in the fields of attention, mystical perception, hallucinogenic drugs, and psychosis. Although states of consciousness associated with the receptive mode are often pejoratively labeled as "regressive" or "unreal," there is evidence for considering such modes of consciousness to be mature organismic options appropriate to particular dimensions of reality.*

WHEN WE consider the psychological and physiological variations that occur from day to day and from minute to minute as we work, eat, play, or respond to

Accepted for publication Feb 22, 1971.

From the Department of Psychiatry, University of Colorado Medical Center, Denver. Dr. Deikman is currently with the Langley Porter Neuropsychiatric Institute.

An earlier version of this paper was read before the Conference on Voluntary Control of Internal States, Council Grove, Kan, April 16, 1970.

Reprint requests to 15 Muir Ave, Mill Valley, Calif 94941.

emergencies or drugs, or to radical shifts in our environment or goals, we are presented with a confusing mass of observations that are difficult to organize. Changes occur in body boundaries, in muscle tension, in sensory vividness, in electroencephalograms, in imagery, in logic, and in self-awareness. Some of these changes are slight, others can be extreme. Discussions of states of consciousness usually do not integrate these many physiological and psychological variables and, in addition, it is usually assumed that unusual states of consciousness are pathological or unreal. This paper will present a model in which psychological and physiological variations are viewed as manifestations of two basic organismic states or modes that are coordinated to a particular function. The model will be used to clarify phenomena in the fields of attention, mystical perception, hallucinogenic drugs, and psychosis.

### Action Mode and Receptive Mode

Let us begin by considering the human being to be an organization of components having biological and psychological dimensions. These components are coordinated in two primary modes of organization: an "action" mode and a "receptive" mode.

The action mode is a state organized to manipulate the environment. The striate muscle system and the sympathetic nervous system are the dominant physiological agencies. The EEG shows beta waves and baseline muscle tension is increased. The principal psychological manifestations of this state are focal attention, object-based logic, heightened boundary perception, and the dominance of formal characteristics over the sensory; shapes and meanings have a preference over colors and textures. The action mode is a state of striving, oriented toward achieving personal goals that range from nutrition to defense to obtaining social rewards, plus a variety of symbolic and sensual pleasures, as well as the avoidance of a comparable variety of pain.

The attributes of the action mode develop as the human organism interacts with its environment. For example, very early in life focusing attention is associated not only with the use of the intrinsic muscles of the eyes, but also becomes associated with muscle movements of the neck, head, and body, whereby visual interest is directed toward objects. Likewise, thinking develops in conjunction with the perception and manipulation of objects and, because of this, object-oriented thought becomes intimately associated with the striate muscle effort of voluntary activity, particularly eye muscle activity.[1] Specific qualities of perception, such as sharp boundaries, become key features of the mode because sharp boundaries are important for the perception and manipulation of objects and for acquiring knowledge of the mechanical properties of objects. Sharp perceptual boundaries are matched by sharp conceptual boundaries, for success in acting on the world requires a clear sense of self-object difference. Thus, a variety of physiological and psychological processes develop together to form an organismic mode, a multidimensional unity adapted to the requirements of manipulating the environment.

In contrast, the receptive mode is a state organized around intake of the environment rather than manipulation. The sensory-perceptual system is the dominant agency rather than the muscle system, and parasympathetic functions tend to be most prominent. The EEG tends toward alpha waves and baseline muscle tension is decreased. Other attributes of the receptive mode are diffuse attending, paralogical thought processes, decreased boundary perception, and the dominance of the sensory over the formal. The receptive mode is aimed at maximizing the intake of the environment and this mode would appear to originate and function maximally in the infant state. The receptive mode is gradually dominated, if not submerged, however, by the progressive development of striving activity and the action mode.

In the course of development the action mode has priority to insure biological survival. The receptive mode develops also—but it occurs as an interlude between increasingly longer periods of action mode functioning. This developmental preference for the action mode has led us to regard the action mode as the proper one for adult life, while we have tended to think of the more unusual receptive states as pathological or "regressive."

Within each mode the attributes or components are interrelated to form a system, so that a shift in any one component can affect any of the others. For example, a decrease in muscle tension can decrease anxiety because of a shift in mode. Depending on the relative strength of competing motives and functional orientation, a change in one component of a mode may or may not bring about a noticeable shift to the other mode and with that shift a change in other components. The components are not independent of each other or caused by each other (eg, lowering muscle tension lowers anxiety; muscle tension, therefore, equals anxiety), but are related through the pattern or mode of organization in which they participate. If the balance of motivational force is very strong in favor of a particular mode that mode will be quite resistant to change, even if a component is changed.

A very commonplace instance can be given of these two different modes in daily experience. Try thinking about a problem while lying flat on your back and then contrast that with thinking about the same problem while sitting upright. You will notice that maintaining a directed, logical stream of thought is much easier in the upright position. This can be understood as a function of two different organismic states, initiated by postural changes, but not determined by postural changes alone. It is possible to think logically while supine but it is more difficult. Our action mode activities develop in conjunction with an upright posture while receptivity originated in the reclining, infant state.

Language, it should be noted, is the very essence of the action mode; through it we discriminate, analyze, and divide up the world into pieces or objects which can then be grasped (psychologically and biologically) and acted upon. The richness of our vocabulary reflects the extent to which we apply the action mode to a particular sector of our environment. For example, the average person has only one word for snow, the skier has several, and the Eskimo many. It is not just a matter of how much we detect differences between varieties of snow or any other dimension. Consider the experience of "love." Here again, the average person has only one word for love, yet he has probably experienced a variety of love states. We have not developed words for these states because love is experienced in the receptive mode; indeed, it requires the receptive mode for its occurrence. Color *experience* (rather than color as a sign) requires the receptive mode; colors have only a few names compared to the vast variety of hues to which we are sensitive. In the case of the artist, however, who *works* with, *manipulates,* and *makes* color objects, the case is different. An artist's vocabulary is much expanded. The Whorfian hypothesis, that we are unable to think outside of our language structures, has relevance only for the action mode. We manipulate our environment through language-directed strategies.

To illustrate the modes more concretely, consider a cab driver in heavy traffic, struggling to get a passenger to the airport in time. He is in the action mode, contending maximally with his environment, trying to direct and control what happens, and focusing intensely on a goal located in future time. His conscious experience features sharp boundary perception, high field articulation, and verbal, logical thought patterns. His EEG is desynchronized and his baseline muscle tension is high. At the opposite pole is the monk in meditation who is in a receptive mode with a corresponding state of consciousness that may feature merging of the self with the environment or an ineffable (nonverbal) perception of unity, or both. Muscle relaxation, cortical synchrony, and sensory dominance are principal features of his state. The monk endeavors to adopt an attitude of selflessness and abandonment of personal striving. To this end, he gives up personal choice and material gain. Language and thinking are given low priority and a vow of silence may be taken.

These two modes are not to be equated with activity and passivity. The functional orientation that determines the mode has to do with the *goal* of the organism's activity: whether or not the environment is to be acted upon, or whether stimuli or nutriment are to be taken in. "Letting it" is an activity, but a different activity than "making it." Likewise, it is not the presence or absence of physical activity per se that is the mode determinant. In the pure state of the receptive mode the organism does seem helpless to act on the environment, as in states of ecstasy or drug intoxication. In most receptive mode conditions, however, an active relationship with the environment takes place, as in the case of the monk working in the garden or lovers in sexual intercourse. Characteristically, the relationship to the environment in the receptive mode is what Buber describes as the "I-Thou," in contrast to the "I-It" of the action mode.[2] For example, the monk at work in the garden could have two quite different *experiences* depending on which mode is dominant. Likewise, the lovers may be "screwing" rather than "making love." In most cases, we are talking about a modal balance or mixture, whose characteristics depend on the extent of dominance of a particular mode. The enlightened

monk, working in the garden, operates in the action mode only to the extent needed to conduct his work activity, and the receptive mode can thereby still play a prominent role in his conscious experience.

Just as the action mode and the receptive mode are not the equivalents of activity and passivity, they are also not to be equated with the secondary and primary process of psychoanalytic theory. There is some similarity between aspects of the receptive mode and the cognitive style associated with the primary process. The bimodal model, however, addresses itself to a functional orientation—that of taking in versus acting on the environment. The receptive mode is not a "regressive" ignoring of the world or a retreat from it—although it can be employed for that purpose—but is a different strategy for engaging the world, in pursuit of a different goal.

The choice of mode is determined by the motives of the individual organism. Motivations exist, however, at different levels and with different time scales. It is hard to say much about the specific hierarchy of motives that affect the choice of mode. It is my impression, however, that the baseline of mode choice is set by the general orientation of the individual's culture. In Western civilization, that orientation is toward the individual's exerting direct, voluntary control over all phases of his life. This orientation of control is enhanced by the ideal of the self-made man and by the pursuit of material and social goals—all of which call for manipulation of the environment and of the self. The action mode dominates our consciousness. Men, however, have been concerned for many years with ways to shift to what I have described as the receptive mode. Later on I will discuss an example of a system that was developed to make the receptive mode the dominant orientation.

Although this bimodal analysis of organismic states at first may seem to be quite arbitrary and make little theoretical difference, I will now show how this model is very useful in clarifying a number of problems that otherwise would remain obscure.

**Poetzel Effect.**—Poetzel observed a difference in what happens to stimuli that are perceived in the periphery of awareness as compared to those in the center.[3] A stimulus that is incidental, on the margin of the field of awareness, is "processed" differently than stimuli in the center. In the former case, dream processes dominate, in the latter case, rational logic holds sway. This phenomenon can be understood in terms of the two organizational modes. Stimuli at the center of awareness are subject to the organizational mode associated with object manipulation—the action mode. In terms of thought processes, this means object-based logical thought. Stimuli in the periphery are processed according to the more indirect, sensually oriented, intake goal of the receptive mode. This mode of thought uses paralogical strategies.

**Silverman's Chronicity Study.** —Silverman and his colleagues have described changes in the cognitive style of schizophrenic patients as their stay in the hospital increases.[4,5] They report that with confinement of three years or more the attentional style of schizophrenic patients changes toward diminished field articulation and diminished scanning. Similar results were found in prison inmates.[6] These findings are not easy to explain on the basis of chemical deficits or "deterioration." The mode

model does, however, suggest a way of understanding the shift. Diminished field articulation means that an object is less sharply differentiated from its surroundings, and diminished scanning means that fewer objects in the visual field have awareness centered on them. On the other hand, where field articulation is sharp and scanning is wide, the subject is in the best position to encounter and manipulate, to actively engage the object environment. This active striving style, however, is specifically defeated by the hospital environment if the patient must stay in it over several years. Such long-term frustration of active striving would be expected to result in diminished striving and a shift to the receptive mode.

**Gaffron Phenomenon.**—Gaffron has described different modalities of conscious experience according to where on the object attention is focused.[7] For example, if visual awareness is centered on the near side of an object, ("grasping") the object is perceived "exteriorly" and the dominant qualities of the experience are form, surface, distance, and separateness from the observer. Awareness centered on the far side of an object ("mere looking") features "proprepceptive" qualities of volume, weight, and "interior" feelings of tension and inner movement. The object seems to intrude or extend into the boundaries of the self. The reader can observe this for himself if he stops for a moment and looks at a nearby object in these two ways.

It is most instructive to observe this shift of mode in situations such as eating a pear. In reaching for the pear, the focus is on the near side, in preparation for grasping it. As the pear is brought to the mouth, the focus shifts to the far side and beyond. In the act of eating, the pear is inside the zone of focus and, literally, being incorporated into the organism. The grasping of the pear is associated with the action mode and the intake of the pear with the receptive. The accompanying visual shifts are integral parts of the change in mode so that a shift of visual activity is accompanied by a shift in other components of the mode involved, for example, muscle relaxation and parasympathetic stimulation. The developmental coordination of the visual focus and body activity persist even though the objects involved may not be ones that can be eaten.

**Neurotic Styles.**—Shapiro has presented evidence that the characteristic way an individual attends to stimuli, his attentive *style,* has important effects on his conscious experience.[8] Shapiro distinguishes between two main groups—sharply focused attention (obsessive-compulsive and paranoid styles) and diffuseness of attention with absence of sharp focus (hysterical styles). His conclusions are as follows: "the most conspicuous characteristic of the obsessive-compulsive's attention is its intense, sharp focus. These people are not vague in their attention, they concentrate and particularly do they concentrate on detail . . . (they) seem unable to allow their attention simply to wander or passively permit it to be captured. Thus, they rarely seem to get hunches, they are rarely struck or surprised by anything." The consequence of such a pervasive style of attention is that "he will often miss those aspects of a situation that give it its flavor or its impact; thus, these people often seem quite insensitive to the 'tone' of social situations." "Certain kinds of subjective experiences, affect experiences, particularly require, by their nature, an abandonment or at least a relaxation of the attitude of deliberateness and where such relaxation is impossible, as in the obsessive-compulsive style, those areas of psychological life tend to shrink."

Shapiro's conclusions support the concept of different organizational modes. In the case of the obsessive-compulsive, his thought and style is focused on object manipulation, an activity at which he is usually quite successful. Hunches or moments of inspiration that come about involuntarily in creative states or moments of mystical revelation are, however, quite absent from the experience of persons rigidly committed to the object-manipulative mode of cognition and perception. Likewise, rich affective experience is not found with that mode because "abandonment" and "relaxation of the attitude of deliberateness" is not compatible with the action mode. In the diffuse, hysterical style, however, we see the counterpart to the receptive-sensory mode. Here, sensory details, inspiration, and affect dominate the experience.

**Body Boundaries, Muscle Relaxation, and Perception.**—Reports of subjects undergoing autogenic training, a European treatment technique of self-suggested relaxation, and reports of subjects undergoing relaxation training by means of feedback devices, indicate the frequent occurrence of body boundary changes correlated with deep levels of muscle relaxation[9,10] (and J. Stoyva and Budzynski, personal communication). Similar phenomena are noted under conditions of sensory isolation and in the induction phase of hypnosis. These correlations become understandable when we identify fluid boundaries and muscle relaxation as components of the receptive mode, components that tend to vary as a group when a shift in mode takes place. The conditions of autogenic training, sensory isolation, and hypnosis all predispose to a taking in of the environment rather than an orientation towards acting on the environment. Although the direct influence on muscle tension or sensory input is important, the shift in mode may be due as much to the accompanying shift in the orientation of the subject.

This line of reasoning also suggests an explanation for instances of reduction of anxiety as a consequence of muscle relaxation. Insofar as anxiety is an affect linked to future action (eg, "If I perform this destructive or forbidden act, I will be destroyed"), the shift to the receptive mode could be expected to decrease anxiety because the state of receptivity is not organized around action to be directed at the environment. In the time dimension, the action mode is the Future and the receptive mode is the Now.

**Experimental Studies of Meditation.**—For many centuries contemplative meditation has been prescribed as a technique for bringing about an altered perception of the world and of the self. This different mode of perception is characterized by a sense of unity of the person with his environment. In some cases, heightened sensory vividness is part of the description as well as timelessness, exultation, strong affect, and a sense that the horizon of awareness has been greatly expanded. In an attempt to study the possible connection between contemplative meditation and mystical experiences, I instructed a group of normal subjects in a basic procedure adapted from the Yoga of Pantanjali[11,12]:

The purpose of the sessions is to learn about concentration. Your aim is to concentrate on the blue vase. By concentration I do not mean analyzing the different parts of the vase, or thinking a series of thoughts about the vase, or associating ideas to the vase; but rather, trying to see the vase as it exists in itself, without any connections to other things. Exclude all other thoughts or feelings or sounds or body sensations. Do not let them distract you, but keep them out so that you can concentrate all your attention, all your awareness on the vase itself. Let the perception of the vase fill your entire mind.

Each subject performed this exercise for one-half hour at a time, for 40 or more sessions spread over several months. The subjects' perceptions of the vase changed in the following directions: (1) an increase in the vividness and richness of the vase percept (for example, they described it as "luminous," "more vivid"); (2) the vase seemed to acquire a kind of life of its own, to be animated; (3) there was a decrease in the sense of being separate from the vase, occurring in those subjects who continued longest in the experiment (eg, "I really began to feel, you know, almost as though the blue and I were perhaps merging or that the vase and I were. It was as though everything were sort of merging"); and (4) a fusing and alteration of normal perceptual modes (eg, "when the vase changes shape, I feel this in my body," "I began to feel this light going back and forth").

As I have discussed in an earlier paper, these data are not easily explained by the usual concepts of suggestion, projection, autohypnosis, or sensory isolation.[11] I interpreted these changes as being a "deautomatization," an undoing of the usual ways of perceiving and thinking due to the special way that attention was being used. The meditation exercise could be seen as withdrawing attention from thinking and reinvesting it in percepts—a reverse of the normal learning sequence. However, the concept of modes serving a particular function clarifies the phenomenon even further. It was required that the subjects adopt a particular *attitude*, that of a passive abandonment. This attitude represented an important shift for the subject away from the action mode and towards the receptive mode. Instead of grasping, manipulating, or analyzing the object in front of him, he was oriented to a different function. Instead of isolating and manipulating the object, he becomes one with it or takes it into his own space. Then sensuous attributes of the object, which are ordinarily of little importance, became enhanced and tend to dominate.

It is of interest that after the experiments subjects tended to report that they had learned something important in that experience but could not specify what it was. "I've experienced . . . new experiences, and I have no vehicle to communicate them to you. I expect that this is probably the way a baby feels when he is full of something to say about an experience or an awareness and he has not learned to use the words yet." The experience was ineffable in the sense of not being suited for verbal communication, not fitting the customary categories of language of the action mode.

Physiological studies of Yogis, Zen masters, and students of transcendental meditation indicate that proficiency in meditation is characterized by a predominance of alpha waves plus such changes as a lowered respiratory rate.[13-15] Beginning students, intermediate students, and masters could be separated on the basis of their EEG during the meditation state —the further advanced the student, the greater the dominance of alpha waves. These data can be understood if we regard meditation training as developing the receptive mode.

**Zen Consciousness.**—Zen Buddhism aims at changing the experience of a person to that particular view of himself and the world which is called "enlightenment." If one looks closely at the psychosocial system of a Zen monastery, it becomes clear that different aspects of that system are coordinated towards changing the individual's usual orientation of striving for personal goals. The monastery aims at producing a state of acceptance and "nondiscrimination." The principal means by which this is accomplished are meditation, communal living, and an ascetic way of life.

The highest form of Zen meditation is *shikan-taza* or "just sitting." At first it is hard to grasp the literalness of the instruction to "just sit." But it means exactly what it says. A person meditating is "not supposed to do" anything except to *be* sitting. He is not to strive for enlightenment because if he is truly "just sitting," he *is* enlightened. That state of beingness is enlightenment itself. During meditation, thinking and fantasy are treated as intruders or distracting influences, to be patient with until they go away. Pain from the crosslegged sitting posture is regarded as part of the sitting and not to be avoided or categorized or even fought. "Be the pain" might be the instruction given to a student. The "being" that is referred to is essentially a sensory-perceptive experience. The teaching is aimed specifically at doing away with categorizing and classifying, an activity that is felt to intervene between the subject and his experience.

In meditation, the sense of time can change to what might be called timelessness. Again, the urgency to accomplish things is undermined by this timeless orientation. Furthermore, during meditation the subject may experience a sense of total satisfaction with his moment-to-moment experience so that the need to strive for a distant satisfaction is diminished once again.

The sessions of sitting meditation take place three or more times daily within the setting of a communal society. No one accrues profits in that society. There are some status rewards but these tend to be minimized. The students share in whatever work needs to be done, share the same daily routine, the same daily food, and the same discipline. Every activity is represented as being equally important as any other. Thus, washing dishes is held to be as "good" as an activity as walking in the woods. Once again, such an attitude and structure militates against an orientation towards the future, because the future contains nothing intrinsically more satisfying than what is contained in the present.

I stress the matter of the shift in functional orientation because the concept of an organizational mode is based on the idea that psychological and biological activities are integrated in the service of the total organism and the functional attitude of that organism is the crucial determinant of which mode is adopted. To take another example, the wish for perpetual survival is perhaps the most powerful desire motivating the ordinary person's life. It is very interesting to see how this problem is handled in the Zen system. To begin with, the idea of

being dead versus being alive is labeled a fallacious concept based on dualism. The Buddhist cosmology of constant change, of a basic Nothing that takes an endless variety of forms, says that the student is part of a process that does not end but simply changes or flows. Most important of all, the student is taught that his notion of a soul, of an enduring self, is erroneous. Indeed, the concept of a self is held to be the cause of all suffering. During meditation the student may have the concrete experience that his sense of separateness is arbitrary and an illusion.

The principal purpose or goal held out for the students as legitimate and worthwhile is that of the Buddhist vow "to save all sentient beings" from the suffering of delusion. It should be noticed that this is a selfless goal. The student will not be rewarded by having a special place in heaven if he accomplishes this, but rather that purpose is the purpose of the universe of which he is a part. Such an ethic of action directed toward the good of others (the basic ethic of almost all religions) provides a dimension for participation in the world in an active and energetic way but one that attempts to minimize the mode of consciousness associated with striving for one's own personal goals.

The asceticism of the Zen community is not that of the anchorite who despises sensual pleasure as an enemy, but an asceticism that forms a backdrop against which the student can see clearly the role that his desires play in his suffering. In this connection it should be noted that a contemporary Zen master described renunciation as, "We do not give them up, but accept that they go away."[16] This open-handed approach to life means that any sensual pleasure that comes along is to be enjoyed for its own sake, but there is to be no attempt to hang on, to grasp, to strive for, to reach for. If we look at the goals around which we organize many of our activities, we see that they are often oriented towards prolonging or bringing back a particular pleasure that we have had, often at the detriment of the pleasure available at the moment. This lesson of nongrasping is brought home to the student over and over again in the different situations that arise at the monastery.

Thus, the emphasis on experiencing, or enduring, and on being —rather than on avoiding pain or seeking pleasure—provides the groundwork for a mode of consciousness that Zen texts describe as nondualistic, timeless, and nonverbal. It is part of the mode of organismic being that I have categorized as the receptive mode.

**Mystical Psychosis.**—One of the puzzling phenomena of psychosis is that of the mystical state preceding or marking the onset of many cases of acute schizophrenia. As Bowers and Freedman have described,[17] the specific configurations of these states vary from case to case but they share basic features: marked heightening of sense perception; a feeling of communion with people, the world, God; intense affective response; and blurring of perceptual and conceptual boundaries. First-person accounts of this type of psychotic experience are strikingly similar to reports of sensate mystical experience and suggest a similar process. In terms of the bimodal model, the experience is one of a sudden, sharp, and extreme shift to the receptive mode: decreased self-object differentiation, heightened sensory intake, and nonverbal, nonlogical thought process.

Both mystical and psychotic states appear to have arisen out of a situation in which the individual has struggled with a desperate problem, has come to a complete impasse, and given up hope, abandoned the struggle in despair.[18] For the mystic, what emerges from the "cloud of unknowing" or the "dark night of the soul" is an ecstatic union with God or Reality. For the psychotic person, the world rushes in but does not become integrated in the harmony of *mystico unio* or *satori*. Instead, he creates a delusion to achieve a partial ordering and control.

As I have discussed earlier, mystical practice can be viewed as a cultivation of the receptive mode by means of a particular functional orientation and control of thought and environment. No such training program precedes the many examples of mystical psychotic episodes cited above. How are we to understand them then? Maternal deprivation in the case of children and loss or rejection by a loved person in the case of adults are frequently reported as precursors or precipitants of psychosis.[19] In my own experience and in that of others, therapeutic investigation reveals intense hatred and destructive fantasies directed towards the loved person but not acknowledged by the patient. The emergence into consciousness of the anger directed towards the appropriate person is usually accompanied by a dramatic improvement in the patient's condition and marks the demise of the psychotic defense. This suggests the possibility that the psychotic alteration in consciousness is a defensive shift to a mode that will preclude destructive action on the other person. If someone is ecstatic, Christlike, overcome with the significance of a thousand details, buffeted by alternate winds of fear, exultation, grief, and rapture, he is in a state that maximizes what comes in and minimizes the possibility of aggressive action on someone else. Not incidentally, maximum sensory intake can be viewed as dealing with the painful emptiness following deprivation of love.

Although such a person may pass to a phase of tightly ordered paranoid delusion in which he can be dangerous, in the mystical, flooded stage he is helpless, like an infant. The shift to the mystical state is a functional shift on the part of an organism desperately concerned over final loss of nutriment. The control gates are thrown down and the world floods in through the senses and through the inner stores of affect and memory. The action mode is abandoned. When the person begins to drown in the overload, he asserts control in a delusional compromise that to some extent restores order and effectiveness while providing a substitute object.

The mystics' success in achieving a harmonious integration of self and world may be explained by a consideration of the many factors that differentiate the life and practice of the mystic from that of the psychotic. But the similarity of the initial experience that occurs when striving towards the world is abandoned suggests a similar basic organismic shift— the giving up of the action mode in favor of the receptive. In the case of acute mystical psychosis, a crucial rejection or life impasse triggers a collapse of the action mode and a sudden rush of receptive mode cognition and perception ensues for which the person is unprepared and unsupported. Delusional reordering then takes place to solve the affective impasse.

**Lysergic Acid Diethylamide LSD).**—Accounts of LSD experiences reveal a cluster of characteristics identifying it with the receptive mode: a marked decrease in self-object distinction; a loss of control over attention; the dominance of paralogical thought forms; intense affect and vivid sensory experience; decreased field articulation and increased parasympathetic stimulation; plus a reification of thought and feeling with a corresponding decrease in "reality testing."

As in the case of meditation, I hypothesized that the general effects of LSD and related drugs were those of "deautomatization," an undoing of the automatic psychological structures that organize, limit, select, and interpret perceptual stimuli.[20] In considering the problem of explaining the perceptual and cognitive phenomena of mystic experience as a regression, I stated, "One might call the direction regressive in a developmental sense, but the actual experience is probably not within the psychological scope of any child. It is a de-automatization occurring in an adult mind, and the experience gains its richness from adult memories and functions now subject to a different mode of consciousness." That mode of consciousness I would now designate as the receptive mode and consider it to be a mature cognitive and perceptual state, one that is not ordinarily dominant, but is an option that has developed in richness and subtlety in parallel with the development of the action mode that is our customary state of consciousness. Reports of the LSD experience show the complex possibilities of thought and perception that can occur in the receptive mode.[21,22]

It is noteworthy that one of the

effects of widespread use of LSD and other psychedelics has been to stimulate a revival of interest in Eastern religions. This orientation towards Eastern mysticism can be understood if Yoga and Zen are viewed as developments of the receptive mode: a perception and cognition that features the blurring of boundaries; the merging of self and environment, coupled with affective and sensory richness and marked by a detachment from the object-oriented goals of the action mode.

**Physiological Dimensions in Psychosis and LSD.**—The physiological data pertaining to meditating Yogis and Zen monks are clear and support the mode hypothesis. In the case of acute and chronic schizophrenia, however, the data are ambiguous or contradictory. Chronic schizophrenic patients tend to have EEGs suggesting cortical activation and high anxiety levels.[23-25] A study of hospitalized schizophrenic patients undergoing acute decompensation shows an increase and wide variability of muscle tension, rather than the decreased muscle tension predicted on the basis of the receptive mode model.[26] On the other hand, Salamon and Post,[27] using a special method of measuring alpha waves, found increased alpha-wave production in schizophrenic patients as compared to controls. Studies of autonomic function are likewise variable and unclear. Issues of diagnosis, chronicity, and drug effects undoubtably confound the data. In the case of LSD states, there is not much data to work with, but the clinical variability of the states and the frequent occurrence of anxiety suggest a situation similar to the psychoses. Although a more detailed and systematic physiological investigation needs to be done to solve this problem, in these instances we are probably dealing with an unintegrated mixture of modes. One way of understanding this is to consider the fact that, in the case of schizophrenia, the shift to the receptive mode may arouse great anxiety and a compensatory attempt to control the receptive mode experience, an attempt that is an action mode response. That such a response creates a problem is suggested by the lore of LSD users whose standard advice for those about to take LSD is not to fight the experience, but to "go with it," to "float downstream," and abandon oneself to what feels like "ego death." It is said that if one can do this, chances are good that the experience will be beatific. On the other hand, if the subject attempts to control or fight the experience, a "bad trip" is the likely result. Giving oneself up to an unusual experience, abandoning oneself to "ego death," is precisely what Yogis and Zen monks are trained to do, but what schizophrenic persons find most difficult. Perhaps this difference underlies the different physiological portraits accompanying these different situations.

**Implications**

**Control of Psychological and Physiological Dimensions.**—The concept that dimensions of a state of consciousness are components of organismic modes suggests the possibility of indirect control over specific aspects of each mode. For example, it becomes reasonable to affect the sharpness of perceptual boundaries by increasing muscle tension or to decrease anxiety by lowering it. Similarly, by restricting analytic thinking and attending to a sensory mode, alterations in muscle tension, EEG, and galvanic skin response can be obtained. By delineating other dimensions of the modes we may be able to widen our repertoire of techniques for change along a variety of organismic dimensions.

**Strategic Options.**—The receptive mode seems to be one in which certain *activities* are facilitated. The examples below are assumed to involve instances of the receptive mode by virtue of their emphasis on relinquishing conscious striving and intellectual control:

Subjects who learn to control functions of the autonomic nervous system, such as alpha-wave production or finger temperature, learn that they must let it happen rather than make it happen. In the case of temperature control, Green et al[28] have termed this activity "passive volition."

Accounts of the process of creative synthesis show several distinct stages: first a stage of directed intellectual attack on the problem leading to a feeling of impasse, then the stage of "giving up," in which the person stops struggling with the problem and turns his attention to other things. During this unfocused rest period the solution to the problem manifests itself as an "Aha!" or "Eureka!" experience —the answer is suddenly there of itself. The final stage sees a return of directed intellectual activity as the "answer" is worked over to assess its validity or fit with the object world. In terms of the mode model, the first stage is one in which the action mode is used, followed by the receptive mode in which the creative leap is made, followed by a return to the action mode to integrate the discovery with the object world.

It may be that paranormal phenomena require the development of the receptive mode. Such a possibility fits well with assertions of classical Yogic literature and with contemporary dream research.[29]

A prosaic example of the need to switch to the receptive mode to achieve a particular aim is the attempt to recover a forgotten name. Typically, the person struggles with it and then gives up, saying, "It will come to me in a minute"—and it does. What could not be gained by a direct effort was accomplished by relinquishing effort and becoming relatively receptive.

In ordinary life circumstances, the receptive mode probably plays its most important role in sexual intercourse. Erikson describes the psychological importance of the healthy sexual act as ". . . a supreme experience of the mutual regulation of two beings (that) in some way breaks the point off the hostilities and potential rages caused by the oppositeness of male and female, of fact and fancy, of love and hate. Satisfactory sex relations thus make sex less obsessive, overcompensation less necessary, sadistic controls superfluous."[30] Psychotherapeutic investigation shows that an individual's capacity for such a satisfying sexual experience is in proportion to his or her capacity to relinquish control, to allow the other person to "enter in," to adopt what I have termed the receptive mode orientation. It is of interest to this discussion that sexual climax in persons with such a capacity is associated not only with intensely heightened sensation and diffuse attention, but with a decrease in self-other boundaries that in some cases results in experiences properly classified as mystical.[31] An inability to shift to the receptive mode, however, results in a serious impairment of the sexual act. Sensation, release, and feelings of closeness become attenuated or absent.

**Knowledge.**—Although this discussion of modes began with a simple dichotomy of action—namely, manipulating the environment versus taking it in—the study of mystical consciousness suggests that the receptive mode may provide a way of "knowing" certain aspects of reality not accessible to the action mode. The "knowing" that takes place is usually a nonverbal experience, although it may later be translated into words in order to be shared with others. Thus, what is taken in is not only those aspects of the environment with which we are familiar but other aspects as well.

Contemporary psychological models, such as primary process theory, view the object world as the standard by which to judge the realism of perception and cognition. The receptive mode and other modes yet to be discerned or utilized can, however, be conceptualized as modes by which the organism addresses itself to reality dimensions other than those of the object world associated with the action mode and logical thinking. The "thinking" of the receptive mode may be organized in terms of a *different* logic in pursuit of aims located along different dimensions of reality than those to which we ordinarily address ourselves.

It may be felt that to talk of other dimensions of reality is to indulge in romantic thinking, but however it may be judged the idea of other dimensions is not illogical. Considerations of developmental psychology provide the basis for the possibility that the organism has exercised a considerable selection over what features of the world it gives the priority of its attention and the structuralization of its language. That the view of the world thus obtained is relative, rather than absolute, and incorrect in certain applications is held by many theoretical physicists. Furthermore, it has been noted that the correspondence between the cosmology of mystics and that of contemporary physicists is striking.[32] Such a correspondence suggests that the receptive mode of mystic consciousness may have validity in terms of the "external world" if the sector of reality being considered is different from that of the biological with which we are familiar and in which we developed.

**Values.**—The crises now facing the human race are technically solvable. Controlling population, reducing pollution, and eliminating racism and war do not require new inventions. Yet these problems may prove fatally insolvable because what is required is a shift in values, in self-definition, and in world view on the part of each person—for it is the individual consciousness that is the problem. Our survival is threatened now because of our great success in manipulating our environment and acting on others. The action mode has ruled our individual lives and our national politics and the I-It relationship that has provided the base for technical mastery is now the primary obstacle to saving our race. If, however, each person were able to feel an identity with other persons and with his environment, to see himself as part of a larger unity, he would have that sense of oneness that supports the selfless actions necessary to regulate population growth, minimize pollution, and end war. The receptive mode we have been discussing is the mode in which this identification—the I-Thou relationship—exists and it may be needed to provide the experiential base for the values and world view now needed so desperately by our society as a whole.

## Conclusion

I believe it is important that we recognize the relativity of different modes of consciousness rather than assign an absolute primacy and validity to that mode with which we are familiar. The simple dichotomy of receptive and action modes is undoubtably not a complete inventory of the options available to the human organism. Whether or not we are successful in adopting a variety of appropriate modes of consciousness may well depend on factors with which psychoanalysis is very familiar: defenses against the unknown, against relinquishing conscious control, against the blurring or loss of self boundaries. Perhaps the first step in awarding ourselves new options is to make them legitimate. The limits of what is thinkable tend to be prescribed by the assumptions that permeate a culture. In our own culture mystical means unreal or "kooky," altered states of consciousness are considered "regressive" or pathological, "spiritual" wishes and intuitions are labeled "omnipotent." There are instances where these cultural assumptions are justified but the area encompassed by unusual experiences is much larger than that allotted by such pejorative categories. I hope I have been able to indicate how different states of consciousness can be viewed as organismic modes that may have an important reality-based function necessary for our growth, our vitality, and our survival as a species. Instead of "regression" or "unrealistic" or "autistic," we might better term our organismic options "alternate modes" and be receptive to what they have to teach us.

This study was supported by research grant MH 16793-02 from the Public Health Service and by the Department of Psychiatry, University of Colorado Medical Center.

Drs. I. Charles Kaufman, David Metcalf, and Robert Emde advised in the preparation of this manuscript.

## References

1. Piaget J: *The Construction of Reality in the Child.* New York, Basic Books Inc Publishers, 1954.
2. Buber M: *I and Thou.* New York, Charles Scribner's Sons, 1958.
3. Poetzl O, et al: Preconscious stimulation in dreams, associations, and images. *Psychol Issues* 2:1-18, 1960.
4. Silverman J: Variations in cognitive control and psychophysiological defense in the schizophrenias. *Psychosom Med* 29:225-251, 1967.
5. Silverman J: A paradigm for the study of altered states of consciousness. *Brit J Psychiat* 114:1201-1218, 1968.
6. Silverman J, Berg P, Kantor R: Some perceptual correlates of institutionalization. *Nerv Ment Dis* 141:656-657, 1965.
7. Gaffron M: Some new dimensions in the phenomenal analysis of visual experience. *J Personality* 24:285-307, 1956.
8. Shapiro D: *Neurotic Styles.* New York, Basic Book Inc Publishers, 1965.
9. Schultz J, Luthe W: *Autogenic Training: A Psychophysiologic Approach in Psychotherapy.* New York, Grune & Stratton Inc, 1959.
10. Kleinsorge H, Klumbies G: *Technique of Relaxation.* Bristol, England, John Wright & Sons Ltd, 1964.
11. Deikman AJ: Experimental meditation. *J Nerv Ment Dis* 136:329-343, 1963.
12. Deikman AJ: Implications of experimentally induced contemplative meditation. *J Nerv Ment Dis* 142:101-116, 1966.
13. Bagchi B, Wenger M: Electrophysiological correlates of some Yogi exercises. *Electroenceph Clin Neurophysiol* 7:132-149, 1957.
14. Akishige Y (ed): Psychological studies on Zen. *Kyushu Psychological Studies* 5:1-280, 1968.
15. Wallace RK: The physiological effects of transcendental meditation. *Science* 167:1751-1754, 1970.
16. Suzuki S: Lecture given at Zen Mountain Center, July 1968. *Wind Bell* 7:28, 1968.
17. Bowers MB, Freedman DX: Psychedelic experiences in acute psychoses. *Arch Gen Psychiat* 15:240-248, 1966.
18. Bowers MB: Pathogenesis of acute schizophrenic psychosis. *Arch Gen Psychiat* 19:348-355, 1968.
19. Mednick SA, Schulsinger F: Factors related to breakdown in children at high risk for schizophrenia, in

Roff M, Ricks DF (eds): *Life History Research in Psychopathology*. Minneapolis, University of Minnesota Press, 1970, pp 87-88.

20. Deikman AJ: De-automatization and the mystic experience. *Psychiatry* 29:324-338, 1966.

21. Masters REL, Houston J: *The Varieties of Psychedelic Experience*. New York, Dell Publishing Co Inc, 1967.

22. Harman W, et al: Psychedelic agents in creative problem solving: A pilot study, in Tart C (ed): *Altered States of Consciousness*. New York, John Wiley & Sons Inc, 1969, pp 445-461.

23. Lindsley D: Electroencephalography, in Hunt J McV (ed): *Personality and the Behavior Disorders*. New York, Ronald Press Co, 1944, pp 1081-1083.

24. Venables PH: Input dysfunction in schizophrenia, in Maher B (ed): *Progress in Experimental Personality Research*. New York, Academic Press Inc, 1964, p 41.

25. Kennard M: The EEG in schizophrenia, in Wilson W (ed): *Applications of Electroencephalography in Psychiatry*. Durham, NC, Duke University Press, 1965, pp 168-184.

26. Whatmore G: Tension factors in schizophrenia and depression, in Jacobson E (ed): *Tension in Medicine*. Springfield, Ill, Charles C Thomas Publisher, 1967.

27. Salamon I, Post J: Alpha blocking and schizophrenia. *Arch Gen Psychiat* 13:367-374, 1965.

28. Green EE, Green AM, Walters ED: Voluntary control of internal states: Psychological and physiological. *Psychologia* 12:107, 1970.

29. Ullman M, Krippner S: A laboratory approach to the nocturnal dimension of paranormal experience: Report of a confirmatory study using the REM monitoring technique. *Biol Psychiat* 1:259-270, 1969.

30. Erikson E: *Childhood and Society*. New York, WW Norton & Co Inc Publishers, 1950, p 230.

31. Laski M: *Ecstasy*. London, Cresset Press Ltd, 1961, pp 145-153.

32. LeShan L: Physicists and mystics: Similarities in world view. *J Transpersonal Psychology*, fall, pp 1-20, 1969.

# The Esoteric and Modern 5
## Psychologies of Awareness

Robert E. Ornstein

**T**hese natural questions arise:

Why do these disciplines seem to share the common aim of "turning off" ordinary awareness of the external world for a short period of time?

What is the experience of meditators after that of "darkness"?

What are the general effects of the practice of meditation on awareness?

What is the relationship of the "turning-off" form of meditation to the "opening-up" form?

With the viewpoint adopted in this essay, we may be able to provide appropriate answers to these questions.

If we are to determine the aftereffects of concentrative meditation on awareness, it would be useful to review some aspects of the psychology and physiology of consciousness. Though we should not expect that the practice of meditation will necessarily change every aspect of ordinary consciousness, we may be able to determine more clearly the effect and aftereffect of meditation in terms of our knowledge of the psychology and physiology of consciousness.

Contemporary psychology provides several different viewpoints from which to characterize awareness. Some are completely independent of one another, some are complementary, some intersect.

We normally consider that the single function of our sensory systems is to gather information about the world: we see with our eyes, we hear with our ears. Gathering information is certainly a major function of sensation, but sensory systems also act in just the opposite way. Our ordinary awareness of the world is selective and is restricted by the characteristics of sensory systems. Many philosophers have stressed a similar view, but only recently has precise physiological evidence been available. Huxley and Broad have elaborated on Bergson's general view of the mind as a "reducing valve." In *The Doors of Perception and Heaven and Hell*, Huxley quotes Dr. D. C. Broad, the eminent Cambridge philosopher:

> The function of the brain and nervous system is to protect us from being overwhelmed and confused by this mass of largely use-. less and irrelevant knowledge, by shutting out most of what we should otherwise perceive and remember at any given moment, leaving only that very small and special selection that is likely to be practically useful.

And then Huxley comments:

> According to such theory each one of us is potentially Mind at Large. But insofar as we are animals our business is at all costs to survive. To make biological survival possible, Mind at Large has to be funneled through the reducing valve of the brain and nervous system. What comes out at the other end is a measly trickle of the kind of consciousness which will help us to stay alive on the surface of this particular planet. To formulate and express the contents of this reduced awareness man has invented and endlessly elaborated those symbol-systems and implicit philosophies that we call languages. Every individual is at once the beneficiary and the victim of the linguistic tradition into which he has been born— the beneficiary inasmuch as language gives access to the accumulated records of other people's experience, the victim insofar as it confirms him in the belief that reduced awareness is the only awareness and as it bedevils his sense of reality, so that he is all too apt to take his concepts for data, his words for actual things. That which, in the language of religion, is called "this world" is

the universe of reduced awareness expressed, and, as it were, petrified by language. The various "other worlds" with which human beings erratically make contact, are so many elements in the totality of awareness belonging to Mind at Large. Most people most of the time know only what comes through the reducing valve and is consecrated as genuinely real by their local language. Certain persons, however, seem to be born with a kind of bypass that circumvents the reducing valve. In others temporary bypasses may be acquired either spontaneously or as the result of deliberate "spiritual exercises" or through hypnosis or by means of drugs. Through these permanent or temporary bypasses there flows, not indeed the perception of everything that is happening everywhere in the universe (for the bypass does not abolish the reducing valve which still excludes the total content of Mind at Large), but something more than, and above all something different from, the carefully selected, utilitarian material which our narrow individual minds regard as a complete, or at least sufficient, picture of reality.[1]

Huxley writes more elegantly and less quantitatively than do most researchers and theorists in the fields of psychology and physiology, but much modern work in these disciplines tends to support the same general view that ordinary awareness is a personal construction. If awareness is a construction and not a "registration" of the external world, then by altering the nature of the construction process our awareness can be changed.

The normal view outside of the philosophical tradition, psychology, and the esoteric disciplines is that we experience *what exists*, that the external world is completely and perfectly reflected in our subjective experience. This idea is quite impossible to maintain even at the simplest level if we consider the many different forms of energy that impinge upon us at any moment. Sounds, electricity, light waves, magnetism, smells, chemical and electrical impulses within ourselves, thoughts, internal muscular sensations, all constantly bombard us. An appropriate question on the nature of our "ordinary" consciousness should be one that reflects a view quite different from the common one. How do we ever achieve a stable consciousness in the face of all this fantastic amount of stimulation?

There are two major ways in which we "make sense" out of the world. First, we use our sensory systems to discard and to simplify the incoming information, allowing only a few of the possible dimensions of sensation into our awareness. Second, we further sort the amount of information that does come in along a very limited number of dimensions, out of which we construct our awareness. These dimensions have been called in psychology "unconscious inferences," "personal constructs," "category systems," "efferent readinesses," or "transactions," depending on the writer's style and his level of analysis.

Quite obviously, each individual receptor is equipped physiologically to receive information only within certain limits. We wouldn't expect our eyes, for instance, to respond to the low bass note of an organ, or our ears to the taste of noodles. The eyes are "tuned" by their physiological structure to receive only a certain limited frequency range of stimulation and to send messages to the brain when energy in the appropriate frequency range reaches them—and so with the ears, the tongue, etc. That sensory receptors function to reduce the incoming information can be better understood if we study animals who are lower on the phylogenetic continuum and whose receptors discard even more information than do our own. It is difficult, otherwise, to conceive of the amount of stimulation to which we ourselves do not respond.

Perhaps the most cogent illustration of this point has been in the study of the visual system of the frog. The eye of the frog was studied by Lettvin, Maturana, McCulloch, and Pitts at the Massachusetts Institute of Technology. They were interested, essentially, in the same point made by Huxley, that sensory systems serve mainly for data *reduction*.[2]

They devised an experiment in which visual stimulation could be offered to one of the eyes of an immobilized frog. The frog was seated so that its eye was at the center of a hemisphere with a radius of seven inches. On the inner surface of this hemisphere small objects could be placed in different positions by means of magnets or moved around in space. The investigators implanted micro-electrodes into the frog's optic nerve to measure, as they called it, "what the frog's eye tells the frog's brain"—the electrical impulses sent to the brain by the eye. Since the frog's eye is somewhat similar to our own, these investigators hoped that electrical recording from the optic nerve would show the different kinds of "messages" that the eye sends to the brain. They studied the relationship of the evoked patterns of electrical activity to the different objects displayed on the hemisphere. There are thousands, millions, of different visual patterns that one could present to a frog—colors, shapes, movements, in various combinations, the almost infinite richness of the visual world of which we are normally aware. However, in presenting a large number of different objects, colors, movements, to the frog, a remarkable phenomenon was observed: from all the different kinds of stimulation presented only four different kinds of "messages" were sent from the retina to the brain. In other words, no matter the complexity and subtle differences in the environment, the frog's eye is "wired up" to send only this extremely limited number of different messages. The frog's eye presumably evolved to discard the remainder of the information available. The structure of its eye limits the frog's awareness to only four different kinds of visual activity. Lettvin and the others termed the four related systems: sustained contrast detectors; moving edge detectors; net dimming detectors; and net convexity detectors.

The first provides the general outline of the environment; the second seems to enhance response to sudden moving shadows, like a bird of prey; the third responds to a sudden decrease in light, as when a large enemy is attacking. These are systems that have presumably evolved to abstract information relevant to survival and to discard the rest, in the manner described by Huxley.

The fourth type of "message," conveyed by the net convexity detectors, is the most obviously related to survival and the most interesting of all. The net convexity detectors do not respond to any general change in light or to contrast; they respond only when small dark objects come into the field of vision, when these objects move at a closer distance, wriggling in front of the eye. It is quite clear, then, how the frog gets its food, how it can see flying bugs in front of it even with its limited visual system. The frog has evolved its own subsystem, which is wired up to ignore all other information except that of bugs flying around close to it—a very specialized "bug-perceiving" subsystem.

So, out of the complexity and richness of the information presented to the eye, the frog extracts only images with four dimensions. Higher-level animals exhibit similarities to this kind of process but on a much more complicated level. This type of dimensional analysis has been extended to cats and monkeys by David Hubel and Torsten Weisel at Harvard University and by many other investigators, who have determined that different cells in the brain respond to different types of stimulation. They found that certain cells detect edges and corners, others respond to movement on the retina, etc. Although vision has been the sensory system generally studied, since it is much easier to record from and much easier to specify what the dimension is, one would also expect that other sensory modalities would show the same kinds of relationships.

Sensory systems by "design" reduce the amount of useless and irrelevant information. We can then say that the function of our receptors and sensory systems is not only to gather information but to *select* and discard it.

If we consider more and more complicated organisms, their capacity to "retune" their sensory systems becomes greater. If the visual world of a goldfish is turned upside down by surgically inverting its eyes, it never learns to adjust to the new situation, swimming continuously in a circle until death, or until a kind surgeon reorients its eyes. If the visual field of a human is turned around by wearing inverting lenses, he can, in a few weeks, perform actions as complicated as riding a bicycle through town. To make use of the familiar machine analogies, the sensory systems of some animals are like permanently wired-up simple machines. In a mousetrap or a pencil sharpener or even in a telephone or an automobile, a change in one part throws everything else out of adjustment, since it has no built-in capacity for self-alteration. As we consider more complicated animals, more and more advanced all the way up to man, their nervous systems seem to be more computer-like—machines, to be sure but ones that can alter the relationship between input and performance by a change in the "program." The higher mammals can be regarded as machines that are capable of "retuning" themselves in accordance with alterations in the external environment. This is not to say that there are no limits to their performance. Even the most sophisticated current computer has its physical limitations. No matter how the computer alters its own programs, it will never learn to fly. But it can alter itself within the limits of its own structure, as we can.

We can easily demonstrate this computer-like, higher-level selectivity and tuning. At a party or at a place where several people are talking at the same time, we close our eyes and listen to just one person speaking, then tune him out and listen to another person. We are able to do this, to listen to one person's speech and then suppress it as it comes into our ears and hear another person's speech that we have previously ignored. It is very easy to do. We shouldn't really be surprised since we tune ourselves continuously to suit our needs and expectations, but we are not usually aware of it. When we perspire during the summer we like the taste of foods that are more salty than usual. We don't think consciously that we need salt and we should take more salt in our foods; we *simply like* foods that at other times we would consider quite oversalted. The character in the middle of Figure 2 can be seen either as a number or as a letter depending upon the context, which governs how we tune ourselves.

Some examples from our everyday existence show how we become more sensitive to portions of our environment when we are in need. When we are hungry we see more restaurants, see more food, smell more aromas than when we are not. When we

*Figure 2*

are awaiting someone we immediately notice anyone who resembles the other person, in his hair color, general appearance,
clothes, or because he is coming out of the door through which
we expect the person to arrive. When we are interested in the
ópposite sex, we perceive them differently than when we are not.
When after a meal our need for food has diminished, so does the
attractiveness of food. We are able continuously to reprogram
and reconstruct our awareness, based, at least in part, on our intent.

Many contemporary psychologists have investigated this "tune-
ability." Some have made use of a "tachistoscope," a visual display device that allows figures, objects, pictures, to be presented
for short and measurable periods of time. One interesting series
of experiments based on the tachistoscope demonstrated that we
recognize familiar objects or words with less time exposure than
unfamiliar ones. Our past experiences can tune input processing
so that we can construct an image based on a small amount of
input information. A coherent sentence, for instance, is much
more easy to recognize and to remember than just a random combination of words. Again, our past experience "tunes" us to have
some idea of what should follow what, and we need much less
information to construct an image. Jerome Bruner calls this
"going beyond the information given."[3]

A major way in which we create our awareness is by tuning

out the constancies in our environment. While we are learning a new skill, like skiing, all the complex adjustments and motor movements are somewhat painfully in our awareness. As we progress, as skill becomes "automatic," the movements no longer enter consciousness. Compare the first time you tried to drive a car, especially one with a gear shift, with how it feels to drive a car now, after you've learned. When we drive to work the first time, everything appears quite new and interesting—a red house, a big tree, the road itself—but gradually, as we drive the same route over and over, we "get used" to everything on the way. We stop "seeing" the trees, the bridges, the corners, etc. We become "automatic" in our response to them. When we enter a room and a fan is turning, creating a buzzing sound, we are aware of it for the first few moments and then the sound seems to go out of awareness.

Many of the producers of the objects we buy take into account that we constantly need new stimulation, and that we adapt to and tune out the old. When we buy a new phonograph record, we play it over and over again for a period, then leave it on the shelf unplayed. We get bored, the record no longer seems "new"; it is out of our awareness—on "automatic.". Most of the Market products are periodically changed slightly (automobiles, for instance), so that we begin to "see" them again, and presumably buy them.

In psychology and physiology, the phenomenon we have described is termed "habituation." The "response" in this case is one of the physiological components of the "orienting reaction" to new stimuli, the reaction that involves our registering of input. The physiological indicators of such reaction include EEG, heart rate, and skin resistance. Suppose we measure the resistance of the skin, for example, and repeat a click every five seconds. The first tone will cause a sharp drop in skin resistance. There will be less skin resistance change caused by the second tone, still less by the third, until, depending on the parameters of the particular experiment, the skin resistance no longer drops with each click.

The response of the skin to this stimulus has been "habituated." When, after hearing for a while the sound of a clock ticking, we then turn the sound off, we no longer show the "orienting" or registering reaction. This does not merely involve a simple process of raising the threshold for stimuli entering into awareness and thus tuning the click out. Our computer is capable of a more sophisticated selective tuning. It is true that if we substitute a louder click, we will begin to hear it again. And if we substitute a *softer* one, the orienting reaction also returns and we will hear it again. If we change the interval between the appearances of the tone—if it appears a little bit later than we expect, or a little bit sooner, even slightly—the tone returns to our awareness, and the orienting reaction reappears.

Karl Pribram has pointed out another example of this phenomenon, which he called the "Bowery El" effect. In New York City an elevated railroad once ran along Third Avenue. At a certain time late each night a noisy train would pass through. The train line was torn down some time ago with some interesting aftereffects. People in the neighborhood called the police to report "something strange" occurring late at night—noises, thieves, burglars, etc. It was determined that these calls took place at around the time of the former late-night train. What these people were "hearing," of course, was the *absence* of the familiar noise of the train. We have a similar experience, although much simpler, when a noise that has been going on suddenly stops.[4]

If we look at the same object over and over again, we begin to look in the same way each time. We do this with the constancies of our world, our ordinary surroundings—the pictures in our house, the route we drive every day, etc. Charles Furst has studied the effect of repeated viewing of the same picture on the way we look at it.[5] He found that eye movements tend to become more and more stereotyped as the same visual stimulus is presented. When we see a new image our eyes tend to move in a new pattern around it, but as we see it again and again, like the rooms in our house, we tend to look in a fixed way at fixed portions of it and ignore or tune out the rest. The "Bowery El" effect, the "Furst" effect, and the more precise studies on habituation suggest that we tune out the recurrences of the world by making a "model" of the external world within our nervous system, and testing input against it.[6] We somehow can program and continuously revise or reprogram conception or models of the external world. If the input and our model agree, as they do most often with the constancies of the world, then the input stays out of consciousness. If there is any disagreement, if the new input is *even slightly* different, slower, softer, louder, a different form, color, or even if it is absent, we become aware of the particular input once again. This "programing" forms an additional reducing valve behind the fixed reducing valves of the senses.

Perhaps the most clear and striking trend in the psychology and physiology of perception in the past few years has been our increasing understanding of the interactive and constructive nature of our "ordinary" awareness. One of the leaders in this investigation, Jerome Bruner, has emphasized that perception involves acts of categorization.[7] As we become experienced in dealing with the world we attempt to make more and more consistent "sense" out of the mass of information arriving at our receptors. We develop stereotyped systems or categories for sorting the input that reaches us. The set of categories we develop is limited, much more limited than the richness of the input. Simple categories may be "straight," "red," or "animal." More complex ones may be "English," "rectilinear," or "in front of." In social situations categories may be personality traits. If we come to consider a person "aggressive," we then consistently tend to sort all his actions in terms of this particular category. Personality traits seem to exist mainly in the category system of the perceiver.[8]

Our previous experience with objects strengthens our category systems. We expect cars to make a certain noise, traffic lights to be a certain color, food to smell a certain way, and certain people to say certain things. But what we actually experience, according to Bruner and to others, is the *category* which is evoked by a particular stimulus, and *not* the occurrence in the external world.

Bruner and his associates conducted an extensive series of studies on the effects of category systems on awareness. In his review "On Perceptual Readiness," he suggests that "correct" perception is

> . . . not so much a matter of representation as it is a matter of what I shall call model-building. In learning to perceive we are learning the relations that exist between the properties of objects and events that we encounter and learning appropriate categories and category systems. *Learning to predict and project what goes with what.* A simple example illustrates the point. I present for tachistoscopic recognition two nonsense words, one a zero-order approximation to English, constructed according to Shannon's rule, and a four-order approximation, w-r-u-l-p-z-o-c and v-e-r-n-l-a-t, 500 ms of exposure one perceives correctly and in their place about 48 per cent of the letters in zero-order words. And about 93 per cent of the letters of the four-order words; . . . the difference in perception is a function of the fact that individuals learn the traditional probability mode, what goes with what in English writing."[9]

Bruner, Postman, and Rodrigues attempted to demonstrate the effects of our well-learned categories on the contents of awareness.[10] They used ordinary playing cards familiar to most people in our culture. Our past experience with playing cards evokes categories in which the colors and the forms of playing cards are "supposed" to fall. We expect shapes like ♣ and ♠ to be black and ♦ and ♥ to be red.

Subjects in this experiment looked at the cards one at a time. A few of the cards were "anomalous," "wrong" colors for their shapes—a red ace of spades, a black eight of diamonds, etc. Subjects tended not to see the miscolored cards as anomalous, thus "correcting" the image. They would call a red ace of spades an ace of hearts, for instance. Not until it was expressly pointed out to the subjects that the colors might not necessarily, in this situation, be those usually associated with the shapes were the anomalous cards seen for what they were. The import of these and others of Bruner's interesting demonstrations is that we expect certain correspondences of objects, colors, forms, to occur, and we tune ourselves to see them. Newspaper editors often note that numerous typographical errors go unnoticed. The reader does the "correcting" within himself, merely by selecting the category "correct English."

At about the time Bruner was studying the effects of categories, another group of psychologists, led by Adelbert Ames, was exploring a similar viewpoint on the nature of awareness. Ames characterized the nature of ordinary awareness as a "transaction" between the perceiver and the environment. In spite of the overflow of information available to our sense organs at any given time, *relevant* information is often lacking. We cannot, for instance, determine tri-dimensionality directly. We cannot tell whether a room is "really" rectangular or not, or whether a given chair is physically closer than others, since we do not possess a direct sense of distance. There are, however, perceptible dimensions usually associated with closeness of objects. If we assume constant size, an image that seems larger is closer to us. So if we are trying to determine closeness, we "bet" that the larger object is the closer. This is, again, not a conscious process of correction. We *directly experience* the larger object as closer. The Ames group set out to demonstrate the nature of the bet we make with the environment.[11]

By manipulating our "unconscious inference," as Helmbolz called it, we can become aware of the bets or, in Bruner's term, the "categories" that constitute our awareness. To give another example, normally when we see a line drawing of a room as in Figure 3, we bet that in a top view it would be shaped like Figure 4, a rectangle. But a rectangle is only one of the many possible forms that could be derived from the two-dimensional drawing. One side may not be at all parallel with the other. The top view might look like either of the drawings in Figure 5, or any of many other shapes. We bet that the room is rectangular because almost all the rooms in our experience are rectangular. But if the room is not in fact rectangular, our bet causes us to "see"

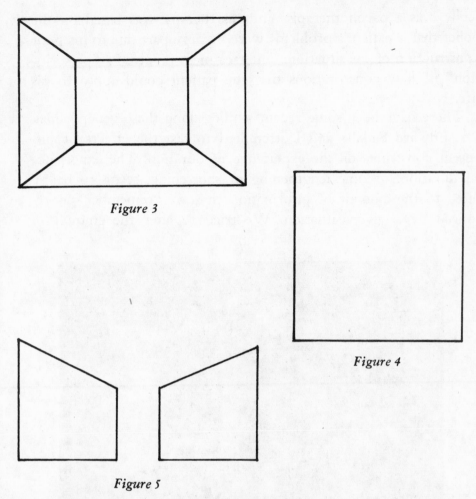

Figure 3

Figure 4

Figure 5

objects or people in the room in a very strange way. (See Figure 6.)

George Kelly pursued a similar line of investigation, concerned more with the psychology of ordinary experience and with clinical psychology. His conception was that each man *creates* his own world by means of his "personal constructs." He considered these "constructs" as scientific hypotheses, in that they are generated on the basis of our past experience and are applied to new experiences as long as they seem to work. So, for Kelly, our experience of the world consists of our constructs, as it consists of categories for Bruner and of transactions for the Ames group.

Kelly was a psychotherapist and his therapy was based on the belief that a patient's problems were in large part due to his poor construction of the situation. The treatment involved a "prescription" of new constructions that the patient could apply to his life.[12]

There have been some recent studies along these general lines. Dr. Edward Sadalla and I attempted to test the effects of different constructs on the experience of duration. The experience of duration, of time lengthening or shortening, seems to be related to the amount of information that we "remember" as required by a given situation. We tried to alter the amount of

*Figure 6.* The distorted room

information that a person would assume to be present in a constant situation. We made a film of a modern dancer performing several movements in a series. These movements were rather abstract to most people except modern dancers, and the interpretation could be easily altered. We trained one group of people to code the dance into two segments or constructs, another to code six segments, and a third, eleven segments. Those who were trained to code eleven segments (occurrences) perceived the dance as much longer than those who coded six, who in turn experienced the dance as longer than those who coded two.[13]

In a later study, Sadalla has shown that training to code different constructions has a basic effect on the recognition of various individual components of the dance.[14] Albert Hastorf and Hadley Cantril of the Ames group studied an even more complex effect. It is clear that we can tune ourselves on the basis of our needs and on the basis of our conception of past experience, and even on the basis of our expectations of future occurrences. Hastorf and Cantril demonstrated that people "tune" their perception on the basis of a quite complex expectation—by being "for" a team in a football game, for instance. The perception of the same events (a play in a football game, a verbal interchange) can be quite different in different people, depending upon these very general biasing factors, which can completely change the nature of the experience of a given series of events.

Since we can tune ourselves on the basis of our category systems, there must be physiological mechanisms that allow us to tune our awareness. Pribram and Spinelli have set out to demonstrate an analogue of this process on the physiological level.[15] They recorded from cells in the frontal cortex of the brain while stimulating other areas, and showed that the pattern of the receptive fields to external stimuli can be altered by the brain. The way in which stimuli are received, even as far out as on the retina itself, is "reprogrammable" on a moment-to-moment basis, and this can be demonstrated physiologically. These and other experiments demonstrate that the output system of the brain (efference) has an effect on the input (afference), the brain "selecting its input."

The investigation of the active role of the brain's output in determining the contents of awareness has been a recent major trend in the psychophysiology of perception. The work of Bruner, of the transactionists, and of Kelly demonstrate this active role on a psychological level; that of Pribram and Spinelli on the physiological. Some investigators have been explicitly concerned with the relationship between the input processing and the output systems of the brain in determining awareness. One test that we can try ourselves is that of closing one eye and pushing the other eye with a finger to a side. The visual world seems to "jump" a bit, it seems discontinuous. But if we make an eye movement in the usual manner over the same space, the world doesn't seem to jump. This difference indicates that in constructing our awareness we must also take our own movements into account and correlate them with the changes in input. If we didn't have a record somewhere of our efference, in this case our eye movements, the visual world would be constantly jumping around.

Some have gone so far as to maintain that consciousness depends *solely* upon the output of the brain, regardless of which input keys off a given output. Roger Sperry emphasized this point,[16] and after him Taylor and Festinger have provided some experimental demonstrations of this idea. Their statement that awareness depends solely on the output regardless of the input is not at all inconsistent with Bruner's contention that the category activated will determine awareness. In one case, if one is "ready" to see a black ace of spades or a red ace of hearts when a red ace of spades is shown, one will see one of the two choices one has set for himself. On the other hand, if one is "ready" to make a straight eye movement in response to a curved line, one will see the curved line as straight.

We ordinarily speak of "seeing an image" on the retina of our eyes. More properly, we do not really "see" with our eyes but, rather, with the help of our eyes. The eyes and other sense organs should be considered information selection systems. We can trick the eye, for instance, in several ways. If we press on our eyelids with our eyes closed, we "see" a white light, and yet there is no physical light energy present. What we have done is to cause the cells in the retina to fire by pressure instead of by their usual source of stimulation, light energy. The cells in the retina fire and send signals up to the brain. Messages from the retina are interpreted as light by the brain, no matter how the message was brought about, and so we are tricked into "seeing." There are times when we do not even need our eyes to "see"—for instance, when we dream at night, or in the case of hallucinations, there is no light energy reaching our eyes.

Wilder Penfield, a Canadian neurosurgeon, demonstrated the same point.[17] He performed brain surgery for patients with epilepsy and, as part of this procedure, electrically stimulated various areas of the brain. His patients would often report conscious experiences without any input at all. In addition, stimulation of the visual cortex usually leads to the experience of vision. We can understand, then, that seeing is not a process which takes place *in* our eyes but, rather, *with the help* of our eyes. It is a process that occurs in the brain and is determined by the category and output systems of the brain. Vision is a process that is fed only by the input that comes through our eyes, and our awareness is constructed from this input and from our past experience.[18]

Our eyes are also constantly in motion, in large eye movements (saccades) as well as in eye tremors (nystagmus). We blink our eyes every second, move our eyes around, move our heads, our bodies, and we follow moving objects. The view of an object is never constant, and the very receptive fields on the eyes are changing all the time. Yet our visual world remains very stable. We can walk around a horse, for instance, and although our view is constantly changing—we sometimes see the tail, sometimes the back, a side view, a three-quarter view, a straight front view—we always see the same horse. If we "saw" an "image" on our retina, the visual world would be different each second. We must then *construct* our awareness from the selected input sorted into categories and in this way achieve some stability of our awareness out of the rich and continuously changing flow of information reaching our receptors.

We might briefly review some of these general characteristics of our awareness. Our senses receive information from the external world but, for the most part, are built to discard much of the continuously changing stimulation that reaches them. We

also possess the ability to restrict further and modify the information that reaches awareness, by "reprograming." The brain
selects and modifies input. We build "models" or representations
of the world based on our past experience. We can, therefore,
tune our awareness on the basis of past experience, expectation,
and needs. We use this ability to tune out the constancies of
the world, the clock ticking, the route over which we normally
drive, our living room, an old phonograph record. Our experience is therefore an interactive process between the external
world and the continuously revised models of our categories. We
can select input, tune ourselves to relevant input, categorize,
and finally construct our awareness from these and from our
past experiences, our associations, thoughts, and emotional state.

Similar analyses of normal awareness appear in literature. Lawrence Durrell's four novels of the *Alexandria Quartet* investigate
the interactive nature of awareness. Durrell explores the same
series of events as they appear to different people. For Durrell,
as for Kelly, it is not important what actually happens, but what,
rather, is construed to have happened. The world of Durrell's
novels reflects the richness and complexity of life itself.

The current work in American academic psychology provides
a useful means of understanding normal awareness as a constructive process. One dimension, though, that is lacking in the current
characterization is an analysis of the continuous flow of awareness. The writers cited provide a useful series of metaphors for
the frame-by-frame components of awareness, but this is a
segmented analysis. There is no doubt that at any instant our
awareness is a construction based on past experience, but a more
general characterization of the continuing nature of our awareness is needed. A more suitable metaphor was given by William
James in his *Principles of Psychology*. He considered awareness
a stream, continuously flowing, continuously changing direction. James said:

Consciousness then does not appear to itself chopped up in bits.
Such words as chain or train do not describe it fitly, as it presents

itself in the first instant. It is nothing joined, it flows, a river or a stream are the metaphors by which it is naturally described. In talking of it thereafter, let us call it the stream of thought, of consciousness, or of subjective life.[19]

Our thoughts are in constant change. Awareness shifts from one aspect of the stimuli surrounding us to another, to a thought of the past, to a bodily sensation, to a plan, to a change in external stimulation, back and forth. The stream carves its own new path continuously. James would have agree with the more recent and precise analysis that awareness is a simplification and a construction. He said:

> Looking back, then, over this review, we see that the mind is at every stage a theatre of simultaneous possibilities. Consciousness consists in the comparison of these with each other, the selection of some, and the suppression of others, of the rest by the reinforcing and inhibiting agency of attention. The highest and most celebrated mental products are filtered from the data chosen by the faculty next beneath, out of the mass offered by the faculty below that, which mass was in turn sifted from a still larger amount of yet simpler material, and so on. The mind, in short, works on the data it received much as a sculptor works on his block of stone. In a sense, the statue stood there from eternity. But there were a thousand different ones beside it. The sculptor alone is to thank for having extricated this one from the rest. Just so the world of each of us, however different our several views of it may be, all lay embedded in the primordial chaos of sensations, which gave the mere matter to the thought of all of us indifferently. We may, if we like, by our reasoning unwind things back to that black and jointless continuity of space and moving clouds of swarming atoms which science calls the only real world. But all the while the world we feel and live in will be that which our ancestors and we, by slowly cumulative strokes of choice, have extricated out of this, like sculptors, by simply rejecting certain portions of the given stuff. Other sculptors, other statues from the same stone! Other minds, other worlds, from the same monotonous and inexpressive chaos! My world is but one in a million, alike embedded and alike real to

those who may abstract them. How different must be the world in the consciousness of ants, cuttlefish or crab![20]

A similar characterization of awareness is offered by the Indian yogi, Vivikenanda. He more negatively compares ordinary awareness to a "drunken monkey." He calls up images of awareness moving from one random thought to another—thinking about hunger, thinking about the past, glimpsing an aspect of the present, thinking of the future, planning an action—continuously bouncing around like a monkey from one thing to another.

The esoteric traditions in general have characterized consciousness in terms similar to those of modern psychology. The Sufis are the clearest precursors of modern psychology's conceptions of awareness. Sufi teaching stories frequently focus on men who are too preoccupied to hear what is being said, or who misinterpret instructions because of their expectations, or who do not see what is in front of them, because of the limited nature of their constructs.[21] The Sufis emphasize the constantly changing biases that constitute our normal awareness. "What a piece of bread looks like depends on whether you are hungry," says a Sufi poet, Jallaudin Rumi. The Sufis quite explicitly consider the effects of our limited category system on awareness. Many of the Sufis' descriptions of awareness could have been a statement of Bruner's about category systems, or a summary by Lettvin of his research on the frog, e.g., "Offer a donkey a salad, and he will ask what kind of thistle it is." They emphasize that we can be aware of only that which we conceive to exist, and that which our senses will transmit to us.

The Sufi and other traditions contend that the selective and restricted nature of awareness is an obstacle to be overcome and that the process of meditation, among other exercises, is a way of turning down the restrictions that normally limit awareness. One specific aim in these traditions is the removal of the automaticity and selectivity of ordinary awareness. The Sufis characterize man's usual state as one of "deep sleep" or "blindness," as one of being concerned with the irrelevant dimensions of the world. Gurdjieff's image is that of man placing shock absorbers between himself and the world. "We must destroy our buffers, children have none, therefore we must become like little children."[22] In Indian thought, as we have seen, ordinary awareness is a "drunken monkey" living solely in his constructs—the world of "illusion." This same thought is the metaphorical meaning of the "fall" of man in the Christian tradition. All these metaphors, without their derogatory connotation, can be understood in terms of modern psychology as depicting our selective awareness, our model-building, our automaticity, our limited category systems.

An aim of meditation, and more generally of the disciplines involving meditation, is the removal of "blindness," or the illusion, and an "awakening" of "fresh" perception. Enlightenment or illumination are words often used for progress in these disciplines, for a breakthrough in the level of awareness—flooding a dark spot with light. The Indian tradition speaks of opening the third eye, seeing more, and from a new vantage point. *Satori,* the desired state in Zen, is considered an "awakening." The Sufis speak of growing a new organ of perception.

Reports of the experiences of practitioners of the disciplines of meditation indicate that a primary aftereffect of the concentrative meditation exercises is an "opening up" of awareness, a "deautomatization," as Deikman calls it, which may be considered as involving a reduction of the processing of input. Deikman's own subjects, who gazed at a blue vase for a half-hour at a time over a number of sessions, reported that the vase appeared "more vivid" and "more luminous."[23] Deikman quotes Augustine Poulain, who emphasized that concentrative meditation is a temporary process of withdrawal, a blank-out, in other terms, of awareness with the intent to become deautomatized or dishabituated.

It is the mysterious darkness wherein is contained the limitless Good. To such an extent are we admitted and absorbed into something that is one, simple, divine, and illuminable that we seem no longer distinguishable from it. . . . In this unity the feeling of multiplicity disappears. When afterwards these persons come to themselves again, they find themselves possessed of a more distinct knowledge of things, some luminous and more perfect than that of others.[24]

Some speak of seeing things "freshly" or as if for the first time. To William Blake, "if the doors of perception were cleansed, everything would appear to man as it is, infinite." Others, like Gurdjieff, use a loose metaphor and compare their experiences to that of a child who presumably has not yet developed many automatic ways of tuning out the world. In Zen, one speaks similarly of seeing something the five hundredth time in the same way one saw it the first time.

All of these descriptions are understandable and easily translatable into the more precise psychological terms of building a model of the environment and testing and selecting input against the model. When we see something for the five hundredth time we have developed a model for it and tune out the input.

These characterizations of consciousness represent a point of encounter between the concepts of contemporary psychology and the metaphors of the esoteric disciplines. We speak of man as controlling his input, building models, responding "automatically" to the external environment. The esoteric traditions refer to this process as man's lacking awareness of his surroundings and consider this "blindness" the barrier to his development. The practice of meditation, then, can be considered as an attempt to turn off conceptual activity temporarily, to shut off all input processing for a period of time, to get away for a while from the external environment.

A result of this "turning off" of our input selection systems is that, when we introduce the same sensory input later, we see it differently, "anew."

When we leave our normal surroundings and go on a vacation we usually return to find ourselves much more aware of the immediate environment. We play many of our old records, which we haven't "heard" in a while. We look anew at the plants in our garden, the paintings on our walls, our friends. Getting away and returning seems to have the same effect on awareness as presenting new stimuli.*

We can consider the process of meditation as similar to that of taking a vacation—leaving the situation, "turning off" our routine way of dealing with the external world for a period, later returning to find it "fresh," "new," "different," our awareness "deautomatized."

Contemporary psychology recognizes that we easily adapt to most anything new. New technology, the changes in our environment, quickly become an integral part of our lives, part of our model. The model-building process is specifically what is to be dismantled through the practice of meditation. In Zen, one is instructed to stop conceptualizing while remaining fully awake. In Yoga, the aim is to leave the "illusion"—to cease identifying the external world with our models.

The three major traditions that we've considered each speak of developing an awareness that allows every stimulus to enter into consciousness devoid of our normal selection process, devoid of normal tuning and normal input selection, model-building, and the normal category systems.

The same metaphor is used in many traditions to describe the desired state of awareness. The Sufi poet Omar Khayyám says: "I am a mirror and who looks at me, whatever good or bad he speaks, he speaks of himself." The contemporary Zen master, Suzuki Roshi says: "The perfect man employs his mind as a mirror, it grasps nothing, it refuses nothing, it receives but does not keep." Christ said in prayer: "A mirror I am to thee that perceivest me." The metaphor of consciousness as a mirror fits well with some of the psychologists' own metaphors. A mirror allows every input to enter equally, reflects each equally, and cannot be tuned to receive a special kind of input. It does not

* Cf. the phenomenon of "spontaneous recovery" in habituation.

add anything to the input and does not turn off repetitive stimuli; it does not focus on any particular aspect of input and retune back and forth, but continuously admits all inputs equally.

This metaphor leads to another consideration. Many of the traditions claim to allow men to experience the world *directly*. The Sufis speak of attaining an "objective consciousness," others of "cosmic consciousness," and the statement is often made that one can have *direct* perception of reality. Whether one can perceive "reality" directly is not yet a question for science, but some comment within the terms of psychology might be made. The ability to be a mirror, to be free of the normal restrictions, of the tuning, biasing, and filtering processes of awareness, may be part of what is indicated by "direct" perception. This state can perhaps be considered within psychology as a diminution of the interactive nature of awareness; a state in which we do not select, nor do we bet on the nature of the world, nor do we think of the past, nor do we compel awareness by random associations, nor do we think of the future, nor do we sort into restrictive categories, but a state in which all possible categories are held in awareness at once. It has been described also as living totally in the present; not thinking about the future or of the past; a state in which everything that is happening in the present moment enters into awareness.

There have been some studies of the state of awareness of practitioners in and after meditation. These studies have used the EEG to measure the response of the brain of meditators to the external stimulation.

When we enter a room and hear a clock ticking we ordinarily learn to tune it out fairly quickly. If we study this process physiologically, the normal orienting response to new stimulation would begin to disappear after a few moments and wouldn't reappear. We would have built a model to tune it out.[25] The response would have habituated. But if one's consciousness were like a mirror, then each time the clock ticked we would "reflect" the tick.

The Indian psychologists' studies on Yoga meditation showed this result. In testing the yogi's brain response to external stimuli, the current contention on the effects and aftereffects of meditation was confirmed. During the meditation and during the withdrawal there was no response in the yogi's brain to external stimuli. When the yogi was not meditating, repetition of the external stimulus showed no habituation, as it presumably would have occurred in other subjects.[26]

The Japanese neuropsychiatrists Kasumatsu and Hirai studied the habituation of the orienting response to a repeating click in ordinary people and in Zen masters. The subjects in this experiment sat in a soundproof room and listened to a click repeated each fifteen seconds while an EEG was being taken. The normal subjects showed the customary phenomenon of habituation. There was a decrease in the response of the brain's electrical activity to the click after the third or fourth click. After habituation, each time the click occurred there was no response in the brain of the subject: the click had been tuned out of awareness. When the Zen masters were exposed to this same repetitive click over a period of five minutes, they did not show the customary habituation but responded to the last click in the same way as they did to the first.[27] They did not seem therefore to make a "model" of the repetitive stimulation and tune it out.

There are important differences in intent in the particular forms of Zen and Yoga meditation, which would lead us to expect different kinds of responses to the external world during the meditation exercise and after. The early and beginning forms of Zen are similar to Yoga; the breath counting, the koan, etc., involve an attempt to restrict awareness to a single process. We remember that Rahula indicates that one will not be aware of the external world if one does the breath-counting meditation successfully. These exercises are similar to the use of the *mandala, mantra, mudra*, etc. in Yoga. In the more advanced forms of Zen in the Soto sect, once the breath-counting is mastered, the

second form of meditation exercises, shikan-taza, is practiced—
"just sitting." Yasutani Roshi describes this exercise as follows:

> Up to now you have been concentrating on following your
> breaths with your mind's eye, trying to experience vividly the in-
> haled breath as only inhaled breath and the exhaled breath as only
> exhaled breath. From now on I want you to practice shikan-taza,
> which I will shortly describe in detail. . . .
>
> *Shikan* means "nothing but" or "just," while *ta* means "to hit"
> and *za* "to sit." Hence shikan-taza is a practice in which the mind
> is intensely involved in just sitting. In this type of Za-Zen it is all
> too easy for the mind, which is not supported by such aids as
> counting the breath or by a koan, to become distracted. The cor-
> rect temper of mind therefore becomes doubly important. Now, in
> shikan-taza the mind must be unhurried yet at the same time firmly
> planted or massively composed, like Mount Fuji let us say. But it also
> must be alert, stretched, like a taut bowstring. So shikan-taza is a
> heightened state of concentrated awareness wherein one is neither
> tense nor hurried, and certainly never slack. It is the mind of some-
> body facing death. Let us imagine that you are engaged in a duel
> of swordsmanship of the kind that used to take place in ancient
> Japan. As you face your opponent, you are unceasingly watchful,
> set, ready. Were you to relax your vigilance even momentarily,
> you would be cut down instantly. A crowd gathers to see the fight.
> Since you are not blind you see them from the corner of your
> eye, and since you are not deaf you hear them. But not for an in-
> stant is your mind captured by these sense impressions.
>
> This state cannot be maintained for long—in fact, you ought not
> to do shikan-taza for more than half an hour at a sitting. After
> thirty minutes get up and walk around in kinhin [Zen moving
> meditation] and then resume your sitting. If you are truly doing
> shikan-taza, in half an hour you will be sweating, even in winter
> in an unheated room, because of the heat generated by this intense
> concentration. When you sit for too long, your mind loses its vigor,
> your body tires, and your efforts are less rewarding than if you
> had restricted your sitting to thirty-minute periods.[28]

We can then consider two basic types of meditation exercises
—both concerned with a common effect—those which "turn

off" input processing for a period of time to achieve an *after-effect* of "opening up" of awareness, and those which consist in the active practice of "opening up" during the period of the exercise.

To return for a moment to the studies of the response of Zen and Yoga meditators to external stimuli, we can expect dishabituation *during* the advanced form of Zen meditation—that is, a consistent response to a stimulus which continues—and a shutting down of awareness of external stimuli during Yoga meditation. When the yogin is not in meditation, we might expect no habituation to a repetitive stimulus (if he is advanced enough in his practice).

Active practice in opening up awareness is a part of all the traditions, but in Zen it is a specific meditation exercise. A less demanding Buddhist practice stems from one component of the Buddha's Eightfold Path and is usually termed "right-mindedness." It requires that one be "conscious" of everything one does, to attend very closely to ordinary activities, and to open up awareness to these activities while engaged in them. Rahula says:

> Another very important, practical and useful form of "meditation" (mental development) is to be aware and mindful of whatever you do, physically or verbally, during the daily routine of work in your life, private, public or professional. Whether you walk, stand, sit, lie down or sleep, whether you stretch or bend your limbs, whether you look around, whether you put on your clothes, whether you talk or keep silent, whether you eat or drink—even whether you answer the calls of nature—in these and other activities you should be fully aware and mindful of the act performed at the moment, that is to say, that you should live in the present moment, in the present action. This does not mean that you should not think of the past or the future at all. On the contrary, you should think of them in relation to the present moment, to the present action, when and where this is relevant. People do not generally live in their actions in the present moment. They live in the past or the future. Though they seem to be doing some-

thing now here, they live somewhere else in their thoughts, in their problems and worries, usually in the memories of the past or in desires and speculations about the future. Therefore, they do not live in nor do they enjoy what they do at the moment, so they are unhappy and discontented with the present moment with the work at hand. Naturally, they cannot give themselves fully to what they appear to be doing.[29]

Spiegelberg gives an example of a similar practice in the Tibetan tradition. The Tibetan "Stories of the 84 Magicians" exercises, analogous to those described by Rahula, deal for the most part with the daily occupation of the meditator.

> The street cleaner has to take his task of sweeping as the starting point for meditation. So, likewise, must the potter take his task of producing clay utensils on his potter's wheel and the cobbler, his handicrafts. Here, again, therefore, it is evident that one may do what he will so long as he is clearly aware of what he is doing. Every activity is of equal value as a basis for a dharana exercise.[30]

In Yoga, self-observation is called "the Witness." The attempt is to observe oneself as if one were another person. One tries to notice exactly what one is doing—to invest ordinary activtiy with attention. The witness does not judge action or initiate action. The witness simply observes.

In Zen, this practice is highly developed. Right-mindedness or attention to what one is doing can be a part of almost any activity that one performs, no matter how degrading. There is no action that cannot be used for the purposes of the alteration of one's consciousness. One simply need be mindful of what one is doing. One can be performing actions that are quite degrading to a Buddhist, such as butchering an animal, but simply by paying close attention to what one is doing, one's awareness can be developed.

In Sufism, at least in the version that is attributed to Gurdjieff, there are similar practices, one of which is called "self-remembering." As in Zen, no special constraints are put on action. There are no prohibitions as to what can be eaten or general rules of conduct. The attempt is simply to be aware of oneself. Gurdjieff's students are constantly instructed to "remember themselves" wherever they are, remember that they are present, and notice what they do. When one is "remembering oneself in Gurdjieff's terms one is considered to be "awake."[31]

A similar exercise attributed to Gurdjieff consists simply in maintaining continuous awareness on a part of one's body—an elbow, hand, leg. Another exercise of this tradition is to perform ordinary habitual actions slightly differently, such as putting shoes on in the opposite order, shaving the other side of the face first, eating with the left hand. These can be seen as attempts to return the habitual "automatic" actions into full awareness.

Recall the phenomenon of habituation. A slight change in the input is enough to "dishabituate" and to return the stimulus to awareness. Similarly, slightly altering our usual "automatic" behavior, such as tying shoes or driving cars, can return it again into awareness.

In Yoga itself there is a tradition called *Karma Yoga*. The attempt is to treat everyday activities as a sacrament and to give them full attention. This exercise performs a function similar to "right-mindedness" and "self-remembering," and is perhaps a less extreme version of *shikan-taza*.

Many schools within these traditions combine the two major awareness exercises devoting a half-hour or so twice a day to the "shutting-down" form of meditation and as much as possible of the remainder of the day to a form of self-observation.

We mentioned earlier that the other major practice which often accompanies both forms of meditation is that of a renunciation of or a non-attachment to external objects. There are several different types of these practices, involving either prohibitions on behavior or the cultivation of a psychological state that combines renunciation and non-attachment. In the Judeo-Christian tradition, these practices usually involve behavioral restrictions. For example, some churchgoers are required during Lent to abstain from eating meat. The usual result of this kind of practice is that awareness is focused on the forbidden object. Most people find themselves craving meat, thinking about it, devising substitutes (meatless meals, for instance), waiting until the period of prohibition is over.

But the practice of renunciation, according to the various esoteric traditions, is intended to create a psychological state of *cessation*, not enhancement, of desire, and it is not necessarily tied to any change in external behavior. Most of the traditions emphasize that merely abstaining in practice while desiring, planning to consume the object, is worthless—perhaps worse than not giving it up at all. Christ himself made this point, although his followers do not always seem to be mindful of it.

Renunciation is the process, it is said, of conquering desire, of not requiring or needing anything. The Indian practices emphasize the cultivation of a psychological state of non-attachment as well as prohibitions on actual behavior. Most yogis are vegetarian, chaste, and live in poverty. Often yogic practice involves a withdrawal from society and its "temptations" into an *ashram*, in which one lives as a monk on a simple diet. Christian monasteries also emphasize psychological non-attachment as well as the actual cessation of certain "impure" behavior—the vows of poverty, chastity, solitude—a separation from the culture in order to "purify" oneself.

In the Zen and Sufi traditions the emphasis is solely on the psychological state of non-attachment and not on prohibitions in actual practice. Both Zen and Sufism emphasize, as they do in the exercise of self-awareness, that one can do whatever one wants as long as one is not attached to it.

The difference between the Sufis and Zen on the one hand, and much of Yoga and Christian tradition on the other, is illustrated in some advice given to Rafael Lefort, who traveled to the Mideast in search of the teachers of Gurdjieff—the Sufis—and was asked:

> "Are you prepared to leave the world as you know it and live in a mountain retreat on a very basic diet?" I signified that I was.

"You see," he nodded his head regretfully, "you still feel that to find knowledge you must seek a solitary life away from impure things. This is a primitive attitude and one satisfactory for savages. . . . Can you comprehend the uselessness of abandoning the world for the sake of your selfish development?

"You may need a course," he went on," at a Sarmoun Centre, but that will not mean total abandonment of your mundane worldly activity provided you do not allow it, nay invite it, to corrupt you. If you have enough skill you can actually harness the negative forces to serve you . . . but you must have enough skill."[32]

Zen also points out that "worldly" activity can be a perfect vehicle for development as long as one is free from attachment. Worldly activity and pleasures are legitimate in Zen as long as one is not in their service. The Sufis admonition is: "Be *in* the world but not *of* the world." The attempt is to isolate the important aspect of renunciation, the psychological state of non-attachment, from the external behavior. This is illustrated by a student's experience with Gurdjieff, when she felt that she was a "slave" to her habit of cigarette smoking. Gurdjieff, who stressed that men were often the slaves of their habits, instructed her to give up smoking. On returning to him a year later, she told Gurdjieff triumphantly that she had given up smoking and was no longer a slave to her cigarette habit. Gurdjieff smiled and immediately offered her a very expensive Turkish cigarette, indicating that it was not her behavior but the fact that she had been slave to her cigarette habit that was important. Only when she no longer needed to smoke was it permissible to smoke again.[33] Gurdjieff himself kept a quite well-known larder stocked with delicacies from all parts of the world.

But why is non-attachment to "worldly" pleasures a major part of the meditative disciplines? One answer can be given in terms of our analysis of ordinary consciousness. Recall that normal consciousness is constructed from our past experience, our expectations, and our needs. When we are hungry we are likely to search out food, or to *create* food images or smells, or to en-

hance food images that are present, or to think about food. A
Sufi tale illustrates this general point:

> Two men were sitting in a cafe and a camel walked past.
> "What does that make you think of?" said one.
> "Food," said the other.
> "Since when are camels used for food?" said the first.
> "No, you see, everything makes me think of food."[34]

The meditative traditions consider that one major barrier to
the development of expanded awareness is that we continuously
tune out those portions of the external environment that do not
suit our needs at the moment. If we are hungry we would be
very unlikely to notice the river around us or the people whom
we see. We are concerned solely with food and construct our
world around food.

In its effect on awareness, the practice of non-attachment can
be considered as an additional way to remove the normal restrictions on input. If there are no desires, there is less of a
bias at any one moment to "tune" perception. Our awareness of
the external environment becomes less restricted, less of an
interaction, less solely a function of our desire at the moment,
and more like a mirror.

There is another function of non-attachment. If, for instance,
one *needs* nothing from another person or from the external
environment—prestige, sex, food, love—one can exist "for them"
as a mirror, as do Omar Khayyám, Suzuki Roshi, and Christ.
We sometimes reach this state when our needs are satisfied. We
all have observed that the world appears different when we are in
love or are a success.

It is also commonplace to observe, however, that the sensualist
is often the one who becomes the renunciant, a "worldly" man
who gives up all for his religion—a Thomas à Becket.

In many ways the aims of the disciplines of meditation—
total attention to the moment, "dishabituation," "extended"
awareness—are the same ones we seek in many of our "ordinary"

activities. We buy new products, new clothes, new records; we slightly change our surroundings to attempt to return them to awareness. Dangerous sports, for example, engage our awareness and bring us into the present moment in which we think of nothing else but the activity in which we are engaged. We arrange the conditions so that it is *absolutely necessary* for us to pay full attention to what is taking place at that moment. When we race a sports car or motorcycle, or ski or ride a toboggan down a slope, or sky-dive, anything less than complete awareness to the moment may lead to injury or to death. The necessity of opening up our awareness is perhaps one of the reasons people are willing to risk injury or even their lives in dangerous sports. A particularly good example is the sort of rock climbing that requires intense concentration over a prolonged period of time. Doug Robinson writes in *Ascent*, the journal of the Sierra Club:*

> . . . to take a familiar example, it would be hard to look at Van Gogh's "The Starry Night" without seeing the visionary quality in the way the artist sees the world. He has not painted anything that is not in the original scene, yet others would have trouble recognizing what he has depicted. The difference lies in the intensity of his perception, at the heart of his visionary experience, he is painting from a higher state of consciousness. Climbers too have their "starry nights." Consider the following from an account by Alan Steck of the Hummingbird Ridge Club on Mount Logan. "I turned for a moment and was completely lost in silent appraisal of the beautifully sensuous simplicity of windblown snow. The beauty of that moment, the form and motion of the blowing snow was such a powerful impression, and so wonderfully sufficient that the climber was lost in it. It is said to be only a moment and yet by virtue of total absorption he is lost in it and the winds of eternity blow through it!"

A second example comes from an account of the 7th day and the 8th day of the first ascent under trying conditions on El Capitan's Muir Wall. Yvon Chouinard relates, in the 1966 *American Alpine Journal*: ". . . with our more receptive senses we now ap-

* I would like to thank Dr. E. K. Sadalla for pointing this example out to me.

preciated everything around us. Each individual crystal in the granite stood out in bold relief. The varied shape of the clouds never ceased to attract our attention. For the first time we noticed tiny bugs that were all over the walls, so tiny they were barely noticeable. While belaying, I stared at one for fifteen minutes, watching him move and admiring his brilliant red color. How could one ever be bored with so many good things to see and feel? This unity with our joyous surroundings, this ultra penetrating perception gave us a feeling of contentment that we had not had for years."

In these passages the quality that makes up the climber's visionary experience are apparent: the overwhelming beauty of most ordinary objects—as clouds, granite, and snow—of his experience, the sense of the slowing down of time to the point of disappearing, and the "feeling of contentment" and an oceanic feeling of supreme sufficiency of the present, and while delicate in substance these feelings are still strong enough to intrude firmly into the middle of dangerous circumstances, and remain there temporarily superceding even apprehension and the drive for achievement."[35]

Much of Western art is similarly an attempt to "cleanse" perception, to return our awareness to things that are seen automatically. One critic considers the function of art to "make strange" ordinary objects, to allow us to see our usual surroundings as if they were "strange"—as if for the first time. The recent trend in Pop Art is an example. There is an important difference in the way we look at a Warhol sculpture of a Campbell's soup can in a gallery and at the same object at home. By presenting ordinary objects in a context that demands that we attend to them, we "see" them in a new way. We do not immediately call up our customary category of "soup can," in which we ignore everything but the particular label ("is it vegetable or noodle?"). We now "look" at the shape, the lettering, the way the light falls on the surface of the can. We are brought out of our ordinary responses of ignoring the object. Looking at a common object in a gallery is a means of deautomizing our awareness of it.

We could give many more examples from the fields of art, music, and literature. There are many essayists and poets who have written directly about meditative experiences and traditions; among them, William Blake, Herman Hesse, Aldous Huxley, T. S. Eliot; but it would be useful here to consider a writer whose work is quite different and who is not usually associated with this subject.

The sensualist Henry Miller would seem to share little with Huxley, Hesse, Eliot, the traditions of meditation, the rock climber, or the visual artist. But, in a volume of *The Rosy Crucifixion* (*Sexus*), Miller states the aim of his work and life in terms almost identical to those of the esoteric traditions, namely, that men are "blind" and have first to acquire "vision."

> . . . the world is not to be put in order: the world *is* order incarnate. It is for us to put ourselves in unison with this order, to know what is the world order and in contradistinction to the wishful thinking orders that we seek to impose on one another. The power which we long to possess in order to establish the good, the true and the beautiful would prove to be, if we could have it, but the means of destroying one another. It is fortunate that we are powerless. We have first to acquire vision, then discipline and forbearance until we have the humility to acknowledge a vision beyond our own, and until we have faith and trust in superior powers, the blind must lead the blind. Men who believe that work and brains will accomplish must ever be deceived by the quixotic and every unforeseen turn of events.[36]

In the *World of Sex*, Miller makes the point, which could have been made by a Zen monk, that any ordinary activity, if one is mindful (in the Zen sense), can lead to a breakthrough. He also recalls Spiegelberg's comments that "every hallucination, every unappeasable hatred, every amorous attachment provides a certain power of concentration to him who cherishes it and helps to direct the forces of his being to a similar goal."

Life moves on whether we act as cowards or heroes. Life has no other discipline to impose, if we could but realize it, but to accept life unquestioningly. Everything we shut our eyes to, everything we run away from, everything we deny, denigrate or despise, serves to defeat us in the end. What seems nasty, painful, evil can become a source of beauty, joy, and strength if faced with an open mind. Every moment is a golden one for him who has the vision to recognize it as such. Life is now, every moment, no matter if the world be full of death. Death triumphs only in the service of life.[37]

In "*Creative Death*" Miller writes:

Strange as it may seem today to say, the aim of life is to live, and to live is to be aware, joyously, drunkenly, divinely, serenely aware. In this state of godlike awareness one sings, and in this realm the world exists as poem, no why or wherefore, no direction, no goal, no striving, no revolving. Like the enigmatic Chinaman, one is rapt by the ever-changing spectacle of changing phenomenon; this is the sublime, the amoral state of the artist, he who lives only in the moment, the visionary moment of utter far-seeing lucidity. Such clear icy sanity that it seems like madness.* [38]

Although many of our endeavors are directed toward achiev-

---

* I was beginning to wonder whether the contention that much of our endeavors are directed to the same end as that of the disciplines of meditation is exaggerated. Perhaps I was forcing some of these into a mold. Then I happened to pick up two of the most popular magazines in this country, *Life* and *Look*, and read them at about the same time as this chapter was being prepared. In *Life* we read, in the introduction to a photographic essay; "Imprisoned in the narrowness of our human scale, we are blind to the vast reaches of reality. Mysteries lie all around us, even within us, waiting to be revealed by a new way of seeing." Then, in *Look* magazine: "Up, quick if you can it's long past time to do. You've stayed so long you've lost yourself and now exist cut off from all that is around you, from all of you that's human, you're civilized beyond your senses: out of touch, narcotized, mechanized, Westernized, with bleached out eyes that yearn for natural light. The intellects turn tyrant on us all and make our daily lives neatly laid-out, over-intellectualized, over-technological exercises in sinister lunacy. . . . We are severed from ourselves and alien to our sensibilities, fragmented, specialized, dissected, pidgeonholed into smothering." In popular music, a friend recalled the Beatles' song "Tomorrow Never Knows," which begins, "Turn off your mind, relax and float downstream,/it is not dying,/lay down all thoughts, surrender to the void/that you may see the meaning of within/it is shining."

ing a meditation-like state of awareness, these means are held to be inefficient by the esoteric traditions. If we actually do achieve states of total awareness to the moment by ordinary means, this achievement does not last for long, does not carry with it a permanence. Our success fades, our love ends, we must come down from the mountain.

Noting the common aim of many of our interests and that of the disciplines of meditation, another function of detachment becomes more clear. The practice can be seen as an attempt to separate the subjective state produced by sports, sex, love, music, art, etc., from that of its usual object, and to detach the effect—the resultant internal state—from the usual cause, the stimulus object. The person works then within himself to attempt to generate the internal state directly. "What need have I of an external woman when I have an internal woman," says a practitioner of *Tantra*. The "worldly" sensualist perhaps sees the same possibility—to achieve a result that is similar to what he seeks in sensual activity, but one more permanent and under his control. He then gives up the outward manifestations of what he is seeking. The process involves a detachment from the usual triggers to this state—sex, love, prestige, power, money, food, etc.—and an attempt to concentrate upon internal "centers," which are held to give rise to these and to "higher" experiences. The energy force is called *kundalini* in Yoga, and these centers termed *chakras* in Yoga and *lataif* in the Sufi tradition. There are some differences in the two systems but these two centers are for this consideration analogous.*[39]

In the terms of this essay, detachment and concentration on these internal centers can be considered as an attempt to stimulate internally the structures that are usually associated with the experiences of dishabituation, pleasure, etc. We can consider the process as learning to stimulate the "reward" circuits of the brain.

Physiologists working with animals have implanted electrodes

---

* This energy system is not at all understood in science. The exercises are almost always given a secret and little is ever written of them.

in those parts of the brain in which stimulation seems to serve as a reward, and they have had interesting results. In a situation where animals can continue the stimulation of these systems themselves, they will do so at the expense of everything else. Some actually worked to stimulate these circuits until they died, even though food and drink were available freely. They had no need of external stimulation because they could do it internally.[40]

The second function of renunciation and the concomitant concentration on various parts of the body can then be considered as a functional training technique in self-stimulation of the centers of the nervous system.[41]

These first two sections of this essay have covered a lot of ground, so it should be of some use to recall briefly some of their major points.

If we ignore our preconceptions about the function of meditation and overcome both attraction and repulsion toward the exotic and esoteric, it is clear that the practices of meditation can be analyzed in terms of modern psychology. The repetitive or concentrative form of meditation can be seen as an exercise in "turning off" awareness of the external environment, inducing a central state in the nervous system equivalent to that of no external stimulation. In the traditions we are considering, this state is known as the "void" or the "darkness." If restriction of awareness is accomplished by other means, such as that of a ganzfeld, there is a similar result—the "blank-out" of experience of the external environment.

The production of a state in which one is insulated from the external world has some consistent aftereffects on awareness. Many meditators report seeing the world "anew," "fresh," seeing everything "glowing," illuminated, enlightened. A metaphor used in most traditions for this state is that of a "mirror."

It is interesting to note the similarities between the esoteric and the modern psychologies of consciousness. Both stress that our awareness of the environment is a process of selection and categorization, that our sensory systems serve the purpose of discarding much of the information that reaches us, and that we finally construct our awareness from this heavily filtered input. The "shutting-down" form of meditation can be compared to taking a vacation. We often leave a situation to "get out of our rut." When we return we see things differently.

The meditation exercises can be seen as attempts to alter the selective and limited nature of our awareness, to change the habitual way in which we respond to the external world. In physiological terms it might involve a reduction in the efferent modification of input and in the "models" that we usually make of the external world.

Another form of these meditation exercises consists in the active practice of "opening-up" awareness. *Shikan-taza* in Zen is one of the most difficult of these exercises. Sufi, Zen, and Yoga followers emphasize the process of self-observation. In some of the traditions specific exercises are performed for the purpose of returning awareness to actions that usually occur "automatically," a practice analogous to "dishabituation."

The third major technique in these systems involves renunciation and detachment from "worldly" pleasures. Detachment can affect awareness by removing one of the components that serve to tune awareness: our needs and desires. By removing our needs with their biasing function, our awareness can be more like a mirror.

The second function of renunciation involves the consideration that many of our ordinary pursuits are attempts to reach a state similar to that produced by the practice of meditation. Dangerous sports, sex, food, art, etc., at their best moments, produce a state in which we exist just then, totally in the moment, devoid of our automatic way of responding. This has been termed a state of increased receptivity or expanded awareness.*

---

* Within psychology this state is not well defined as yet. It is hardly clear whether "being like a mirror" involves an actual increase in the amount of information that reaches awareness, or whether it involves a leveling of

The problem of reaching this state in the usual way, say the spokesmen of the disciplines of meditation, is that ordinary means are inefficient, that men usually concern themselves with irrelevant dimensions, that the subjective state desired is not often produced by the ordinary means themselves, and that, if produced, its aftereffects do not persist.

Detachment can be seen, then, as an attempt to reach a similar state *within* by separating the state itself from the stimuli that usually trigger it, and by the conjoint practice of concentrating on the parts of the nervous system that produce this experience. These exercises, the centers upon which one concentrates, the *chakra* and the *lataif* in the Yoga and Sufi traditions, can be considered as techniques for inducing a state in the nervous system similar to that which may be transiently produced by external means.

The attempt in these two chapters has been to begin the process of extracting the psychological aspects of these Eastern meditative disciplines. No attempt has been made to provide an airtight case sealed by relevant experiments at each point. But we may begin most usefully by the simple process of translating the metaphors of the esoteric traditions into those of contemporary psychology and physiology, and noting the overlap.

the normal filtering processes—letting no more information into awareness, but simply letting the same amount in with less bias. The only evidence on this question so far is that relating to the brain response of meditators to quite simple stimulation. It will be necessary to extend these studies to get a measure of the "channel capacity" within and across sensory modalities, before, during, and after meditation, and, perhaps, to follow practitioners longitudinally as they progress in meditation training.

# Notes

1. Aldous Huxley, *The Doors of Perception and Heaven and Hell* (New York: Harper & Row, 1954).
2. J. Y. Lettvin, H. R. Maturana, W. S. McCulloch, and W. H. Pitts, "What the Frog's Eye Tells the Frog's Brain," *Proceedings of the Institute of Radio Engineers,* 47 (1959): 1940-51.
3. Jerome Bruner, "On Perceptual Readiness," *Psychological Review,* 64 (1957): 123-52.
4. Karl H. Pribram, "The Neurophysiology of Remembering," *Scientific American,* January 1969, pp. 73-86.
5. Charles Furst, "Automatization of Visual Attention," *Perception and Psychophysics* (1971).
6. For a development of this idea, see Y. N. Sokolov, *Perception and the Conditioned Reflex* (London: Pergamon, 1960).
7. Bruner, *op. cit.*
8. See Walter Mischel, *Personality & Assessment* (New York: John Wiley & Sons, 1968).
9. Bruner, *op. cit.*
10. *Ibid.*
11. W. H. Ittleson and F. P. Kilpatrick, "Experiments in Perception," *Scientific American,* August 1951.
12. George Kelly, *The Psychology of Personal Constructs,* Vols. 1 and 2 (New York: Norton, 1955).
13. Robert E. Ornstein, *On the Experience of Time* (New York: Penguin Books, 1969).
14. E. K. Sadalla, (Ph.D. diss., Stanford University, 1970).
15. D. N. Spinelli and K. H. Pribram, "Changes in Visual Recovery Functions and Unit Activity Produced by Frontal and Temporal Cortex Stimulation," *Electroencephalography and Clinical Neurophysiology,* 22 (1967): 143-49.
16. Roger W. Sperry, "Neurology and the Mind-Brain Problem," *American Scientist,* 40 (1951): 291-312.
17. W. Penfield and L. Roberts, *Speech and Brain Mechanism* (Princeton University Press, 1959).
18. For current psychology's most sophisticated account on the "con-

structive" nature of awareness, see Ulric Neisser, *Cognitive Psychology* (New York: Appleton-Century-Crofts, 1967).

19. William James, *The Principles of Psychology* (New York: Dover Publications, 1950).

20. *Ibid*.

21. See Shah, *The Way of the Sufi, Caravan of Dreams*, and *The Exploits of the Incomparable Mulla Nasrudin*.

22. K. Walker, *A Study of Gurdjieff's Teachings* (London: Jonathan Cape, 1957).

23. Arthur Deikman, "Experimental Meditation," *Journal of Nervous and Mental Disease*, 136 (1963) 329-43. Reprinted in Tart, Supra, Ch. 2, note 4. Also, A. Deikman, "Implications of Experimentally Produced Contemplative Meditation," *Journal of Nervous and Mental Disease*, 142 (1966): 101-116.

24. Quoted in Deikman, "Deautomatization and the Mystic Experience."

25. Y. N. Sokolov, *Perception and the Conditioned Reflex* (New York: Macmillan Co., 1963).

26. Anand, Chhina, and Singh, *op. cit.*

27. Kasamatsu and Hirai, *op. cit.*

28. Quoted in Kapleau, *op. cit.*

29. Rahula, *op. cit.*

30. Spielberg, *op. cit.*

31. Walker, *op. cit.*

32. Rafael Lefort, *The Teachers of Gurdjieff* (London: Gollancz, 1966).

33. K. Hulme, *Undiscovered Country* (Boston: Atlantic–Little, Brown, 1966).

34. Shah, *The Way of the Sufi*.

35. Doug Robinson, "The Climber as Visionary," *Ascent, The Sierra Club Mountaineering Journal*, Vol. 64, No. 3, May 1969.

36 Henry Miller, *Sexus* (Paris: Obelisk Press, 1949); also, Lawrence Durrell, ed., *The Henry Miller Reader* (New York: New Directions, 1959).

37. Henry Miller, *The World of Sex*, rev. ed. (Paris: Olympia Press, 1957); also, Durrell, *op. cit.*

38. Henry Miller, "Creative Death: An Essay," *The Henry Miller Reader*, ed. Lawrence Durrell.

39. See Shah, *The Sufis.*

40. For a full discussion of the science of electrical brain stimulation, see Jose Delgado, *Physical Control of the Mind: Toward a Psychocivilized Society* (New York: Harper & Row, 1969).

41. For experiments related to these considerations, *see* W. Wyrwicka and M. B. Sterman, "Instrumental Conditioning of Sensorimotor Cortex EEG Spradles in the Walking Cat," *Physiology and Behavior*, 3, (1968): 703-707.

# A Cartography of the Ecstatic 6
## and Meditative States

### Roland Fischer

In this age so concerned with travel in outer as well as inner space, it is strange that, while we have detailed charts of the moon, we have no cartography of the varieties of human experience. In order to draft a map of inner space, I am ready to be your travel guide and take you on two voyages: one along the perception-hallucination continuum of increasing ergotropic (1) arousal, which includes creative, psychotic, and ecstatic experiences; and another along the perception-meditation continuum of increasing trophotropic (1) arousal, which encompasses the hypoaroused states of Zazen and Yoga samadhi.

Along the perception-hallucination continuum of increasing arousal of the sympathetic nervous system (ergotropic arousal), man—the self-referential system—perceptually-behaviorally (corti-

The author is professor of experimental psychiatry and associate professor of pharmacology at the Ohio State University College of Medicine, Columbus 43210. (Address after 1 January: Drug Treatment and Research Center, Veterans Administration Hospital, 50 Irving Street, NW, Washington, D.C. 20422.) This article is adapted from a paper presented at the AAAS symposium on "Mood, Behavior, and Drugs" in Chicago, Illinois, 28 December 1970, and from a seminar given on 20 January 1971 at the department of psychiatry, Johns Hopkins University, Baltimore, Maryland.

cally) interprets the change (drug-induced or "natural") in his subcortical activity as creative, psychotic, and ecstatic experiences (2). These states are marked by a gradual turning inward toward a mental dimension at the expense of the physical. The normal state of daily routine, our point of departure, is followed by an aroused, creative state, which can be characterized by an increase in both data content (a description of space) and rate of data processing ["flood of inner sensation" (3), or most intense time] (4). However, in the next aroused state on the continuum, the acute schizophrenic [or rather, "hyperphrenic" (5)] state, a further increase in data content may not be matched by a corresponding increase in the rate of data processing. While the creative state is conducive to the evolution of novel relations and new meaning, the psychotic "jammed computer" state interferes with the individual's creative interpretation of the activity of his central nervous system (CNS). At the peak of ecstatic rapture, the outside (physical) world "retreats to the fringe of consciousness" (6), and the individual reflects himself in his own "program." One can conceptualize the normal, creative, "hyperphrenic," and ecstatic states along the perception-hallucination continuum as the ledges of a homeostatic step function (7). While the creative person may travel freely between "normal" and creative states, the chronic schizophrenic patient is stranded in the "jammed computer" state. And the talented mystic, of course, does not need to go through every intermediate step to attain ecstasy.

The mutually exclusive relationship between the ergotropic and trophotropic systems (8) justifies a separate perception-meditation continuum of increasing trophotropic arousal (hypoarousal) that is continuous with, and to the right of, the perception-hallucination continuum (Fig. 1). The course of our second trip, therefore, will take us in the opposite direction, along the tranquil perception-meditation continuum, where man may symbolically interpret his gradually increasing trophotropic arousal as Zazen, and, ultimately, samadhi.

That the two continua in Fig. 1 represent two mutually exclusive states of arousal has been well documented by Hess (1) and Gellhorn (8, 9). The mutual exclusiveness of the ergotropic and trophotropic systems can also be illustrated by characteristic changes in the frequency of the small, involuntary, micronystagmoid movements of the eye. These rapid scanning movements (with a mean frequency of one per second and an amplitude of 5 to 10 minutes of arc) are regarded as a prerequisite for the fixation of an object in physical space-time (10). The frequency of saccadic movements is increased five- to eightfold in response to the ergotropic arousal induced by moderate doses of mescaline, psilocybin, or LSD (D-lysergic acid diethylamide) (10). This increase is also present without drugs in acute schizophrenics (11)

[that is, patients in a state of ergotropic arousal, the "alarm reaction" (12) stage of Selye's general adaptation syndrome (13)].

On the other hand, 0.9 gram of alcohol per kilogram of body weight, and even sleepiness and fatigue, decreases saccadic frequency (14); more precisely, 0.01 milligram of Valium (diazepam) per kilogram of body weight reduces the saccadic frequency by 9 degrees per second (15). Such a progressive decrease seems to be a characteristic feature of trophotropic arousal along the perception-meditation continuum. That the alpha rhythm appearing on the electroencephalogram (EEG) appears to be phase-locked to the onset of saccades (16) may also be of significance, since states of progressively greater trophotropic arousal along the perception-meditation continuum are characterized by EEG waves of progressively lower frequencies (measured in hertz) (17) (see Fig. 1, right). Moreover, since a complete arrest of saccadic frequency, [for example, by optical immobilization of the retinal image (18)] results in periodic fading, disintegration, and fragmented reconstruction of the image, we may postulate that reduced saccadic frequency may be linked with the Yogi's comment that, at the peak of a meditative experience, he can still see "objects," but they have no predicative properties (19).

## What Are Hallucinations and How Can They Be Measured?

The hallucinatory or waking-dream states along the perception-hallucination continuum can best be described as experiences of intense sensations that cannot be verified through voluntary motor activity. Note that such a

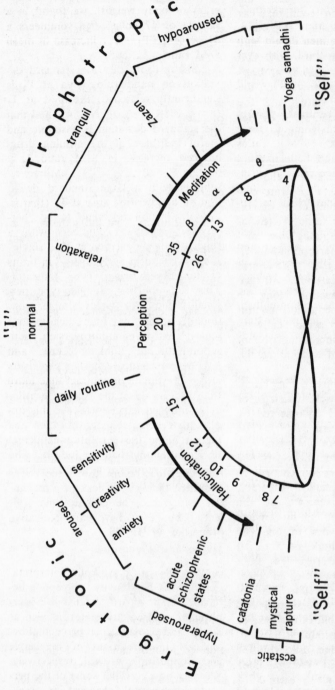

Fig. 1. Varieties of conscious states mapped on a perception-hallucination continuum of increasing ergotropic arousal (left) and a perception-meditation continuum of increasing trophotropic arousal (right). These levels of hyper- and hypoarousal are interpreted by man as normal, creative, psychotic, and ecstatic states (left) and Zazen and samadhi (right). The loop connecting ecstasy and samadhi represents the rebound from ecstasy to samadhi, which is observed in response to intense ergotropic excitation. The numbers 35 to 7 on the perception-hallucination continuum are Goldstein's coefficient of variation (46), specifying the decrease in variability of the EEG amplitude with increasing ergotropic arousal. The numbers 26 to 4 on the perception-meditation continuum, on the other hand, refer to those beta, alpha, and theta EEG waves (measured in hertz) that predominate during, but are not specific to, these states (17).

definition does not differentiate between dreams and hallucinations; for example, see the "Three Wise Men" (Fig. 2). Two of the three wise men dream with eyes closed, while the third, with eyes open, hallucinates the angel who carries all three away from the "real" world into a mental dimension.

We can describe verifiable perceptions, therefore, by assigning to them low sensory-to-motor (S/M) ratios (20), while nonverifiable hallucinations and dreams can be characterized by increasing S/M ratios as one moves along the perception-hallucination or perception-meditation continuum toward ecstasy or samadhi, the two most hallucinatory states (21) (Fig. 1, left and right, respectively). Moderate doses of the hallucinogenic drugs LSD, psilocybin, and mescaline (22) can get one "moving" along the perception-hallucination continuum, whereas minor tranquilizers and some muscle relaxants may initiate travel along the perception-meditation continuum.

If high S/M ratios do, indeed, reflect hallucinatory experiences, as my definition of hallucinations would imply, it would be important to quantify S/M ratio as a measure of hallucinatory intensity. In fact, a quantitative meaning has been given to the S/M ratio by measuring the components of a psychomotor performance, specifically, handwriting area and handwriting pressure (20), in volunteers during a psilocybin-induced waking-dream state.

The techniques for measuring handwriting area (S) (in square centimeters), as well as for obtaining handwriting pressure (M) (in $10^4$ dynes averaged over time), with an indicator that operates on a pressure-voltage-to-frequency basis, have been described elsewhere (20). Using these two parameters prior to ($T_1$) and at the peak ($T_2$) of a psilocybin-induced experience [160 to 250 micrograms of psilocybin per kilogram of body weight], we found in a sample of 47 college-age volunteers a 31 percent ($T_2 - T_1$) increase in mean S/M ratio.

I should note that the standard deviation on handwriting area at $T_1$ is significantly related to the S/M at $T_1$ ($r = 0.4888$, $P < .01$, $N = 47$) and that the standard deviation is a simple and useful indicator of the ensuing drug-induced increase in S/M ratio ($r = 0.372$, $P < .01$, $N = 47$). Moreover, subjects with a large standard deviation on handwriting area at $T_1$ (that is, "variable" subjects), tend to be "perceivers," whereas volunteers with a small standard deviation at $T_1$ ("stable" subjects) tend to be "judgers," in terms of the Myers-Briggs Type Indicator. This self-reporting, Jungian-type personality indicator yields simple, continuous scores on four dichotomous scales: extroversion-introversion, sensation-intuition, thinking-feeling, and judging-perceiving (23). The perceivers also overestimate or contract time more than judgers do at the peak of a psilocybin-induced experience (4); this implies that perceivers move faster and farther along the perception-hallucination continuum than do judgers, who apparently require a larger dose for a comparable experience.

## Space and Increasing
## Hyper- and Hypoarousal

We call man's symbolic interpretation of his CNS activity "perception-behavior" and regard creative, "hyperphrenic," and ecstatic states, as well as Zazen and samadhi, as perceptual-behavioral interpretations of ergotropic and trophotropic arousal, respectively. We may now consider some of the perceptual-behavioral changes, or trans-

Fig. 2. Gislebertus' "Three Wise Men," in the Cathedral of Autun in the south of France, dramatizes the intense sensations and concomitant loss of voluntary motor activity which are the common features of both hallucinations (see the wise man with eyes open) and dreams (see the two dreaming wise men).

formations, that gradually develop as the level of arousal increases and decreases along each continuum. One of the most conspicuous transformations is that of "constancies" (24), which in the normal state of daily routine form a learned structure of primary ordering of space and time "out there." Although the newborn infant's only reality, in the beginning, is his CNS activity, he soon learns, by bumping into things, to erect a corresponding model "out there." Ultimately, his forgetting that his CNS activity had been the only reality will be taken by society as proof of his maturity, and he will be ready to conduct his life "out there" in (container) space and (chronological) time (4). This gradually learned and projected model, then, is the re-presentation of a world ordered and stabilized by self-programmed invariances. The adult interprets his CNS activity within this structure of similarity criteria, or "constancies," and thus experience can be said to consist of two processes: the programmed (subcortical) CNS activity; and the symbolic or perceptual-behavioral (cortical) interpretation, or metaprograms, of the CNS activity.

I have studied the transformation of certain constancies along the perception-hallucination continuum and find, for example, that the ability to readapt to optically induced spatial distortions, or to maintain the constancy of the visual world, gradually diminishes as a subject turns inward under the influence of psilocybin (25). Another finding revealed that the preferred level of (the constancy of) brightness increases under the influence of hallucinogenic drugs (26), but only in "variable" subjects (20, 27)—that is, those subjects whose large standard deviations on a variety of perceptual and behavioral tasks indicate a large and varied interpretive repertoire. However, in "stable" subjects, who are characterized by small standard deviations and, thus, by smaller and more predictable interpretive repertoires, the level of preferred brightness decreases when they are under the influence of hallucinogenic drugs. In addition, nearby visual space was found to gradually close in as subjects moved along the perception-hallucination continuum under the influence of moderate doses of psilocybin. This contraction of nearby visual space was observed with two different techniques: monitoring the apparent fronto-parallel plane (*28*), and handwriting measurements (*29*).

The transformation of constancies under ergotropic arousal—specifically, as manifested in the psilocybin-induced contraction of nearby visual space— can also be observed in acute schizophrenics under "natural" ergotropic arousal (that is, without hallucinogenic drugs). The transformation of constancies during acute psychotic episodes apparently gives rise to a "vertical displacement of the visual angle," which is implicit in a contraction of visual space and which results in an elevation of the horizon (*30*). Rennert (*30*), who for years has studied the angle of perspective in the drawings of schizophrenic patients, finds the acuteness of a schizophrenic episode to be significantly related to the height of the horizon in the patient's drawings. In fact, using a ruler, Rennert can predict remission or relapse from the position of the horizon in a drawing: the more severe the schizophrenic episode, the higher the position of the horizon—ultimately, it may even disappear. At the same time (see cover), a map-like perspective, or bird's-eye view, of the landscape results, with houses and other significant figures appearing in the foreground. The cover etching, made during an acute (hyper-

aroused) schizophrenic episode, demonstrates the contraction of nearby visual space, resulting in a raised horizon. Note that the elevation of the horizon forces the animals to walk at a steep angle. Compare with the low horizon in another etching by the same patient after remission (*31*).

I have also observed that the just-noticeable difference (JND) in taste, expressed as Weber fraction, becomes smaller with increasing ergotropic arousal: subjects need fewer molecules of a sapid substance (such as sucrose, quinine, and so on) to taste a JND in sweetness or bitterness. On the other hand, under the influence of tranquilizers of the phenothiazine type, the Weber fraction becomes larger: more molecules are needed to taste a JND (*32*). Since the Weber fraction is constant at levels of arousal associated with daily routine (within the customary middle range of taste sensitivity) (*33*), I interpret the above as examples of arousal-induced transformations of constancies. Because the number of molecules necessary to elicit the sensation of a JND gradually decreases during a voyage from the physical to the mental dimension along the perception-hallucination continuum, it might be extrapolated that no sapid molecules at all are needed for the experience of taste during ecstasy, the most hyperaroused hallucinatory state.

It should be emphasized that the projection of our CNS activity as location in the physical dimension of space and time "out there" was learned at, and is hence bound to, the lower levels of arousal characteristic of our daily survival routines. That this projection is gradually learned can be supported by Bender's observation that schizophrenic children "do not experience hallucinations of the projected type like adults, but only of the introjected type. They hear voices inside their head or other parts of the body, feel that they originate inside themselves and do not feel persecuted by them" (*34*).

The constancy of corporeal awareness also undergoes transformations as one moves along the perception-hallucination continuum. For instance, phantom sensations [that is, readaptation phenomena compensating for and correcting distortions of corporeal awareness in physical space-time (*35*)] gradually diminish and disappear as one moves into the mental dimension under the influence of hallucinogenic drugs (*36*). Depersonalization phenomena, on the other hand, manifest themselves as changes in body image, and usually accompany the dissolution of ego boundaries during creative, psychotic, ecstatic, or meditative states—whether "natural" or drug-induced—as well as while falling asleep. All of this is to say that the constancy of the "I" is interfered with as one moves along the perception-hallucination continuum from the "I" of the physical world to the "Self" of the mental dimension. Analogously, the perception-meditation continuum (Fig. 1, right) also involves a departure from the "I" to the "Self." These two continua can thus be called "I-Self" continua. As will become clear later, the "Self" of ecstasy and the "Self" of samadhi are one and the same "Self."

The further we progress on the perception-hallucination continuum from the normal through the creative, psychotic, and, ultimately, to the ecstatic state (Fig. 1), the more complete is the transformation, or "unlearning," of the constancies of the physical dimension. Input, or outside information in general, is gradually reduced along this continuum. Thus, Saint Teresa of Avila tells us in her autobiography that, at the peak of a mystical experience, ". . .

the soul neither hears nor sees nor feels. While it lasts, none of the senses perceives or knows what is taking place" (*6*). Space, then, which was gradually established in ever-widening circles during childhood, gradually contracts with increasing arousal and ultimately disappears.

## Time and Increasing Hyper- and Hypoarousal

A gradual contraction and ultimate disappearance is also the fate of chronological time in the physical dimension (of the "I" state) as one progresses along the perception-hallucination or the perception-meditation continuum. In particular, we find that LSD (*37*) and psilocybin (*4*) cause an overestimation of time, the magnitude of which is related to a subject's variability on a perceptual or behavioral test before ingesting the given drug. The greater a subject's variability before ingesting a drug—for example, the retest-variance on his quinine taste-threshold or the standard deviation on his handwriting area—the greater will be his contraction or overestimation of time at drug peak [that is, 150 minutes after the oral administration of 160 to 200 micrograms of psilocybin per kilogram of body weight, when 63 minutes of chronological time (in geometrically increasing intervals) are estimated and recorded (*4*)]. Moreover, the greater the subject's variability, and thus his contraction of time, the greater will be his "rebound effect" 24 hours after; that is, his underestimation or expansion of time (*4*).

Dividing people, according to the magnitude of their perceptual variability, into "maximizers" ("stable" subjects) and "minimizers" ("variable" subjects) assists one in resolving the hotly debated question of whether time "flies" or "drags" during a hallucino-genic drug–induced experience. Actual-ly, as we have found, it does both: it is overestimated (it "flies" or contracts) by the minimizers, the subjects with a large standard deviation, who prefer to de-crease (visual) sensory data content and its rate of processing at drug peak; and it is underestimated (it "drags" or ex-pands) by the maximizers, the subjects with a small standard deviation, who prefer to increase data content and its rate of processing at drug peak.

Such contraction of time parallels the already described contraction of nearby visual space. By "time-contraction," I mean an increase in data content within a chronological time span, or, in experi-ential terms, "the flood of inner sensa-tion" (*3*); and I imply that, during such an experience, the subject, if without a watch, would arrive early for an ap-pointment. Under the impact of an acute, hallucinogenic drug–induced ex-perience, the subject usually compares the time-contraction or increased data content of the mental dimension with his past and present routine perform-ance in physical space-time and has, therefore, to conclude that "time" passes slowly. Note, for instance, Hof-mann's classical description of riding home on his bicycle under the influence of LSD: "The trip is about four miles and I had the feeling of not getting ahead, whereas my escort stated that we were rolling along at a good speed" (*38*). By comparing the usual rate of revolution of the spokes, as well as the usual rate at which the roadside "passed him by," with his experience of an in-creased data content or "flood of inner sensation," he had to conclude that he was not getting ahead and that time was dragging. Thus, there is only an apparent contradiction in terms: while experience is shifting from the physical toward the mental dimension, physical or chronological time becomes less and less important. Still, this transitional state can only be described in Aristo-telian [dualistic, or two-valued (true-false)] terms of chronological time (*39*) and by comparing experimental with experiential data. This contradiction re-solves itself at the peak of ergotropic or trophotropic arousal, since these purely mental states are timeless and spaceless and in no need of comparative verifica-tion.

## Increasing Cortical-Subcortical Integration with Increasing Arousal

If we assume that man, the self-refer-ential system, creates experience through the cortical (that is, perceptual-behav-ioral) interpretation of his subcortical activity, we may ask about the extent of freedom, or relative independence, of the mind (cortex) from the subcor-tical substratum. Indeed, man is to a large extent free to interpret his sub-cortical activity in a variety of ways at levels of arousal associated with daily routine. That this freedom is implicit in the functional independence of the lim-bic and neocortical systems is dramat-ically demonstrated by the fact that the electrical discharges resulting from hip-pocampal seizures are confined to the limbic system (*40*).

We can find no relation between the extent of psilocybin-induced perceptual and behavioral (or cortical) change and a drug-induced increase in pupillary diameter (*41*), which is a drug dose–de-pendent parameter of autonomic activity (*20, 42*). This lack of a relation points to a large degree of freedom of cortical interpretive activity, even under mod-erate hyperarousal.

The cortical-subcortical independence at the level of daily routine and even moderate levels of arousal is also implicit in the results of Marañon's (43) and Schachter and Singer's (44) experiments, in which the set and setting determined the particular cortical interpretation (from "good trip" to "bad trip") of each subject after his subcortical activity had been altered by an injection of 0.5 cubic centimeter of a 1 : 1000 solution of epinephrine.

It is now common knowledge that the set and setting, as well as the personality, decisively influence the cortical interpretation of hallucinogenic drug–induced changes in subcortical activity (45). What is not fully realized is that set, setting, personality, expectations, and past experiences determine the cortical "effects" of most of the psychoactive drugs when they are used in medically endorsed dosages. In fact, except for the anesthetics and hypnotics, there are no drugs that selectively direct human cognitive (psychological, or, in our terms, cortical) functions.

With rising levels of ergotropic and trophotropic arousal, however, perception-behavior becomes increasingly dependent upon (or less free of) the subcortical substratum that generates it. A cat responds to ergotropic hyperarousal with rage, while at the peak of trophotropic arousal the animal always yawns, curls up, and falls asleep. But man may be compelled to interpret these two extreme states of hyper- and hypoarousal as ecstasy and samadhi. This increasing stereotypy (loss of freedom) with increasing ergotropic arousal can be observed, for example, as a decrease in the variability of the EEG amplitude, which Goldstein and others have measured with a Drohocki integrator (46). A decrease in variability is expressed as the coefficient of variation (see the coefficient of variation values for states ranging from relaxation to catatonia in Fig. 1) (46, 47). Increasing stereotypy also manifests itself as an increase in the S/M ratio (20), thus indicating an intensification of inner sensations, accompanied by a loss in the ability to verify them through voluntary motor activity. Such high S/M ratios are implicit in the statements uttered during both drug-induced hallucinations and the hallucinations of schizophrenics: "of being hypnotized," "of being not free," "of being overpowered," "of being paralyzed," and so on, and in the mystic's inability to experience the subject-object dichotomy of daily routine in the physical dimension.

Apparently, then, an increase in ergotropic arousal is paralleled by a restriction in the individual's repertoire of available perceptual-behavioral interpretations. This restriction implies that certain levels can *only* be interpreted as creative (artistic, scientific, religious) or psychotic experiences (48). Although a religious interpretation is a common feature of catatonia (49), ecstasy, which is the mystical experience of the Oneness of everything, results from a creative breakthrough out of catatonic hyperarousal. During the ecstatic state, there is neither capacity nor necessity for motor verification of the intense sensations. In the mental dimension, in contrast to the physical, the all-pervasive experience of absolute certainty does not require further verification (50) and will be structured according to current mythology or the belief system of a St. Francis, Pascal, or Ramakrishna. What is one man's loss of freedom, therefore, may be another's gain in creativity.

An increasing stereotypy can also be observed along the perception-meditation continuum of increasing trophotropic arousal (see Fig. 1, right); this enables one to gradually exclude stimulation from without and turn attention inward. Continuous trains of alpha waves accompany these changes, and the dominant frequency of the alpha pattern decreases toward the alpha-theta border region, until some subjects, in a state of reverie, produce long trains of theta waves (*51*) [see the beta, alpha, and theta waves (*52*), measured in hertz, in Fig. 1, right]. According to Green *et al.* (*17*), the "alert inner-focused state is associated with the production of alpha rhythm"; in this state Zen masters show an alpha-blocking response to auditory clicks, but, in contrast to normal controls, do not habituate to these stimuli (*51*). Since the alpha rhythm is not altered or blocked by flashing lights, sounding gongs, or the touch of a hot test tube during the deep meditation of Indian Yoga masters (*53*), the Yoga samadhi apparently represents a more intense state of trophotropic arousal than Zazen does and must also express a greater inability to function in physical space-time than Zazen does. In fact, a Yoga master denies noticing *any* outside stimuli during deep meditation, whereas control subjects show alpha-blocking with as little stimulus as a flashing light (as do the Yoga masters themselves when not meditating).

## "Self": The Knower and Image-Maker; and "I": The Known and Imagined

We have seen that the departure from the physical dimension during a voyage on the perception-meditation continuum is accompanied by a gradual loss of freedom, which is manifested in the increasing inability to verify the experience through voluntary motor activity (*53*). At the peak of trophotropic arousal, in samadhi, the meditating subject experiences nothing but his own self-referential nature, void of compelling contents. It is not difficult to see a similarity between the meditative experience of pure self-reference and St. Teresa's description of her ecstasy: in both timeless and spaceless experiences,

the mundane world is virtually excluded. Of course, the converse is true of the mundane state of daily routine, in which the oceanic unity with the universe, in ecstasy and samadhi, is virtually absent. Thus, the mutual exclusiveness of the "normal" and the exalted states, both ecstasy and samadhi, allows us to postulate that man, the self-referential system, exists on two levels: as "Self" in the mental dimension of exalted states; and as "I" in the objective world, where he is able and willing to change the physical dimension "out there." In fact, the "I" and the "Self" can be postulated on purely logical grounds. See, for instance, Brown's reasoning (*54*) that the universe is apparently

. . . constructed in order (and thus in such a way as to be able) to see itself. But in order to do so, evidently it must first cut itself up into at least one *state which sees*, and at least one other *state which is seen*. In this severed and mutilated condition, whatever it sees is only partially itself . . . but, in any attempt to see itself as an object, it must, equally undoubtedly, act so as to make itself distinct from, and therefore, false to, itself. In this condition it will always partially elude itself.

In our terminology, the "Self" of exalted states is that which sees and knows, while the "I" is the interpretation, that which is seen and known in the physical space-time of the world "out there." The mutually exclusive relation between the "seer" and the "seen," or the elusiveness of the "Self" and the "I," may have its physiological basis in the mutual exclusiveness of the ergotropic and trophotropic systems (*8*).

A discernible communication between the "Self" and the "I" is only possible during the dreaming and hallucinatory states, whether drug-induced or "natural." These states can be located approximately between coefficients of variation 10 and 13 on the perception-hallucination continuum (Fig. 1, left) and in the 9 to 12 hertz EEG range on the perception-meditation continuum (Fig. 1, right). Such "I"-"Self" communication is the creative source of art, science, literature, and religon.

In spite of the mutually exclusive relation between the ergotropic and trophotropic systems, however, there is a phenomenon called "rebound to superactivity," or trophotropic rebound, which occurs in response to intense sympathetic excitation (55), that is, at ecstasy, the peak of ergotropic arousal (56). A rebound into samadhi at this point can be conceived of as a physiological protective mechanism; Gellhorn (8, 9) was among the first to notice that the rebound of the trophotropic system is not confined to the autonomic branches, but also causes significant changes in behavior. Thus, repetitive stimulation of the reticular formation in the midbrain increases the arousal level in awake cats, but this phase is followed by one in which the animal yawns, lies down, and finally falls asleep. This rebound phase is associated with the appearance of theta potentials in the hippocampus (57), just as the corresponding human trophotropic rebound—samadhi—is characterized by theta potentials (17) (see Fig. 1, right). These rebound or reversal phenomena between ecstasy and samadhi (8, 9) are illustrated by the loop (58) connecting the two extreme exalted states in Fig. 1.

The "Self" of ecstasy and samadhi are one and the same, as if the reflecting surface of a lake in Fig. 1 embraced both exalted states. If the level of water in such a lake were gradually raised, it would intersect successive and corresponding hyper- and hypoaroused states. The intersected states represent levels of gradually diminishing subjectivity (less "Self") and increasing objectivity (more "I"), until eventually the objective "I"-state of the world is reached.

Thus, each level of water would connect a hyper- and hypoaroused state with a specific subjectivity/objectivity (or "Self"-to-"I") ratio, implying a similarity between those pairs of hyper- and hypoaroused states that are connected by gradually raised levels of water. This similarity might, for example, be used to account for the success of the widely practiced narcoanalytic technique of abreacting a traumatic, hyperaroused experience in a hypoaroused state of similar "Self"-to-"I" ratio. The similarity between corresponding hyper- and hypoaroused states could also account for the hypermnesic phenomena of the hypoaroused elderly, who clearly recall the hyperaroused experiences of their youth, but do not recall more recent experiences (59).

During the "I"-state of daily routine, the outside world is experienced as separate from oneself, and this may be a reflection of the greater freedom (that is, separateness or independence) of cortical interpretation from subcortical activity. With increasing ergotropic and trophotropic arousal, however, this separateness gradually disappears, apparently because in the "Self"-state of ecstasy and samadhi, cortical and subcortical activity are indistinguishably integrated. This unity is reflected in the experience of Oneness with everything, a Oneness with the universe that is oneself.

### Sign-Symbol-Meaning Transformations

The separateness of subject and object during the daily routine levels of arousal (in the "I"-state) has been elaborated in our customary, rational, Aristotelian logic and language—a two-valued (either-or, true-false) logic that discounts the interaction between observer (subject) and observed (object) (60). This separateness of object and subject, as we have seen, is a reflection of the relative independence of cortical interpretation from subcortical activity and is of survival value in the "I"-state, where the subject must make decisions of life and death by manipulating objects (through voluntary motor activity).

But when we depart along either continuum from the "I" toward the "Self," the separateness of object and subject gradually disappears and their interaction becomes the principal content of the experience. This interaction, again, is a reflection of the gradually increasing integration of cortical and subcortical activity. In this state of Unity, the separateness of subject and object that is implicit in dualistic, Aristotelian logic and language becomes meaningless; only a symbolic logic and language can convey the experience of intense meaning. Apparently, then, meaning is "meaningful" only at that level of arousal at which it is experienced, and every experience has its state-bound meaning. During the "Self"-state of highest levels of hyper- or hypoarousal, this meaning can no longer be expressed in dualistic terms, since the experience of unity is born from the integration of interpretive (cortical) and interpreted (subcortical) structures. Since this intense meaning is devoid of specificities, the only way to communicate its intensity is the metaphor; hence, only through the transformation of objective sign into subjective symbol in art, literature, and religion can the increasing integration of cortical and subcortical activity be communicated.

The transformation of sign to symbol is also apparent in the visual realm, where the constancies of space and time are replaced by geometric-ornamental-rhythmic structures, the "hallucinatory form constants" of Klüver (*61*). In the light of my own experience, I would extend Klüver's observations to include hyper- and hypoaroused hallucinatory

experiences in general, whether electrically (*62*), "naturally," or drug-induced (*63*). The hallucinatory constancies are "magical symbols," visible or audible metaphors within a structure of symbolic logic and language, the language of hyper- and hypoaroused hallucinatory states, and are at the base of the general tendency toward geometric-rhythmic ornamentalization. For example, both the rose windows of Gothic cathedrals and the mandalas of Tantric religious art (*64*) are ritualized hallucinatory form constants. The tendency toward ornamentalization, however, is not reserved to visual imagery, but also governs the order of poetic and musical rhythm, imposing an all-pervasive metrum and harmony on the hallucinatory creative-religious states (*65*); the rhythm of music, poetry, and language corresponds to the geometric-ornamental rhythm of the visual realm. Therefore, the manneristic (*66*) hallucinatory-creative style of art and literature is regarded as a projection and elaboration of the geometric-rhythmic-ornamental fabric of hyper- and hypoaroused states.

### State-Boundaries

Inasmuch as experience arises from the binding or coupling of a particular state or level of arousal with a particular symbolic interpretation of that arousal, experience is state-bound; thus, it can be evoked either by inducing ("naturally," hypnotically, or with the aid of drugs) the particular level of arousal, or by presenting some symbol of its interpretation, such as an image, melody, or taste. "Acquired aversions to tastes following illness are commonplace in humans. The knowledge that the illness was caused by the stomach flu and not the Sauce Bernaise does not prevent the sauce from tasting bad in the future" (*67*).

Alcohol induces the state of arousal necessary for the recall of a state-bound experience in the film *City Lights*. Here, Charlie Chaplin saves a drunken millionaire from attempted suicide, and so becomes his good friend. When sober, however, the millionaire does not remember Charlie. However (*68*):

. . . the millionaire does not stay sober long. When he is drunk again, he spots Charlie and treats him like a long-lost friend. He takes Charlie home with him, but in the morning, when he is again sober, he forgets that Charlie is his invited guest and has the butler throw him out.

Evidently, consciousness extends either between states of drunkenness, or between states of sobriety, but there is complete amnesia between the two discontinuous states of sobriety and drunkenness, states with characteristic and different "Self"-to-"I" ratios.

Charlie's story has been recently remodeled and scientifically validated by Goodwin *et al.* (*69*), who had 48 subjects memorize nonsense syllables while drunk. When sober, these volunteers had difficulty recalling what they had learned, but they could recall significantly better when they were drunk again. Bustamante *et al.* (*70*) also observed amphetamine-induced (20 milligrams) excitatory, and amobarbital-induced (200 milligrams), "inhibitory," state-dependent recall of geometric configurations. His volunteers both memorized and later recalled the configurations under one of the two drugs. I submit, however, that while remembering from one state to another is usually called "state-dependent learning" (*71*) (implying that the individual was confronted with a learning task), extended practice, learning, or conditioning is *not* necessary for producing "state-boundness." On the contrary, a single experience may be sufficient to establish state-boundness.

Déjà vu experiences and the so-called

LSD flashbacks are, I believe, special cases of the general phenomenon of state-boundness. Note that neither focal lesions nor molecules of a hallucinogenic drug are necessary for the induction of a flashback—a symbol evoking a past drug experience may be sufficient to produce an LSD flashback (*72*).

An 18-year-old boy had a "bum trip" on "acid" and could not "come down" for two weeks. After he drank wine with a group of friends and was told by one of them that the wine contained a high dose of LSD (which it did not), he experienced hallucinations continuously for 14 days.

And here is the story of a "flashback" involving no drugs whatsoever (*73*).

I was in love with a college classmate, but he married someone else. I also married, and even after four years and a beautiful baby I still dreamed about this fellow. Whenever I saw a car like his, my heart would pound even though he had left town years before and I knew it couldn't possibly be his.

It follows from the state-bound nature of experience, and from the fact that amnesia exists between the state of normal daily experience and all other states of hyper- and hypoarousal, that what is called the "subconscious" is but another name for this amnesia. Therefore, instead of postulating *one* subconscious, I recognize as many layers of self-awareness as there are levels of arousal and corresponding symbolic interpretations in the individual's interpretive repertoire. The many layers of self-awareness, each with its characteristic "Self"-to-"I" ratio, remind one of the captain with girl friends in many ports, each girl unaware of the existence of the others, and each existing only from visit to visit (that is, from state to state). This is how multiple existences become possible: by living from one waking state to another waking state; from one dream to the next; one amobarbital narcoanalysis session to the next (74); from LSD to LSD (75); from epileptic aura to aura (76); from one creative, artistic, religious, or psychotic inspiration or possession to another creative artistic, religious, or psychotic experience; from trance to trance; and from reverie to reverie.

### References and Notes

1. W. Hess, *Das Zwischenhirn und die Regulierung von Kreislauf und Atmung* (Thieme, Leipzig, 1938); *Das Zwischenhirn* (Schwabe, Basel, 1949). Ergotropic arousal denotes behavioral patterns preparatory to positive action and is characterized by increased activity of the sympathetic nervous system and an activated psychic state. These states may be induced either naturally or, for example, through hallucinogenic drugs. Trophotropic arousal results from an integration of parasympathetic with somatomotor activities to produce behavioral paterns that conserve and restore energy, a decrease in sensitivity to external stimuli, and sedation. During ergotropic and trophotropic arousal, "alterations in autonomic activity are not confined to the visceral organs, but induce changes in cortical activity" [W. Hess, cited by Gellhorn (9)].
2. R. Fischer, in *Psychiatry and Art*, vol. 2, *Art Interpretation and Art Therapy*, I. Jakab, Ed. (Karger, Basel, 1969), p. 33.
3. R. Gelpke, quoted by A. Hofmann, in *Sonderabdruck aus dem Basler Stadtbuch* (Basel, 1964).
4. R. Fischer, in *Proceedings of the 4th International Congress of Pharmacology* (Schwabe, Basel, 1970), vol. 3, p. 28; *Ann. N.Y. Acad. Sci.* **138**, 440 (1967).
5. The word "hyperphrenic" was suggested to me by Dr. Alfred Bader, Lausanne, Switzerland.
6. Saint Teresa, *The Life of Saint Teresa*, J. M. Cohen, Transl. (Penguin, Baltimore, 1957), p. 142.
7. W. Ashby, *Design for a Brain* (Wiley, New York, 1960), p. 88.
8. E. Gellhorn, *Psychol. Forsch.* **34**, 48 (1970).
9. ———, *J. Nerv. Ment. Dis.* **147**, 148 (1968).
10. E. Hebbard and R. Fischer, *Psychopharmacologia* **9**, 146 (1966).
11. J. Silverman and K. Gaarder, *Percept. Mot. Skills* **25**, 661 (1967).
12. R. Fischer, *J. Nerv. Ment. Dis.* **119**, 492 (1954).
13. H. Selye, *J. Clin. Endocrinol. Metab.* **6**, 117 (1946).
14. M. C. Franck and W. Kuhlo, *Arch. Psychiat. Nervenkr.* **213**, 238 (1970).
15. J. Aschoff, *ibid.* **211**, 325 (1968).
16. K. Gaarder, R. Koresko, W. Kropfl, *Electroencephalogr. Clin. Neurophysiol.* **21**, 544 (1966).
17. E. Green, A. Green, E. Walters, *J. Transpersonal Psychol.* **1**, 1 (1970).
18. R. Ditchburn and D. Fender, *Opt. Acta* **2**, 128 (1955). Immobilization is accomplished by attaching a tiny mirror to a contact lens in such a way that the image will follow the micronystagmoid movements of the eye. Also see R. Pritchard, W. Heron, D. Hebb [*Can. J. Psychol.* **14**, 67 (1960)].
19. K. Behanan, *Yoga, A Scientific Evaluation* (Dover, New York, 1937), p. 223. The cobra has fixed eyes to begin with; therefore, to compensate for the lack of scanning eye movements, it must sway its head rhythmically to fixate the image of its victim. (If nothing else, one practical application of this paper may be the following: whenever you meet a cobra, swing along with him and he won't be able to locate you.)
20. R. Fischer, T. Kappeler, P. Wisecup, K. Thatcher, *Dis. Nerv. Syst.* **31**, 91 (1970); K. Thatcher, T. Kappeler, P. Wisecup, R. Fischer, *ibid.*, p. 181.
21. R. Fischer, *ibid.* **30**, 161 (1969). J. Strauss's evidence also supports this concept of the continuous, nondiscrete nature of perceptual and hallucinatory experience [*Arch. Gen. Psychiat.* **21**, 581 (1969)]. Our definition of hallucinations or dreams as experiences characterized by a high S/M ratio is free of value judgment, thus implying that hallucinatory experience can be labeled pathological, artistic, religious, and so on, according to one's taste [and taste threshold: see R. Fischer, in *Gustation and Olfaction*, G. Ohloff and A. E. Thomas, Eds. (Academic Press, New York, 1971), pp. 187–237].
22. The cross-tolerance between LSD, psilocybin, or mescaline [H. Isbell, A. Wolbach, A. Wikler, E. Miner, *Psychopharmacologia* **2**, 147 (1961); A. Wolbach, H. Isbell, E. Miner, *ibid.* **3**, 1 (1962)] as well as the characteristic square-wave pattern of saccadic movement they elicit [E. Hebbard and R. Fischer, *ibid.* **9**, 146 (1966)] mark these drugs as *the* hallucinogenic, psychotomimetic, psychodelic, or psychodysleptic drugs. It is implied, therefore, that any state which can be induced by one of these drugs can be duplicated by the others as well.
23. R. Corlis, G. Splaver, P. Wisecup, R. Fischer, *Nature* **216**, 91 (1967).
24. "Constancies" assure the recognition of identity; they refer to what Piaget meant by the "conservation" of area, distance, length, volume, and so on [J. Piaget, B. Inhelder, A. Szeminska, *The Child's Conception of Geometry*, E. A. Luzer, Transl. (Routledge, London, 1960), p. 390]. For example, wearing prism spectacles results in a variety of visual distortions which, due to the cortical transformation of subcortical (retinal) information, gradually disappear with time. Perceptual-behavioral constancies can be formalized as information (or signal to noise) ratios; that is, as dimensionless quantities [R. Fischer, F. Griffin, R. C. Archer, S. C. Zinsmeister, P. S. Jastram, *Nature* **207**, 1049 (1965)].
25. R. Hill, R. Fischer, D. Warshay, *Experientia* **25**, 171 (1969).
26. R. Fischer, R. Hill, D. Warshay, *ibid.*, p. 166. (1969).
27. R. Fischer, P. Marks, R. Hill, M. Rockey, *Nature* **218**, 296 (1968); R. Fischer, in *Origin and Mechanisms of Hallucinations*, W. Keup, Ed. (Plenum, New York, 1970), pp. 303–332.

28. R. Fischer, R. Hill, K. Thatcher, J. Scheib, *Agents Actions* **1**, 190 (1970).
29. R. Hill and R. Fischer, *Pharmakopsychiat. Neuro-Psychopharmakol.* **3**, 256 (1970).
30. H. Rennert, *Confin. Psychiat.* **12**, 23 (1969).
31. L. Navratil, *ibid.*, p. 30.
32. R. Fischer and R. Kaelbling, in *Recent Advances in Biological Psychiatry*, J. Wortis, Ed. (Plenum, New York, 1967), vol. 9, p. 183; R. Fischer, L. Ristine, P. Wisecup, *Biol. Psychiat.* **1**, 209 (1970).
33. R. Fischer, H. Dunbar, A. Sollberger, *Arzneimittel-forschung* **21**, 135 (1971).
34. L. Bender, in *Psychotomimetic Drugs*, D. Efron, Ed. (Raven, New York, 1969), p. 267.
35. R. Fischer, *Perspect. Biol. Med.* **12**, 259 (1969). The loss of a limb or an organ, for instance, can be regarded as a distortion of corporeal awareness; the phenomenon that corrects for this distortion results in a very real feeling that the lost limb or organ is still there, but this is only a phantom sensation.
36. S. Kuromaru, S. Okada, M. Hanada, Y. Kasahara, K. Sakamoto, *Psychiat. Neurol. Jap.* **64**, 604 (1962).
37. R. Fischer, *Ann. N.Y. Acad. Sci.* **96**, 44 (1962).
38. A. Hofmann, in *Discoveries in Biological Psychiatry*, F. Ayd and Blackwell, Eds. (Lippincott, Philadelphia, 1970), chap. 7.
39. R. Fischer, in *The Voices of Time*, J. Fraser, Ed. (Braziller, New York, 1966), p. 357.
40. P. MacLean, *J. Neurosurg.* **11**, 29 (1954); *Amer. J. Med.* **25**, 611 (1958).
41. The mean increase in pupillary diameter induced by 160 micrograms of psilocybin per kilogram of body weight in 34 college-age male volunteers was 0.93 millimeter, standard deviation = ± 0.52; whereas in 13 females, the mean increase was 0.56 millimeter, standard deviation = ± 0.27.
42. R. Fischer and D. Warshay, *Pharmakopsychiat. Neuro-Psychopharmakol.* **1**, 291 (1968); R. Fischer, *Perspect. Biol. Med.* **12**, 259 (1969).
43. G. Marañon, *Rev. Fr. Endocrinol.* **2**, 301 (1924).
44. S. Schachter and J. Singer, *Psychol. Rev.* **69**, 379 (1962).
45. H. Lennard, L. Epstein, A. Bernstein, D. Ransom, *Science* **169**, 438 (1970).
46. L. Goldstein, H. Murphree, A. Sugerman, C. Pfeiffer, E. Jenney, *Clin. Pharmacol. Ther.* **4**, 10 (1963).
47. K. Thatcher, W. Wiederholt, R. Fischer, *Agents Actions* **2**, 21 (1971); G. Marjerrison, A. Krause, R. Keogh, *Electroencephalogr. Clin. Neurophysiol.* **24**, 35 (1967).
48. R. Fischer, in *Genetic Factors in "Schizophrenia,"* A. Kaplan, Ed. (Thomas, Springfield, Ill., in press).
49. B. Pauleikhoff, *Fortschr. Neurol. Psychiat.* **37**, 476 (1969). The distinction between a genuine religious and a psychotic religious conversion experience is pointed out by H. Weitbrecht [*Beiträge zur Religionspsychopathologie, insbesondere zur Psychopathologie der Bekehrung* (Scherrer, Heidelberg, 1948)]. His four schizophrenics experienced a religious conversion during their psychoses. Although after remission they had insight into the diseased nature of their psychoses, they continued to regard their conversion experiences as valid turning points. We conceptua-

lize conversion experiences as confrontation and dialogue between a man's wordly "I" and his ecstatic (or meditative) "Self," resulting in the creation of a more consistent personality—one that has "found its style" [R. Fischer, *Confin. Psychiat.* **13**, 1 (1970); *ibid.*, in press].
50. Pascal recorded, at the peak of his decisive religious illumination: "Fire./God of Abraham, God of Isaac, God of Jacob,/not of the philosophers and the scientists./Certainty. Certainty." [M. Arland, *Pascal* (l'Enfant Poête, Paris, 1946), pp. 120–121].
51. A. Kasamatsu and T. Hirai, *Psychologia* **6**, 89 (1963); *Folia Psychiat. Neurol. Jap.* **20**, 315 (1966).
52. It is likely that these parietal, low-frequency EEG waves are related to dendritic field-potential charges.
53. B. Anand, G. Chhina, B. Singh, *Electroencephalogr. Clin. Neurophysiol.* **13**, 452 (1961).
54. G. Brown, *Laws of Form* (Allen, London, 1969), p. 105. Saint Teresa elegantly expressed this partial elusiveness: "There remains the power of seeing and hearing; but is as if the things heard and seen were at a great distance far away" [in E. Underhill, *Mysticism* (Methuen, London, 1912), p. 450].
55. E. Gellhorn, *Acta Neuroveg.* **20**, 181 (1959).
56. Such rebound would be called "inhibition" in Pavlovian terminology [I. Pavlov, in C. Murchison, *Psychologies of 1930* (Clark Univ. Press, Worcester, Mass., 1930), p. 213], and "phase of resistance" by Selye [*Stress* (ACTA, Montreal, 1950), pp. 15–43]. It can also be accounted for within the frame of Wilder's Law of Initial Value, which states that "the higher the initial value of a measured function, the lower is the tendency of the system to respond to furthering stimuli, while the highest as well as the lowest values tend to result in a *reversal of action* (italics mine)" [J. Wilder, *J. Psychother.* **12**, 199 (1958)].
57. P. Parmeggiani, *Brain Res.* **7**, 350 (1968).
58. The "loop" in Fig. 1 has also been independently suggested to me (on experiential grounds alone) by both Dr. J. H. M. Whiteman, University of Cape Town, South Africa, and Marilyn Delphinium Rutgers, Glen-Ellen, California. I am gratefully indebted to them, as well as to Primarius Dr. Leo Navratil, Gugging, Austria, for sharing with me their intuition and scholarship.
59. This example was suggested to me by Primarius Dr. Leo Navratil, Gugging, Austria.
60. For example, neither quinine molecules nor a subject's taste receptors are bitter per se—bitterness results only during interaction of the two. Therefore, no taster, no bitterness (just as there can be no image or sound of a falling tree without a viewer or listener). [See R. Fischer, *Dis. Nerv. Syst.* **30**, 161 (1969)]. The interactional nature of reality is already implicit in the fact that the brain is the only organ that develops through experiencing itself. [See H. Ey, *La Conscience* (Presses Universitaires de France, Paris, 1963), p. 64.]
61. H. Klüver, *Mescal and Mechanism of Hallucinations* (Phoenix, Univ. of Chicago Press, Chicago, 1966), p. 66.
62. M. Knoll, J. Kugler, D. Höfer, S. Lawder,

*Confin. Neurol.* **23**, 201 (1963).

63. W. Keup, Ed., *Origin and Mechanisms of Hallucinations* (Plenum, New York, 1970), pp. 95–210.

64. A. Mookerjee, in *Tantra-Kunst*, R. Kumar, Ed. (Basilius, Basel, 1967–1968), p. 11.

65. R. Fischer, *Confin. Psychiat.* **13**, 1 (1970).

66. See L. Navratil, *Schizophrenie und Kunst* (Deutsches Taschenbuch Verlag, München, 1965), p. 35; *Schizophrenie und Sprache* (Deutsches Taschenbuch, München, 1966), p. 162.

67. M. Seligman, *Psychol. Rev.* **77**, 416 (1970).

68. G. McDonald, M. Conway, M. Ricci, Eds. *The Films of Charlie Chaplin* (Citadel, New York, 1965), p. 191.

69. D. Goodwin, B. Powell, D. Bremer, H. Hoine, J. Stern, *Science* **163**, 1358 (1969).

70. J. Bustamante, A. Jordan, M. Vila, A. Gonzalez, A. Insua, *Physiol. Behav.* **5**, 793 (1970).

71. R. Fischer, *Dis. Nerv. Syst.* **32**, 373 (1971); ——— and G. M. Landon, *Brit. J. Psychiat.*, in press. The latter paper also includes an extensive discussion of state-dependent learning in human beings and animals. Note that this term could just as well be "state-dependent adaptation," since learning and adaptation are as indistinguishable from each other as hallucinations and dreams.

72. L. Tec, *J. Amer. Med. Ass.* **215**, 980 (1971).

73. From "Dear Abby," in *Citizen Journal*, Columbus, Ohio, 13 January 1971, p. 21.

74. Primarius Dr. Raoul Schindler, Vienna, informed me at Linz in 1969 that a patient's thread of thought in narcoanalysis resumes, after an injection of amobarbital, exactly where it left off at the end of the previous session.

75. Dr. Hanscarl Leuner, Göttingen, Germany, also confirms (1970) that his patients in LSD-supplemented or psycholytic therapy regard each LSD experience as a continuation of the last.

76. M. Horowitz, J. Adams, and B. Rutkin [*Arch. Gen. Psychiat.* **19**, 469 (1968)] report from the case history of an epileptic girl that the imagery of every aura consisted of "pigs walking upright like people." In early grade school the girl would rip open her blouse during a seizure, but, of course, she would not remember this after the seizure. Nevertheless, her classmates called her a pig, and it was this pig which she saw "walking upright" in each aura.

77. Supported in part by National Institute of Mental Health grant 1 RO3 MH17633-01 and general research support grants. I am indebted to Sandoz Pharmaceuticals, Basel, Switzerland, and to Dr. John A. Scigliano, former executive secretary, FDA-PHS Psychotomimetic Agents Advisory Committee, Bethesda, Maryland, for generously providing me with psilocybin (under IND-3530). I am also grateful to Dr. Peter Gwynne, James Scheib, and Pamela Furney for their devoted competence and to my creative artist wife, Trudy, for vital perceptual as well as cognitive illumination.

# A Wakeful Hypometabolic  7
## Physiologic State

### Robert Keith Wallace, Herbert Benson and Archie F. Wilson

WALLACE, ROBERT KEITH, HERBERT BENSON, AND ARCHIE F. WILSON. *A wakeful hypometabolic physiologic state.* Am. J. Physiol. 221(3): 795–799. 1971.—Mental states can markedly alter physiologic function. Hypermetabolic physiologic states, with in creased oxygen consumption, accompany anticipated stressful situations. Hypometabolic physiologic changes, other than those occurring during sleep and hibernation, are more difficult to produce. The present investigation describes hypometabolic and other physiologic correlates of a specific technique of meditation known as "transcendental meditation." Thirty-six subjects were studied, each serving as his own control. During meditation, the respiratory changes consisted of decreased $O_2$ consumption, $CO_2$ elimination, respiratory rate and minute ventilation with no change in respiratory quotient. Arterial blood pH and base excess decreased slightly; interestingly, blood lactate also decreased. Skin resistance markedly increased, while systolic, diastolic, and mean arterial blood pressure, arterial $P_{O_2}$ and $P_{CO_2}$, and rectal temperature remained unchanged. The electroencephalogram showed an increase in intensity of slow alpha waves and occasional theta-wave activity. The physiologic changes during meditation differ from those during sleep, hypnosis, autosuggestion, and characterize a wakeful hypometabolic physiologic state.

behavior; hypometabolism; $O_2$ consumption; $CO_2$ elimination; minute ventilation; respiratory quotient; blood pressure; pH; $P_{O_2}$; $P_{CO_2}$; base excess; blood lactate; heart rate; rectal temperature; skin resistance; electroencephalogram; meditation; respiratory rate

**134**

MENTAL STATES can markedly alter physiologic function. Hypermetabolic physiologic states, with associated increased oxygen consumption, accompany anticipated stressful situations (34, 61). Hypometabolic physiologic changes, other than those occurring during sleep and hibernation, are more difficult to produce, but may accompany meditational states.

Physiologic changes during meditation have been investigated, (1–4, 6, 11, 14, 15, 23, 29, 30, 38, 42–44, 46, 53, 55, 56, 58, 59), but interpretation of the results has been problematic because of difficulties of subject selection. It was difficult to evaluate which subjects were expert in the investigated technique and therefore could be expected to produce physiologic changes (4, 53); many so-called experts were located in geographic areas where adequate research facilities were not available; the magnitude of physiologic changes was sometimes dependent upon the length of time the subject had been practicing a particular technique and his personal aptitude for the specific discipline (30, 53). However, consistent physiologic changes have been observed during the practice of certain mental techniques of meditation (1–3, 30, 46, 53, 56). Oxygen consumption and respiratory rate have decreased markedly, while the electroencephalogram has shown increased alpha- and occasional theta-wave activity. The present study confirms and extends earlier physiologic observations during the practice of one of these techniques, taught by Maharishi Mahesh Yogi, known as "transcendental meditation" (56).

Transcendental meditation was investigated because: *1)* consistent, significant physiologic changes, characteristic of a rapidly produced wakeful hypometabolic state, were noted during its practice (2, 46, 56); *2)* the subjects found little difficulty in meditating during the experimental measurements; *3)* a large number of subjects were readily available who had received uniform instruction through an organization specializing in teaching this technique (Student's International Meditation Society, National Headquarters located at 1015 Gayley Avenue, Los Angeles, Calif. 90024). The technique comes from the Vedic tradition of India made practical for Western life (36). Instruction is given individually and the technique is allegedly easily learned, enjoyable, and requires no physical or mental control. The individual is taught a systematic method of perceiving a "suitable" sound or thought without attempting to concentrate or contemplate specifically on the sound or thought. The subjects report the mind is allowed to experience a thought at a "finer or more creative level of thinking in an easy and natural manner." There is no belief, faith, or any type of autosuggestion involved in the practice (37). It involves no disciplines or changes in life style, other than the meditation period of 15 or 20 min twice a day when the practitioner sits in a comfortable position with eyes closed.

METHODS

Thirty-six subjects were studied with each serving as his own control. Informed consent was obtained from each. The subjects sat quietly in a chair with eyes open for 10–30 min prior to the precontrol measurements. During the precontrol period, all subjects continued to sit quietly with eyes open or closed for 10–30 min. The subjects were then instructed to start meditating. After 20–30 min of meditation, they were asked to stop. During the postcontrol period, they continued to sit quietly with eyes closed for 10 min and then with eyes open for another 10 min. Blood pressure, heart rate, rectal temperature, and skin resistance and electroencephalographic changes were measured continuously. Other measurements were made and samples taken every 10 min throughout the precontrol, meditation, and postcontrol periods. Mean values were calculated for each subject in each period. The data from the precontrol period were then compared to those during meditation by use of a paired $t$ test (52).

Oxygen consumption was measured in five subjects by the closed- (7) and in 15 subjects by the open-circuit methods (13). In the open-circuit method, expired gas was collected in a Warren E. Collins, Inc. 120 l Tisot spirometer for 6- to 10-min periods. The expired gas was analyzed in triplicate for $P_{O_2}$ and $P_{CO_2}$ with a Beckman Instruments, Inc. physiological gas analyzer model 160. Oxygen consumption, $CO_2$ elimination, and respiratory quotient were calculated according to standard formulas (13). In all subjects tested by the closed-circuit method and in four subjects tested by the open-circuit method, a standard mouthpiece and nose clip were used. A tight-fitting face mask was made for use in 16 subjects. The face mask contained two one-way low-resistance inspiration valves (id 1.5 cm) in its sides and a one-way expiration valve (id 2.3 cm) in its front. The Tisot spirometer was weighted to ensure adequate collection, regardless of tidal volume or rate of respiration. Total ventilation was measured in the four subjects with the unweighted Tisot spirometer. Respiration rate was recorded during the closed-circuit method measurements.

Systemic arterial blood pressure was measured and arterial blood samples were obtained from a polyethylene or Teflon catheter inserted percutaneously via a no. 18 Cournand or a Becton, Dickinson & Co. Longwell 20-g 2-in catheter needle, respectively, after local anesthesia with 5–10 ml of 1 % procaine HCl (novocaine; Winthrop Laboratories, Inc.) or 2 % lidocaine HCl (Xylocaine, Astra Pharmaceutical Products, Inc.). The catheters were filled with a dilute heparin saline solution (5,000 USP units Na heparin per 1 0.9 % NaCl) and connected to a Statham P23Db strain-gauge pressure transducer. Systolic and diastolic or mean arterial blood pressure were recorded on either a Hewlett-Packard Co. Sanborn recorder, model 964, or a Brush Instruments Division, Clevite Corp. Mark 240 polygraph. Mean pressures were obtained by low-pass filtering in the driver amplifier. Average values for mean and systolic and diastolic blood pressure were calculated using horizontal lines of best fit drawn through records every 100 sec. Arterial blood samples were taken in heparinized syringes for determination of pH, $P_{CO_2}$, and $P_{O_2}$ with a Sanz pH glass microelectrode and Radiometer (Copenhagen), model pH M4; a Severinghaus $P_{CO_2}$ electrode system (49); and a Clark $P_{O_2}$ Instrumentation Laboratory, Inc. ultramicro system, model 113-S1, respectively. Base excess was calculated for each of the arterial blood samples (51). Blood lactate concentration was determined by enzymatic assay from unheparinized arterial blood samples (48). Lactate determinations for each sample were performed in duplicate and the results averaged.

Electrocardiograms were recorded with a Grass Instruments Co. polygraph, model 5, or the Hewlett-Packard

Sanborn recorder, model 964. Heart rate was calculated by counting the number of QRS electrocardiogram spikes occurring during two out of every five consecutive minutes. Rectal temperature was continuously measured with a Yellow Springs Instruments, Inc. telethermometer, model 44TA, utilizing a flexible probe inserted 2.5–3.0 cm into the rectum. The values for rectal temperature were recorded every min. Skin resistance was measured with Beckman Instrument, Inc. silver-silver chloride electrodes placed 0.5 cm apart on the left palm (40) and recorded continuously on the Grass Instrument Co. polygraph, model 5 at a current of 50 $\mu$a. Values for skin resistance were recorded every min.

Electroencephalograms (EEG) were recorded with a Grass Instrument Co. electroencephalograph model 6. The EEG traces were recorded with an Ampex Corp. tape recorder, model FR-1300. The skin electrodes were placed, according to the International 10–20 system, at Fpl, Cz, T3, P3, 01, 02, and A2 (26). Grass Instruments Co. gold-plated cup electrodes and EEG electrode cream were employed. Recordings were monopolar with A2 acting as the reference electrode, and the ground electrode was placed over the right mastoid bone. The EEG tracings were recorded as analog data on tape and then were converted to digital data by a Systems Data, Inc. SDS 930 computer with a nominal accuracy of one part in 2048, operating at 256 samples/sec on each channel. These digital data were subsequently processed by an IBM 360-91 computer with spectral analysis computed by the BMD X92 program (19), sampling 2 of every 15 sec of data with a resolution of 1 c/sec for 32 frequencies. Every 10 samples were averaged and displayed as a time history of intensity (mean square amplitude) for each frequency and as a contour map of time vs. frequency with a representation of intensity (57). The sampling of short periods of data was used to increase the likelihood of including temporary frequency changes which might have occurred during the meditation period. Eye movements (electro-oculograms), were recorded in five subjects with the electrodes placed at E1 and A1, and E2 and A1 (45).

RESULTS

The age of the subjects ranged from 17 to 41 years with a mean of 24.1 years. There were 28 males and eight females. The length of time practicing transcendental meditation ranged from 0.25 to 108.0 months, with a mean of 29.4 months. Oxygen consumption averaged 251.2 ml/min prior to meditation, with small variation between the two mean precontrol measurements (5.3 ml/min) (Table 1). During meditation, $O_2$ consumption decreased 17% to 211.4 ml/min, and gradually increased after meditation to 242.1 ml/min. Carbon dioxide elimination decreased from 218.7 ml/min during the precontrol period to 186.8 ml/min during meditation. Respiratory quotient prior to meditation was in the normal basal range (0.85) and did not change significantly thereafter. Minute ventilation decreased about 1 liter/min and respiratory rate decreased about three breaths per min during meditation.

Systolic, diastolic, and mean arterial blood pressure changed little during meditation (Table 1). Average systolic blood pressure before meditation was 106 mm Hg; average diastolic blood pressure 57 mm Hg; average mean blood pressure 75 mm Hg. The arterial pH decreased slightly in almost all subjects during meditation, while $P_{CO_2}$ and $P_{O_2}$ showed no consistent or significant changes during meditation. The average base excess decreased about 1 unit during meditation.

Mean blood lactate concentration decreased from the precontrol value of 11.4 to 8.0 mg/100 ml (Table 1). In the 10 min following meditation, lactate continued to decrease to 6.85 mg/100 ml, while in the next and final 10 min it increased to 8.16 mg/100 ml. During the 30-min precontrol period, there was a slow decrease in lactate concentration of 2.61 mg/100 ml per hr. At the onset of meditation, the rate of decrease markedly increased to 10.26 mg/100 ml per hr.

During meditation, the average heart rate decreased by 3 beats/min (Table 1). Rectal temperature remained essentially constant throughout the meditation period (Table 1). Skin resistance increased markedly at the onset of meditation, with a mean increase of about 140 kilohms (Table 1).

## WAKEFUL PHYSIOLOGIC HYPOMETABOLISM

TABLE 1. *Physiologic changes before, during, and after meditation*

| Measurement | No. of Subjects | Precontrol Period, mean ± SD | Meditation Period, mean ± SD | Postcontrol Period, mean ± SD |
|---|---|---|---|---|
| Oxygen consumption, ml/min | 20 | 251.2 ±48.6 | 211.4 ±43.2* | 242.1 ±45.4 |
| $CO_2$ elimination, ml/min | 15 | 218.7 ±41.5 | 186.8 ±35.7* | 217.9 ±36.1 |
| Respiratory quotient | 15 | 0.85 ±0.03 | 0.87 ±0.04 | 0.86 ±0.05 |
| Respiratory rate, breaths/min | 5 | 13 ±3 | 11 ±3† | 11 ±3 |
| Minute ventilation, l/min | 4 | 6.08 ±1.11 | 5.14 ±1.05† | 5.94 ±1.50 |
| Blood pressure, mm Hg | | | | |
| Systolic | 6 | 106 ±12 | 108 ±12 | 111 ±10 |
| Diastolic | 6 | 57 ±6 | 59 ±5 | 60 ±5 |
| Mean | 9 | 75 ±7 | 75 ±7 | 78 ±7 |
| pH | 10 | 7.421 ±0.022 | 7.413 ±0.024† | 7.429 ±0.025 |
| $P_{CO_2}$, mm Hg | 10 | 35.7 ±3.7 | 35.3 ±3.7 | 34.0 ±2.9 |
| $P_{O_2}$, mm Hg | 10 | 103.9 ±6.4 | 102.8 ±6.2 | 105.3 ±6.3 |
| Base excess | 10 | −0.5 ±1.5 | −1.3 ±1.5* | −1.0 ±1.8 |
| Blood lactate, mg/100 ml | 8 | 11.4 ±4.1 | 8.0 ±2.6* | 7.3 ±2.0 |
| Heart rate, beats/min | 13 | 70 ±8 | 67 ±7† | 70 ±7 |
| Rectal temperature, °C | 5 | 37.5 ±0.4 | 37.4 ±0.3 | 37.3 ±0.2 |
| Skin resistance, kilohms | 15 | 90.9 ±46.1 | 234.6 ±58.5* | 120.5 ±92.0 |

*P* is the probability of the mean value of the precontrol period being identical to the mean value of the meditation period. *$P < 0.005$.    †$P < 0.05$.

After meditation skin resistance decreased, but remained higher than before meditation.

The EEG pattern during transcendental meditation showed increased intensity (mean square amplitude) of 8–9 cycles/sec activity (slow alpha waves) in the central and frontal regions (Fig. 1). The change in intensity of 10–11 'cycles/sec alpha waves during meditation was

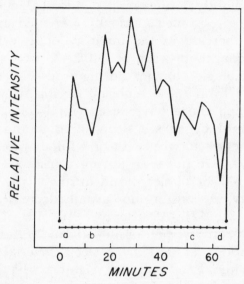

FIG. 1. Relative intensity of 9 cycles/sec activity (alpha-wave activity) in lead FP1 (see text) in a representative subject. *a-b:* premeditation control period with eyes closed. *b-c:* meditation period. *c-d:* postmeditation period with eyes closed. During meditation period, relative intensity of alpha-wave activity increased.

variable. In five subjects, the increased intensity of 8–9 cycles/sec activity was accompanied by occasional trains of 5–7 cycles/sec waves (theta waves) in the frontal channel (Fig. 2). Intensity of 12–14 cycles/sec waves and 2–4 cycles/sec waves either decreased or remained constant during meditation. In three subjects, who reported feeling tired and drowsy at the beginning of meditation, flattening of the alpha activity and low voltage mixed frequency waves with a prominence of 2–7 cycles/sec activity was noted. As meditation in these three subjects continued, the pattern was replaced by regular alpha activity. In the five subjects in whom electro-oculograms were recorded, no changes were observed.

DISCUSSION

Consistent and pronounced physiologic changes occurred during the practice of a mental technique called transcendental meditation (Table 1). The respiratory changes consisted of decreased $O_2$ consumption, $CO_2$ elimination, respiratory rate, and minute ventilation, with no change in respiratory quotient. Arterial blood pH and base excess decreased slightly; interestingly, blood lactate also decreased. Skin resistance markedly increased and the EEG showed an increase in the intensity of slow alpha waves with occasional theta-wave activity.

The physiologic changes during transcendental meditation differed from those reported during sleep. The EEG patterns which characterize sleep (high-voltage slow-wave activity, 12–14 cycles/sec sleep spindles and low-voltage mixed-frequency activity with or without rapid eye movements) (45), were not seen during transcendental meditation. After 6–7 hr of sleep, and during high-voltage slowwave activity, $O_2$ consumption usually decreases about 15 % (8, 10, 20, 33, 47). After only 5–10 min of meditation, alpha-wave activity predominated and $O_2$ consumption decreased about 17%. During sleep, arterial pH slightly decreases while $P_{CO_2}$ increases significantly, indicating a respiratory acidosis (47). During meditation, arterial pH also decreased slightly. However, arterial $P_{CO_2}$ remained constant while base excess decreased slightly, indicating a mild condition of metabolic acidosis. The skin-resistance changes during meditation were also different from those observed during sleep (22, 54). In sleep, skin resistance most commonly increases continuously, but the magnitude and rate of increase are generally less than that which occurred during meditation.

The consistent physiologic changes noted during transcendental meditation also differed from those reported during hypnosis or autosuggestion. During hypnosis, heart rate, blood pressure, skin resistance, and respiration either increase, decrease, or remain unchanged, approximating changes which normally occur during the states which have been suggested (5, 25, 32). During so-called hypnotic sleep, in which complete relaxation has been suggested, no

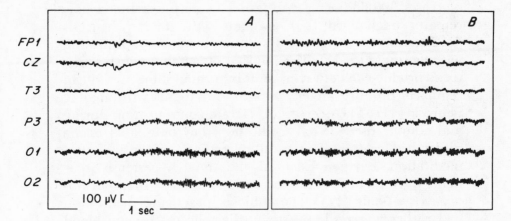

FIG. 2. EEG records of a subject with theta-wave activity during meditation. A: EEG record close to start of meditation period. B: EEG record during middle of meditation period. EEG leads are noted on vertical axis (see text). In A, alpha-wave activity is present as shown in leads P3, 01 and 02. In B, prominent theta-wave activity is present in lead FP1 simultaneous with alpha-wave activity in leads T3, P3, 01, and 02.

noticeable change in $O_2$ consumption occurs (5, 24, 60). EEG patterns occurring during hypnosis are usually similar to the suggested wakeful patterns and therefore differ greatly from those observed during meditation (32).

Operant conditioning procedures employing physiologic feedback can also alter autonomic nervous system functions and EEG patterns (9, 21, 28, 31, 39, 50). Animals can be trained to control autonomic functions, such as blood pressure, heart rate, and urine formation (9, 18, 39). Human subjects can alter their heart rate and blood pressure by use of operant conditioning techniques (31, 35, 50) and can be trained to increase alpha-wave activity through auditory and visual feedback (21, 28). However, the physiologic changes during transcendental meditation occurred simultaneously and without the use of specific feedback procedures.

The relative contribution of various tissues to lactate production has not been established, but muscle has been presumed to be a major source (16). The fall in blood lactate observed during meditation might be explained by increased skeletal muscle blood flow with consequent increased aerobic metabolism. Indeed, forearm blood flow increases 300% during meditation while finger blood flow remains unchanged (46). Patients with anxiety neurosis develop an excessive rise in blood lactate concentration with "stress" (12, 27). The infusion of lactate ion can sometimes produce anxiety symptoms in normal subjects and can regularly produce anxiety attacks in patients with anxiety neurosis (41). The decrease in lactate concentration during and after transcendental meditation may be related to the subjective feelings of wakeful relaxation before and after meditation. Further, essential and renal hypertensive patients have higher resting serum lactate levels than normotensive patients (17). The subjects practicing meditation had rather low resting systolic, diastolic, and mean blood pressures.

A consistent wakeful hypometabolic state accompanies the practice of the mental technique called transcendental meditation. Transcendental meditation can serve, at the present time, as one method of eliciting these physiologic changes. However, the possibility exists that these changes represent an integrated response that may well be induced by other means.

The authors thank Mr. Michael D. Garrett, Mr. Robert C. Boise, and Miss Barbara R. Marzetta for their competent technical assistance; Dr. Walter H. Abelmann and Dr. J. Alan Herd for their review of the manuscript; and Mrs. G. Shephard for typing the manuscript.

This investigation was supported by Public Health Service Grants HE 10539-04, SF 57-111, NIMH 2-T01, MH 06415-12, and RR-76 from the General Clinical Research Centers Program of the Division of Research Resources; the Council for Tobacco Research; and Hoffmann-LaRoche, Inc., Nutley, N. J. 07110.

Some of these data were submitted by R. K. Wallace in partial fulfillment of the requirements for the degree of Doctor of Philosophy in physiology at the University of California, Los Angeles. A preliminary report of another part of these experiments was presented at the April, 1971, meeting of the Federation of American Societies for Experimental Biology.

Received for publication 22 February 1971.

# REFERENCES

1. AKISHIGE, Y. A historical survey of the psychological studies in Zen. *Kyushu Psychol. Studies, V, Bull. Fac. Lit. Kyushu Univ.* 11: 1–56, 1968.

2. ALLISON, J. Respiration changes during transcendental meditation. *Lancet* 1: 833–834, 1970.

3. ANAND, B. K., G. S. CHHINA, AND B. SINGH. Some aspects of electroencephalographic studies in Yogis. *Electroencephalog. Clin. Neurophysiol.* 13: 452–456, 1961.

4. BAGCHI, B. K., AND M. A. WENGER. Electrophysiological correlates of some Yogi exercises. *Electroencephalog. Clin. Neurophysiol.* Suppl. 7: 132–149, 1957.

5. BARBER, T. X. Physiological effects of "hypnosis." *Psychol. Bull.* 58: 390–419, 1961.

6. BEHANAN, K. T. *Yoga, a Scientific Evaluation.* New York: Macmillan, 1937.

7. BENEDICT, F. G., AND C. G. BENEDICT. *Mental Effort in Relation to Gaseous Exchange, Heart Rate, and Mechanics of Respiration.* Washington, D.C.: Carnegie Inst. Washington, 1933, p. 29–39.

8. BENEDICT, F. G., AND T. M. CARPENTER. *The Metabolism and Energy Transformation of Healthy Man During Rest.* Washington, D.C.: Carnegie Inst. Washington, 1910, p. 179–187.

9. BENSON, H., J. A. HERD, W. H. MORSE, AND R. T. KELLEHER. Behavioral induction of arterial hypertension and its reversal. *Am. J Physiol.* 217: 30–34, 1969.

10. BREBBIA, D. R., AND K. Z. ALTSHULER. Oxygen consumption rate and electroencephalographic stage of sleep. *Science* 150: 1621–1623, 1965.

11. BROSSE, T. A psycho-physiological study. *Main Currents Modern Thought* 4: 77–84, 1946.

12. COHEN, M. E., AND P. D. WHITE. Life situations, emotions and neurocirculatory asthenia (anxiety neurosis, neurasthenia, effort syndrome). *Res. Publ. Assoc. Res. Nervous Mental Disease* 29: 832–869, 1950.

13. CONSOLOZIO, F., R. E. JOHNSON, AND L. J. PECORA. *Physiological Measurements of Metabolic Functions in Man.* New York: McGraw-Hill, 1965, p. 1–30.

14. DAS, N. N., AND H. GASTAUT. Variations de l'activité electrique due cerveau, du coeur et des muscles squelletiques au cours de la meditation et de l'extase Yogique. *Electroencephalog. Clin. Neurophysiol.* Suppl. 6: 211–219, 1957.

15. DATEY, K. K., S. N. DESHMUKH, C. P. DALVI, AND S. L. VINEKAR. "Shavasan": a yogic exercise in the management of hypertension. *Angiology* 20: 325–333, 1969.

16. DECKER, D. G., AND J. D. ROSENBAUM. The distribution of lactic acid in human blood. *Am. J. Physiol.* 138: 7–11, 1942–43.

17. DEMARTINI, F. E., P. J. CANNON, W. B. STASON, AND J. H. LARAGH. Lactic acid metabolism in hypertensive patients. *Science* 148: 1482–1484, 1965.

18. DiCARA, L. V., AND N. E. MILLER. Instrumental learning of systolic blood pressure responses by curarized rats: dissociation of cardiac and vascular changes. *Psychosomat. Med.* 30: 489–494, 1968.

19. DIXON, W. J. (Editor). *BMD: Biomedical Computer Programs: X-Series Programs Supplement*. Los Angeles, Calif.: Univ. of California Press, 1969.

20. GROLLMAN, A. Physiological variations in the cardiac output of man. *Am. J. Physiol.* 95: 274–284, 1930.

21. HART, J. T. Autocontrol of EEG alpha. *Psychophysiology* 4: 506, 1968.

22. HAWKINS, D. R., H. B. PURYEUR, C. D. WALLACF, W. B. DEAL, AND E. S. THOMAS. Basal skin resistance during sleep and "dreaming." *Science* 136: 321–322, 1962.

23. HOENIG, J. Medical research on Yoga. *Conf. Psychiat.* 11: 69–89, 1968.

24. JANA, H. Energy metabolism in hypnotic trance and sleep. *J. Appl. Physiol.* 20: 308–310, 1965.

25. JANA, H. Effect of hypnosis on circulation and respiration. *Indian J. Med. Res.* 55: 591–598, 1967.

26. JASPER, H. H. The ten twenty electrode system of the international federation. *Electroencephalog. Clin. Neurophysiol.* 10: 371–375, 1958.

27. JONES, M., AND V. MELLERSH. Comparison of exercise response in anxiety states and normal controls. *Psychosomat. Med.* 8: 180–187, 1946.

28. KAMIYA, J. Operant control of the EEG alpha rhythm and some of its reported effects of consciousness. In: *Altered States of Consciousness*, edited by C. T. Tart. New York: Wiley, 1969, p. 507–517.

29. KARAMBELKAR, P. V., S. L. VINEKAR, AND M. V. BHOLE. Studies on human subjects staying in an airtight pit. *Indian J. Med. Res.* 56: 1282–1288, 1968.

30. KASAMATSU, A., AND T. HIRAI. An electroencephalographic study on the Zen mediation (Zazen). *Folia Psychiat. Neurol. Japon.* 20: 315–336, 1966.

31. KATKIN, E. S., AND E. N. MURRAY. Instrumental conditioning of autonomically mediated behavior: theoretical and methodological issues. *Psychol. Bull.* 70: 52–68, 1968.

32. KLEITMAN, N. *Sleep and Wakefulness*. Chicago: Univ. of Chicago Press, 1963, p. 329–330.

33. KREIDER, M. B., AND P. F. IAMPIETRO. Oxygen consumption and body temperature during sleep in cold environments. *J. Appl. Physiol.* 14: 765–767, 1959.

34. LANDIS, C. Studies of emotional reactions IV. Metabolic rate. *Am. J. Physiol.* 74: 188–203, 1925.

35. LEVENE, H. I., B. T. ENGEL, AND J. A. PEARSON. Differential operant conditioning of heart rate. *Psychosomat. Med.* 30: 837–845, 1968.

36. MAHARISHI MAHESH YOGI. *Maharishi Mahesh Yogi on the Bhagavad*

*Gita: A New Translation and Commentary*. Baltimore: Penguin, 1969, p. 10–17.

37. MAHARISHI MAHESH YOGI. *The Science of Being and Art of Living*. London: Intern. SRM Publ. 1966, p. 50–59.

38. MILES, W. R. Oxygen consumption during three yoga-type breathing patterns. *J. Appl. Physiol.* 19: 75–82, 1964.

39. MILLER, N. E., AND L. V. DiCARA. Instrumental learning of urine formation by rats; changes in renal blood flow. *Am. J. Physiol.* 215: 677–683, 1968.

40. O'CONNELL, D. N., AND B. TURSKY. Silver-silver chloride sponge electrodes for skin potential recording. *Am. J. Psychol.* 73: 302–306, 1960.

41. PITTS, F. N., JR., AND J. N. McCLURE, JR. Lactate metabolism in anxiety neurosis. *New Engl. J. Med.* 277: 1329–1336, 1967.

42. RAO, S. Metabolic cost of head-stand posture. *J. Appl. Physiol.* 17: 117–118, 1962.

43. RAO, S. Cardiovascular responses to head-stand posture. *J. Appl. Physiol.* 18: 987–990, 1963.

44. RAO, S. Oxygen consumption during yoga-type breathing at altitudes of 520 m and 3800 m. *Indian J. Med. Res.* 56: 701–705, 1968.

45. RESCHTSCHAFFEN, A., AND A. KALES, R. J. BERGER, W. C. DEMENT, A. JACOBSON, L. C. JOHNSON, M. JOUVET, L. J. MONROE, I. OSWALD, H. P. ROFFWARD, B. ROTH, AND R. D. WALTER. *A Manual of Standardized Terminology, Techniques and Scoring System for Sleep Stages of Human Subjects*. Washington, D. C.: U. S. Govt. Printing Office, 1968.

46. RIECHERT, H. Plethysmograpische Untersuchungen bei Konzentrations-und Meditationsübungen. *Ärztliche Forsch.* 21: 61–65, 1967.

47. ROBIN, E. D., R. D. WHALEY, C. H. CRUMP, AND D. M. TRAVIS. Alveolar gas tensions, pulmonary ventilation and blood pH during physiologic sleep in normal subjects. *J. Clin. Invest.* 37: 981–989, 1958.

48. SCHOLZ, R., H. SCHMITZ, T. BUCHLER, AND J. O. LAMPEN. Über die Wirkung von Nystatin auf Bäckerhefe. *Biochem, Z.* 331: 71–86, 1959.

49. SEVERINGHAUS, J. W., AND A. F. BRADLEY. Electrodes for blood $Po_2$ and $Pco_2$ determination. *J. Appl. Physiol.* 13: 515–520, 1958.

50. SHAPIRO, D., B. TURSKY, E. GERSHON, AND M. STERN. Effects of feedback and reinforcement on the control of human systolic blood pressure. *Science* 163: 588–590, 1969.

51. SIGGARD-ANDERSEN, O. *The Acid-Base Status of the Blood*. Baltimore: Williams & Wilkins, 1963.

52. SNEDECOR, G. W., AND W. G. COCHRAN. *Statistical Methods*. Ames, Iowa: Iowa State Univ. Press, 1960, p. 91–119.

53. SUGI, Y., AND K. AKUTSU. Studies on respiration and energy-metabolism during sitting in Zazen. *Res. J. Phys. Ed.* 12: 190–206, 1968.

54. TART, C. T. Patterns of basal skin resistance during sleep. *Psychophysiology* 4: 35–39, 1967.

55. VAKIL, R. J. Remarkable feat of endurance of a Yogi priest. *Lancet* 2: 871, 1950.

56. WALLACE, R. K. Physiological effects of transcendental meditation. *Science* 167: 1751–1754, 1970.

57. WALTER, D. O., J. M. RHODES, D. BROWN, AND W. R. ADEY. Comprehensive spectral analysis of human EEG generators in posterial cerebral regions. *Electroencephalog. Clin. Neurophysiol.* 20: 224–237, 1966.

58. WENGER, M. A., AND B. K. BAGCHI. Studies of autonomic functions in practitioners of Yoga in India. *Behavioral Sci.* 6: 312–323, 1961.

59. WENGER, M. A., B. K. BAGCHI, AND B. K. ANAND. Experiments in India on "voluntary" control of the heart and pulse. *Circulation* 24: 1319–1325, 1961.

60. WHITEHORN, J. C., H. LUNDHOLM, E. L. FOX, AND F. G. BENEDICT. The metabolic rate in "hypnotic sleep." *New Engl. J. Med.* 206: 777–781, 1932.

61. WHITEHORN, J. C., H. LUNDHOLM, AND G. E. GARDNER. The metabolic rate in emotional moods induced by suggestion in hypnosis. *Am. J. Psychiat.* 86: 661–666, 1929–30.

# CENTRAL NERVOUS SYSTEM ACTIVITY:
# HUMAN

# Awareness of EEG-Subjective Activity Relationships Detected Within a Closed Feedback System

**8**

Barbara B. Brown

## ABSTRACT

The present report summarizes results from feedback experiments using the three EEG frequency ranges of theta, alpha, and beta to operate lights of three different colors. The subjects were requested to try to isolate and identify feeling (and/or thought) activity which they felt caused successful operation of the lights. Written descriptions of this experience from one subject group (26 Ss) were compared to evaluations of subjective activity obtained in a second group of subjects (45 Ss) determined using a color Q-sort technique. Results from the latter technique were controlled for effects of color and for effects of the feedback experience using a control subject group (45 Ss). Results established two sets of relationships with subjective activity: color and EEG frequency. Each set could exist independently or in relationship to the other. Several characteristics were postulated to account for development of the subjective–biological relationships in this feedback system, e.g., that generation of "stimulus" and "response" were both internal events; that both reinforcement of the process and the behavior reinforced were selected by subjective activity of the subject; and that positive reinforcement did not occur without effort by the subject to define it.

DESCRIPTORS: Awareness, EEG feedback, Pre-conscious factors in voluntary control, Operant conditioning, Color perception. (B. B. Brown)

Recently the research of a number of psychophysiologists with widely varying interests has converged upon defining a physiologic function referred to as auto-regulation of internal functions, or "feedback" physiology. This area of research specifically explores the ability to control physiologic functions which occur when indicators of the functions are presented in a form which can be perceived by the subject.

Earlier studies have employed the experimental structures of both classical and operant conditioning techniques, e.g., Hart (1968), Stoyva and Kamiya (1968), Engel and Chism (1967), Kimmel and Kimmel (1963), and Delse and Feather (1968), and the interpretation of the auto-regulation phenomenon has rested upon the experimental contingencies. Largely because of this the automatic features of

This research was supported in part by NIH Grant No. MH-17678-01.

The author gratefully acknowledges the cooperation of John R B Whittlesey in defining some of the conceptualizations presented in this paper.

Address requests for reprints to: Barbara B. Brown, Ph.D., Experiential Physiology, Veterans Administration Hospital, Sepulveda, California 91343.

**151**

the phenomena have been emphasized and relationships to conscious activity have not generally been explored. Experimental emphasis has been directed toward control of behavior by means of the environmental determinants.

Bio-feedback techniques augment the investigation of behavior–environment relationships by providing conditions under which shaping is controlled by subjective responses of the subject. The experiments described in this paper provide a technique in which subjective activity is a major determinant of changes in physiologic activity. The subject is provided with environmental factors which can be altered by his perceptual and neural information processing activity as well as by his physiological responses. The physiologic responses are experimentally limited by the environmental (perceptual) devices provided. The sum of the internal events thus can be measured in fairly precise terms both by measurements of the physiologic responses as they control the external aspects, and further, by relating measurements of subjective changes to the physiologic responses or to their physical indicators.

The present report summarizes results from feedback experiments using the three EEG frequency ranges of theta, alpha, and beta to operate lights of three different colors. The subjects were requested to try to isolate and identify feeling (and/or thought) activity which they felt caused successful operation of the lights. A control study of color–feeling or thought associations provided a baseline for quantification of the subjective activities related to operation of the EEG feedback circuit.

The rationale for the present study developed from earlier work (Brown, 1966, 1968, 1969) in which brain electrical responses to color were found to differ between visualizer and non-visualizer subjects. Experiment 1 reported in this paper was originated to test the hypothesis that such differences might relate to different sets of subjective associations to color. The first requirement of the investigation was to determine average relationships between EEG frequency and subjective activity under those special conditions in which the external indicator (color) reflected the EEG frequency range. The positive results of Experiment 1 prompted Experiment 2 which included more extensive control procedures and an independent technique for evaluation of subjective activity, and which confirmed results of Experiment 1.

## METHOD

EEGs were recorded by conventional techniques on a Grass Model 6 machine and on analog tape. The amplified signal from the right parieto-occipital electrodes was fed to active band pass filters which simultaneously filtered the three ranges: theta (3.5–7.5 Hz), alpha (7.5–13 Hz), and beta (13–28 Hz). The output from each filter was connected through a variable attenuator to a low level preamplifier. These outputs were then rectified and smoothed by RC filters with variable time constants which were set so that the output of each circuit was a smooth voltage proportional to the envelope of the filtered output. Activation of a circuit threshold required 1.5 theta waves of 20 $\mu$v, 2.5 alpha waves of 10 $\mu$v, and 4 beta waves of 5 $\mu$v amplitude. Thus one envelope corresponded to the amplitude of the original signal. The intensity of the feedback light signal was directly proportional to the amplitude of the original signal such that, e.g., at 20 $\mu$v of alpha activity the light was very dim, and moderate to maximal brightness occurred when alpha amplitude reached 80 to 100 $\mu$v. The voltages were then further amplified to drive three 6 volt lamps (red, blue, and green) in the subject's room.[1]

Practice sessions were 60 min long. The experiments were conducted with the eyes open. Eye movements were recorded continuously. The colored lights were projected from behind onto a large diffusion screen placed 4 ft in front of the *S*. Each spot of light was about 5 in. in diameter. The *S*s were seated in a comfortable chair in a small isolated room with moderate ambient lighting. All recording instruments and circuitry were contained in a separate room equipped with open two-way communication with the *S*'s room.

*S*s were informed that each of the three lights was being operated by their brain electrical activity and that each light could represent one or more feeling states. Their task was to find subjective states or feelings which would selectively operate the lights and to find a way mentally to keep specific lights on as much of the time as possible. Only 2 *S*s had more than a casual reading knowledge of brain wave activity.

Subjective activity associated with the three EEG frequency ranges was evaluated by two different techniques in two separate experiments.

### Experiment 1

In Experiment 1 the three colors of lights were paired with the three EEG frequency ranges in two different arrangements (see below, Table 1) such that 13 *S*s for each of the two pairings were obtained. All 26 *S*s received the feedback experience. Immediately following the 60 min session they were asked to write a description of any thoughts, emotions, or feelings which they associated to each color.

### Experiment 2

In Experiment 2 a group of 90 *S*s (aged 21–62; 48 males) was employed, none of whom had participated in Experiment 1. One-half of the *S*s (45) received the feedback experience; the remaining 45 *S*s did not receive feedback and were tested for color–feeling associations away from the EEG laboratory. All 90 *S*s were asked to sort 105 descriptors of feeling or thought activity to red, blue, green, or white bins. The white bin was used to indicate no association between descriptor and color. The descriptors were obtained from various published lists, such as the Clyde Mood Check List, with many additions made by the investigator (available upon request). The 45 *S*s of the experimental group sorted the descriptors as rapidly as possible immediately after the first session, and were asked to sort according to the color–feeling associations made during the feedback experience.

The significance of the association between subjective activities and EEG frequencies in Experiment 2 was estimated by $\chi^2$ values obtained by comparing the

[1] During Experiment 2, "inhibit" circuits were added which turned off the visual displays when the DC EEG voltage level exceeded 120 $\mu$v.

sorts to color for each descriptor against expected sort values based upon results of the color sorts by the control *S*s, e.g. in Table 3, below, the observed frequencies to red, blue, and green for beta activity were 9, 3, and 5 respectively, giving a total of 17; whereas taking the relative proportion scored by the controls to the descriptor "angry" and multiplying this by 17 (experimental total for beta) results in expected values of 16.6, 0.4, and 0.0.

EEG analysis was conducted by filtering the taped records for theta, alpha, and beta frequencies in 5 min samples from the initial, middle, and final thirds of the 60 min EEG record. Interval histograms of wave periods were derived for each frequency range by means of the C.A.T. 400 and its amplitude discriminator accessory. Counts were made of the intervals between positive-going wave-crossings occurring within a 125 msec (for beta), 250 msec (for alpha), or 500 msec (for theta) analysis time, discriminating to 0.362, 0.625, and 1.25 msec intervals respectively. Instead of zero-crossings, wave-crossings amplitudes (voltage) were used which were identical to those used to drive the lights. Abundance of each range was measured in terms of peak area of the histogram calculated by multiplying the peak height measured in mm by the width at half the peak height (giving an area equal to one-half the base of the triangle times its height). Mean frequencies in Hz for each sample were determined by measuring the interval to the peak of the histogram, converting to msec, and calculating the reciprocal. Variation of frequency was determined by measuring the intervals at both edges

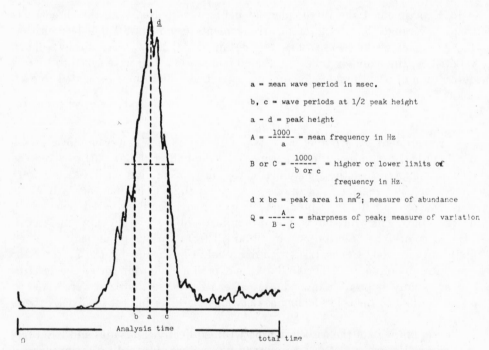

FIG. 1. Example of interval histogram and calculations used for analysis of EEG theta, alpha, and beta activity. Total analysis times were 500, 250, and 125 msec respectively. See text (Method) for details.

TABLE 1

*Extracted descriptions of subjective thought or feeling activity which Ss reported using to activate colored lights operated by EEG frequency ranges (N = 26 Ss)*

| Number of Subjects | Descriptions | | |
| --- | --- | --- | --- |
| | Beta (Red or Green) | Alpha (Blue or Red) | Theta (Green or Blue) |
| Methods Reported 9–14 Ss | Worry, anger, fear, frustration (9) | Pleasant feeling, well-being, pleasure, tranquillity, relaxation (14) | Memory of problems, uncertainty, problem solving, future planning, switching thoughts, solving mechanical or financial problems, day dreaming (10) |
| 5–7 Ss | Tension, alertness, excitement (5) | Increased awareness of thoughts and feelings (7) | — |
| 1–3 Ss | Contentment, warmth, love (3); hunger, surprise (1) | Reviewing personal experiences (2) | Restful-alertness (2); frustration, tenseness (1) |
| No Methods Reported[a] | (8)[a] | (3)[a] | (13)[a] |

Note.—Number of Ss is given in parenthesis.

[a] Includes 5 Ss who ignored the red light, 1 S who ignored the blue light, and 5 Ss who ignored the green light.

of the width of the histogram at half the peak height and calculating the reciprocals in Hz. The Q values ("peakedness" of the histograms) were used as the measure of variation of frequency. Amplitudes were measured directly from the records.

EEG analysis was completed for 36 Ss. Analysis of relationships between subjective activity and EEG parameters is indicated in the Results. A "score" was determined for each S by calculating the number of descriptor–EEG frequency associations made which agreed with the descriptors found to be significantly related to each of the three EEG frequency ranges. This was expressed as percent of number of choices agreeing with the consensus (i.e., for descriptors associated with an EEG frequency having a $p$ of $< .01$, $\chi^2$ statistic) out of the total number of sorts made by each S. These scores and the EEG variables measured were compared between the highest and lowest scoring Ss (12 Ss each).

## RESULTS

### Experiment 1

Extracts of the exact words written by the 26 Ss to describe their associations between subjective activity and colors of lights representing their EEG activity are given in Table 1. Descriptions were often brief.

Naive Ss appeared to associate alpha activity either with pleasant feelings or

TABLE 2

*Distribution of descriptors sorted by color for all Ss*

(A) Distribution of Descriptors to Color

| Subject Group | N and Percent of Descriptors | | | | | | | |
| | Red | | Blue | | Green | | No-Color | |
| | N | % | N | % | N | % | N | % |
| Controls (Non-EEG Ss, 45) | 1,125 | 24 | 1,249 | 26 | 945 | 20 | 1,407 | 30 |
| EEG Ss (45) | 937 | 20 | 931 | 20 | 828 | 17 | 2,030 | 43 |

(B) Distribution of Descriptors to EEG Frequency Ranges by EEG Ss (45)

| | Alpha | | Beta | | Theta | | None | |
| | N | % | N | % | N | % | N | % |
| EEG Ss | 1,088 | 23 | 881 | 19 | 727 | 15 | 2,030 | 43 |

(C) Distribution of Card Sorts to EEG Frequency by Color by EEG Ss (45)

| EEG Frequency | Number of Descriptors | | |
| | Red | Blue | Green |
| Alpha | 433 | 349 | 306 |
| Beta | 262 | 301 | 318 |
| Theta | 242 | 281 | 204 |

with increased inner awareness and tranquillity, and tended to associate beta activity with unpleasant thoughts and feelings, and with excitement. There were three exceptions to the latter. The greatest difficulty in formulating an adequate unifying description occurred with theta activity. This was to be expected on the basis of its relatively low incidence in the EEG. Nonetheless, 10 of 13 Ss who did define feelings related theta activity to the general mental activity of problem solving or orienting in the sense of adjusting to surroundings.

The results in Table 1 show, first, that the majority of descriptions were quite different for each of the three EEG frequency ranges, regardless of color of light used to display the frequency. Second, for each frequency range, the majority of descriptions connoted similar concepts, and third, the greatest number of descriptions or associations occurred with alpha and the fewest with theta activity.

Post-session comments concerning the experience as a whole were unexpectedly uniform. Fourteen Ss reported the experience as "interesting and relaxing," 7 Ss as "interesting and curious," and 5 Ss as "no special feeling."

*Experiment 2*

*Discussion of Table 2.* The descriptors sorted by the two subject groups were first tabulated by color. Those sorted by the experimental group were then decoded and tabulated according to the EEG frequency range which had been represented by the different colors of lights. Table 2 summarizes the total distributions of the sorted descriptors.

The $\chi^2$ statistic derived from results in Table 2A indicated that the difference between the sorts by color for the two groups was significant at $p < .01$ (3 df). The differences occurred both for the individual colors to which the descriptors were sorted as well as for the no-color choice.

All descriptors sorted to colors representing the three EEG frequency ranges are tabulated in Table 2B for the 45 $S$s of the EEG feedback experiment. More descriptors were sorted to alpha than to either of the other EEG frequencies, and the fewest number of sorts were made when the colors represented theta activity. The results are consistent with those of Experiment 1.

Table 2C shows the total sort of descriptors by color to the EEG frequency ranges. Descriptors were sorted more frequently to red when alpha activity was represented by a red light ($p \leq .01$) and were sorted more frequently to beta when beta activity was represented by either a blue or green light. Subsequent analysis revealed no relationships between the number of descriptors sorted to a color and statistically significant correlations between descriptors and EEG frequency ranges. The sort to theta activity appears random.

*Color and Subjective Activity.* Of the 105 descriptors of aspects of subjective activity, 67 were sorted to color significantly differently by the two subject groups. A comparison of the distribution of the color sorts revealed two types of differences. First, the experimental $S$s generally failed to agree about the colors that they associated with the descriptors, and second, they more frequently sorted descriptors to the white bin (indicating no association with color) than did the control group.

A total of 48 descriptors were significantly associated with color ($p \leq .01$, $\chi^2$ statistic) by the control subject group. These were: 24 with red, 14 with blue, 1 with green, and 9 associated equally with blue and green. The experimental group agreed about the color association for only 4 descriptors, 1 each to red and blue, and 2 to green.

The strongest color–descriptor associations for the control subjects to red were: angry, aggravated, excited, intense, impulsive, impatient, frustrated, powerful, and threatened ($p \leq .001$). The EEG-feedback subject group related only the descriptor angry to red.

The strongest associations with blue for the control group were: dreamlike, moody, sad, unhappy, fatigued, sleepy, and sluggish, while for the experimental group the single association to blue was the descriptor 'transcendental thinking.'

The control subjects agreed that 'able to concentrate' was associated with green, while the EEG-feedback subject group selected the 2 descriptors vacillating and investigative as related to the color green.

Control subjects sorted the following descriptors roughly equally to blue and green: calm, complacent, at-ease, contemplative, passive, pleasant, and peaceful. For the experimental group none of the sorts for any descriptor approached approximate equality between any two colors, but roughly equal distribution often occurred among the three colors.

TABLE 3

*Two examples of results of sorting descriptors of subjective activity to colors representing the three EEG frequency ranges*

*Fifteen Ss received the color–EEG frequency combinations indicated by each cell*

| EEG Frequency | Number of Descriptors | | | |
|---|---|---|---|---|
| | Red | Blue | Green | Total |
| **Angry** | | | | |
| Alpha | 5 | 0 | 1 | 6 |
| Theta | 3 | 0 | 1 | 4 |
| Beta* | 9 | 3 | 5 | 17 |
| Beta$_E$[a] | 16.6 | 0.4 | 0 | 17 |
| Experimental Total | 17 | 3 | 7 | 27 |
| Control E[a] | 26.3 | 0.7 | 0 | 27 |
| **Peaceful** | | | | |
| Alpha* | 6 | 12 | 3 | 21 |
| Alpha$_E$[a] | 0 | 10.7 | 10.3 | 21 |
| Beta | 0 | 4 | 1 | 5 |
| Theta | 4 | 6 | 1 | 11 |
| Experimental Total | 10 | 22 | 5 | 39 |
| Control E[a] | 0 | 20 | 19 | 39 |

[a] Expected values were calculated from the percentage distribution by color of the sort of the individual descriptors by the control group of 45 Ss.

* $p < .001$; C.C. = .27 for beta, .96 for alpha.

*Associations Between Subjective Activity and EEG Frequencies.* Of the 105 descriptors, 28 were found to be significantly associated with a specific EEG frequency range ($p \leq .01$). Seven additional descriptors were associated approximately equally with two frequencies.

The specificity of a descriptor for an EEG frequency range was determined by calculating expected frequencies for the three EEG frequencies on the basis of the sort distribution by color found for the control Ss, and using the $\chi^2$ statistic. Examples of results are given in Table 3.

Significant relationships between descriptors and EEG frequencies are listed below. Descriptors suggesting similar connotations are grouped together. Those descriptors found to be specific for a color by the control Ss are indicated by superscripts: R refers to red, B to blue, and BG to both blue and green.

Alpha: calm[BG], peaceful[BG], pleasant[BG], at-ease[BG], neutral; illusion, dreamlike[B], mysterious, uncertainty; contemplative[BG], association of ideas, transcendental thinking, remembering; drowsy[B], tired[B], sluggish[B].

Beta: angry[R], aggravated[R], irritated[R], impatient[R], unhappy[B], troubled[R], frustrated[R], touchy[R], shaky, investigative, feel-a-void inside.

Theta: vacillating.

Alpha and beta: intense[R], talkative, disgusted.

Alpha and theta: conjuring up, wish fulfillment, passive[BG], sleepy[B].

*Relationship Between EEG Activity and the Subjective–EEG Associations.* An

TABLE 4

*Average values for parameters of EEG activity compared between 12 Ss identifying the greatest numbers and 12 Ss identifying the smallest numbers of descriptors which were significantly associated to each of the EEG frequencies*

| EEG Parameters | Mean Values | | | | | |
| --- | --- | --- | --- | --- | --- | --- |
| | High Scorers Average 'Score' = 13 Average % with Agreement = 23 | | | Low Scorers Average 'Score' = 4 Average % with Agreement = 7 | | |
| | Alpha | Beta | Theta | Alpha | Beta | Theta |
| Average frequency in Hz | 10.5 | 19.1[a] | 5.6 | 10.6 | 20.5 | 5.4 |
| Average Q[b] | 4.6 | 5.8 | 4.2 | 4.6 | 4.3 | 4.0 |
| Average amplitude in $\mu$v | 28.5 | 16.3* | 28.0 | 19.5 | 9.9 | 18.1 |
| Average % of total abundance measured as peak area[b] | 42 | 31 | 27 | 48 | 32 | 20 |

[a] Two distinct frequencies of beta activity, one between 13–16 Hz and the other between 19–23 Hz, were found in 7 of 12 of the high scoring Ss and in 2 of 12 of the low scoring Ss.

[b] Q = a measure of variation of frequency, and peak area = the measure of abundance, both derived from interval histograms.

* Significantly different from value for low scorers, $p = .01$ (Student's $t$).

index for this relationship was constructed by determining the number of EEG-specific descriptors (as above) identified by each S. This was expressed as percent of the total number of descriptors each S sorted to the colors representing the EEG frequencies. Values of the EEG parameters were then compared between the 12 Ss with the highest "scores" and the 12 Ss with the lowest "scores."

Results are summarized in Table 4. Those Ss who agreed with the consensus about descriptor–EEG frequency associations were found to exhibit generally larger amplitudes of all three frequency ranges, but the difference was statistically significant only for the amplitude of the 13–28 Hz beta activity. High scorers also tended to have two different frequency levels of beta activity more frequently than low scoring Ss.

Relatively high amplitude of alpha waves (60–100 $\mu$v) was required to activate the feedback system for bright light and the values in Table 4 do not reflect the low amplitude alpha activity present in many Ss. The rather large values for abundance of theta activity are due to the fact that abundance for the three frequency ranges only was considered and peak areas for these three were summed and the individual ranges then expressed as percentages of the total.

*Relationship Between Color and the Association Between Subjective Activity and EEG Frequency Range.* Table 5 indicates the relationships found between different pairs of color–EEG frequencies and the average percent of EEG-specific descriptors selected from the total number sorted to each color.

The largest number of EEG-specific descriptors selected occurred when blue represented alpha activity and when either red or green represented beta activity.

The total number of descriptors sorted to each color representing an EEG fre-

TABLE 5

*Number of descriptors of subjective activity sorted to color and percent of those agreeing with the statistical consensus for association between descriptors and EEG frequencies when the colors represented different EEG frequency ranges*

| Groups | Color Representing EEG Frequency | Number of Descriptors | | | | | |
|---|---|---|---|---|---|---|---|
| | | Mean Total No. of Descriptors Selected | | | Mean % Agreeing with Consensus | | |
| | | Alpha | Beta | Theta | Alpha | Beta | Theta |
| 1 | Red | 29 | 16 | 16 | 21 | 17 | 4 |
| 2 | Blue | 23 | 20 | 18 | 30 | 8 | 3 |
| 3 | Green | 20 | 22 | 14 | 20 | 15 | 5 |

quency ranged between 14 and 23 for all combinations except when red represented alpha activity where an average of 29 sorts were made (this effect is also noted in Table 2C). The greatest agreement among *S*s about color–descriptor associations occurred when blue represented alpha activity, and the lowest agreement when any of the three colors represented theta activity. A low order of agreement also was found when blue represented beta activity.

## Discussion

Naive *S*s can quickly relate sets of subjective activities to different ranges of their own EEG frequencies when these are displayed as light signals. Support for this conclusion is three-fold.

First, the sorting of descriptors of subjective activity by color differed significantly between the subject group who had received the EEG feedback experience and the control group who sorted only against color. The ability to associate feelings with EEG activity during the feedback experience was often dominant over commonly held color–feeling associations, many subjects identifying feeling concepts by colors diametrically opposed to color associations made by the control subjects.

Second, experimental subjects sorted the descriptors to specific EEG frequencies, namely alpha and beta, while failing to agree about subjective–color associations, regardless of the color of light which represented the EEG frequencies. Moreover, descriptors specific for an EEG frequency range were similar in connotation, but differed markedly across ranges. Consensus of color–feeling associations thus provided a convenient baseline by which changes in subjective activities were quantified.

Third, there was a marked agreement in content between written descriptions and the descriptors of subjective activity found to be significantly related to the same EEG frequency range.[2]

The delineation of concepts resulting from written descriptions indicated a

[2] Similar descriptions of subjective states related to alpha activity derived in feedback experiments were reported at the Second Annual Conference on Brain Research, Aspen, Colorado, 1969. (Kamiya, Nowlis, Mulholland).

greater underlying unity of concepts than did results from the card sorts. Subjects writing descriptions may have focused upon key words and used these to construct unifying concepts. The difference in types of information obtained from the two types of reporting was most marked with respect to theta activity; written descriptions bore considerable resemblance to behavioral activities reported for theta in animal studies. The card sorting technique failed to elicit similar aspects of subjective activity although descriptors of such activities were available for sorting.

On the other hand, data obtained from the descriptor color-sort technique indicate that aspects of pre-conscious activity may be identified objectively since many descriptors sorted distinctively to color by the EEG subjects were not associated with a specific EEG frequency. The card sort technique also elicited some subjective–EEG associations which were not found in the written descriptions (e.g. illusion and dream-like with alpha). Since the descriptor cards were sorted quickly, opportunities to form unifying concepts were limited. This may also account for the lack of agreement about subjective association to theta activity.

*Relationship to Color*

Although identification of aspects of subjective activity with EEG frequency did occur independently of color–subjective biases, color–feeling associations were factors in relating feeling states to EEG frequencies, and may in themselves be intimately related to EEG activity.

The results revealed two sets of relationships with subjective activities: color–subjective activity and EEG–subjective activity. The interrelationships among color, EEG frequency, and (aspects of) subjective activity are easily demonstrated using Venn diagrams. The color blue was most frequently associated with descriptors which the consensus related to alpha activity (regardless of light color used). Descriptors significantly related to alpha activity were about equally associated with blue and green by the control subjects. The difference, i.e., the lack of consensus about associations between green and alpha, indicates the effect of the EEG feedback experience. The majority of descriptors associated with beta activity by the EEG subjects (regardless of light color used to display beta) were those associated with the color red by the control subjects. The types of feeling associations to blue and to red are almost universal in our culture. The partial overlap of these associations and the subjective associations with alpha and beta respectively suggest the possibility that subjective activity related to these colors may originate from the same underlying processes as the EEG activity. The area of overlap in associations among subjective activity aspects, color, and EEG components may provide a bridge between the pre-conscious associations among perceptual and experiential data and the synthesis of conscious meanings and symbols.

*Correlation With EEG Activity*

Currently available techniques for EEG analysis provide only a fraction of the information about brain electrical activity which might be found to relate to complex subjective activities of the type represented in the experiments reported. None of the parameters measured (Table 4) appeared to relate convincingly to the subjective aspects elicited. The fact remains, however, that subjects were able to identify in a quantifiable way some aspects of subjective activity associated with specific aspects of brain electrical activity. It may be deduced that if the parameters measured are involved in the phenomenon, they must be involved in a different order or arrangement than the one analyzed. Other factors of importance may be temporal or spatial patterning, space-time event patterning, or ranges and mixtures of identifiable EEG components which were not measured.

### Inferences[3]

The unique characteristic of the experimental situation was that it allowed the subject to interact with aspects of his own physiologic functioning in the absence of either directed or preformed concepts.

The light monitors of the EEG activity provided perceptual information about the experience, and instructions to the subjects generated some degree of subjective exploratory activity. The subject's task was to identify relationships between his subjective and EEG activities. The subjective activity accompanying a specific EEG frequency presumably was identified by light intensity and the temporal aspects of the on-ness or off-ness of the light signals.

The general agreement among subjective reports about subjective aspects associated with each EEG frequency suggests that the perceptual and experiential data are organized similarly in the majority of individuals, and that similar chains of mechanisms process the data of both active perception and feeling states generated by prior life experiences. Experimental evidence obtained in the earlier study suggested that these two sets of information undergo organization at a pre-conscious level since production of alpha activity increased significantly prior to awareness of a conscious concept of how this was effected (Brown, 1970). Results of the present study confirm the formation of EEG–feeling relationships below the level of communicated awareness.

The attempt to quantify pre-consciously organized associations provides a paradigm for studying relationships between experiential and perceptual data. Variations in the degree of organization may account for differences in abilities to conceptualize the relationships. The pre-conscious associations provide a structure by which perceptual and experiential relationships can be verified, leading to conscious recognition and finally, voluntary control of these inner aspects. In the latter stage no external signals are necessary to sustain the relationships between feeling states and EEG activity (Brown, 1970).

[3] A portion of the following discussion is based on results of an earlier experiment (Brown, 1970) in which subjects were asked to isolate subjective activity which would keep on a blue light operated by the subject's alpha activity. It was found that (a) a significant increase in alpha activity preceded an EEG discrimination response, and (b) voluntary control over the alpha activity developed during three training sessions could be elicited in the absence of the light signal.

### Differences from Characteristics of Conditioning

In the feedback circuits of this study, the elements of "response" and "reinforcement" cannot be identified as separate entities. Any identifiable relay of the circuit (feeling state, EEG frequency, light signal) can be considered as at least two of these three elements.

The techniques further differ in that in operant conditioning, the response (and response set) is either directed or matched by a judgment external to the system, i.e., the experimentor selects both the criteria for reinforcement and the behavior to be reinforced. Subjective activity arises either from unconsciously associated response–reinforcement relationships or from the process of recognizing formation of these relationships.

In the feedback system used, programming of the reinforcement is internal, and is a function of actively relating subjective activity to an external indicator which operates only when a specific EEG activity is present. Successful operation appears to require some internal effort by the subject: he generates both the "response" (identification of a subjective state) and the reinforcement signal, and in addition selects the criteria for significant values of the reinforcement indicator. The subject selects the criteria for reinforcement (color, light on-ness or off-ness, intensity, temporal sequencing, etc.) such that he generates a signal appropriate to produce that reinforcement. The circuit of the feedback system either is closed and operating or is not closed and not operating. Reinforcement cannot occur in the absence of a continued effort both to specify and generate it, and cannot be separated from the EEG "response." The reinforcements are, in fact, externalized EEG events.

In the feedback system the entire learning process is internally directed. Subjective attributes of motivation, reward, error, anticipation, etc., stem from the verification of an internal event. The characteristics and attributes of the phenomenon classify it as an awareness or cognitive function. It is, ultimately, the awareness of the relationship between subjective activity and the light signals operated by EEG activity which is the "response." The unconscious awareness of this relationship or its formation may serve as a bridge or "temporary connection" needed to complete formation of the response.

Finally, as noted in the earlier paper (Brown, 1970), extinction of the response either does not occur or diminishes slowly over time, and in contrast to conditioning mechanisms, does not appear to relate to continued presence of the reinforcing signal.

In conditioning terminology the phenomenon may describe the first demonstrable operant which involves consciousness.

### REFERENCES

Brown, B. B. Specificity of EEG photic flicker responses to color as related to visual imagery ability. *Psychophysiology*, 1966, *2*, 197–207.

Brown, B. B. Subjective and EEG responses to LSD in visualizer and non-visualizer subjects. *Electroencephalography & Clinical Neurophysiology*, 1968, *25*, 372–379.

Brown, B. B. Effect of LSD on visually evoked responses to color in visualizer and non-visualizer subjects. *Electroencephalography & Clinical Neurophysiology*, 1969, *27*, 356–363.

Brown, B. B. Recognition of aspects of consciousness through association with EEG alpha activity represented by a light signal. *Psychophysiology*, 1970, *6*, 442–452.

Delse, F. C., & Feather, B. W. The effect of augmented sensory feedback on the control of salivation. *Psychophysiology*, 1968, *5*, 15–21.

Engel, B. T., & Chism, R. A. Operant conditioning of heart rate speeding. *Psychophysiology*, 1967, *3*, 418–426.

Hart, J. T. Autocontrol of EEG alpha. *Psychophysiology*, 1968, *5*, 506. (Abstract)

Kimmel, E., & Kimmel, H. D. A replication of operant conditioning of the GSR. *Journal of Experimental Psychology*, 1963, *65*, 212–213.

Stoyva, J., & Kamiya, J. Electrophysiological studies of dreaming as the prototype of a new strategy in the study of consciousness. *Psychological Review*, 1968, *75*, 192–205.

# Effects of Initial Alpha Wave 9
## Abundance and Operant Training
## Procedures on Occipital Alpha
## and Beta Wave Activity

### Jackson Beatty

Operant methods were used to increase differentially the abundance of occipital EEG waves in the alpha (8-12 Hz) and beta (above 13 Hz) frequency bands of naive undergraduate Ss in the presence of a discriminative stimulus. Ss were grouped by the amount of alpha wave activity in their pretraining EEG. Operant training with continuous reinforcement produced reliable and orderly changes in EEG spectra as a function of reinforcement contingency. Baseline alpha abundance predicted only the mean level of alpha output over trials, not the efficiency of training. Matched yoked controls showed no difference in EEG spectra between the two reinforcement conditions.

It has been reported recently that human Ss may alter the spectra of their EEG activity if they are provided feedback indicating the level of activity in the frequency band which is to be augmented or reduced (Kamiya, 1968; Nowlis & Kamiya, 1970; Green, Green, & Walters, 1969; Brown, 1970). Previous attempts to condition cortical alpha activity classically met with limited success (Jasper & Shagass, 1941a, b; Shagass, 1942; Shagass & Johnson, 1943; Wells & Wolff, 1960; Albino & Burnand, 1964; Torres, 1968). In the current work of Kamiya (1968), Nowlis & Kamiya (1970), and Green et al (1969), the training methodology is presented primarily in terms of feedback operating in a cybernetic control system. Ss are presented with displays which indicate the amount of alpha band activity in

S's recent EEG. Other models also fit this methodology. Since Ss in these experiments are presumably motivated to control their EEG patterns, feedback may be considered to operate as a reinforcer in an operant conditioning paradigm with a continuous schedule of reinforcement.[1]

The present study is based on the operant model of response modification. It represents an attempt to gather basic data on the control of EEG alpha and beta activity in a normal and relatively unselected population of undergraduate students. The use of the operant theoretical framework suggests some appropriate control procedures which have not been previously employed. To show experimental control of EEG activity, Ss were trained in a mixed set of trials to increase either occipital alpha or beta activity, contingent on the state of a visual discriminative stimulus (SD). To show that it was, in fact, the contingency of response and reinforcement that was responsible for

*This research was supported by the Advanced Research Projects Agency of the Department of Defense and was monitored by the Office of Naval Research under Contract N00014-70-C-0350 to the San Diego State College Foundation.

any observed alteration in the experimental groups, a group of yoked controls which received noncontingent reinforcement was also employed. Since a fairly large number of Ss was studied, the suggestion that the efficiency of training is related to the initial abundance of alpha activity (Nowlis & Kamiya, 1970) was systematically tested.

### SUBJECTS

Thirty-six undergraduate students served as Ss in order to partially satisfy the requirements of an introductory psychology course. Ss were assigned to this experiment without prior knowledge of its nature. This procedure was thought to minimize problems stemming from the self-selection of Ss.

### ELECTRICAL RECORDING

Occipital EEG was recorded from position $O_z$ of the 10-20 system (Jasper, 1958) referred to the right earlobe. S's left earlobe was grounded. The EEG was first amplified by a Grass P-15 amplifier and then by a series of integrated circuit amplifiers with active filters. The frequency response of the total system was essentially flat between 2 and 20 Hz, with ½ amplitude attenuation at 0.6 and 32 Hz. This signal was monitored on an oscilloscope and was available at the analog/digital converter of the computer.

### DESIGN AND PROCEDURE

The Ss were first told that they were participating in a study of brain wave activity. After the recording electrodes were attached, Ss were seated in an electrically shielded room with a low level of ambient lighting. They were asked to keep their eyes open and refrain from moving for a 300-sec period, during which the computer calculated the baseline spectra of their EEG. Ss were then instructed as to the nature of their task, in words similar to the following: "While you have been sitting here, the computer has made a number of measurements of your EEG activity. You now have the opportunity to learn to control your own brain waves. The EEG is a complex waveform which may be thought to show many different patterns. From all these patterns we have arbitrarily selected two for today's study. Each second the computer will sample your EEG, looking for one of the two selected wave patterns. Light 1 signifies that the computer is looking for Pattern 1, and Light 2 means Pattern 2. When Light 3 is on, you may rest. When it finds what it is looking for, the loudness of the background tone will be increased for 1 sec. Your job is to learn to produce the kinds of wave patterns which will keep the tone on. If you succeed in doubling either kind of EEG activity from your baseline level, you will receive an extra hour of experimental credit. If you double both, you will receive 2 free hours of credit. As before, keep your eyes open and refrain from moving."

Twenty-seven Ss were then run for 10 experimental training trials of 200-sec duration. Training was divided into five blocks of two trials, one with alpha reinforcement and one with beta. The ordering of trials within a block was random. Between blocks, Ss were forced to get up and walk around for a period of not less than 1 min. No mention was ever made of alpha waves, cortical desynchronization, or similar matters during training, nor was there any discussion of the psychological states which are thought to be associated with these phenomena. Between trials, Ss were given general indications of their success in achieving control.

The 27 experimental Ss were divided, on the basis of baseline data, into low, medium, and high alpha groups of nine Ss each. Nine additional Ss served as yoked controls. They were treated in exactly the same manner as experimental Ss, except that their pattern of reinforcement was not contingent upon their EEG. Instead, their baseline spectra were used to match them with a single experimental S. The paper-tape record of that experimental S's reinforcements was used by the computer to generate the reinforcement pattern for the control S.

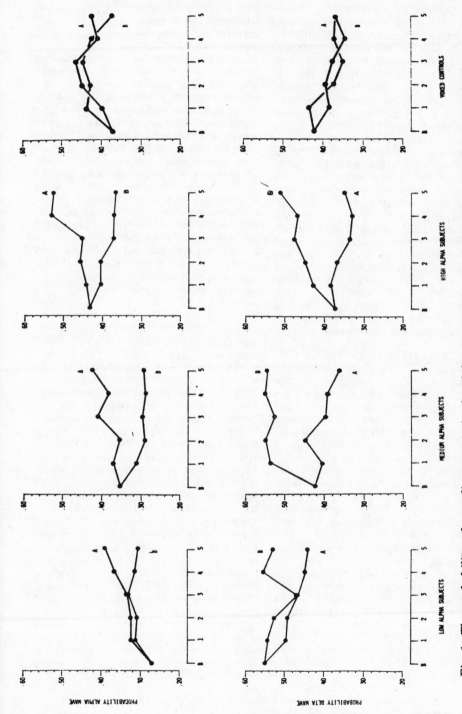

Fig. 1. The probability of sampling a wave in the alpha (top row) or beta (bottom row) frequency band is given for experimental Ss with low, medium and high levels of baseline alpha and for control Ss as a function of baseline or trial block. "A" curve denotes alpha and "B," beta, reinforcement contingency.

## COMPUTER CONTROL

The entire experiment was run under digital computer control. During a trial or baseline period, the EEG was sampled each second for one complete wave, referenced to 0 potential and beginning with a positive deflection. The period of this wave was then measured and classified by the method of Legewie & Probst (1969) as a single wave at X Hz. If the wave was within the criterion frequency band (8-12 Hz for alpha, 13 Hz or more for beta), the intensity of a quiet 400-Hz tone was augmented for 1 sec. During that second, the sampling and measurement procedure was repeated and, if that wave was also within the criterion bounds, the tone intensity remained high for another second. During the baseline trial, the tone was totally suppressed. After each trial, a count of the number of waves at each frequency was printed out and a record of the temporal pattern of reinforcement was punched on paper tape.

## RESULTS

The data of this investigation are summarized in Fig. 1, which shows the probability of obtaining an alpha (top row) or a beta wave (bottom row) for each group, reinforcement contingency, and trial block. It can be seen that all experimental groups show differentiation of their EEG activity between the alpha and beta trials. Thus, alpha wave activity (seen in the top row of Fig. 1) is more probable during alpha than during beta reinforcement. Further, these differences increase with practice, as a function of trial block. These conclusions are supported by an analysis of variance (ANOVA) for the probability of alpha waves in the experimental groups. In the alpha ANOVA the effect of reinforcement contingency is clearly significant ($F = 21.84$, df = 1/24, $p < .001$), indicating that our Ss had shown differential control of alpha wave production as a function of the state of the discriminative stimulus. The significant interaction of Reinforcement Contingency by Trial Block ($F = 4.49$, df = 4/96, $p < .0025$) supports the conclusion that this differentiation increases reliably with practice.[2]

It appears that the baseline level of alpha activity is related to the mean level of alpha wave production on the subsequent trial blocks ($F = 4.64$, df = 2/24, $p < .025$). But the lack of a significant interaction between alpha wave abundance, group, and trials ($F = 0.487$, df = 8/96) fails to support the view that initial alpha wave abundance is a major determinant of the relative efficiency of learning differential control. Similarly, the correlations are neither large nor positive between baseline alpha wave abundance and either the change in alpha activity between baseline and Block 5 ($r = -0.15$, n.s.) or the difference in probability of alpha activity between alpha and beta trials in Block 5 ($r = -.20$, n.s.). The probability of alpha wave on the last alpha reinforcement trial is, of course, significantly related to level of baseline alpha ($r = .43$, $p < .05$).

Reinforcement contingency also effects occipital desynchronization. It may be seen in the bottom row of Fig. 1 that for experimental Ss the probability of beta frequency activity is greater during beta than during alpha reinforcement. The ANOVA for the beta wave probabilities in the experimental groups reveals less order in this data than was seen above with the alpha probabilities. As with alpha wave activity, the effect of reinforcement contingency is highly significant ($F = 26.13$, df = 1/24, $p < .001$). Ss showed more beta wave activity on those trials in which it was reinforced. No other main effect or interaction approached significance. There is no evidence in this analysis for systematic effects of any consequence of trial block or baseline level of alpha on the probability of beta frequency activity. Similarly, no significant correlation was found between alpha or beta baseline and any of the measures of beta activity used (probability of beta activity in Block 5, the difference in the probability of beta activity between the reinforcement contingencies in Block 5, or the change in the probability of beta activity during beta reinforcement between Blocks 1 and 5). Knowledge of the baseline spectra is of little use in predicting the probability of beta frequency activity and its changes in this task.

Separate analyses of the variance of the probability of alpha and beta activity were computed for Ss in the yoked control condition. Neither analysis reveals a significant effect of reinforcement contingency, trials, or their interaction. The yoked controls, unlike the experimental Ss, fail to show any differential response between alpha and beta trials. This argues that the contingency of reinforcement and response is necessary for the development of EEG control in our situation.

## DISCUSSION

As has been previously reported, Ss can significantly and differentially increase the amount of alpha and beta activity in their occipital EEG when given feedback information or immediate reinforcement. Several aspects of the present study, however, should be emphasized. First, the amount of time spent in training was relatively short—16.6 min under each reinforcement contingency. Nevertheless, the effects of training are quite reliable and reasonably large. Differential responsiveness is evident after the first trial block.

Second, care was taken not to inform our Ss that the states to be discriminated were occipital alpha and desynchronization. These words currently trigger explicit expectations among a considerable subset of the undergraduate population, the effects of which upon the learning situation would be unclear.

Third, the suggestion that initial alpha wave abundance is related to the efficiency of training is not empirically verified. Although an examination of Fig. 1 suggests that the medium and high groups show a more reliable differentiation between conditions, the correlational analysis does not

support this view. One can predict reliably only that the final level of alpha wave activity will depend on the pretraining level. The efficiency of training does not depend in any important way upon initial alpha abundance, within the normal range of variability.

Fourth, the total failure of the yoked control Ss to learn or to show a significant response change with trials provides good evidence that it is, in fact, the response-contingent feedback or reinforcement which is responsible

## REFERENCES

ALBINO, R., & BURNAND, G. Conditioning of the alpha rhythm in man. Journal of Experimental Psychology, 1964, 67, 539-544.

BROWN, B. B. Recognition of aspects of consciousness through association with E.E.G. alpha activity represented by a light signal. Psychophysiology, 1970, 6, 442-452.

GEISSER, S., & GREENHOUSE, S. W. An extension of Box's results on the use of the F distribution in multivariate analysis. Annual of Mathematical Statistics, 1958, 29, 885-891.

GREEN, E. E., GREEN, A. M., & WALTERS, E. D. Self-regulation of internal states. Proceedings of the International Congress of Cybernetics, London, 1969. J. Rose (Ed.). London: Gordon & Breach, 1970.

JASPER, H. H. The ten-twenty electrode system of the International Federation. Electroencephalography & Clinical Neurophysiology, 1958, 10, 371-375.

JASPER, H. H., & SHAGASS, C. Conditioning the occipital rhythm in man. Journal of Experimental Psychology, 1941a, 28, 373-388.

JASPER, H. H., & SHAGASS, C. Conscious time judgements related to conditioned time intervals and voluntary control of the alpha rhythm. Journal of Experimental Psychology, 1941b, 28, 503-508.

KAMIYA, J. Conscious control of brain waves. Psychology Today, 1968, 1, 57-60.

LEGEWIE, H., & PROBST, W. On-line analysis of EEG with a small computer (period-amplitude analysis). Electroencephalography & Clinical Neurophysiology, 1969, 27, 533-536.

NOWLIS, D. P., & KAMIYA, J. The control of electroencephalographic alpha rhythms through auditory feedback and the associated mental activity. Psychophysiology, 1970, 6, 476-484.

SHAGASS, C. Conditioning the human occipital alpha rhythm to a voluntary stimulus. A quantitative study. Journal of

Experimental Psychology, 1942, 31, 367-379.

SHAGASS, C., & JOHNSON, E. P. The course of acquisition of a conditioned response of the occipital alpha rhythm. Journal of Experimental Psychology, 1943, 33, 201-209.

TORRES, A. A. Sensitization and association in alpha blocking "conditioning." Electroencephalography & Clinical Neurophysiology, 1968, 24, 279-306.

WELLS, C. E., & WOLFF, H. G. Electrographic evidence of impaired brain function in chronically anxious patients. Science, 1960, 131, 1671-1672.

NOTE

1. The meaning of "continuous reinforcement" becomes less clear when the response to be reinforced is a particular configuration of a continuous analog signal such as the EEG. Nonetheless, the notion of scheduling reinforcement may be applied to such data as we show in a forthcoming paper, "Control of occipital EEG activity: Effects of the schedule of reinforcement."

2. The univariate ANOVA is biased toward overestimating the significance level of data based on repeated measures, if the correlations between these measures are not equal. To guard against this possibility, the Geisser-Greenhouse convervative F test (1958), which assumes the worst case of unequal correlation, was also used to estimate the minimal level of significance of the Trials by Reinforcement Contingency interaction. This interaction remains significant with $p < .05$.

# 10

# Occipital Alpha
# and Accommodative Vergence, Pursuit
# Tracking, and Fast Eye Movements

## Thomas B. Mulholland and Erik Peper

### ABSTRACT

The parietal–occipital EEG was recorded while subjects performed various fixation, accommodation, and tracking maneuvers with stationary and moving targets. For some experiments the target was continuously in view and independent of the EEG; in others, a feedback path connected the occurrence of parietal–occipital alpha with the visibility of the target. The results show that alpha attenuation or blocking is *not* due to "visual attention" but to processes of fixation, lens accommodation, and pursuit tracking. Saccadic movements were not reliably linked to alpha or alpha "blocking." The utility of feedback methods for testing the hypotheses that visual control processes are linked to the parietal–occipital alpha rhythms was demonstrated.

DESCRIPTORS: EEG, Alpha rhythms, Oculomotor functions, Alpha feedback methods, Visual attention, Visual controls. (T. B. Mulholland & E. Peper)

The close association of vision and the EEG occipital alpha rhythm was recognized forty-one years ago (Berger, 1930 (trans., 1969); Adrian & Matthews, 1934; Durup & Fessard, 1935; Adrian, 1943). In a lecture, "The Dominance of Vision," Adrian (1943) clearly pointed to changes of lens accommodation and eye fixation as salient variables involved in the desynchronization or "blocking" of the occipital EEG. Nevertheless, these early researchers and those who followed them stressed the role of "visual attention," or simply "attention," as the variable that was associated with the "blocking" of the occipital alpha rhythm. Measurements or observations of the position and movement of the eye or of the accommodation of the lens were rarely compared with simultaneous EEG recording. One feature of this history was the emergence of a definition of the electroencephalographic alpha rhythm which included a psychological concept, e.g., "alpha rhythm: rhythm, usually with a frequency 8–13 cps in adults, most prominent in posterior areas, present most markedly when eyes are closed and attenuated during attention, especially visual [Storm Van Leeuwen, Bick-

Address requests for reprints to: Thomas B. Mulholland, Perception Laboratory, Veterans Administration Hospital, Bedford, Massachusetts 01730.

ford, Brazier, Cobb, Dondey, Gastaut, Gloor, Henry, Hess, Knott, Kugler, Lairy, Loeb, Magnus, Oller Daurella, Petsche, Schwab, Walter, & Widén, 1966, p. 306]."

Recently, the concept of attention in neurophysiology has been criticized (Evans & Mulholland, 1969). Mulholland (1968, 1969a) offered an explanation of the "blocking" of the occipital alpha rhythm as a result of visual receptor adjusting and positioning processes occurring in the parietal and occipital cortex in addition to the activation or "arousal" processes following sensory stimulation.

This paper presents results obtained by recording the parietal–occipital EEG simultaneously with electro-oculographic recordings during accommodative vergence, slow pursuit tracking, and fast eye movements. The results suggest some directions that neurophysiological studies might take in order to resolve the questions that are raised. For the psychologist, the results are a comment on the oversimplification and ambiguity involved in the statement that "visual attention" causes the blocking of occipital alpha rhythms. Some of the results were briefly reported previously (Mulholland, 1969b; Peper, 1970). We shall present more detailed results and a comprehensive discussion of those and subsequent studies. Part A describes studies in which the stimulus is not controlled by the subject's EEG; Part B describes the "Feedback" method, in which the occurrence of a visual stimulus is controlled by the occurrence of parietal–occipital alpha rhythms.

## Part A

### *Method and Materials*

Adult humans with normal corrected vision and who had recordable occipital alpha with eyes open were studied. Recordings were made in a quiet audiometric test room. Three kinds of data were obtained: EEG and EOG recordings, and a marker controlled by the $S$ which indicated the apparent clearness or subjective clarity (SC) of the target. EEGs were obtained from parietal–occipital electrodes, $P_3$–$O_1$, $P_4$–$O_2$, or occipital $O_1$–$O_2$, in the International Nomenclature (Jasper, 1958). The EEG electrodes were attached to the scalp with electrolytic paste and connected to a Grass Model 5 polygraph. An electrode over the mastoid was ground.

The EEG was automatically classified into intervals of "alpha" and "no-alpha" (Mulholland, 1968). The definition of "alpha" was accomplished by means of a bandpass filter, amplifier, and "state" relay circuit. The frequency of the occipital alpha was determined during a prior "resting" recording with eyes closed. The filter was set to $\pm 1$ or $\pm 0.5$ Hz of the "resting" alpha frequency. The apparatus was set so that alpha having an amplitude greater than 25% of the maximum "resting" alpha recorded with eyes closed caused the state relay to be ON. At less than 20% resting it was OFF. Between 20–25% the relay was unpredictably ON or OFF. ON and OFF defined "alpha" and "no-alpha." The definition of "alpha" was not evidently different for the two filter settings.

The target moved laterally at eye level in the frontal plane through a distance of 5 to 6 inches. Movement of the target was controlled by two variable-speed motors. These were connected by cams to rigid levers which were linked to the target holder. The levers and motors were noisy when the target was moving. By varying the speed of the motors with a manual control, simple and complex movements could be generated. Target motion was recorded from a potentiometer linked to the movement of the target holder. As the target moved, it turned the potentiometer through a small angle. The change of resistance was recorded as a voltage deflection by connecting the potentiometer between the polygraph driver amplifier and ground. The beginning, direction, and end of target motion was recorded, which was sufficient for these studies.

The EOG was recorded with nonpolarizing AgCl (Beckman) electrodes from the inner and outer canthi for each eye. The EOG showed the beginning, direction, and end of eye movements. At the beginning and end of each trial the EOG for extreme left, right, upward, and downward ocular deviation was recorded. A head or jaw support was used for all $S$s. When necessary a bite board was used.

Three kinds of eye movements were recorded: slow accommodative vergence, slow tracking movements, and fast movements. To record accommodative vergence the target was viewed monocularly, one eye being occluded. When the target was brought near the viewing eye, the occluded eye moved inward (convergence) while the viewing eye showed no such movement. When the far field was viewed, the occluded eye moved outward (divergence). Four $S$s were tested (P.W., S. L., R. H., A. M.). For the other 5 $S$s the target was viewed binocularly and both eyes showed the symmetrical movements of binocular convergence. Change in vergence was usually associated with a change in subjective clearness of the target. The $S$ was instructed to press a telegraph key whenever the target appeared to be unclear or blurred, and not to press the key when it appeared clear and focussed. The key position was marked on the EEG record. Sometimes the report of subjective clarity (SC) lagged behind the recorded change of vergence.

Pursuit tracking movements were distinguished from fast movements by a slower velocity and close correspondence with target motion. Pursuit movements were faster than vergence movements and each eye moved in the same direction. Vergence movements were slower and the eyes moved in opposite directions.

The EEG, EOG, and subjective clarity data (SC) were recorded during four experiments: 1) target stationary; 2) target moving laterally in a predictable, nearly sinusoidal trajectory; 3) target moving laterally in a complex, less predictable trajectory; and 4) target moving laterally in a variable frequency sinusoidal trajectory. Velocity of motion was gradually increased, then gradually decreased by manually controlling the speed of one of the motors controlling target movement.

Two viewing conditions were tested for Experiment 1. The $S$ was instructed to "focus the target" (focus, F) or to "let it blur" (blur, B), that is, to relax accommodation until the target was blurred. In the other experiments the target was moving. Three conditions were tested in each experiment: focus and track the target (focus-track, FT); relax accommodation until the target is subjectively blurred and continue tracking (blur-track, BT); and relax accommodation and do not track (blur-no-track, BNT).

Within each experiment the viewing conditions were F, B, FT, BT, and BNT, and the number of trials sometimes varied from S to S. For this reason, data for each S are presented separately. Fourteen Ss were tested. Two Ss showed no alpha under any of the conditions; 3 did not monitor target clearness reliably. The EEG results for the last 3 were similar to those obtained by the majority of the remaining 9 Ss whose results are presented here.

The quantification of the EEG was based on measures made on the ink tracing: 1. Alpha index. "State" relay ON defined "alpha"; OFF defined "no-alpha." From these the series of durations of "alpha" and "no-alpha" events were obtained and an estimate of percent-time "alpha." 2. Maximum alpha amplitude. In each trial the maximum peak-to-peak amplitude of alpha associated with "state" relay ON was measured in millimeters. 3. Alpha delay. The delay between the beginning of an experiment trial and the first state relay ON ("alpha") was measured. 4. Total time. The total time (sec) for each trial was measured.

The beginning of a trial was defined as the ON or OFF interval during which the brief instructions were given over the intercom as prearranged with the S. These were "focus," "blur," "focus-track," "blur-track," or "blur-no-track." The total time in each trial was also measured. The means, for each S, of total time, percent-time "alpha," maximum "alpha" amplitude, and "alpha" delay were analyzed by analysis of variance.

## Results

*Experiment 1. Stationary Target.* Ss were instructed to focus the target or to relax accommodation; this resulted in a blurred image of the target. These trials were alternated. The target was stationary, in the line of sight of Ss viewing monocularly or in the median plane for those viewing binocularly. Seven of the 9 Ss had a greater percent-time "alpha" for "blur," compared with "focus" trials. Seven of the 9 had a greater maximum alpha amplitude during the blur trials. The delay between the beginning of the condition and the occurrence of "alpha" was longer during "focus" trials for 6 of the 9 Ss. The delay between the shift from "focus" to "blur" and the first alpha burst was usually longer than 1.0 sec and sometimes longer than 15 sec (see Table 1). This contrasts with the brief delay between the shift from "blur" to "focus" and the first interval of "no-alpha." This could be evaluated only if "alpha" were present at the time of the shift from Blur to Focus. This delay was never longer than 0.5 sec (see Fig. 1). Analysis of variance indicated that the differences between Focus and Blur conditions were significant ($p < .05$) for percent-time alpha measures and for maximum alpha amplitude.

*Experiment 2. Predictably Moving Target.* The EEG was evaluated in the same way as in Experiment 1. Table 2 presents the various measures for the focus-track (FT), blur-track (BT), and blur-no-track (BNT) conditions. As can be seen, there is a clear trend toward increased percent-time alpha as the target appears to be blurred, divergence occurs, and pursuit tracking is stopped. For

TABLE 1

*Experiment 1*

*Stationary target*

| Subjects | N Trials | | Total Time | | X̄ Percent-Time Alpha | | X̄ Max. Alpha Amplitude (mm) | | X̄ Alpha Delay (sec) | |
|---|---|---|---|---|---|---|---|---|---|---|
| | Focus | Blur | Focus | Blur | Focus | Blur | Focus | Blur | Focus | Blur |
| P. W. | 6 | 6 | 197 | 262 | 4.6 | 3.1 | 6.3 | 5.2 | 15.6 | 18.4 |
| W. C. | 7 | 6 | 164 | 173 | 15.1 | 10.1 | 4.5 | 4.6 | 3.2 | 3.4 |
| S. F. | 5 | 5 | 75 | 84 | 2.3 | 8.4 | 4.0 | 6.0 | 9.1 | 9.1 |
| S. L. | 3 | 3 | 87 | 80 | 2.5 | 10.2 | 3.5 | 8.5 | 14.6 | 11.8 |
| R. H. | 7 | 7 | 101 | 120 | 22.9 | 69.5 | 19.0 | 34.5 | 4.5 | 1.0 |
| R. D. | 5 | 6 | 50 | 116 | 14.3 | 22.2 | 12.5 | 25.0 | 4.5 | 2.4 |
| W. P. | 2 | 2 | 34 | 56 | 13.3 | 40.9 | 4.0 | 11.5 | 2.4 | 1.9 |
| R. G. | 3 | 3 | 60 | 63 | 0.7 | 13.0 | 6.5 | 7.5 | 9.1 | 2.8 |
| A. M. | 9 | 7 | 145 | 89 | 1.1 | 6.2 | 6.0 | 6.5 | 14.4 | 8.6 |
| X̄ | | | 101.4 | 115.8 | 8.5 | 20.4 | 7.4 | 12.1 | 8.6 | 6.6 |

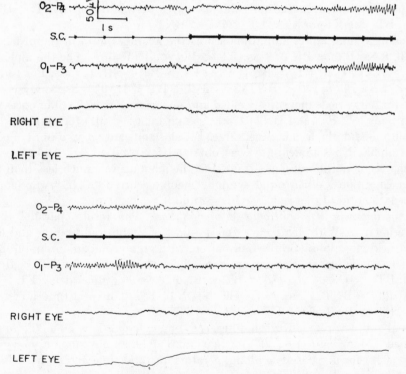

FIG. 1. Top half: Alpha occurs with a delay, after a shift from convergence and a report of a clearly focussed target to divergence and a report of a blurred target. Bottom half: Alpha is blocked just prior to a shift from divergence and report of blurred target to convergence and report of a focussed target. Tracings are R P–O EEG, subjective clarity of the target superimposed on a 1 sec time mark, L P–O EEG, right EOG, and left EOG. See text.

TABLE 2

*Experiment 2*

*Predictably moving target*

| Subjects | N Trials | | | Total Time | | | X̄ Percent-Time Alpha | | | X̄ Maximum Alpha Amplitude (mm) | | | X̄ Alpha Delay (sec) | | |
|---|---|---|---|---|---|---|---|---|---|---|---|---|---|---|---|
| | FT | BT | BNT | FT | BT | BNT | FT | BT | BNT | FT | BT | BNT | FT | BT | BNT |
| P. W. | 3 | 3 | 3 | 164 | 185 | 96 | 7.3 | 10.1 | 34.1 | 9.0 | 9.0 | 12.0 | 4.4 | 6.9 | 2.8 |
| W. C. | 4 | 4 | 4 | 185 | 296 | 158 | 10.5 | 10.6 | 35.1 | 3.6 | 4.5 | 6.0 | 4.6 | 2.2 | 0.5 |
| S. F. | 3 | 3 | 3 | 59 | 56 | 40 | 2.7 | 3.5 | 41.3 | 4.0 | 5.0 | 8.0 | 6.8 | 10.4 | 0.8 |
| S. L. | 3 | 3 | 3 | 96 | 101 | 114 | — | 2.1 | 20.5 | — | 4.5 | 11.5 | — | 20.3 | 3.4 |
| R. H. | 8 | 7 | 7 | 141 | 185 | 206 | 42.4 | 78.0 | 79.7 | 31.0 | 39.0 | 41.5 | 0.4 | 0.8 | 0.6 |
| R. D. | 4 | 4 | 4 | 98 | 131 | 112 | 4.9 | 10.9 | 41.6 | 10.5 | 10.0 | 19.5 | 14.6 | 7.0 | 2.7 |
| W. P. | 3 | 3 | 3 | 136 | 152 | 142 | 15.7 | 31.3 | 42.3 | 10.5 | 16.0 | 15.5 | 7.4 | 4.4 | 4.0 |
| R. G. | 3 | 3 | 3 | 116 | 121 | 129 | 9.9 | 12.7 | 12.4 | 11.0 | 7.5 | 10.5 | 2.1 | 1.2 | 2.7 |
| A. M. | 5 | 4 | 4 | 149 | 111 | 50 | 1.3 | 6.6 | 40.5 | 8.0 | 5.5 | 10.5 | 20.6 | 13.5 | 1.7 |
| X̄ | | | | 127.1 | 148.6 | 116.3 | 10.5 | 18.4 | 38.6 | 9.7 | 11.2 | 15.0 | 7.6 | 7.4 | 2.1 |

the percent-time alpha the individual averages were in the order FT < BNT for 9 *S*s; BT < BNT for 8 *S*s; FT < BT < BNT for 7 *S*s.

For maximum alpha amplitude scores the averages were in the order FT < BNT, 8 *S*s; BT > BNT, 8 *S*s; FT < BT < BNT, 5 *S*s. For the alpha delay FT > BNT, 7 *S*s; BT > BNT, 8 *S*s; FT > BT > BNT, 5 *S*s. For total time FT < BNT, 5 *S*s; BT < BNT, 3 *S*s; FT < BT < BNT, 3 *S*s. Analysis of variance for the various measures yielded an *F* associated with the differences among conditions FT, BT, and BNT. *F* was significant ($p < .01$) for maximum alpha amplitude and alpha delay measures. *F* was significant ($p < .001$) for percent-time alpha. No significant *F* was obtained for total time. "Alpha" occurred during the condition of focus-track, but the amount was much less than for the other conditions. When rapid eye movements occurred "alpha" was sometimes present, at other times not. See Figs. 2 and 3.

*Experiment 3. Unpredictably Moving Target.* The results parallel those of Experiment 2. With divergence and a report of a "blurred" target and no pursuit tracking, "alpha" occurs more often, with greater maximum amplitude and sooner (see Table 3). For percent-time alpha the averages for FT < BNT for 9 *S*s; BT < BNT, 7 *S*s; FT < BT < BNT, 6 *S*s. For alpha delay FT > BNT, 8 *S*s; BT > BNT, 7 *S*s; FT > BT > BNT, 5 *S*s. For total time FT < BNT, 3 *S*s; BT < BNT, 5 *S*s; FT < BT < BNT, no *S*s.

Analysis of variance for the differences among conditions FT, BT, and BNT yielded *F* significant ($p < .05$) for maximum alpha amplitude, and *F* significant ($p < .001$) for percent-time alpha. *F* ratios for total time and alpha delay were not significant. Fig. 4 illustrates these results. Saccadic eye movements were not clearly associated with an increase or a decrease of "alpha" occurrence.

*Experiment 4. Predictably Moving Target: Speed Increased Then Decreased.* The results generally parallel those of Experiment 3. The levels of significance were lower. *F* ratios for the differences among conditions were significant for percent-

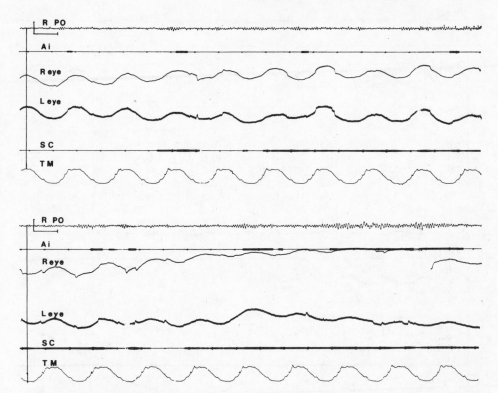

FIG. 2. P–O EEG while tracking a moving target. Tracings: R P–O is right parietal oc⁻
cipital EEG; Ai is alpha index superimposed on a 1 sec time marker; R eye EOG, L eye
EOG; SC is report of subjective clarity; and TM is an analog of target motion. EEG calibration is 50 μⅤ and 1 sec. In the beginning eyes are converged. Pursuit tracking is associated with a report of a focussed target. Minimal alpha occurs. Target is reported as blurred,
and the eyes diverge. Pursuit tracking occurs. More alpha occurs. Target is reported blurred
and pursuit tracking ceases. This is associated with ocular drift toward the right and divergence. Most alpha occurs.

time alpha ($p < .01$), alpha delay ($p < .05$), and maximum alpha amplitude
($p < .05$). (See Table 4.) There were some results occurring with rapidly moving
targets which showed that even when pursuit tracking was not evident in the
record, less "alpha" occurred compared with the record obtained while tracking
a slowly moving target. To evaluate this result, an interval 12 sec before and 12
sec after the faster target movement (briefest period) was measured in units of 1
sec. A given second was scored 1 if "alpha" occurred or 0 if it did not. This was
done for every second and each subject. The cumulative number of $S$s, who had
in a 1-sec interval "alpha," was calculated through the 24-sec interval for each
of the three conditions FT, BT, and BNT. This gave an estimate of the rate of
alpha occurrence during the 24 sec. The estimated rate of "alpha" occurrence
was relatively less near the middle of the 24-sec interval when the target was
moving rapidly, even for BNT. The average rate of alpha occurrence was low
for FT, higher for BT, and highest for BNT.

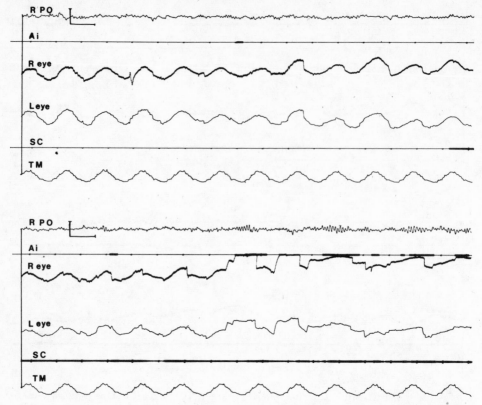

Fɪɢ. 3. Same as Fig. 2 but illustrating that rapid eye movements which followed a cessation of pursuit tracking are associated with either occurrence or non-occurrence of alpha as defined by the alpha index.

## Part B

In the previous studies, targets were used whose luminosity was constant and did not change as a function of the occipital alpha EEG occurrence. In Experiment 5 the link between oculomotor processes and the occipital EEG response was explored by connecting target visibility to the occurrence of the occipital alpha rhythm and to eye tracking by the instructions, "When you see the moving target, track it." It was expected that feedback, that is, target visibility controlled by the S's own alpha EEG, would demonstrate a tight link between oculomotor functions and occipital alpha occurrence.

### Methods and Materials

Twelve Ss who had recordable alpha with eyes open were tested. The occipital or parietal–occipital EEG and EOG were recorded as described previously. The target was controlled as described in Experiment 1. It moved with a quasi-sinusoidal velocity, laterally. The period of motion was unstable so that the target would gradually speed up or gradually slow down. The external path connecting the occurrence of "alpha" to the target visibility was similar to that described previously (Mulholland, 1968) (see Fig. 5).

Alpha was defined as in Experiment 1. When "alpha" occurred the EEG "state" relay was ON, when "no-alpha" occurred it was OFF. This relay controlled the lamp that illuminated the target in two ways. In Loop 1 state relay

TABLE 3

*Experiment 3*

*Unpredictably moving target*

| Subjects | N Trials | | | Total Time | | | $\bar{X}$ Percent-Time Alpha | | | $\bar{X}$ Maximum Alpha Amplitude (mm) | | | $\bar{X}$ Alpha Delay (sec) | | |
|---|---|---|---|---|---|---|---|---|---|---|---|---|---|---|---|
| | FT | BT | BNT | FT | BT | BNT | FT | BT | BNT | FT | BT | BNT | FT | BT | BNT |
| P. W. | 3 | 3 | 3 | 117 | 114 | 102 | 23.3 | 16.2 | 28.9 | 10.6 | 9.0 | 10.0 | 1.6 | 3.3 | 1.4 |
| W. C. | 4 | 3 | 3 | 65 | 98 | 80 | 10.8 | 17.1 | 38.8 | 4.8 | 4.3 | 7.0 | 3.8 | 2.3 | 2.0 |
| S. F. | 3 | 3 | 3 | 68 | 64 | 86 | 3.8 | 5.2 | 34.3 | 6.3 | 4.6 | 10.3 | 7.7 | 2.1 | 1.8 |
| S. L. | 3 | 3 | 3 | 112 | 85 | 107 | 1.8 | 3.4 | 20.5 | 4.0 | 8.0 | 11.5 | 9.9 | 9.2 | 3.8 |
| R. H. | 2 | 2 | 2 | 51 | 68 | 41 | 48.7 | 80.7 | 75.4 | 11.0 | 8.2 | 8.0 | 1.6 | 0.6 | 0.5 |
| R. D. | 2 | 2 | 2 | 91 | 71 | 79 | 6.6 | 9.9 | 46.3 | 8.0 | 7.5 | 9.5 | 8.5 | 1.1 | 4.4 |
| W. P. | 3 | 3 | 3 | 132 | 171 | 132 | 15.1 | 41.9 | 44.7 | 12.0 | 15.0 | 16.5 | 7.6 | 3.9 | 1.3 |
| R. G. | 3 | 3 | 3 | 180 | 149 | 258 | 9.4 | 15.1 | 12.2 | 10.0 | 7.5 | 10.0 | 3.1 | 5.2 | 4.6 |
| A. M. | 3 | 3 | 3 | 106 | 59 | 70 | 2.1 | 13.9 | 41.1 | 7.3 | 11.6 | 10.6 | 4.7 | 6.3 | 2.6 |
| $\bar{X}$ | | | | 102.4 | 97.6 | 106.1 | 13.5 | 22.6 | 38.2 | 8.2 | 8.4 | 10.4 | 5.4 | 3.8 | 2.5 |

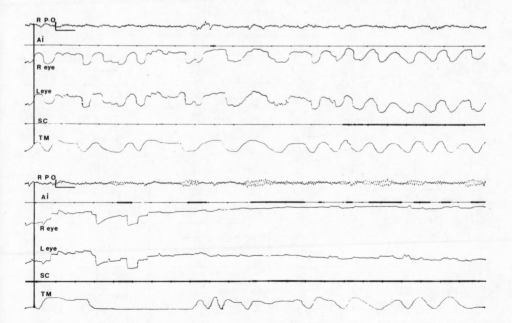

Fig. 4. Same as Fig. 3 but with an unpredictable target. Note that alpha recurs in "bursts" following a cessation of pursuit tracking.

ON ("alpha") was associated with target light ON; with state relay OFF ("no-alpha") target light was OFF. In Loop 2 with state relay ON, target light was OFF; with state relay OFF, target light was ON.

*Procedure.* Each *S* was tested in the same way. First was an interval of eyes open with monocular viewing (left eye occluded). This was followed by 8 1-min trials: Loop 1, Loop 2, Loop 1, Loop 2, Loop 1, Loop 2, Loop 1, Loop 2. To re-

TABLE 4

*Experiment 4*

*Variable speed target*

| Subjects | N Trials | | | Total Time | | | $\bar{X}$ Percent-Time Alpha | | | $\bar{X}$ Maximum Alpha Amplitude (mm) | | | $\bar{X}$ Alpha Delay (sec) | | |
|---|---|---|---|---|---|---|---|---|---|---|---|---|---|---|---|
| | FT | BT | BNT | FT | BT | BNT | FT | BT | BNT | FT | BT | BNT | FT | BT | BNT |
| P. W. | 1 | 1 | 1 | 73 | 88 | 122 | 7.5 | 22.6 | 57.9 | 8.0 | 14.0 | 16.0 | 1.2 | 0.4 | 0.1 |
| W. C. | 1 | 1 | 1 | 60 | 38 | 37 | 15.6 | 17.6 | 23.7 | 3.0 | 6.0 | 5.5 | 3.0 | 1.3 | 0.6 |
| S. F. | 2 | 2 | 2 | 96 | 105 | 114 | 3.5 | 4.2 | 31.1 | 3.5 | 8.5 | 11.0 | 14.4 | 7.6 | 1.0 |
| S. L. | 2 | 2 | 1 | 69 | 187 | 72 | — | 2.5 | 31.1 | — | 7.0 | 5.0 | — | 10.6 | 1.5 |
| R. H. | 1 | 1 | 1 | 31 | 78 | 86 | 29.3 | 75.7 | 63.5 | 11.0 | 9.5 | 8.0 | 1.5 | 0.8 | 0.2 |
| R. D. | 1 | 1 | 1 | 59 | 60 | 80 | 9.4 | 12.5 | 23.2 | 3.5 | 5.0 | 4.5 | 8.7 | 1.0 | 0.4 |
| W. P. | 1 | 1 | 1 | 58 | 74 | 74 | 10.3 | 33.2 | 38.6 | 4.0 | 4.0 | 5.0 | 3.6 | 0.8 | 0.4 |
| R. G. | 2 | 2 | 2 | 197 | 176 | 81 | 10.3 | 18.7 | 17.4 | 5.0 | 6.0 | 6.5 | 1.8 | 4.5 | 2.3 |
| A. M. | 2 | 2 | 2 | 32 | 27 | 88 | — | 0.7 | — | — | — | — | — | — | — |
| $\bar{X}$ | | | | 75.0 | 92.5 | 83.7 | 9.5 | 20.8 | 31.8 | 4.2 | 6.7 | 6.8 | 5.5 | 3.0 | 0.7 |

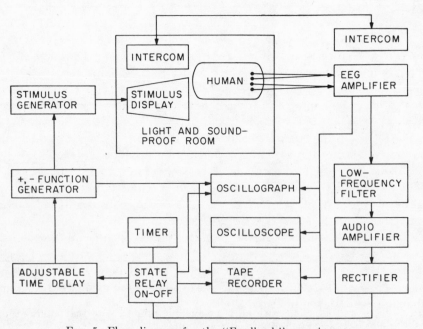

Fig. 5. Flow diagram for the "Feedback" experiment

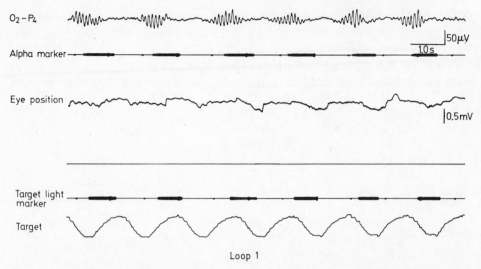

$O_2 - P_4$

50μV

Alpha marker

1.0 s

Eye position

0.5mV

Target light marker

Target

Loop 1

FIG. 6. The EEG and EOG during Loop 1 feedback with instructions to track the target when it was visible. Note stable alternation between alpha and no-alpha. When the eyes begin to track the target alpha is blocked; when it is not tracked alpha recurs. Tracings are: right parietal–occipital EEG; alpha index superimposed on a 1 sec time mark; L and R eye EOG; target light marker superimposed on a 1-sec time mark; and analog of target motion. (From Peper, 1970)

emphasize: in Loop 1, the visibility of the target depended upon the $S$'s occipital alpha EEG. Namely, "alpha" was present in order for the target to be visible. In Loop 2, "alpha" was absent for the target to be visible.

### Results

All 12 $S$s behaved identically and showed two extremes. During Loop 1, regenerative feedback developed in which there was a regular alternation between "alpha" and "no-alpha." An example is shown in Fig. 6. The frequency of alternation is dependent upon the fixed system delays (0.3 sec) and two variable delays: the time between stimulus ON and "alpha" OFF, and the time between stimulus OFF and the "alpha" recurrence in the dark. In *no* case could a subject initiate or continue to track without blocking his occipital alpha EEG.

With loop 2, erratic alternation between longer intervals of "alpha" and "no-alpha" occurred. No $S$ could initiate tracking without "blocking" the alpha rhythm. A typical result is shown in Fig. 7. The change in the EEG following a change from Loop 2 to Loop 1 clearly is shown in Fig. 8.

The average duration of "alpha" and "no-alpha" events was calculated for each $S$ and each trial. These were analyzed with analysis of variance. The differences between the two responses (R), "alpha" vs "no-alpha"; Loop (L), Loop 1 vs Loop 2; trials (T); and the interaction of these, were evaluated. A summary of the analysis is shown in Table 5.

Table 6 presents the mean "alpha" and "no-alpha" durations for each trial

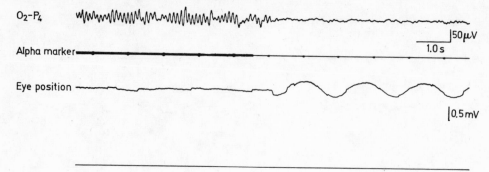

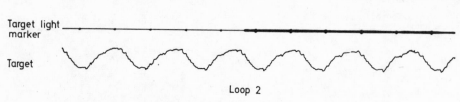

Loop 2

FIG. 7. Same as Fig. 6 but during Loop 2. (From Peper, 1970)

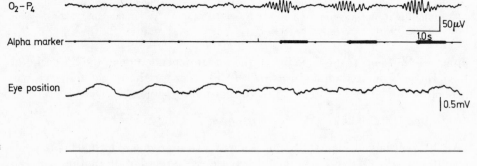

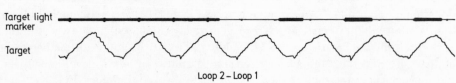

Loop 2 – Loop 1

FIG. 8. Same as Fig. 6 but showing the effects on the EEG and EOG of a shift from Loop 2 to Loop 1. (From Peper, 1970)

and each loop. The two different feedback loops have different effects on the mean duration of EEG "alpha" and "no-alpha" events (Mulholland, 1968).

The sequential durations of each "alpha" and "no-alpha" interval were calculated for Loop 1 and Loop 2 across all *S*s. These were pooled to obtain an average series. The onset of Loop 1 produced initially long "no-alpha" intervals followed by a decrease of successive intervals. Intervals of alpha, which were brief at first, gradually increased. For Loop 2, the average durations were longer and the variability greater (see Fig. 9).

TABLE 5

*Summary analyses of variance*

| Source of Variance | df | Mean Square | F |
|---|---|---|---|
| Subjects | 11 | 2389 | 2.8* |
| Trials (T) | 3 | 135 | $< 1.0^b$ |
| Loop (L) | 1 | 35059 | $40.5^b$ ** |
| Response (R) | 1 | 40272 | $46.6^b$ ** |
| T × L | 3 | 98 | $< 1.0^a$ |
| T × R | 3 | 200 | $< 1.0^a$ |
| L × R | 1 | 27020 | $38.3^a$ ** |
| T × L × R | 3 | 484 | $< 1.0^a$ |
| Residual$^a$ | 165 | 705 | — |
| Residual$^b$ | 166 | 864 | — |

NOTE.—Residual b is (Residual a + L × R).

$^a$ F tested against Residual a.

$^b$ F tested against Residual b.

* $p < .05$.

** $p < .001$.

TABLE 6

*Mean durations (sec) of "alpha" and "no-alpha" events*

| Events | Trial 1 | | Trial 2 | | Trial 3 | | Trial 4 | |
|---|---|---|---|---|---|---|---|---|
| | Loop 1 | Loop 2 | Loop 1 | Loop 2 | Loop 1 | Loop 2 | Loop 1 | Loop 2 |
| $\bar{\Delta}t$ "alpha" | 0.7 | 4.6 | 0.7 | 0.9 | 0.8 | 1.3 | 0.7 | 1.4 |
| $\bar{\Delta}t$ "no-alpha" | 3.9 | 19.5 | 2.8 | 22.3 | 2.5 | 25.8 | 2.0 | 24.8 |

Distributions of the durations were obtained by counting the number of $\Delta t$ "alpha" and $\Delta t$ "no-alpha" which fell within class intervals of 0.4 sec. The results are shown in Fig. 10. Loop 2 has time durations for both "alpha" and "no-alpha" which are longer and more variable than those in Loop 1.

DISCUSSION

The first conclusion to be drawn from these studies is that the "visual attention" hypothesis, which has been advanced to account for the "blocking" of the occipital alpha rhythm, is incorrect. In Experiments 1–4, the subject had to visually monitor the apparent clarity of the target and its position. Also, in the condition Blur-No-Track he had to inhibit tracking movements, and maintain a degree of accommodation associated with an apparently blurred target. This task clearly involved a high level of visual attention. Compared with the condition Blur-Track, the amount of visual attention was no less for Blur-No-Track. Yet there were evident and reliable increases in the alpha rhythm. If attention means selective scrutiny and differential emphasis on visual stimuli, that is, an

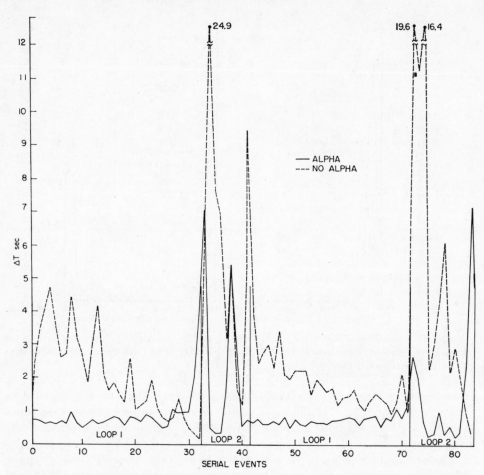

F<small>IG</small>. 9. Average time series of Δt "alpha" and Δt "no-alpha" events. During Loop 1 Δt alpha are brief and stable. Δt "no-alpha," initially longer, decrease in an irregular way. With Loop 2 both "alpha" and "no-alpha" vary over a wide range between very long and brief intervals. Loop 1 again exhibits the typical "disturbance and recovery," Δt alpha are brief and stabilized while Δt no-alpha, initially longer, decrease; another shift to Loop 2 produces unstable alternations between longer and briefer values.

on-going selective monitoring of the visible environment, then "attention" cannot account for the large changes in alpha rhythm observed in these experiments.

Clearly, the occurrence of the alpha rhythm is related to changes in the visual control systems which include afferent, integrative, and efferent processes. This is hardly a surprise, since these processes are occurring in the same general regions of cortex from which the occipital or parietal–occipital EEG is derived. The changes in the EEG previously attributed to "visual attention" can be explained in terms of changes occurring in cortical regions that are important for visual control processes. The reported decreases of alpha attributable to "visual imagery" and the blocking of alpha in response to auditory stimulation can be

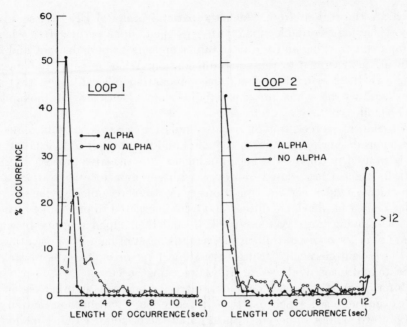

FIG. 10. Distribution functions for Δt "alpha" and Δt "no-alpha." The distributions for Loop 1 are different from those in Loop 2. More than 25% of Δt "no-alpha" are greater than 12 sec for Loop 2 while none are greater than 12 sec for Loop 1.

interpreted in terms of the visual orienting processes that are associated with imagery and audition (Mulholland, 1968, 1969). Zickmund (1969) has shown that an auditory stimulus presented in darkness is followed by a series of eye movements.

The occipital EEG is a gross, general record from an extensive cortical region; the oculomotor system has extensive representation in brain regions 17, 18, and 19 (Robinson, 1968). Conversely, oculomotor or visual functions that do not involve areas 17, 18, and 19 in a continuing and extensive process would not have an observable effect on the occipital EEG. For instance, episodic, saccadic movements involving primarily the frontal eye fields (Robinson, 1968) may not be associated with changes in the recorded occipital EEG alpha rhythm. No reliable change in the occipital EEG in association with saccadic movements was observed in these studies. However, a more precise quantification of occipital alpha and the fast eye movements may reveal some relationship.

The occipital alpha "blocking" response involves processes in the reticular substance of the brain-stem tegmentum. Stimulation of this region produces a desynchronized EEG (Morruzzi & Magoun, 1949). The oculomotor pathway is located in the same zone of the brain-stem tegmentum as the reticular activation system, and stimulation which can cause cortical desynchronization also causes alterations in eye movements (Bender & Shanzer, 1964).

The occipital alpha rhythm is markedly reduced during ocular fixation and pursuit tracking (Adrian & Matthews, 1934; Durup & Fessard, 1935; Mulholland, 1968). These processes involve regions 17, 18, and 19 (Robinson, 1968), which are the regions from which the parietal–occipital EEG is recorded. For subjects having recordable alpha with eyes open, alpha occurs often when there is no pursuit tracking and the near target appears to be indistinct and blurred following instructions to relax accommodation. When pursuit tracking occurs, even with the target blurred and accommodation relaxed, alpha rhythms are "blocked," as these and previous studies show (Dewan & Mulholland, 1969; Mulholland, 1968). ·

The continuous reception of visual stimulation *per se* is not sufficient to cause continuous desynchronization of the EEG and the concept of "visual attention" has been used to convey the idea of a higher-level selective process, presumably cortical, which is associated, however, with eye movements, fixation, and lens adjustment. Under certain conditions, e.g., trained subjects viewed a target under Loop 1 feedback conditions and were instructed to press a key when they saw the moving target yet *not* track it, and their alpha was not blocked. See Fig. 11. Yet for many untrained subjects the onset of light is an orienting stimulus which "automatically" causes the subject to direct his eyes toward it and to fixate and focus it, therefore alpha "blocking" occurs.

Motor functions or sensory-motor integrative functions in other regions of the cortex can cause a desynchronization or reduction of synchronous activity in the EEG record similar to desynchronization of the occipital EEG. Directed movement of the limbs desynchronizes the central $m\mu$ rhythm (Chatrian, Magnus, Petersen, & Lazarte, 1959). See Fig. 12. Recordings from the precentral gyrus in man show that voluntary movement blocks the precentral beta rhythms (Jasper & Penfield, 1949). These authors stated, "It would seem that the beta rhythm is characteristic of the activity of the "resting" motor cortex in a manner analogous to the alpha rhythm for the occipital cortex. Activation by voluntary movement seems, therefore, to block the beta rhythm in a manner similar to the well-known effect of visual stimuli upon the occipital alpha rhythm [p. 171]." Here we emphasize the possibility that the analogy drawn by Jasper and Penfield is valid because *oculomotor* processes are involved in the response of the parietal–occipital EEG to visual stimuli.

The paradoxical facilitation of EEG alpha rhythms by extreme ocular deviation may be interpreted in terms of visual control processes. Vertical, lateral, and downward deviation of the eyes greater than 30–40° produces, in some sub-

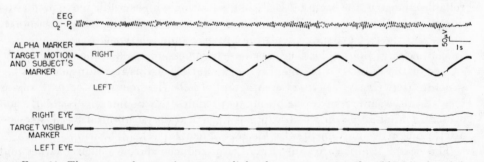

FIG. 11. The onset of a moving target light does not necessarily "block" the alpha rhythm if no tracking occurs.

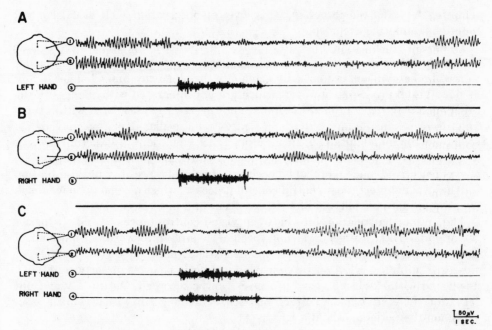

FIG. 12. From Chatrian et al., 1959, Fig. 6. Motor responses are associated with disappearance of synchronous activity (central mμ). Note that blocking begins in the contralateral recording when one hand is involved; blocking occurs at the same time on each side when both hands are involved. The blocking reaction on the contralateral side clearly occurs *before* the hand response is given.

jects, a loss of fixation and relaxation of accommodation which can result in a marked increase of occipital or parietal–occipital EEG alpha (Mulholland & Evans, 1965, 1966; Kris, 1968; Dewan, 1967; Fenwick & Walker, 1969; Mulholland, 1969). For deviations less than 30–40° the facilitation of alpha may not occur (Fenwick & Walker, 1969; Chapman, Shelburne, & Bragdon, 1970) presumably because fixation and accommodation of the lens to visible targets can occur with smaller deviations. In an experiment on himself Dewan (1967) reported that extreme deviations of the eyes did not facilitate alpha if he did not also avoid focussing and convergence. Eberlin (1969) reported that eye deviation *per se* was not associated with alpha facilitation; ocular instability associated with eye deviation as indicated by ocular drift was associated with alpha. Reymond (1968) has stated that the topography of activity in the alpha frequency band when eyes are deviated clearly indicated its independence from the subjects' spontaneous alpha activity. This result may also be interpreted as evidence that the distribution of alpha activity is influenced by ocular deviation.

In Experiment 4, Part A, the speed of the target movement was gradually increased and then decreased. For some subjects, when the target movement was too speedy the eye could not follow and no evident pursuit movement was recorded. Alpha still did not occur for some subjects. Those subjects may have been fixating a point in the movement path of the target or may have been attempting to track the target. At this level of observation such visual control functions cannot be excluded.

The most general hypothesis to account for the results reported here is that the combined processes of pursuit tracking, convergence, and lens accommodation will reliably block or markedly attenuate the alpha rhythm. Changes in any of these visual processes, however, which are not integrated with changes in the others in a way that optimizes vision are not necessarily associated with recordable decreases in the alpha rhythm; e.g., extreme ocular deviation may be associated with abundant alpha. In the Blur-Track conditions of Experiments 2, 3, and 4 in Part A, pursuit tracking occurred with relaxed accommodation and no convergence, and much more alpha occurred. In the absence of visual stimulation for the awake subject those central control processes which depend upon feedback from the target position and blur do not occur and most alpha occurs.

The reason that relationships between visual control processes and the parietal–occipital EEG are general—not specific—is straightforward. Visual control processes are occurring extensively in the parietal–occipital cortex. Because of the gross nature of EEG only extensive, large-scale changes of cortical activity associated with extensive visual processes can be recorded. On this level of observation there are reliable correlations between changes in visual control processes and the parietal–occipital EEG.

The feedback experiment described in Part B was not only a demonstration of the link between visual control processes and the occipital alpha rhythms. It also illustrated the utility of feedback methods for testing hypotheses. The use of feedback methods to test hypotheses rests on an analogy between control systems and the formal properties of two sets of experimental variables—a "cause" set and an "effect" set. In a control system the transfer function relating the input to the output is produced by the particular design and operating characteristics of the system. The chain of events beginning with an input and ending with an output can be described as a causal chain that is unidirectional. Of course, the best design does not produce a perfectly predictable relationship between input and output. There is always unpredictable variation or "noise." By analogy, independent variables and dependent variables are linked in a causal chain. Moreover, there is unpredictable variation in the relationship between the independent variable ("cause") and dependent variable ("effect").

In linear control systems, the responses to negative and positive feedback are different. Negative feedback reduces the unwanted or unpredictable variations of the output so that output "follows" the controlling function of the input. With positive feedback the output may go to some limiting minimum or maximum value or unpredictably swing between the limits.

By analogy, an external path between the dependent variable (alpha) and the independent variables (target visibility and eye-tracking behavior) may produce different effects on the output (alpha), depending on the sign of the feedback. Thus, Loop 1 produced a relatively stable alternation between "alpha" and "no-alpha," while Loop 2 produced an unstable alternation. These different effects are consistent, reproducible, and reliable. If these different effects occur with Loop 1, as compared with Loop 2, then obviously there must be a feedforward connection between independent and dependent variables; that is, in Part B, initiation of tracking blocked alpha, cessation of tracking facilitated alpha. In summary, when the link between independent and dependent variables is "noisy," then feedback methods can be useful in testing the hypothesis that there is a causal link, a "feedforward" path from the independent to the dependent variable. In the experiments reported here the "feedback" variables were complex and cannot be rigorously defined as either negative or positive feedback. The demonstration of a link between dependent and independent variables was made, even though the experimental situation was less than ideal.

These experiments demonstrate a tight relationship between oculomotor efferent "commands" and the occurrence of the parietal–occipital alpha rhythms. "Visual attention" as indicated by alpha blocking is, operationally, oculomotor change. Further detailed neurophysiological investigations using feedback methods[1] and direct recordings from brain and ocular muscle processes involved in visual control will be required to resolve the ambiguities and questions that these studies raise concerning the neurological and neurophysiological relationship between vergence, accommodation, pursuit tracking, and alpha occurrence. Finally, autoregulation of the alpha rhythm by alpha feedback training is likely to be mediated by learned control of oculomotor and lens adjustment processes. However, the learner may not be aware of the mediating process.

## REFERENCES

Adrian, E. D. The dominance of vision. *Ophthalmological Society, U.K.*, 1943, *63*, 194–207.

Adrian, E. D., & Matthews, B. H. C. The Berger rhythm: Potential changes from the occipital lobes in man. *Brain*, 1934, *57*, 356–385.

Bender, M. D., & Shanzer, S. Oculomotor pathways defined by electric stimulation and brain stem lesions in the monkey. In M. B. Bender (Ed.), *The oculomotor system.* New York: Harper & Row, 1964. Pp. 81–140.

Berger, H. In P. Gloor (Trans. & Ed.), Hans Berger on the electroencephalogram of man. *Electroencephalography & Clinical Neurophysiology*, 1969 (Suppl. 28), 84, 86, 106, 248–252, 315–316.

Chapman, R. M., Shelburne, S. A., & Bragdon, H. R. EEG alpha activity influenced by visual input and not by eye position. *Electroencephalography & Clinical Neurophysiology*, 1970, *28*, 183–189.

Chatrian, G. E., Magnus, M. D., Petersen, C., & Lazarte, J. A. The blocking of the rolandic wicket rhythm and some central changes related to movement. *Electroencephalography & Clinical Neurophysiology*, 1959, *11*, 497–510.

Dewan, E. D. Occipital alpha rhythm, eye position and lens accommodation. *Nature*, 1967, *214*, 975–977.

Dewan, E. D., & Mulholland, T. B. The visual control system and the occipital alpha rhythm: An hypothesis. *Electroencephalography & Clinical Neurophysiology*, 1969, *26*, 633. (Abstract)

Durup, G., & Fessard, A. L'electrencephalogramme de l'homme. Observations psycho-

---

[1] For example, application of "feedback" method to the study of the relationship between parameters of brain-stem stimulation and activity in the dorsal hippocampus (rabbits) was reported by Traczyk, Whitmoyer, and Sawyer (1969). Activity of the dorsal hippocampus was connected back to the brain-stem stimulator by an external path, thereby giving a convincing demonstration of the association between brain-stem processes and hippocampal activity.

physiologiques relatives a l'action des stimuli visuels et auditifs. *L'Annee Psychologique*, 1935, *36*, 1–35.

Eberlin, P. The effects of the oculomotor system on the electroencephalogram. Unpublished Masters thesis, Miami University, Oxford, Ohio, 1969.

Evans, C. R., & Mulholland, T. B. (Eds.) *Attention in neurophysiology*. London: Butterworths, 1969.

Fenwick, P. B. C., & Walker, S. The effect of eye position on the alpha rhythm. In C. R. Evans & T. B. Mulholland (Eds.), *Attention in neurophysiology*. London: Butterworths, 1969. Pp. 128–141.

Jasper, H. H. Report of the committee on methods of clinical examination in electro-encephalography. *Electroencephalography & Clinical Neurophysiology*, 1958, *10*, 371–375.

Jasper, H. H., & Penfield, W. Electrocorticograms in man: Effect of voluntary movement on the electrical activity of the precentral gyrus. *Archiv fur Psychiatrie und Zeitschrift Neurologie*, 1949, *183*, 163–174.

Kris, C. EOG and EEG measurement while learning to position the eyes when the lids are open and closed. *Electroencephalography & Clinical Neurophysiology*, 1968, *24*, 189. (Abstract)

Moruzzi, G., & Magoun, H. W. Brain stem reticular formation and activation of the EEG. *Electroencephalography & Clinical Neurophysiology*, 1949, *1*, 455–486.

Mulholland, T. Feedback electroencephalography. *Activitas Nervosa Superior* (Prague), 1968, *10*, 410–438.

Mulholland, T. Occipital alpha activity during accommodative vergence, pursuit tracking and saccadic eye movements. *Electroencephalography & Clinical Neurophysiology*, 1969, *27*, 548. (Abstract) (a)

Mulholland, T. B. The concept of attention and the electroencephalographic alpha rhythm. In C. R. Evans & T. B. Mulholland (Eds.), *Attention in neurophysiology*. London: Butterworths, 1969. Pp. 100–127. (b)

Mulholland, T., & Evans, C. R. An unexpected artefact in the human electroencephalogram concerning the alpha rhythm and the orientation of the eyes. *Nature*, 1965, *207*, 36–37.

Mulholland, T., & Evans, C. R. Oculomotor function and the alpha activation cycle. *Nature*, 1966, *211*, 1278–1279.

Peper, E. Feedback regulation of the alpha electroencephalogram activity through control of internal and external parameters. *Kybernetik*, 1970, *7*, 107–112.

Reymond, A. The importance of topographic data in EEG phenomena and an electrical model to reproduce them. In D. O. Walter & M. A. B. Brazier (Eds.), Advances in EEG analysis. *Electroencephalography & Clinical Neurophysiology*, 1968 (Suppl. 27), 32.

Robinson, D. A. Eye movement control in primates. *Science*, 1968, *161*, 1219–1224.

Storm Van Leeuwen, W., Bickford, R., Brazier, M., Cobb, W. A., Dondey, M., Gastaut, H., Gloor, P., Henry, C. E., Hess, R., Knott, J. P., Kugler, J., Lairy, G. C., Loeb, C., Magnus, O., Oller Daurella, L., Petsche, H., Schwab, R., Walter, W. G., & Widén, L. Proposal for an EEG terminology by the terminology committee of the IFSECN. *Electroencephalography & Clinical Neurophysiology*, 1966, *20*, 293–320.

Traczyk, W. Z., Whitmoyer, D. I., & Sawyer, C. H. EEG feedback control of midbrain electrical stimulation inducing sleep or arousal in rabbits. *Acta. Biol. Exp.*, 1969, *29*, 135–152.

Zickmund, V. The time course of the oculomotor component of orienting reaction. In C. R. Evans & T. B. Mulholland (Eds.), *Attention in neurophysiology*. London: Butterworths, 1969. Pp. 247–257.

# Comment on Feeback Training of Parietal-Occipital Alpha Asymmetry in Normal Human Subjects

11

Erik Peper

*Abstract.* Experiments with feedback regulation of normal subjects' parietal-occipital alpha electroencephalographic asymmetry have shown that subjects learned to optimize the conditions under which symmetry and asymmetry occurred. Asymmetry was defined as the difference in the occurrence of the two hemispheres' alpha EEG activity. The results of this experiment can be interpreted to mean that the subjects did not learn alpha asymmetry *per se*, but instead learned to increase their percent time of alpha and increase the alternations between alpha and no alpha. This condition is optimized when the subject has his eyes closed and is not performing a visual search. On the other hand, symmetry is optimized when the subject performs a visual task. Methodological problems in feedback training are discussed.

With the advent of feedback training, autoregulation of various physiological processes has been explored. Subjects have learned to control and/or recognize the occurrence of their alpha, beta, and theta EEG patterns (Mulholland, 1968; Kamiya, 1969; Dewan, 1964; Brown, 1968; Peper and Mulholland, 1970). There is also some evidence that certain subjects can control the occurrence of epileptic discharges (Tassinari, 1968). Little feedback training has been done with the interesting phenomenon of alpha asymmetry, in which the two hemispheres of the brain produce different EEG alpha patterns, on one side compared with the other. Asymmetry is clinically important, since "Unilateral depression of alpha rhythm is an important diagnostic sign but experience

Perception Laboratory, Veterans Administration Hospital, Bedford, Mass.

suggests that only extreme asymmetry on more than one occasion can safely be given much diagnostic weight in the absence of confirmatory EEG, clinical or radiological signs" (Cobb, 1963). This condition is found infrequently in normals, but is associated with cerebral pathology. The possibility exists that if normals could learn to voluntarily control alpha asymmetry (through feedback training) one could investigate their subjective learning experiences and thereby understand the mechanism of EEG asymmetry. Furthermore, a knowledge of the conditions under which alpha asymmetry in normal human subjects occur or does not occur could be used in the clinical setting to investigate pathological conditions.

With these considerations in mind, the author conducted an experiment to explore regulation of alpha EEG asymmetry in the parietal-occipital regions. The results not only point out the methodological problems but also the potential usefulness of EEG feedback for studying the optimum conditions for asymmetry.

## *Method*

*Apparatus.* The EEG was recorded from $O_2$–$P_4$ and $O_1$–$P_3$ with standard scalp electrodes (Grass); the ground electrode was over the right mastoid. Two parallel alpha triggering circuits were used, as shown in Fig. 1. Each circuit similar to that described by Mulholland (1968) detected independently the presence of alpha in either the right or left parietal-occipital EEG.

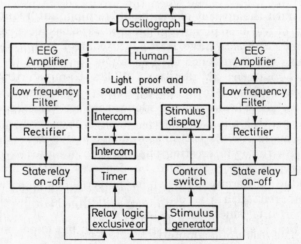

Fig. 1. Flow diagram of electroencephalographic alpha feedback system used for asymmetry training

The input to the Grass Model 5 preamplifiers was so adjusted that the maximum "resting" alpha was approximately 1 cm p-p deflection on the oscillograph tracing using standard calibration of the Grass Model 5 E driver, and the bandpass filter was set $\pm 0.5$ Hz of each subject's individual alpha frequency, to define the triggering frequency.

Asymmetry was defined by a logic relay circuit that triggered whenever one or the other side, but not both, produced alpha or no-alpha. This was used to drive a tone and record cumulative asymmetry duration on a clock.

The tone was a 300 Hz $< 50$ dB presented by a speaker. Both the subject and speaker were in a sound-attenuated lightproof room. An intercom linked the experimental chamber with the experimenter.

To reemphasize, tone "ON" meant there existed gross alpha asymmetry between the right and left parietal-occipital EEG recording.

### Procedure

Six subjects were tested under basically similar procedures. One subject's exact procedure is detailed below.

The experimenter instructed the subject (J.B.) about the method of reporting over the intercom, the requirement for remaining silent, and so forth. To calibrate the alpha trigger circuit, a single EEG signal was passed through both circuits which were adjusted until they triggered identically. The input was then shifted to EEG from both sides. Baseline recordings were obtained without tone feedback with eyes open and closed for 2 min each. The subject was then instructed to keep her eyes closed, and was told that a sound would occur when the produced a particular brain-wave pattern. The subject was further instructed to attempt to discriminate her subjective states during tones ON and OFF. An 8-min practice session was given. After this, the subject, on command from the experimenter, was asked to keep the tone ON for 2 min, OFF for 2 min, etc., for a total of 12 two-minute trials. At the end of the training trials, two-minute trials were given without feedback to test "learning to control symmetry and asymmetry from inner cues." Final baseline conditions with the eyes open and closed were also recorded.

*Results.* Of the 6 subjects, 2 subjects (J.B. and J.D.) learned to "control" asymmetry. Detailed results will be presented only of J.B. (J.D. performed similarly.)

The result of asymmetry training is shown in Fig. 2. Learning is clearly demonstrated and is shown distinctly during asymmetry ON and OFF when the feedback tone is not given. Therefore, the subject did respond differently during the condition for maintaining symmetry compared with that for maintaining asymmetry. The amount of alpha during each condition was also measured as shown in Fig. 3. Fig. 4 shows the frequency distribution of the sum of alpha and no-alpha for each condition.

The subject J.B. reported that to keep the tone ON she "relaxed" and did not "concentrate," while to keep the tone OFF she "concentrated hard,"

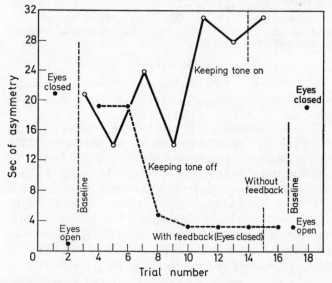

Fig. 2. Seconds of asymmetry between the left and right EEG recording for each condition

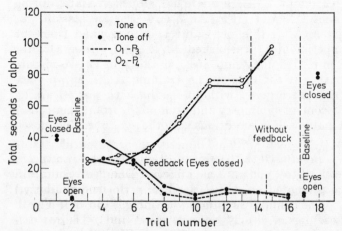

Fig. 3. Total seconds of alpha from each side for each condition

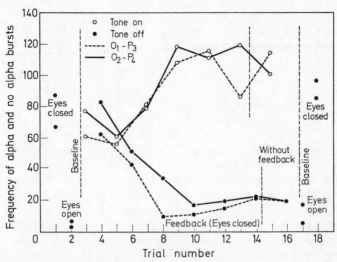

Fig. 4. Number of alpha and no-alpha occurrences from each
side for each condition

attempting to look at the point of her nose even
though her eyes were closed and the room was dark.
A similar mechanism was reported by subject J.D.
who reported that to keep the tone ON he did not
think about anything and kept his eyes closed while
to keep the tone OFF he opened his eyes and kept
looking around for light, even though the room was
lightproof. (This subject had not been instructed to
keep his eyes closed.)

*Discussion.* On initial inspection of the asymmetry
curve, it appears that a subject can "learn" asymmetry. This is indicated by the fact that the subject
was able to increase the amount of asymmetry above
the constant baseline level of "eyes closed."

On closer consideration this conclusion appears
somewhat unjustified. The requirement for efficient
learning is the knowledge of the correct results. We
need the feedback to tell us that we have made a
correct response. In this case, the feedback signal
for the subject did not actually train asymmetry, even
though much more asymmetry occurred during training than under baseline conditions. Instead it appears
that the subject learned to optimize the condition
under which asymmetry can occur; the subject learned
to autoregulate those unknown processes that mediate
the alpha rhythms, as was shown in Fig. 2. The successful results can be explained through probability. Given

a certain probability that when alpha bursts occur, they will occur asymmetrically, then if we increase the number of alpha bursts, the number of instances of asymmetry should also increase. The same applies to the condition of no-alpha. Basically, the more frequently the subject changes EEG patterns, the greater will be the cumulative duration of asymmetry.

The subject learned to optimize the probability that one side or the other would produce alpha, consequently most asymmetry occurred when the number of bursts was greatest. This can be shown by comparing the frequency distribution of alpha and no-alpha (Fig. 4) with the asymmetry learning curve (Fig. 2).

This pilot experiment pointed out the methodological error inherent in many studies of autoregulation by means of physiological feedback systems. The subject may correctly control his alpha and the stimulus, but he really learns to regulate an unknown mediating response. To correct for this error, the format of future experiments should be changed, so that two different tones independently indicate each hemisphere's presence of alpha. This learning task, to keep both tones ON (symmetry) or only one ON (asymmetry) has not yet been demonstrated. Since under the original experimental conditions, however, long asymmetries ($>1$ sec) did occur for some subjects as is shown in Fig. 5, there are valid grounds for continuing the exploration of asymmetries using a more precise feedback system which may facilitate true autoregulation of the asymmetries in which the subject can associate different subjective mechanisms with each tone.

The present study illustrates the methodological difficulty in training asymmetry. No insight was discovered in the mechanism of asymmetry. This appears due to the feedback signal because the tone did not

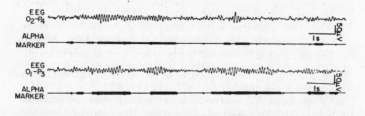

Fig. 5. Example of alpha asymmetry between the two sides

discriminate between right and left asymmetry, only

absolute asymmetry. Nevertheless, the results are promising for two reasons.

First, previous work has demonstrated that parietal-occipital alpha blockage occurs always with visual commands (Mulholland, 1968; Peper, 1970). Therefore, the presence of asymmetry should indicate some change in visual commands. What those specific parameters are would explain the mediation of visual control signals related to alpha blockage in one hemisphere or the other.

Second, the results demonstrate that subjects learned to optimize the conditions under which asymmetry and symmetry occurred. Obviously, normative data on alpha asymmetries varies when seeing and looking are required. These data should be utilized in the diagnosis of pathological asymmetry. Because asymmetries occurred minimally under conditions of visual search, under this condition they should then always be suspect, expecially in those cases that may appear to be "borderline."

*Acknowledgement.* The author would like to thank Dr. Thomas B. Mulholland for his cooperation and discussion of this work, and Mr. David Goodman for his assistance.

## References

Brown, Barbara, B.: Recognition of associations between aspects of consciousness and EEG frequencies using colored lights operated by specific EEG components. Presented at the Society for Psychophysiological Research Meeting, held in Washington, D.C., Oct. 17–20, 1968.

Cobb, W. A.: The normal adult EEG. In: Electroencephalography, p. 238 (Denis Hill and Geoffrey Parr, eds.). New York: Macmillan Company 1963.

Dewan, E. M.: Communication by electroencephalography. Air Force Cambridge Research Laboratories, Special Report No 12, 1–7 (1964).

Kamiya, J.: Operant control of the EEG alpha rhythm and some of its reported effects on consciousness. In: Altered states of consciousness, pp. 507–517 (Charles T. Tart, ed.). New York: John Wiley and Sons, Inc. 1969.

Mulholland, T.: Feedback electroencephalography. Activ.nerv. sup. (Praha) 10, 410–438 (1968).

— Occipital alpha activity during accommodative vergence, pursuit tracking and saccadic eye movements. Electroenceph. clin. Neurophysiol. 27, 548 (Abstract) (1969).

Peper, E.: Feedback regulation of the alpha electroencephalogram activity through control of internal and external parameters. Kybernetik 7 (3), 107–112 (1970).

— Mulholland, T.: Methodological and theoretical problems in the voluntary control of electroencephalographic occipital alpha by the subject. Kybernetik 7, 10–13 (1970).

Tassinari, C. A.: Supression of focal spikes by somato-sensory stimuli. Electroenceph. clin. Neurophysiol. 25, 574–578 (1968).

# On the Mechanisms of the 12
## Feedback Control of Human
## Brain Wave Activity

### James J. Lynch and David A. Paskewitz

The recent attention given to the feedback control of human brain wave activity and the implications of such control prompts a careful analysis of this phenomenon. Particular emphasis is placed on the learned control of the alpha rhythm. A review of possible factors which might influence the density of alpha rhythms led to the differentiation of three general sources of influence: constitutional, physiological, and cognitive-attentional factors. Each of these factors is discussed as a possible mediator of the learned control of the alpha rhythm. The view is advanced that increases in alpha density during feedback training arise from a diminution of those factors which block this rhythm, and some implications of such a view are discussed. Several of the issues raised appear generalizable to the whole question of the operant control of autonomic activity.

In recent years an ever growing number of studies have reported the possibility of using operant conditioning techniques to control a wide variety of physiological and neurophysiological processes (15, 48, 49, 67, 68, 112). Of special interest are reports that the human $S$ can learn to control various electroencephalographic (EEG) waveforms by these operant techniques. Clinical applications of these techniques have been suggested by several authors. Miller (67) has, for instance, suggested the possibility of using operant techniques to train epileptic patients to suppress the abnormal paroxysmal spiking in their EEG. In addition to the potential therapeutic application of operant techniques to the human EEG, an ever increasing number of studies have presented evidence to suggest that the amount of alpha activity which occurs in the human can, through appropriate feedback conditions, be either increased or decreased (14, 31, 38–41, 76–78, 80, 84, 85, 96, 97). These reports have stimulated a great deal of excitement, not only because of the potential of controlling specific neurophysiological processes, but also in regard to the potential of this approach in gaining an understanding of the relationship between alpha activity and subjective mood states (40). Further, it has been suggested that these techniques may lead to a more precise definition of the various states of consciousness (13, 105).

Kamiya (40) has, for instance, reported the possibility of changing the mood state of a $S$ by having the $S$ "turn on his alpha." The possibility of not only controlling brain

[1] The Institute of Psychiatry and Human Behavior, Department of Psychiatry, University of Maryland School of Medicine, Baltimore. Maryland.

[2] The Institute of the Pennsylvania Hospital, Unit for Experimental Psychiatry, 111 North 49th Street, Philadelphia, Pennsylvania.

wave activity itself, but also influencing subjective feelings associated with brain wave activity has naturally elicited a wave of enthusiasm among behavioral scientists. In commenting on this research, Maslow (65) recently stated:

What is seminal and exciting about this research is that Kamiya discovered quite fortuitously that bringing the alpha waves to a particular level could produce in the subject a state of serenity, meditativeness, even happiness. Some follow-up studies with people who have learned the Eastern techniques of contemplation and meditation show that they spontaneously emit EEG's that are like the "serene" ones to which Kamiya was able to educate his subjects. That is to say, that it is already possible to teach people how to feel happy and serene. The revolutionary consequences not only for human betterment, but also for biological and psychological theory, are multitudinous and obvious. There are enough research projects here to keep squadrons of scientists busy for the next century. The mind-body problem, until now considered insoluble, does appear to be workable after all. (p. 728)

Gardner Murphy (83) suggests that by using Kamiya's techniques: "before the year 2000, there will be both identification of many kinds of phenomenological states that are anchored upon particular types of EEG's and the invention of appropriate names, appropriate language, to describe the newly identified and newly integrated components." (p. 526)

Because of the broad implications of controlling the human alpha rhythm, both as a process in and of itself, and because of the stated implications that such control may lead to the altering and control of subjective mood states, it is imperative that a very close analysis be made of the phenomenon. Specifically, at least four questions are elicited by the previous research. 1) First, what is alpha activity? 2) What factors influence the production of alpha activity and how might control be gained over it? 3) How does one evaluate the acquisition of control? 4) How and to what extent does the control of alpha activity influence the subjective mood state of the individual?

## THE NATURE OF ALPHA ACTIVITY

Among the intrinsic rhythms of the human brain, perhaps the most widely investigated has been the alpha rhythm, a rhythm of 8 to 13 Hz, usually averaging around 30 $\mu$v, and occurring most frequently in the human during the state of relaxed wakefulness (57). One of the first reported characteristics of the alpha rhythm was the fact that it would block when the human was presented with any of a variety of sensory or attentional stimuli, but that after a few repetitions of these stimuli, this rhythm would no longer block (10). Berger (10) believed that alpha blocking resulted from the focus of attention upon the specific sensory system being stimulated, with inhibition then spreading to other systems. This view was subsequently supported in studies by Adrian and Matthews (2), and has ultimately led to the inclusion of attention as part of the official definition of alpha activity by the terminology committee of the International Federation for Electroencephalography and Clinical Neurophysiology; "alpha rhythm: rhythm, usually with a frequency 8-13 c/sec in adults, most prominent in the posterior areas, present most markedly when eyes are closed, and attenuated during attention, especially visual." (104)

The relationship of alpha activity to the visual system has even led recently to the suggestion that the alpha rhythm is an artifact produced by a tremor of the extraocular muscles (58), but alpha activity has also been recorded in humans even when these muscles have been eliminated (102). The possibility that the alpha rhythm is an artifact is by no means a recent suggestion (66). The proposal was made some years ago that alpha rhythm recordings were an artifact produced by mechanical pulsation (choroid plexus pump) of a gel, in this case the human brain, causing differential electrical pulsations (46). Lindsley (56) and Mundy-Castle (82) have suggested that alpha rhythms reflect a fluctuation in the excitability of individual neurons, with fluctuations then synchronized for many neurons. Bard (9) suggests that alpha rhythms represent basic cellular metabolic processes. Eccles (20) has suggested that the alpha rhythms are due to reverberating chains in the cortex. Recently the possibility that alpha rhythms are generated by thalamic activity has gained widespread neurophysiological support. In a comprehensive textbook review of the physiological basis of alpha rhythms, Andersen and Andersson (5) have concluded: "The available evidence strongly indicates that the thalamus is the prime mover of the thalamocortical rhythmic activity...The large degree of thalamic control over the cortical alpha rhythm advocates that studies on this rhythm and the control of it should be directed toward the thalamic mechanisms involved." (p. 209)

One of the most perplexing aspects of the alpha rhythm is the high degree of variability found both within and between Ss. Although it is generally agreed that an individual's EEG is characteristic (33), Davis and Davis (17) summing up the then available evidence, stated: "All of the features of the EEG show variations from person to person, even when the records are taken under strictly standard conditions. Most of the features, however, are quite stable and characteristic for each individual person on successive tests. The least stable feature is the amount of alpha rhythm" (p. 53).

In spite of the many factors contributing to alpha rhythm variability, however, the within S stability of alpha activity has been sufficiently high to suggest a constitutional basis for difference among Ss (16). Grey Walter (114) has stated:

These observations have shown clearly that, unlike most physiological phenomena, the alpha rhythms must be considered in relation to each individual of a given species, and not merely as a specific or genetic character. In other words the alpha rhythm patterns, in terms both of spatial distribution, frequency and relation to function, are highly characteristic of every individual. The variation is so wide that classification of alpha type must include a class of normal persons in whom no alpha activity whatever is visible even in those conditions which are most favorable to the appearance of these rhythms in other people. At the other extreme there are people in whom alpha rhythms persist even in circumstances which are most inclined in other subjects to interrupt or suppress this activity. (p. 287)

The hypothesized consititutional basis for differences in alpha density has led to a variety of schemata for classifying individuals on this dimension (16, 29, 95). For example, Golla, Hutton and Walter (29) have divided Ss as follows: 1) those with no alpha, even with eyes closed and their mind at rest; 2) those with alpha only with their eyes closed and their mind at rest; 3) those with alpha present even with their eyes open and their mind active.

Numerous reports have attempted to link alpha activity to various personality traits, but in this complex area no clear definitive results have yet emerged (22, 24, 30, 55, 99).

### FACTORS IN THE PRODUCTION AND CONTROL OF ALPHA ACTIVITY

There are several aspects to the feedback control of alpha activity which require further elucidation, but none seems more central to understanding the phenomenon of alpha control than the suggestion that this control occurs as the result of operant conditioning (39).

In a recent review of the operant control of autonomic responding, Katkin and Murray (43) have proposed a set of criteria for evaluating whether the autonomic response observed is truly an example of operant conditioning. Briefly, they pointed out that if a response is mediated, either cognitively or physiologically by some other system, then it is that system that is being conditioned and not the autonomic response system one happens to be measuring. While this proposal seems simple enough, the thrust of their argument is perhaps deceptively so.

A pair of analogies may serve to illustrate both the proposal and the dilemma it creates. No one would be surprised if an individual claimed he could control his heart rate by jumping up or down, or by running, or holding his breath; in such cases the mediation of heart rate activity *via* other physiological mechanisms would be clear to us all. In such a case it is also clear that the individual has not "learned" to control his heart rate directly, rather he has altered other mechanisms which in turn reflexively affect heart rate. What is "learned" in such a case is an operationally bewitching problem, but clearly one did not learn to control his heart rate directly. But the alternative question, albeit pushed to its logical extreme, is equally bewitching. Is it ever possible for a physiological system to be conditioned without some sort of mediation? Can we, for instance, increase heart rate without affecting changes in blood flow, blood pressure. or peripheral vasomotor tone? This would seem to be a hydraulic impossibility and, therefore, following the strictest interpretation of Katkin and Murray's (43) proposals, heart rate cannot be operantly conditioned in any direct sense. Furthermore, in light of the many variables affecting alpha activity, it is equally unlikely that alpha activity may be operantly conditioned according to such a proposed criterion.

Even the Pavlovian conditioning of alpha activity has been questioned. It was the observation of the sensory blocking of alpha activity which led to the investigation of whether this blocking response could be classically conditioned. Indications that conditional alpha blocking was possible first came with reports by Durup and Fessard (19), and Loomis, Harvey and Hobart (59). Following these initial reports, a more detailed analysis of a variety of conditioning parameters of alpha blocking was made by Jasper and Shagass (36). Since these reports, a large number of studies have indicated that alpha blocking responses could be obtained with Pavlovian conditioning techniques, and that various types of alpha blocking and alpha enhanced responses could be elicited with various conditioning contingencies (115). The Pavlovian methodology for eliciting these changes has been, however, usually restricted to very short

time periods (1 to 10 seconds) during the conditional stimulus, and, in addition, the changes are subject to a great deal of variability caused both by environmental and organismic influences (50, 51, 71, 72). Much of this classical conditioning literature, however, has evoked questions as to whether or not the alpha blocking observed is really a "conditional response" (4, 50, 109).

Although a number of authors (45, 47, 53, 74, 75, 103), have held that autonomic functions could be conditioned only through the use of Pavlovian techniques, this assumption has been challenged by evidence indicating that autonomic and neurophysiological responses can be conditioned by operant or instrumental techniques (15, 48, 49, 67, 68, 112). It appears, however, that the recent avalanche of reports on the successful operant conditioning of autonomic systems, rather than convincing large numbers of people that such a phenomenon can occur, has instead elicited an operational crisis in psychology as to just what is meant by conditioning. An in-depth discussion of this problem would take us far from the central theme of this article, but the general question cannot be avoided. It is becoming abundantly clear that the very nature of the meaning of conditioning is being cast in doubt, and this doubt extends to both classical and operant conditioning (21, 26, 62, 63, 94, 100, 101). One aspect of this operational crisis is exemplified in the recent discussions of the proper controls necessary in conditioning (43, 44, 94) and the suggestion that there are limits to the usefulness of such controls (101). One conclusion does seem apparent, however, alpha activity is mediated by a whole host of factors, and the likelihood of ever controlling or eliminating all these factors to observe only simple alpha conditioning is extremely small. Thus, in the more restricted sense, any discussion of the "operant control of alpha activity" seems to us, operationally indefensible.

Having then for the moment assumed that any demonstration of the operant control of "non-mediated alpha activity" is highly unlikely, it becomes necessary to understand those factors, both physiological and cognitive, which mediate alpha activity and which are possible mechanisms by which a $S$ could control such activity.

### GENERAL FACTORS WHICH INFLUENCE ALPHA ACTIVITY

A large number of environmental and organismic variables have previously been documented as altering the density of alpha activity observed in the human EEG. These may be roughly broken down into two major categories, physical or somatic influences, and attentional-arousal factors.

#### PHYSICAL OR SOMATIC INFLUENCES ON ALPHA ACTIVITY

Perhaps the most dominant influence on alpha activity and its variability is the visual system, either through direct visual stimulation, attention to visual stimuli, or through oculomotor activity. It has long been recognized that visual stimulation and oculomotor activity can markedly affect alpha levels (1, 2, 19). Recently this oculomotor activity has been implicated as a major mediating mechanism for how some $Ss$ "learn" to control their own alpha activity during feedback training (18, 79, 92). On the other hand, it has also been reported that in some $Ss$ alpha activity is not significantly related to eye position (25) and that $Ss$ can control their alpha activity with their eyes in either an up or a down position (39).

In addition to this type of movement, the ambient illumination of the room and the concomitant possibility of visual scanning and fixation clearly influence the amount of alpha activity observed, with significantly greater densities being seen when a $S$ is in a dark room or has his eyes closed (57). In fact, the entire visual system, whether muscular activity, visual stimulation, or visual attention, appears to have such massive effects on alpha activity, that a close analysis must be made to assess the degree to which the visual system can be controlled adequately in order to assess the learned control of alpha activity. Whether other systems are involved in the mediation of alpha

activity in the feedback situation, systems such as respiration, muscle tension, cardiovascular activity, and so forth, is, as yet, unclear. Changes in respiration rate, tidal volume, and $O_2$ consumption during Zen meditation have been linked to the occurrence of more alpha activity during meditative states (8, 34, 107) but whether these changes occur during alpha feedback is again not certain. In all, few attempts have been made, thus far to critically evaluate the possibilities in the somatic mediation of alpha activity.

#### ATTENTIONAL-AROUSAL FACTORS IN ALPHA ACTIVITY

From the extant research data on human alpha activity, it appears that some type of "optimal level of arousal" exists for the occurrence of alpha activity. If the $S$ is too aroused, alpha activity will be diminished, and conversely, if the $S$ becomes too drowsy, alpha will be diminished. When a $S$ passes into this optimal level, from either a state of alertness or a drowsy state, alpha activity tends to be activated almost in proportion to the amount that the individual $S$ is constitutionally able to produce it. A large and varied assortment of research data seems to reinforce this statement (56).

Alpha activity tends to occur most frequently when an individual is in a state of relaxed awakening, either with eyes closed or when the individual is in a dark room. It is usually diminished either in states of extreme arousal or in sleep (37, 52, 90).

Related to the state of arousal of an individual is the fact that ongoing alpha activity will usually block when an awake individual is presented with a variety of environmental stimuli, with visual stimulation usually eliciting the most marked blocking (2, 10). However, the rate of extinction of this alpha blocking orienting response depends on a number of organismic and environmental variables; for example, the type of sensory stimulus used, the definition of an alpha blocking response, the number of times the sensory stimulus is presented, the length and intensity of the stimulus, and the emotional state of the organism (7, 23, 51, 70, 111, 113). Furthermore, it appears that this alpha blocking response can also be elicited by conditional signals paired with these unconditional alpha blocking stimuli (115).

While factors which block alpha activity have received the greatest amount of research interest, numerous reports since the first observations on the existence of alpha activity have also noted the frequent occurrence of the reverse of alpha blocking, *i.e.*, stimulus-induced alpha activity (2, 7, 117). In reviewing this phenomenon Lenore Morrell (69) has identified at least four situations in which stimulus-induced alpha enhancement has been observed; during sleep, during aspects of Pavlovian conditional inhibition, during studies on attention, and during periods in which no alpha activity is occurring just prior to stimulation. She notes that this phenomenon has been frequently observed and given a variety of labels, including paradoxical activity, inverted reaction, alpha activation, alpha enhancement, alpha facilitation, alpha augmentation, or stimulus-provoked alpha activity (69). Alpha activity labeled as paradoxical or inverted reaction is that which occurs against a background which contains no alpha activity (11, 28). A series of studies have also noted that if stimuli are presented to *S*s who are going to sleep (12, 60, 89), or if stimuli are presented to *S*s who have been sleep deprived (6) alpha activity can be elicited. Alpha enhancement has been frequently noted in studies involving Pavlovian conditional inhibition, including inhibition of delay, differential conditioning, and extinction (27, 35, 72, 73, 98, 115). Research on aspects of sustained attention, such as prolonged visual attention or prolonged mental arithmetic have also noted the phenomenon of alpha enhancement (61, 108, 116). A similar phenomenon has been reported in studies of directed or focused attention (54, 81). Noting that all of these various situations involve some type of inhibition, Morrell hypothesizes that "stimulation-provoked alpha activity may be an electrical sign of central inhibitory processes" (69, p. 560). Perhaps

stimulus-evoked alpha is an indication that the *S* has been aroused to a level where alpha activity would normally occur.

Because of the paucity of evidence concerning the role of cognitive factors in the alpha feedback situation, we can only suggest some of the factors which may influence the production of alpha activity. Among them is the feedback situation itself, the attention which it demands of the *S*, the eventual boredom of the task, and the feeling he has about being evaluated by the experimenter. The amount of success which a *S* experiences in the form of trial-to-trial increases also determines, in part, his cognitive-emotional state during the feedback situation, not only relative to the point at which he starts, but also in relation to his expectations concerning his performance. Previous research with other physiological systems, such as the galvanic skin response, has clearly indicated that the *S*'s experiences, feelings of success, and motivations can interact with each other to influence the physiological responses observed (32, 88). The whole fact of being in a particular place for the purpose of participating in an experiment can have subtle and far-reaching effects on physiology (3). The method of feedback, whether visual, auditory, tactual or otherwise, will lead to certain variable difficulties in habituating to its presence. It has long been known, for instance, that when a stimulus is first presented to a *S*, any alpha activity which is occurring will usually be blocked (10). Adrian and Mathews (2) as early as 1934 noted that focusing of attention, or any "disturbance of the mind" such as mental arithmetic, will usually block the alpha rhythm. As noted earlier, the rate at which this alpha blocking orienting response will extinguish is contingent upon a number of variables; the type of sensory stimulus used, the definition of a blocking response, the length and intensity of the stimulus, and the emotional state of the organism (23, 51, 70, 111, 113). The number of factors which enter into the rate of extinction of the alpha blocking orienting response have to be considered in the feedback situation, if for no other reason than the fact that the changing feedback stimuli can themselves be partly considered as orienting stimuli to which the $S$ must habituate.

EVALUATING RESPONSE ACQUISITION
AND CONTROLS IN THE FEEDBACK
CONTROL OF ALPHA ACTIVITY

In addition to their comments on mediation in operant conditioning, Katkin and Murray (43) discuss two additional factors to be considered in evaluating evidence that conditioning has occurred. First of all, they point out that an increase in the response should be demonstrated above the level observed during a base line period, that is, an increase should really be an increase. Secondly, appropriate controls should be present such that the procedure can be related to observed increases directly, and that increases are not merely a chance or natural occurrence.

The problem of defining response acquisition is perhaps one of the most difficult methodological problems to appear in evaluating the feedback control of alpha activity. There are two basic strategies which have been employed. The first of these is to define the desired result of the experimental procedure in terms of demonstrating that a $S$ can gain control over the production of alpha activity, and to seek significant differences between periods when $Ss$ are told to keep their alpha activity on and periods when they are instructed to keep the activity off. Such differential control in the density of alpha activity as the result of instructions has been demonstrated by a number of studies (18, 39, 40, 85, 93). Some authors have noted, however, that although $Ss$ can very quickly learn to suppress their alpha activity, often within the first trial, increases during instructions to augment alpha densities are far more difficult to achieve, and rarely rise above alpha levels which naturally occur under optimal conditions (91, 93). In light of the many known factors which may block alpha activity, such differential control, while of interest, indicates only that $Ss$ can bring these factors into use with little difficulty. The other

side of the coin, that is, the degree to which such factors may be voluntarily excluded, has perhaps, more important consequences.

In such a case, it is imperative to know whether or not a $S$ has, by means of the feedback procedure, increased alpha density above that observed during optimal base line periods. In light of the many factors influencing alpha density, however, the establishment of appropriate or optimal base line conditions from which to measure increases becomes difficult. Almost any initial base line will be contaminated by apprehensions about the forthcoming experiment, the novelty of the situation, or other such influences. As a result, unless measurements of base line density are obtained during the course of the feedback training, it is impossible to establish whether or not any increase is due to training, or only to factors involved in the situation which relate to the rapport or ease of the $S$. Indeed, $Ss$ who receive false feedback, or those who are simply told at the end of each session how well they did have been shown to increase their alpha densities (31, 64, 91). Even the procedure of including frequent base line determinations, however, has been questioned as a method for establishing differences between base line and feedback conditions. Noting that his $Ss$ do not exceed base line levels during periods when they were getting the feedback stimulus, Kamiya (41) suggests that the procedure itself alters the base line:

> The increase in the curve for the Enhance Alpha condition is much more striking, (than the suppress Alpha Condition), and it is clear that there is a very significant difference in percent alpha time between the enhance and suppress conditions for these $Ss$. Thus it's not merely a function of alpha decreasing with the passage of time; there does seem to be some measure of volitional control. Now, consider the third curve (labeled basal level) which represents the percent alpha score $Ss$ got in the rest periods when they weren't getting the tone; as a matter of fact they were specifically told not to try producing tones, they were told that the tones would be switched off and just merely to wait until we got our machine aligned. This curve shows a generally upward trend, yet if

this were really a baseline sort of thing one would have expected it to have stayed level. My interpretation of this upward trend is that the experimental tasks apparently set them into certain preferred modes of waiting, and the preferred mode is the higher alpha state. (p. 513)

Such an explanation appears to be based on the assumption that all increases in alpha density arise from training, rather than from the sorts of rapport factors considered earlier. Irrespective of the various interpretations of the source of base line shifts in alpha density, it is clear that no proper controls have been established. Unless the task of the S can be specified during base line periods in a way which allows a standard assessment of resting alpha level which will be stable from time to time, there appears little possibility of conclusively demonstrating that Ss can be trained to increase their alpha densities above those observed during optimal resting conditions. To our knowledge no such demonstration has yet appeared.

SUBJECTIVE MOODS AND

ALPHA FEEDBACK

Much of the interest in the relationship between alpha activity and subjective mood has come from reports that Zen and Yoga practitioners show high and almost continuous levels of alpha activity during meditation, usually slowing in frequency during the course of a session (8, 42, 86). Additional interest has been generated by reports that Ss in the feedback situation generally find the experience pleasant, relaxing, and wish to return, often reporting dissociative phenomena such as feelings of floating, being unaware of the immediate environment, and distorted time perception (13, 31, 39–41, 85).

The source of these feedback mood statements and the process through which they come about are both somewhat obscure. Although the study of the relationship between brain wave activity and mental processes began quite early in the EEG literature, and subjective reports of mental blankness and abstract thinking were asso-

ciated with alpha activity (110), to say, as does Maslow (65) that we can now "teach people how to feel happy and serene" appears premature. Certainly no simple and direct relationship exists between alpha density and subjective feelings. Individuals with high chronic alpha density have not been shown to be markedly different from others with lower levels. Simple physical maneuvers like closing or opening the eyes have not been related to mood changes of the sort reported in feedback situations and yet such eye maneuvers markedly affect alpha density. It would appear fruitful to examine some aspects of the feedback situation itself in some detail.

Subjective reports are frequently influenced by the experimental setting and the course of the experiment itself. It is certainly possible that some of the reports of Ss in the feedback situation are influenced by what Orne (87) has called the "demand characteristics" of the situation, that is, Ss enter the experiment expecting to experience alterations in mood, expecting the session to be pleasant, perhaps a "high," or if they don't feel this way initially, the experimenter may reinforce such feelings, both in the pre-experimental interview and in the actual instructions given during the experiment. It would be interesting to speculate on the effects of an alternative orientation, that alpha feedback would permanently warp one's personality, for instance. It is, indeed, somewhat surprising to find such general agreement on the pleasantness of the situation, since some Ss with naturally low alpha densities can be expected to fail at the task of increasing alpha density; conversely, some of the positive affect in the situation may arise from the S's feelings of success at the task. Some of the dissociative phenomena, however, are less easily explained by S expectations.

One aspect of the situation which bears consideration is its similarity to perceptual and sensory deprivation environments where Ss are cut off from patterned external stimulation. Many of the effects which have been reported by Ss in the feedback situation have also been noted as concomitants of sensory deprivation experiments, even with durations as short as 1 hour (106, 118). Although noted after several days, rather than the shorter time span common in feedback experiments, a slowed alpha frequency with sensory deprivation may suggest common aspects between this and the meditative situation.

One aspect of the feedback task that must be considered as a possible source of subjective reports is that a great deal of literature, as noted earlier, stresses the importance of attention in blocking alpha activity. It is likely that those who exhibit alpha activity during feedback sessions do so, in part, through a process of "unfocusing" attention, that is, trying not to attend to any one aspect of the surroundings, thus creating a sort of perceptual deprivation. Whether this may have psychological or physiological effects which contribute to subjective mood states is certainly unclear at present.

A VIEWPOINT TOWARD ALPHA DENSITY
INCREASES DURING FEEDBACK

A consideration of the phenomena of the feedback control of alpha activity, based on previous data and consideration of the many factors which can influence alpha density, has led us to formulate a hypothesis to account for the trial-to-trial increases in alpha activity noted in previous research, as well as other related effects. We suggest that *alpha activity occurs in the feedback situation when an individual ceases to pay attention to any of a number of stimuli which normally block this activity.* These stimuli may be cognitive, somatic, emotional, or anything, in fact, which will lead to alpha blocking. The alpha densities which can occur in the feedback situation may approach those seen in that same individual under optimal base line conditions, but will not significantly exceed them. While the feedback process may yield trial-to-trial increases which resemble learning curves, these curves are the result of inhibition, as the S gradually removes from his attention most, or all of the influences which block the production of alpha

activity. The resulting density is limited only by the S's own natural ability to generate this activity. In addition to the feedback process, any other process by which these influences may be removed will result in increased alpha activity, and the process need not be an active one. It may be a process similar to falling asleep, or something analogous to "highway hypnosis," that is, something which occurs naturally unless blocked. Working at the task may, indeed, lead to a result quite the opposite of that intended by focusing attention on those aspects of the situation which lead to alpha blocking.

The implications of this approach to the study of alpha activity are several. One implication is that the feedback situation may not necessarily be the best method for producing a high index of alpha activity in a S, but only one way of producing it in a situation which would not normally be expected to yield a great deal of alpha activity. If the feedback situation could be shown to produce amounts significantly greater than those achieved in other conditions, it would deserve special attention, but such demonstrations have not been reported.

A second implication is that not every S can be expected to successfully inhibit blocking influences, particularly in the feedback situation, and thus feedback may not assure high alpha densities. A corollary to this implication is that those Ss having a high degree of naturally occurring alpha activity would probably be less able to block such activity for sustained periods of time, compared to those with low alpha densities; that is, some Ss would be able to generate alpha activity better than they could block it. Yet another implication of this approach is that much of the literature on attentional processes, orienting, habituation, and the factors which influence these processes becomes relevant to the question of alpha control. A fourth implication concerns the etiology of the subjective mood states which are reputed to accompany the control of alpha activity. If, as hypothesized, the lack of attention to blocking stimuli results in alpha increases, and other methods may produce similar increases in alpha levels, than these other methods should lead to changes in mood states similar to those reported during feedback control.

## REFERENCES

1. Adrian, E. D. The dominance of vision. Trans. Ophthal. Soc., U.K., *63*: 194–207, 1943.
2. Adrian, E. D. and Matthews, B. H. C. The Berger rhythm: Potential changes from the occipital lobes in man. Brain. *57*: 355–385. 1934.
3. Agnew, H. W., Webb. W. and Williams. R. L. The first night effect: An EEG study of sleep. Psychophysiology, *2*: 263–266. 1966.
4. Albino, R. and Burnand, G. Conditioning of the alpha rhythm in man. J. Exp. Psychol.. *67*: 539–544, 1964.
5. Andersen, P. and Andersson, S. A. *Physiological Basis of the Alpha Rhythm*. Appleton-Century, New York, 1968.
6. Armington, J. C. and Mitnick, L. L. EEG and sleep deprivation. J. Appl. Physiol.. *14*: 247–250, 1959.
7. Bagchi, B. K. The adaptation and variability of response of the human brain rhythm. J. Psychol., *3*: 463–485, 1937.
8. Bagchi, B. K. and Wenger. M. A. Electrophysiological correlates of some Yogi exercises. In *EEG, Clinical Neurophysiology and Epilepsy*, pp. 132–149. Pergamon Press, London, 1959.
9. Bard, P. B. Some further analyses of the functions of the cerebrum. In Bard, P. B., ed. *Medical Physiology*, 11th ed. Mosby, St. Louis, 1961.
10. Berger, H. Über das Elektrenkephalogramm des Menschen. Arch. Psychiat. Nervenkr., *87*: 527–570, 1929.
11. Bjerner, B. Alpha depression and lowered pulse rate during delayed reactions in serial reaction test. Acta Physiol. Scand.. *19* (suppl. 65): 1–93, 1949.
12. Blake, H. and Gerard, R. W. Brain potentials during sleep. Amer. J. Physiol., *119*: 692–703, 1937.
13. Brown, B. Recognition of aspects of consciousness through association with EEG alpha activity represented by a light signal. Psychophysiology, *6*: 442–452. 1970.
14. Bundzen, P. V. Autoregulation of functional state of the brain: An investigation using photostimulation with feedback. Fiziologicheskii Shurnal SSSR imeni I. M. Sechenova, *51*: 936, 1965. (Republished: Fed. Proc. [Transl. Suppl.], *25*: T551–T554, 1966.)
15. Crider, A., Shapiro, D. and Tursky, B. Reinforcement of spontaneous electrodermal activity. J. Comp. Physiol. Psychol., *61*: 20–27, 1966.
16. Davis. H. and Davis. P. A. Action potentials of the brain in normal persons and in normal states of cerebral activity. Arch. Neurol. (Chicago), *36*: 1214–1224, 1936.
17. Davis. P. A. and Davis, H. Electrical activity of the brain, its relation to physiological states and to states of impaired consciousness. Res. Publ. Ass. Res. Nerv. Ment. Dis., *19*: 50–80, 1939.
18. Dewan, E. M. Occipital alpha rhythm, eye position and lens accommodation. Nature (London), *214*: 975–977, 1967.
19. Durup, G. and Fessard, A. L'électroencephalogramme de l'homme. Année Psychol., *36*: 1–32, 1935.
20. Eccles, J. C. *The Neurophysiological Basis of Mind*. Clarendon Press, London, 1953.
21. Efron, R. The conditioned reflex: A meaningless concept. Perspect. Biol. Med., *9*: 488–514, 1966.
22. Ellingson, R. J. Brain waves and problems of psychology. Psychol. Bull., *53*: 1–34, 1956.
23. Esecover, H. B., Torres, A. A., Taylor, R. M., Wilkens, B. and Malitz, S. Contingent alpha blocking and sensitization. Nature (London), *201*: 1247–1248, 1964.
24. Fenton, G. W. and Scotton, L. Personality and the alpha rhythm. Brit. J. Psychiat., *113*: 1283–1289, 1967.
25. Fenwick, P. B. The effects of eye movement on alpha rhythm (abstract). Electroenceph. Clin. Neurophysiol., *21*: 618, 1966.
26. Gantt, W. H. B. F. Skinner and his contingencies. Cond. Reflex, *5*: 63–74, 1970.
27. Gastaut, H., Jus, A., Jus, C., Morrell, F., Storm van Leeuwen, W., Dongier, S., Naquet, R., Regis, H., Roger, A., Bekkering, D., Kamp, A. and Weere, J. Etude topographique des réactions d'electroencéphalographiques conditionées chez l'homme. Electroenceph. Clin. Neurophysiol., *9*: 1–34, 1957.
28. Goldie, L. and Green, J. M. Paradoxical blocking and arousal in the drowsy state. Nature (London), *187*: 952–953, 1960.
29. Golla, F. L., Hutton. E. L. and Walter, W. G. The objective study of mental imagery: I. Physiological concomitants. J. Ment. Sci., *89*: 216–223, 1943.
30. Gottlober, A. B. Relationship between brain potentials and personality. J. Exp. Psychol., *22*: 67–74, 1938.
31. Hart, J. T. Autocontrol of EEG alpha. Presented at the Seventh Annual Meeting of the Society for Psychophysiological Research. San Diego, October 20–22. 1967.
32. Hicks, R. G. Experimenter effects on the physiological experiment. Psychophysiology, *7*: 10–17, 1970.
33. Hill, D. The EEG in psychiatry. In Hill, D. and Parr, G., eds. *Electroencephalography: A Symposium on Its Various Aspects*. Macmillan, New York, 1963.
34. Hirai, T. Electroencephalographic study on the Zen meditation (Japan). Psychiat. Neurol. Jap., *62*: 76–105, 1960.
35. Iwama, K. Delayed conditioned reflex in man and brain waves. Tohoku J. Exp. Med., *52*: 53–62, 1950.
36. Jasper, H. and Shagass, C. Conditioning occipital alpha rhythm in man. J. Exp. Psychol., *28*: 373–388, 1941.

Central Nervous System Activity: Human

37. Johnson, L., Lubin, A., Naitoh, P., Nute, C. and Austin, M. Spectral analysis of the EEG of dominant and non-dominant alpha subjects during waking and sleeping. Electroenceph. Clin. Neurophysiol., *26:* 361–370, 1969.

38. Kamiya, J. Conditional discrimination of the EEG alpha rhythm in humans. Presented at the Meeting of the Western Psychological Association, San Francisco, April 1962.

39. Kamiya, J. EEG operant conditioning and the study of states of consciousness. In Freedman, D. X., (Chairman), Laboratory Studies of Altered Psychological States. Symposium at American Psychological Association, Washington, D.C., September 4, 1967.

40. Kamiya, J. Conscious control of brain waves. Psychol. Today, *1:* 57–60, 1968.

41. Kamiya, J. Operant control of the EEG alpha rhythm and some of its reported effects on consciousness. In Tart, C., ed. *Altered States of Consciousness: A Book of Readings.* Wiley, New York, 1969.

42. Kasamatsu, A. and Hirai, T. An electroencephalographic study on the Zen meditation (Zazen). Folia Psychiat. Neurol. Jap., *20:* 315–336, 1966.

43. Katkin, E. S. and Murray, E. N. Instrumental conditioning of autonomically mediated behavior: Theoretical and methodological issues. Psychol. Bull., *70:* 52–68, 1968.

44. Katkin, E. S., Murray, E. M. and Lachman, R. Concerning instrumental autonomic conditioning: A rejoinder. Psychol. Bull., *71:* 462–466, 1969.

45. Keller, F. L. and Schoenfeld, W. N. *Principles of Psychology.* Appleton-Century, New York, 1950.

46. Kennedy, J. L. A possible artifact in electroencephalography. Psychol. Rev., *66:* 347–352, 1959.

47. Kimble, G. A. *Hilgard and Marquis, Conditioning and Learning.* Appleton-Century, New York, 1961.

48. Kimmel, H. D. and Hill, F. A. Operant conditioning of the GSR. Psychol. Rep., *7:* 555–562, 1960.

49. Kimmel, E. and Kimmel, H. D. A replication of operant conditioning of the GSR. J. Exp. Psychol., *65:* 212–213, 1963.

50. Knott, J. R. Electroencephalography and physiological psychology: Evaluation and statement of problem. Psychol. Bull., *38:* 944–974, 1941.

51. Knott, J. R. and Henry, C. E. The conditioning of the blocking of the alpha rhythm of the human EEG. J. Exp. Psychol., *28:* 134–143, 1941.

52. Knott, J. R., Gibbs, F. A. and Henry, C. E. Fourier transformations of the EEG during sleep. J. Exp. Psychol., *31:* 465–477, 1942.

53. Konorski, J. and Miller, S. Further remarks on two types of conditioned reflex. J. Gen. Psychol., *17:* 405–407, 1937.

54. Kreitman, N. and Shaw, J. C. Experimental enhancement of alpha activity. Electroenceph. Clin. Neurophysiol., *18:* 147–155, 1965.

55. Lemere, F. The significance of individual differences in the Berger rhythm. Brain, *59:* 366, 1936.

56. Lindsley, D. B. Basic perceptual processes and the EEG. Psychiat. Res. Rep., *6:* 161–170, 1956.

57. Lindsley, D. B. Attention, consciousness, sleep and wakefulness. In Field, J., ed. *Handbook of Physiology, Section 1: Neurophysiology,* vol. 1. American Physiological Society, Washington, D. C., 1960.

58. Lippold and Novotny, G. E. K. Is alpha rhythm an artefact? Lancet, 976–979, 1970.

59. Loomis, A. L., Harvey, E. N. and Hobart, G. A. Electrical potentials of the human brain. J. Exp. Psychol., *19:* 249–279, 1936.

60. Loomis, A. L., Harvey, E. N. and Hobart, G. A. Distribution of disturbance patterns in the human electroencephalogram with special reference to sleep. J. Neurophysiol., *1:* 413–430, 1938.

61. Lorens, S. A. and Darrow, C. W. Eye movements, EEG, GSR, and EKG during mental multiplication. Electroenceph. Clin. Neurophysiol., *14:* 739–746, 1962.

62. Lynch, J. J. The stimulus-the ghost-the response: The carousel of conditioning. Cond. Reflex, *5:* 133–139, 1970.

63. Lynch, J. J. and Kakigi, S. Some theoretical implications of CS-UCS intervals in classical conditioning. Presented at the Annual Meeting of the Society for Psychophysiological Research, Washington, D. C., October 1968.

64. Lynch, J. J., Paskewitz, D. A., Orne, M. T. and Costello, J. An analysis of the feedback control of alpha activity (abstract). Cond. Reflex, *5:* 185–186, 1970.

65. Maslow, A. Toward a humanistic biology. Amer. Psychol., *24:* 724–735, 1969.

66. Miller, H. L. Alpha waves: Artifacts. Psychol. Bull., *69:* 279–280, 1968.

67. Miller, N. E. Learning of visceral and glandular responses. Science (Washington), *163:* 434–445, 1969.

68. Miller, N. E. and Carmona, A. Modification of a visceral response, salivation in thirsty dogs, by instrumental training with water reward. J. Comp. Physiol. Psychol., *63:* 1–6, 1967.

69. Morrell, L. K. Some characteristics of stimulus-provoked alpha activity. Electroenceph. Clin. Neurophysiol., *21:* 552–561, 1966.

70. Morrell, F. and Jasper, H. H. Electrographic studies of the formation of temporary connections in the brain. Electroenceph. Clin. Neurophysiol., *8:* 201–215, 1956.

71. Morrell, F., Roberts, L. and Jasper, H. H. Effect of focal epileptogenic lesions and their ablation upon conditioned electrical responses of the brain in the monkey. Electroenceph. Clin. Neurophysiol., *14:* 724–730, 1962.

72. Morrell, F. and Ross, M. Central inhibition in cortical conditioned reflexes. Arch. Neurol. (Chicago), *70:* 611–616, 1953.

73. Motokawa, K. and Huzimori, B. EEG and conditioned reflexes. Tohoku J. Exp. Med., *50:* 214–234, 1949.

74. Mowrer, O. H. On the dual nature of learning: A reinterpretation of "conditioning" and "problem-solving." Harvard Educat. Rev., *17:* 102–148, 1947.

75. Mowrer, O. H. *Learning Theory and Personality Dynamics. Selected Papers.* Ronald Press, New York, 1950.

76. Mulholland, T. Variations in the response duration curve of successive cortical activation by a feedback stimulus. Electroenceph. Clin. Neurophysiol., *16:* 394–395, 1964.

77. Mulholland, T. The concept of attention and the electroencephalographic alpha rhythm. In Evans, C. R. and Mulholland, T.. eds. *Attention in Neurophysiology,* 100–127. Butterworths, London, 1969.

78. Mulholland, T. Feedback electroencephalography. Activitas Nervosa Superior *10:* 410–438, 1968.

79. Mulholland, T. and Evans, C. R. An unexpected artefact in the human electroencephalogram concerning the alpha rhythm and the position of the eyes. Nature (London), *207:* 36–37, 1965.

80. Mulholland, T. and Evans, C. R. Oculomotor function and the alpha activation cycle. Nature (London), *211:* 1278–1279, 1966.

81. Mulholland, T. and Runnals, S. Increased occurrence of EEG alpha during increased attention. J. Psychol., *54:* 317–330, 1962.

82. Mundy-Castle, A. C. An appraisal of electroencephalography in relation to psychology (monograph suppl.). J. Nat. Inst. Personnel Res., 1958.

83. Murphy, G. Psychology in the year 2000. Amer. Psychol., *24:* 523–530, 1969.

84. Nowlis, D. P. Early observations on a system providing EEG alpha feedback. Hawthorne House Res. Memorandum 78, 1968.

85. Nowlis, D. P. and Kamiya, J. The control of electroencephalographic alpha rhythms through auditory feedback and the associated mental activity. Psychophysiology, *6:* 476–484, 1970.

86. Okeima, T., Kogu, E., Ikeda, K. and Sugiyama, H. The EEG of Yoga and Zen practitioners. Electroenceph. Clin. Neurophysiol., *51* (suppl. 9): 1957.

87. Orne, M. T. On the social psychology of the psychological experiment: With particular reference to demand characteristics and their implications. Amer. Psychol., *17:* 776–783. 1962.

88. Orne, M. T., Thackray, R. I. and Paskewitz. D. A. On the detection of deception: A model for the study of the physiological effects of psychological stimuli. In Greenfield, N. and Sternbach, R., eds. *Handbook of Psychophysiology.* Holt, Rinehart and Winston, New York. In press.

89. Oswald, I. *Sleeping and Waking.* Elsevier, Amsterdam, 1962.

90. Paskewitz, D. A. The Quantification of Nocturnal Electroencephalographic Patterns in Man. Doctoral Dissertation, University of Oklahoma, Ann Arbor, Michigan: University Microfilms, No: 67-14140, 1967.

91. Paskewitz, D. A., Lynch, J. J., Orne, M. T. and Costello, J. The feedback control of alpha activity: Conditioning or disinhibition. Psychophysiology, *6:* 637–638, 1970.

92. Peper, E. Feedback regulation of the alpha electroencephalogram activity through control of the internal and external parameters. Kybernetik. *7:* 107–112, 1970.

93. Peper, E. and Mulholland, T. Methodological and theoretical problems in the voluntary control of electroencephalographic occipital alpha by the subject. Kybernetik, *7:* 10–13, 1970.

94. Rescorla, R. A. Pavlovian conditioning and its proper control procedures. Psychol. Rev., *74:* 71–80, 1967.

95. Rubin. M. A. The distribution of the alpha rhythm over the cerebral cortex of normal man. J. Neurophysiol., *1:* 313–323, 1938.

96. Runnals, S. and Mulholland, T. A method for the study of bilateral asymmetry of cortical activation. Amer. J. EEG Techn., *4:* 15–18, 1964.

97. Runnals, S. and Mulholland, T. Selected demonstrations of voluntary regulation of cortical activation. Bedford Res., *11:* 26, 1965.

98. Rusinov, V. S. General and localized alterations in the electroencephalogram during the formation of conditioned reflexes in man. Electroenceph. Clin. Neurophysiol., (suppl. 13): 309–320, 1960.

99. Saul. L. J., Davis, H. and Davis. P. A. Correlations between electroencephalograms and psychological organization of the individual. Trans. Amer. Neurol. Ass., *63:* 167, 1937.

100. Schoenfeld, W. N. Some old work for modern conditioning theory. Cond. Reflex, *1:* 219–223, 1966.

101. Seligmann. M. E. Control group and conditioning: A comment on operationism. Psychol. Rev., *76:* 484–491, 1969.

102. Shaw, J. C., Foley, S. and Blowers, G. H. Alpha rhythm: An artefact? Lancet, 1173, 1970.

103. Skinner. B. F. *The Behavior of Organisms: An Experimental Analysis.* Appleton-Century, New York. 1938.

104. Storm van Leeuwen, W. (Chairman), Bickford, R., Brazier, M. A. B., Cobb, W. A., Dondey, M., Gastaut, H., Bloor, P., Henry, C. E., Hess, R., Knott, J. R., Kugler, J., Lairy, G. C., Loeb, C., Magnus, O., Oller Daurella, L., Petsche, H., Schwab, R., Walter, W. G. and Widen, L. Proposal for an EEG terminology by the terminology committee of the International Federation for Electroencephalography and Clinical Neurophysiology. Electroenceph. Clin. Neurophysiol., *20:* 293–320, 1966.

105. Stoyva, J. and Kamiya, J. Electrophysiological studies of dreaming as the prototype of a new strategy in the study of consciousness. Psychol. Rev., *75:* 192–205, 1968.

106. Suedfeld, P. Changes in intellectual performance and in susceptibility to influence. In Zubek, J. P., ed. *Sensory Deprivation: Fifteen Years of Research.* Appleton-Century, New York, 1969.

107. Sugi, Y. and Akutsu, K. *Science of Zagen— Energy Metabolism.* Tokyo, 1964.

108. Toman, J. E. P. The electroencephalogram during mental effort. Fed. Proc., *2:* 49, 1943.

109. Torres, A. A. Sensitization and association in alpha blocking "conditioning." Electroenceph. Clin. Neurophysiol., *24:* 297–360, 1968.

110. Travis, L. E. Brain potentials and the temporal course of consciousness. J. Exp. Psychol., *21:* 302–309, 1937.

111. Travis, L. E. and Egan, J. B. Conditioning of the electrical response of the cortex. J. Exp. Psychol., *22:* 524–531, 1938.

112. Trowill, J. A. Instrumental conditioning of the heart rate in the curarized rat. J. Comp. Physiol. Psychol., *63:* 7–11, 1967.

113. Visser, S. L. Correlations between the contingent alpha blocking EEG characteristics and clinical diagnosis. Electroenceph. Clin. Neurophysiol., *13:* 538–548, 1961.

114. Walter, W. G. Intrinsic rhythms of the brain. In Field, J., ed. *Handbook of Physiology: Section I, Neurophysiology,* vol. 1, chap. 11, pp. 279–313. American Physiological Society, Washington, D.C., 1959.

115. Wells, C. E. Electroencephalographic correlates of conditioned response. In Glasser, G. H., ed. *EEG and Behavior.* Basic Books, New York, 1963.

116. Williams, A. C. Some psychological correlates of the electroencephalogram. Arch. Psychol., *240:* 1–48, 1939.

117. Williams, A. C. Facilitation of the alpha rhythm in the electroencephalogram. J. Exp. Psychol., 26: 413–422, 1940.

118. Zubek, J. P. Physiological and biochemical effects. In Zubek, J. P., ed. *Sensory Deprivation: Fifteen Years of Research.* Appleton-Century, New York, 1969.

# IV

## CENTRAL NERVOUS SYSTEM ACTIVITY: ANIMAL

# The Direct Control of Neural Processes by Reward and Punishment    13

Abraham H. Black

Recent experiments have begun to explore the use of reward to obtain direct control over the electrical activity of the brain. In this paper, I shall describe some of the research my co-workers and I have been doing in this field, with a word about its wider social implications.

Using reward to change behavior is called *operant conditioning*. The basic principle is simple: to increase the probability of a certain response, a reward is presented *immediately* after the response. This elementary concept

*A. H. Black, professor of psychology, McMaster University, received his Ph.D. in 1956 at Harvard University. His early research interests focused on behavioral analysis of fear and anxiety with particular attention to the possibility that responses controlled by the autonomic nervous system could be employed as measures of anxiety. This work led to an interest in the control of autonomic responding by operant conditioning procedures and in the direct operant conditioning of central neural processes that might control both autonomic and skeletal responses. This article is an adapted version of the author's 1970 Sigma Xi National Lecture. The research discussed was carried out in collaboration with G. Young and L. Grupp, and was supported by grants from the Ontario Mental Health Foundation and the National Research Council of Canada. The author also wishes to acknowledge the assistance of F. Brandemark and A. Dalton. Address: Department of Psychology, McMaster University, Hamilton, Ontario, Canada.*

is one of the most powerful procedures used to change behavior. Judicious application of reward can produce long sequences of complex, and novel, patterns of responding.[1]

Although much of human behavior can be operantly conditioned, many people feel that certain areas—private thoughts in particular—are safe from such manipulation. Recent research, however, has cast doubt on these assumptions about covert processes and has indicated that the regions of the mind and behavior beyond the reach of psychological control by operant conditioning are fewer than previously supposed.

Consider, for example, the responses of visceral muscles, cardiac muscles, and glands regulated by the autonomic nervous system. It is generally believed that because these responses are involuntary, they cannot be changed to obtain a reward. Experiments have shown, however, that increases and decreases in blood pressure, heart-rate, stomach contractions, salivary flow, and similar processes can be operantly conditioned (Kimmel 1967; Miller 1969).

**213**

Another internal response that research has shown can be operantly conditioned is the electrical activity of the brain (Black, Young, and Batenchuk 1970; Carmona 1967; Dalton 1969; Dewan 1967; Fetz 1969; Fox and Rudell 1968; Kamiya 1969; Miller 1966; Olds 1967; Sterman, Wyrwicka, and Roth 1969; Stoyva and Kamiya 1968; and Wyrwicka and Sterman 1968). This discovery will be useful only if we establish that a particular type of electrical activity in a particular location of the brain indicates a psychological or neural process important in the functioning of the brain.[2] When this proves to be the case, we might be able to condition thoughts or brain processes directly by rewarding the electrical activity of the brain. For example, as Miller (1969) suggested, epileptic seizures might be prevented by operantly conditioning subjects to refrain from producing the brain wave patterns that always precede a seizure. Similarly, insomnia might be cured by conditioning the production of brain wave patterns that are necessarily related to sleep.

Both of these examples demonstrate that the usefulness of operant conditioning depends upon knowing what central nervous system state or process a brain wave pattern indicates. In some cases, such as the distinction between the waking and sleeping states, we already have some knowledge about the related brain wave patterns. In many others, however, we do not know the functional significance of the patterns. In our experiments, we found that the task of operantly conditioning brain waves itself helps us to obtain the information we need to relate the brain wave to neural or psychological processes.

A "case history" from our experiments

will illustrate this idea. The first section below gives an example of the operant conditioning of brain waves; the following section describes research on what central nervous system processes the conditioned changes in brain waves might indicate. In the final section is a discussion of the operant conditioning of brain waves as a practical means of obtaining direct control over neural and psychological processes that we have been unable to control directly before.

## Hippocampal electrical activity in dogs

My interest in the hippocampus was first aroused by C. Vanderwolf, when he was on the faculty at McMaster University. I had been concerned with the neural structures underlying operantly conditioned skeletal responses, such as running and lever pressing, and was, therefore, intrigued by Vanderwolf's observations that led him to believe that the hippocampus is involved in the initiation of these voluntary skeletal movements (Vanderwolf 1967, 1968, 1969).

The hippocampus is shaped like a pair of C's joined at the top and spread apart at the bottom. It lies near the center of the brain, one C on each side of the midline, the opening of the C facing forward. It is usually described as a component of the limbic system, a more primitive part of the mammalian brain than the neocortex which lies over it. In the first experiment I shall describe, we attempted to reward different patterns of electrical activity in the dorsal or upper part of the hippocampus.[3] The electrical activity of the dorsal hippocampus was recorded from permanently implanted, stainless steel needle electrodes that permitted the dog to move about normally during record-

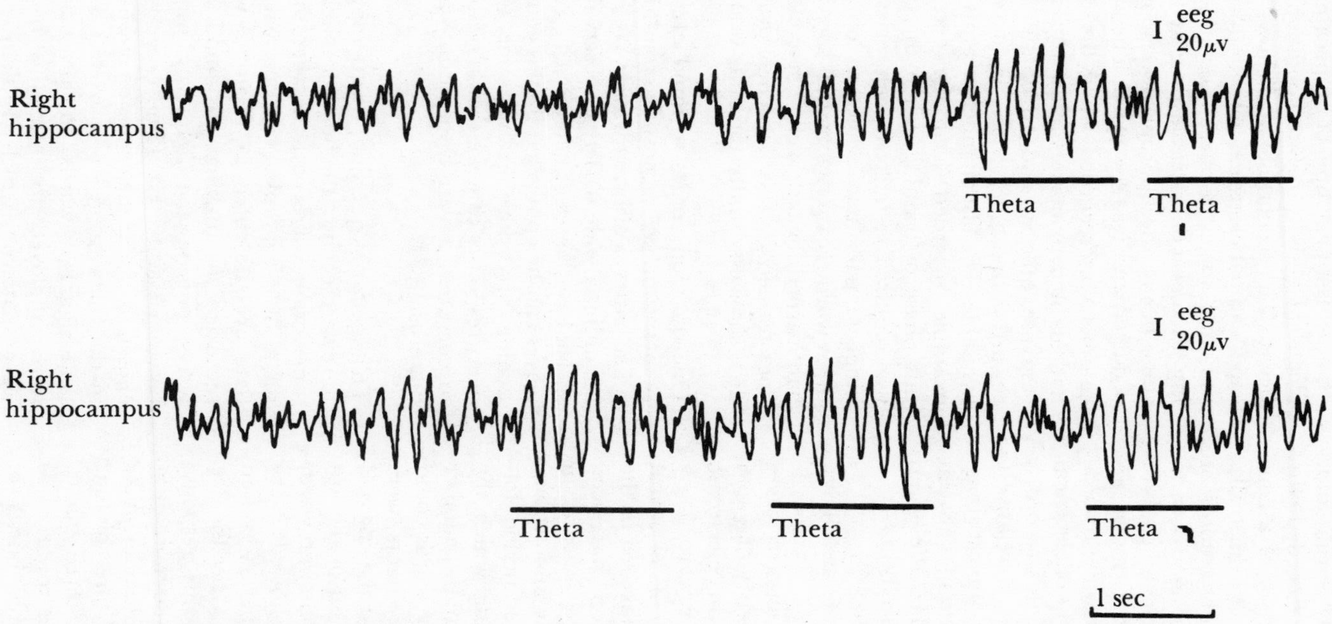

Figure 1. Records of the electrical activity of the right dorsal hippocampus of a single dog. Underlining indicates examples of theta activity (regular sinusoidal waves, 4 to 6 Hz).

ing. The electrodes, which were insulated except for a small area at the tip, were relatively large and, therefore, presumably recorded the aggregate electrical activity of a considerable number of brain cells. "Brain waves" are simply records of the fluctuations in voltage over a period of time between a pair of these electrodes. Figure 1 shows an example of such a brain wave record. One of the typical patterns of electrical activity that appears in this record is called the theta rhythm, a relatively high amplitude, regular, almost sinusoidal brain wave pattern between approximately 4 and 6 Hz. We began by rewarding this theta rhythm.

Briefly, the procedure was as follows.

On each trial, when a burst of waves of the appropriate frequency of 4 to 6 Hz was detected by an electronic circuit, the dog was rewarded by passing a brief pulse of electrical current through the septal area of the brain. (Such stimulation has been shown to function as a reward in other experiments [Olds and Milner 1953].) A 10-second rest period followed the reward, during which the lights in the experimental chamber were turned off and no rewards could be obtained. Then the lights were turned on, indicating that the dog had another opportunity to make the appropriate response and obtain reward. At first, the reward followed every burst of three or four theta waves in the presence of the light. Once the dog had learned to make this response quickly, his task was made more difficult. The dog was required to make two successive bursts of three or four theta waves, and then three bursts, and so on. Finally, the reward was given after 15 successive bursts of three or four theta waves.

Figure 2 shows data for one dog trained by this procedure. The top channel is an example of hippocampal electrical activity before conditioning began. The second channel shows the hippocampal electrical activity during the early stages of operant conditioning. It took considerable time at this stage before the appropriate response occurred and was rewarded. The next channel was recorded when the dog had learned to make the appropriate response quickly and to obtain the reward almost as soon as it was available. The last channel presents an example recorded near the end of this phase of training, when the dog was required to make a long series of hippocampal theta waves to obtain the reward. It is obvious that the dog had learned his task well. Three other dogs trained by this particular procedure show essentially the same results.

One question comes to mind at this point: Can we operantly condition other patterns of brain waves? We can condition a wide variety of observable skeletal responses. Therefore, if brain waves can be controlled by this conditioning procedure in the same way overt responses can, we should be able to condition a variety of brain wave patterns.

To answer this question, we attempted to reward each of the dogs for making some brain wave pattern other than theta. For example, the dog whose data are presented in Figure 2 was rewarded for making low amplitude waves outside the frequency range between 3 and 7 Hz. (This range was chosen to ensure the exclusion of waves in the theta range—4 to 6 Hz.) The same signals, rewards, and procedure were employed to train this brain wave pattern (which I shall call "non-theta") as were used to train the

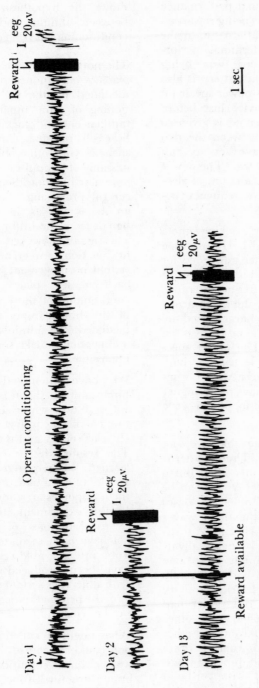

Before operant conditioning

Operant conditioning

Day 1

Reward | eeg
         I | 20 μv

Day 2

Reward | eeg
         I | 20 μv

Day 13

Reward | eeg
         I | 20 μv

Reward available

1 sec

Figure 2. Records of electrical activity from the dorsal hippocampus for a single dog being trained to produce theta waves. Samples are presented from the period before training and from the 1st, 2nd, and 13th days of training. The onset of the period during which reward was available is indicated by the vertical line. Rewards are indicated by labels.

theta pattern. Figure 3 presents an example of the terminal performance of the dog when it was being rewarded for the non-theta pattern; to make comparison easier, terminal performance when the dog was being rewarded for the theta pattern is also shown. In addition, a power spectrum of the electrical activity just before the reward was presented is given so that the differences between the two patterns of brain wave activity can be more readily observed. (The power spectrum presents the amount of electrical activity at each frequency between 1 and 25 Hz.)

When rewarded for making theta waves between 4 and 6 Hz, the dog learned to do so. When rewarded for making the low amplitude brain wave pattern outside the frequency range between 3 and 7 Hz, the dog learned to make a pattern characterized by low amplitude, irregular waves of various frequencies. The power spectrum shows that the electrical activity in the non-theta pattern was concentrated at frequencies lower and higher than those observed for theta-wave conditioning.

These results indicate that we can operantly condition different patterns of electrical activity in a dog. But a further question arises. A dog can be making a variety of other responses simultaneously with the theta waves and non-theta waves. He can be turning his head, focusing his eyes, salivating, and so on. This might tempt one to conclude that we had not really directly conditioned electrical activity of the hippocampus, but rather had inadvertently conditioned some other response, and feedback from this other response elicited the appropriate brain wave patterns in the hippocampus. This idea is illustrated in the left-hand section of Figure 4 and is labelled

"peripheral mediation." The diagram shows the hypothesized connections between stimulus and response after conditioning has been completed.

The notion that the electrical activity was not conditioned directly but was mediated by the inadvertent conditioning of some other response is a familiar one and, luckily, one that can be easily rejected. Curare-like drugs, such as Gallamine, block the transmission of impulses at the neuromuscular junction. Sensory input and central processing of that input can go on, as well as the transmission of signals from the brain to the muscles. The signals, however, are blocked at the junction between nerve and muscle so that no movement or related feedback can take place. If the operant conditioning of the electrical activity of the hippocampus is peripherally mediated, the administration of Gallamine should make such conditioning impossible.

We have attempted to condition hippocampal theta and non-theta waves in dogs whose skeletal musculature had been paralyzed by Gallamine (Black, Young, and Batenchuk 1970). The results are clear-cut: the dogs learned the required response. Examples of conditioned theta and non-theta responses are shown in Figure 5. In this experiment, the conditioned electrical response of the dog could not have been mediated by feedback from an observable response; it must have been produced directly by a central nervous system process. Therefore, the peripheral mediational model can be rejected.[4]

What might be called central mediation could, of course, have occurred; we might have conditioned some other brain structure (one that controls movement, for example), and the output from this structure could have elicited the appropriate pattern of brain waves in the hippocampus as a by-product. This possibility is illustrated in the right-hand panel of Figure 4. To find out whether this is the case, we must determine whether a simple central mediational system or some other complex central control system is involved. (An example of another possible control system is

shown in the center panel of Figure 4, in which there is a direct connection between input and output through the hippocampus.) We do not have enough information yet to choose among these and other central models. Whatever model prevails, the available data demonstrate that we can directly operantly condition the electrical activity of the brain.

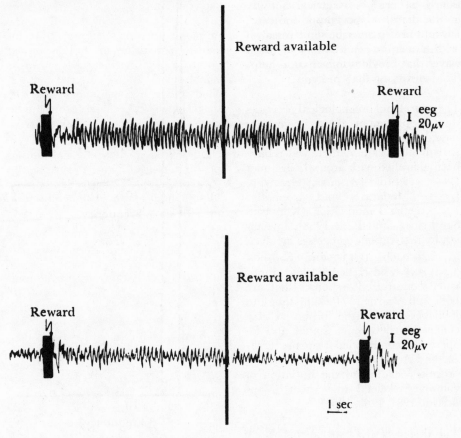

Figure 3. Samples of electrical activity from the dorsal hippocampus during the terminal stages of operant conditioning. The upper record presents a sample for a dog trained to make hippocampal theta waves to obtain reward. The lower record presents data for the same dog when it was subsequently trained to make "non-theta" waves. To the right of each sample is a power spectrum indicating the amount of power at each frequency between 1 and 25 Hz. The power spectrum was computed over a 25-second period during the terminal stages of each phase of conditioning.

## Functional significance

As I mentioned in the introduction, there would be little point in demonstrating that we can condition the electrical activity of the brain if we did not have some idea of the functional significance of the particular patterns of electrical activity we have conditioned. What neural or psychological processes do operantly conditioned patterns of electrical activity in the dorsal hippocampus indicate? I would like to describe some research on the operant conditioning of brain waves that provides information helpful in answering that question.

The neural and psychological processes that hippocampal theta waves are thought to reflect are astonishingly varied. Hippocampal theta waves have been identified with arousal (Bremner 1964), orienting responses (Grastyan, Lissak, Madarasz, and Donhoffer 1959), general motivation (Konorski, Santibanez, and Beck 1968), low intensity motivational processes involved in approach (Grastyan, Karmos, Vereczkey, and Kellenyi 1966), motivated conditioned responses that are not well learned (Pickenhain and Klingberg 1967), the formation of a connection between a signal and an operantly conditioned response (Elazar and Adey 1967), and with neural processes leading to the initiation of voluntary skeletal movement (Vanderwolf 1967, 1968, 1969).

The design of the experiments which led to the formulation of these hypotheses about the functional significance of hippocampal theta waves was straightforward. Observations were made of brain wave patterns that accompanied behavior in natural settings, such as walking, eating, and sleeping, or that accompanied condi-

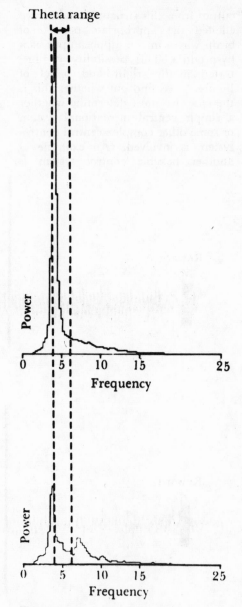

Figure 3.

tioned responses, such as lever pressing. In the first experiment that I will describe, we reversed this procedure. We observed the overt behavior that accompanied operantly conditioned brain wave patterns.[5]

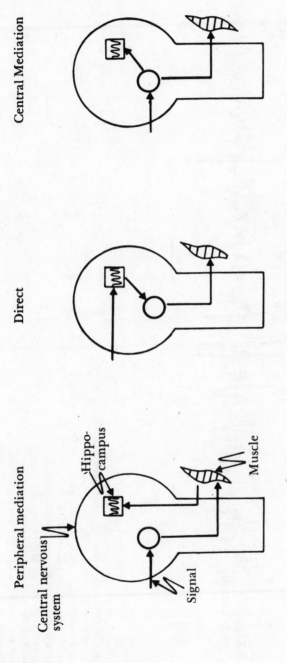

**Peripheral mediation**　　　　**Direct**　　　　**Central Mediation**

Central nervous
system

Hippo-
campus

Signal

Muscle

**Excitatory models**

Figure 4. Schematic diagrams illustrating the and circles within it represent structures campus is assumed to have an excitatory possible connections between the signal and within the central nervous system that might effect; similar models can be constructed in behavior after operant conditioning has been be involved in the stimulus response connec- which the role of the hippocampus is in- completed. The key-slot form represents the tion. One of these structures is the hippo- hibitory. The various models are discussed central nervous system; the small squares campus. In the models shown, the hippo- in the text.

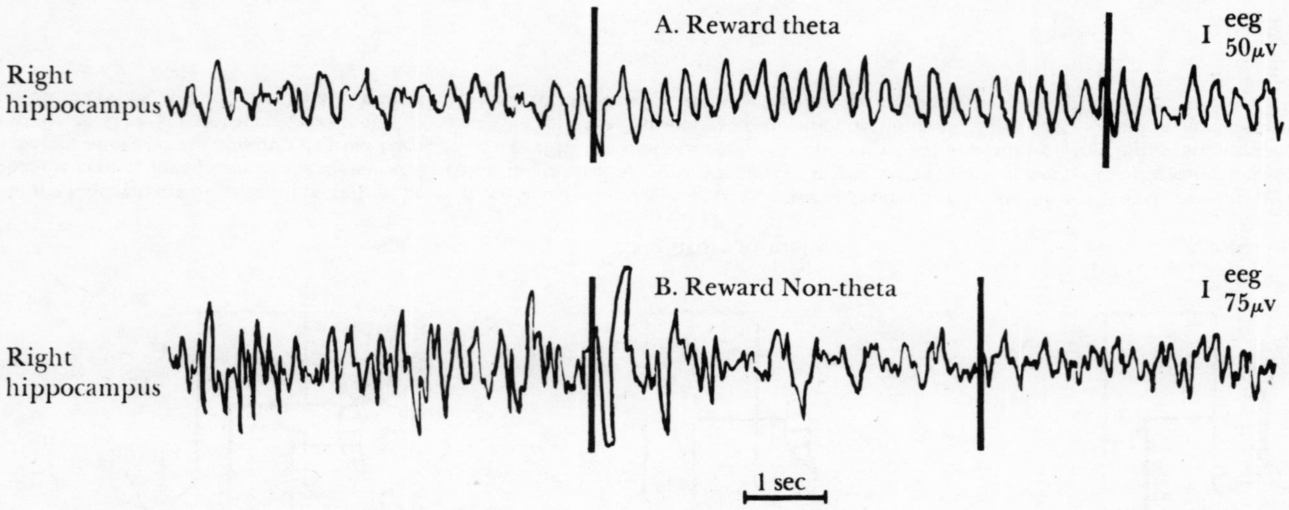

Figure 5. A recording of electrical activity for a single trial for a dog that was rewarded for making theta waves (A) while a signal was present, and for a dog that was rewarded for refraining from making theta waves (B) while a signal was present. In both cases, the skeletal musculature of the dog was paralyzed by Gallamine. The vertical lines indicate the beginning and the termination of the signal.

We began by comparing the overt skeletal behavior observed during the operant conditioning of theta waves with that observed during the conditioning of what I have called non-theta waves. The data were obtained in the first experiment described above. We watched videotapes of the dogs' behavior during the last second before a reward was given, and classified the behavior in terms of type and intensity.

When trained to make hippocampal theta waves, the dogs were very active and displayed a characteristic pattern of responding. The dog would turn to one side with its head over the edge of the hammock, lift its legs, strain against the restraining tapes, and make darting movements of the head, turning it from side to side. Let me label these "manipulative" responses for the moment. The dogs trained to make low amplitude waves outside the 3 to 7 Hz frequency range displayed two patterns of responding. One was holding still[6]; the other was making a reflex or consummatory response, such as licking or yawning. The results for two typical dogs are presented in Figure 6.

These data indicate that when we reward different patterns of hippocampal electrical activity, we obtain correlated changes in overt skeletal behavior. Another question arises at this point. We have shown that there are correlated changes in overt behavior when particular brain wave patterns are rewarded. Suppose we were to reward these changes in overt behavior. Would we find correlated changes in brain wave patterns?

We have carried out two experiments on this question. In one experiment, six dogs were trained to avoid shock

by making two different responses. In the presence of one danger signal, each dog had to press a pedal rapidly for approximately five seconds to avoid shock; in the presence of the second danger signal, the dog had to hold still for approximately five seconds to avoid shock. Figure 7 presents data for all six dogs on the electrical activity recorded from the dorsal hippocampus in the presence of each danger signal. In every case, there was more hippocampal theta activity in the presence of the signal requiring the dog to press a pedal than in the presence of the signal that required the dog to hold still.

In the second experiment, we attempted to compare the electrical activity of the hippocampus in rats which were operantly conditioned to press a lever in the presence of one signal and to drink water in the presence of a second signal. Two rats were trained to avoid shock, and two to obtain a food reward.

Normally, an animal drinks when deprived of water and does not drink when satiated. In the present experiment, the role of drinking was not to regulate water intake as a function of deprivation level, but to obtain some other reward, such as food or the avoidance of shock. Drinking that functions to regulate water intake is not accompanied by hippocampal theta waves. We wanted to find out whether drinking would be accompanied by theta waves when it played the role of an operant response.

Again, it is clear from the results, presented in the right-hand section of Figure 7, that the rats who were bar pressing, either for food or to avoid shock, displayed more theta activity than the rats who were drinking for

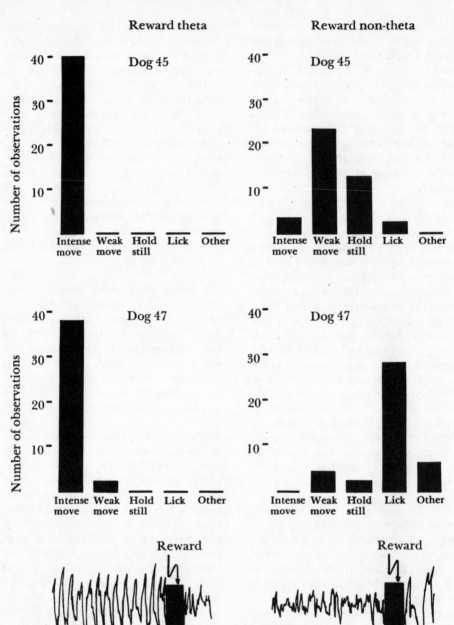

Figure 6. The frequency of various types of activity while two dogs were being rewarded for specific patterns of hippocampal electrical activity. Data for the two dogs when they were being rewarded for making theta waves are on the left; data for the same two dogs being rewarded for making non-theta waves are on the right. Examples of theta and non-theta patterns of electrical activity are given under the appropriate graphs. Forty observations were made for each graph. The categories of movement are: *Intense*, clear-cut movement of the head, body, and limbs; *Weak*, slight head movements, twitches, and eye blinks; *Hold still* and *Lick* are self-explanatory. Most of the responses in the *Other* category were yawning.

either reward. These results, along with those of the previous experiment, are most consistent with the hypothesis on the functional significance of theta waves suggested by Vanderwolf. His hypothesis is that dorsal hippocampal theta waves reflect neural processes involved in the initiation of what I have called manipulative[7] phasic skeletal movement, such as running, pedal pressing, and jumping; they do not reflect processes leading to consummatory or reflex responses, such as licking and drinking, nor do they occur when an animal is holding still, whether with muscles tense or relaxed.

The data do not provide support for any of the other hypotheses mentioned earlier. Consider, for example, the hypothesis that hippocampal theta waves reflect a motivational process. According to this hypothesis, dorsal hippocampal theta should occur whenever an organism is motivated. However, in a number of examples in our research in which it seems safe to assume that the subjects were motivated, little theta occurred. One example is the experiment in which rats were operantly conditioned to drink to avoid shock; another is the experiment in which dogs were trained to make non-theta waves to obtain food. Of the other hypotheses listed above, only the one proposed by Vanderwolf seems to be supported by the data.

It is obvious that we must attempt to specify more precisely the relationship between hippocampal electrical activity and behavior. Most of the evidence we have presented is relative— more theta under one condition, less under another. Therefore, we must ask whether there actually is a one-to-one relationship between theta waves and manipulative responding, or whether theta occurs without

manipulative responding, and vice versa, under certain circumstances. There are, of course, reports of manipulative responding when the subject is not producing theta waves (Pickenhain and Klingberg 1965) and of the occurrence of theta waves when the subject is not moving (Grastyan et al. 1966). These reports are difficult to interpret, however, since the discrepant results may have been produced by differences in methodology (for example, differences in electrode location and in response definition[8]) rather than by differences in the relationship between theta waves and manipulative behavior.

To rule out the effects of discrepancies produced by methodological variables, the following operant conditioning procedure was devised: first, find a preparation in which the normal correlation between theta waves and manipulative responding is observed, and then try to break this relationship by operant conditioning procedures. If the relationship is more complex than a simple one-to-one correspondence, the subject should be able to learn to produce theta waves while holding still or to refrain from producing theta waves while making manipulative responses. In a sense, this procedure employs operant conditioning to "dissect" a relationship.

For example, in one experiment, we rewarded the response of "simultaneously holding still and making hippocampal theta waves." First, we trained rats to remain absolutely motionless for a food reward. Then we attempted to train the rats to make hippocampal theta waves by rewarding brain wave patterns that were closer and closer to the theta pattern. So far, we have trained three rats to emit bursts of theta waves of approximately 0.5 second's

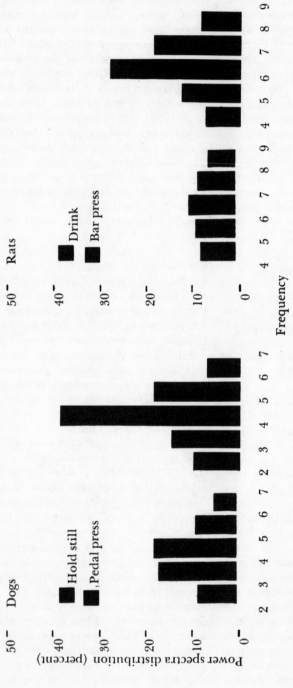

Figure 7. The graph on the left presents data for six dogs that were rewarded for pressing a pedal in the presence of one stimulus and holding still in the presence of another. Records of electrical activity under each condition were obtained from the dorsal hippocampus. The mean power in the frequency range between 2 and 7 Hz is presented for each condition. On the right-hand side are data for four rats that were rewarded for pressing a bar in the presence of one stimulus and for drinking water in the presence of another. Records of electrical activity under each condition were obtained from the dorsal hippocampus. The mean power in the frequency range between 4 and 9 Hz is presented for each condition. (It is important to note that the frequency ranges labeled "theta" are higher in the rat than in the dog—6 to 11 Hz for the rat and 4 to 6 Hz for the dog.)

duration at a frequency of just over 6 Hz while holding still. Also, the three rats failed to learn to make longer bursts of theta waves.

At first glance, these results do not seem to support the view of a one-to-one relationship between dorsal hippocampal theta waves and manipulative responding. There is, however, an explanation of the results that requires very little modification of this view. Vanderwolf (1969) has shown that a few low-frequency theta waves immediately precede the onset of a movement, such as jumping, in the rat. He has also noted that the greater the intensity of the movement, the higher the frequency of theta. Our results are consistent with these observations. The theta frequency during holding still was low.[9] Also, the rats failed to learn to make longer bursts of theta waves, which is what we would expect if rats can make only a few very low frequency theta waves just before the onset of movement. To provide further evidence relevant to this explanation, we need to find out whether we can train rats to make higher frequency theta waves while motionless, since it is the higher frequency waves that actually accompany movement. This has not been done yet.

We have a long way to go before we will have a satisfactory understanding of the functional significance of the electrical activity of the hippocampus. Nevertheless, I think we can attempt to answer the question posed at the beginning of this section. Since the electrical activity of the dorsal hippocampus does seem to be related to neural processes that control certain classes of behavior, it appears that we are changing important psychological and neural processes when we reward certain patterns of central

nervous system electrical activity. Sterman (1969) has carried out research on other brain wave patterns which makes the same point. He has shown, for example, that a pattern which he calls the sensory-motor rhythm is associated with holding still and with sleep behavior.

Also, the operant conditioning of brain waves seems to provide a technique for analyzing the nature of the psychological and neural processes that may be related to particular brain waves. The data, for example, on the correlations between operantly conditioned brain wave patterns and associated changes in overt responding proved to be helpful in understanding the functional significance of hippocampal theta waves. In addition, the procedure of rewarding combinations of brain wave patterns and overt behavior that we do not normally observe seems to have special potential as a dissecting tool for determining more precisely the nature of the relationship between the electrical activity of the brain and behavior.

## Practical uses

There is a tendency today to condemn scientists who do their research, publish the results, and stop there, without worrying about the consequences of their findings. It is not always possible, especially in basic research work, for all scientists to be concerned with the practical implications of their research; but in some cases there seem to be special reasons to give a good deal of thought to practical consequences.

Such seems to be the case with our work. In evaluating the practical applications, we must first determine whether the control achieved by rewarding brain waves is different from, or more efficient than, that achieved by rewarding overt skeletal behavior. If there are no differences between the two, there will be no practical advantage to operantly conditioning brain waves rather than overt observable behavior.

Two relevant examples come from laboratories other than my own. Sterman and his colleagues (1969) studied what they call a "post-reinforcement rhythm" recorded from the cortex of cats. This rhythm normally occurred during and just after the consumption of a reward. During the operant conditioning of this post-reinforcement brain wave pattern, the cats began to display a somewhat strange pattern of behavior. When the reward was presented, the cats would continue to make the brain wave pattern and sit there placidly without bothering to obtain the reward. It was as though the brain wave pattern itself led to a state of satiation or, perhaps, euphoria, so that the cats either did not need the reward or preferred the neural state associated with the post-reinforcement brain wave pattern to the reward.

Kamiya (1969), who has pioneered research on the operant conditioning of the surface electrical activity of the cortex in human subjects, suggests that he can alter mood states by rewarding appropriate brain wave patterns. Human subjects conditioned to produce a cortical alpha rhythm (regular waves between 8 and 12 Hz) report that they are in a "tranquil, calm, and alert" state. Kamiya speculated that this state might be similar to Zen and Yoga meditation and suggested that operant conditioning may be a more efficient way of learning to

achieve this state than the usual protracted Zen or Yoga training procedures—a method, perhaps, for attaining instant Nirvana.

These examples suggest that new and more efficient types of control can be achieved by rewarding brain waves. This conclusion will be tentative, however, until more data are available comparing the conditioning of various brain wave patterns with the conditioning of overt behavior, similar to the data we obtained with theta waves. It may be, for example, that some of these effects obtained by Sterman and Kamiya could be obtained just as easily by rewarding overt behavior.

Even if it develops that there are possible applications of the operant conditioning of brain waves that are related to psychological processes, a number of questions must still be answered before we know whether the method can be successfully applied. We have to find out about the limits on our ability to condition neural patterns of electrical activity. It is incorrect to assume that we can condition all patterns because we can condition some of them. Furthermore, even though certain patterns can be operantly conditioned, they may differ with respect to the range of circumstances under which they can be conditioned. For example, we might be able to condition one pattern only when the subject was serene and calm, and another pattern during a much wider variety of emotional states.

Also, we need to find out whether the operantly conditioned brain wave pattern generalizes beyond the training laboratory. There would be little point, for example, in curing stutterers by operant conditioning if the subjects spoke normally only in the laboratory. Therefore, in certain cases, we must find out how to produce stable generalization of operant conditioning beyond the laboratory.

In other cases, we may not be searching for a stable change in responding that generalizes to a variety of situations but rather for a response to come under self or voluntary control. For example, we might want a subject to be able to change his level of anxiety at will, instead of having it conditioned to some fixed level. Many assume that operant conditioning is a means of bringing responses under such voluntary control. In fact, some seem to believe that the simple demonstration of operant conditioning is enough to establish that a response has been brought under voluntary control. This is an incorrect assumption for several reasons. First, it is hard to find any response these days that cannot be operantly conditioned under some circumstances, and I do not think that we would call all responses voluntary. Second, the concept of voluntary control is a complex and difficult one; we do not have two simply defined categories—voluntary and involuntary.

To label a response voluntary, we must demonstrate not only that we can operantly condition subjects to make the response in situations which normally do not elicit it but also that we can condition them to refrain from making the response in situations which normally elicit it. We would be loath to call a response voluntary if the subject could not "turn it off" as well as "turn it on." Also, within the limits set by the ability to perform or to refrain from performing a response, there is a wide range of voluntary

control. At one extreme, we have the awkward initiation or inhibition of a response with little control over its intensity and direction; at the other extreme we have a precise, skilled mastery over graded movements. In addition, if the subject can perform a response in a variety of situations using a variety of rewards, we would be more likely to consider that he has voluntary control over that response than if his ability to initiate or inhibit it were limited to one class of situations or rewards. Therefore, to determine the degree of voluntary control, we must demonstrate a great deal more than the simple operant conditioning of a response. Because very little work has been done on any of these questions we cannot be sure at present how useful the method will be.

Although the use of the operant conditioning of brain waves in everyday affairs lies in the future, it is worthwhile for us to consider it seriously. The first reaction of many people is to start worrying about possible dangerous applications of the method—brainwashing, thought control, and so on. The first advice that usually follows this reaction is to stop the research. This, I think, would be unwise for two reasons. First, there is the possibility of favorable consequences.

Consider, for example, the use of operant conditioning techniques to obtain control over brain wave patterns to prevent epileptic seizures or to treat insomnia (Miller 1969). Also, we may be better able to resist attempts by others to control us if we have learned to obtain better voluntary control over internal processes and states. Second, even if the dangerous possible consequences outweighed the beneficial ones, the attempt to stop the research would be, I think, a futile gesture.

One of the characters in Durrenmatt's play *The Physicists* says: "Our knowledge has become a frightening burden. Our researches are perilous, our discoveries are lethal. We have to take back our knowledge, and I have taken it back." This scientist took back his knowledge by pretending to be insane and allowing himself to be incarcerated in an asylum. This did not work for him, and a similar strategy will not work for us. Man is amenable to the kinds of psychological control that I have been talking about, and this reality will not be changed by denying it. The attempt to become aware of the possibilities of the future and to work to avoid the dangers is better than to try to escape into ignorance.

## Footnotes

1. Novel patterns of response can be produced by a procedure called "shaping"—rewarding closer and closer approximations to the desired pattern of behavior. Complex sequences of responses can be produced by chaining one response to another; the subject is rewarded for making response A, then for making response B just before response A, and so on. (For more detailed descriptions of these techniques see, for example, Skinner, 1953, and Reynolds, 1968.)

2. We might, for example, state that a particular brain wave pattern in a particular location of the brain indicated the occurrence of some specific type of perception, thought, or desire or, in other terms indicated the occurrence of some central nervous system process, such as excitation or inhibition, which played an important role in the functioning of the brain. However one prefers to say it, the important point is that in some cases specific patterns of electrical activity in the brain may be indices of important neural and psychological processes.

3. All results described here were obtained from electrodes located in the dorsal hip-

pocampus; those in the ventral or lower parts of the hippocampus give different results.

4. One could argue, of course, that the brain waves were mediated by responses of the smooth muscles or by glandular responses. The former seems unlikely, since in many of our experiments the behavior of the smooth muscles differed greatly in the paralyzed and normal states. Also, the rapidity of the brain wave response to conditioned stimuli suggests that glandular secretions could not have mediated it.

5. In these experiments, we have measured a number of other responses in addition to those of the skeletal musculature. We have considered electrical activity of parts of the brain other than the hippocampus and also responses of the autonomic nervous system. We will not describe these because of the limitations of space, and also because, as it has turned out, the skeletal responses are most important for our purposes in this paper. One further point about these experiments must be made. The interpretation of correlations between the electrical activity of the brain and behavior is a difficult task. Fox and Rudell (1968) have documented the problems which arise when we attempt to study the neural correlates of observable skeletal conditioned responses. Similar difficulties arise when we study the behavioral correlates of neural conditioned responses (Mulholland 1969).

6. Holding still is an ambiguous term; an animal may be holding still with muscles flaccid and relaxed, or tense and rigid. Dorsal hippocampal theta does not occur in either case.

7. Vanderwolf has labeled the responses with which dorsal hippocampal theta waves are presumed to be correlated as "voluntary," I have used the term "manipulative" here because of the difficulties associated with the definition of voluntary behavior. It should be pointed out that the class of voluntary responses as defined by Vanderwolf is not identical with the class of responses that can be operantly conditioned, since drinking can be operantly conditioned but is not voluntary according to Vanderwolf.

8. One important task in studying a relationship is to establish more refined definitions of the classes of events to be related—the brain wave patterns and the behavior patterns. It may be that apparent exceptions to

the relationship occur because one or the other is incorrectly defined

9. The model theta frequency that we recorded while rats were bar pressing was between 6 and 7 Hz (see Fig. 7). This seems to disagree with Vanderwolf's observations. However, Vanderwolf recorded only during the actual movement, while we recorded continuously—not only while the rat was bar pressing but also while the rat was holding still between bar presses, approaching the bar, and so on.

*References*

Black, A. H., G. A. Young, and C. Batenchuk. 1970. The avoidance training of hippocampal theta waves in Flaxedilized dogs and its relation to skeletal movement. *Journal of Comparative and Physiological Psychology* 70:15–24.

Bremner, F. J. 1964. Hippocampal activity during avoidance behavior in the rat. *Journal of Comparative and Physiological Psychology* 58:16–22.

Carmona, A. 1967. Trial and error learning of the voltage of the cortical EEG activity. *Dissertation Abstracts* 28:1157B–58B.

Dalton, A. J. 1969. Discriminative conditioning of hippocampal electrical activity in curarized dogs. *Communications in Behavioral Biology* 3:283–87.

Dewan, Edmond M. 1967. Occipital alpha rhythm, eye position and lens accommodation. *Nature* 214:975–77.

Elazar, Z., and W. R. Adey. 1967. Spectral analysis of low frequency components in the electrical activity of the hippocampus during learning. *Electroencephalography and Clinical Neurophysiology* 23:225–40.

Fetz, E. E. 1969. Operant conditioning of cortical unit activity. *Science* 163:955–7.

Fox, S. S., and A. P. Rudell. 1968. Operant controlled neural event: Formal and systematic approach to electrical coding of behavior in brain. *Science* 162:1299–1302.

Grastyan, E., G. Karmos, L. Vereczkey, and L. Kellenyi. 1966. The hippocampal electrical correlates of the homeostatic regulation of motivation. *Electroencephalography and Clinical Neurophysiology* 21:34–53.

Grastyan, E., K. Lissak, I. Madarasz, and H. Donhoffer. 1959. Hippocampal electrical activity during the development of conditioned reflexes. *Electroencephalography and Clinical Neurophysiology* 11:409–30.

Kamiya, J. Paper presented at the meetings of the Feedback Society, Los Angeles, California, 1969.

Kimmel, H. D. 1967. Instrumental conditioning of autonomically mediated behavior. *Psychological Bulletin* 67(5):337–45.

Konorski, J., G. Santibanez, and J. Beck. 1968. Electrical hippocampal activity and heart-rate in classical and instrumental conditioning. *Acta Biologiae Experimentalis* 28:169–85.

Miller, N. E. 1966. Experiments relevant to learning theory and psychopathology. Proceedings of the 18th International Congress of Psychology, Moscow.

Miller, Neal E. 1969. Learning of visceral and glandular responses. *Science* 163:434–45.

Mulholland, Thomas B. Problems and prospects for feedback electroencephalography. Presented at the meetings of the Feedback Society, Los Angeles, California, 1969.

Olds, J. 1967. The limbic system and behavioral reinforcement. In W. R. Adey and T. Tokizane (eds.), *Progress in Brain Research*, Vol. 27, Structure and Function of the Limbic System. Elsevier, Amsterdam.

Pickenhain, L., and F. Klinberg. 1965. Hippocampal slow wave activity as a correlate of basic behavioral mechanisms in the rat. In W. R. Adey and T. Tokizane (eds.), *Progress in Brain Research*, Vol. 27, Structure and Function of the Limbic System, pp. 218–27. Elsevier, Amsterdam.

Reynolds, G. S. 1968. *A Primer of Operant Conditioning*. Scott, Foresman and Company.

Skinner, B. F. 1953. *Science and Human Behavior*. New York: MacMillan Press.

Sterman, M. B. Paper presented at the meetings of the Feedback Society, Los Angeles, California, 1969.

Sterman, M. B., W. Wyrwicka, and S. Roth. 1969. Electrophysiological correlates and neural substrates of alimentary behavior in the cat. *Annals of the New York Academy of Sciences* 157:723–39.

Stoyva, J., and J. Kamiya. 1968. Electrophysiological studies of dreaming as the prototype of a new strategy in the study of consciousness. *Psychological Review* 75:192–

205.

Vanderwolf, C. H. 1967. Behavioral correlates of "theta" waves. *Proceedings of the Canadian Federation of Biological Sciences* 10:41–2.

Vanderwolf, C. H. 1968. Hippocampal electrical activity and voluntary movement in the rat. Technical Report No. 17, Department of Psychology, McMaster University.

Vanderwolf, C. H. 1969. Hippocampal electrical activity and voluntary movement in the rat. *Electroencephalography and Clinical Neurophysiology* 26:407–18.

Wyrwicka, W., and M. B. Sterman. 1968. Instrumental conditioning of sensorimotor cortex EEG spindles in the waking cat. *Physiology and Behavior* 3:703–7.

# Operant Conditioning of Specific Patterns of Neural and Muscular Activity

# 14

## Eberhard E. Fetz and Dom V. Finocchio

**Abstract.** *In awake monkeys we recorded activity of single "motor" cortex cells, four contralateral arm muscles, and elbow position, while operantly reinforcing several patterns of motor activity. With the monkey's arm held semiprone in a cast hinged at the elbow, we reinforced active elbow movements and tested cell responses to passive elbow movements. With the cast immobilized we reinforced isometric contraction of each of the four muscles in isolation, and bursts of cortical cell activity with and without simultaneous suppression of muscle activity. Correlations between a precentral cell and specific arm muscles consistently appeared under several behavioral conditions, but could be dissociated by reinforcing cell activity and muscle suppression.*

In investigating the possible role of precentral "motor" cortex cells in generating voluntary movements, previous experimenters trained monkeys to perform specific motor responses by making operant reinforcement contingent on the position and force trajectories of the responding limb (*1, 2*). Such response patterns involved coordinated activity of many muscles of the responding limb (*2, 3*) and therefore were not designed to resolve the question of which specific muscles a given cortical cell may influence. To determine the degree to which precentral cell activity may be correlated with specific limb muscles and to test the stability of such correlations during different behaviors, we recorded the activity of single precentral cells and four major arm muscles (a flexor and extensor of wrist and elbow) while reinforcing specific patterns of activity in these elements.

Experiments were performed with a fluid-deprived monkey (*Macaca mulatta*) seated in a restraint chair with his head immobilized and a juice-dispensing tube in his mouth. The monkey's arm could be held semiprone in a molded cast pivoted at the elbow, allowing measurable flexion and extension of the elbow but no gross movement of the wrist. The cast could also be locked in place (elbow at 90°, wrist at 180°), rendering all muscle contractions isometric (*4*). Electromyographic (EMG) activity of major flexors and extensors of the wrist (flexor carpi radialis and extensor carpi radialis) and elbow (biceps and triceps) was recorded through pairs of braided stainless steel wires permanently implanted in the belly of each muscle and led subcutaneously to a connector implanted on the skull. Activity of single precentral cells in contralateral cortex was recorded with tungsten microelectrodes. For about a month prior to the data-recording sessions, the monkey was trained in several behavior performances: (i) He was reinforced with fruit juice for sitting quietly while we tested the cells' responses to passive movement of the arm and cutaneous stimulation. (ii) With his arm in the position monitor he was reinforced for active flexion and extension of the elbow. (iii) With the position monitor locked in place, reinforcement was made contingent upon isometric contraction of any one of the muscles with simultaneous suppression of activity in the other three.

Specific patterns of cell and muscle activity were monitored and reinforced with an electronic "activity integrator" which continuously integrated a weighted sum of voltages proportional to cortical cell and muscle activity, and delivered a reinforcement when the resultant voltage exceeded a preset threshold (Fig. 1). The activity integrator had several input channels which accepted either voltage pulses triggered from the cell's action potentials or rectified EMG activity from specific muscles. A summing network produced a weighted sum

$$V(t) = \sum_i a_i v_i(t)$$

of these input voltages; the algebraic sign and magnitude of each weighting factor $a_i$ were determined by the experimenter through a polarity switch and gain control for each channel. This summed voltage was temporally integrated with a parallel resistor-capacitor network with a time constant of 50 to 100 msec to generate the "integrator voltage." When this integrator voltage reached a preset threshold level $V_T$ the feeder discharged and the integrator voltage was briefly reset to zero.

To illustrate a typical application, consider reinforcing the activity of a specific muscle, say biceps, in isolation. When cortical unit activity did not enter into the reinforcement contingency,

its contribution to the integrator voltage was switched off ($a_5 = 0$). The polarity switches that were on the muscle channels were set such that activity in the biceps drove the integrator voltage toward threshold ($a_3 > 0$), while activity in the other three muscles drove the voltage away from threshold ($\alpha_i < 0$; $i = 1,2,4$). When reinforcement became available, the monkey typically began to emit bursts of EMG activity in several arm muscles every few seconds. The gain controls ($a_i$) were set such that approximately half of these burst responses were reinforced. After several minutes the proportion of reinforced responses typically increased. By reducing the gain on the biceps channel we could require the monkey to produce more biceps activity to reach threshold; by increasing the gains on the other muscle channels we could require a greater suppression of activity in these muscles in order to prevent reinforcement from being withheld. Thus, separation of activity in different muscles was accomplished by selectively reinforcing better successive approximations to the required pattern. Terminal performance typically consisted of repeated bursts of EMG activity in the reinforced muscle with negligible coactivation of the other three muscles.

During reinforcement periods a meter in front of the monkey was illuminated and its needle deflection was made proportional to the integrator voltage. Extreme rightward deflections were consistently correlated with juice reinforcement; thus the meter deflections could become a conditioned reinforcer. During reinforcement of isolated activity of specific muscles a set of colored lights indicated which muscle was being reinforced, and the amplified EMG activity of the reinforced muscle was audible to the monkey (5).

The results from one 8-hour experi-

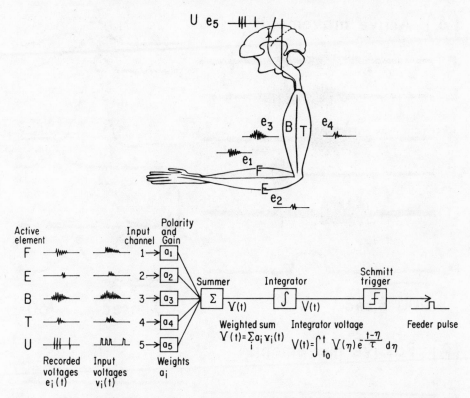

Fig. 1. (Top) Schematic diagram of monkey, showing location of arm muscles and precentral cell, with typical recorded potentials ($e_i$). *F*, flexor carpi radialis; *E*, extensor carpi radialis; *B*, biceps; *T*, triceps; *U*, precentral cell. (Bottom) Schematic of "activity integrator" used to reinforce patterns of activity under isometric conditions. Input voltages ($v_i$) were rectified EMG activity for muscles or voltage pulses triggered from the cell's action potentials. The weighted sum was temporally integrated in a parallel resistance-capacitance network; when the integrator voltage reached the Schmitt trigger threshold, the feeder discharged and a relay (not shown) briefly reset the integrator voltage to zero.

ment are presented in detail to illustrate the relation between a precentral cell and major flexors and extensors of elbow and wrist during passive and active elbow movements (Fig. 2) and under isometric conditions while reinforcing isolated muscle activity or cortical unit activity (Fig. 3).

Passive movements of the contralateral elbow and wrist reliably evoked responses from this cell, but cutaneous stimulation (brushing hairs or touching skin) did not. The cell responded re-

peatedly to passive extension of the elbow (Fig. 2B) and to passive flexion of the wrist without overt signs of resistance or gross EMG activity (6). When *active* movements of the elbow were reinforced, the cell invariably fired in relation to active flexion (Fig. 2A). Flexion was also accompanied by activity in both wrist muscles as well as biceps, but the bell-shaped average of cell activity more closely resembled that of biceps than the averages of either wrist muscle. The peak discharge

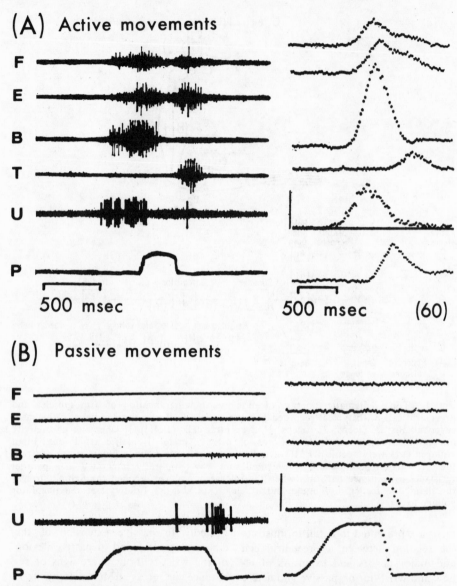

Fig. 2. Responses of precentral cell and arm muscles during active and passive elbow movements. Successive lines from top to bottom show activity of flexor carpi radialis (*F*), extensor carpi radialis (*E*), biceps (*B*), triceps (*T*), cortical unit (*U*), and the position of the elbow (*P*). A single trial is shown at left, and the averages over 60 successive trials at right. This cell fired before active flexion of the elbow (A) and responded to passive extension of the elbow (B). All EMG averages were computed at identical gains. Time histogram of cell activity is shown with a zero baseline; vertical calibration bar equals 50 impulses per second. Upward deflection of the position monitor represents flexion.

frequency of the cell occurred approximately 100 msec before peak activity of the biceps (7).

With the monkey's arm cast locked in place and with appropriate discriminative stimuli, we reinforced the monkey for isometric contractions of a particular muscle when accompanied by concomitant suppression of activity in the three remaining muscles. After a brief practice period, such differential reinforcement resulted in repeated bursts of activity predominantly or exclusively in the reinforced muscle. Selective reinforcement of isolated activity in flexor carpi radialis resulted in bursts of activity in that muscle without appreciable cocontraction of the other three muscles (Fig. 3A). Some cell activity accompanied the wrist flexor bursts, but this was more variable and less intense than that accompanying biceps bursts. Bursts of extensor carpi radialis activity were difficult to obtain without some concurrent activity in the wrist flexor (Fig. 3B). However, negligible cell activity accompanied this pattern of wrist muscle activity. Isolated bursts of biceps activity were emitted with minimal cocontraction of wrist muscles or triceps (Fig. 3C). In this case the cell began to fire well in advance of the biceps activity and reached its peak frequency coincident with the maximum muscle activity. Reinforcing isolated triceps activity resulted in sharp bursts of activity in this muscle with some coactivation of both wrist muscles (Fig. 3D). Relatively little cell activity accompanied this pattern. Analysis of the relationships between the precentral cell activity and isometric contraction of the four arm muscles suggests that the activity of this cell was most strongly correlated with contraction of the biceps muscle.

Next, with his arm still immobilized in the cast, the monkey was reinforced for bursts of cortical cell activity with no contingency imposed on the EMG activity. Under these conditions bursts of cell activity were repeatedly accompanied by bursts of EMG activity in the biceps and both wrist muscles (Fig. 3E). The amount of EMG activity accompanying successive unit bursts fluctuated by a small amount, but some degree of muscle activity was invariably associated with each burst of cell activity. The previously observed correlation between cell and biceps activity was again apparent, with peak cell activity preceding peak biceps activity by 70 msec.

We then attempted to dissociate the correlation between cell and muscle activity by reinforcing bursts of cell activity with simultaneous suppression of all muscle activity (8). After approximately 15 minutes of reinforcing successively better approximations to the required pattern—involving about 100 reinforced response patterns and an equal number of unreinforced responses—the monkey repeatedly emitted bursts of cortical cell activity without any measurable EMG activity (Fig. 3F).

The reverse dissociation of cell and biceps activity was attempted next by reinforcing isometric biceps activity accompanied by simultaneous suppression of cortical cell activity. This schedule was imposed after 7 hours of conditioning, involving some 3000 reinforcements, and the monkey's rate of responding was clearly decreasing. In 25 minutes of reinforcing the closest approximations to the required pattern, the monkey emitted about 200 reinforced responses and about 60 unreinforced patterns. At the end of this period the response patterns consisted of intense biceps bursts, with some remaining concomitant cell activity, as well as wrist muscle activity. Averages of unit and muscle activity over the last 50 reinforced responses, computed

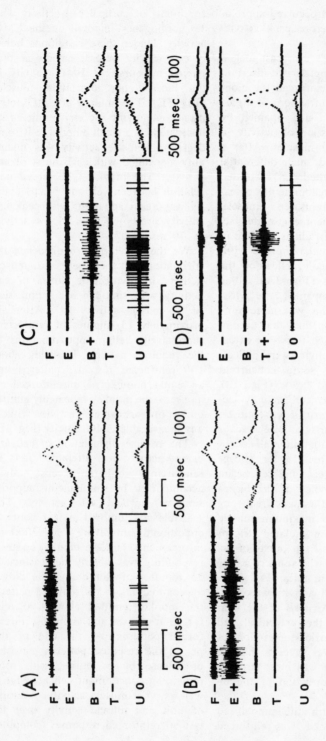

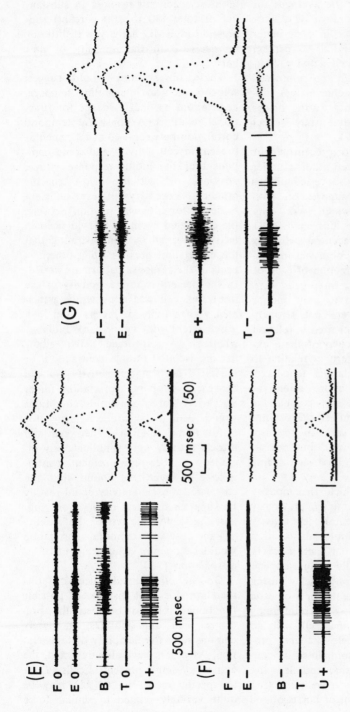

Fig. 3. Operant reinforcement of patterns of neural and muscular activity under isometric condition. (The labels of the horizontal lines are as in Fig. 2.) Muscles and unit are labeled "+" or "−" to indicate whether their activity drove the integrator voltage toward (+) or away (−) from threshold, or with a "0" if their activity was not included in the reinforcement contingency. For (A) to (D) the monkey was reinforced for isometric contractions of each specific muscle in isolation: flexor carpi radialis (A), extensor carpi radialis (B), biceps (C), and triceps (D). Averages for (A) to (D) were computed for 100 responses, with the vertical scale of all EMG averages identical except for a reduction of (D) by one half. In (E) and (F) the monkey was reinforced for bursts of cortical cell activity, first with no contingency on the muscles (E), then requiring simultaneous suppression of all muscle activity (F). In (G) biceps activity and unit suppression were reinforced. Averages for (E) to (G) were computed for 50 successive responses, with identical vertical scale on EMG averages. Vertical bars on time histograms of unity activity represent 50 impulses per second; the scale for (B) and (D) is the same as (C).

at the same gains as the averages for reinforced unit bursts (Fig. 3G), show a 300 percent increase in area under the biceps average and a 10 percent decrease in average cell activity, indicating a net change in the reinforced direction. Failure to achieve total suppression of cell activity during biceps bursts on this schedule may reflect fatigue or satiation (9).

Of a large number of precentral cells observed, 16 have been studied under at least half of the above conditions (not counting unit suppression with muscle activation, which was only documented for the illustrated cell) (10). Of the nine precentral cells (six pyramidal tract cells) observed in relation to isometric contraction of each of the four arm muscles, three cells were predominantly related to only one or two muscles, two were not strongly related to any, and four fired in relation to all four muscles (two of these exhibited the same pattern in relation to all four muscles). Relations to antagonistic muscles were more often the same (six cases) or not comparable (five) than reciprocal (three). Unit-muscle correlations seen in the isometric case were usually, but not always, consistent with those seen during active movements.

The ease with which the monkey suppressed muscle activity previously associated with precentral cell activity led us to attempt similar dissociation with five other cells. In each case (i) the cell fired repeatedly before a specific muscle or group of muscles during active elbow movements, or isometric contraction, or both; (ii) reinforcing bursts of activity of that cell, with no contingency on muscle activity, produced unit bursts accompanied by contraction in those same muscles and often in other muscles as well; and (iii) selective reinforcement of bursts of cell activity with simultaneous suppression

of muscle activity resulted in substantial or total (80 to 100 percent) suppression of EMG activity with little or no decrease in the intensity of unit bursts.

These observations would suggest some caution in interpreting temporal correlations as final evidence for functional relations. A consistent temporal correlation between two events, such as precentral cell activity and some component of the motor response (force, position, or activity of a specific muscle) is necessary but never sufficient evidence for a causal relation between the correlated events. The evidence can be strengthened by demonstrating that the correlation persists while other aspects of the response pattern are varied. In the present example, activity of the illustrated cell was consistently associated with activity of biceps (and to a lesser extent with flexor carpi radialis) whether we reinforced active elbow flexion, isolated muscle contraction, or bursts of cortical cell activity. Such a consistent temporal correlation under a variety of behavioral conditions would seem to be strong evidence for a functional relation. When cell and muscle activity were simultaneously included in the reinforcement contingency, however, we found that the correlated muscle activity could readily be suppressed. These observations suggest that a possible test of the stability of an observed temporal correlation would be operant reinforcement of its dissociation (11).

On the other hand, successful dissociation does not disprove a possible functional relation between the precentral cell and muscles; it merely demonstrates the flexibility of that relation. As others have already noted, the activity of single precentral cells (1, 2) or specific motor units (12) may be quite variably related to similar force or position trajectories in successive motor responses. To what extent our EMG recordings are representative of the activity of these and synergistic muscles remains to be documented. These preliminary results suggest that a useful approach to investigating relationships between central cells and muscles is to study the activity of the same elements under as many different behavioral conditions as possible, including operant reinforcement of specific response patterns.

EBERHARD E. FETZ
DOM V. FINOCCHIO
*Regional Primate Research Center*
and *Department of Physiology and Biophysics,* and *Department of Neurological Surgery, University of Washington, Seattle 98195*

**References and Notes**

1. E. V. Evarts, *J. Neurophysiol.* **29**, 1011 (1966); E. S. Luschei, R. A. Johnson, M. Glickstein, *Nature* **217**, 190 (1968); E. S. Luschei, C. R. Garthwaite, M. E. Armstrong, *J. Neurophysiol.* **34**, 552 (1971).
2. E. V. Evarts, *J. Neurophysiol.* **31**, 14 (1968); in *Neurophysiological Basis of Normal and Abnormal Motor Activity,* M .D. Yahr and D. P. Purpura, Eds. (Raven, Hewlett, N.Y., 1967), .p 215; D. R. Humphrey, E. M. Schmidt, W. D. Thompson, *Science* **170**, 758 (1970).
3. W. T. Thach, *J. Neurophysiol.* **333**, 527 (1970).
4. Under isometric conditions integrated EMG activity has been demonstrated to be proportional to muscle tension [V. T. Inman *et al., Electroencephalogr. Clin. Neurophysiol.* **4**, 187 (1952); O. C. J. Lippold, *J. Physiol.* **117**, 492 (1952); B. Bigland and O. C. J. Lippold, *ibid.* **123**, 214 (1954)].
5. A seven-channel FM tape system recorded the activity of the precentral cell and four arm muscles, the position of the elbow during passive and active movements, and a delayed trigger pulse 1 second after the occurrence of each reinforced response pattern. Playing the tape backward, we used these delayed pulses to trigger a Nuclear-Chicago Data Retrieval Computer, which computed averages of the full-wave rectified EMG activity of each muscle and time histograms of unit activity over 2-second intervals around the reinforced responses.
6. A small, brief EMG response of biceps during passive elbow extension, seen on close inspection of single trials, was probably due to the myotatic stretch reflex; this response was not large enough to appear on the averages at the same gain used for active movements.
7. Active elbow extension was accompanied by some triceps activity, but due to unequal loading, required somewhat less force than active flexion. Note that cell activity accompanying *active* extension was negligible compared to the response evoked by comparable rates of *passive* extension.
8. While voltage pulses triggered by the cell's action potentials drove the integrator voltage toward reinforcement threshold, activity of any muscles drove the integrator voltage away from threshold. The relative contribution of the EMG activity was minimized initially so that only those unit bursts accompanied by lesser amounts of EMG activity were reinforced. As the monkey emitted less EMG activity with successive unit bursts the gains on the EMG channels were gradually increased to require further EMG suppression for reinforcement.
9. After a rest period, however, the monkey still performed the active flexions and extensions of the elbow. The actual sequence of the described observations was: passive movements of elbow and wrist; isometric contraction of biceps, triceps, extensor carpi radialis, flexor carpi radialis; reinforced unit bursts; unit bursts with EMG suppression; biceps bursts with unit suppression; passive elbow movements; active elbow movements.
10. Eight of these cells were identified as pyramidal tract (PT) cells on the basis of an invariant antidromic response to stimulation of the medullary pyramids. Three cells did not respond to PT stimulation, and five cells, including the one illustrated, were studied before the pyramidal tract electrode was implanted.
11. By showing that specific components of the visual evoked response may be altered by operant reinforcement, S. S. Fox and A. P. Rudell [*J. Neurophysiol.* **33**, 548 (1970)] demonstrated that consistent correlations between neural responses in a sensory system and the evoking stimulus may be operantly dissociated.
12. J. V. Basmajian and A. Latif, *J. Bone Joint Surg.* **39A**, 1106 (1957); J. V. Basmajian, *Muscles Alive* (Williams & Wilkins, Baltimore, 1967).
13. Supported by NIH grant FR 00166 and PHS 5 FO3MH35745-02 and PHS 5T1 NB5082-13. We thank Dr. E. S. Luschei for suggestions concerning the chronic unit recording techniques, Mr. F. Spelman for assistance with electronic instrumentation, and Mrs. B. Klompus for computing the averages.

25 February 1971; revised 28 June 1971    ∎

# V

## AUTONOMIC RESPONSES: HUMAN

# Learned Control 15
## of Cardiovascular Integration in Man
## Through Operant Conditioning

Gary E. Schwartz, David Shapiro, and
Bernard Tursky

In previous research, it has been shown that subjects can learn to increase or decrease their systolic blood pressure without corresponding changes in heart rate, or they can learn to increase or decrease their heart rate without corresponding changes in blood pressure. The present paper outlines a method for directly conditioning a combination of two autonomic responses. A system was developed which, at each heart cycle, determines on line whether heart rate *and* blood pressure are integrated (both increasing or both decreasing) or differentiated (one increasing and one decreasing). To test this method, 5 subjects received a brief light and tone feedback only when their heart rate *and* blood pressure were simultaneously increasing, and 5 subjects received the feedback only when their heart rate *and* blood pressure were simultaneously decreasing. Subjects earned rewards consisting of slides and monetary bonuses each time they produced 12 correct heart rate-blood pressure combinations. Significant cardiovascular integration was obtained in a single session. Subjects rewarded for simultaneous increases in heart rate *and* blood pressure showed small, comparable increases in both, while subjects rewarded for simultaneous decreases showed sizeable decreases in both. Applications of the method in research and treatment are discussed.

Many papers have been published which demonstrate that by providing subjects with feedback of their autonomic activity

From the Department of Psychiatry, Harvard Medical School, at Massachusetts Mental Health Center, Boston, Mass.

Supported by NIMH Research Scientist Award K5-MH-20,476; NIMH Research Grants MH-08853-06 and MH-04172-09; Milton Fund of Harvard University; and Office of Naval Research Contract N00014-67-A-0298-0024, Physiological Psychology Branch.

The integration research represents a portion of the first author's doctoral dissertation in the Department of Social Relations, Harvard University. The assistance of Mrs. Margaret Chartres is gratefully acknowledged.

Presented in part at the annual meeting of the American Psychosomatic Society, Washington, DC, March 20, 1970.

Received for publication May 13, 1970; revision received Sept 14, 1970.

and rewarding specific changes, it is possible to modify responses in the autonomic nervous system (1–4). The theoretical and practical significance of this research stems in large part from data showing that learning is specific to the autonomic response that is directly reinforced—ie, the rewarding of one autonomic response does not seem to produce learning in others.

A series of experiments by Shapiro and associates illustrates the extent of learned autonomic differentiation in man within the cardiovascular system. In one experiment (5), subjects were given feedback and reward for increasing or decreasing systolic

Address for reprint requests: Gary E. Schwartz, Massachusetts Mental Health Center, 74 Fenwood Rd, Boston, Mass 02115.

blood pressure while heart rate was simultaneously monitored. Significant blood pressure differences were obtained between increase and decrease subjects without corresponding differences in heart rate. After replicating this result in a second sample of subjects (6), a similar experiment was performed (7), except that this time feedback and reward were given for increasing or decreasing heart rate while systolic blood pressure was simultaneously monitored. The results indicated significant heart rate conditioning without corresponding changes in blood pressure.

These data indicate that learned control of blood pressure or heart rate is possible in man, an encouraging finding concerning the application of operant procedures for the treatment of certain forms of hypertension or tachycardia. However, there arises a related question of whether it is possible to control a combination of responses at the same time. For example, if reinforcing blood pressure leads to learned blood pressure control and reinforcing heart rate leads to learned heart rate control, then what procedure is necessary to produce simultaneous learning of *both* blood pressure and heart rate? It would seem that this particular combination of responses should be relatively easy to learn since heart rate is itself one physiologic determinant of systolic blood pressure (8).

The approach taken in the present paper is that it is possible to condition a combination of autonomic responses by rewarding a subject *only* when he shows the desired pattern. This requires a methodology for measuring *on line* the phasic interrelationships of autonomic activity. Toward this end, instrumentation was developed, which, at each heart cycle, determines whether heart rate and blood pressure are integrated—ie, both going in the same direction, either both increasing or both decreasing, or whether the responses are differentiated—ie, both going in opposite directions, one increasing and the other simultaneously decreasing, as measured from median levels.

To test the system as well as to attempt the direct conditioning of heart rate-blood pressure integration in man, the following experiment was performed.

## METHOD

### Subjects

The subjects were 10 normotensive males between the ages of 21 and 30. All subjects were in good physical health and were paid for participating in the experiment.

### Physiologic Measures

Systolic blood pressure, heart rate and respiration were recorded on an Offner Type R Dynagraph. The electrocardiogram was measured using standard plate electrodes and was displayed on one channel of the polygraph. An electronic switch was used to trigger Grason-Stadler (Model 1200) solid state programming equipment at each heart cycle (R spike). The procedure for measuring median systolic blood pressure and median heart rate is based on the method developed in the earlier studies (5–7). Median systolic pressure is defined as the constant cuff pressure level at which 50% of possible Korotkoff sounds occur. By displaying the Korotkoff sounds on one channel of the polygraph in conjunction with a second electronic switch, it is possible, through appropriate logic modules, to track the number of heart beats accompanied by a Korotkoff sound, and the number of heart beats followed by the absence of a Korotkoff sound. Similarly, median heart rate is defined as the heart rate level (detected by a third electronic switch calibrated in beats per minute) at which 50% of possible fast (above the level) heart beats occurred. This is accomplished by displaying beat-by-beat heart rate on one channel of the polygraph through a cardiotachometer (Lexington Instrument Model 107) and, using appropriate logic modules in conjunction with the third (cardiotachometer) electronic switch, by tracking the number of heart beats (R to R intervals) that are faster than the cardiotachometer level detector. It has been empirically determined that if 36 or more of 50 possible Korotkoff sounds (or fast heart beats) occur, the applied cuff pressure (or cardiotachometer electronic switch) is raised 2 mmHg (or 2 bpm) on the next trial. If 14 or fewer of 50 possible sounds (or fast heart beats) occur, the applied pressure (or the cardiotachometer electronic switch) is lowered by 2 mmHg (or 2 bpm) on the next trial. This procedure provides an accurate means for independently tracking both median systolic pressure and median heart rate at the same time, and for obtaining comparable beat-by-beat information about relative increases or decreases in both responses.[*]

The tracking of blood pressure-heart rate integration and differentiation at each heart beat is obtained by a program which detects the four possible combinations of these two responses *relative to their median values*. Figure 1 shows a representative portion of a polygraph record of the system in operation. Shown are the electrocardiogram, heart rate displayed through a cardiotachometer, the presence or absence of Korotkoff sounds measured at a constant cuff pressure, and two marker channels. The presence or absence of a Korotkoff sound, relative to the constant pressure in the cuff, indicates whether blood pressure is up or down for each heart cycle, while up and down heart rate is relative to the median heart rate. After each heart cycle, one of four possible marks appears on the integration-differentiation (ID) marker. The longest and shortest marks reflect integration—ie, *up* blood pressure and *up* heart rate produce the longest mark, while *down* blood pressure and *down* heart rate produce the shortest mark. The other two marks reflect differentiation—ie, *up* blood pressure and *down* heart rate produce the third longest mark, while *down* blood pressure and *up* heart rate produce the second shortest mark. The bottom channel indicates which of the four possible combinations is receiving feedback and reward. In this example, feedback is occurring for *up* blood pressure-*up* heart rate integration.

The extent of beat-by-beat integration, as defined here, becomes the percentage of beats in which both heart rate and blood pressure are simultaneously up or down. Therefore, for a given trial, 100% would reflect complete integration and 0% would reflect complete differentiation. The system is purposefully complicated by the fact that if tonic levels of physiologic activity change, the integration values change accordingly. Consequently, a subject can best succeed at producing rewards in, for example, a *down-down* condition, by lowering both his *median* heart rate and blood pressure, as opposed to changing only the more phasic characteristics of the two responses. Since the ultimate clinical goal in this research is to affect *tonic* levels of physiologic activity, the ID system proves very satisfactory.

In addition to heart rate and blood pressure, respiration was recorded on the polygraph, using a strain gauge device placed around the subject's chest.

---

*See Tursky, Shapiro and Schwartz: *An Automated Constant Cuff-pressure System for Measuring Average Systolic and Diastolic Blood Pressure in Man* (submitted for publication) for a complete description of the blood pressure system. Included in their article are data validating the system against blood pressures recorded by surgical catheterization.

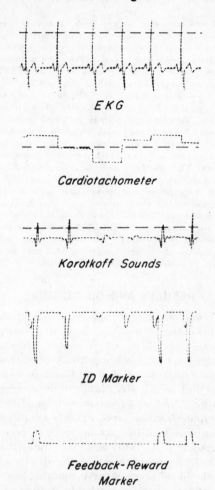

EKG

Cardiotachometer

Korotkoff Sounds

ID Marker

Feedback-Reward Marker

**Fig 1.**   Segment of polygraph record of subject rewarded for increasing both his heart rate and systolic blood pressure simultaneously (up-up integration). Horizontal dashed lines indicate level detectors.

## Design and Procedure

On entering the laboratory, subjects were seated in a lounge chair in a sound- and temperature-controlled room, and were connected to the physiologic recording devices. Subjects were told that the purpose of the experiment was to determine if they could learn to control certain physiologic responses that are considered involuntary. They were instructed to refrain from moving and to breathe regularly. Half the subjects received a brief light and tone as feedback each time their blood pressure and heart rate were simultaneously increasing; the other half received the light-tone feedback only when their blood pressure and heart rate were simultaneously decreasing. For every 12 correct responses, a reward in the form of a slide was shown for 3 seconds. In working with normal males, we have found that a potpourri of rewards provides the most interest and incentive. The slides included landscapes, pictures of attractive nude females, and monetary bonuses for succeeding at the task.

All subjects received five adaptation and 40 conditioning trials, each trial being 50 beats in length. Variable rest periods of 20–30 seconds' duration separated each trial. Initial blood pressure levels between groups were made comparable by matching subjects (±4 mmHg) on the adaptation values. The matching procedure also served to eliminate potential experimenter bias effects (9), since the experimenter did not know what condition the subject would receive until after he read the instructions, left the subject room, and obtained the adaptation data. At the end of conditioning, the experimenter re-entered the subject room and interviewed all subjects concerning what they were doing to control their physiologic activity.

## RESULTS AND DISCUSSION

The results of this experiment (Fig 2) are quite different from the previous research wherein specificity was obtained when a single response was rewarded. As predicted, significant control of *both* blood pressure *and* heart rate was obtained in a single session. Analyses of variance (Biomed 08V computer analysis) reveal highly significant groups by trial interactions for both blood pressure ($p < 0.001$) and heart rate ($p < 0.001$), demonstrating that the divergence of the blood pressure curves and that of the heart rate curves are reliable. Subjects rewarded for simultaneous increases show small comparable increases in both systems (maximum increase at trial 40 for a single subject of +6 mmHg and +2 bpm), while subjects rewarded for simultaneous decreases show larger decreases in both systems (maximum decrease at trial 40 for a single subject of −12 mmHg and −8 bpm).

Potential respiratory influences on blood pressure and heart rate were considered. As in our previous work, analysis of respiration revealed no systematic differences between groups. Interestingly, there was some tendency for the up-up subjects to report more active mental and task involvement than the down-down subjects. However, these data are too variable to warrant firm conclusions about cognitive correlates of the conditioned autonomic activity.

Analysis of the frequency of the four possible combinations of heart rate and blood pressure revealed that on the average, subjects' blood pressure and heart rate were both simultaneously above or below their respective medians only about 50% of the time (during adaptation, the 10 subjects ranged from 25 to 60%). This fact may explain why when blood pressure or heart rate is singularly rewarded, learning does not occur in the other. In other words, if increased blood pressure is being rewarded, from the heart's point of view, half the time it receives reward when it is increasing and half the time it receives reward when it is decreasing. The hypothesis is put forth that it should be theoretically possible to predict the amount of relationship over time between two autonomic responses by rewarding one and determining the extent to which the other shows simultaneous learning. The reverse hypothesis is that when a single autonomic response is rewarded, the extent to which it is related over time to any other autonomic response is the extent to which those responses will also show learning similar to the response controlling the reward.

The data and theory may have important implications for treatment. If it is clinically desirable to lower the activity of only one response without affecting others, care should be taken to make sure that the other responses are not highly correlated with the symptom in question. If it should be desirable to lower two autonomic responses, it may be necessary to reward the patient directly for the integration of this activity, as in the present experiment. For example, one application of operant autonomic integration may be in the treatment of angina pectoris, where lowering the combination of blood pressure and heart rate can result in reduced cardiac oxygen requirements and therefore in reduced pain (10, 11). Finally, if two responses are partially correlated, and it is still desirable to lower only one, it may be necessary to

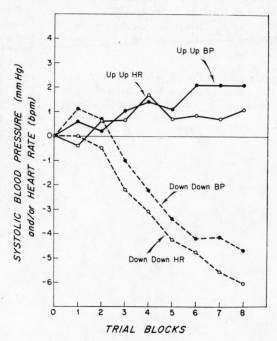

**Fig 2.** Average heart rate (HR) and systolic blood pressure (BP) in subjects rewarded for simultaneously increasing both HR and BP (up-up integration) and for simultaneously decreasing both HR and BP (down-down integration). Each point is mean of 5 subjects, five trials each. Ordinate is both beats/min and mmHg. All values were adjusted for initial adaptation levels and were set to zero.

reward the patient directly for the differentiation of this activity. The doctoral research of the first author (12), just completed, not only demonstrates the direct conditioning of cardiovascular integration on a second sample of subjects, but further demonstrates that the direct operant conditioning of cardiovascular *differentiation* is possible in man.

These data, in conjunction with those in our previous research (5–7), offer strong evidence for human operant autonomic control. Man can learn to increase both his blood pressure and his heart rate, lower both his blood pressure and his heart rate, or raise and lower his blood pressure or his heart rate. This degree of *learned* autonomic specificity raises important questions as to what controls what in the autonomic nervous system. The present paper offers a method for the study of autonomic integration and differentiation, and outlines a new technic for the control of multi-autonomic responses in man.

## REFERENCES

1. Kimmel HD: Instrumental conditioning of autonomically mediated behavior. Psychol Bull 67:337–345, 1967
2. Katkin ES, Murray EN: Instrumental conditioning of autonomically mediated behavior: theoretical and methodological issues. Psychol Bull 70:52–68, 1968
3. Miller NE: Learning of visceral and glandular responses. Science 163:434–445, 1969
4. DiCara LV: Learning in the autonomic nervous system. Scientific American 222: 30–39, 1970
5. Shapiro D, Tursky B, Gershon E, et al: Effects of feedback and reinforcement on the control of human systolic blood pressure. Science 163:588–590, 1969
6. Shapiro D, Tursky B, Schwartz GE: Control of blood pressure in man by operant conditioning. Circulation Res 271:27–32, 1970
7. Shapiro D, Tursky B, Schwartz GE: Differentiation of heart rate and blood pressure in man by operant conditioning. Psychosom Med 32:417–423, 1970

8. Berne RM, Levy MN: Cardiovascular Physiology. St. Louis, C. V. Mosby, 1967

9. Rosenthal R: Experimenter Effects in Behavioral Research. New York, Appleton-Century-Crofts, 1966

10. Braunwald E, Epstein SE, Glick G, et al: Relief of angina pectoris by electrical stimulation of the carotid-sinus nerves. New Eng J Med 277:1278–1283, 1967

11. Sonnenblick EH, Ross J, Braunwald E: Oxygen consumption of the heart: newer concepts of its multifactoral determination. Amer J Cardiol 22:328–336, 1968

12. Schwartz GE: Operant conditioning of human cardiovascular integration and differentiation. Unpublished doctoral dissertation, Harvard University, 1971

# Unidirectional and Large 16
# Magnitude Heart Rate Changes with
# Augmented Sensory Feedback

Mary W. Headrick, Ben W. Feather,
and David T. Wells

## ABSTRACT

In the first of two studies, subjects (Ss) were required to either raise or lower heart rate (HR) relative to pre-trial baseline by altering a tone which changed frequency with HR. Reliable increases but no decreases in HR were found. In a second study extended training of a single S with visual feedback resulted in consistent sustained HR increases of 15 to 35 beats per minute (bpm), but only slight decreases. Sustained elevated rate was accompanied by anxiety. No reliable changes in breathing occurred in either study.

DESCRIPTORS: Voluntary control, Instrumental autonomic conditioning, Heart rate. (M. W. Headrick)

The possibility that responses mediated by the autonomic nervous system (ANS) might be instrumentally conditioned has recently gained strong support from experiments reported by Miller and his colleagues (Miller & DiCara, 1967; DiCara & Miller, 1968; Miller & Banauzizi, 1968). These studies have demonstrated that the activity of the cardiac, vasomotor, and digestive systems of curarized rats can be instrumentally modified and that the observed changes are not readily attributable to peripheral striate muscle activity. In view of these data, the theoretical generalization that instrumental conditioning is effective only with voluntary, striate muscle responses (Kimble, 1961) appears increasingly untenable and the theoretical and practical implications of instrumental ANS conditioning are being recognized (Miller, 1969).

Evidence of instrumental control of ANS responses in humans is much less clear or convincing. Reports of successful instrumental HR conditioning, with which this paper is concerned, are difficult to interpret due to several methodological problems. First, yoked-control procedures have been employed by several investigators (Engel & Hansen, 1966; Engel & Chism, 1967; Shearn, 1962) to demonstrate both HR increases and decreases. Detailed examination of reports based on yoked-control procedures (Katkin & Murray, 1968) indicates that the direction and relative magnitude of HR changes in experimental and control groups have not been consistent across studies. These inconsistencies might be

This research was supported by NIMH PHS Grant MH 08394-05, NIMH Grant 5 K02 MH-19523, and NIMH Grant 2 R01 MH-11549.

Address requests for reprints to: M. W. Headrick, P. O. Box 3812, Duke University Medical Center, Durham, North Carolina 27706.

**251**

due to the use of the yoked-control design in situations where large individual differences rather than reinforcement or feedback may produce significant results (Church, 1964).

A second source of difficulty is the failure of previous investigators to assess HR change relative to prestimulus level. This problem is particularly crucial when determining the bidirectional conditionability of HR. Typically, HR change has been assessed by comparing samples taken during free operant or discrete trial conditioning with a "resting" sample taken prior to conditioning. This procedure has made it difficult to differentiate the effects of baseline changes from those of reinforcement. Brener and Hothersall (1966) utilized such a measure in their report of bidirectional stimulus control of HR on alternating increase and decrease trials. In that study each interbeat interval (IBI) during each trial was classified as longer or shorter than a modal value obtained for each S during an initial rest period. While HR increases were clearly demonstrated, the reported data indicate a general decrease in HR during the experiment and it is not possible to determine whether decreases from baseline occurred or whether performance on decrease trials reflects a decline in baseline HR. In order to determine whether HR decreases occur under stimulus control it must at least be shown that no baseline decline occurred during conditioning. A more suitable method of assessing HR change is the comparison of HR during discrete trials with HR immediately preceding each trial.

A final problem concerns the amount of training necessary to demonstrate reliable instrumental control of HR. The relatively small changes in HR which have been reported may be due to insufficient opportunity for learning. In most studies only a single training session has been given and the maximum number reported has been six to ten (Levene, Engel, & Pearson, 1968). In view of the complexity of the response required of Ss and of the probable lack of practice prior to conditioning, it may be necessary to extend training over a longer time period. If increased response magnitude could be obtained with extended practice, statistical reliability might be demonstrated consistently across studies and the examination of possible concomitant striate muscle activity might be facilitated.

In view of these methodological problems, as well as reports of failure to demonstrate instrumental HR control (Harwood, 1959, 1962), it is apparent that instrumental control of HR in humans requires further examination. The present report consists of two studies, the first of which was designed to determine whether reliable increases and decreases in HR can be demonstrated in human Ss when adequate samples, controls, and analyses are employed. The second study, employing a single S, was an attempt to produce large-magnitude HR changes as the result of extended training.

EXPERIMENT 1

### Method

*Subjects.* Twenty-four male undergraduate psychology students participated in the study for class credit. All Ss were free from respiratory, cardiovascular, and psychiatric disorders and were not taking any drugs.

*Apparatus.* Electrocardiogram (EKG), cardiotachometer detection of inter-pulse (R–R) intervals, breathing responses (chest wall expansion), and trial periods were recorded on a Grass Model 7 Polygraph. The EKG was detected with Industrial Medical Instrument fluid-type electrodes placed on the extreme lateral margins of the chest. A voltage-to-frequency converter coupled to the output of the cardiotachometer was used to provide continuous auditory feed-back to Ss about their HR. The feedback to Ss was a moderately soft tone, pre-sented through earphones, which varied in pitch as a function of instantaneous bpm rate. The relationship between bpm and tone frequency was reversible, i.e., high-pitched tones could be produced by either faster or slower rates de-pending upon the position of a manually operated switch. Tone frequency varied non-linearly from 880 to 4400 Hz in the range between 40 and 120 bpm such that relatively less change in tone frequency occurred with extreme HR.

Breathing was monitored with an air-filled rubber tube encircling the chest below the sternum and coupled to a Grass PT5 pressure transducer. Intertrial intervals and auditory feedback were controlled electronically. All equipment was located outside a sound-attenuated chamber (Industrial Acoustics Corpora-tion) and pre-taped instructions and communication between experimenter and S were provided by intercom.

*Procedure.* Twelve Ss were randomly assigned to each of two conditions, Increase HR and Decrease HR. Half the Ss in each group were instructed to raise and half to lower the frequency of the tone, and the contingency between HR and tone frequency was adjusted so that half the Ss receiving each instruc-tion had to raise and half to lower HR in order to alter the tone frequency ap-propriately.

Subjects were seated in a comfortable, reclining chair and were told that several physiological measures would be recorded. The breathing tube and EKG leads were attached with the EKG ground lead placed behind the right ear. In addition, a second "dummy" lead was placed behind the left ear and a metal disc was taped on the dorsal surface of the right hand. A brief explanation of each transducer was given as it was attached and the head and hand leads were falsely described as detecting brain waves and temperature, respectively. Sub-jects were misled concerning the response being conditioned on the basis of observations by other investigators (Engel & Hansen, 1966) that awareness of the contingency between HR and feedback tended to result in poorer perform-ance.

The experiment consisted of a 5-min rest period, 10 adaptation trials, and 10 training trials. All trials consisted of a 30-sec pre-feedback and 60-sec feedback period during which HR and breathing were measured. Intertrial intervals ranged from 30 to 90 sec and averaged 1 min. Adaptation and training trials differed only in instructions. Prior to adaptation Ss were told that they would hear a tone which would change in pitch and that they should simply listen to the tone. After adaptation and prior to training, the following taped instructions were given to Ss:

We are going to ask you during the second half of the experiment to try to influence the tones coming through the earphones. The tone will vary in frequency as a function of one aspect of your brainwaves or EEG. It has been noted by researchers in this field that the various waves coming from the two halves of a person's brain are sometimes in phase and sometimes out of phase. There is no evidence so far that this variation is correlated with any particular mental process or thought patterns. The purpose of this experiment is to make you aware of this aspect of your EEG to see whether it can be brought under your control. Your only measure of success at this task is how high (or low) the tone in your earphones is. Therefore, you should put all your attention on the tone. The higher (or lower) the tone, the greater the amount of similarity in the EEG from the two halves of your brain. While the tone is on, concentrate on making the tone as high (or low) as you can for as long as you can. The purpose of the various devices attached to you is simply to provide us with a simultaneous record of their functions besides your EEG. In order that these measures may be as free from artifact as possible, we ask that you remain as still as possible. If you become uncomfortable wait until the tone has gone off before moving or changing position. Just remember, concentrate on making the tone as high (or low) as possible for as long as possible.

*Data Quantification and Analyses.* The 60-sec feedback period of each trial was divided into 2 30-sec measurement periods in order to obtain equal-interval samples in comparing trial and pre-trial HR. The bpm value and msec equivalent of each IBI during the 30-sec pre-trial and 2 30-sec trial periods were recorded for all training trials. Average bpm HR for each of these 3 measurement periods was derived by taking the reciprocal of the mean msec IBI values within each period, i.e. the reciprocal of the harmonic mean. The percentage change in HR from pre-trial rates was computed separately for each of the 2 30-sec trial periods for each $S$ by the formula (Post − Pre)/Pre. These scores were averaged across blocks of 5 trials to obtain 2 scores for each $S$ for each of 2 trial blocks.

Breathing frequency and amplitude were also obtained for the 30-sec pre-trial and 2 30-sec trial periods for each trial. Breathing frequency was defined as the number of breaths in each measurement period in which inspiration was completed during the period. Breathing frequency was averaged into 2 trial blocks for each of the 3 measurement periods. Breathing amplitude was expressed as the mean mm pen deflection of all breaths in each measurement period. Percentage change scores were computed for the breathing amplitude data using the same formula as was used for HR and were similarly averaged into 2 blocks of 5 trials.

Multivariate analyses of variance were performed separately on HR, breathing amplitude, and breathing frequency. For HR and breathing amplitude the 2 percentage-change scores for each $S$ for each of 2 trial blocks comprised the 4 elements of the vector in the analyses; for breathing frequency the pre-trial period was included to comprise a 6-element vector. For each contrast the analyses yielded (1) univariate $F$-ratios for each vector element, and (2) exact likelihood ratio $F$s for the overall effect.

## *Results*

All results will be discussed in terms of the Increase and Decrease groups pooled across instruction conditions, since there were no significant interactions ($F < 1$) between instructions (raise or lower tone) and direction of HR change for either the HR or breathing data.

*Heart Rate.* It can be seen in Figure 1 that HR increases occurred in both the Increase and Decrease groups with relatively substantial increases occurring only in the Increase group. Multivariate analyses of variance revealed that the slight increase in HR occurring in the Decrease group was not significantly different from pre-trial level (overall $F = 2.06$, $p < .13$, $df = 4,17$). In contrast, HR in the Increase group was significantly higher than pre-trial level during both 30-sec trial periods (3.29 and 4.10 bpm, respectively) in the first half of the experiment and during the first 30-sec trial period (3.40 bpm) during the second half of the experiment ($F = 8.49$, $p < .008$; $F = 7.23$, $p < .013$; and $F = 12.92$, $p < .002$, respectively; $df = 1,20$). The magnitude of HR change declined somewhat during the second 30-sec period (2.30 bpm) in the second half of the experiment, but remained marginally significant ($F = 3.47$, $p < .074$, $df = 1,20$). The overall increase in HR across all trial periods was highly reliable ($F = 5.04$, $p < .0075$, $df = 4,17$). The difference in HR increase between the Increase and Decrease groups approached significance during the first 30-sec trial period in the first half of the experiment ($F = 3.87$, $p < .06$, $df = 1,20$) but was less reliable during subsequent periods ($F = 2.08$, $p < .161$; $F = 2.31$, $p < .140$; and $F < 1$). The overall difference between groups was not significant ($F = 1.23$, $p < .34$, $df = 4,17$).

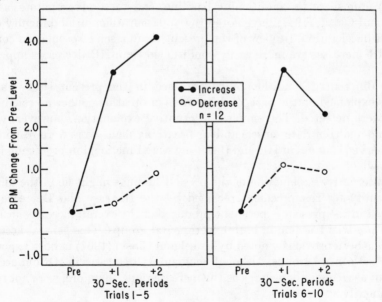

FIG. 1. Changes in HR from baseline during periods of auditory feedback for *S*s required to increase or decrease HR.

Pre-trial HR failed to change significantly in either the Increase or Decrease group during the 10 training trials.

*Breathing*. Multivariate analyses of variance revealed no significant changes in breathing amplitude in either the Increase or Decrease group. Further analyses of the relationship between breathing and HR revealed that the product-moment correlation between changes in breathing amplitude and HR across trial periods was significant for only one $S$ ($r = +.998$, $p < .05$, $df = 1$). Using an $r$-to-$z_r$ conversion, the average correlation across all $S$s was $+.30$, which was not significant. Furthermore, the correlation between changes in breathing amplitude and HR was positive for half the $S$s and negative for half the $S$s in each group. Multivariate contrasts of breathing frequency showed that, relative to pre-trial frequency, breathing rate decreased in the Increase group and increased in the Decrease group during the first 30 sec of the first block of trials ($F = 4.29$, $p < .048$, $df = 1,20$). No significant changes in breathing rate occurred during the remainder of the experiment in either group. The overall difference in breathing frequency between the Increase and Decrease groups was not significant ($F < 1$).

## Discussion

The finding that $S$s increased but failed to decrease HR when change in rate was assessed relative to pre-trial HR raises questions concerning the bidirectional conditionability of HR with instrumental techniques. Although HR decreases have previously been reported (Brener & Hothersall, 1966; Engel & Hansen, 1966), no studies have assessed change relative to pre-trial HR. Only Levene, Engel, and Pearson (1968) have attempted statistical evaluation of change relative to immediate preconditioning baseline, and these investigators, as well as Engel and Chism (1967) have noted the apparent differential difficulty of learning HR deceleration. In view of the present results, some speculation concerning why HR increases are more easily conditioned than HR decreases appears warranted.

The differential conditionability obtained in the present study cannot be readily explained on the basis of differences in breathing, since no reliable differences were detected. The simplest alternative explanation, however, would be that undetected striate muscle and/or breathing maneuvers were responsible for the observed changes in HR and that they were functional in producing increases but not decreases.

An alternative explanation of the present findings might lie in the differential opportunity for reinforcement received by the Increase and Decrease groups. The task in the present experiment produced slight overall increases in HR relative to pre-trial baseline in both experimental groups. This general acceleratory effect has been previously noted by Engel and Chism (1967) in both experimental and yoked-control groups. Although momentary decreases in HR did occur, they were not as frequent or as large as the increases and, therefore, were not rewarded as frequently.

As Katkin and Murray (1968) have pointed out, there is utility in conceptually separating the questions of physiological mechanisms and experimental control.

While questions of mechanism remain highly speculative at this point, it is apparent that the experimental parameters of reinforcement contingency, feedback quality, motivation, and amount of training must be explored in more detail in order to clarify the bidirectional conditionability of HR responses.

## Experiment 2

Two observations were made during Experiment 1 which prompted a second experiment designed to determine whether large-magnitude changes in HR could be produced with modified procedures. The first of these observations, based upon post-experimental interviews, was that the majority of $S$s in Experiment 1 reported becoming disinterested in the task and being dubious about the purpose of the experiment and the veridicality of the instructions. The second observation was the occurrence of large-magnitude changes in HR on the second and subsequent trials of one $S$ in the Increase group. Figure 2 shows a typical trial selected from this $S$'s record. The maximum increase over baseline HR was approximately 35 bpm and the average increase across all trials was 19.8 bpm. Maximum rate change was usually achieved within a few seconds after trial onset. Neither the data nor interviews with the $S$ revealed evidence of muscle tension or breathing maneuvers which could account for these marked changes in HR. The $S$ reported that he simply concentrated intensely on raising the frequency of the tone. Additional testing of this $S$ revealed that his ability to elevate HR was reproducible and independent of the direction of tone frequency change produced by HR increases. He was unable to produce decreases of similar magnitude. The performance of this $S$ indicated that large-magnitude, discrete-trial HR changes were physiologically possible under the existing experimental conditions. The second experiment was undertaken to determine whether similar large-magnitude HR changes could be produced by a randomly selected $S$ if he were highly motivated and given extended training with augmented sensory feedback.

### Method

*Subjects.* The final subject run in Experiment 1 was interviewed and agreed to participate in the second experiment as a paid volunteer. During Experiment 1

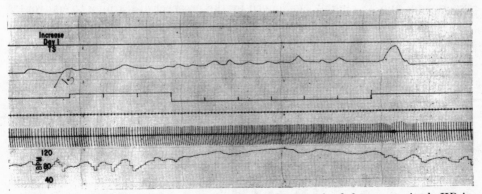

Fig. 2. Polygraph record of a typical trial showing sustained, large magnitude HR increases occurring during Experiment 1 in one $S$.

he had been in the Increase group and his performance was below average showing a net increase of 3 bpm during the first 5 trials and a decrease of 1 bpm during the second 5 trials of the experiment.

*Apparatus.* During the first 4 training sessions all apparatus was identical with that used in the first experiment. As a result of interviews with the $S$ it became apparent that, although the continuous auditory feedback had advantages over binary feedback contingent upon a criterion, the quality of the auditory feedback was not adequate. Specifically, continuous auditory feedback required the $S$ to judge relative pitch over a 60-sec period. This proved to be very difficult and the $S$ reported not being able to judge whether the tone was actually higher or lower than the initial pitch he had heard at the onset of each trial. Therefore, on the subsequent 8 sessions of the experiment the auditory feedback was replaced by a meter display of instantaneous HR change relative to pre-trial HR. The meter (Simpson Model 29 DC microammeter) was mounted inside a metal box placed 2 feet in front of the $S$. The face of the meter measured $2\frac{1}{2}$ in. by 4 in. and was covered with one-way glass so that the meter was not visible except when lighted from within during trials. The meter was connected with the output of the Grass Model 7 tachograph by a circuit providing both gain and balance adjustments. Programming equipment operating on this output counted the number of heart beats in the 30 sec immediately prior to each trial and automatically changed the balance of the meter such that the average pre-trial HR was equivalent to a meter reading at center scale during a trial. By adjusting the gain any change from 8 to 100 bpm could be selected to produce a full-scale pointer deflection from center-scale on the meter. At the onset of each trial the meter was illuminated and read center-scale as the result of balancing during the pre-trial period. The relationship between direction of pointer deflection (left or right of center) and direction of HR change was manually reversible.

*Procedure.* The $S$ was fully informed of the nature of the procedures and their theoretical and practical implications. The responses being measured and the feedback contingencies were explained in detail and the $S$ was encouraged to pay attention to and increase his awareness of his HR. His comments were fully transcribed after each training session. This $S$ became extremely interested in the experiment, and was highly challenged by the prospect of learning to control his HR and to match the performance of the $S$ whose polygraph record is shown in Fig. 2. He was consistently early for his appointments and gave many other indications of continued high interest in the task throughout the 6 weeks of the experiment.

The experiment consisted of a total of 12 sessions averaging 2 hours each, including a post-testing interview. Trial duration was 1 min and sessions had a variable number of trials, either increase, decrease, or both. A total of 64 increase trials were administered over 6 sessions and 100 decrease trials over 8 sessions. Procedures for applying electrodes were identical with those described in Experiment 1, except that no "dummy" leads were used.

### Results
During the first 34 increase trials over 4 sessions HR increases of approximately

5 to 10 bpm occurred regularly. During the fifth session (after a total of 42 trials) the magnitude of HR acceleration suddenly increased. On trial 43 HR increases as great as 44 bpm occurred and averaged 30 bpm until the end of the trial period. The $S$ immediately reported having experienced "tension," "uneasiness," and a feeling "like being anxious" during the trial. The session was terminated at $S$'s request. During the sixth increase session the $S$ was somewhat reluctant to reproduce the large magnitude HR changes produced in the previous session, but felt he could do it "at will." He agreed to continue in the experiment and, again, altered HR by over 30 bpm on each of several trials. The pattern of HR change was characterized by rapid onset and rapid return of rate to pre-trial levels upon trial termination. Feelings of anxiety and uneasiness again were reported as a concomitant of trial periods. The experiment was terminated after this session.

Examination of the polygraph records indicated that breathing during sustained elevated rate failed to deviate markedly from pre-trial patterns. No gross muscle activity was apparent in the EKG although momentary low-amplitude R-waves occurred resulting in failure to trigger the tachograph periodically.

After 100 trials on which $S$ attempted to decrease HR, no decreases of large magnitude occurred. During some sessions $S$ was able to lower HR by approximately 5 bpm, but performance was not consistent either from trial to trial or from session to session.

## DISCUSSION

The large magnitude HR changes noted in one $S$ in Experiment 1 and produced with extended training by the $S$ in Experiment 2 suggest that the characteristics of ANS mediated responses such as HR can be grossly modified voluntarily by humans. The short latency and rapid offset of the response are not typical of the slower HR changes produced by circulating neurohormones. The ability of these $S$s to produce large magnitude responses, "at will," without marked skeletal muscle changes is of special interest.

Whether such large magnitude increases in HR can be generally produced in a more extensive sample of human $S$s is under current investigation in this laboratory. The failure to obtain similarly large HR decreases with extended training lends verification to the findings of Experiment 1, and the apparent differential conditionability of HR increases and decreases poses some interesting problems for future research. While questions of mechanism remain largely speculative, it is apparent from the results of the present studies that the process of achieving effective control over HR in humans is a long and difficult one. At least three factors appear to be of critical importance in future experiments designed to demonstrate extensive control. First, the amount of training required to produce effective voluntary control may be in the range of 50 to 100 trials of at least 1-min duration. Only two experiments have reported training times of this length (Engel & Hansen, 1966; Engel & Chism, 1967). Neither experiment (the former attempting HR slowing, the latter HR speeding) showed changes greater than 10 bpm. The absence of greater changes in these studies may have been the result of using long periods of continuous reinforcement rather than discrete trials. On the other hand, shorter periods of large-magnitude changes may have occurred in some $S$s in those studies which do not appear in the results due to the averaging of performance over the entire reinforcement period for each session.

A second factor involved in producing large-magnitude HR changes is the type of feedback given $S$s. With the exception of reports by Lang and his co-workers (Hnatiow & Lang, 1965; Lang, Sroufe, & Hastings, 1967; Sroufe, 1969), previous experiments have usually used a criterion system of reward which gave $S$ no feedback unless his rate changed in the proper direction from the criterion. In addition, even if the direction of rate change was appropriate, $S$ was given no information concerning the magnitude of his response relative to the criterion. In contrast, the meter employed in Experiment 2 of the present report informed $S$ continuously of whether he was above or below his pre-trial rate and the magnitude of the change on each beat. It may be that amount of training time interacts with the information content of the feedback such that less training is required when the information content of the feedback is high.

The final factor involved in effective HR control is that of motivation. In order for a $S$ to devote sufficient concentration to the task to utilize the training time and feedback available, his motivation and interest in the task must be high. If $S$s are selected randomly and no attempt is made to produce high motivation in them, it seems likely that performance will be poorer than with highly motivated $S$s. Furthermore, since the process of learning to achieve voluntary control over HR is a long and demanding one, a few dollars probably will not be sufficiently motivating. On the other hand, a high degree of personal involvement and challenge, induced by fully informing the $S$ of the nature and import of the experiment, seems to be a sustaining source of motivation.

In spite of the special attention given these experimental factors in the second experiment reported here, large magnitude HR decreases failed to occur. Additional features of the experimental procedures might possibly be manipulated in such a way that HR decreases can be learned. It may be that substantial HR decreases can only be obtained when baseline activity is considerably above "normal" levels.

In view of the implications of effective voluntary control of ANS mediated responses for the treatment of a number of functional disorders, it appears that extensive investigation of the experimental factors involved in control be undertaken, not only with HR but also with other physiological systems such as blood pressure. Similar intensive study of mechanisms underlying the conditionability of bidirectional response systems also seems of great importance to our understanding ANS mediated responses.

## REFERENCES

Brener, J., & Hothersall, D. Heart rate control under conditions of augmented sensory feedback. *Psychophysiology*, 1966, *3*, 23–28.

Church, R. M. Systematic effect of random error in the yoked control design. *Psychological Bulletin*, 1964, *62*, 122–131.

DiCara, L. V., & Miller, N. E. Instrumental learning of vasomotor responses by rats: Learning to respond differentially in the two ears. *Science*, 1968, *159*, 1485–1486.

Engel, B. T., & Chism, R. A. Operant conditioning of heart rate speeding. *Psychophysiology*, 1967, *3*, 418–426.

Engel, B. T., & Hansen, S. P. Operant conditioning of heart rate slowing. *Psychophysiology*, 1966, *3*, 176–187.

Harwood, C. W. Operant autonomic conditioning. In *Research in progress*. Bellingham, Washington: Western Washington College of Education, 1959. Pp. 31–37.

Harwood, C. W. Operant heart rate conditioning. *The Physiological Record*, 1962, *12*, 279–284.

Hnatiow, M., & Lang, P. J. Learned stabilization of cardiac rate. *Psychophysiology*, 1965, *1*, 330–336.

Katkin, E. S., & Murray, E. N. Instrumental conditioning of autonomically mediated behavior: Theoretical and methodological issues. *Psychological Bulletin*, 1968, *70*, 52–68.

Kimble, G. A. *Hilgard and Marquis' conditioning and learning*. New York: Appleton-Century-Crofts, 1961.

Lang, P. J., Sroufe, L. A., & Hastings, J. E. Effects of feedback and instructional set on the control of cardiac-rate variability. *Journal of Experimental Psychology*, 1967, *75*, 425–431.

Levene, H. I., Engel, B. T., & Pearson, J. A. Differential operant conditioning of heart rate. *Psychosomatic Medicine*, 1968, *30*, 837–845.

Miller, N. E. Learning of visceral and glandular responses. *Science*, 1969, *163*, 434–445.

Miller, N. E., & Banuazizi, A. Instrumental learning by curarized rats of a specific visceral response, intestinal or cardiac. *Journal of Comparative & Physiological Psychology*, 1968, *65*, 8–12.

Miller, N. E., & DiCara, L. V. Instrumental learning of heart rate changes in curarized rats: Shaping, and specificity to discriminative stimulus. *Journal of Comparative & Physiological Psychology*, 1967, *63*, 12–19.

Shearn, D. W. Operant conditioning of heart rate. *Science*, 1962, *137*, 530–531.

Sroufe, L. A. Learned stabilization of cardiac rate with respiration experimentally controlled. *Journal of Experimental Psychology*, 1969, *81*, 391–393.

# The Effects of Instructional Set and Autonomic Perception on Cardiac Control

17

### Joel S. Bergman and Harold J. Johnson

#### ABSTRACT

Fifty-four Ss were divided into three instructional groups. One group was instructed to increase their heart rate (HR) every time a signal was presented; a second group was told to decrease their HR; and a control group was not instructed to change their HR in any direction. Results indicate that Ss can increase or decrease their HR in the absence of externalized feedback. These HR changes do not appear to be mediated by respiration or skin resistance variations. In addition, Ss were divided into groups on the basis of their APQ scores. The group with middle APQ scores displayed more HR control in both directions than Ss with high or low APQ scores. The study was replicated with 42 Ss and results support the HR increase but not the HR decrease findings.

DESCRIPTORS: Heart rate, Instructions. (J. Bergman)

Recent studies have suggested that under certain conditions Ss can learn to control their cardiovascular responses. In some of these studies, Ss are instructed to produce changes in cardiac behavior (Donelson, 1966; Engel & Chism, 1967; Hnatiow & Lang, 1965; Lang, Sroufe, & Hastings, 1967). The experimental Ss are also given feedback of their cardiac activity in some external (visual or auditory) form to facilitate their task. When experimental and control Ss are subsequently compared, the experimental Ss perform their task more adequately than control Ss. Differences in performance between these two groups are viewed as a function of the external feedback given to the experimental group.

The contribution of instructional set alone in facilitating cardiac control is obscured in the above studies by the use of external feedback. That is, the degree to which instructional set and external reinforcement of cardiac responses independently contribute to cardiac control is difficult to assess. Therefore, the present study attempted to determine the effects of instructional set on cardiac control. By varying only the instructional set, the degree of cardiac control produced by these sets could be determined.

The investigation of instructional set does not rule out the role of feedback in cardiac control. In fact, the instructional set given to Ss very probably enhances or at least focuses the S's attention on naturally occurring feedback. This is in

This research was supported by MH Grant 13373 awarded to the second author.

The senior author is now at Smith College.

Address requests for reprints to: Harold J. Johnson, Department of Psychology, Bowling Green State University, Bowling Green, Ohio 43402.

contrast to enhancing such feedback through artificial means of amplification or display. Thus, the present study examined whether instructional set emphasizing the use of naturally occurring feedback would be sufficient for *S*s to attain cardiac control.

The use of naturally occurring feedback in HR control presupposes some accurate perception of autonomic activity on the part of the *S*. If HR control without external feedback is possible, then the veridicality of autonomic perception might be related to the degree of control. A monotonic relationship was predicted between the accuracy of perception of autonomic functions and HR control.

EXPERIMENT I

*Method*

*Design.* The experiment used a 3 × 3 × 6 design. The first variable consisted of three instructional groups: HR increase, HR decrease, and no HR instructions. The increase instructions were oriented toward HR acceleration; the decrease instructions were oriented toward HR deceleration; and the control instructions were not oriented toward any changes in HR. The instructions for these groups were as follows:

Increase group:

> This study deals with controlling your HR. The majority of people can increase their HR when they are given a signal to do so. Increasing your HR is possible if you concentrate on your heart and try very hard to make your HR go faster. In this experiment, you will hear tones lasting for six seconds. During the time interval that you hear the tone, I want you to try to make your HR go faster. There will be a number of tones presented, and I would like to see if you can increase your heart rate during each of these tones. You might notice that as the experiment progresses, your HR will go faster with each successive tone.

Decrease group: Instructions for the decrease group were identical to those of the increase group except the word "decrease" was substituted for the word "increase."

Control group:

> This study deals with the effects of hearing tones on your HR. In the experiment, you will hear tones lasting for six seconds. During the time interval that you hear the tone, we will be measuring the reaction of your HR to the tone. There will be a number of tones presented.

The second variable consisted of three levels of autonomic perception. Mandler's *Autonomic Perception Questionnaire* (APQ) scores were used as a measure of perception (Mandler, Mandler, & Uviller, 1958), and high, middle, and low APQ groups were constructed by dividing an APQ distribution into upper, middle, and lower thirds, respectively.

The third factor consisted of HR difference scores in beats/minute (bpm) for the first 6 heart beats following onset of a stimulus, and the first 6 heart beats following the termination of a stimulus. The HR difference scores were obtained by subtracting HRs occurring during and following a tone from a mean pre-tone HR.

*Subjects.* The Ss in this experiment consisted of 54 female undergraduates who received credit in their introductory psychology course for participating in the study. The Ss were randomly assigned to one of the three instructional groups by the order in which they arrived for the experiment.

*Procedure.* All Ss were tested individually in a sound- and electrostatically-shielded booth, and had physiological recording devices attached. A 10-min adaptation period served to obtain baseline readings. This period also was used to allow Ss to practice the technique of paced-respiration (Wood & Obrist, 1964) by matching their respiration rate (RR) to a flashing light which went on and off at a frequency approximating S's normal RR.

All Ss were given general introductory instructions about the recording devices, and were given time to practice the paced-respiration procedure. Following these introductory remarks, Ss were given one of three instructional sets, which resulted in three different instructional groups consisting of 18 Ss in each group.

Following the administration of the instructional sets, the tones were presented. A 1000 Hz tone of 60 db intensity was presented through earphones for a duration of 6 sec. The tones were presented 30 times, with an inter-tone-interval randomly ranging from 35–65 sec.

After the 30 tones were presented, Ss were given the 21 items dealing with anxiety of the APQ. An extensive post-experimental questionnaire was also given to determine S's impressions about the experiment, and the ways in which Ss thought they obtained HR control.

*Apparatus.* Heart rate was measured with electrodes attached to S's forearm and ankle and recorded on a Grass Model 7D polygraph. Respiration was measured with a strain gauge transducer attached to S's chest and recorded on the polygraph. Exosomatic measurements of galvanic skin response (GSR) and skin resistance level were obtained with Beckman Biopotential skin electrodes placed on the S's palm. A constant 50 $\mu$a current was used. These skin resistance measures were taken to determine whether the predicted changes in HR would be associated with changes in level of arousal.

The paced-respiration technique was used to reduce HR variation caused by RR changes. Two timers and a light signal were used to signal a RR which was to be matched by the Ss. The RR to be matched was S's normal rate obtained during the adaptation period of the experiment. The frequency of light changes was continuously recorded on the polygraph.

## Results

*Heart Rate.* Heart rate scores in bpm were taken from a cardiotachogram. These rate scores were taken for the 6 heart beats preceding, during, and following the 6 sec tone. Final HR scores were the mean HRs across the 30 tones for each particular beat. A mean HR was calculated from the 6 HR means preceding the tone. This prestimulus mean HR was subtracted from each of the 6 mean HR scores during and following the tone, which resulted in 12 difference scores. A constant was added to the difference scores to keep the scores positive integers.

The first 6 difference scores during the tone were then used as the repeated measure in a $3 \times 3 \times 6$ design using Winer's (1962) Case II as a model.

The first analysis included the three instructional groups and the three APQ score groups. The mean prestimulus HRs for Ss in the increase, decrease, and control groups were 77, 78, and 73 bpm, respectively. The effects of instructional sets were significant, $F(2,45) = 11.34, p < .001$. The increase group ($\bar{X} = 11.14$) showed a higher HR than the control group ($\bar{X} = 9.52$), $t(45) = 2.79, p < .01$, and the decrease group ($\bar{X} = 8.39$) showed a lower HR than the control group, $t(45) = 2.06, p < .05$. These differences are illustrated in Figure 1. The effects of APQ scores were not significant, $F(2,45) = 0.46, p > .25$. Although the Instruction $\times$ APQ interaction was also nonsignificant, $F(4,45) = 1.92, p > .1$, examination of the mean profiles showed that Ss with instructions to increase HR ($\bar{X} = 12.72$) and with middle APQ scores obtained higher HRs than control Ss ($\bar{X} = 9.54$) with middle APQ scores, $F(1,45) = 23.83, p < .001$. Subjects with middle APQ scores who were instructed to decrease their HR ($\bar{X} = 7.83$) showed a lower HR than control Ss with middle APQ scores, but this difference only approached significance, $F(1,45) = 2.60, p > .1$. The Instructions $\times$ Heart Beat Number interaction was significant, $F(10,495) = 4.54, p < .001$. The increase group ($\bar{X} = 12.00$) showed a higher HR than the control group ($\bar{X} = 9.33$) during the 3rd beat while the tone was on, $F(1,495) = 6.03, p < .05$, and the increase group ($\bar{X} = 12.16$) had a higher HR than the control group ($\bar{X} = 9.72$) during the 5th beat, $F(1,495) = 4.85, p < .05$.

A separate analysis was performed to show that the instructional set finding was not caused by very large HR changes occurring in only a few Ss. Of the 18 Ss instructed to increase their HR, 11 showed increases, 6 decreases, and 1 no

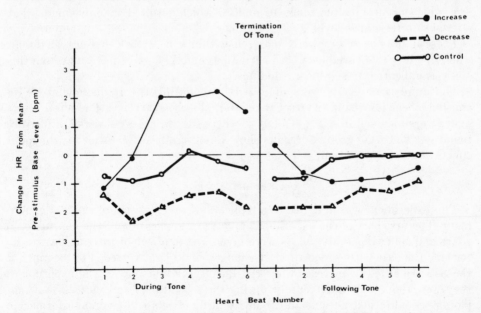

FIG. 1. Changes in HR across the 6 heart beats during and following the tone

change in HR. The decrease group showed 16 $S$s decreasing their HR, and 2 $S$s showing no change. Of the 18 control $S$s, 11 showed decreases, 4 increases, and 3 no change in HR. These differences in the direction of HR change between instructional groups were significant, $\chi^2(2) = 15.8$, $p < .001$.

*Respiration.* Respiration was scored by taking the peak amplitude values of the first 2 inspirations before, during, and after the tone. These peak amplitude values were averaged across the 30 tones. A mean score was obtained from the 2 prestimulus inspirations. This mean score was then subtracted from the 2 mean values during and after the tone, which resulted in 4 difference scores. A constant was added to these difference scores to maintain positive integers.

A $3 \times 3 \times 4$ Winer Case II analysis was performed where the first two factors represented instructions and APQ levels, respectively, and the last factor represented the 2 amplitude peaks during and following the tone. Analysis of the data indicated that there were no significant changes in respiration due to instructional sets, $F(2,45) = 0.50$, $p > .5$. The analysis also indicated a significant decrease in RR amplitude for all groups as a function of time, $F(3,135) = 3.11$, $p < .05$. The second peak inspiration ($\bar{X} = 1.90$) during the tone across all trials showed a decrease in amplitude compared with the first inspiration peak during the tone ($\bar{X} = 1.97$), $t(135) = 3.94$, $p < .01$, and compared with the last peak inspiration following the tone ($\bar{X} = 1.96$), $t(135) = 3.31$, $p < .01$.

*Skin Resistance.* Three scores for each $S$ were used in an analysis of skin resistance level. The first score was a difference score between skin resistance levels at tones 10 and 1. The second score was a difference score of resistance at tones 20 and 11. The third score was a difference score between tones 30 and 21. These scores were used to measure resistance level because of rest periods of 1 min duration which occurred after tones 10 and 20 which resulted in movements that altered skin resistance level.

These difference scores were analyzed within a $3 \times 3 \times 3$ Case II design where the first two variables were instructions and APQ scores. Results from this analysis indicated no significant findings.

The number of GSRs were analyzed by counting the frequency of GSRs emitted by each $S$ within the 6 sec tone interval for the 30 tones. These frequency scores were included in a $3 \times 3$ analysis where the variables consisted of instructional sets and APQ groups. Results showed nonsignificant $F$ ratios for the main effects and the interaction.

## Experiment II

This experiment was designed as a replication and extension of the first experiment. The first part of the experiment involved a replication of the instructional effect and following that, the $S$s were given a second set of instructions to determine the ease with which the HR changes could be reversed. For example, if the $S$s were asked to increase their HR during the first part of the experiment, they were requested to decrease it during the second part and vice versa. Complete reversal of instructions and their resulting effects will provide information regarding the nature and permanence of the HR changes.

*Method*

*Subjects.* The $S$s in this experiment consisted of 42 female undergraduates who received credit in their introductory psychology course for participating in the study. The $S$s were randomly assigned to one of the three instructional groups by the order in which they arrived for the experiment.

*Procedure.* Subjects were tested under the same conditions as the first study, and were given opportunities to practice the paced-respiration technique. The instructional sets were then administered, followed by the tones to which $S$s were to change their HR. This latter sequence is the exact replication of the first experiment and is called Phase 1. Following Phase 1, $S$s were told to change their HR in a direction opposite to the originally instructed direction. Instructing $S$s to produce HR changes in the opposite direction will be called Phase 2 of the replication. For example, the increase group was given the following instructions for Phase 2:

> In the beginning I said that people can control their heart rate. Decreasing your HR is also possible if you concentrate on your heart and try very hard to make your HR go slower. This part of the experiment is the same as the first part, except I would like to see if you can decrease your heart beat during each of the tones.

Thus 14 $S$s were first instructed and tested for increases in HR followed by instructions and tests for decreases in HR. The decrease group was first asked to decrease their HR followed by instructions to increase their HR. A control group received the same instructions that were given in the first experiment for both phases.

Following the administration of the instructional sets, the tones were presented. A 1000 Hz tone of 60 db intensity was presented through earphones for a duration of 6 sec. The tones were presented 20 times during each phase, with an inter-tone-interval randomly ranging from 35–65 sec.

*Apparatus.* Heart rate, respiration amplitude, and GSR were measured and recorded as in the first experiment.

*Results*

*Phase 1. Heart Rate.* Difference scores from the prestimulus mean HR were used in a $3 \times 6$ design where the first variable consisted of the three instructional sets, and the second variable was the repeated measure of the 6 heart beat numbers during the tone. The mean prestimulus HRs for $S$s in the increase, decrease, and control groups were 76, 68, and 76 bpm, respectively. These prestimulus HRs are comparable to the rates in the first study, with the exception of the decrease group which showed a 10 bpm lower baseline during the replication.

The effects of the instructional sets were significant, $F(3,39) = 8.26, p < .001$. The increase group ($\bar{X} = 11.26$) showed a higher HR than the control group ($\bar{X} = 9.84$), $t(39) = 2.82, p < .01$, and a higher HR than the decrease group ($\bar{X} = 9.37$), $t(39) = 5.52, p < .001$. No differences were found between the decrease and the control group ($\bar{X} = 9.84$), $t(39) = 0.93, p > .2$. Group differences due to instructional sets are illustrated in Figure 2. The Instructions $\times$ Heart Beat Number interaction was significant, $F(10,195) = 2.69$, $p < .01$, where the increase group showed higher HRs than the control group for the 6th, $F(1,26) = 10.56$, $p < .01$; 5th, $F(1,26) = 11.56$, $p < .001$; and 3rd, $F(1,26) = 4.79$, $p < .05$, heart beat number. No differences were found between the control and decrease $S$s for any of the heart beat intervals.

A separate analysis was performed to show that the instructional set finding was not caused by very large HR changes occurring in only a few $S$s. Of the 14 $S$s instructed to increase HR, 9 showed increases and 5 showed no change in HR. The decrease group showed 3 $S$s increasing, 6 decreasing, and 5 not changing HR. Of the 14 control $S$s, 3 showed increases, 5 decreases, and 5 no change in HR. Differences in the direction of HR change between instructional groups were significant, $\chi^2(4) = 9.52$, $p < .05$.

*Phase 1. Respiration.* Respiration amplitude was scored and analyzed using the procedure described in the first study. The analysis showed a significant Instruction $\times$ Peak Inspiration interaction, $F(2,39) = 11.70$, $p < .01$. No differences in respiration amplitude were found between the increase ($\bar{X} = 20.15$) and control $S$s ($\bar{X} = 20.03$), $t(26) = 0.87$, $p > .15$. A comparison between the decrease ($\bar{X} = 19.08$) and control ($\bar{X} = 20.03$) groups showed a decrement in respiration amplitude for the decrease group, $t(26) = 2.25$, $p < .05$. Since these same decrease $S$s subsequently showed increments in respiration amplitude when they were asked to increase their HR in Phase 2, an analysis was performed to look at HR changes which normally accompany changes in respiration amplitude.

The analysis was performed by looking at changes in HR during spontaneous changes in respiration which were unaccompanied by a tone. For example, 10

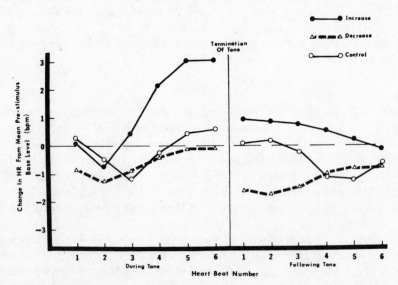

FIG. 2. Changes in HR across the 6 heart beats during and following the tone during Phase 1 of Experiment II.

spontaneous increases in respiration amplitude were looked for in the records of
Ss who were told to increase their HR. The HR for the 6 beats before and during
these increases in respiration were recorded. Heart rate means were then calculated from the 10 intervals. Difference scores were obtained by subtracting the
mean of the 6 HRs preceding the respiration increase from the 6 HRs during the
increase in respiration. A similar procedure was performed for the decrease Ss
except that decreases in respiration amplitude were recorded with the corresponding HR changes for the 10 intervals.

The HR difference scores from the increase and decrease respiration change
groups were then compared with the HR difference scores occurring during the
tone in the replication study. Thus, if the HR changes in the replication were
due to changes in respiration amplitude rather than to the tone (instructional
sets), then the HR patterns to the tone and to the respiration changes should be
similar. The 6 HR scores during the tone and the 6 scores during the "no tone"
intervals for each S were included in a $2 \times 2 \times 6$ Winer Type I design where
the first variable was instructional sets, the second variable was the presence or
absence of the tone, and the third variable was the 6 HR difference scores. Group
means from the analysis are illustrated in Figure 3, where the HR configurations
across heart beat number for the tone and no tone intervals are markedly and
significantly different, $F(5,130) = 5.20$, $p < .01$. The increase-no tone group
showed higher HRs than the increase-tone group at the 3rd heart beat, $t(6) =$
13.9, $p < .01$, and the increase-tone group had higher HRs than the increase-no
tone group at the 5th heart beat, $t(6) = 20.46$, $p < .01$. The decrease-tone
group showed higher HRs than the decrease-no tone group at the 1st, $t(6) =$
17.27, $p < .01$, and at the 6th heart beat, $t(6) = 7.23$, $p < .01$. Thus, the different HR configurations between the tone and no tone conditions suggest that HR

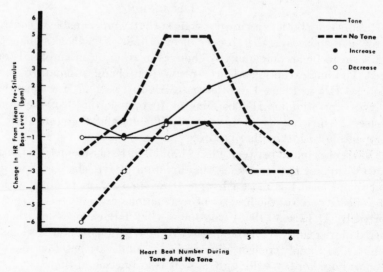

FIG. 3. Changes in HR during the tone and no tone conditions

changes during the replication were due to the effects of the instructional set rather than to changes in respiration amplitude.

*Phase 1. Skin Resistance.* Skin resistance level and the number of GSRs were scored and analyzed in the same way as the first study. No significant differences were found for either measure.

*Phase 2.* This phase investigated changes in HR due to giving instructional sets which were opposite to the instructions given in Phase 1. Thus, the increase group in Phase 1 was given decrease instructions in Phase 2, and in Phase 2 is called the decrease group, while the decrease group in Phase 1 was given increase instructions in Phase 2, and is called the increase group. Scoring and analysis of HR, respiration, and GSR data was the same as performed in Phase 1.

*Phase 2. Heart Rate.* The main effect of instructional set was not significant, $F(2,39) = 2.11$, $p > .25$. Since the instructional variable was significant during Phase 1, one can infer that the order in which Ss receive instructional sets does influence the divergence of HRs for instructional groups. In other words, Ss show greater HR changes in both directions for the first set of instructions than for the second set. The Instructions $\times$ Heart Beat Number interaction was significant, $F(10,195) = 2.60$, $p < .01$, and showed that increase Ss had higher HRs than controls for the 5th, $F(1,26) = 7.17$, $p < .05$, and 6th, $F(1,26) = 7.17$, $p < .05$, heart beat number.

*Phase 2. Respiration.* No differences in respiration amplitude were found between groups except for the increase group ($\bar{X} = 4.04$) which showed a slight but significant increase in amplitude over control Ss ($\bar{X} = 3.99$), $t(26) = 2.69$, $p < .05$. This is the same group which showed a decrease in respiration amplitude during the first phase.

*Phase 2. Skin Resistance.* No differences were found between groups for either skin resistance level or number of GSRs.

DISCUSSION

Results from both experiments suggest that Ss are capable of controlling cardiovascular responses in the absence of externalized feedback. Changes in HR did not seem to be accompanied by changes in respiration amplitude or skin resistance. The one exception was the respiration changes found for Ss who were to decrease HR in Phase 1 and increase HR in Phase 2. However, this group displayed a prestimulus HR baseline of 10 bpm lower than the other groups in Phase 1, which made the task more difficult, and therefore their behavior incomparable with the other groups.

Differences found between Phase 1 and 2 in Experiment II in the degree of HR control suggest that reversing the direction of HR changes is a difficult task, and that Phase 1 is more effective than Phase 2 in producing these changes. The effectiveness of the first set of instructions over the second set has been reported by Donelson (1966) who found that HR changes in either direction occurred more readily with the first set of instructions. Differences between phases might also simply reflect differences in motivational factors, where the Ss become bored or less willing to do well as a function of time.

The greater degree of HR control displayed by middle APQ score Ss over the high and low APQ groups may have been due to the greater accuracy of these *S*s in perceiving autonomic activity. This hypothesis is supported by data showing that high APQ scorers overestimate and low APQ scorers underestimate their autonomic activity (Mandler, Mandler, & Uviller, 1958). The APQ may also be measuring *S*'s willingness to report anxiety or anxiety reactions involving the autonomic rather than some somatic system. Subjects with middle anxiety scores have been shown to produce more adaptive autonomic responses than high or low anxious groups (Fenz & Dronsejko, 1969).

The precise way in which the instructional sets led to the changes in HR observed in these two experiments is an open question. Rather intensive but unstructured post-experimental interviewing of *S*s led to a variety of hypotheses, but various attempts to categorize the *S*s' responses did not yield significant clustering between groups who were attempting to influence their HRs in different directions.

One obvious hypothesis is that some *S*s were in some way altering their general states of arousal by thinking about exciting or frightening things while other *S*s were attempting to relax. Indeed, some *S*s did report going through this sort of procedure. This was by no means a universally used procedure. An attempt to categorize all *S*s' responses along this type of arousal dimension did not differentiate the treatment groups.

Two other closely related but more specific hypotheses concerning the changes should be considered. First, the actual presence or absence of thoughts and covert verbalization might operate to produce changes in HR. Here the emphasis is not on the actual content of the thoughts, but whether or not they occur and thereby influence cardiac functioning during the tones. Again, the presence or absence of thoughts alone did not differentiate the increase and decrease groups.

Secondly, the presence or absence of muscular activity either mediated by central processes or induced in some other manner may have led to the changes. The recent work of Obrist and his colleagues (Obrist, Webb, Sutterer, & Howard, 1970) demonstrates the striking covariation between muscular and cardiovascular responses. It is entirely possible that such a covariation exists in these studies, but few *S*s reported using this technique and little movement was observed on the polygraph record in the visual monitoring of the *S*s. However, the level of muscular activity which would accompany HR changes of the magnitude observed here are admittedly very small and might well be overlooked without more sophisticated monitoring.

It is also possible that some sort of reinforcement paradigm is operating in this situation. The nature of such reinforcement is obscure, however, as the *S*s received no external feedback or cues related to their success or failure. The *S*s may be relating perceived changes to success or failure and in a sense reinforcing themselves. Some *S*s made statements which suggested such a procedure. They cheered themselves on and essentially gave themselves "pep" talks concerning the task.

The final determination of the relationship between the above hypotheses and the changes in HR must await future studies. More detailed, structured, and perhaps forced-choice questionnaires should be employed in the questioning of Ss. Careful monitoring of EMG activity would also aid in evaluating the hypotheses. Furthermore, different Ss may be using different techniques to control HR and thus all of the above mentioned hypotheses and others may have some validity. If this turns out to be the case, then the emphases in future studies should be placed on the relationship between the magnitude of the cardiac response and the technique employed. In any case, careful studies dealing with a number of possible mechanisms should be carried out to more clearly delineate the factors operating in this paradigm.

## REFERENCES

Donelson, E. F. Discrimination and control of human heart rate. Unpublished doctoral dissertation, Cornell University, 1966.

Engel, B. T., & Chism, R. A. Operant conditioning of heart rate speeding. *Psychophysiology*, 1967, *3*, 418–426.

Fenz, W. D., & Dronsejko, K. Effects of real and imagined threat of shock on GSR and heart rate as a function of trait anxiety. *Journal of Experimental Research in Personality*, 1969, *3*, 187–196.

Hnatiow, M., & Lang, P. J. Learned stabilization of cardiac response. *Psychophysiology*, 1965, *1*, 330–336.

Lang, P. J., Sroufe, L. A., & Hastings, J. E. Effects of feedback and instructional set on the control of cardiac-rate variability. *Journal of Experimental Psychology*, 1967, *75*, 425–431.

Mandler, G., Mandler, J. M., & Uviller, E. T. Autonomic feedback: The perception of autonomic activity. *Journal of Abnormal & Social Psychology*, 1958, *56*, 367–373.

Obrist, P. A., Webb, R. A., Sutterer, J. R., & Howard, J. L. The cardiac somatic relationship: Some reformulations. *Psychophysiology*, 1970, *6*, 569–587.

Winer, B. J. *Statistical principles in experimental design.* New York: McGraw-Hill, 1962.

Wood, D. M., & Obrist, P. A. Effects of controlled and uncontrolled respiration on the conditioned heart rate response in humans. *Journal of Experimental Psychology*, 1964, *68*, 221–229.

# 18

# Operant Conditioning
# of the Human Salivary Response

## Daniel A. Frezza and James G. Holland

### ABSTRACT

To demonstrate operant conditioning of the human salivary response, stimulus control was attempted. Unstimulated parotid saliva was collected from 4 Ss under two reinforcement schedules. Continuous reinforcement (CRF) alternated at regular intervals with differential reinforcement for zero responding (DRO)— reinforcement for non-responding during a specified time period. Cumulative records revealed an increase in responding under CRF and a decrease in responding under DRO for 3 of the 4 Ss. Swallowing was recorded. The conditioned salivary response appeared not to be mediated by muscle response.

DESCRIPTORS: Operant conditioning, Salivation, Stimulus control. (D. Frezza)

Following Skinner's (1937) distinction between operant and classical conditioning, it has been assumed that the classical procedure would condition only responses mediated by the autonomic nervous system while the operant procedure would condition only responses mediated by the cerebrospinal system. But the question arises whether classical and operant conditioning result in two basically different kinds of learning or in essentially the same kind of learning (Miller, 1969; Rescorla & Solomon, 1967). The single-kind-of-learning theory would be supported if a response mediated by the autonomic nervous system could be operantly conditioned.

The idea that autonomic responses cannot be operantly conditioned has recently been subjected to a critical second look. Kimmel (1967) reported that his search of the literature of the 1920's, 1930's, and 1940's revealed "not one systematic experiment [p. 337]" to support this idea. Since the early 1960's, a number of autonomic operant conditioning experiments have been done with both humans and animals (Birk, Crider, Shapiro, & Tursky, 1966; Brown & Katz,

This article is based on a thesis submitted by the senior author to the University of Pittsburgh in partial fulfillment of the requirements for the M.S. degree. The research was supported by a fellowship from the National Institute of Dental Research and by the Learning Research and Development Center, which is supported as a research and development center by funds from the United States Office of Education, Department of Health, Education, and Welfare.

Address requests for reprints to: James G. Holland, 211 Mineral Industries Bldg., University of Pittsburgh, Pittsburgh, Pennsylvania 15213.

1967; Kimmel & Kimmel, 1963; Miller, 1969; Miller & Carmona, 1967; Rice, 1966; Van Twyver & Kimmel, 1966).

A difficult problem in experiments of this type is controlling for the possibility of inadvertently conditioning skeletal muscle mediators for the autonomic response instead of the autonomic response itself. Miller (1969) effectively controlled for this possibility by first paralyzing the animals' skeletal muscle systems with curare. He and his associates conditioned such responses as heart rate, intestinal contractions, urine formation by the kidney, and vasomotor activity; these experiments provide the strongest evidence to date that autonomically mediated responses can be operantly conditioned in animals.

Miller and Carmona (1967) operantly conditioned salivation in thirsty dogs using water as a reinforcer. Preliminary tests showed that water did not elicit salivation. One group, reinforced for salivating, increased salivation; a second group, reinforced for not salivating, decreased salivation. The authors did not control for, nor record, possible skeletal muscle mediators of salivation like chewing or swallowing, although they did state that they observed no such activity. They were unable to use the curare control since this drug stimulates a copious flow of saliva which would mask any conditioned response. Subtle, undetected, muscle movements may have mediated the conditioned increase and decrease in salivation.

Brown and Katz (1967) experimented with operant conditioning of salivation in humans and found an increase in salivation when reinforcement followed bursts of three or more drops occurring within 5-sec periods. However, a second group, reinforced during the absence of such bursts, failed to show the expected decrease in response rate. Presenting reinforcement at any time except after periods of burst responding would allow responses below burst level to be reinforced and maintained. The authors suggested that if the group had been reinforced for a specific low rate of responding instead of for absence of bursts, the rate might have decreased.

The present experiment was an attempt to gain sufficient operant control of salivation so that conditioning could be seen in individual subjects rather than in statistical analysis of the pooled results of many subjects, and to better assess the role of skeletal muscle involvement by automatically monitoring swallowing. Second, each subject served as his own control; he was exposed to reinforcement both for responding and for not responding. Third, following Brown and Katz' suggestion, the relationship between response and reinforcement was sharpened: in periods of reinforcement for salivation, reinforcement immediately followed a single drop of saliva (CRF) rather than a time period which included a burst of responses. During periods of differential reinforcement for zero responding (DRO), reinforcement occurred only when S did not salivate at all for a given number of seconds. Fourth, instead of looking simply for a general increase and decrease in salivation rate as a result of reinforcement, stimulus control was introduced to determine if salivation would increase and decrease on cue. Two different colored lights indicated when responding or non-responding would be reinforced. Appropriate response rates in the presence of the two different stimuli would indicate stimulus control.

## Method

### Apparatus

Saliva was collected from the parotid gland by a double-chambered capsule similar in design to one used first by Carlson and Crittenden (1910) and later by Lashley (1916). The clear plastic capsule measured 19.5 mm in diameter. A negative pressure of 150 mm Hg applied to the outer chamber from a vacuum system held the inner chamber of the capsule directly over Stensen's duct. The inner chamber was connected via polyethylene tubing to a sialometer modified in design from that used by Feather and Wells (1966; see also Feather, 1965). This sialometer consisted of a dropper, made from an 18 gauge hypodermic needle with a specially lengthened bevel, inserted through a rubber stopper in the neck of a 1 liter Florence flask. A negative pressure of 15 mm Hg was applied to the sialometer via another tube inserted in the stopper of the flask. Clamped to the neck of the flask ¼ inch below the end of the dropper was a photoelectric cell. The tube connecting the capsule to the dropper was filled with water to eliminate the dead space. A drop of saliva entering the capsule displaced an equal volume of water from the tube and through the dropper. The drop of water fell past the photoelectric cell and was recorded on a Gerbrands cumulative recorder and a Gerbrands event recorder.

Reinforcement was provided by a counter placed within view of the subject. S was told he would receive, in addition to his base pay, one cent for every point the counter recorded. During CRF intervals the counter advanced with every drop recorded by the photoelectric cell. During DRO periods the counter advanced when a time period elapsed A response recorded by the photoelectric cell would reset the timer and prevent reinforcement. Attached to the counter were the two colored lights that were the discriminative stimuli for the two schedules of reinforcement.

A microswitch attached to a Thomas neck brace and adjusted to contact S's neck, recorded swallowing movements. With each swallow the cartilage is raised; this movement depressed the microswitch which was wired to a Gerbrands event recorder. From the record it was possible to determine if S was swallowing on the prescribed schedule. The neck brace also helped keep S's head still. A sign reading "swallow" was located in front of S. A perforated tape timer controlled it. It would light once during each CRF interval and not at all during DRO intervals.

White noise masking sound was delivered via headphones.

### Procedure

Subjects were 4 male university students. They were told that the study concerned salivation but were given no further information. After S was seated, the left Stensen's duct was located visually, the surrounding mucosa dried with gauze, and the capsule placed over the duct. S was instructed to avoid making sudden or large movements, also to swallow only when the sign was lit.

During the first two experimental sessions no stimuli were presented. S's response rate during these sessions was taken to be his base rate of salivation.

Beginning with the third session, the counter was placed in view and *S* was reinforced for every response emitted to determine whether reinforcement would increase the rate above base level. When *S* reached a moderately high and constant level of responding, the discrimination task was introduced. Each discrimination session began with about 10 min of CRF to determine whether there was a gross drop in response in comparison with the rate in the preceding session, as sometimes happened. If the response rate was satisfactory, periods of reinforcement for salivation (indicated by a red light) alternated with periods of reinforcement for not salivating (indicated by a green light). If the rate was not satisfactory, the discrimination task was postponed.

The DRO interval was set by *E* to last 2½ min. The exact length, however, depended upon an appropriate non-response from *S*; the change from DRO to CRF occurred only after a period of no salivation for 10 sec. This prevented an inappropriate response at the very end of the DRO interval from being accidently reinforced by its proximity to the first reinforced response of the new CRF interval.

Extinction sessions began when discrimination was achieved, i.e., when *S* responded at a low rate to the DRO stimulus and at a higher rate to the CRF stimulus. During the first extinction sessions the stimulus lights continued to alternate but reinforcement was not given at any time. For the last two sessions the lights and counter were not present.

## Results

### Conditioning

The data are the cumulative records of drops of saliva secreted by each *S*. Three of the 4 *S*s showed conditioning and stimulus discrimination. For subject T.B., the base level of responding was low and *S* was slow to reach a consistent, moderately high rate of responding to CRF. The DRO stimulus was first presented in session 14. Discrimination first occurred at point *a* in session 15 and continued to the end of the session (Fig. 1). There was discrimination at the beginning and end of sessions 18 and 20. Throughout session 21 discrimination was clear and consistent. Extinction with stimuli began in session 23. The overall rate in sessions 23 and 24 returned to base level and discrimination disappeared. An extinction session without stimuli was not run since the rate had already returned to base level.

Subject T.C. was the quickest to condition. By the end of session 7 there were two consecutive DRO intervals when response rate was lower than surrounding CRF rates. By session 9 there was consistent discrimination; the DRO rate was lower than base level while the CRF rate remained at base level. Extinction with stimuli present began in the second half of session 16. Discrimination disappeared early in session 17; the rate during CRF was lower than usual and the rate during DRO began to increase. Session 19 was extinction without stimuli. The response rate was regular and lower than base level.

For subject M.C., presentation of DRO began in session 10 but discrimination did not appear regularly until session 16; the response rate during DRO was

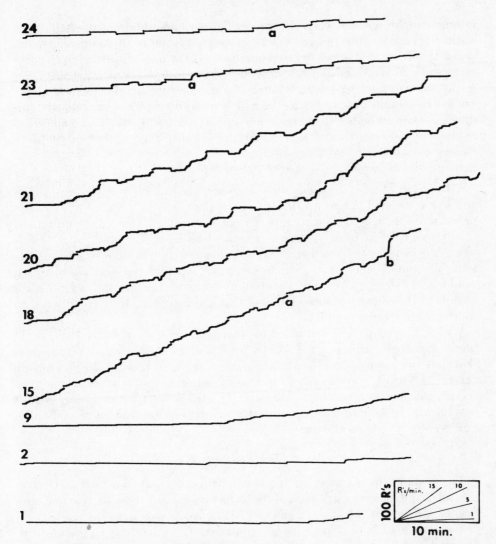

Fig. 1. Cumulative records for $S$, T.B., for acquisition of a CRF-DRO schedule. 1 and 2 are base levels. 23 and 24 are extinction with the discriminative stimuli. The pen deflected upward to indicate DRO intervals. (The bursts of response in session 15 at point $b$ and in sessions 23 and 24 at points $a$ are artifacts caused by coughing.)

consistently lower than in previous sessions. In session 17, the response rate to the two stimuli became clearly different as the rate during CRF increased. Extinction with stimuli began in session 20. Discrimination persisted in session 22 (except in the middle) and occurred occasionally in sessions 23 and 24. The response rate in these two sessions was less regular than in previous sessions. In the final session (25), extinction without stimuli, the response rate was moderately high and regular.

The fourth subject, D.G., did not condition. His base rate was extremely low; no more than 5 or 6 drops of saliva occurred during the 30 min. This low rate alternated with sessions when the rate was rather high (30 drops per half hour). Large fluctuations in rate from day to day were typical of this subject. The increase in rate seemed unrelated to reinforcement. During extinction the response rate remained high and did not decrease to the base level as expected. (This might indicate false base-level readings except for the fact that several of the reinforced sessions were as low as the base-level sessions.) There was no stimulus discrimination. Whether the overall rate was high or low, there was no difference in the response rates to the two stimulus conditions.

### Muscle Response

T.B. began using a conscious skeletal muscle control early in the experiment and was instructed not to continue it. Thereafter, he swallowed only when signalled to do so. His swallowing rate did not increase with his salivation rate.

M.C. also began using a muscular control he later described as a "stifled yawn" to increase the number of reinforcements. He was allowed to continue using this muscle control in order to determine whether its effect on salivation would be consistent. Comparison of the records of the muscle activity with records of the salivary response showed that the muscle activity conditioned as well as the glandular activity.

With T.C. the microswitch failed to record any movement although it would function properly when tested at the beginning of each session. When questioned at the completion of the experiment, *S* reported using a skeletal muscle control, a sucking movement, to increase the number of reinforcements even though routinely instructed at the start of each session to avoid any mouth movements. In spite of this muscle activity *S* did not increase his response rate significantly above his already high base level.

### DISCUSSION

The results demonstrated that an operant procedure could establish stimulus control of the salivary response and that a decrease (below base level in one case, below CRF rate in two cases) could be conditioned as well as an increase.

The microswitch proved to be an unsatisfactory method for recording swallows; with subject T.C., it consistently failed to record even though it functioned properly at the beginning of each session. And it was limited in the kinds of movements it could detect. For example, it could not detect sucking or clenching of the jaws. Three of the *S*s consciously began using skeletal muscle controls even though instructed not to before each session. Obviously, more extensive and sophisticated checks on movements of the muscles of the jaw and floor of the mouth must be used.

While skeletal muscle activity appears to increase salivation rate (Kerr, 1961; Lashley, 1916; Winsor, 1930), it is doubtful that it can decrease salivation. Thus, a decrease during DRO is strong evidence for autonomic conditioning free from skeletal muscle mediation. Whether a conditioned increase can be established without concomitant muscle activity is less clear but T.B. seemed to achieve it. These results provide qualified support for the possibility of operant conditioning of salivation without muscular mediation and for the theory that there is one kind of learning.

More conclusive evidence of salivary conditioning free from skeletal muscle control could probably be obtained by reinforcing salivation only in the absence of a muscle response as Rice (1966) did in his experiment with the GSR. This would automatically discourage use of muscle controls.

## REFERENCES

Birk, L., Crider, A., Shapiro, D., & Tursky, B. Operant electrodermal conditioning under partial curarization. *Journal of Comparative & Physiological Psychology*, 1966, *62*, 165–166.

Brown, C. C., & Katz, R. A. Operant salivary conditioning in man. *Psychophysiology*, 1967, *4*, 156–160.

Carlson, A. J., & Crittenden, A. L. The relation of ptyalin concentration to the diet and to the rate of secretion of the saliva. *American Journal of Physiology*, 1910, *26*, 169–173.

Feather, B. W. An improved sialometer. *Psychophysiology*, 1965, *1*, 299–303.

Feather, B. W., & Wells, D. T. Effects of concurrent motor activity on the unconditioned salivary reflex. *Psychophysiology*, 1966, *2*, 338–343.

Kerr, A. C. *The physiological regulation of salivary secretion in man.* New York: Pergamon Press, 1961.

Kimmel, E., & Kimmel, H. D. A replication of operant conditioning of the GSR. *Journal of Experimental Psychology*, 1963, *65*, 212–213.

Kimmel, H. D. Instrumental conditioning of autonomically mediated behavior. *Psychological Bulletin*, 1967, *67*, 337–345.

Lashley, K. S. Reflex secretion of the human parotid gland. *Journal of Experimental Psychology*, 1916, *1*, 461–493.

Miller, N. E. Learning of visceral and glandular responses. *Science*, 1969, *163*, 434–445.

Miller, N. E., & Carmona, A. Modification of a visceral response, salivation in thirsty dogs, by instrumental training with water reward. *Journal of Comparative & Physiological Psychology*, 1967, *63*, 1–6.

Rescorla, R. A., & Solomon, R. L. Two-process learning theory: Relationships between Pavlovian conditioning and instrumental learning. *Psychological Review*, 1967, *74*, 151–182.

Rice, D. G. Operant conditioning and associated electromyogram responses. *Journal of Experimental Psychology*, 1966, *71*, 908–912.

Skinner, B. F. Two types of conditioned reflex: A reply to Konorski and Miller. *Journal of General Psychology*, 1937, *16*, 272–279.

Van Twyver, H. B., & Kimmel, H. D. Operant conditioning of the GSR with concomitant measurement of two somatic variables. *Journal of Experimental Psychology*, 1966, *72*, 841–846.

Winsor, A. L. Factors which indirectly affect parotid secretion. *Journal of Experimental Psychology*, 1930, *13*, 423–437.

# VI

AUTONOMIC RESPONSES: ANIMAL

# Learning of Cardiovascular Responses: A Review and a Description of Physiological and Biochemical Consequences

# 19

### Leo V. DiCara

## INTRODUCTION

Previous work in the Soviet Union, summarized by Bykov,[5] has shown the extent to which visceral and glandular responses under the control of the autonomic nervous system can be modified by classical conditioning. The strong traditional belief has been that these responses are not subject to the instrumental learning that is possible for skeletal muscles under the control of the somatic nervous system. The question whether visceral and glandular responses can be instrumentally conditioned has fundamental theoretical significance for the nature and neurophysiological basis of learning as well as practical significanse for psychosomatic medicine. If visceral and glandular responses can be modified only by classical conditioning, they can be reinforced only by the unconditioned stimuli that elicit responses similar to those to be learned, but if they are subject to instrumental learning, they can be reinforced by any reward. This would allow vastly more flexible possibility for the learning and maintenance of particular psychophysiologic states.

Until recently, the experimental evidence on instrumental learning of visceral responses has been limited to exploratory or unpublished studies and vague references to the Russian literature. Recently, reports of both success and failure have appeared. These experiments are summarized and reviewed by Kimmel[32] and Katkin and Murray.[31]

A major problem encountered in research on the instrumental modification of visceral responses is that the majority of such responses are altered by voluntary responses, such as tensing of specific muscles or changing the rate or pattern of breathing. One way to circumvent this problem, in animals at least, is to abolish skeletal activity by curarelike drugs such as $d$-tubocurarine; these interfere pharmacologically with the transmission of the nerve impulse to the skeletal muscle but do not affect the neural control of autonomically mediated responses.

*This paper was presented at a meeting of the Section of Psychology on October 19, 1970.

†Personal research reported here and the preparation of this paper were supported by U.S. Public Health Service Grants MH 19172, MH 13189, and GM 34,110 and by Grant 69-797 from the American Heart Association.

††Present address: Department of Psychiatry, University of Michigan, Ann Arbor, Mich.

Curarized subjects cannot breathe and must be maintained on artificial respiration, and, because they cannot eat or drink, the possibilities for rewarding them in a training situation are somewhat limited. As is well known, however, training of instrumental skeletal responses can be accomplished either by using direct electrical stimulation of rewarding areas of the hypothalamus or by allowing escape from and/or avoidance of mildly noxious electric shock. Recent experiments in which these techniques have been used with curarized animals have shown that either increases or decreases can be produced by instrumental procedures in visceral responses such as heart rate,[29, 37, 52, 54] intestinal motility,[16, 36] blood pressure,[10] vasomotor responses,[7, 9] urine formation,[38] and contractions of the uterus.[40] Several investigators have reported training cardiovascular responses in noncurarized rabbits,[24] squirrel monkeys,[1, 27] and rhesus monkeys,[21, 42] and in noncurarized human subjects.[2-4, 17, 18, 22, 25, 29, 33, 47-50, 53]

Previous work has shown that visceral learning can be quite specific. In an early experiment, Miller and Banuazizi[36] showed that curarized rats rewarded for either increases or decreases in heart rate learned to change their heart rates in the rewarded direction but did not learn any change in intestinal contraction. That this was not due to any inability of the intestinal contractions to change was shown by the fact that rats rewarded for either increasing or decreasing their intestinal contractions learned the appropriate change without altering their heart rates. The results of this experiment indicated that visceral learning in rats is not mediated by a generalized reaction, such as a shift in overall level of parasympathetic or sympathetic arousal.

In another experiment, Miller and I showed that rewarding increases in the rate of urine formation could produce increases in curarized rats, while rewarding decreases could produce decreases.[38] This learning was relatively specific: The changes in urine formation were not correlated with changes in either heart rate, blood pressure, or peripheral vasomotor responses. Tests with $^3$H-p-aminohippuric acid and $^{14}$C-inulin showed that the increased rate of urine formation was accompanied, presumably produced, by an increased rate of renal blood flow. Since this change in renal blood flow was not accompanied by changes in blood pressure, heart rate, or peripheral vasomotor responses, it must have been produced by vasomotor responses specific to the kidney.

The specificity of cardiovascular learning is important for a number of reasons. For example, it is obvious that highly specific learned changes in the blood supply of internal organs can affect their function, as illustrated by the rate of urine formation. It is possible that such changes can produce psychosomatic symptoms. It is equally possible that such learning can produce therapeutic effects in abnormal organs. Since learned changes in the blood supply of the heart would be especially significant, we plan to investigate the possibilities of using learning to modify coronary circulation.

The striking degree of specificity to which a visceral response can be trained is shown by the results of a recent experiment in which opposite vasomotor responses were learned in the two ears of the curarized rat.[7] Even the form of the electrocardiagram (ECG) of a curarized rat can be modified by instrumental learning. Fields has shown[19] that either learned increases or decreases in the P-R interval of the ECG can be produced independently of changes in the P-P or R-R intervals.

It has also been shown that the instrumental learning of visceral responses displays a number of the same characteristics that the instrumental learning of skeletal responses displays, such as the ability to be brought under the control of a discriminative stimulus.[8, 37] In a different experiment, we demonstrated that heart-rate learning showed another of the important properties of the instrumental learning of skeletal responses; it could be remembered.[11] Similar results have been reported by Hothersall and Brener.[30] These investigators also reported results that indicate evidence of successive improvement of heart-rate performance as a function of daily training sessions. Additional work has shown that changes in heart rate learned in the curarized state transfer to the noncurarized state[8] and that changes in heart rate[12] or blood pressure[39] can be learned in the noncurarized state, although such learning is more difficult.

## PHYSIOLOGICAL AND BIOCHEMICAL CONSEQUENCES OF CARDIOVASCULAR LEARNING

The demonstration that visceral responses are subject to instrumental learning means that it is theoretically possible that such learning can be carried far enough to create a psychosomatic disorder. Similarly, the success of techniques for training animals to change visceral responses raises the intriguing possibility that these techniques may be used to produce therapeutic changes in human patients with psychosomatic symptoms.

In view of the relevance and implication of the learned modifications of autonomic functions for psychosomatic medicine, my colleagues and I have recently undertaken a series of experiments to determine the biochemical, physiological, and behavioral consequences of the instrumental learning of cardiovascular responses. Neal E. Miller and his associates in the Department of Medicine at Cornell and New York University Medical Centers have recently initiated experiments on the therapeutic learning of responses in human patients with cardiac and gastrointestinal disorders.

The description of current research in this laboratory will be subdivided into four areas: the effects of instrumental heart-rate training on catecholamine metabolism in the heart and brain, the biasing of emotional responses to stress by cardiac training, the experimental induction of cardiovascular disorders, and possibilities for therapeutic human visceral learning.

### Instrumental Heart-Rate Learning and Catecholamine Metabolism

Catecholamines, substances such as epinephrine and norepinephrine that are synthesized in the brain and in sympathetic nerve tissues are vital in the coordination of neural and glandular activity, influencing the blood vessels, the heart, and several other organs.

It is known that the noradrenergic nerve endings in the heart synthesize norepinephrine as well as take it up from the circulating blood and that alterations in myocardial contractility produced by an increasing frequency of cardiac sympathetic nerve stimulation is accompanied by an increased synthesis and liberation of norepinephrine in the heart as well as an increase in cardiac phosphylorase activity.[28] It has also been demonstrated that catecholamine-induced augmentation of cardiac work can produce enough intraventricular pressure to compress subendocardial layers of the myocardium and produce myocardial hypoxia and associated metabolic disorders.[44]

The foregoing results suggest that it may be possible to influence catecholamine metabolism and associated cellular and metabolic events in the heart by the instrumental learning of cardiovascular responses. Such a demonstration would have important implications in view of the possible role of catecholamines in the pathogenesis of essential hypertension,[51] coronary artery disease,[23] clinical and experimental congestive heart failure,[6] and Raynaud's disease.[41]

Eric Stone and I conducted an experiment to determine if cardiac catecholamine metabolism can be influenced by instrumental heart-rate training.[14] In this experiment, separate groups of curarized rats subjected to artificial respiration were rewarded, by direct electric stimulation of the medial forebrain bundle in the hypothalamus, for either increases or decreases in heart rate. After this training, the rats were sacrificed and their hearts assayed for endogenous catecholamines. The results are shown in FIGURE 1. Rats that learned significant

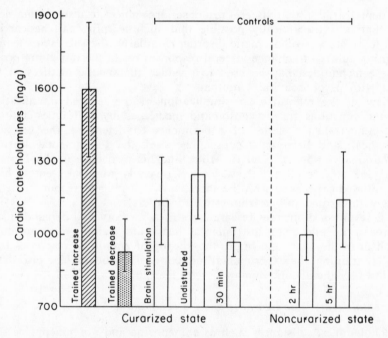

FIGURE 1. Level of endogenous cardiac catecholamines in experimental and in curarized and noncurarized control groups.[14] Standard error of measurements given. By permission of the publishers of Psychosomatic Medicine.

increases in heart rate showed significantly higher cardiac catecholamine levels than subjects trained to decrease heart rate (t = 2.26, df = 14, p < 0.05). Yoked control rats receiving brain stimulation had relatively normal endogenous catecholamine levels. There were no significant differences between either of the experimental groups and the brain-stimulation control group. Taken together with the results of other control experiments on curarized and noncurarized rats, the results indicated that it is the learning of heart-rate responses that is associated with the changes in cardiac catecholamines and not the short- or long-range effects of curarization and/or brain stimulation. Two hours before the start of curarization, each rat was administered, via an indwelling jugular catheter, 20 $\mu$C of tritiated norepinephrine. Analysis of the retention of cardiac [3]H-norepinephrine suggests that rats trained to decrease heart rate under curare were subjected to greater stress than rats trained to incease heart rate.

Some of the foregoing results fit in nicely with the results on catecholamine metabolism that are observed in congestive heart failure.[6] They also bear on a number of the details of the electrocardiographic changes and symptoms of sudden death exhibited by rats trained to decrease their heart rate and in the incidental observation I made that hyperemotional rats are more prone to develop electrocardiographic irregularities and cardiac arrhythmias and to die of sudden congestive heart failure during heart-rate training than are normal rats. Experiments are now under way to determine how long cardiac differences between the two groups persist after training and whether the heart-rate conditioning has long-range effects on the heart and on the excitability of the sympathetic nervous system.

In addition to differences in cardiac catecholamines, a significant difference was obtained in endogenous brainstem norepinephrine concentration between rats trained to increase and those trained to decrease heart rate. This part of the brain is known to contain the majority of norepinephrine-containing cell bodies, as well as the important centers for control of cardiovascular responses. Because of the importance of brain norepinephrine in emotional behavior, as well as its possible role in the development of essential hypertension, we have started experiments to determine whether changes in sympathetic excitability obtained by the prolonged training of heart rate in noncurarized rats are related to changes in the metabolism of norepinephrine and, if so, in which areas of the brain these metabolic changes are most apparent.

## Biasing Emotional Responses to Stress by Cardiac Training

One of the most prominent features of adaptive reactions is that they involve autonomic changes. The following question then arises: If an animal learns to regulate autonomic responses, will this affect subsequent adaptive reactions? In a recent experiment, Jay Weiss and I investigated how instrumentally learning to increase or decrease heart rate to avoid and/or escape electric shock would affect subsequent acquisition of one type of adaptive reaction, a skeletal avoidance response.[15] Rats were initially trained to increase or decrease their heart rates under curare, then tested in the free-moving state for transfer of heart-rate learning, and finally trained in a modified one-way skeletal avoidance situation.

The results are presented in FIGURE 2. It can be seen that large, significant differences in avoidance learning were obtained between heart-rate condition groups. Slow heart-rate learners acquired the skeletal avoidance rapidly, while fast subjects generally failed to learn even to escape. A striking aspect of the skeletal avoidance learning was the rats' reaction to shock. Fast heart-rate subjects were extremely reactive to the shock, generally jumping into the air, squealing, and turning toward their tails with each pulse of shock, while between shocks they remained immobile, frozen. This sequence of responses greatly reduced forward locomotion and prevented either escape or avoidance learning. Slow heart-rate subjects, in contrast, showed much more inhibited reactions to shock pulses, consisting of mild jerks forward, with slow walking between shocks.

These patterns of behavior suggested that fast heart-rate animals were hyper-

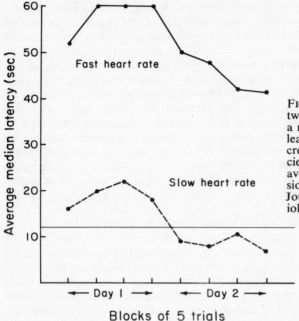

FIGURE 2. Latency to cross during two days of avoidance training in a modified shuttle in rats that had learned either to increase or to decrease their heart rates.[15] Latencies falling below 12 sec are avoidance responses. By permission of the publishers of the Journal of Comparative and Physiological Psychology.

excitable in comparison to subjects that had learned to slow their heart rates. In view of the inverse relationship between strong emotional responses and many types of avoidance learning, it seems likely that the fast heart-rate subjects were

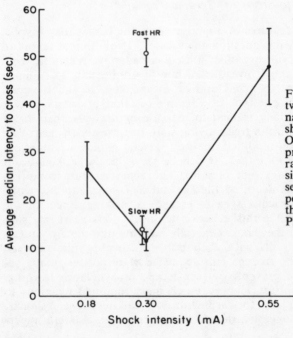

FIGURE 3. Latency to cross during two days of avoidance training in naïve rats trained at different shock intensities (closed circles). Open circles represent rats with previous training to modify heart rate (run at 0.30 ma shock intensity).[15] Latencies falling below 12 sec are avoidance responses. By permission of the publishers of the Journal of Comparative and Physiological Psychology.

too fearful to learn efficiently, whereas slow heart-rate subjects were less fearful and learned well. The inability of fast heart-rate subjects to perform the correct response is consistent with the notion that poor avoidance learning under conditions of strong fear is often produced by interfering responses. One test of this hypothesis is the following: If fast heart-rate subjects had learned the skeletal avoidance response poorly because thaey were hyperreactive or hyperemotional, then learning of the avoidance task should be optimal at a moderate fear level and become progressively poorer at higher fear levels. In order to test this hypothesis, naïve rats were given avoidance training in the same apparatus at different shock intensities. The results of the avoidance learning of these three groups of naive rats is shown by the closed circles in FIGURE 3. As can be seen, learning was best at the moderate (0.30 ma) intensity, poor at the low (0.18 ma) intensity, and very poor at the high intensity (0.55 ma). An analysis of variance showed that the three shock groups differed significantly from one another ($F = 10.1$, df $= 2/15$, $p < 0.001$), and, most importantly, that the group means fit a highly significant quadratic function ($F = 39.45$, df $= 1$, $p < 0.001$). The subjects trained at .55 ma showed hyperreactivity to the shock—jumping and turning to the unconditioned stimulus and freezing between shock pulses. This response pattern was similar to that shown by fast heart-rate subjects in the first experiment of this study. The open circles in FIGURE 3 illustrate the fact that the fast heart-rate subjects, while trained at 0.30-ma shock intensity, performed as did naïve subjects trained at 0.55 ma. Experiments are in progress to learn more about the nature of the emotional motor response pattern: How long does it last; can it be demonstrated across a variety of behaviors, such as open-field behavior; will it apply equally to performance on passive and active avoidance learning tasks; are both negative and positive reward effective in producing emotional changes; can classical conditioning procedures produce similar effects; does it affect the animal's subsequent reactions to stress, such as proneness to stomach lesions under the stress of retrain and/or electric shocks;[55] does it change the proneness to "sudden death" in Richter's swimming situation?[43]

## *Experimental Induction of Cardiovascular Disorders*

It has been postulated that such chronic diseases as peptic ulcer, hypertension, hyperthyroidism, ulcerative colitis, and rheumatoid arthritis result when disturbances in the activity of the automatic nervous system, especially the hypothalamus, are prolonged.[26] Despite the intriguing implications for psychosomatic medicine, relative few attempts have been made to influence cardiovascular function by means of conditioning procedures that produce prolonged sympathetic discharge, and what experiments have been conducted have produced conflicting results. Miminoshvili and colleagues[35] reported that their conditioning procedures produced neurotic behavior in their monkeys, accompanied by a fixed arterial hypertension. Similar disturbances in automatic regulation have been reported by Gantt[25] and Masserman and Pechtel.[34] More recently, Herd and associates[27] and Benson and co-workers[1] have reported that, in squirrel monkeys, mean arterial blood pressure can be made to rise or fall predictably in association with certain patterns of operant behavior. Similarly, Forsyth has reported[21] the results of experiments indicating that chronic Sidman shock-avoidance conditioning can lead to increased levels of arterial pressure in rhesus monkeys. On the other hand, in other experiments on cats[45] and rats,[46] it has not been possible to produce significant increases in arterial blood pressure by means of conditioning procedures.

This laboratory has started experiments to determine if it is possible to induce sustained disorders of heart rate or blood pressure by prolonged instrumental training of these responses. We already have some highly relevant incidental evidence. For example, during the past three years, a total of nine out of 52 rats rewarded for slowing their heart rates under curare have died suddenly during training, with only the pathology of acute passive congestion that is frequently found with terminal cardiac failure; none of 48 rats has died during training for increasing their heart rate. Was this a chance occurrence ($p < 0.02$), or can death be produced in this way, similar to Richter's results on sudden death in wild rats subjected to acute stress by immobilization or forced swimming?[43] While these data may be interpreted to mean that rewarding fast heart rate helps the rat to overcome the stress of a long experiment under curare whereas rewarding slow heart rate does not, it is clear that the deaths were not due to anoxia, because it was possible to disinhibit the extreme slowing and save the animal's life by opening the door to the experimental chamber and stroking the rat's vibrissae. Opening the door, by itself, had no effect. Furthermore, a controlled attempt to initiate similar slowing by gradually reducing respiration parameters of pressure, volume, and rate was without effect until such parameters were drastically reduced, and in such cases it was impossible to return the rat's heart rate to normal by stroking the vibrissae. The majority of surviving rats rewarded for decreases in heart rate showed disturbances in conduction and rhythm that included frequent sinoauricular block, first- and second-degree auriculoventricular block, and a variety of arrhythmias.

*Possibilities for Therapeutic Learning of Visceral Responses*

Instrumental learning techniques have proved to be highly effective in teaching animals to modify functions controlled by the autonomic nervous system. These results suggest that these techniques may be of potential value in the modification of symptoms in human disorders mediated by the autonomic nervous system. Since visceral learning can be made highly specific, success in therapeutic learning of cardiovascular responses would provide the physician with an entirely new treatment technique free from the troublesome side effects characteristic of certain drugs.

Such therapeutic learning should be worth trying on any symptom that is under neural control, that can be continuously monitored, and for which a certain direction of change is clearly advisable from a medical point of view. Engel and Melmon have reported[56] teaching four patients with cardiac arrhythmias to control them. This training, extending over from 10 to 25 sessions, resulted in significant, medically beneficial changes. More recently, Engel has succeeded in training a number of patients with ectopic beats to eliminate them. Similarly, Solomon and colleagues have observed a reduction in tachycardia during an extended period of heart-rate training,[57] the reduction being maintained for a period of a few months during which time the subject practiced daily to maintain his newly achieved rate control.

In a different but related direction, Dworkin and Miller have developed a system for the indirect measurement of blood pressure that can be used to track either slightly below systolic or slightly above diastolic blood pressure. Using this system, they have secured data of the type illustrated in FIGURE 4. In this preliminary experiment, the reward was a tone that told the subject that he had succeeded in changing his blood pressure in the desired direction. When a reduction in blood pressure was rewarded by the tone, the reduction was learned. Then, when increases were rewarded by the tone, they occurred during each of the subsequent two sessions. The subject was not told when a different direction of change was rewarded. As can be seen, the changes in blood pressure were not consistently correlated with heart rate. Nor did they appear to be accompanied by observable changes in respiration, muscular tension, or other skeletal responses. These results are highly encouraging, and work has been initiated with

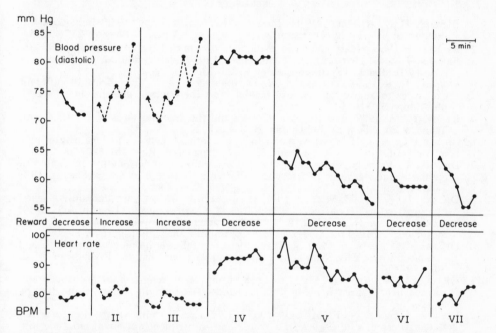

FIGURE 4. Effect of reward for changes in diastolic blood pressure on it and on heart rate.[58]

patients in the labile, premorbid stages of hypertension to see whether they can be trained to achieve reductions in blood pressure that are large and persistent enough to have therapeutic significance.

The possibility of using the instrumental learning of visceral responses for therapeutic purposes is exciting. However, it is far too early to promise any cures, and it remains for vigorous clinical and experimental research to demonstrate that any therapeutic results obtained are indeed the effect of the specific training procedures rather than being placebo effects and to test the long-term therapeutic effectiveness of such training by objective evaluation of the symptom during both pretraining and posttraining test periods.

## CONCLUSIONS

By proving that autonomic responses are subject to instrumental learning and that the learning of visceral responses has significant behavioral, physiological, and biochemical consequences, work in this new area of investigation has significance for learning theory and for the etiology and therapy of psychosomatic symptoms. These experimental results also force us to think of the behavior of the internal visceral organs in the same way that we think of the externally observable behavior of the skeletal musculature. This profound orientation opens up many new opportunities and possibilities for basic research on basic problems of emotion, motivation, and learning.

## REFERENCES

1. BENSON, H., J. A. HERD, W. H. MORSE & R. T. KELLEHER. 1969. Behavioral induction of arterial hypertension and its reversal. Amer. J. Physiol. **217**: 30–34.
2. BRENER, J. 1966. Heart rate as an avoidance response. Psychol. Rec. **16**: 329–336.
3. BRENER, J. & D. HOTHERSALL. 1966. Heart rate under conditions of augmented sensory feedback. Psychophysiology **3**: 23–28.
4. BRENER, J., R. A. KLEINMAN & W. J. GOESLING. 1969. The effects of different exposures to augmented sensory feedback on the control of heart rate. Psychophysiology **5**: 510–516.
5. BYKOV, K. M. 1957. The Cerebral Cortex and the Internal Organs. W. H. Gantt, Trans. & Ed. Chemical Publishing. New York, N.Y.
6. CHIDSEY, C. A. & E. BRAUNWALD. 1966. Sympathetic activity and neurotransmitter depletion in congestive heart failure. Pharmacol. Rev. **18**: 685–700.
7. DiCARA, L. V. & N. E. MILLER. 1968. Conditioning of vasomotor responses in curarized rats: Learning to respond differentially in the two ears. Science **159**: 1485–1486.
8. DiCARA, L. V. & N. E. MILLER. 1968. Changes in heart rate instrumentally learned by curarized rats as avoidance responses. J. Comp. Physiol. Psychol. **65**: 8–12.
9. DiCARA, L. V. & N. E. MILLER. 1968. Instrumental learning of peripheral vasomotor responses in the curarized rat. Commun. Behav. Biol. Part A, **1**: 209–212.
10. DiCARA, L. V. & N. E. MILLER. 1968. Instrumental conditioning of systolic blood pressure in rats: Dissociation of cardiac and vascular changes. Psychosom. Med. **30**: 489–494.
11. DiCARA, L. V. & N. E. MILLER. 1968. Long term retention of instrumentally learned heart-rate changes in the curarized rat. Commun. Behav. Biol. Part A, **2**: 19–23.
12. DiCARA, L. V. & N. E. MILLER. 1969. Heart-rate learning in the noncurarized state, transfer to the curarized state, and subsequent retraining in the noncurarized state. Physiol. Behav. **4**: 452–456.
13. DiCARA, L. V. & N. E. MILLER. 1969. Transfer of conditioned heart-rate changes from curarized to noncurarized state: Implications for a mediational hypothesis. J. Comp. Physiol. Psychol. **68**: 159–162.
14. DiCARA, L. V. & E. A. STONE. 1970. The effect of instrumental heart-rate training on rat cardiac and brain catecholamines Psychosom. Med. **32**: 359–368.
15. DiCARA, L. V. & J. M. WEISS. 1969. Effect of instrumental heart-rate learning under curare on subsequent noncurarized avoidance learning. J. Comp. Physiol. Psychol. **69**: 368–374.
16. DiCARA, L. V., J. BRAUN & B. PAPPAS. 1970. Classical conditioning and instrumental learning of cardiac and gastrointestinal responses following removal of neocortex in rats. J. Comp. Physiol. Psychol. **76**: 208–216.
17. ENGEL, B. T. & R. A. CHISM. 1967. Operant conditioning of heart rate speeding. Psychophysiology **3**: 418–426.
18. ENGEL, B. T. & S. P. HANSEN. 1966. Operant conditioning of heart rate slowing. Psychophysiology **3**: 162–187.
19. FIELDS, C. 1970. Instrumental conditioning of the rat cardiac control systems. Proc. Nat. Acad. Sci. U.S.A. **65**: 293–299.
20. FORSYTH, R. P. 1968. Blood pressure and avoidance conditioning. Psychosom. Med. **30**: 125–135.

21. FORSYTH, R. P. 1969. Blood pressure responses to long term avoidance schedules in the restrained rhesus monkey. Psychosom. Med. 31: 300–309.
22. FRAZIER, T. W. 1966. Avoidance conditioning of heart rate in humans. Psychophysiology 3: 188–202.
23. FRIEDMAN, M., S. M. ST. GEORGE, S. O. BYERS & R. H. ROSENMAN. 1959. Excretion of epinephrine, norepinephrine and other hormones in men exhibiting behavior patterns associated with coronary artery disease. Circulation 20: 689–703.
24. FROMER, R. 1963. Conditioned vasomotor responses in the rabbit. J. Comp. Physiol. 56: 1050–1055.
25. GANTT, W. H. 1953. Principles of nervous breakdown, schizokinesis and autokinesis Ann. N.Y. Acad. Sci. 56: 143–181.
26. GELLHORN, E. & G. N. LOOFBOURROW. 1963. Emotions and Emotional Disorders. Harper and Row, Hoeber Medical Division. New York, N.Y.
27. HERD, J. A., W. H. MORSE, R. T. KELLEHER & L. G. JONES. 1969. Arterial hypertension in the squirrel monkey during behavioral experiments. Amer. J. Physiol. 217: 24–29.
28. HESS, M. E., J. SHANFELD & N. HAUGAARD. 1962. The role of the autonomic nervous system in the regulation of heart phosphorylase in the open chest rat. J. Pharmacol. Exp. Therap. 135: 191–196.
29. HNATIOW, M. & P. J. LANG. 1965. Learned stabilization of cardiac rate. Psychophysiology 1: 330–336.
30. HOTHERSALL, D. & J. BRENER. 1969. Operant conditioning of changes in heart rate in curarized rats. J. Comp. Physiol. Psychol. 68: 338–342.
31. KATKIN, E. S. & E. N. MURRAY. 1968. Instrumental conditioning of autonomically mediated behavior. Theoretical and methodological issues. Psychol. Bull. 70: 52–68.
32. KIMMEL, H. D. 1967. Instrumental conditioning of automatically mediated behavior. Psychol. Bull. 67: 337–345.
33. LEVENE, H. I., B. T. ENGEL & J. A. PEARSON. 1968. Differential operant conditioning of heart rate. Psychosom. Med. 30: 837–845.
34. MASSERMAN, J. H. & C. PECHTEL. 1953. Neuroses in monkeys: A preliminary report of experimental observations. Ann. N.Y. Acad. Sci. 56: 253–256.
35. MIMINOSHVILI, D. I., G. O. MAGAKIAN & G. IA. KOKAIA. 1960. Attempts to obtain a model of hypertension and coronary insufficiency in monkeys. *In* Problems of Medicine and Biology in Experiments on Monkeys. I. A. Utkin, Ed.: 103–121. Pergamon Press. New York, N.Y.
36. MILLER, N. E. & A. BANUAZIZI. 1968. Instrumental learning by curarized rats of a specific visceral response, intestinal or cardiac. J. Comp. Physiol. Psychol. 65: 1–7.
37. MILLER, N. E. & L. V. DiCARA. 1967. Instrumental learning of heart rate changes in curarized rats: Shaping, and specificity to discriminative stimulus. J. Comp. Physiol. Psychol. 63: 12–19.
38. MILLER, N. E. & L. V. DiCARA. 1968. Instrumental learning of urine formation in curarized rats; changes in renal blood flow. Amer. J. Physiol. 215: 677–683.
39. PAPPAS, B. A., L. V. DiCARA & N. E. MILLER. 1970. Learning of blood pressure responses in the noncurarized rat: Transfer to the curarized state. Physiol. Behav. 5: 722–725.
40. PAPPAS, B. A., L. V. DiCARA & N. E. MILLER. Instrumental learning of uterine contraction and relaxation in curarized rats. (In preparation).
41. PEACOCK, J. 1959. Peripheral venous blood concentrations of epinephrine and norepinephrine in primary Raynaud's disease. Circulation Res. 7: 821–835.
42. PLUMLEE, L. A. 1969. Operant conditioning of increase in blood pressure. Psychophysiology 6: 283–307.
43. RICHTER, C. 1957. On the phenomenon of sudden death in animals and men. Psychosom. Med. 19: 191–198.
44. SABISTON, B. C. & D. E. GREGG. 1957. Effect of cardiac contraction on coronary blood flow .Circulation 15: 14–28.
45. SHAPIRO, A. P. & P. HORN. 1955. Blood pressure, plasma pepsinogen, and behavior in cats subjected to experimental production of anxiety. J. Nerv. Ment. Dis. 122: 222–231.

46. SHAPIRO, A. P. & J. MELHADO. 1958. Observations on blood pressure and other physiologic and biochemical mechanisms in rats with behavioral disturbances. Psychosom. Med. **20**: 303–312.
47. SHAPIRO, D., B. TURSKY & G. E. SCHWARTZ. 1970. Differentiation of heart rate and systolic blood pressure in man by operant conditioning. Psychosom. Med. **32**: 417–423.
48. SHAPIRO, D. B. TURSKY, E. GERSHON & N. STERN. 1969. Effects of feedback and reinforcement on the control of human systolic blood pressure. Science **163**: 588–589.
49. SHEARN, D. W. 1962. Operant conditioning of heart rate .Science **137**: 530–531.
50. SHMAVONIAN, B. M. 1959. Methodological study of vasomotor conditioning in human subjects. J. Comp. Physiol. Psychol. **52**: 315–321.
51. SJOERDSMA, A. 1960. Relationship between alterations in amine metabolism and blood pressure in hypertension. Chemical and hormonal factors. Circulation Res. **9**: 734.
52. SLAUGHTER, J. S., W. W. HAHN & P. RINALDI. 1970. Instrumental conditioning of heart rate in the curarized rat with varied amounts of pretraining. J. Comp. Physiol. Psychol. **72**: 356–359.
53. SNYDER, C. W. & M. E. NOBLE. 1968. Operant conditioning of vasoconstriction. J. Exp. Psychol. **77**: 263–268.
54. TROWILL, J. A. 1967. Instrumental conditioning of the heart rate in the curarized rat. J. Comp. Physiol. Psychol. **63**: 7–11.
55. WEISS, J. M. 1968. Effects of coping responses on stress. J. Comp. Physiol. Psychol. **65**: 251–260.
56. ENGEL, B. T. & K. L. MELMON. Personal Communication.
57. SOLOMON, H., J. M. WEISS & N. E. MILLER. Unpublished observations.
58. DWORKIN, B. & N. E. MILLER. Unpublished data.

# Instrumental Conditioning 20
## of Blood Pressure Elevations in the Baboon

Alan H. Harris, Jack D. Findley,
and Joseph V. Brady

**Abstract**—Two adult male baboons were surgically prepared with arterial catheters which provided a continuous measure of blood pressure and heart rate. Environmental consequences (food and electric shock) were made contingent upon prespecified increases in diastolic blood pressure levels. Continued exposure to these contingencies resulted in substantial increases in both diastolic and systolic pressures. The results demonstrated that blood pressure changes are highly susceptible to both operant "shaping" and stimulus control procedures and extend the range of instrumental conditioning effects upon the cardiovascular system.

THE RESULTS of several recent experimental studies have clearly established that both heart rate (Engel and Chism, 1967; Engel and Hansen, 1966; Miller and Di Cara, 1967; Engel and Melmon, 1968) and blood pressure (Di Cara and Miller, 1968; Plumlee, 1969; Benson, *et al.*, 1969), among a wide range of other visceral and glandular responses (Miller, 1969), can be modified by instrumental conditioning procedures involving contingent environmental consequences. For the most part, the reported changes have been limited in both magnitude and duration, and numerous theoretical and methodological questions have been raised concerning the role of "voluntary mediators" (*e.g.*, respiratory or skeletal responses) in the development and maintenance of such operant autonomic conditioning effects (Katkin and Murray, 1968).

The present report describes an extension of such instrumental autonomic conditioning procedures with the dog-faced baboon in a continuously programmed experimental environment. Specifically,

* This work was supported by National Heart and Lung Inst. Grant HE-06945, U. S. Army Medical Research and Development Command, DADA-17-68-C8133, and San Diego State College Contract N-00014-70-C-0350.

the effects of food reward and shock avoidance programmed as environmental consequences contingent upon elevations in diastolic blood pressure have been studied in relationship to changes in both heart rate and blood pressure.

## Methods and Materials

### Subjects and Apparatus

Two male dog-faced baboons, weighing approximately 25 lbs at the start of the experiment, were restrained in specially designed primate chairs (Findley, Robinson and Gilliam, 1971), and housed in sound-resistant wooden chambers ($3' \times 4' \times 5'$). One of the animals (Baboon One) was experimentally naive, while the other (Baboon Two) had been previously trained to obtain food and avoid shock by lever pulling.

Each baboon was surgically implanted with a polyvinyl catheter employing a modification of the techniques described by Perez-Cruet, *et al.* (1966) and Werdegar, *et al.* (1964). Approach to the abdominal aorta was via the left femoral artery, with the beveled tip of the catheter passed to a position just above the bifurcation of the common iliac arteries. The distal end of the catheter was tunneled under the skin, up the leg, around the side just below the waist, and up the body to a point of exit just below the shoulders. Extending beyond the skin, the catheter was fitted with an 18 gauge Luer stud adapter and attached through a system of valves and fittings to the transducer (Statham P23De) which was shock-mounted on the outside top of the experimental chamber. Patency of the catheter was maintained by continuous flushing of heparinized saline solution (10,000 units/liter) at a very slow rate (approximately 100 ml per 24 hours) and by a more rapid flush once per day. A series of 3-way valves and a mercury manometer provided for daily calibration of the system without dismantling the components (Findley, Brady, Robinson and Gilliam, 1971), and the output of the transducer was cabled to a polygraph recorder, Offner Type R, which provided a continuous display of the heart rate and beat-by-beat blood pressure signal. Additionally, the blood pressure and heart rate signals were averaged electronically (Swinnen, 1968) over prespecified time intervals and printed-out in the form of mean systolic and mean diastolic pressures as well as mean heart rate.

Adjustable meter relays were integrated with the automatic programming equipment to permit systematic selection and variation of criterion diastolic blood pressure levels and activation of the food-reward and shock-delivery devices. One-gram food pellets (P. J. Noyes) were delivered through a tube from an automatic feeder mounted on top of the chamber to a tray on the work panel (also containing multiple stimulus lights, push-button switches, and a Lindsley lever manipulandum) which faced the animal in the enclosure. Shock was administered through a stainless-steel band fitted around the animal's abdomen as a waist electrode with the remaining metal portions of the chair (*i.e.*, cuffs, seat, supports) serving as the grounded second electrode.

All programming of the experimental procedures and recording of both physiological and behavioral responses was accomplished automatically and remotely using a system of relays, timers, switches, and cumulative event markers.

*Experimental Procedure*

Figure 1 summarizes graphically the general procedure which established and maintained the relationship between blood pressure, on the one hand, and the contingent programming of food and shock consequences, on the other. Both animals were initially trained, using an operant "shaping" procedure, to raise and maintain diastolic pressure levels above 125 mm Hg for periods of at least 5 seconds at a time. Two feedback lights, which signalled when diastolic blood pressure was either above or below a prescribed criterion, were provided to the animals. After shaping, the animals were put in the presence of one of three added light conditions: "white," during which food could be obtained and no shocks ever occurred, "green," an intermediate condition which was followed by the "white" or "red" condition; and "red," a condition during which shocks could occur and no food was available.

All changes from "white" to "red" or from "red" to "white" were made through the intermediate "green" condition during which two contingencies obtained: (i) if diastolic blood pressure remained *below* criterion (125 mm Hg) for 90 consecutive seconds (momentary rises above criterion reset the 90 sec clock), the condition

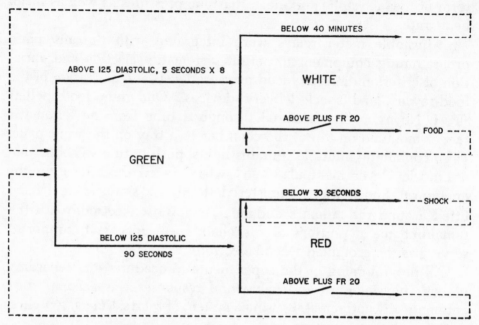

Fig. 1.   Diagram of programmed procedure for arranging behavior and blood pressure contingencies.

changed from "green" to "red"; and (ii) for every five consecutive seconds the diastolic blood pressure remained *above* criterion, a "unit" was earned. Momentary drops in diastolic blood pressure (below 125 mm Hg) reset the 5 sec unit clock. Accumulation of a prescribed number of 5 sec units changed the condition from "green" to "white."

In the "red" condition: (i) every 30 consecutive seconds below criterion produced a 9 ma, 1/4 sec electric shock delivered via the stainless-steel waistband. Momentary rises above criterion reset the 30 sec clock; (ii) twenty responses (FR 20) when the pressure was above criterion changed the condition back to "green." In the "white" condition: (i) lever responses earned food (5 pellets) on a fixed ratio (FR) 20 reinforcement schedule only when diastolic blood pressure was *above criterion* (same contingency as for escape from the shock condition in "red"); falls in pressure below criterion not only made the lever functionally inoperative, but also reset any count already accumulated toward the FR 20 requirement; (ii) when 40 minutes of accumulated "down" time (time below criterion) was reached, the condition changed back to "green." If diastolic blood pressure remained above criterion, the "white" condition (including the food schedule) remained in effect indefinitely.

Stimulus changes were programmed in such a way as to establish an environment in which elevated diastolic blood pressure was rewarded by both food delivery and safety from electric shock. Low pressure (*i.e.*, below criterion), on the other hand, resulted in frequent shocks and no food. During the course of the experiment, the duration requirement of the blood perssure response was systematically increased. For Baboon One, the number of required units was increased to 32 through the following steps: 1, 2, 4, 8, 16, 20, 24, 28, 32. For Baboon Two, the number of required units was increased to 14 through the steps of 1, 2, 4, 8, 12, 14. Increments for both subjects were made at approximately 10-day intervals.

The procedure illustrated in Figure 1 remained in effect continuously (except for 1-hour maintenance and data recording periods each day) for Baboon One and for 12 hours each day for Baboon Two. Additionally, the procedure for Baboon Two differed from that for Baboon One in the following respects: (i) the "white" condition was a fixed (independent of blood pressure) 10-minute period with no food contingencies, which served as a time out (TO) or intertrial interval (ITI) between presentations of "green"; (ii) conditioning sessions ("red"-"green"-"white") were 6 hours long two times a day (at 10 AM and 6 PM), and there were separately programmed 6-hour periods of sleep and food (FR 150 for 10 pellets). These separate food and sleep periods served, in part, as a control for the effects of lever pulling per se, and to establish baseline (sleep) pressures and heart rate levels.

## Results

Figures 2 and 3 show typical polygraph recordings for each of the two baboons under the various stimulus conditions with progressively increasing unit number requirements. Both animals produced the required elevations in diastolic blood pressure above 125 mm Hg and maintained this 50–60 mm Hg rise above resting levels for the specified intervals. Elevations of similar magnitude (60 mm Hg) were also observed in systolic blood pressure, as illustrated in Figures 2 and 3, and both baboons maintained an essentially shock-free, food-abundant environment throughout the experimental period.

Figure 2 shows a sample of four separate record strips illustrating characteristic performances under each of four progessively higher unit requirement conditions. With four 5-sec intervals of elevated diastolic pressure (125 mm Hg) required (top panel), the rise in

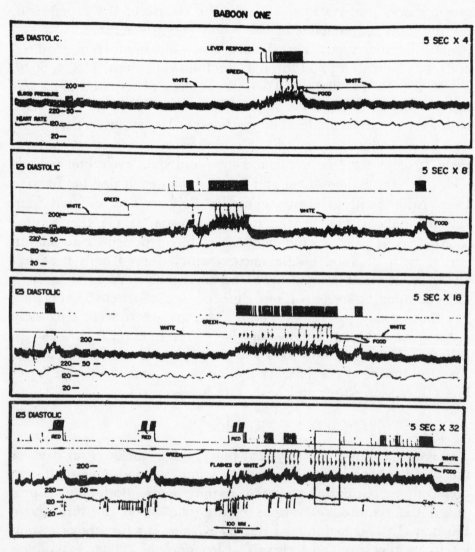

FIG. 2. Sample polygraph recordings for Baboon One showing changes in blood pressure and heart rate in response to four progressively higher contingency unit requirement conditions.

both heart rate (bottom line) and blood pressure (2nd line from bottom) can be seen to develop soon after presentation of the "green" panel light following termination of the "white" condition. Within 30 to 40 sec, the diastolic pressure rose above 125 mm Hg, remained at that level for the required four 5-sec units, and reinstated the "white" condition. Following completion of the FR 20 for food with the pressure remaining above 125 mm Hg as required, a precipitous drop in pressure accompanied by a more gradual decline in heart rate can be seen to have occurred. Similar changes are shown in the 2nd and 3rd panels of Figure 2 for the same animal with unit requirements of eight and sixteen 5-sec intervals, respectively. These two panels also show additional instances of food-reinforced performances with diastolic blood pressure levels above the required 125 mm Hg criterion. Significant variations in the strength of the performance did appear, however, when the requirement was increased to 32 5-sec units as shown in the bottom panel of Figure 2. Alternations between the "red" (shock) condition and the intermediate "green" condition can be seen to predominate in contrast to the previously observed alternation between "green" and "white" conditions. Although the animal did in fact meet the stringent unit requirement on this occasion, the performance could not be reliably maintained at this increased level. The animal thus received frequent shocks, failed to obtain enough food to meet adequate body weight requirements, and was terminated on the program at this point.

Figure 3 shows a similar series of record strips for Baboon Two. The onset of the green light can be seen to have produced a somewhat more gradual increase in pressure until the diastolic level reached 125 mm Hg. This was maintained until the unit requirement indicated for each panel (*e.g.*, "5 sec × 4") was satisfied and the "white" condition was reinstated. Heart rate increases usually accompanied at least the onset of the blood pressure rise but there were instances (*e.g.*, point marked "C" in the second panel from the top of Figure 3) when heart rate actually declined during periods of heightened blood pressure. Appearance of the "white" light, however, invariably resulted in a precipitous fall in blood pressure accompanied by more gradual heart rate decreases. And at a requirement level of fourteen 5 sec units (bottom panel, Figure 3), Baboon Two showed a deterioration in performance similar in virtually all

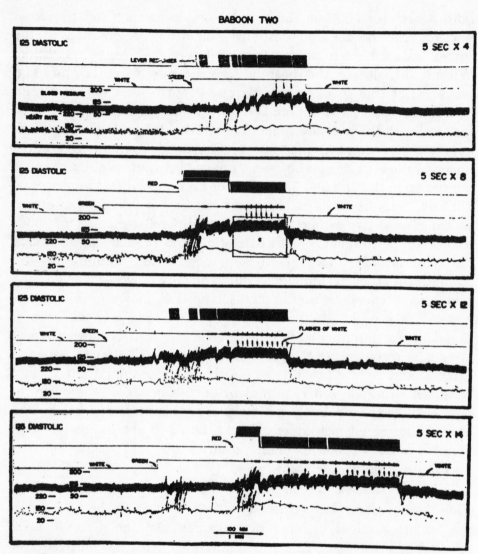

FIG. 3.    Sample polygraph recordings for Baboon Two showing changes in blood pressure and heart rate in response to four progressively higher contingency unit requirement conditions.

respects to that observed with Baboon One at a criterion level requiring thirty-two 5 sec units: the number of "red" periods increased, more frequent shocks occurred, and food intake decreased sharply.

It is perhaps worthy of note that both animals emitted relatively high rates of responding on the lever manipulandum in the presence of the green light early in the experiment even though no reinforcement contingencies were programmed. That the physical activity associated with this generalized responding was neither a necessary or sufficient condition for the recorded blood pressure changes, however, is indicated by two additional observations. One of the animals (Baboon One) showed a gradual reduction in this "superstitious" lever pulling with the result that periods of maintained pressure elevation with virtually no associated lever responding (*e.g.*, point marked "C," bottom panel, Figure 2) occurred with increasing frequency as the experiment progressed. Additionally, the second animal (Baboon Two), trained to obtain food by pulling the lever 150 times for each 10 pellets, showed relatively little change in blood pressure despite even vigorous and sustained responding during such separately programmed food periods. Sample polygraph records for Baboon Two during food and rest periods are shown in Figure 4. It is clear from these records that the change in heart rate and blood pressure associated with lever pulling cannot be solely responsible for the large magnitude cardiovascular changes shown previously.

Figure 5 summarizes for Baboons One and Two the effects of

**BABOON TWO**

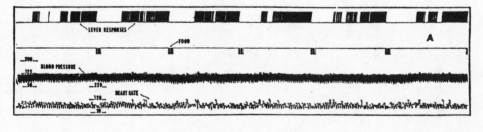

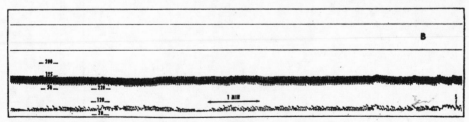

Fig. 4. Sample polygraph recordings for Baboon Two showing blood pressure and heart rate during (A) food period, and (B) rest period.

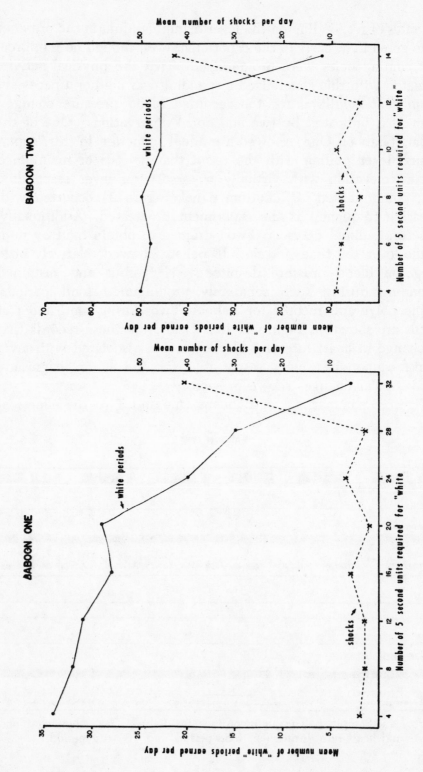

Fig. 5. Changes in the number of "white" (shock-free, food available) periods earned each day and the number of shocks received each day by Baboons One and Two as a function of the number of 5-sec contingency units required.

unit number increases upon the number of "white" (shock-free, food available) periods earned per day and upon the number of shocks received each day. As the unit number increased, Baboon One maintained a low (2–3 shocks/day) shock rate despite a gradually decreasing number of earned "white" periods. When 32 5-sec units were required to earn a "white" period, however, the performance of Baboon One deteriorated rapidly and shock frequency rose sharply. Similar results were obtained with Baboon Two, although the performance deterioration can be seen to have occurred by the time only 14 5-sec units were required to earn a "white" period with this animal.

## Discussion

The results of this experiment clearly show that substantial elevations in blood pressure can be established and maintained in baboons by an operant conditioning procedure involving food reward and shock avoidance programmed as environmental consequences contingent upon increases in diastolic pressure levels. Under these conditions, both systolic and diastolic blood pressure levels were observed to increase 50 to 60 mm Hg above resting levels and to remain elevated for intervals of 5 minutes or longer in order to produce food and/or avoid shock. Heart rate changes, on the other hand, were more variable and appeared to bear rather complex relationships to the conditioned blood pressure response. For the most part, marked elevations in heart rate accompanied at least the onset of the instrumentally conditioned blood pressure rise, but independent variations in the heart rate (*e.g.*, decelerations in heart rate during periods of heightened blood pressure; gradual heart rate decreases following precipitous drops in blood pressure, etc.) were frequently observed.

The present findings substantially extend the range of instrumental conditioning effects upon the cardiovascular system, particularly as these relate to the control of blood pressure. Although contingent increases of similar amplitude (50–60 mm Hg) have been reported in Rhesus monkeys (Plumlee, 1969) and rats have been shown to develop operant blood pressure elevations approximating 30–40 mm Hg (Di Cara and Miller, 1968), the duration of such changes appears to have been limited to periods of a few seconds. Performance deterioration did occur in the present study, however, when extended unit requirements were programmed at the diastolic blood pressure criterion level of 125 mm Hg. The difference between the unit number limit for the two animals (*i.e.*, 32 5-sec units for Baboon One, 14 5-sec units for Baboon Two) suggests that the work schedule per se may play a role in determining such treatment effects. Baboon One had to fulfill his work unit requirement every 40 minutes during a 23-hour day for a total of approximately 35 unit performances per day. Baboon Two, on the other hand, was required to perform a work unit every 10 minutes during two six-hour sessions for a daily total of 72 performance units. Significantly, this 2:1 "work ratio" between the performance schedule requirements corresponds closely to the ratio of unit number limits (*i.e.*, 32 for Baboon One to 14 for Baboon Two) attained by the two experimental subjects.

Direct observation of the two baboons participating in the present study failed to reveal any obvious or systematic changes in posture or respiration accompanying the extensive blood pressure elevations herein described. The effects of somatic mediation, however, were not the object of study in this investigation, and the present data do not permit detailed analysis of the limits of even those interacting respiratory and somatic effects which have been previously investigated (Engel and Chism, 1967; Brener and Hothersall, 1967; Brady, 1971). Indeed, the contributions of other less easily measured "cognitive" and "emotional" mediators which can be presumed to participate in the control of cardiovascular conditioning effects would seem to require at least as much experimental attention in the continuing analysis of the behavioral and physiological conditions under which such extreme cardiovacular modulations can occur.

# References

Benson, H., Herd, J. A., Morse, W. H., and Kelleher, R. T.: Behavioral inductions of arterial hypertension and its reversal. *Amer. J. Physiol.*, 217:30-34, 1949.

Brady, J. V.: Emotion revisited. *J. Psychiat. Res.*, In press, 1971.

Brener, J., and Hothersall, D.: Paced respiration and heart rate control. *Psychophysiology*, 4:1-6, 1967.

Di Cara, L. V., and Miller, N. E.: Instrumental learning of systolic blood pressure responses in curarized rats: Dissociation of cardiac and vascular changes. *Psychosom. Med.*, 5:489-494, 1968.

Engel, B. T., and Chism, R. A.: Effects of increase and decrease in breathing rate on heart rate and finger pulse volume. *Psychophysiology*, 4:83-89, 1967.

Engel, B. T., and Chism, R. A.: Operant conditioning of heart rate speeding. *Psychophysiology*, 3:418-426, 1967.

Engel, B. T., and Hansen, S. P.: Operant conditioning of heart rate slowing. *Psychophysiology*, 3:176-187, 1966.

Engel, B. T., and Melmon, K. L.: Operant conditioning of heart rate in patients with cardiac arrhythmias. *Cond. Reflex*, 3:130, 1968.

Findley, J. D., Brady, J. V., Robinson, W. W., and Gilliam, W. J.: Continuous cardiovascular monitoring in the baboon during long-term behavioral performances. *Comm. Behav. Biol.*, Part A, No. 2, 6: June, 1971.

Findley, J. D., Robinson, W. W., and Gilliam, W. J.: A restraint system for chronic study of the baboon. *J. Exper. Anal. Behav.*, 15:69-71, 1971.

Katkin, E. S., and Murray, E. N.: Instrumental conditioning of autonomically mediated behavior: Theoretical and methodological issues. *Psychol. Bull.*, 70:52-68, 1968.

Miller, N. E.: Learning of visceral and glandular responses. *Science*, 163:434-445, 1969.

Miller, N. E., and Di Cara, L.: Instrumental learning of heart rate changes in curarized rats: Shaping, and specificity to a discriminative stimulus. *J. Comp. Physiol. Psych.*, 63:12-19, 1967.

Plumlee, L. A.: Operant conditioning of increases in blood pressure. *Psychophysiology*, 6:283-290, 1969.

Perez-Cruet, J., Plumlee, L., and Newton, J. E.: Chronic basal blood pressure in unanesthetized dogs using the ring-catheter technique. *Proc. Symp. Biomed. Engr.*, 1:383-386, 1966.

Swinnen, M. E. T.: Blood pressure digitizer. *21st ACEMB*, p. 18.4, 1968.

Werdegar, D., Johnson, D. G., and Mason, J. W.: A technique for continuous measurement of arterial blood pressure in unanesthetized monkeys. *J. Appl. Physiol.*, 19:519-521, 1964.

William W. Hahn and John Slaughter

ABSTRACT

Heart rate of curarized and non-curarized rats was recorded while both groups
were exposed to classical conditioning procedures with tone as the conditional
stimulus (CS) and shock as the unconditional stimulus (UCS). The unconditional HR response of curarized animals to the tone was significantly greater than
that of the non-curarized animals, while the HR response to shock of the curarized animals was significantly less than that of the non-curarized group. Both
groups showed evidence of conditioning over 30 conditioning trials.

DESCRIPTORS: Heart rate, Autonomic conditioning, Curare. (W. W. Hahn)

Recent work on instrumental conditioning of autonomic responses has concentrated on shaping heart rate (HR) responses in the curarized rat (Trowill,
1967; DiCara & Miller, 1968; Hothersall & Brenner, 1969; Slaughter, Hahn, &
Rinaldi, 1969). Despite the apparent simplicity of the methods used, obtaining
reliable HR responses under curare is a difficult procedure (cf. Hahn, 1970) and
there are some indications from previous experiments that central nervous system (CNS) and cardiac reactivity are altered in the curarized state (Gellhorn,
1958; Black, 1967).

Earlier work from this laboratory suggested that no reliable HR response
could be obtained from the curarized rat when heat and cold stimuli were used,
even though the same stimuli evoked significant changes in HR of non-curarized
rats (Hahn, Slaughter, & Rinaldi, 1969). Nevertheless, it was observed that
simple sensory stimuli such as tone and light evoked marked responses in some
animals, and others have reported consistent HR responses to shock in curarized
dogs (Black, 1967; Church, LoLordo, Overmier, Solomon, & Turner, 1966). To
study the effects of these stimuli on HR of the curarized rat the present study
was initiated, using tone and shock in a classical conditioning format.

METHOD

*Subjects*

Subjects were 20 naive, male Sprague-Dawley rats 500–600 grams.

*Procedure*

One week prior to testing all animals were lightly anesthetized with ether and
stainless steel recording electrodes were inserted in their back according to the

This research was supported in part by NIMH Grant No. 16791.

Address requests for reprints to: William W. Hahn, Department of Psychology, University of Denver, Denver, Colorado 80210.

TABLE 1

*Heart rate difference scores: Reaction to stimuli*

| Condition | Statistic | HR Difference Scores | | C vs NC | |
|---|---|---|---|---|---|
| | | Curare | No Curare | $t$ | $p$ |
| Tone | $\bar{X}$ | 20.41 | 4.57 | 6.51 | .001 |
| | S | 9.89 | 10.10 | | |
| Shock | $\bar{X}$ | −5.22 | 76.64 | 20.82 | .001 |
| | S | 13.08 | 18.67 | | |
| Tone vs Shock | $t$ | 9.07 | 19.63 | | |
| | $p$ | .001 | .001 | | |

method of Stern and Word (1961). At this time two stainless steel shock electrodes were inserted dorsal to the thigh. Subjects (Ss) were divided into 10 pairs and one member of each pair was assigned to the control and the other to the experimental group. Experimental and control Ss were run in alternating order with equal numbers from each group being run in morning and afternoon to control for possible diurnal variations in HR.

Experimental Ss were injected with an initial dose of .2 cc of a 3.0 mg/ml solution of d-tubocurarine chloride and given additional doses of .05 cc every half hour for the duration of the training session. Ss were then placed in a small animal test chamber and artificially respirated in the manner described by Hahn (1970). Training began after an adaptation period of approximately 30 min during which time necessary adjustments were made in the respirator to maintain HR at approximately "normal" levels of 350–420 bpm and with a beat-by-beat variability of 20–40 bpm. Control Ss were injected with .2 cc saline and then placed in a plexiglass restraining cage inside the test chamber and given a 30 min adaptation period before training.

The training session consisted of 30 shock trials with predetermined intertrial intervals of 60, 90, or 120 sec, in fixed random order. At the beginning of each trial a 1000 Hz tone at approximately 75 db (CS) was turned on for 10.5 sec and followed by a .5 ma shock (UCS) delivered to the S for .5 sec. Both EKG and a beat-by-beat cardiotachograph were recorded on a Beckman-Offner Type R Dynograph.

## RESULTS

The unconditioned HR responses to tone and shock summed over all 30 trials for both groups are presented in Table 1. These data were obtained by sampling HR for each of 10 1-sec periods pre-tone, pre-shock, or post shock. To evaluate response to tone the mean HR during the last second of pre-tone was subtracted from the mean HR for the first second of tone. Although this is a relatively brief measure it does accurately reflect the initial orienting response (OR) to the stimuli used. The complete OR to tone lasts about 5 sec in both curarized and non-curarized animals and is reported in more detail in a forthcoming paper.[1]

[1] Manuscript in preparation entitled "The Effects of Curare on Orienting, Conditioned and Unconditioned Heart Rate Responses," by W. W. Hahn and P. Rinaldi.

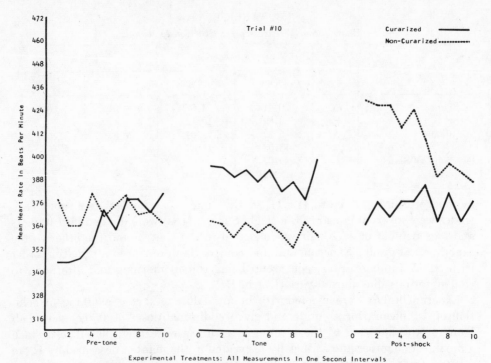

Fig. 1. Heart rate responses during conditioning, Trial 10

Reaction to shock was also evaluated by comparing the HR level during the first second post-shock with the last second of tone or pre-shock. These results are not noticeably altered if a mean of 10 sec pre-tone HR is used as the base level. It is important to evaluate responses in this manner to avoid contamination of the unconditioned response to tone by the decelerative CR which develops; and, in the shock response, the very rapid recovery which occurs after onset would mask or reduce the initial response if an average of 10 sec were used (see below, Figs. 1 and 2).

The mean HR response to tone of the curarized animals was significantly higher than their response to shock and significantly greater than the non-curarized animals' reaction to tone; but the non-curarized animals' reaction to shock was significantly higher than that of the curarized group and significantly higher than their own reaction to the tone stimulus (see Table 1). It appears that the curarized *S*s are hyper-reactive to the tone and hypo-reactive to the shock stimulus.

HR responses for both groups on trial 10 are shown in Fig. 1, and on trial 30 in Fig. 2. Both groups demonstrated an apparent conditioning effect by trial 30 which was seen as a decreasing HR response during tone. Two techniques were used to evaluate this response. The first was a difference score of the first second of tone minus the tenth second of tone; group responses were compared on this measure for the first 5 trials vs the same measure for the last 5 trials (26–30). According to this index both groups showed significant evidence of condi-

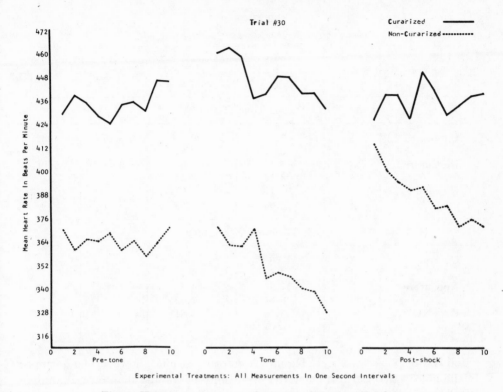

Fig. 2. Heart rate responses during conditioning, Trial 30

tioning, i.e., a greater decrease in HR during tone on the later trials than on the earlier trials (see Table 2).

Because this response measure could be influenced by the initial OR to tone onset and by habituation of this OR, a second method of analysis was used. A difference score was derived by subtracting the mean HR during the tenth second of tone from the mean pre-tone HR for each group. This measure would be less influenced by the initial reaction to tone and it also showed significant conditioning effects in both groups (see Table 2).

## DISCUSSION

The data suggest that curarized rats are hyper-reactive to onset of a tone stimulus; mean HR response for this group was $+20.4$ bpm compared to $+4.6$ bpm for the non-curarized group; yet the same animals appear to be *hypo-reactive* to the shock stimulus, yielding a mean HR response of $-5.2$ bpm compared to $+76.6$ bpm for the non-curarized group. These results suggest that curare, and/or the procedures associated with its administration, alters the "normal" HR reactivity to stimuli.

It may not be the results of curare *per se* that lead to such results but rather the effects of controlled respiration, reduced proprioceptive feedback, etc., or one might suggest that escape attempts in the non-curarized *S*s produced ele-

TABLE 2

*Heart rate difference scores: Conditioning effects*

| Condition | Statistic | HR Difference Scores | | Trials 1–5 vs Trials 26–30 | |
|---|---|---|---|---|---|
| | | Trials 1–5 | Trials 26–30 | $t$ | $p$ |
| $\Delta$ During Tone $(T_{10} - T_1)$ | | | | | |
| Curare | $\bar{X}$ | −7.3 | −30.4 | 8.19 | .002 |
| | S | 8.87 | 6.84 | | |
| No Curare | $\bar{X}$ | −7.1 | −35.5 | 9.48 | .001 |
| | S | 3.42 | 8.33 | | |
| C vs NC | $t$ | .173 | .954 | | |
| | $p$ | .05 | .05 | | |
| $\Delta$ $T_{10}$ minus $\bar{X}$ pre-tone | | | | | |
| Curare | $\bar{X}$ | 17.6 | −4.0 | 6.37 | .01 |
| | S | 7.83 | 9.15 | | |
| No Curare | $\bar{X}$ | −11.9 | −34.4 | 7.63 | .002 |
| | S | 6.81 | 7.92 | | |
| C vs NC | $t$ | 5.18 | 3.84 | | |
| | $p$ | .01 | .02 | | |

vated HR responses to shock. Results from other studies, however, lend support to the notion that cardiac reactivity itself may be altered in curarized animals. Black (1967), for example, reported a "reversal" in HR response to vagal stimulation under deep curarization in some animals and attenuation of response to sympathetic stimulation in another $S$. Black also comments on the changes in cardiac responsivity as an animal passes from light to deep curarization, noting that the parasympathetic components of the vagus nerve are readily blocked by d-tubocurarine while sympathetic components are not blocked easily and perhaps only some animals show the sympathetic block.

Gellhorn (1958) has reported reduced CNS activation to noxious stimuli with curarization. Pilot work for this study (Hahn, Slaughter, & Rinaldi, 1969) indicated that no reliable response to painful heat and cold stimuli could be obtained in curarized rats and the lowered reaction of curarized animals to shock in this study is consistent with such data. It is clear that some formulation which can account for different cardiac reactivity to certain stimuli is needed to explain the results obtained.

Although the curarized animals showed a minimal unconditioned HR response to shock, they showed a conditioned response very similar to that of the noncurarized group. This response was a HR deceleration during tone that was significantly greater on the last 5 trials than on the first 5 trials. It is interesting that an "ineffective" UCS by one criterion (the mean HR response to shock, −5.2 bpm, was not significantly different from chance probability for this group) was nevertheless an effective stimulus in that it produced a conditioned response. Although there has been some disagreement about the nature of the classically conditioned HR response, these results agree with a recent study by Hein (1969) in which a shock UCS led to a decelerative HR response in cats when succinylcholine was used to induce muscular paralysis.

In this study there were not the proper control groups for sensitization and pseudoconditioning; and it is possible that these results are due only to changing rates of habituation to the tone or to sensitization effects due to administration of shock. However, initial HR response to tone did not change significantly over trials for either group and this might be a more typical measure of habituation or sensitization effects.

There was an increase in HR over trials for the curarized animals. The total recording time under curare was over 2 hours and it is difficult to maintain steady HR in the rat over this period even when additional doses are administered regularly. The present authors, as well as others,[2] have observed an increase in resting HR of 60–100 bpm when curare is administered. However, it does not seem that this trend was a significant contributor to either conditioned or unconditioned HR responses in this group. A Law of Initial Value effect would have led to a greater likelihood of obtaining decreases to stimulation under these higher basal levels, but there was *less* of a decrease to shock over trials and no change in the response to tone. The conditioned response was evaluated as a change from both pre-tone levels and first second of tone and the decrease was significantly greater for the later trials in both cases. While this could conceivably be a result of elevated base levels it seems unlikely in view of the unconditioned responses of the curarized *S*s and the similarity of the conditioned response of the non-curarized *S*s which showed a much smaller rise in HR over trials.

## REFERENCES

Black, N. Operant conditioning of heart rate under curare. Technical Report No. 12, 1967, Department of Psychology, McMaster University, Hamilton, Ontario.

Church, R., LoLordo, V., Overmier, B., Solomon, R. L., & Turner, L. H. Cardiac responses to shock in curarized dogs: Effects of shock intensity and duration, warning signal, and prior experience with shock. *Journal of Comparative & Physiological Psychology*, 1966, *62*, 1–7.

DiCara, L. F., & Miller, N. E. Changes in heart rate instrumentally learned by curarized rats as avoidance responses. *Journal of Comparative & Physiological Psychology*, 1968, *65*, 8–12.

Gellhorn, E. The influence of curare on hypothalamic excitability and the electroencephalogram. *Electroencephalography & Clinical Neurophysiology*, 1958, *10*, 697–703.

Hahn, W. W. Apparatus and technique for work with the curarized rat. *Psychophysiology*, 1970, *7*, 283–286.

Hahn, W. W., Slaughter, J. S., & Rinaldi, P. Some methodological difficulties in obtaining heart rate in the curarized rat. Paper presented at the meeting of the Rocky Mountain Psychological Association, Albuquerque, New Mexico, 1969.

Hein, P. L. Heart rate conditioning in the cat and its relationship to other physiological responses. *Psychophysiology*, 1969, *5*, 455–464.

Hothersall, D., & Brenner, J. Operant conditioning of changes in heart rate in curarized rats. *Journal of Comparative & Physiological Psychology*, 1969, *68*, 338–342.

---

[2] J. Trowill, personal communication, September 11, 1969.

Slaughter, J. S., Hahn, W. W., & Rinaldi, P. Instrumental conditioning of heart rate in the curarized rat with varied amounts of pre-training. *Journal of Comparative & Physiological Psychology*, 1970, *72*, 356–359.

Stern, J. A., & Word, T. J. Changes in cardiac response of the albino rat as a function of electroconvulsive seizures. *Journal of Comparative & Physiological Psychology*, 1961, *54*, 389–394.

Trowill, J. Instrumental conditioning of heart rate in the curarized rat. *Journal of Comparative & Physiological Psychology*, 1967, *63*, 7–11.

# Apparatus and Technique 22

## for Work with the Curarized Rat

### William W. Hahn

**ABSTRACT**

Apparatus for respirating the curarized rat is described. Important variables in obtaining a stable curarized rat preparation are the volume and pressure of air with which the animal is respirated. Heart rate is a convenient indicator of the adequacy of respiration and a bleed valve added to the respirator allows fine volume adjustments which result in a stable, moderate level HR of 350–420 bpm and a variability of 20–40 bpm. It is also important to keep the animal at a steady depth of curarization, and maintain adequate body temperature.

DESCRIPTORS: Heart rate, Curarized rat, Respiration. (W. Hahn)

The use of neuromuscular blocking agents in psychophysiological experiments provides control over two important variables—respiration and striate muscle activity. Most previous studies that have appeared in psychological journals have used cats or dogs as experimental subjects (Black, Carlson, & Solomon, 1962; LoLordo, Overmier, Solomon, & Turner, 1966; Hein, 1969), but recently reports using the curarized rat have appeared (Miller & DiCara, 1967; Trowill, 1967; DiCara & Miller, 1968). The maintenance of a relatively normal and stable physiological state in the curarized rat is difficult to obtain and the recording of any physiological measures may be contaminated if adequate ventilation and body temperature are not maintained. It is important to establish

This work was supported in part by NIMH Grant 16791-01 and by GRS PHS Grant No. 5-S01-FR05523-03 to the Children's Asthma Research Institute and Hospital.

Address requests for reprints to: Dr. William W. Hahn, Department of Psychology, University of Denver, Denver, Colorado 80210.

techniques for study of the curarized rat in order to avoid reporting of artifactual results. The following suggestions may be helpful to investigators attempting to obtain physiological measures in the curarized rat.

While intubation is the method of choice for respirating a curarized animal, it is very difficult to achieve adequate ventilation of the rat by this method. A tracheal tube must be no larger than 2.5 mm in diameter and is difficult to insert properly as it tends to enter the esophagus. If intubation is attempted, the tube may irritate the trachea and this mechanical irritation plus increased mucus flow due to curare may lead to clogging of the tube and, of course, impaired ventilation of the animal. Recently a report of intubation of the anesthetized rat has appeared (Palacek, 1969) but one wonders if the trauma of this procedure might not have serious effects on the non-anesthetized (curarized) rat.

An alternative to intubation is the use of some kind of face mask such as that mentioned briefly by Wurtz (1966). Ideally this should be a small air-tight chamber with minimal dead space which can be affixed quickly and painlessly to the animal. The face mask which we have found most suitable is made from the suction piece of a rubber eye-dropper. One end is cut in an oval beveled shape so that it fits the contour of the rat's snout; the common joint of a "y" tube is fitted into the opposite end for attachment to the respirator, and a small rubber band is attached to the lower side of the "y" tube (see Fig. 1). When the animal begins to show the effects of a curare injection the rubber band is slipped over his upper incisors to hold the face mask against the nose; then both animal and nose-piece are taped to a small platform which has a 4 cm × 6 cm surface raised 10 mm for support of the animal's head and nose piece. A small hole has been drilled into the raised portion and the subject's upper incisors are fitted into this notch; this

prevents the animal's head from slipping away from the face mask. This surface also keeps the animal's head raised and stretched slightly forward and anchors the nose-piece in a direct line with the subject's nostrils and trachea—see Fig. 1.

It is important to avoid pinching the subject's nostrils with the nose-piece, misalignment of the nose-piece and subject, or exerting pressure on the subject's trachea. The rat has small flexible epidermal flaps over each nostril and if mechanical pressure or air pressure hits these from above they may close over the nostrils and occlude the air flow.

Pressure-volume characteristics of the respirating air flow are critical in obtaining proper respiration of the animal. Too little air will quickly lead to a hypoxic animal, slowed HR, and death, while too much air may lead to hyperoxemia, bloating of the animal,

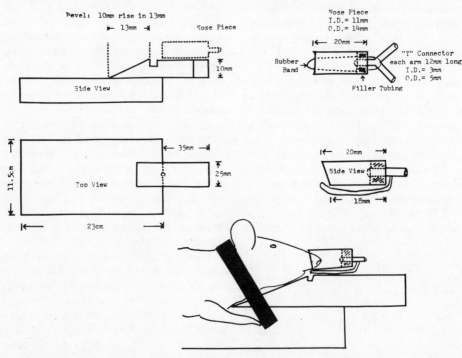

FIG. 1. Apparatus for respiration of the curarized rat

possible pneumothorax, and high, un-varying HR. Respiration rate should be maintained between 68–72 cycles/min and slight variations in rate will not have marked effects on HR. A 1:1 inspiration-expiration ratio is accept-able. Pressure readings of the respirat-ing system we have used vary from 15 to 23 mm Hg with the subject at-tached; lower pressures have been used successfully[1]. One of the most con-venient indicators of the animal's status is HR. This measure should be obtained as an index of the adequacy of respiration even if an investigator is not concerned with HR as an ex-perimental variable. We have found empirically that an animal's HR usually stabilizes between approxi-mately 350 and 420 bpm with a variability of 20–40 bpm. (Variability here refers to the maximum and minimum values read on a beat-by-beat cardiotachograph.) If the volume of air delivered to the animal is too large one observes first a decrease in variability to <10 bpm and then a steady rise in mean HR reaching a level between 440–480 bpm in 5–15 min. HR is "locked in" under these conditions and the animal will be relatively unresponsive to stimuli, a somewhat exaggerated heaving of his thorax and/or abdomen may be noted, and skin color will be a bright pink. A slight reduction in volume may lead to the opposite symptoms, greying or bluing of the skin, increased variability of HR, a few long R–R intervals of .5 to .80 seconds, and a decline in mean HR to levels below 300 bpm.

Volume of the Phipps and Bird[2] small animal respirator cannot be adjusted without stopping the ap-paratus. If this is done the animal

builds up a large oxygen debt and it is practically impossible to obtain a normal physiological condition. We have found it necessary, therefore, to add a "relief" valve to the system which permits very slight adjustments of pressure and volume without inter-rupting the respiratory cycle. The respirator is set at approximately 25% of maximum volume (range is .5 to 80 cc); opening this valve decreases volume and pressure in amounts which vary with the back-pressure exerted by the animal on the system.

It is advisable to maintain a steady depth of curarization with as little variation as possible. An initial dose of 3.0 mg/kg d-tubocurarine chloride[3] given intraperitoneally (IP) is sufficient to paralyze the animal rapidly and deeply; thereafter additional doses of .05 cc of 3 mg/ml d-tubocurarine chloride every one-half hour or an intravenous infusion of a comparable amount is adequate to maintain a 400–600 gm animal in a deeply curarized condition. Occasionally excessive saliva and/or mucus build-up may develop in the curarized animal. Elevating the animal's rear quarters or the use of a negative pressure tube may alleviate this condition.

Exposure to the curarized condition for two hours or more may lead to a "shock"-like reaction with decreased blood-flow and a fall in body tempera-ture. We have found it helpful to keep a 75 watt light bulb on in the small ventilated recording chamber; this maintains the environmental tempera-ture at approximately 28° C.

Recovery from the deeply curarized state may take from 1–5 hours for the rat. This may be hastened by keeping the animal warm, and by injections of neostigmine or endrophonium. The use of Prostigmin[4] only partially

---

[1] N. Miller, personal communication, July 1, 1969.

[2] We have used the Phipps and Bird Small Animal Respirator #70-886, Phipps and Bird, Inc., Richmond, Virginia.

[3] Abbott Laboratories, Chicago, Illinois.

[4] Neostigmine Methylsulfate, Roche Lab-oratories, Nutley, New Jersey.

counteracts the effects of curare and will not result in a complete recovery of a deeply curarized rat. The rat will begin to struggle, show spasmodic respiratory attempts and overt reactions to stimuli 15–50 min before he is able to provide adequate ventilation for himself. At this time Prostigmin may be administered to aid recovery.

## REFERENCES

Black, A. H., Carlson, N. J., & Solomon, R. L. Exploratory studies of the conditioning of autonomic responses in curarized dogs. *Psychological Monographs*, 1962, *76* (29, Whole No. 548).

DiCara, L. V., & Miller, N. E. Changes in heart rate instrumentally learned by curarized rats as avoidance responses. *Journal of Comparative & Physiological Psychology*, 1968, *65*, 8–12.

Hein, P. L. Heart rate conditioning in the cat and its relationship to other physiological responses. *Psychophysiology*, 1969, *5*, 455–464.

LoLordo, V., Overmier, J. B., Solomon, R. L., & Turner, L. H. Cardiac responses to shock in curarized dogs: Effects of shock intensity and duration, warning signal and prior experience with shock. *Journal of Comparative & Physiological Psychology*, 1966, *62*, 1–7.

Miller, N. E., & DiCara, L. V. Instrumental learning of heart rate changes in curarized rats: Shaping and specificity to a discriminative stimulus. *Journal of Comparative & Physiological Psychology*, 1967, *63*, 12–19.

Palacek, F. Measurement of ventilatory mechanics in the rat. *Journal of Applied Physiology*, 1969, *27*, 149–156.

Trowill, J. Instrumental conditioning of heart rate in the curarized rat. *Journal of Comparative & Physiological Psychology*, 1967, *63*, 7–11.

Wurtz, R. H. Steady potential correlates of intracranial reinforcement. *Electroencephalography & Clinical Neurophysiology*, 1966, *20*, 59–67.

# Effects of Coping Behavior 23
## in Different Warning Signal Conditions
## on Stress Pathology in Rats

### Jay M. Weiss

Rats received electric shock that was preceded by either a warning signal, a series of signals forming an "external clock," or no signal at all. In all conditions, subjects which could avoid and/or escape shock developed less ulceration than did yoked "helpless" animals which received exactly the same shock (through fixed electrodes wired in series) but had no control over shock. Presence or absence of a warning signal did, however, have an effect: A discrete warning signal reduced the ulceration both of subjects having control over shock and of yoked helpless subjects. A theory is proposed to explain how psychological factors determine the development of gastric ulceration in stress situations, and the present results are examined in relation to it.

In 1968 I reported that rats which could avoid or escape electric shocks lost less body weight, developed fewer stomach ulcers, and showed less fear in a stressful situation (as measured by a CER test) than did rats which received exactly the same electric shocks but could not avoid or escape them (Weiss, 1968a). A previous study which had also examined the effects of coping behavior on the development of psychosomatic pathology obtained results opposite to these. Brady, Porter, Conrad, and Mason (1958), in a study which became known as the "executive" monkey experiment (Brady, 1958), found that in four pairs of monkeys, animals which could avoid electric shocks eventually developed severe gastrointestinal pathology and died, while animals which received the same electric shocks but could not perform the avoid-

ance response developed no discernible disorders. In the 1968a paper, I discussed the possible reasons why my results were opposite to those of Brady et al. Although the studies in question were carried out on different species, and there was an unfortunate selection factor in the executive monkey experiment (i.e., the avoidance and yoked subjects were not chosen at random but, rather, a 2-4 hr. avoidance pretest was given to each pair and the monkey responding at the higher rate was always made the avoidance animal), nevertheless it was plausible that the opposite results were due largely to different experimental conditions used in the two studies. The present experiment investigated this possibility.

This experiment examined the importance of warning signals in the coping situation. In the original studies I carried out, where the animal able to perform the coping response developed less severe symptomatology than its helpless partner, the shock was always preceded by a tone signal, a standard avoidance procedure. Thus, the tone always predicted the occurrence of

[1] This study was supported by United States Public Health Service Research Grant MH-13189 from the National Institute of Mental Health.

[2] Requests for reprints should be sent to Jay M. Weiss, Rockefeller University, New York, New York 10021.

**319**

shock and could serve as a signal for the animal to respond at the appropriate time. In the executive monkey experiment, on the other hand, shock was not preceded by a signal, for a Sidman avoidance schedule was used. In this avoidance situation, the animal postponed (avoided) shock with each response but it had no external signal to inform it that shock was imminent so it had to make a temporal discrimination in order to predict when shock would occur and respond appropriately. This Sidman avoidance response may be considerably more difficult to maintain than is a signaled avoidance response; therefore, having to maintain a coping response in an unsignaled shock situation might be more stressful than being unable to perform any effective response, whereas the reverse is true when the impending shock is clearly signaled. If this were correct, it would afford an explanation for why the effects of coping behavior were opposite in my studies and in the executive monkey experiments.

In the present experiment, the effects of three different warning signal conditions were studied. In each of these conditions, matched triplets of animals underwent experimental treatment simultaneously, each triplet consisting of an animal which could avoid or escape shock, a yoked animal which received exactly the same shocks (and warning signals) as the avoidance-escape subject but which had no control over shock, and a nonshock control animal. In the first warning signal condition, a signal (beeping tone) preceded shock by several seconds, which formed a signaled coping-response situation for those subjects able to avoid and escape shock. In the second condition, no signal preceded shock, which formed an unsignaled, or Sidman-type, coping-response situation for avoidance-escape subjects. In the third condition, called the progressive-signal condition, the beep signal preceded shock as in the first condition but, in this case, a series of tones, each increasing in frequency and amplitude, led up to the beep. Thus, animals in this condition were provided with an "external clock" giving them even more information to predict the occurrence of shock than was present in the signal condition. The effect of these conditions was examined primarily upon the development of gastric ulcers. Steroid con-

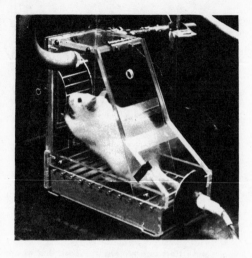

Fig. 1. The Plexiglas chamber, in which an animal is performing the wheel-turning response in the experimental situation. The tubing leading from the top of the chamber is the air exhaust outlet. The graduated cylinder seen in the rear contains water; the drinking spout protrudes into the chamber through a small hole.

centration in the blood was also measured since steroids may participate in the ulcero-genic process. The amount of body weight lost during the stress session was observed as well.

## METHOD

### Subjects

The subjects were 180 male albino Sprague-Dawley rats obtained from Hormone Assay Laboratories (Chicago, Illinois). The animals weighed approximately 180–250 gm. at the time of the experiment.

### Apparatus

The apparatus consisted of individual Plexiglas avoidance-escape chambers housed in soundproof compartments (Industrial Acoustics, Inc., New York; Model AC-1) as shown in Figure 1. The wheel at the front of the avoidance-escape chamber, when rotated by the animal, tripped a switch that could be activated to produce escape from, or avoidance of, electric shock delivered to the tail. The shock source was a high-voltage ac step-up transformer (1,200-v. peak output) with a 300 K external resistance in series with the subjects, and the current was varied by regulating the primary voltage input to the transformer. Auditory signals originated from Ameco Code practice oscillators and were delivered through 4-in. Lafayette 8-ohm speakers (No. 99-0172) with three speakers (one in each of three compartments) wired in parallel.

## Procedure

All experimental procedures were carried out simultaneously on three animals (a triplet). The three animals of each triplet were matched for body weight (within 15 gm. of one another) when drawn from the colony and were then housed together in one cage where they had access to water but no food. Twenty-four hours later, each animal was weighed and placed into a chamber inside an individual soundproof enclosure (described above). Prior to each subject's being placed into its chamber, a lightweight aluminum disk was slipped onto the animal's tail and a piece of tubing was secured to the tail behind the disk (see Figure 1); this assembly prevented the animal from pulling its tail completely into the chamber while permitting the animal to turn over, move backward, and also move forward up to the point where the tubing came in contact with the disk. Behind the disk and tubing, shock electrodes, consisting of two 2-cm. lengths of 18-gauge stainless-steel tubing, were placed onto the tail after electrode paste was rubbed lightly onto the site of electrode contact. The three subjects were then randomly assigned to three different groups, one being designated as the avoidance-escape subject, which controlled the frequency and duration of shock by its responses, another as the yoked subject, which received exactly the same shocks as the avoidance-escape subject but had no control over shocks, and a nonshock control subject.[3] The tail electrodes of the avoidance-escape animal and its matched yoked animal were wired in series, so that the shocks received by these two subjects were identical in number, duration, and current intensity throughout the entire experiment. The electrodes of the nonshock subject were bypassed in the circuit so that this subject was never shocked.

*Warning signal conditions.* Each triplet was also assigned randomly to one of the three warning signal conditions (signal, progressive signal, no signal) which are diagrammed in Figure 2a. In the signal condition, a beeping tone preceded shock by 20 sec. The beep was produced by .1-sec. pulses of a 555-cps tone with .3 sec. between pulses. In the progressive-signal condition, shock was also preceded by the beep as in the signal condition. In this case, however, an ascending series of tones oc-

[3] It is necessary to point out that the present experiment does not utilize the yoked-*control* design which has been criticized by Church (1964). The yoked groups in the present experiment are in no way a control condition. "Yoked" is a specific condition in which animals receive shocks but have no control over them. This is, in fact, precisely the point Church made: He correctly pointed out that yoked is a specific condition in which animals are helpless so that stimuli (or reinforcements) are imposed on such animals regardless of their physiological state, level of arousal, etc. This condition is, of course, specifically one that I wished to study in the present experiment, which was designed to compare the effects of having a coping response with the effects that occur when no such response is available and stimuli therefore occur arbitrarily.

curred in the 180-sec. period prior to the beep. This 180-sec. period was divided into six 30-sec. periods. Following the first 30-sec. period, during which no tone occurred, the tones commenced, each lasting 30 sec. and each increasing in frequency and amplitude with respect to the previous one. The frequencies for the ascending tones in this series were 250, 275, 333, 385, and 555 cps. In the no-signal condition, no signal of any kind preceded shock.

The effect of these different warning signal conditions on the avoidance-escape schedules was as follows: *The basic response-shock contingency was the same in all three warning signal conditions. In all conditions, if the avoidance-escape animal turned the wheel at the front of its apparatus, the signal-shock sequence was immediately terminated and begun again;* i.e., the signal-shock sequence was reset to the time marked "0" in Figure 2a. Thus, if shock had begun, a response terminated shock immediately and delayed the next shock for 200 sec.; if shock had not yet begun, the response postponed shock for 200 sec. An avoidance-escape response therefore had the same effect on shock frequency regardless of the warning signal condition—the response always delayed the next shock for 200 sec. A response, in resetting the signal-shock sequence, also immediately terminated any warning signal (or CS) that was present, as is standard procedure in signaled avoidance-escape situations. Thus, if an animal in the signal condition responded during the beep prior to shock, the beep immediately terminated, and if an animal in the progressive-signal condition responded during one of the ascending tones or the beep preceding shock, the tone or the beep immediately terminated. Figure 2b shows the effect of the same hypothetical response pattern on stimuli (tones and shocks) in the signal condition (upper section), progressive-signal condition (center), and no-signal condition (lower). A total of 60 triplets (20 in each condition) were used.

*Stress-session procedure.* At the beginning of the session, the avoidance-escape animal received a brief period of training (30 min.) in wheel turning. The shock, which was administered in pulses (pulse duration, .2 sec.; interpulse interval, .6 sec.), was kept at a low intensity during this phase (not exceeding 1.0 ma.). On the initial trials, the shock was reduced or terminated whenever the avoidance-escape animal moved toward the wheel and increased slightly when the animal moved away from the wheel. Once the animal had learned to turn the wheel, the shock was set at a low level (.5-.6 ma.) for the remainder of the training period. Trials were presented at the rate of 1/min during this training phase. It should be noted that yoked animals, being wired in series with avoidance-escape animals, received all shocks that were received by avoidance-escape animals during all phases of the experiment, including the training period.

At the conclusion of the initial training period, standard conditions (as described in the previous section on warning signal conditions) were initiated. The shock, delivered in pulses as described in the previous paragraph, was initially set at an intensity of 1.6 ma., and every 12 hr. the intensity was increased by .6 ma. The stress session lasted for 48 hr. Water was available ad lib throughout the session, and the amount consumed was recorded.

At the end of the stress session, the animals were quickly removed from the apparatus, weighed, and sacrificed by decapitation. Blood was collected for plasma corticosterone determination. (The time required to remove an animal from the apparatus—from the opening of the compartment door to decapitation—did not exceed 1 min., so that steroid levels were not affected by the re-

moval procedures.) Stomachs were removed, opened. and mounted for inspection (see Weiss, 1968a, for details of the procedure).

### Measures and Statistics

Stomach ulceration was the primary stress symptom measured in this experiment. Stomachs were examined under a dissecting microscope and lesions were counted. The criteria for identification of lesions by gross inspection of tissue can be found in an earlier paper (Weiss, 1968a). Recent experi-

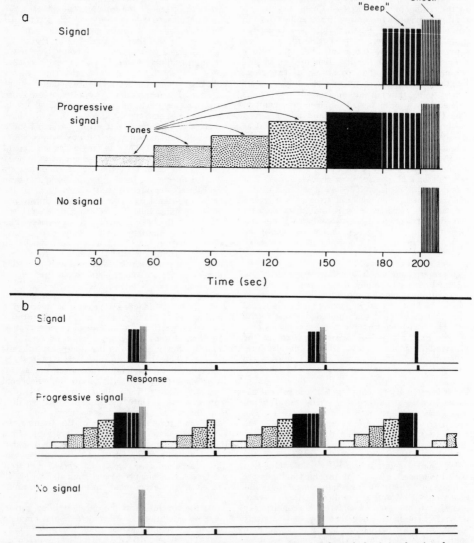

FIG. 2. At top (a) is shown the basic arrangement of warning signals and shock in the signal, progressive, and no-signal conditions. At bottom (b) is shown the effect of one hypothetical avoidance-escape response pattern on shock and warning signals in each of these conditions.

ments (Ganguly, 1969; Sethbhakdi, Pfeiffer, & Roth, 1970) have demonstrated the importance of quantifying the amount of the gastric mucosa which is ulcerated, having shown that measures which do not reflect this are insensitive to differences produced by known ulcerogenic conditions. Therefore, the length of each lesion was measured, a method used previously in this laboratory (Weiss, 1968a, 1970); the total length of lesions found in each subject constituted the principal measure of amount of ulceration. In addition to gastric lesions, body weight change during the session and plasma corticosterone concentration at the time of sacrifice were measured. Plasma corticosterone was determined by the method of Guillemin, Clayton, Smith, and Lipscomb (1958).

Statistical analysis was carried out using nonparametric tests of significance, since the scores on most measures were not normally distributed. The following statistical tests were used: For comparisons between avoidance-escape, yoked, and nonshock subjects of the same warning signal condition, Wilcoxon signed-ranks tests for matched subjects were used. (Since one subject from each of these groups was included in each triplet. these groups all contained matched subjects.) For comparisons between groups that were not of the same signal condition, Mann-Whitney $U$ tests were used.

## RESULTS

### *Wheel-Turning Behavior (Avoidance-Escape Responding)*

Table 1 shows the median number of wheel-turning responses for all groups and the median number of shocks received by animals in each condition. As expected, avoidance-escape animals made significantly (at least $p < .05$) more responses than yoked animals in each signal condition.

Avoidance-escape subjects showed a wide variety of response patterns, particularly in conditions where a signal preceded shock (signal and progressive-signal conditions). The total number of responses made by avoidance-escape subjects in the signal condition ranged from slightly over 1,500 to more than 20,000, and the range was similar for subjects in the progressive-signal condition. Approximately 70% of the avoidance-escape animals in these two signaled-shock conditions did not often respond during the beep signal preceding shock but responded quickly after the shock began, thus terminating it; i.e., they primarily escaped from shock. This accounts for the high number of shocks in these conditions. The remaining 30% of the animals in each of these conditions, on the other hand, consistently re-

sponded during the beep prior to the shock, terminating this signal and avoiding the impending shock. In the no-signal condition, avoidance-escape animals also showed considerable variation in responding (range: 3,200–31,000 responses) but the most striking feature of this group was its generally high response rate. These avoidance-escape animals made more responses than avoidance-escape subjects in the signal

TABLE 1

MEDIAN NUMBER OF WHEEL-TURN RESPONSES AND SHOCKS RECEIVED BY ALL GROUPS DURING THE STRESS SESSION

| Condition | Group | | |
|---|---|---|---|
| | Avoidance-escape | Yoked | Non-shock |
| Signal | | | |
| Responses | 3,717 | 1,404 | 60 |
| Shocks[a] | 705 | 705 | |
| Progressive signal | | | |
| Responses | 4,418 | 2,678 | 74 |
| Shocks[a] | 702 | 702 | |
| No signal | | | |
| Responses | 13,992 | 4,357 | 51 |
| Shocks[a] | 516 | 516 | |

[a] Since avoidance-escape and yoked animals are wired in series, the number of shocks received is necessarily identical in these groups.

condition ($p < .001$) and progressive-signal condition ($p < .005$), which accounts for the lower number of shocks received by animals in the no-signal condition. Yoked animals in the no-signal condition also showed more wheel-turning behavior than yoked animals in the signal condition ($p < .001$) but not significantly more than yoked subjects in the progressive-signal condition.

### *Stomach Ulceration*

Gastric lesions, commonly called stress ulcers, were found in the lower, glandular area of the stomach. Figure 3 shows such a lesion as it appeared in the stomach, and also a histological section of this lesion. No lesions were found in the upper, rumenal area of the stomach.

Figure 4 shows the amount of lesioned gastric tissue (length of lesions) found in each group, and the confidence levels for all significant comparisons. Figure 5 shows the same for number of lesions.

Within all three signal conditions, avoidance-escape animals showed less extensive gastric ulceration than did yoked animals. The difference between the avoidance-escape and yoked groups was statistically significant in each condition on at least one of the two measures, with the largest difference between these groups clearly occurring in the progressive-signal condition. Nonshock animals, which developed a small

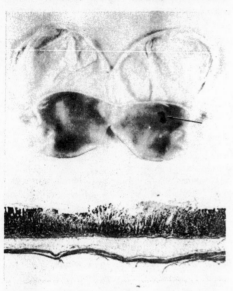

FIG. 3. At top is shown a gastric lesion (indicated by arrow) as it appeared in a rat's stomach. The lesion lies in the lower, glandular part of the stomach. The upper, rumenal part of the stomach, which has not been removed in this case, shows no lesions, as usual. At bottom is shown a histological section of the lesion seen above.

amount of ulceration as a result of the 48-hr. restraint in the apparatus, showed less ulceration than the animals which received shock (avoidance-escape and yoked groups), as expected.

Examining differences between warning signal conditions showed that avoidance-escape animals developed more ulceration in the no-signal condition than they did in either the signal or progressive-signal condition, in which avoidance-escape animals developed similar amounts of ulceration. Thus, animals able to avoid and escape shock developed more ulceration when shock was not preceded by a signal than they did when shock was signaled, though,

as stated in the previous paragraph, in no case did avoidance-escape animals develop more ulceration than matched yoked subjects. Comparing yoked animals across conditions, ulceration was also more extensive in the no-signal condition than it was in the signal condition. Ulceration of yoked animals in the progressive-signal condition, however, was almost as severe as that which occurred in the no-signal condition.

It should be noted that the ulceration of avoidance-escape animals which consistently terminated the beep signal before shock did not differ markedly from those avoidance-escape animals in the same signal conditions which did not do so. In the signal condition, for example, the median amount of ulceration for the entire group was 1.12 mm.; for subjects with a large number of beep terminations (150 or more; $n = 5$), it was 1.25 mm.

### Body Weight Loss

Figure 6 shows body weight loss during the stress procedure for all groups. Yoked animals in the progressive-signal and no-signal conditions lost significantly more weight than did avoidance-escape animals;

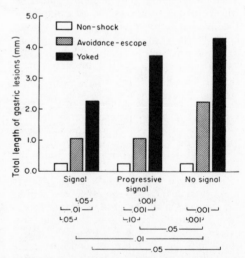

FIG. 4. The median total length of gastric lesions for the nonshock, avoidance-escape, and yoked groups in the signal, progressive-signal, and no-signal conditions. Also shown are the confidence levels of all comparisons between groups for which the chance probability was .10 or less. Twenty matched triplets were used in each signal condition.

the weight loss difference between these groups in the signal condition was quite small and did not approach significance. Nonshock animals lost less weight than shocked groups (avoidance-escape and yoked subjects) in all conditions.

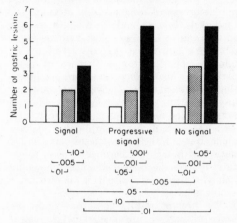

Fig. 5. The median number of gastric lesions for the nonshock, avoidance-escape, and yoked groups in the signal, progressive-signal, and no-signal conditions. Also shown are the confidence levels for all comparisons between groups for which the chance probability was .10 or less. See Figure 4 for key.

Significance of comparisons across conditions are shown, but because of the variation in weight loss observed across conditions (e.g., compare nonshock groups), care should be taken in interpreting differences on this measure which are not based on comparison of groups of the same signal condition which had matched subjects.

It should be noted that prestress weight, which was taken prior to the placement of the animals into the apparatus for the stress procedure, was highly similar for all groups. The average weight across the nine groups of the experiment showed a range of only 3 gm.; the average weight of the lightest group was 212.5 gm.[4] compared with 215.5 gm. for the heaviest group; no difference approached significance.

---

[4] Weight includes the tail-guard assembly, which was in position on the tail when this weight was taken. The entire assembly contributed approximately 21.0 gm. to this weight. The animal did not, however, support the weight of the assembly in the apparatus, as can be seen in Figure 1.

## Plasma Corticosterone

Levels of plasma corticosterone at the termination of the stress session are shown for all groups in Figure 7. Individual variation was considerable, which is not surprising for the level of steroid in the blood, particularly under stress conditions (e.g., Friedman, Ader, Grota, & Larson, 1967); for example, within the yoked group of the signal condition, values ranged 6.3–102.0 μg. per 100-ml. plasma. The only statistically significant difference between matched subjects was the difference between nonshock and yoked animals in the no-signal condition.

Plasma steroid level did, however, correlate with amount of ulceration. The average correlation for all groups which received shock (avoidance-escape and yoked subjects in each of the three signal conditions) was $r = .52$. This correlation was mainly attributable to subjects with very high steroid levels which invariably showed extensive ulceration—in those subjects where the steroid level exceeded 70 μg. per 100-ml. plasma, the amount of ulceration averaged 21.2 mm.

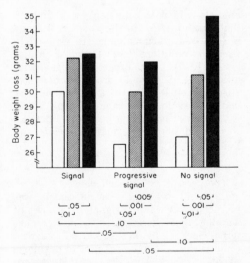

Fig. 6. The median amount of body weight lost during the stress session by the nonshock, avoidance-escape, and yoked groups in the signal, progressive-signal, and no-signal conditions. Also shown are the confidence levels for all comparisons between groups for which the chance probability was .10 or less. See Figure 4 for key.

## Water Intake

In all signal conditions, avoidance-escape and yoked animals drank significantly (at least $p < .01$) more water than nonshock

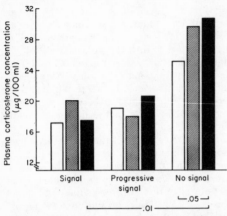

FIG. 7. The median concentration of corticosterone in the blood at the conclusion of the stress session for the nonshock, avoidance-escape, and yoked groups in the signal, progressive-signal, and no-signal conditions. Also shown are the confidence levels for all comparisons between groups for which the chance probability was .10 or less. See Figure 4 for key.

animals, which is consistent with findings that water intake (in the absence of food) is increased when animals are exposed to stressful conditions (e.g., Deaux & Kakolewski, 1970). In the progressive-signal condition, yoked animals drank more water ($Mdn = 40.0$ ml.; $p < .02$) than did matched avoidance-escape subjects ($Mdn = 33.0$ ml.); no other significant difference was found between avoidance-escape and yoked groups.

## DISCUSSION

The present experiment showed that regardless of whether electric shock was preceded by a warning signal, by a series of warning signals forming, so to speak, an external clock, or by no signal at all, rats that could perform coping responses to postpone, avoid, or escape shock developed less severe gastric ulceration than matched subjects which received the same shocks but could not affect shock by their behavior. Thus, altering the predictability of shock by means of external signals did not change

the basic effect of being able to perform a coping response compared with not being able to perform one—being able to perform an effective coping response was less pathogenic under all conditions studied. Thus, the possibility discussed in the introduction—namely, that the absence of a warning signal before shock might result in more pathology in animals able to avoid or escape shock than in helpless yoked animals—was not borne out. Since the executive monkey phenomenon, i.e., the occurrence of more pathology in avoidance-escape subjects than in yoked animals, was not found in any condition, the present results offer no rationale for reconciling my earlier results with those of the executive monkey experiment. Instead, the present results, in combination with earlier experiments, serve to establish that the beneficial effect of coping behavior in stressful situations is of considerable generality.

The present results point out again the extraordinary significance of psychological factors in the production of stomach ulcers. If, in Figure 4, we compare the gastric ulceration of any nonshock group with that of the avoidance-escape animals in the signal and progressive-signal conditions, we can see that simply receiving shock was not necessarily very harmful in and of itself. These avoidance-escape animals clearly ulcerated more than did nonshock controls; however, the amount of ulceration in these avoidance-escape animals was not very large. Now let us compare either of these avoidance-escape groups with the yoked animals in the no-signal condition. The difference here was produced by psychological variables, by differences in warning signals and the ability to control shock, and not by the presence or absence of the shock stressor, since all subjects in this comparison received shock (in fact, the yoked animals in this comparison received 25% *fewer* shocks than either of the avoidance-escape groups). The size of this difference (even ignoring the difference in shock frequency) tells us that the psychological characteristics of the stressful situation—the predictability, avoidability, and escapability of shock—primarily determined how pathological the stress situation was, not whether the animal was exposed to the stressor. I have noted this observation before (Weiss,

1968a, 1968b, 1970); initially, it was surprising but it has proved to be a consistent feature of the results.

In regard to the other measures, the amount of body weight lost during the stress session by the various groups showed a pattern roughly comparable to that seen for stomach ulceration. Significant differences between avoidance-escape and yoked animals, with yoked animals losing more weight than avoidance-escape animals, appeared in the progressive-signal and no-signal conditions, although this difference did not reach significance in the signal condition.

For plasma corticosterone levels, the variation between individual rats was so large that this measure did not differentiate the groups. This variation, however, makes the steroid measure a good one for correlational analysis, and a correlation between steroid level and ulceration was observed which is of particular interest. Administration of exogenous steroids, both in humans and in rats, often leads to gastric ulceration, so that steroids are thought to be involved in the causal sequence by which gastric ulcerations develops (Roberts & Nezamis, 1964; Spiro & Milles, 1960). However, when exogenous steroid is given, the quantity is often so large, the introduction of steroid into circulation is so abrupt, etc., that we wish to know whether steroids secreted normally by the adrenal cortex play a role in the ulcerogenic process. Results in the present experiment showed that very high *endogenously produced* steroid levels were accompanied by severe gastric ulceration; this lends support to the possibility that steroids, in quantities that the animal is capable of secreting, may contribute to the production of ulcers.

### A Theory to Explain How Coping Behavior Affects Ulcer Development

While a number of significant conclusions are clearly evident from the present results, puzzling aspects also remain. For example, why was the difference between avoidance-escape and yoked subjects consistently larger in the progressive-signal condition than it was in either of the other signal conditions? Based on data from the present experiment, I have been able to generate a theory which attempts to answer this and other questions relating to how coping behavior regulates the development of gastric ulceration in stressful situations. The derivation of the hypotheses will not be presented here; I shall simply state the theory and show how it conforms to the present results.

Stress ulceration is said to be a function of two variables: the number of coping attempts an animal makes, and the amount of appropriate feedback which these coping attempts produce. Figure 8 shows how these variables interact. On the left side of the solid line is represented the relationship between the first variable, number of coping attempts, and ulcerogenic (ulcer-producing) stress. When an animal is presented with a stressor, or stimuli associated (by contiguity) with the stressor, the animal will emit coping attempts which we measure as responses. The number of responses emitted and the amount of ulcerogenic stress directly covary; that is, the more responses we observe, the more likely the animal is to develop ulcers. Hence, the first proposition is that ulceration tends to increase monotonically as the number of responses, or coping attempts, increases.

The theory states, however, that expression of the foregoing relationship is completely dependent on a second variable—the consequences of coping attempts, or, in operational terms, the stimulus feedback from responses. The effect of this variable is shown on the right side of the solid line in

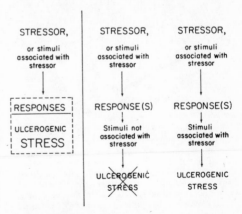

Fig. 8. Factors which determine the presence or absence of an ulcerogenic condition.

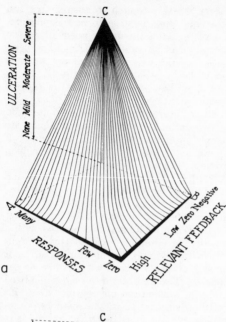

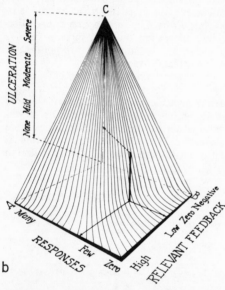

Figure 8. If responses immediately produce stimuli that are not associated with the stressor, ulcerogenic stress will not occur. If, on the other hand, responses fail to produce such stimuli, then ulcerogenic stress will occur. Stimuli that are not associated with the stressor and that follow a response are called *relevant feedback*, since their occurrence is said to negate ulcerogenic stress. Thus, the more the relevant feedback, i.e., the more responses produce stimuli that are not associated with the stressor, the less the ulceration. The second proposition is, therefore, that ulceration tends to decrease monotonically as the amount of relevant feedback from coping attempts increases.

Combining these two propositions generates a function (a plane) such as is shown in Figure 9a. Figure 9b shows how, given the number of responses which an animal makes and the amount of relevant feedback it experiences from these responses, we can predict the amount of ulceration which will develop. Where number of responses and amount of feedback intersect, we simply project upward until we reach the plane; the height of this point represents the amount of ulceration which occurs.

This theory generates some interesting predictions. First, if an animal does not make coping attempts, it will not ulcerate regardless of what the feedback circumstances are. (See in Figure 9 that at all feedback values intersecting with "zero" responses, the plane shows no elevation.) Also, if relevant feedback is maximally high, an animal will not ulcerate regardless of how many responses it makes. (See in Figure 9 that at all response values intersecting with maximally high feedback, the plane also shows no elevation.) As number of responses increases and amount of feedback decreases, the point where these quantities intersect moves closer and closer to the intersection of the three axes, above which the plane progressively rises higher, denoting that ulceration is expected to become progressively more severe.

Fig. 9. At top (a) is shown the three-dimensional figure which describes the proposed relationship between responses, feedback, and ulceration. This relationship is a plane which shows how the two independent variables, responses and feedback, are related to the dependent variable, ulceration. At bottom (b) is shown how this plane is used. Where a hypothetical number of responses and amount of feedback intersect, the amount of ulceration is determined by the height of the plane above this point. (For ease of reading this figure, responses and feedback are labeled across the axes in the foreground. These labels are customarily placed along the axes in the background which are parallel to the ones bearing the labels. It therefore should be noted that feedback designations apply to the axis from Point A to the intersection of the three axes, and response designations apply to the axis from Point B to the intersection.)

To apply this framework, it is necessary to keep clearly in mind what is meant by relevant feedback. The principle to be remembered is that relevant feedback consists of *stimuli* which immediately follow a response. The *amount* of relevant feedback is the extent to which a response produces stimuli that are not associated with the stressor. To avoid the stressor is not relevant feedback; in fact, more relevant feedback will occur from escape responses than from many types of avoidance responses. For example, in the present experiment the stimulus event of shock termination is further removed in time from the onset of the shock (i.e., less associated with the stressor) than is any other external stimulus in the environment (see Figure 2b). Moreover, shock termination is a very large change in the external stimulus situation and is, therefore, an extremely conspicuous event. These factors make shock termination excellent feedback, and this results from every escape response. In contrast, consider the feedback from avoidance responses in the no-signal condition. These responses postpone shock, thus producing kinesthetic and proprioceptive stimuli from responding which are always at least 200 sec. removed from the onset of shock (good feedback), but such responses produce no change at all in the external stimulus situation; hence, the amount of feedback from this type of avoidance response is considerably less than that of an escape response even though it avoids the stressor.

Figure 10 shows the present results in relation to the framework I have suggested.

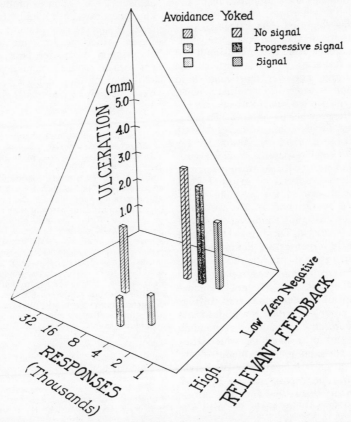

FIG. 10. The figure shows the results obtained in the present experiment in relation to the proposed theory. For each group which received shock, the amount of ulceration (height of bar) is shown at the point where responding and feedback for that group intersect.

One can fix the position of any group with regard to the two important variables (responses and feedback) since the responding of each group was directly measured and the amount of feedback in each condition can be ascertained, which is done as follows: The best response feedback occurred for avoidance-escape animals in the progressive-signal condition. In this case, any response made more than 30 sec. after shock terminated a tone of some sort and immediately produced a stimulus condition (silence) which was not closely associated with the onset of shock. The only responses in this condition that failed to produce relevant feedback via external stimulus change were those that occurred within the first 30 sec. after shock. Avoidance-escape animals in the signal condition experienced less feedback than this since responses made before the beep produced no external feedback event in this condition. Nevertheless, feedback in the signal condition was quite good; relevant feedback from external stimuli did arise from responses which terminated the beep signal and, moreover, most animals in this condition responded to terminate shock, which provided excellent feedback as explained in the previous paragraph. The poorest feedback for avoidance-escape animals occurred in the no-signal condition. In this case, only escape responses provided substantial relevant feedback since responses prior to shock produced no external feedback, as explained in the previous paragraph. As a result, most of the responses made in the no-signal condition produced rather low feedback. Turning to the yoked animals, their responses, by definition, had no effect on external stimuli and so could not produce any stimuli consistently unrelated to the stressor; relevant response feedback for all such groups is zero. In Figure 10, all groups lie along the appropriate feedback coordinate at points corresponding to the amount of responding which they showed. At these points, the amount of observed ulceration is indicated by the height of each bar. The correspondence of these values with the theoretical function can be assessed by comparing their fit with the function in Figure 9. We can now see why, for example, the difference between avoidance-escape and yoked animals was so large

in the progressive-signal condition, for animals in this condition made a substantial number of responses, with very good feedback occurring for avoidance-escape subjects in contrast to the zero feedback for yoked subjects.[5]

One of the most significant aspects of the theory proposed is that it does away with any *qualitative* distinction between animals which can avoid and escape shock and animals which are helpless; the difference between such conditions is expressed *quantitatively*. If we consider the two dimensions which are functionally related to ulceration (responding and feedback), we see that avoidance-escape and yoked groups differ quantitatively with respect to both—these groups differ in the *amount* of responses they emit and in the *amount* of relevant feedback these responses produce. Thus, we can incorporate both avoidance-escape and yoked (helpless) conditions into a common schema, which we see done in Figure 10. The primary distinction between an avoidance-escape condition and a yoked condition lies along the feedback continuum; for yoked, or helpless, animals, relevant feedback for responding is zero, while for avoid-

---

[5] It is important to note that the small amount of ulceration which developed in nonshock control animals is not an exception to the theory set forth above but is also explained by using the same principles. A minimum stress condition was imposed on all subjects, including nonshock controls, since all subjects were restrained in the apparatus for 48 hr. without food. Any attempt that a subject made to get out of this stressful situation necessarily produced zero relevant feedback because no response ever produced escape from the chamber (i.e., no response produced any stimuli that were not associated with the chamber). Since attempts to escape from the apparatus produce zero feedback, simply being in the experimental situation is, according to the proposed theory, potentially ulcerogenic, and subjects will ulcerate in accordance with the number of escape attempts emitted. It was found, in fact, that the wheel-turning behavior of nonshock control subjects, which would reflect escape attempts, correlated with the amount of ulceration these subjects developed ($r = .66$). Thus, the ulceration of nonshock animals can be seen to develop as a function of coping attempts for which feedback is low, and consequently fits into the framework presented above. If we examine Figure 9, it is equally evident why the ulceration of nonshock groups was quite mild since, in the absence of the major stressor of electric shock, the number of responses emitted by these subjects was very low.

ance-escape animals, feedback occurs in some amount greater than zero depending upon the stimulus characteristics of the situation. This difference explains why animals which have control over a stressor generally ulcerate less than do helpless animals: Animals which have control generally receive a considerably greater amount of relevant feedback for their coping attempts than do helpless animals. Thus, the value of control for ameliorating ulcerogenic stress is said to lie essentially in the ability to produce relevant feedback from responses. Using this approach, we can analyze a wide variety of circumstances and predict their effects, which has been done in generating further experiments (Weiss, 1971a, 1971b).

## REFERENCES

BRADY, J. V. Ulcers in "executive" monkeys. *Scientific American*, 1958, **199**, 95–100.

BRADY, J. V., PORTER, R. W., CONRAD, D. G., & MASON, J. W. Avoidance behavior and the development of gastroduodenal ulcers. *Journal of the Experimental Analysis of Behavior*, 1958, **1**, 69–72.

CHURCH, R. M. Systematic effect of random error in the yoked control design. *Psychological Bulletin*, 1964, **62**, 122–131.

DEAUX, E., & KAKOLEWSKI, J. W. Emotionally induced increases in effective osmotic pressure and subsequent thirst. *Science*, 1970, **169**, 1226–1228.

FRIEDMAN, S. B., ADER, R., GROTA, L. J., & LARSON, T. Plasma corticosterone response to parameters of electric shock stimulation in the rat. *Psychosomatic Medicine*, 1967, **29**, 323–328.

GANGULY, A. K. A method for quantitative assessment of experimentally produced ulcers in the stomach of albino rats. *Experientia*, 1969, **25**, 1224.

GUILLEMIN, R., CLAYTON, G. W., SMITH, J. D., & LIPSCOMB, H. S. Measurement of free corticosteroid in rat plasma: Physiological validation of a method. *Endocrinology*, 1958, **63**, 349–358.

ROBERT, A., & NEZAMIS, J. Histopathology of steroid-induced ulcers. *Archives of Pathology*, 1964, **77**, 407–423.

SETHBHAKDI, S., PFEIFFER, C. J., & ROTH, J. L. A. Gastric mucosal ulceration following vasoactive agents: A new experimental approach. *American Journal of Digestive Diseases*, 1970, **15**, 261–270.

SPIRO, H. M., & MILLES, S. S. Clinical and physiologic implications of the steroid-induced peptic ulcer. *New England Journal of Medicine*, 1960, **26**, 286–294.

WEISS, J. M. Effects of coping responses on stress. *Journal of Comparative and Physiological Psychology*, 1968, **65**, 251–260. (a)

WEISS, J. M. Effects of predictable and unpredictable shock on development of gastrointestinal lesions in rats. *Proceedings of the 76th Annual Convention of the American Psychological Association*, 1968, **3**, 281–282. (b)

WEISS, J. M. Somatic effects of predictable and unpredictable shock. *Psychosomatic Medicine*, 1970, **32**, 397–408.

WEISS, J. M. Effects of punishing the coping response (conflict) on stress pathology in rats. *Journal of Comparative and Physiological Psychology*, 1971, **77**, 14–21. (a)

WEISS, J. M. Effects of coping behavior with and without a feedback signal on stress pathology in rats. *Journal of Comparative and Physiological Psychology*, 1971, **77**, 22–30. (b)

(Received January 18, 1971)

# Effects of Coping Behavior 24
# With and Without a Feedback Signal
# on Stress Pathology in Rats

Jay M. Weiss

When rats avoid and/or escape electric shock that is not preceded by a warning signal, considerable gastric ulceration normally develops under conditions used previously in this laboratory. In the present experiment, very little ulceration developed under these conditions when animals were given a brief feedback signal after each avoidance-escape response. These animals showed only slightly more ulceration than nonshock controls and much less ulceration than either animals which could also avoid and escape shock but had no feedback signal or yoked "helpless" animals. These results, showing that excellent response feedback will greatly reduce or even eliminate ulceration, is predicted by a proposed theory. This theory can also account for the "executive" monkey phenomenon, and the explanation for this atypical effect is presented.

In a previous paper (Weiss, 1971a), a theory was presented which attempts to explain why rats develop stomach ulceration in stressful situations. Stomach ulceration is said to be a function of two variables: the number of coping attempts an animal makes and the feedback which coping attempts produce. Ulceration will increase as (a) the number of coping attempts increases and (b) the amount of relevant feedback decreases, so that ulceration will be severe when responding is high and relevant feedback is low, and will be progressively less severe as responding decreases and relevant feedback increases.

The theory described above has been applied in a number of situations. Initially, it was used to explain why animals which are able to perform effective coping responses usually do not ulcerate as severely as helpless (yoked) animals when exposed to the

same stressor. The theory could account for this effect, and its magnitude, in a variety of experimental conditions (Weiss, 1971a). A second experiment was then carried out to determine if the normally beneficial effect of coping behavior could be reversed by applying feedback principles derived from the theory (Weiss, 1971b). It was found that animals having an effective coping response indeed could be made to ulcerate very severely if the relevant feedback for responding was made extremely low; such animals, in fact, ulcerated more severely than did helpless animals. The present experiment was conducted to determine if ulceration can also be reduced, and possibly eliminated, by manipulation of psychological feedback contingencies. In this experiment, the amount of relevant feedback for responding was greatly increased, which, according to the proposed theory, should prevent ulceration.

The attempt was made to prevent ulceration from developing in rats that could avoid or escape electric shocks but without a warning signal before shock. Animals in this situation will normally develop a con-

[1] This study was supported by United States Public Health Service Research Grant MH-13189 from the National Institute of Mental Health.

[2] Requests for reprints should be sent to Jay M. Weiss, Rockefeller University, New York, New York 10021.

siderable amount of ulceration (Weiss, 1971a), which is why this condition was chosen for the present study, since it will permit us to assess just how effective a psychological feedback manipulation could be.

Let us consider why, according to the proposed theory, ulceration develops when animals avoid and escape unsignaled shock and, consequently, how this ulceration ought to be reduced by increasing relevant feedback. It is first necessary to understand what is meant by feedback. Feedback consists of stimuli that occur contingent upon, i.e., immediately follow, a response. A certain kind of feedback stimuli are considered to be particularly significant for an animal in a stress situation, those being *stimuli that are not associated with the stressor*. These stimuli are defined as *relevant feedback*. The amount of relevant feedback from a response, therefore, is determined by the extent to which a response produces stimuli that are not associated with the stressor.

Ulceration is thought to develop, as stated in the first paragraph, when an animal performs many responses for which relevant feedback is low. Such is the case for avoidance-escape animals in the unsignaled-shock condition. These animals receive a low amount of relevant feedback from responding because whenever they respond prior to shock, the response postpones shock for 200 sec. but produces no alteration in the external stimulus situation. As a result, the only relevant feedback for this avoidance response comes from proprioceptive stimuli (internal response-produced stimuli) that have not been closely associated with the onset of shock, since no feedback at all comes from the external stimulus situation. When we consider that avoidance-escape animals in the unsignaled-shock condition emit a great many of these responses, we can explain why these animals ulcerate.

If animals which avoid and escape unsignaled shock indeed ulcerate because they perform many responses which produce low relevant feedback, clearly one way to reduce ulceration is to increase the relevant feedback for responding. The proposed theory states, in fact, that if relevant feedback is extremely high, animals will not ulcerate at all regardless of how many responses they make. Therefore, in the present experiment a feedback stimulus was introduced into the unsignaled-shock condition. This stimulus was a brief (5-sec.) tone that followed each avoidance-escape response. The presence of such a stimulus will substantially increase relevant feedback for the following reasons: Since every avoidance-escape response postpones shock for 200 sec., the feedback tone, occurring after each response and lasting 5 sec., must always be at least 195 sec. removed from the onset of the shock stressor. No external stimulus in any of my experiments, with the exception of shock termination itself, represented a longer delay between the stimulus and the stressor. In addition, the tone constitutes an external stimulus that is distinct from any stimulus preceding the shock, so that each avoidance-escape response, even a response which simply postpones shock, will produce a conspicuous external stimulus event which is not closely associated with the stressor.

To test the effect of this feedback stimulus or, in other words, of greatly increasing relevant feedback for responding, two avoidance-escape animals were exposed to experimental treatment at the same time. Both animals were subjected to the same unsignaled-shock conditions except that for one subject the feedback tone was present, while for the other it was not. To each of these avoidance-escape animals was matched a yoked animal, which received the same shocks as the avoidance-escape subject and also the tone if it were present, as well as a nonshock control animal. This experiment enables us to (a) assess the effect of the feedback stimulus by comparing avoidance-escape animals performing simultaneously with and without the feedback stimulus, and (b) determine the importance of these feedback conditions relative to receiving no relevant feedback from responding, i.e., helplessness, by comparing avoidance-escape animals with matched yoked animals. The measures taken included, in addition to the amount of gastric ulceration produced by these conditions, the level of corticosterone in the blood at the conclusion of the experiment, since steroids appear to be involved in the ulcerogenic process, and also body weight loss during the stress procedure.

## METHOD

### Subjects

The subjects were 96 male albino Sprague-Dawley rats obtained from Hormone Assay Laboratories (Chicago, Illinois), weighing 180–250 gm. at the time of the experiment.

### Apparatus

The apparatus was the same as described in Weiss (1971a); it basically consisted of several small chambers. each of which had a wheel mounted at the front which the animal in the chamber could rotate. Each chamber was housed in a separate soundproof compartment.

### Procedure

Six animals, comprising two triplets, were treated simultaneously. The animals, matched for body weight, were drawn from the colony and housed without food for 24 hr. Each animal was then placed into a chamber and tail electrodes were affixed as described previously (Weiss, 1971a). Just prior to the first trial, the six animals were divided into two triplets of three animals each. Within each triplet, one subject was randomly designated as the avoidance-escape subject, whose responses controlled the frequency and duration of shock; another was designated as the yoked subject, which received exactly the same shock as the avoidance-escape subject but had no control over shock; and the third was designated as the nonshock control. The tail electrodes of the avoidance-escape and yoked subjects in each triplet were wired in series, so that the shocks received by both of these subjects were identical in number, duration, and current intensity throughout the entire experiment.

The stress session was conducted using the parameters and procedure (shock level, pulse duration, initial training of avoidance-escape subjects, etc.) of the unsignaled condition in Weiss (1971a). Whenever the avoidance-escape animal turned the wheel at the front of its cage, the onset of the next shock was postponed for 200 sec. Thus, if the avoidance-escape animal responded during the shock, the shock terminated and did not occur again for 200 sec. If the avoidance-escape animal responded prior to shock, the next shock was simply postponed by 200 sec.

### TABLE 1
MEDIAN NUMBER OF WHEEL-TURN RESPONSES AND SHOCKS RECEIVED BY ALL GROUPS DURING THE STRESS SESSION

| Condition | Group | | |
|---|---|---|---|
| | Avoidance-escape | Yoked | Non-shock |
| No signal | | | |
| Responses | 13,504 | 5,517 | 139 |
| Shocks[a] | 384 | 384 | |
| No signal + Feedback | | | |
| Responses | 15,133 | 3,938 | 130 |
| Shocks[a] | 383 | 383 | |

[a] Since avoidance-escape and yoked animals are wired in series, the number of shocks received is necessarily identical in these groups.

As stated above, two matched triplets were run simultaneously. For one triplet, the conditions were exactly as described above; i.e., normal unsignaled-shock conditions. For the second triplet, each response by the avoidance-escape animals produced a tone (feedback stimulus) 5 sec. in duration. A delay of 650 msec. was placed between activation of the response relay and tone onset, in order to reduce any possibility that aversive aftereffects from initial shocks would be associated with the tone. If the avoidance-escape subject performed a wheel-turning response while the 5-sec. feedback-tone stimulus was on, the tone stimulus simply remained on for a period of 5 sec. following this response. Yoked animals in this feedback condition also received the tone stimulus whenever the avoidance-escape animal produced it, as did nonshock animals also. The experimental design, therefore, consisted of two independent triplets run simultaneously, both in the unsignaled-shock condition, one with feedback stimulus and one without it. Figure 1 shows the effect of the same hypothetical avoidance-escape response pattern on stimuli in these two conditions. A total of 32 triplets were used, so that 16 received the feedback stimulus and 16 did not.

The stress session lasted for 48 hr. after which the animals were removed from their cages, weighed, and sacrificed by decapitation. Blood was collected for plasma corticosterone determination,

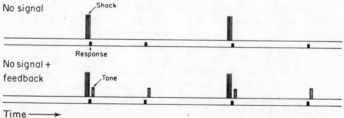

FIG. 1. This shows the effect of a hypothetical avoidance-escape response pattern on external stimuli (shock and tone) in the normal unsignaled-shock condition (top) and in the same condition with the feedback stimulus present (bottom).

which was carried out by the method of Guillemin, Clayton, Smith, and Lipscomb (1958). Each animal's stomach was opened and inspected for ulceration. Because of the stringent predictions generated by the theory in question (see introduction), the evaluation of ulceration in this experiment was carried out by the scorer without his knowing which group the animals had been in. Lesions were counted. They were also measured (to the nearest .25 mm.) so that total amount (length) of ulcerated tissue could be ascertained;

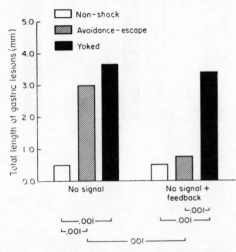

FIG. 2. The median total length of gastric lesions for the nonshock, avoidance-escape, and yoked groups in the unsignaled-shock condition (left) and in the same condition with the feedback stimulus added (right). Also shown are the confidence levels for all comparisons between groups for which the chance probability was .10 or less. Sixteen triplets were used in each of the two conditions.

this constituted the principal measure of ulceration.

Statistical analysis for all measures was based on Wilcoxon signed-ranks tests for matched subjects. For details of stomach preparation, ulcer identification, and statistical analysis, see earlier papers (Weiss, 1968, 1971a).

## Results

### Wheel-Turning Behavior (Avoidance-Escape Responding)

Table 1 shows the median number of responses made by all groups, and also the number of shocks received. Avoidance-escape animals, as expected, made significantly more responses ($p < .001$) than yoked animals in both conditions. Comparing across conditions, responding of avoidance-escape subjects which received the

tone-feedback stimulus did not differ significantly from that of avoidance-escape animals which did not receive this stimulus. Responding of yoked animals in the two conditions also did not differ. The number of shocks received in both conditions was highly similar.

### Stomach Ulceration

Gastric lesions were found in the glandular (lower) portion of the stomach. Figure 2 shows the length of lesions for all groups, and the confidence levels of significant comparisons. Figure 3 shows the same for number of lesions.

It is apparent that the feedback stimulus produced a large reduction in stomach ulceration. Within the normal unsignaled-shock condition (left side of figures), the ulceration of avoidance-escape animals was less than that of yoked animals but the difference between these groups did not reach statistical significance. However, within the unsignaled-shock condition but with the feedback stimulus added (right side), ulceration of avoidance-escape animals was much less than that of matched yoked animals. Avoidance-escape animals in this feedback condition did not ulcerate much

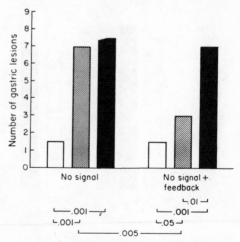

FIG. 3. The median number of lesions for the nonshock, avoidance-escape, and yoked groups in the unsignaled-shock condition (left) and in the same condition with the feedback stimulus added (right). Also shown are the confidence levels for all comparisons between groups for which the chance probability was .10 or less. See Figure 2 for key.

more than nonshock controls; the difference between these groups was significant only for number of lesions and not for total length.

Comparing groups across conditions directly confirmed the large difference between the two avoidance-escape conditions. A highly significant difference was evident between the avoidance-escape group which received the tone-feedback stimulus and the avoidance-escape group which did not. The ulceration of yoked animals did not differ across the two conditions, which showed that simply having the tone stimulus present in the stress situation without its being contingent on responding, as was the case for yoked animals in the tone-feedback condition, produced no reduction in the amount of ulceration.

*Body Weight Loss and Plasma Corticosterone Concentration*

Figure 4 shows the median body weight loss for all groups. For this measure, the only significant differences appeared between animals that received shock (avoidance-escape and yoked groups) and matched nonshock animals.

Figure 5 shows the steroid level at the time of sacrifice for all groups. Within the

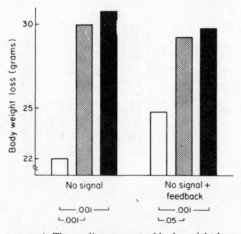

r iG. 4. The median amount of body weight lost during the stress session by the nonshock, avoidance-escape, and yoked groups in the unsignaled-shock condition (left) and in the same condition with the feedback stimulus added (right). Also shown are the confidence levels for all comparisons between groups for which the chance probability was .10 or less. See Figure 2 for key.

normal unsignaled-shock condition, the steroid level for nonshock animals was significantly lower than that of both avoid-

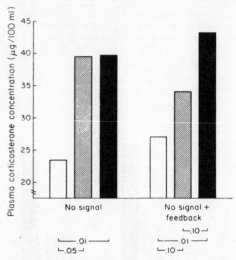

Fig. 5. The median concentration of corticosterone in the blood at the conclusion of the stress session for the nonshock, avoidance-escape, and yoked groups in the unsignaled-shock condition (left) and in the same condition with the feedback stimulus added (right). Also shown are the confidence levels for all comparisons between groups for which the chance probability was .10 or less. See Figure 2 for key.

ance-escape and yoked animals. In the tone-feedback condition, the level for nonshock animals was below that of yoked animals but the difference between nonshock and avoidance-escape animals only approached significance. The difference between avoidance-escape and yoked animals in this condition also approached significance. As in previous studies, steroid level was correlated with ulceration; the correlation between total length of lesions and steroid level averaged $r = .43$ in the groups receiving shock.

Water intake during the stress session, which was also recorded, showed no significant differences between groups which received shock. The shocked groups (avoidance-escape and yoked subjects) drank significantly more water than the nonshock groups, as we have reported previously (Weiss, 1971a, 1971b).

DISCUSSION

The present results clearly show the remarkable influence that feedback from coping attempts has upon the development of stomach ulceration. Two groups of animals were allowed to avoid and/or escape shock in the same unsignaled-shock situation except that for one group a brief tone stimulus was presented whenever a response was made. The amount of responding was similar in both groups so that they received almost identical amounts of shock. Despite the similarity of stressful conditions and the number of shocks received, the animals which could avoid and escape shock under normal unsignaled-shock conditions developed considerable ulceration (as expected), whereas the animals which could avoid and escape shock but with the feedback-tone stimulus present developed less ulceration than has been seen in any previous shock condition. Thus, by increasing the relevant feedback from responding, it was possible to reduce stomach ulceration greatly in a condition which is otherwise quite ulcerogenic.

That high feedback for responding would result in a low amount of ulceration was predicted by a proposed theory (Weiss, 1971a). Why this was expected to occur can be seen by consulting a model of the theory presented in Figure 9 of an earlier paper (Weiss, 1971a). This theory states that ulceration tends to increase as the number of coping attempts increases. But it further states that this tendency diminishes as the appropriate feedback from coping responses (which is called relevant feedback) becomes greater. Thus, when relevant feedback is very high (as it is in the feedback signal condition of the present experiment), ulceration is expected to be low because animals will not ulcerate more severely as they increase the number of responses they make. Conversely, when relevant feedback is low (as it is in the normal unsignaled-shock condition), ulceration is expected to be considerable because animals will indeed ulcerate more severely as their responding increases. The results roughly confirm these predictions. Figure 6 shows the amount of ulceration as a function of the number of responses for all avoidance-escape animals in the experiment. For avoidance-escape animals which did not have the feedback tone, ulceration increased as the number of responses increased. But for avoidance-escape animals which received the tone stimulus, the regression line is almost flat, showing that ulceration did not increase regardless of how many responses these animals made.

The ulceration which developed in avoidance-escape animals that received the tone-feedback stimulus was, in fact, not much more severe than that which was found in nonshock control animals. Ulceration in the tone-feedback condition, as can be seen from the results, consisted almost entirely of small pinpoint lesions less than .25 mm. in size, which avoidance-escape animals developed in slightly greater number than did nonshock controls. Large lesions did not occur in the tone-feedback condition. For example, lesions larger than .25 mm., of which Figure 7 shows an example, were observed in only 31% (5 out of 16) of the avoidance-escape animals in the tone-feedback condition. That this constitutes very mild pathology in the group can be judged by the fact that among the control animals of this study which received no shock at all, 34% showed such lesions. By comparison, 100% of the avoidance-escape animals which did not receive the feedback stimulus developed such lesions. Thus, while

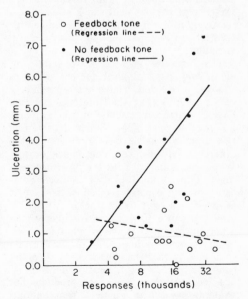

FIG. 6. The amount of ulceration developed by all avoidance-escape animals as a function of the number of avoidance-escape responses.

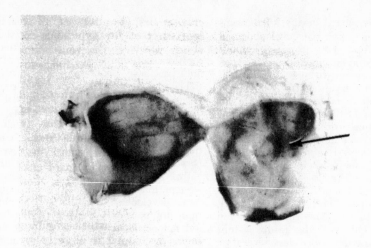

FIG. 7. The stomach of an avoidance-escape animal which received the feedback stimulus, showing a .5-mm. lesion (indicated by arrow). This is one of the five subjects in this group which developed a lesion of this size. The lack of pathology in this group can be judged by the fact that, with the exception of one subject which could not be photographed, the subject shown here had the largest amount of ulceration found in this group.

we can see that the feedback stimulus did not completely reduce ulceration to the level seen in nonshock control animals, the difference between these groups was very small. These findings again reveal that the presence of the physical shock stressor is a relatively minor determinant of stomach ulceration in comparison to psychological variables.

These results also serve to point out again how psychological factors influence stomach ulceration. I have noted previously (Weiss, 1968) that the difference between having control over shock and being helpless is often more important in determining the extent of gastric ulceration than is the difference between receiving shock or not. While this is indeed true, the present experiment shows that this does not occur because having control over shock is, in and of itself, the significant factor; rather, it occurs because having control over shock generally means that the relevant feedback from responses is high. The present results show clearly that the effectiveness of coping behavior in reducing ulceration depends on the feedback that responses produce. For example, we see in Figure 2 that animals which could avoid or escape shock in the normal unsignaled-shock condition developed only slightly less ulceration than yoked animals which were helpless. Thus, being able to control shock was, in this case, not much more beneficial than being helpless. Now if we compare the normal avoidance-escape animals with the avoidance-escape animals that received the feedback stimulus, we note a large difference here. The size of this difference in comparison to the one cited just above illustrates how receiving the appropriate feedback for responding is more important than simply having control over the stressor. This observation is fully in accord with the theory I have proposed, which does not emphasize qualitative differences, such as control or the lack of it, but considers the amount of feedback which responses produce. Keeping in mind that control vs. helplessness does not represent a difference which is per se important for ulceration, but that this distinction becomes important only insofar as a subject which has control over the stressor receives relevant feedback as a consequence of this control, we can now approach the question of why the "executive" monkey results were obtained.

### EXPLAINING THE EXECUTIVE MONKEY RESULTS

The theory presented in Weiss (1971a) offers an explanation for why the executive monkey results (Brady, 1958) occurred. In four pairs of monkeys, the animal which could avoid an electric shock by pressing a lever developed severe gastric ulceration[3] and died, whereas yoked animals that received the same shock showed no evidence of gastric pathology. As the experimenters carefully pointed out in the original report of this effect (Brady, Porter, Conrad, & Mason, 1958), animals chosen as avoidance subjects were placed into this condition because they initially showed a higher rate of responding than their matched partners, which were made yoked subjects. According to the theory I have proposed, ulceration is a function of the number of responses emitted, so that the executive monkeys were therefore more likely to ulcerate than their yoked partners. It is indeed remarkable that the variable inadvertently used to select the executive monkeys turned out to be one which is functionally related to the development of ulceration. Moreover, the executive monkeys were made to perform in a Sidman, or unsignaled-shock, condition which, as was pointed out earlier, can be highly ulcerogenic because the relevant feedback from coping responses is low. The executive monkeys, therefore, were high-rate responders placed into a low-feedback condition, which is just the combination of circumstances that the theory states will produce severe ulceration. In addition to these considerations, the high rate of responding by avoidance monkeys was very effective in avoiding the shock, so that they and yoked partners often received only one or two brief shocks per hour. For this reason, the yoked animals probably did not emit a large number of coping attempts because the situation for them was relatively benign. Under these circumstances, it is not at all surprising that the monkeys which were performing the avoidance response developed severe pathology while the yoked subjects did not.

Although in the present experiments I chose avoidance-escape and yoked animals randomly, it is possible to draw from the already existing data a sample of matched avoidance-escape and yoked rats which bear the same sampling characteristics as did the subjects in the executive monkey experiment. This is done if from these data one selects matched subjects in which the avoidance-escape animal shows a response rate above the median for the avoidance-escape group and the yoked animal shows a response rate below the median for the yoked group; in this population, high and low responders are distributed as avoidance-escape and yoked animals in the same way, on the average, as occurs if one matches two subjects and then selects the higher responder as the avoidance-escape subject, as was done in the executive monkey experiment. Using all 36 triplets that I have exposed to the unsignaled-shock condition in the present experiment and in Weiss (1971a), which is the condition analogous to the one used in the executive monkey experiment, nine of the matched avoidance-escape and yoked pairs should by chance have these characteristics, and nine did. In such a sample, the avoidance-escape animals showed significantly ($p < .05$) more ulceration ($Mdn = 4.0$ mm.) than did their matched yoked partners ($Mdn = 1.8$ mm.), which indicates that I find essentially the same effect as did Brady et al. (1958) if subjects in the present experiments are selected in a manner similar to theirs. Thus, I conclude that the executive monkey results are not anomalous but came about because of most unusual conditions.[4]

### GENERALITY OF THE PROPOSED THEORY

Since the two independent variables used in the proposed theory, responding and feedback, are basic ones in any stressful situation, it is indeed possible that stress responses other than gastric ulceration may be

---

[3] Chronic duodenal lesions were found in this study. It should be noted that the lesions studied in the present experiments are acute lesions of the fundus, and the theory I have proposed has been developed and tested in relation to this type of lesion. Of course, in so far as the theory can be applied to a phenomenon in which duodenal lesions were observed, this is evidence that the theory is not restricted to acute gastric lesions only.

[4] This does not, of course, mean that the executive monkey experiment should be easy to replicate. Replication would depend on using a population of monkeys which were susceptible to development of gastrointestinal ulcers. Monkeys generally used in experimentation appear to be considerably more resistant to development of gastrointestinal ulcers (e.g., Foltz & Millett, 1964) than were the subjects used in the executive monkey experiment.

related to these variables in the manner this theory proposes. There are suggestions of this in other measures taken, one such measure being the plasma level of corticosterone. The level of corticosterone in the blood rises when an animal is exposed to a stressor. This response is, however, a rather sluggish one, the level building up slowly in the blood and also tending to rise substantially regardless of the intensity of the stressor (Friedman & Ader, 1967; Friedman, Ader, Grota, & Larson, 1967), possibly because the function of corticosterone is actually to antagonize excitatory stress reactions (Weiss, McEwen, Silva, & Kalkut, 1970). Despite the nature of this response, it nevertheless showed differences which fit with the expectations of the proposed theory. In addition, Weiss, Stone, and Harrell (1970) reported that brain norepinephrine level can be increased by the ability to perform an effective coping response. In both situations where this effect was found, the feedback for responding was quite high. Results recently obtained in this laboratory indicate that when feedback from avoidance-escape responses is low, as in the unsignaled-shock condition, this norepinephrine increase is not seen but that it does occur when a feedback stimulus is added to such a condition; thus brain norepinephrine metabolism may be responsive to the variables delineated. Whether the proposed theory will, in fact, have a wider application than is seen in the present experiments remains to be determined.

## REFERENCES

BRADY, J. V. Ulcers in "executive" monkeys. *Scientific American,* 1958. **199,** 95–100.

BRADY, J. V., PORTER, R. W., CONRAD, D. G., & MASON, J. W. Avoidance behavior and the development of gastroduodenal ulcers. *Journal of the Experimental Analysis of Behavior,* 1958, **1,** 69–72.

FOLTZ, E. L., & MILLETT, F. E. Experimental psychosomatic disease states in monkeys: I. Peptic "ulcer-executive monkeys." *Journal of Surgical Research,* 1964, **4,** 445–453.

FRIEDMAN, S. B., & ADER, R. Adrenocortical response to novelty and noxious stimulation. *Neuroendocrinology,* 1967, **2,** 209–212.

FRIEDMAN, S. B., ADER, R., GROTA, L. J., & LARSON, T. Plasma corticosterone response to parameters of electric shock stimulation in the rat. *Psychosomatic Medicine,* 1967. **29,** 323–328.

GUILLEMIN, R., CLAYTON, G. W., SMITH, J. D., & LIPSCOMB, H. S. Measurement of free corticosteroid in rat plasma: Physiological validation of a method. *Endocrinology,* 1958, **63,** 349–358.

WEISS, J. M. Effects of coping responses on stress. *Journal of Comparative and Physiological Psychology,* 1968, **65,** 251–260.

WEISS, J. M. Effects of coping behavior in different warning signal conditions on stress pathology in rats. *Journal of Comparative and Physiological Psychology,* 1971, **77,** 1–13. (a)

WEISS, J. M. Effects of punishing the coping response (conflict) on stress pathology in rats. *Journal of Comparative and Physiological Psychology,* 1971, **77,** 14–21. (b) .

WEISS, J. M., McEWEN, B. S., SILVA, M. T., & KALKUT, M. Pituitary-adrenal alterations and fear responding. *American Journal of Physiology,* 1970, **218,** 864–868.

WEISS, J. M., STONE, E. A., & HARRELL, N. Coping behavior and brain norepinephrine level in rats. *Journal of Comparative and Physiological Psychology,* 1970, **72,** 153–160.

# VII

## HYPNOSIS

# An Appraisal of Hypnosis 25

## H. Merskey

'*There is no doubt that Freud is right in his remark that the eager readiness of the medical profession to employ the term "suggestion"' is due not so much to the propagandism of the Nancy school as to the alleviating discovery that a great economy of thought can thereby be effected*' (Jones, 1910).

Hypnosis tends today to be little used in psychiatric practice. Occasionally it is employed, as a useful adjunct to psychotherapy or manipulation of the environment, in the treatment of patients with hysterical conversion symptoms. A relaxation procedure with or without hypnotic suggestions may be followed in the treatment of specific phobias (which are rare), or in the treatment of tension headache—which is common but far more often treated with psychotherapy and medication. Claims are made for its use in psychosomatic conditions, e.g. warts or asthma, and in the treatment of pain in childbirth. But typically, in such instances, warts respond to alternative means of suggestion, whilst asthma benefits most in respect of patients' reports of subjective well-being but very much less in regard to physical indices like vital capacity (Maher-Loughnan & Kinsley, 1968; Maher-Loughnan, 1970). Similarly pain in childbirth is only relieved erratically, and probably not more than moderately, by hypnosis, so that whilst relaxation training is widely practised (Chertok, 1969) hypnosis itself is rarely used. In this country there are one or two research workers in the field of hypnotism and systematic experimental work is conducted by a number of psychologists in North America. In the U.S.S.R. the subject attracts attention, in a framework of Pavlovian theory. The writer only uses the technique occasionally but has employed it from time to time in the past, and many, perhaps most, psychiatrists in the U.K. do not use it at all. Nevertheless the subject remains of considerable theoretical and human interest.

### The common phenomena

The following brief description of the technique and phenomena of induction of a hypnotic state, will serve as an introduction to considering the nature of the condition.

As a preliminary the hypnotist attempts to establish the patient's confidence in him and also his willingness to co-operate, since hypnosis cannot be induced without co-operation. In most techniques the recumbent patient is required to fixate his eyes on a point slightly above and forwards, to breathe slowly and deeply, and to consciously relax his muscles. Suggestions are then given that he will go to sleep: 'Your eyes feel heavy and they are slowly closing. You won't be able to keep them open. The eyelids are getting heavier and heavier and closer and closer together. It is more and more of an effort to keep them open . . . you can't keep them open any longer . . .'. If the patient is susceptible his eyes will close in about 5 or 10 min, sometimes, in fact frequently, if the attempt is made to produce a quick result, he will close them within 2 or 3 min. This is the first stage of hypnosis. Suggestions are then given that the sleep is deepening, the relaxation more profound. In the second stage of hypnosis the subject or patient apparently loses his ability to control his muscles voluntarily. A convenient way to test this is to give the suggestion that one arm is rising from the couch. As this suggestion is repeated, intensively, the arm will rise slowly into the air. At this point the suggestion can be given that the arm has gone stiff when the patient will find that he can no longer move his arm until told to do so. This level of hypnosis is suitable for most treatment. The third stage of hypnosis is the somnambulist, in which the patient can walk about although still hypnotized. It is at this stage that some of the more curious phenomena can be observed, e.g. pinprick is not only unfelt but bleeding may not occur. This level of hypnosis is only attained by a minority of subjects and although it is used in research, it is often not necessary in medical treatment. In the second and third stages of hypnosis, psychogenic paralysis, amnesias, anaesthesias and even hallucinations or false beliefs may be induced or abolished. Suggestions may be given during the session to carry out various actions either immediately or after the session has finished. Those which are intended to take effect later are known as post-hypnotic suggestion and make subsequent induction easier (Merskey & Tonge, 1965). The practice of hypnosis is relatively easy for anyone who has an interest in undertaking it and, despite the potential drama, the procedure seems rather boring after a few occasions. Sim (1968) indeed puts it that 'if trade unions were to rate the practice of hypnotism, it would not rate higher than semi-skilled labour'. However, many striking effects are attributed to hypnosis and it is quite widely accepted that hypnosis can relieve the pain of childbirth and operations in an exceptional way even though the provision of good relief may be unreliable; it is also widely thought that a splitting of consciousness is involved as well as some physiological alterations. Since 1958 evidence has been produced in abundance which challenges the idea that these phenomena are the perquisite of a special trance state (Barber, 1969, 1970). This evidence, supporting an older view, allows a re-interpretation of hypnosis and is, in the writer's opinion, the most important psychological contribution to the topic since Freud discovered the transference in the course of hypnotic treatment. Before attempting to describe Barber's work, an account will be given of some of the history of the subject and the most relevant scientific findings.

### History of hypnosis

The literature and sources on this aspect as on others to do with hypnosis is vast, and even a whole-time student of the subject would probably be unable to achieve comprehensive coverage. The most consistent theme is a relationship between hypnosis and suggestion, it being disputed whether hypnosis is nothing more than suggestion, or else a special trance state in which suggestion readily occurs. It is confidently stated (Ambrose & Newbold, 1968) that the phenomena were known to many ancient civilizations including the early Celtic inhabitants of Britain. Cures by suggestion, perhaps involving some alteration of attitudes or apparent awareness, could probably be found throughout medical writings from antiquity to the present times. In the eighteenth and nineteenth centuries the efficacy of suggestion and hypnotic procedures was ineluctably recognized. The story commonly highlights Franz Anton Mesmer (1734–1815) a physician who combined cures with demonstrations. At first Mesmer attributed his successes to the use of magnets—genuinely believing in their powers. He soon learnt that magnets were unnecessary but continued to believe that 'animal magnetism' caused the various phenomena which he induced and he regarded 'animal magnetism' as a physiological process. The subject was investigated by a Commission appointed by Louis XVI headed by the astronomer Bailly and including Benjamin Franklin, Dr Guillotin and Lavoisier. The Bailly report (1784) described a number of hypnotic phenomena, accepted their reality and attributed their production to imagination not magnetism. '. . . imagination without magnetism can produce convulsions . . . magnetism without imagination has no effect at all'. D'Eslon (1780) had already remarked 'If the medicine of the imagination is best why should we not practice the medicine of the imagination?' Thus the ebb and flow of discussion and investigation resulted in an explicit distinction being made between physical effects due to physiological agents and physical effects due to psychological influences; and the psychological view was established authoritatively. Despite this, controversy and uncertainty continues to the present time. It was in the course of argument about rival explanations that Braid (1843) coined the word 'hypnotism' to emphasize the neurophysiological interpretation.

The course of the nineteenth century discussion could serve as a paradigm for the problems—and also the achievements—of research into psychological phenomena. Apart from the influence of the placebo effect and the difficulty of establishing control procedures there were problems of finding adequate concepts, exemplified by the use of terms like those already mentioned and others such as 'fluidism' and 'animist'. Moreover, as Freud was later to show, the motives of both subject and hypnotist were often neither scientific nor solely directed towards a cure. And the topic is, and was, bedevilled by the ease with which it lends itself to practice by charlatans and the uncritical. Indeed the latter are at a particular advantage since the less sceptical the practitioner is of his powers and results, the easier it is to produce impressive changes. Some of the more extreme examples of behaviour induced under hypnosis, including those alleged to support notions of extra-sensory perception, are to be found in a series of volumes edited by Dingwall (1967), and include items like reading sentences which have been completely covered over, playing cards blindfold, supposed thought-transmission and similar tricks which today would be considered essentially the province of the deliberate stage illusionist. An excellent brief but scholarly account of the history of the scientific issues is given by Chertok (1966).

It is worth remarking also that the school of Charcot noted the apparent identity of many types of hysterical behaviour with hypnosis, the same patterns of response, the same neurological characteristics in the paralysis, the tendency with hypnosis to produce dissociations of consciousness and even multiple personalities, and the particular liability of some patients with hysteria to produce the most extreme examples of hypnotic effects. In consequence hysterics can accept and act upon the most remarkable suggestions under hypnosis but at other times prove very resistant to being hypnotized.

### Suggestion

After the claim that hypnosis was a psychological process the next notable development in the nineteenth century was the increasing recognition of the importance of suggestion as a principal factor in inducing hypnotic phenomena. The development of this viewpoint is particularly credited to Hippolyte Bernheim, Professor of Medicine at Nancy. Associated with his name is that of Liébeault, a country practitioner of wide experience and great skill and integrity. Suggestion— as will be indicated—remains the most solidly established element in the hypnotic procedures. Theories of suggestion had to contend with other evidence emerging from the school of Charcot at the Salpêtrière and a quotation on the matter from William James (1890) is apposite:

'*The Theory of Suggestion* denies that there is any special hypnotic state worthy of the name of trance or neurosis. All the symptoms above described as well as those to be described hereafter, are results of that mental susceptibility which we all to some degree possess, of yielding assent to outward suggestion, of affirming what we strongly conceive, and of acting in accordance with what we are made to expect. The bodily symptoms of the Salpêtrière patients are all of them results of expectation and training. The first patients accidentally did certain things which their doctors thought typical and caused to be repeated. The subsequent subjects "caught on" and followed the established traditions. In proof of this the fact is urged that the classical three stages and their grouped symptoms have only been reported as spontaneously occurring so far, at the Salpêtrière, though they may be superinduced by deliberate suggestion, in patients anywhere found. The ocular symptoms, the flushed face, accelerated breathing etc. are said not to be symptoms of the passage into the hypnotic state as such, but merely consequences of the strain on the eyes when the method of looking at a bright object is used. They are absent in the subjects at Nancy where simple verbal suggestion is employed. The various reflex effects (aphasia, echolalia, imitation, etc.) are but habits induced by the influence of the operator, who unconsciously urges the subject into the direction in which he would prefer to have him go. The influence of the magnet, the opposite effects of upward and downward passes, etc. are similarly explained. Even that sleepy and inert condition the advent of which seems to be the prime condition of further symptoms being developed, is said to be merely due to the fact that the mind expects it to come; whilst its influence on the other symptoms is not physiological, so to speak, but psychical, its own easy realization by suggestion simply encouraging the subject to expect that ulterior suggestions will be realized with equal ease. The radical defenders of the suggestion theory are thus led to deny the very existence of the hypnotic state, in the sense of a peculiar trance-like condition which deprives the patient of spontaneity and makes him passive to suggestion from without. The trance itself is only one of the suggestions, and many subjects in fact can be made to exhibit the other hypnotic phenomena without the induction of this one.

The theory of suggestion may be said to be quite triumphant at the present day over the neurosis theory as held at the Salpêtrière, with its three states, and its definitive symptoms supposed to be produced by physical agents apart from co-operation of the subject's mind. But it is one thing to say this, and it is quite another thing to say that

there is no peculiar physiological condition whatever worthy of the name of hypnotic trance, no peculiar state of nervous equilibrium, 'hypotaxy', 'dissociation', or whatever you please to call it, during which the subject's susceptibility to outward suggestion is greater than at ordinary times. All the facts seem to prove that, until this trance-like state is assumed by the patient, suggestion produces very insignificant results, but that, when it is once assumed, there are no limits to suggestion's power. The state in question has many affinities with ordinary sleep.'

Clearly although the importance of suggestion was well recognized by all workers, James could not rid himself of the idea that a special nervous or trance state might be occurring or some form of dissociation of consciousness. The latter was suggested by Janet, Charcot, Prince, Tuckey and numerous others, who took an active interest at that time in dissociations of the personality and related phenomena, like hysterical fits and trances, similar hypnotically induced states and hypnotic treatment. Bernheim, despite his attack on Charcot, thought that hypnosis was a normal physiological variant of sleep. The belief in a special trance state persisted in the view of many astute workers who considered that hypnosis resembled sleep (Schilder, 1956) and it is still held at least in the form that there is some altered state of consciousness (e.g. Gill & Brenman, 1959; Shor, 1959; Delay & Pichot, 1962; Abse, 1966; Tart, 1969). The reasons why the writer has relinquished this view will appear shortly. In essence they depend on the negative character of relevant neurophysiological data and the positive nature of Barber's experimental work. Before relating this information, it is worthwhile considering the dynamic aspects of hypnosis and the relationship with hysteria, since even though hypnosis may not be a special form of trance state it is important to examine how 'suggestion' may work. As Jones (1910) put it 'to be able to attribute a given occurrence to suggestion is with many a complete solution of the problem, and they do not find it necessary to pursue the matter further . . . it is striking to find what little work has been done on the question of the nature of suggestion'.

### The motives for suggestion

In 1917 Freud remarked that Bernheim 'could never say what suggestion actually was or how it arises . . . he did not recognize the dependence of "suggestibility" on sexuality, or the functioning of the libido. And we have to admit that we only abandoned hypnosis in our methods in order to discover suggestion again in the shape of transference'. Freud abandoned hypnosis primarily because he discovered that it led to a special dependence upon him by the hysterical patients he treated. At first his only complaints were that he could not hypnotize every patient and that he could not always take those who were hypnotized deep enough. Then increasing experience raised doubts. He found 'even the most brilliant results were liable to be suddenly wiped away if my personal relationship with the patient became disturbed'. Then 'one of my most acquiescent patients with whom hypnotism had enabled me to bring about the most marvellous results, and whom I was engaged in relieving of suffering by tracing back her attacks of pain to their origins, as she woke up on one occasion, threw her arms around my neck. The unexpected entrance of a servant relieved us from a painful discussion, but from that time onwards there was a tacit understanding between us that the hypnotic treatment should be discontinued. I was modest enough not to attribute the event to my own irresistible attraction, and I felt that I had now grasped the nature of the mysterious element that was at work behind hypnotism. In order to exclude it or at all events to isolate it, it was necessary to abandon hypnotism.'

The power which motivated the patient to accept the hypnotic procedure was evidently not just a wish to recover, it was sexual love which would attach itself inevitably to the therapist; and hypnosis resembled love with its humble subjection and absence of criticism towards the hypnotist as towards the loved object (Freud, 1921). Moreover, the ability to be hypnotized to a varying depth has to do, as Jones (1910) put it, 'rather with some inherent faculty that varies with different subjects than with any positive action on the part of the hypnotist'. A justification or criticism of these views is beyond the scope of this article. It is sufficient for our purposes to recognize: (1) that the relationship of hypnotizer to subject is most typically, though not invariably, one in which masculine dominance attitudes are adopted by the hypnotizer and feminine-passive-compliant attitudes are displayed by the subject, who is most often female; (2) other motives, less closely tied, if at all, to sexual libido can play an important part in determining hypnotizability, e.g. valid wishes to recover, explore a new experience, or (supposedly) an extra dimension of consciousness, or to assist a scientific investigation; (3) since the ability to be hypnotized depends so much on the individual it is essential to consider the motives that lead to the acceptance of suggestion.

## Physiological observations

The view that hypnosis is a trance state with a specific physiological basis gains credence in part from the supposedly far-reaching effects of hypnosis upon the body. In the sensory systems, deafness, blindness and the ·abolition of pain are notable changes attributed to hypnosis; similarly autonomic changes affecting the bronchioles, circulation and perhaps the skin are widely supposed to occur with hypnosis, and differences in immunological responses have been shown (Black, 1963a, b; Black, Humphrey & Niven, 1963; Black & Friedman, 1965). The regression of a subject to childhood and the production of an extensor plantar response, or the abolition of corneal reflexes have likewise been claimed. There is good reason however, to doubt that any of the more extreme claims of the power of hypnosis are justified. According to this view a very typical result was obtained by Malmo, Boag &

Raginsky (1954) in a study of hysterical deafness and hypnotically induced deafness. Muscle potentials were recorded and also eye-blink, and the authors describing their first hypnotic subject report '. . . in interview following the hypnotic session (she) denied hearing any sounds during the period of hypnotic deafness. Motor data . . . showed clear reaction to the first stimulus'. Subsequent motor responses were reduced significantly apart from blink, but were not wholly abolished. The discrepancy between the absolute subjective loss of hearing and the persistence of reflex response emphasizes the failure of hypnosis to fully inhibit the involuntary mechanisms of the nervous system. Similarly in regard to pain, Barber (1963) in a detailed examination of the evidence finds that 'hypnotic analgesia' may be accompanied by signs of pain and produces an unwillingness to state directly to the hypnotist that pain was experienced. Taking the most famous cases of 'painless' surgery under hypnosis, those of Esdaile, Barber finds such reports as 'she moved and moaned', 'About the middle of the operation she gave a cry', 'The man moved and cried out, before I had finished . . . on being questioned he said that he had felt no pain'. Of six patients on whom Esdaile operated for scrotal tumours, three showed no gross signs of pain, but two of these three showed marked elevations of pulse rate of the order of 40 beats/min. Here and there is more than a hint that many hypnotized patients experience pain which they are reluctant to report. A striking illustration of this is provided in a report by Kaplan (1960) of a deeply hypnotized subject who was traumatized in the left arm. To the experimenter he said 'When are we going to begin?' With his right hand, which was engaged in automatic writing he had written 'Ouch, dammit, you're hurting me!' Kaplan concludes from this that the pain was experienced '*at some level*' and that hypnosis produced an 'artificial repression and/or denial'. Mandy *et al.* (1952) similarly presented evidence that 'natural childbirth' patients who claimed not to have pain would tell independent observers that delivery was painful after all. One patient said she could not admit it to the staff for fear of disappointing them. This is not to say that pain is not susceptible to hypnosis. There is much evidence that pain is reduced by hypnosis and by a variety of other psychological influences (Barber, 1959; Merskey & Spear, 1967). But the extent of the reduction by hypnosis is usually limited and it has not been shown that more can be done by hypnosis, either in causing or alleviating pain, than by the usual forms of psychiatric treatment or by procedures which, either necessarily or deliberately, employ placebos. In the writer's practice, which involves many patients who have pain of psychological origin and others with physical causes for their pain the use of hypnosis is negligible. Authors who have reported on the treatment of the pain in spinal cord lesions (Dorcus & Kirkner, 1948) and in neoplasia (Butler, 1954) find the help given is often incomplete and time-consuming, and perhaps not more than could be obtained by psychological support (Butler, 1954).

Sacerdote (1965) reports partial success in the treatment of two patients with secondary carcinoma, but in one of the cases the patient required daily sessions and had much emotional support of which he was in obvious need. Sacerdote is one of the few making claims for the active use of hypnosis in the treatment of cancer (Sacerdote, 1966) and of patients with chronic protracted pain of organic origin (Sacerdote, 1962). Whilst the benefit of the hypnotist's presence can be readily understood and conceded it is by no means to be supposed that comparable effects were not obtainable by other psychological techniques.

In regard to physiological changes associated with pain Shor (1962a) found experimentally that galvanic skin response, respiration, limb movement and heart rate were favourably influenced by hypnosis and equally by the reduction of anxiety without hypnosis. From this work and from a review of other papers on the physiological variables associated with pain (Shor, 1962b) he concludes that 'hypnotic analgesia is one means of eliminating the incidental anxiety component of the total pain experience'.

As Barber has emphasized there are three conclusions, amongst others, which can be drawn from the quite large number of papers available. Firstly hypnotic subjects do give behavioural evidence of experiencing pain, secondly they tend to deny the experience of pain to the hypnotist—but acknowledge it to others, and thirdly hypnosis has not been shown to produce more effect than other techniques. Where it has been directly compared with them as by Shor (1962a) and Barber & Hahn (1962) the responses of the hypnotic group and of the others are more or less the same.

The limited nature of the hypnotic effect can likewise be seen in studies of the circulation. Black *et al.* (1963) found no interaction between hypnosis and thermal body changes. Only small effects were observed with the induction of hypnosis on hand blood flow, pulse and respiration and none on forearm blood flow. In a few experiments marked changes in forearm blood flow occurred which appeared to resemble changes in the circulation caused by emotional stimuli. A failure to show more than minor physical changes in the vital capacity of asthmatics has already been mentioned. Experiments which claimed to show the unilateral abolition of warts (Sinclair-Gieben & Chalmers, 1959) have not apparently been replicated (the writer once tried this unsuccessfully). There is an impressive report (Black, 1936b) of the effect on hypersensitivity where direct suggestion under hypnosis showed very marked to moderate degrees of instant inhibition, in eight subjects out of twelve, of the immediate-type (Prausnitz-Küstner) hypersensitivity response. Even here however the control comparison was with the normal waking state and not with non-hypnotic suggestion. Thus the peripheral physiological effects of hypnosis, like its effect on pain, are less impressive than is sometimes thought and comparable results appear to be attainable by other psychological techniques.

Another possibly significant area of physiological knowledge has to do with so-called animal hypnosis.

An excellent account of this and of related phenomena is given by Oswald (1962). The classical experiment in this field was conducted in 1646 by the Abbé Kircher who described how a trance state of immobility could be brought about in a chicken by seizing it and holding the head and trunk motionless in an unnatural position. Similar 'death feigning' or 'still reactions' have been reported to occur in all varieties of creatures from cockroach to primate. Oswald states that a response can be provoked by overwhelming fear, monotonous stimulation and imposed restriction either separately or in combination. The initial condition is one of immobility, with extreme alertness and increased muscular tension, passing into a condition of light sleep lasting for a matter of minutes or more. The EEG changes are first those of alertness and then those of sleep. A similar condition has often been induced in animals subjected to insoluble conflict situations in the course of laboratory experiments. This condition is often described as an inhibitory experimental neurosis and was observed first by Pavlov. Some writers have seen a similarity between animal hypnosis and human hypnosis. Chertok (1966) observed that a living organism always requires to react to the outside world, and if this interaction is interrupted or altered, the organism may react by adopting a regressive attitude. He claimed that this is precisely what happens in both animal and human hypnosis, and this common factor provides the basis for a fundamental similarity in the two forms of hypnosis. The writer does not find this view convincing. Animal hypnosis—so-called—is a condition of immobility with tension. Human hypnosis is generally one of relaxation but not necessarily immobility. A varied response is possible for the hypnotized human subject but does not appear to occur in the animal case. Natural sleep seems to be the usual sequel to animal hypnosis and it is a relatively rare one in the human. The biological significance of animal hypnosis is that producing immobility helps in the avoidance of notice by predators. None of this would apply to human hypnosis except by very far-fetched argument. There are conditions in man which seem to resemble animal hypnosis somewhat more, and they are generally forms of stupor. Catatonic stupor and, to a lesser extent, depressive stupor are somewhat like animal hypnosis, in their lack of response to communications and stimuli. Some cases of stupor provoked by organic brain damage, may also be held to resemble animal hypnosis. Again they are distinct from conventional human hypnosis both by virtue of the presence of organic disease and, as with stupors caused by psychosis, in the failure of the affected person to respond to instructions and communications. It seems reasonable to conclude that phenomena of this type are very different from the sort of conditions that are called hypnosis in man.

Hypnosis also differs from natural sleep. The EEG of natural sleep passes through several stages but is different in readily recognizable ways from that of the waking state. The EEG under hypnosis remains little changed from, if not identical with, that of the waking condition, except when after a while the subject may become unresponsive to hypnotic commands or enquiries because natural sleep has supervened. Such small changes as may be seen in the EEG under hypnosis can be related to variations in attention, relaxation and emotion. These simple well-known data were at first very surprising and in some ways a disappointing discovery. It might have been confidently expected that the EEG of the hypnotized subject would show some alteration which enabled us to classify it with organic or physiological disturbances of consciousness, perhaps in the same group but with distinctive features of its own. In that event one of the most fascinating psychological problems could have been understood or re-interpreted in terms of cerebral physiology. So far this has not been possible, and indeed if we take the psychological evidence seriously it is not very likely that it will be possible until we can describe thought processes and the complexities of interpersonal behaviour in physiological terms. An investigation which confirms this lack of recognizable cerebral physiological changes under hypnosis was reported by Halliday & Mason (1964). These investigators recorded somato-sensory and auditory evoked potentials and found no difference in the potentials between the normal state and that following hypnotically induced sensory loss. This negative finding is important, particularly because it was not the result which the investigators might well have anticipated. But it fits extremely well with the view that hypnosis (and hysteria) do not prevent the registration of sensory impulses or even their cerebral processing. And if one accepts that hypnotic subjects are engaging in denial of experience rather than managing to block their sensory input then this result is in precise accordance with expectation. Nonetheless the attempt to find a physical basis for hypnosis in brain activity is not readily jettisoned and authors can still be found who try, much in advance of currently available knowledge, to locate the mechanism of hysteria and hypnosis in the reticular activating system.

### Expectation and hypnotic behaviour

Even if hypnosis is not sleep we are still left with the problem as to whether hypnosis is a special form of trance or altered consciousness. Evidence in regard to this has already been touched on. It is considered in detail by Barber (1969) who on the basis of much experimental evidence offers the view, in essence, that hypnosis is a pattern of behaviour which depends upon expectation and suggestion—and it is nothing more.

Barber's argument runs somewhat as follows:

From the standard accounts of hypnotic behaviour we can abstract two patterns. One, the *response to test-suggestions* is elicited by suggesting that the subject cannot unclasp his hands or bend a knee or feel stimuli. He is told—and acts accordingly—that he will see or hear things not present, forget everything that has occurred and will undertake post-hypnotic acts which are sometimes bizarre or comical. The second pattern is of *limpness–relaxation*, lack of spontaneity, fixity of the eyes and psycho-motor retardation. In addition patients will later state

that they were hypnotized to a light, medium or deep level. From these observations two assumptions are commonly made: (1) that a special trance state occurred and (2) that this state is an instrumental factor in producing the patterns of behaviour described. From the earlier discussions it will be seen how tenuous are these explanations. A scientific approach requires that we specify independent (antecedent) and dependent (consequent) variables and that we determine their relationship empirically. In hypnosis the dependent variables are the well recognized behaviour patterns just mentioned. The independent variables are less obvious. The first group includes the instructions or suggestions employed in hypnotic induction. Besides the usual pattern this means such subtle features as tone of voice, method of presentation (e.g. orally or by tape-recording) and the specific wording of the questions used to elicit subjective testimony. For example, with respect to amnesia the wording of an enquiry may vary from 'Tell me everything that you remember' to 'Have you forgotten everything that occurred?'

A second group of independent variables includes the personality characteristic of the subject, his attitudes and expectations. A third group relates to the experimenter's status, personality, attitudes and expectations. Lastly a fourth group relates to the personality interactions between hypnotist and subject. When these variables are systematically studied it becomes possible to show that each of them influences the outcome of hypnosis. Thus investigators use a more forcible tone with hypnotic than non-hypnotic subjects. If this is controlled by tape-recording the experimental results are the same for hypnotic and non-hypnotic groups. Another example may be found in the way phrasing of questions influences responses (Barber, Dalal & Calverley, 1968). In one group asked 'Did you feel you could *not* resist the suggestions?' the answer is usually 'Yes'. In a second group asked 'Did you feel you could resist the suggestions?' the answer is also usually 'Yes'. These groups will likewise testify appropriately that they felt hypnosis was basically similar to, or different from, the waking state, depending upon the way the question is put to them.

Barber claims that the reasoning which requires us to suppose that these changes depend on a trance state is basically circular and invalid. In effect the subject is told he will feel relaxed and act differently. We see him relax and act differently and we assume that he was 'hypnotized' into a trance state. As Chaves (1968) puts it, the presence of the hypnotic state is inferred from criteria which are inseparable from responses to suggestions, and a circular explanation is difficult to avoid because the hypnotic construct is used to explain responses to suggestions. Trance depth is similarly inferred from the behaviour it is supposed to explain. The more the subject carried out waking suggestions to hallucinate, stand on his head or forget everything that occurred, the deeper we say was the trance depth. Subjects follow the same lead and say they were deeply hypnotized because they followed the various suggestions (Barber &

Calverley, 1966). Yet, if instructions are given which strongly motivate subjects to carry out the tasks set them, results can be achieved comparable with those of suggestion under hypnosis. Barber calls these instructions 'task-motivating'.

For the most economical explanation it is unnecessary to postulate a special trance state. The more one looks at the subject's expectations, the things said to him, and the questions put to elucidate what occurred, the clearer it becomes that hypnotic phenomena are determined by the antecedent variables and not by any other peculiar intervening condition. Not surprisingly these antecedent variables work best to produce 'hypnotic' changes where the result depends most on the subject's agreement and testimony (as with suggested deafness) and less or not at all where the dependent variable is a physiological change, or an independently measurable change for which input has to be abolished. Subjects reporting total or partial deafness produced with, or even without, an hypnotic induction procedure, showed stuttering and mispronunciations under conditions of delayed auditory feedback in the same way as persons with normal hearing (Barber & Calverley, 1964). The phenomena of hypnosis then are to be explained as responses to suggestions carried out in accordance with the subject's initial expectations. Those expectations are determined by his previous idea of what is to happen and especially by the way in which the hypnotist presents the situation. Barber gives credit to Sarbin (1950) and to others for similar prior formulations but there is no doubt that his is the most radical and extensive revision of the concept of the hypnotic state.

Despite the range, skill and logic of Barber's work not everyone has been convinced by it. There is a general recognition that he has shown much of interest concerning the interpersonal factors and other variables promoting change under hypnotic suggestion. Chertok (1966) expresses his reservations by arguing, that as with Bernheim, those who wish to assimilate hypnosis to suggestibility continue to use the techniques of instruction in hypnotic induction, thereby showing a lack of consistency. This does not appear to be true of Barber however since he has carefully used the techniques of hypnosis in order to compare them with non-hypnotic suggestibility. One wonders what he should have been asked to do.

Some criticisms of Barber's work have been made both on theoretical and experimental grounds, but none of them appears weighty. Hilgard (1964) seems to suggest that Barber's control condition, in which subjects may be asked to imagine something, is a type of hypnotic induction and thus that his results with 'control' subjects can be attributed to hypnosis. Evans (1966) offers a similar argument. Evans and also Bowers (1966) argue that Barber's demonstrations that hypnosis and suggestion in the form of task-motivating instructions produce the same results do not disprove the occurrence of a trance state; which is true but scarcely proves the existence of a hypnotic trance state. Chaves (1968) supports Barber and points out that if subjects who are instructed to imagine vividly are being exposed to a hypnotic in-

duction procedure, we cannot draw a line separating those instructions which constitute a hypnotic induction procedure from those which do not. In any case there is little justification for labelling instructions to imagine as a 'hypnotic induction' unless we are able to demonstrate that they produce a state of hypnosis. On the other hand Barber's critique of the methods used so far to infer the presence of the presumed hypnotic state have not been criticized by Hilgard or by Evans.

Conn & Conn (1967) criticized Barber for failing to consider important variables like 'primitive transference motivations', 'need gratifications', 'human variables' and 'the willingness and trust of the subject'. Barber has suggested that these and other variables should be evaluated empirically. It is not a fault in his theories that he has failed to lay much emphasis on these particular motivational variables since his theory can stand with or without discussion of them. However, it would probably help to give a more complete explanation of hypnosis, along the lines which Barber uses, if attention were to be paid in the future to both the unconscious and conscious motivations which incline people to be subjects for 'hypnotic induction'.

Experimentally Hilgard & Tart (1966) have attempted to show that Barber's failure to find differences between the effects of task-motivating instructions and a hypnotic induction procedure was because he did not use a design sensitive enough to detect differences. Their own design and conclusions have been criticized by Chaves (1968) who finds that the most appropriate interpretation is that Hilgard & Tart in fact confirmed Barber & Calverley's (1966) findings that, as compared with an unmotivated control treatment, hypnotic induction procedures produced a small increment in suggestibility.

In essence Barber's argument is that what happens in hypnosis depends on the preconception of the participants.

The writer considers Barber's case to be well-established. A Freudian explanation is helpful in addition in understanding some of the motives involved. Why people accept suggestion must be considered as well as how they respond to it. Further the acceptable physiological evidence shows (a) that hypnosis does not produce results which are unobtainable by other psychological means and (b) there is no detectable change in cerebral activity as a special result of hypnosis.

In these circumstances we can describe the nature of hypnosis as follows:

*The nature of hypnosis. Hypnosis is a manoeuvre in which the subject and hypnotist have an implicit agreement that certain events (e.g. paralysis, hallucinations, amnesias) will occur, either during a special procedure or later, in accordance with the hypnotist's instructions. Both try hard to put this agreement into effect and adopt appropriate behavioural rules and the subject uses mechanisms of denial to report on the events in accordance with the implicit agreement. This situation is used to implement various motives whether therapeutic or otherwise, on the part of both participants. There is no trance* state, no detectable cerebral physiological change, and only such peripheral physiological responses as may be produced equally by non-hypnotic suggestion or other emotional changes.

## References

ABSE, W. (1966) *Hysteria*. John Wright, Bristol.

AMBROSE, G. & NEWBOLD, G. (1968) *A Handbook of Medical Hypnosis*. Baillière, Tindall & Cassell, London.

BAILLY, J.S. (1784) *Rapport des Commissaires Chargés par le Roi de l'Examen du Magnetisme Animale*. Imprimerie Royale, Paris, cit. Chertok, 1966.

BARBER, T.X. (1959) Toward a theory of pain: relief of chronic pain by prefrontal leucotomy, opiates, placebos and hypnosis. *Psychological Bulletin*, **56**, 430.

BARBER, T.X. (1963) The effects of hypnosis on pain. A critical review of experimental and clinical findings. *Psychosomatic Medicine*, **25**, 303.

BARBER, T.X. (1969) *A Scientific Approach to Hypnosis*. Van Nostrand, Princeton.

BARBER, T.X. (1970) Suggested ('hypnotic') behaviour. In: *The Trance Paradigm Versus an Alternative Paradigm*. Harding, Mass. Medfield Foundation.

BARBER, T.X. & CALVERLEY, D.S. (1964) Experimental studies in hypnotic behaviour. Suggested deafness evaluated by delayed auditory feedback. *British Journal of Psychology*, **55**, 439.

BARBER, T.X. & CALVERLEY, D.S. (1966) Effects on recall of hypnotic induction, motivational suggestions, and suggested regression: a methodological and experimental analysis. *Journal of Abnormal and Social Psychology*, **71**, 169.

BARBER, T.X., DALAL, A.S. & CALVERLEY, D.S. (1968) The subjective reports of hypnotic subjects. *American Journal of Clinical Hypnosis*, **11**, 74.

BARBER, T.X. & HAHN, K.W. (1962) Physiological and subjective. responses to pain-producing stimulation under hypnotically-suggested and waking-imagined 'analgesia'. *Journal of Abnormal and Social Psychology*, **65**, 411.

BLACK, S. (1963a) Inhibition of immediate-type hypersensitivity response by direct suggestion under hypnosis. *British Medical Journal*, **1**, 925.

BLACK, S. (1963b) Shift in dose-response curve of Prausnitz-Küstner reaction by direct suggestion under hypnosis. *British Medical Journal*, **1**, 990.

BLACK, S., EDHOLM, O.G., FOX, R.H. & KIDD, D.J. (1963) The effect of suggestion under hypnosis on the peripheral circulation in man. *Clinical Science*, **25**, 223.

BLACK, S. & FRIEDMAN, M. (1965) Adrenal function and the inhibition of allergic responses under hypnosis. *British Medical Journal*, **1**, 562.

BLACK, S., HUMPHREY, J.H., NIVEN, J.S.F. (1963) Inhibition of Mantoux reaction by direct suggestion under hypnosis. *British Medical Journal*, **1**, 1649.

BOWERS, K. (1966) Hypnotic behaviour: the differentiation of trance and demand characteristic variables. *Journal of Abnormal and Social Psychology*, **71**, 42.

BRAID, J. (1843) *Neurypnology*. Churchill, London.

BUTLER, B. (1954) The use of hypnosis in the care of the cancer patient. *Cancer*, **7**, 1.

CHAVES, J.F. (1968) Hypnosis reconceptualized: An overview of Barber's theoretical and empirical work. *Psychological Reports*, **22**, 587.

CHERTOK, L. (1966) *Hypnosis*. Pergamon Press, London.

CHERTOK, L. (1969) *Motherhood and Personality, Psychosomatic Aspects of Personality*. Tavistock, London.

CONN, J.H. & CONN, R.N. (1967) Discussion of. T. X. Barber's 'Hypnosis' as a causal variable in present-day psychology: a critical analysis. *Journal of Clinical and Experimental Hypnosis*, **15**, 106.

DELAY, J. & PICHOT, P. (1962) *Abrégé de Psychologie*. Masson, Paris.

D'ESLON, M. (1780) *Observations sur le Magnétisme Animale*. cit. Chertok, 1966.

DINGWALL, E.J. (1967) *Abnormal Hypnotic Phenomena. A Survey of Nineteenth Century Cases*, Vol. 1 France. Churchill, London.

DORCUS, R.M. & KIRKNER, F.J. (1948) The use of hypnosis in the suppression of intractable pain. *Journal of Abnormal and Social Psychology*, **43**, 237.

EVANS, F.J. (1966) Current developments in experimental hypnosis. *Proceedings of the American Psychological Association*. cit. Chaves, 1968.

FREUD, S. (1917) *Introductory Lectures on Psycho-Analysis*. Allen & Unwin, London, 1922.

FREUD, S. (1921) *Group Psychology and the Analysis of the Ego*. Hogarth, London.

FREUD, S. (1925) *An Autobiographical Study*. Hogarth, London, 1935.

GILL, M. & BRENMAN, M. (1959) *Hypnosis and Related States*. International Universities Press, New York.

HALLIDAY, A.M. & MASON, A.A. (1964) The effect of hypnotic anaesthesia on cortical responses. *Journal of Neurology, Neurosurgery and Psychiatry*, **27**, 300.

HILGARD, E.R. (1964) The motivational relevance of hypnosis. In: *Symposium on Motivation* (Ed. by M. R. Jones), cit. Chaves, 1968. Nebraska Press, Lincoln, Nebraska.

HILGARD, E.R. & TART, C.T. (1966) Responsiveness to suggestions following waking and imagination instructions and following induction of hypnosis. *Journal of Abnormal and Social Psychology*, **71**, 196.

JAMES, W. (1890) *Principles of Psychology*, Vol. 2. Macmillan, London.

JONES, E. (1910) The action of suggestion in psychotherapy. *Journal of Abnormal and Social Psychology*, reprinted as Chap. 12 in: *Papers on Psychoanalysis*. William Wood, New York, 1913.

KAPLAN, E.A. (1960) Hypnosis and pain. *Archives of General Psychiatry*, **2**, 567.

LUDWIG, A.M. & LYLE, W.H. Jr (1964) Tension induction and the hyperalert trance. *Journal of Abnormal and Social Psychology*, **69**, 70.

MAHER-LOUGHNAN, G.P. (1970) Hypnosis and asthma. *International Journal of Clinical and Experimental Hypnosis*, **18**, 1.

MAHER-LOUGHNAN, S.P. & KINSLEY, B.J. (1968) Hypnosis for asthma—a controlled trial: a report to the Research Committee of the British Tuberculosis Association. *British Medical Journal*, **4**, 71.

MALMO, R.D., BOAG, T.J. & RAGINSKY, B.R. (1954) Electromyographic study of human deafness. *Journal of Clinical and Experimental Hypnosis*, reprinted in: *Psychopathology* (Ed. by C. F. Reed, I. E. Alexander & S. S. Tomkins). Science Editions, Harvard University Press, Harvard 1964.

MANDY, A.J., MANDY, T.E., FARKAS, R. & SCHER, E. (1952) Is natural childbirth natural? *Psychosomatic Medicine*, **14**, 431.

MERSKEY, H. & SPEAR, F.G. (1967) *Pain: Psychological and Psychiatric Aspects*. Baillière, Tindall & Cassell, London.

MERSKEY, H. & TONGE, W.L. (1965) *Psychiatric Illness*. Baillière, Tindall & Cassell, London.

OSWALD, I. (1962) *Sleeping and Waking*. Elsevier, Amsterdam.

SACERDOTE, P. (1962) The place of hypnosis in the relief of severe protracted pain. *American Journal of Clinical Hypnosis*, **4**, 150.

SACERDOTE, P. (1965) Additional contributions to the hypnotherapy of the advanced cancer patient. *American Journal of Clinical Hypnosis*, **7**, 308.

SACERDOTE, P. (1966) Hypnosis in cancer patients. *American Journal of Clinical Hypnosis*, **9**, 100.

SARBIN, T.R. (1950) Contributions to role-taking theory. I.

Hypnotic behaviour. *Psychological Review,* **57,** 255.

SCHILDER, P. (1956) *The Nature of Hypnosis.* International Universities Press, New York.

SHOR, R.E. (1959) Hypnosis and the concept of the generalized reality orientation. *American Journal of Psychotherapy,* **13,** 582.

SHOR, R.E. (1962a) Physiological effects of painful stimulation during hypnotic analgesia under conditions designed to minimize anxiety. *International Journal of Clinical and Experimental Hypnosis,* **10,** 183.

SHOR, R.E. (1962b) *On the Physiological Effects of Painful Stimulation During Hypnotic Analgesia.* Basic Issues for Further Research in Hypnosis: Current Problems, 1962 (Ed. by S. H. Estabrooks). Harper & Row, London.

SIM, M. (1968) *Guide to Psychiatry.* Livingstone, Edinbrugh.

SINCLAIR-GIEBEN, A.H.C. & CHALMERS, D. (1959) Evaluation of treatment of warts by hypnosis. *Lancet,* **ii,** 480.

TART, C.T. (1969) *Altered States of Consciousness,* p. 229. John Wiley, New York.

# Barber's Reconceptualization 26
## of Hypnosis: An Evaluation of Criticisms

### Nicholas P. Spanos

Theories of hypnosis which refer to a special state (hypnotic trance) have been seriously challenged by Barber's reconceptualization of the area. His reconceptualization, in turn, has been criticized by proponents of the special-state theories. This paper brings together all criticisms that have been leveled at Barber's theoretical and experimental endeavors and evaluates each criticism. It is concluded that (a) Barber's reformulation of hypnosis capably withstands criticisms and (b) special-state theorists have not as yet satisfactorily answered his challenge to their basic assumptions.

The long history of hypnosis has been characterized by heated controversy. However, as implicit theoretical assumptions have come into sharper focus, the disagreements in this area have gradually consolidated under two major theoretical paradigms. The more dominant of these paradigms, which may be labeled as "hypnotic-state theory," has traditionally viewed hypnotic behavior as being fundamentally different from waking behavior. Acceptance of this paradigm has been fostered by studies which concluded that the behaviors carried out by hypnotic subjects are highly unusual and probably incapable of being performed by waking individuals (Erickson, 1938a, 1938b, 1939). Studies of this type, in turn, have lent credence to the notion that a special state (trance or hypnotic state) has to be postulated in order to explain hypnotic behavior.

The second approach to hypnotic phenomena, which has been traditionally upheld by a relatively small number of investigators, has not drawn a fundamental distinction between hypnotic and other behaviors. Proponents of this alternative paradigm have stressed the similarities between hypnotic and other psychological phenomena and have attempted to explain hypnotic behavior without invoking a special state. Although this approach has historical antecedents in the work of previous investigators (Sarbin, 1962), it has attained maturity largely through the contemporary efforts of T. X. Barber. In recent years, Barber has carried out a systematic program of research and theory construction which has culminated in a reconceptualization of hypnotic phenomena. The focus of this reconceptualization has involved a thoroughgoing critique of the hypothetical construct hypnotic trance and the delineation of objective antecedent variables which functionally relate to hypnotic behaviors.

Proponents of hypnotic-state theory have raised many objections with respect to Barber's reconceptualization of hypnosis. The first major purpose of this paper is to bring these many criticisms together in one place. The second major purpose is to evaluate the criticisms. However, in order to provide a background for understanding the critiques of Barber's formulation, it is necessary first to present a brief overview of his theoretical and experimental endeavors.

[1] I am indebted to Dr. Theodore X. Barber for the many hours he spent with me in discussion of his work and also for reading a preliminary draft of the manuscript. I also thank the following for criticizing the manuscript: Richard F. Johnson, Maurice J. Silver, and John D. McPeake.

Overview of Barber's Work

*Critique of the Hypnotic State Construct*

One of the most important aspects of Barber's work is his critique of the hypothetical construct hypnotic state or trance. Barber has noted that this construct is typically embedded in circular reasoning. A subject is typically considered to be in hypnotic trance if he manifests a high degree of response to suggestions of limb rigidity, hallucination, age-regression, analgesia, amnesia, etc. However, hypnotic trance is considered to be an instrumental factor in producing the high level of response to suggestions. Thus, a person is said to respond to suggestions because he is in a hypnotic trance and, turning around circularly, he is said to be in hypnotic trance because he responds to suggestions.

Two other criteria are also used at times to infer the presence of a hypnotic trance state, namely, (a) subjects' "hypnotic appearance" (e.g., appearance of lethargy, relaxation, and lack of spontaneity) and (b) their testimony of having been hypnotized. Barber has pointed out that the use of these criteria as indices of a hypnotic state is open to at least three criticisms:

1. Both criteria are typically used circularly; for example, hypnotic trance is inferred because the subject appears lethargic and relaxed, and lethargy and relaxation are then explained by stating that the person is hypnotized.

2. Both "hypnotic appearance" and subjects' testimony of being hypnotized can vary independently of subjects' response to test suggestions of amnesia, analgesia, catalepsy, hallucination, and the like. That is, an individual can appear limp and relaxed and also state that he is hypnotized, yet perform quite poorly on test suggestions. Conversely, individuals can respond quite well to test suggestions while stating that they are not hypnotized and without exhibiting the slightest signs of lethargy and relaxation.

3. Both "hypnotic appearance" and subjects' testimony of being hypnotized have been shown to vary as a function of numerous antecedent variables which are difficult to conceptualize under the construct hypnotic state. Some of these antecedent-consequent relations will be specified below.

*Demonstrations of Antecedent-Consequent Relations*

Another important aspect of Barber's work involves his reconceptualization of the behaviors traditionally subsumed by the term "hypnosis." Barber's approach is based on the assumption that an explication of phenomena traditionally associated with this construct requires the establishment of lawful relationships between denotable antecedent and consequent variables. Among the consequent variables Barber includes (a) overt response to test suggestions of muscular rigidity, hallucination, age-regression, amnesia, and so on, (b) subjective reports that the suggested effects were experienced, and (c) testimony from subjects that they entered a trance or were hypnotized.

Much of Barber's work has been devoted to the delineation of numerous antecedent variables that affect the above-mentioned consequent variables. Barber and Calverley (1965a, 1965b) have pointed out that procedures traditionally labeled "hypnotic inductions" are multifaceted and include at least four antecedent variables: (a) The situation is defined to the subject as "hypnosis." (b) Instructions are administered to motivate subjects to accept suggestions. (c) Suggestions of eye-heaviness, eyeclosure, relaxation, drowsiness, and sleep are administered. (d) The subject is told that he can now easily respond to test suggestions and can easily experience the suggested effects. In a series of experiments, Barber and Calverley (1963, 1964g, 1965a, 1965b) demonstrated that the independent and interactive effects of each of these variables play important roles in eliciting response to test suggestion.

Barber and his associates have also demonstrated relationships among various other antecedent variables and the phenomena of hypnosis. These antecedent variables include subjects' attitudes toward hypnosis (Barber & Calverley, 1969b), subjects' base-line levels of response to direct suggestions (Barber, 1965), the tone of voice used by the experimenter in administering the suggestions (Barber & Calverley, 1964c), what subjects are told about the purpose of the experiment (Barber & Calverley, 1964d), whether or not it is implied that the procedure to be used is effective in producing hypnosis (Barber & Calverley, 1965b), and other variables (Barber, 1969a).

Despite the fact that Barber's formulation has been criticized by hypnotic-state theorists, some of his most important findings have become accepted tenets in the area of hypnosis research. These findings have been replicated by investigators of varying theoretical orientation and they must be seriously considered in any attempt at theory construction in the area of hypnosis. Two of these findings will be examined next.

*Reevaluation of Hypnotic Phenomena*

Even after the publication of Hull's (1933) classic monograph, the hypnotic state was thought by many to produce behavioral feats which transcended the capacities of normal nonhypnotized individuals. The trance state was thought to confer on individuals the ability to develop behavioral conditions, such as blindness, color-blindness, deafness, and analgesia, which were indistinguishable from organic disorders bearing the same labels (Erickson, 1938a, 1938b, 1939). Barber's experimentation, and his critical reviews of the literature have played a major role in demonstrating that hypnotic induction procedures simply do not produce conditions such as "genuine" blindness or deafness (McPeake, 1968).

For instance, hypnotic and control subjects who had received suggestions of deafness had their hearing tested by delayed auditory feedback (DAF) (Barber & Calverley, 1964e). This procedure has been found to accurately discriminate deaf subjects from subjects attempting to fake deafness. Although some subjects stated that they could not hear, when hearing was assessed with DAF, Barber and Calverley (1964e) were unable to find a single subject whose behavior resembled that of a genuinely deaf individual. Similar results have been obtained by other investigators who have tested "hypnotically deaf" subjects with the DAF technique (Kline, Guze, & Haggerty, 1954; Kramer & Tucker, 1967; Scheibe, Grey, & Keim, 1968).

Barber's research has also raised serious questions concerning the genuineness of other hypnotic phenomena. For example, the work of Barber and his associates (Barber, 1959; Barber & Calverley, 1969a; Barber & Deeley, 1961; Barber & Hahn, 1962) has indicated that "hypnotic color-blindness" and "hypnotic analgesia" bear little resemblance to organic color-blindness or to analgesia produced by chemical means. Barber's (1962b) work, along with that of other investigators (Edmonston & Erbeck, 1967), has also indicated that "hypnotic age-regression" to childhood is quite different from actual child behavior, and that "hypnotic time distortion" does not produce the same effects that would be expected by an actual slowing of time (Barber & Calverley, 1964f).

*Demonstration of High Base-Level Response*

A second and related empirical finding which has gained support from Barber's experimentation states that behaviors in the repertoire of hypnotic subjects can also be elicited from nonhypnotic subjects. One of Barber's most intriguing findings is that behaviors once thought to result only from disease, drugs, or hypnosis (e.g., amnesia, hallucinations), in fact, have a high baseline rate of occurrence in the general population. That is, subjects not given an hypnotic induction procedure but instead simply instructed to vividly imagine what is suggested to them, typically respond at a higher level (than was previously assumed) to suggestions of catalepsy, hallucinations, amnesia, and the like. For example, Barber and Calverley (1964a) found that one-third to one-half of normal female control subjects, simply instructed to "imagine" the suggestions they were administered, reported the occurrence of vivid auditory and visual hallucinations.

The findings of high base-level response to suggestions has been replicated by a number of experimenters whose theoretical orientations differ from that of Barber. Thus, Sarbin and his associates (Andersen & Sarbin, 1964; Sarbin & Andersen, 1963; Sarbin & Juhasz, 1967) and Hilgard and Tart (1966) have also demonstrated that subjects' response to motoric suggestions such as catalepsy, and to perceptual suggestions such as hallucination, is almost as high under base-line conditions as it is under hypnotic conditions.

The two empirical findings outlined above are no longer problematic. Regardless of their theoretical persuasions, investigators no longer equate "hypnotic" and organically produced disorders, and no longer deny the fact that behaviors traditionally assumed to result only from disease, drugs, or a trance state can be achieved with relative ease by normal control subjects (Hilgard, 1965; Orne, 1966; Sarbin, 1962).

Another interesting generalization resulting from Barber's research is the finding that brief instructions, exhorting subjects to try their hardest, and informing them that the tasks to be performed are easy (task-motivating instructions), raise subjects' level of suggestibility to the same extent as does a traditional hypnotic induction procedure. As will be discussed below, this finding is a controversial one. In examining the controversy, however, it is important to keep in mind that the increments in suggestibility over base-line levels produced by either hypnotic or task-motivation treatments are not very large, and that any possible difference in suggestibility between these two treatments must of necessity be quite small.

We will now turn to an examination of the criticisms that have been leveled against Barber's theoretical formulation and experimental findings. Criticisms of Barber's theoretical formulation will be considered first.

### CRITICISMS OF BARBER'S THEORETICAL FORMULATION

Four basic criticisms of Barber's theoretical formulation have been proffered by hypnotic-state theorists. These criticisms usually involve attempts to reinterpret Barber's findings within the conceptual framework of hypnotic-state theory. Each criticism will be discussed and evaluated below.

*Criticisms 1 and 2. Hypnotic Subjects Remain "Unhypnotized" and Control Subjects "Slip into Trance"*

These criticisms may be stated in the following manner:

(1) Many subjects who are administered hypnotic induction procedures do not enter a "trance state." Because subjects in Barber's experiments are usually randomly selected and randomly assigned to hypnotic and control conditions, many subjects assigned to hypnotic groups are probably "unhypnotizable" and thereby never enter a "trance state." Consequently, any potential differences between "hypnotized" and control subjects will be attenuated in these experiments by the fact that many of the hypnotic subjects are not really in a "trance" (Evans, 1968; Hilgard, 1965, 1969; Hilgard & Tart, 1966).

(2) Susceptible individual's may enter a "trance state" even if they are not administered a traditional hypnotic induction procedure. Therefore, it is quite possible that some of Barber's control subjects actually "slip into a trance state" when they are administered task-motivation or imagination instructions (Evans, 1968; Hilgard, 1969; Hilgard & Tart, 1966; Schneck, 1969; Wachtel, 1969).

Statements to the effect that subjects do or do not enter a "trance state" can be demonstrated empirically only if the presence or absence of a "trance state" can be determined in a reliable and noncircular fashion. Before hypnotic and control subjects can be said to enter or not enter a "trance," a valid criterion of the "trance state," which is independent of subjects' response to suggestion, should be available. As Barber (1964) has pointed out, however, a century of research has failed to provide an unambiguous and nontautological criterion for this construct.

Several hypnotic-state theorists have, in fact, conceded that "hypnosis" is often inferred from heightened response to suggestion in a circular fashion (Edmonston, 1968; Hilgard, 1969; Hilgard & Tart, 1966; McGlashon, Evans, & Orne, 1969; Wachtel, 1969). A number of these investigators have attempted to circumvent this circularity by developing indices of "hypnosis" which are independent of response to test suggestions. For instance, a number of investigators have suggested that subjects' testimony of being in a "hypnotic state" should be employed as a valid index of the presence of a "trance state." Thus, Conn and Conn (1967) contended that, ". . . the subject and only the subject can report whether he is 'in' or 'out' of hypnosis" (p. 108). In like fashion Tart and Hilgard (1966) suggested that, "S's report that he feels hypnotized to some degree is primary data about the presence or absence of hypnosis, if not a criterion of hypnosis" (p. 253). Tart and Hilgard (1966) have suggested that experimental subjects should be periodically questioned concerning their hypnotic depth as a check against the possibility of control subjects slipping into "trance," and as confirmation of the fact that hypnotic subjects really are in a "trance."

Although it may appear reasonable to assume that a subject is in a "trance" because he says he is, this assumption is questionable. An analogy might help to clarify the reasons why. If members of a religious cult, while engaging in a fervent ceremony, were to state that they were "possessed by a spirit," few contemporary scientists would take their testimony as evidence of actual spirit possession. Possession would not be assumed, despite subjects' testimony, because there exist no unambiguous and noncircular criteria for denoting possession by spirits. The fact that subjects' testimony does not lead the scientist to infer the existence of spirit possession does not mean that such testimony is uninteresting, or incapable of scientific study. On the contrary, a legitimate and interesting question to ask would be: What are the factors leading individuals to define themselves as possessed? This question can be answered objectively.

The process of inferring a "trance state" on the basis of subjects' testimony is basically no different from the above-described process of inferring spirit possession. In both cases the inferences are spurious because the concepts being inferred have not been clearly and nontautologically denoted. Interestingly enough, Barber is one of few workers who have attempted to systematically answer the question: What are the variables leading individuals to state that they are hypnotized? As a result of numerous studies he has demonstrated that some of these variables include (a) the definition of the situation as hypnosis (Barber & Calverley, 1965a), (b) the subjects' preconceptions of what hypnosis is supposed to involve (Barber, 1967b), (c) the subjects' self observation that they responded to a certain degree to suggestions of relaxation and drowsiness or to suggestions of limb rigidity, hallucination, anesthesia, amnesia, and so on (Barber & Calverley, 1969b), (d) the wording and tone of questions that are used to elicit subjects' reports (Barber, Dalal, & Cal-

verley, 1968), and (e) whether the hypnotist implies that subjects were or were not hypnotized (Barber, Dalal, & Carverley, 1968). Taken together, this evidence strongly indicates that subjects' testimony of being "hypnotized" cannot be assumed to covary with the presence or absence of a hypothetical "trance state." It also indicates that the delineation of objective antecedent variables, which can be shown to lawfully relate to subjects' verbal reports, constitutes a fruitful approach to this area of inquiry.

The contention that control subjects may spontaneously slip into hypnosis is an interesting example of an *ad hoc* explanation which functions to incorporate anomalous findings into an existing theoretical conceptualization (Chaves, 1968). The notion that subjects might spontaneously "slip into hypnosis" was not a prediction generated by hypnotic state theory. On the contrary, this idea was developed only after it had been discovered that control subjects can sometimes respond as well as hypnotic subjects. Still another *ad hoc* explanation for hypnotic-state theory has been recently suggested by Shor (1962) and by Wacthel (1969). These investigators contend that the notion of a global "hypnotic state" is an anachronism, and that more powerful prediction could be achieved if the "hypnotic state" were viewed as multidimensional rather than unitary. The main difficulty with both of the *ad hoc* explanations outlined above is that neither of them really predicts any new findings, while both of them are formulated in a fashion vague enough to "explain" the most disparate of already existing findings.

Before a construct such as multidimensional trance state can be usefully employed to predict behavior it should be specified in the following manner. (a) Each dimension of the "state" should be denoted independently of other dimensions as well as independently of the behaviors which the dimension is supposed to explain. In order to successfully carry out this procedure each separate dimension should be indexed by at least two reliable empirical operations. These indices should, in turn, meet the criteria for successfully "converging" on a hypothetical construct (Campbell & Fiske, 1959; Garner, Hake, & Eriksen, 1956; Spanos & Chaves, 1969a).

(b) The empirical and theoretical inter-relationships among the various dimensions should be unambiguously specified.

The procedures outlined above for denoting hypothetical constructs have been applied with some success in various areas of psychological research (But & Fiske, 1968; Stoyva & Kamiya, 1968). As yet, they have not been applied by hypnotic-state theorists.

*Criticism 3. Similar Behaviors in Hypnotic and Control Subjects May be Produced by Different Psychological Mechanisms*

A number of investigators (Bowers, 1966, 1967, 1969; Evans, 1968; Gravitz & Hopkinson, 1969; Ludwig & Lyle, 1964; Orne, 1966) have criticized Barber's results by suggesting that "hypnotized" and task-motivated subjects who respond to suggestions in the same overt fashion, do so for very different subjective reasons. These investigators usually contend that "hypnotized" subjects, because they are in a "trance state," really experience the suggestions they are administered and do not simply respond to suggestion because they are expected to do so. Control subjects, on the other hand, are thought to respond to suggestions because of expectations generated by the experimental situation and not because they actually experience the suggestions administered.

One procedure for attempting to determine whether or not hypnotic and task-motivated subjects experience suggestions in the same way is to ask these subjects about their experiences. Barber (1965) has developed a scale for the standardized assessment and quantification of both overt response to test suggestion, and subjects' testimony concerning their experiences. Employing this scale, Barber (1965) found that hypnotic and task-motivated subjects rate their subjective experiences in the same way. These data do not support the contention that the overt responses of hypnotic and task-motivated subjects are a function of different subjective "mechanisms."

Orne (1962, 1966) has noted that the subjective reports of experimental subjects, like their overt behavior, may be a function of their expectations rather than an accurate reflection of what they actually experience. Operating from this premise,

several investigators (Bowers, 1967; Orne, 1966) have suggested that the subjective reports of "hypnotized" subjects accurately reflect their experiences, while the subjective reports of task-motivated subjects are a function of their expectations and do not accurately reflect their experiences. Bowers (1967) attempted to demonstrate that the subjective reports of task-motivated subjects are not an accurate reflection of their subjective experiences by carrying out the following experiment.

Bowers (1967) administered task-motivation instructions followed by suggestions of visual and auditory hallucinations to two groups of subjects. Before rating the vividness of their hallucinatory experiences, one group of subjects was administered instructions requesting that they make their ratings as honestly as possible. The second group received no such instructions. Bowers found that subjects administered suggestions exhorting them to be honest reported their hallucinations to be less real and vivid than did subjects not administered honesty instructions. He interpreted these results as indicating that task-motivated subjects do not actually experience the suggestions that are administered to them but instead, behave as if they experience these suggestions because of the expectations generated by the experimental situation. Bowers (1967) then hypothesized that hypnotic subjects do experience the suggestions administered to them. He predicted that the subjective ratings of hypnotic subjects would be unaffected by honesty instructions. However, he did not subject this prediction to test.

Two recent studies have tested Bower's predictions concerning the subjective reports by hypnotic and nonhypnotic subjects. In the first study (Spanos & Barber, 1968) half of the subjects in both hypnotic and task-motivated groups were administered honesty instructions before rating the vividness of suggested auditory and visual hallucinations. Spanos and Barber found that both hypnotic and task-motivated subjects administered honesty instructions rated their auditory hallucinations as less vivid than did corresponding subjects who were not asked to be honest. Thus, Bowers' (1967) prediction, that the subjective reports of hypnotic subjects would be unaffected by demands for honesty, was not supported with respect to auditory hallucinations. Spanos and Barber (1968) found that Bowers' predictions were supported with respect to visual hallucinations. That is, task-motivated subjects, but not hypnotic subjects, rated their visual hallucinations as being less vivid when honesty was demanded.

The second study (Spanos, Barber, & Lang, 1969) evaluated the effects of demands for honesty on reported analgesia. In this study hypnotic and nonhypnotic subjects were administered a short set of suggestions stating that their hand would become numb, insensitive, and unable to feel pain (analgesia suggestions). After application of the pain stimulus (a sharp, heavy weight applied to one finger) half of the subjects in each group were administered demands for honesty before rating their degree of felt pain. Spanos, Barber, and Lang (1969) replicated earlier results (Barber & Calverley, 1969a) by finding that analgesia suggestions with or without a hypnotic induction procedure, produced significant decrements in reported pain. Surprisingly, Spanos, Barber, and Lang (1969) also found that demand for honesty did not affect ratings of pain for either hypnotic or control groups.

Taken together, these two studies indicate that demands for honesty achieve their effects through complex interactions with numerous variables such as the instructions administered to subjects and the tasks that subjects perform. In these two studies alone, honesty instructions, depending on the tasks performed, were found to (a) produce decrements in performance for both hypnotic and control subjects, (b) produce decrements in performance for control but not for hypnotic subjects, and (c) produce no effect on the performance of either hypnotic or control subjects. Clearly, these complex findings cannot be explained simply by assuming that the subjective reports of hypnotic subjects are an accurate reflection of their experience while those of control subjects are not. Instead, these studies indicate that the effects produced by demands for honesty will be understood only when the interactions between such demands and numerous other independent variables have been specified.

Another study suggesting that the testimony of hypnotic subjects cannot be assumed to accurately reflect their private experiences was carried out by Barber, Dalal, and Calverley (1968). In this study good hypnotic subjects, upon completion of the hypnotic session, were questioned about the similarities and differences between their hypnotic and waking experiences. Some subjects were given questions worded negatively (e.g., Did you experience the hypnotic state as basically different from the waking state?). Other subjects were asked questions worded positively (e.g., Did you experience the hypnotic state as basically similar to the waking state?). The results of this study indicated that one-third to one-half of the variance in the subjects' postexperimental testimony was a function of the direction in which questions were worded. For example, when questions were worded negatively only 28% of the subjects testified that they experienced the hypnotic state as basically similar to the waking state. However, when questions were worded positively 83% of the subjects claimed that they experienced the hypnotic state as basically similar to the waking state.

The question of possible differences in the behaviors produced by an hypnotic induction procedure and by "waking" control procedures, such as task-motivation instructions, involves two separate issues. The first is the purely empirical issue of whether or not such differences can be demonstrated. The second issue is a theoretical one. Hypnotic-state theorists appear to assume that differences in the behavior of hypnotic and task-motivated subjects would indicate the operation of a "trance state" in the hypnotic subjects (Hilgard & Tart, 1966). Such an assumption is unnecessary. There are many differences between hypnotic induction procedures and task-motivation instructions that could lead to differences in behavior. For example, hypnotic induction procedures, but not task-motivation instructions, define the experimental situation for subjects as hypnosis. Barber and Calverley (1965a) have demonstrated that simply telling subjects that they are in a hypnotic situation raises their responsiveness to a wide array of test suggestions. Defining the situation as hypnosis also affects the extent to which subjects display lack of spontaneity, limpness, and other indices of "hypnotic appearance," and the extent to which they report unusual changes in body image (Barber & Calverley, 1969b). Thus, it is likely that the definition of the situation as hypnosis, and other variables unique to the hypnotic situation, may affect behavioral changes that are not produced by task-motivating instructions. Because any differences between the effects of hypnotic and task-motivation treatments might be due to differences in the objective antecedent variables inherent in these treatments, an "hypnotic trance" cannot simply be assumed to be the important factor producing behavioral differences between these treatments. On the contrary, the importance of the "hypnotic trance" in effecting such treatment differences can be judged only when this construct has been objectively specified, and when its relationships to the behaviors in question have been carefully delineated.

In summary, the suggestion that the behavior of hypnotic and control subjects is mediated by different "mechanisms" is an interesting one. However, before this suggestion can be given much credence as an empirical hypothesis, the construct "mediating mechanisms" will have to be objectively specified and lawfully related to the behavior in question. As yet, the only empirical hypothesis generated by the suggestion of different "mechanisms" states that the behavior of hypnotic subjects accurately reflects their subjective experiences whereas the behavior of control subjects does not. The available data, however, do not support this hypothesis and instead suggest that (a) neither the behavior of hypnotic nor that of control subjects can be employed to accurately reflect subject's experiences, and (b) the behavior of both hypnotic and control subjects is a function of numerous antecedent variables.

*Criticism 4. Barber Attempts to Explain All Hypnotic Phenomena in Terms of Increases in Subjects' Motivation*

Several investigators (Evans, 1968; Hilgard, 1969) have characterized Barber's formulation as a motivational view of hypnosis. These investigators are of the opinion that Barber attempts to explain all hypnotic phenomena on the basis of increases in subjects' motivation. Evans (1968) has pointed out that a good deal of research indicates that highly motivated subjects often respond poorly to hypnotic suggestion. This evidence, he contends, indicates that Barber's formulation is incorrect.

The contention that Barber's is simply a motivational view of hypnosis, oversimplifies his theoretical formulation. Although Barber's research has emphasized the importance of motivational instructions, and has demonstrated that these instructions may be sufficient to account for some hypnotic phenomena, this research has, by no means, been restricted to delineating the role played by motivational factors in hypnotic performance. As pointed out in the overview, Barber has delineated the roles played by numerous antecedent variables in affecting hypnotic behavior. He has not attempted to employ motivation, or any other single antecedent factor as a sufficient explanation of hypnotic phenomena.

CRITICISMS OF BARBER'S
EXPERIMENTAL FINDINGS

One technique employed by proponents of established paradigms for reducing the "conceptual dissonance" produced by anomalous findings is to demonstrate that the findings are not real—that they are due to methodological flaws or artifacts and, consequently, do not pose a threat to the prevailing conceptualization (Kuhn, 1962).

Hypnotic state theorists have attempted to show that many of Barber's findings are due to methodological artifacts. Two arguments have been used against these experimental results. The first argument states that Barber's findings concerning the relationship between hypnotic induction procedures, task-motivation instructions, and suggestibility are due to his use of an insensitive experimental design. The second argument contends that many of Barber's results are due to "experimenter bias," and are, therefore, invalid. These criticisms will be discussed in turn.

*Criticism 5. Barber's Results are Due to His Use of an Insensitive Experimental Design*

Hypnotic state theorists have traditionally subscribed to the view that hypnotic induction procedures enhance suggestibility to a greater extent than do more conventional attempts to increase the level of subjects' responding. As pointed out above, Barber and his associates (Barber, 1965; Barber & Calverley, 1964a, 1965a, and 1965b) have reported findings which are inconsistent with this hypothesis. These investigators have found that the administration of task-motivating instructions usually produces increases in suggestibility which parallel the increases obtained with a standard hypnotic induction procedure. In carrying out these studies Barber and his associates consistently employed a randomized groups experimental design, the main features of which is the random assignment of subjects to different treatments.

Hilgard (1965); Hilgard and Tart (1966), and Edmonston and Robertson (1967) suggested that Barber's failure to uncover significant differences between hypnotic and task-motivation treatments stems from the insensitivity of the randomized groups design. These investigators noted that small differences between hypnotic and task-motivation treatments may be masked in experiments which contain a great deal of variability due to subjects. To test these contentions, Hilgard and Tart (1966) and Edmonston and Robertson (1967) went on to conduct experiments which attempted to minimize intersubject variability. These experiments are described next.

Hilgard and Tart (1966) attempted to increase the sensitivity of their experimental procedures by running the same subject under different treatment conditions on different days, thereby eliminating the problem of intersubject variability. On the basis of data gathered in such treatment-by-subject experiments these investigators concluded that hypnotic induction procedures slightly increase suggestibility above the increase produced by task-motivation instructions. Unfortunately, Hilgard and Tart's use of a treatment-by-subjects design in hypnosis research creates more problems than it solves. The use of this design is based on the assumption that the treatments administered to the same subjects at different times in no way affect one another. However, a number of reports (Barber, 1962a; Sutcliffe, 1960) indicate that different treatments administered to the same subjects in hypnotic experiments do affect one another in a number of subtle and complex ways. Because Hilgard and

Tart (1966) did not clearly meet the assumptions underlying the treatment-by-subjects design which they employed, any interpretation of their results must be regarded as equivocal.

Although Hilgard and Tart (1966) implied, and Hilgard (1965) explicitly stated, that the results of the above-described study indicate that an hypnotic treatment procedure produces slightly greater suggestibility than does a task-motivation treatment, this experiment (Hilgard & Tart, 1966) did not compare an hypnotic treatment with a task-motivation treatment. Instead, Hilgard and Tart compared the effects of an hypnotic induction procedure to various procedures in which subjects were asked to "vividly imagine" what was suggested to them. Barber and Calverley (1963, 1964a), employing the supposedly insensitive randomized groups design, had previously demonstrated that both an hypnotic induction procedure and task-motivation instructions produce significantly greater suggestibility than do such "imagination" procedures. Thus, despite their assertions to the contrary, Hilgard and Tart presented no experimental evidence to support the contention that hypnotic induction procedures produce greater increments in suggestibility than do task-motivation instructions. Instead, these investigators have confirmed Barber and Calverley's (1963, 1964a) finding, that an hypnotic induction procedure produces greater suggestibility than do "imagination" instructions.

Edmonston and Robertson (1967) carried out an experiment which reduced intersubject variability by matching subjects on the basis of their base-line levels of response to test suggestion on the Barber Suggestibility Scale (BSS) before assigning them to one of four treatment conditions. In the first session of this experiment subjects in two of the treatment conditions were administered a standard hypnotic induction procedure and subjects in the other two were administered task-motivation instructions. In a second session half of the subjects previously administered an hypnotic induction procedure and half previously administered a task-motivation procedure were given an hypnotic induction procedure. The other half of the subjects (previously administered either an hypnotic or a task-motivation procedure) were administered task-motivation instructions. In both the first and second session suggestibility was measured with form A of the Stanford Hypnotic Suggestibility Scale (SHSS).

The results of the first session in the Edmonston and Robertson (1967) experiment indicated that the hypnotic treatments produced significantly greater suggestibility than did the task-motivation treatments. Edmonston and Robertson also evaluated the changes in suggestibility which occurred between the first and second sessions of their experiment. Although they found that hypnotic procedures usually produced higher levels of suggestibility than did task-motivation instructions, this was not always the case. Instead, the relative effectiveness of these two treatment conditions in raising suggestibility was found to be a function of complex interactions between treatments and the order in which treatments were administered. Before assessing the relevance of Edmonston and Robertson's (1967) findings to Barber's results, the following considerations should be noted. Barber and his associates (Barber & Calverley, 1963, 1964a, 1964e) have compared the effects of an hypnotic procedure to the effects of task-motivation in naive subjects. Edmonston and Robertson's (1967) subjects were not naive; they had been preexperimentally tested on response to suggestions of catalepsy, hallucination, body immobility, etc. Thus, the differences obtained by Barber and his associates and by Edmonston and Robertson may be due to the differences in the preexperimental procedures undergone by their subjects.

It will be recalled that Edmonston and Robertson (1967), after assessing subjects on the BSS and assigning them to different treatment conditions, measured suggestibility with Form A of the SHSS. However, Form A of this scale is worded to apply specifically to subjects who have been administered an hypnotic induction procedure (e.g., You are very relaxed now. Think how hard it might be to talk while so deeply relaxed. . . ." Weitzenhoffer & Hilgard, 1959). Barber and his associates have not assessed the effects of hypnotic and task-motivation treatments with the SHSS. Instead, they have employed the

BSS or have developed new scales for assessment of specific behaviors which can be administered without incongruity to both hypnotic and control subjects. Thus, differences in methods of assessment employed by Edmonston and Robertson and by Barber and his associates may be another factor contributing to the differences in the results obtained by these investigators.

In brief, Hilgard and Tart (1966a) and Edmonston and Robertson (1967) have presented data which suggest that the changes in performance produced by task-motivation instructions may be affected by a number of variables which have yet to be systematically studied. These variables include the pretraining received by subjects and the scales employed to assess response to test suggestion. Although the data reviewed above indicate that the equivalence in the performance of hypnotic and task-motivated subjects may not be as generalizable a phenomenon as Barber has sometimes indicated, these data neither seriously challenge the validity of Barber's original findings, nor indicate a deficiency in the randomized groups design which he has employed.

The controversy concerning the possible differences in suggestibility resulting from hypnotic and task-motivation procedures can be viewed most fruitfully in historical perspective. The major historical impetus for this controversy stems from the claim that certain behaviors (e.g., amnesia, hallucinations) were a unique function of an "hypnotic state." This contention led Barber and others to demonstrate that behaviors traditionally assumed to be the exclusive resultants of "hypnosis" had a rather high base-level rate of occurrence in the general population. Thus, although hypnotic-state theorists once contended that "hypnosis" produced dramatic and unique behavioral changes, even the most ardent of contemporary hypnotic-state theorists now argues that small differences may sometimes occur between hypnotic and task-motivation treatments. The fact that the important research question has changed from the discovery of dramatic behaviors thought to be exclusive of the "trance state," to the delineation of possible small differences between hypnotic and control subjects, is a credit to Barber's experimentation.

### Criticism 6. Barber's Results are Oftentimes a Function of Experimenter-Bias

In a number of publications, Barber (1967a, 1969b) contended that much experimentation carried out by hypnotic state theorists has been "biased" by preconceptions concerning the nature of "hypnosis." By this Barber meant that hypnotic state theorists have often violated fundamental principles of experimental methodology in an attempt to demonstrate some preconceived notion concerning the "hypnotic state." A similar contention has more recently been made by Spanos and Chaves (in press). Examples of some common methodological errors made by hypnotic state theorists include the following: lack of reliable and/or valid dependent measures, lack of necessary control groups, and confounding of antecedent variables (e.g., assigning suggestible subjects to hypnotic groups and nonsuggestible subjects to control groups). All of these methodological errors have been classified under the rubric of "investigator effect" (Barber & Silver, 1968a, 1968b; Silver, 1968; Silver & Barber, 1969). This rubric indicates that the "effect" or "bias" involved in such studies occurs not during the actual running of the experiment, but instead, during the planning of the experiment or during the analysis of its results.

The charge of "bias" is, of course, a two-edged sword, and recently a number of investigators (Rosenhan, 1967; Wachtel, 1969) have suggested that Barber's failure to find significant differences between hypnotic and task-motivation conditions and between taped and orally presented hypnotic induction procedures, might be due to "experimenter-bias." It is important to point out that the concept of "experimenter-bias" differs substantially from the "investigator-bias" described above. "Experimenter-bias" refers to the proposition that experimenters "bias" the responses of their subjects by subtly and unconsciously transmitting their expectations to their subjects. Subjects are, in turn, thought to respond in the experimental situation in accordance with the experimenter's transmitted expectations. Although Barber (1967a) has suggested that much of the research carried out by hypnotic-state

theorists involves "investigator-bias," he has not suggested that these experiments also involve "experimenter-bias." Hypnotic-state theorists, on the other hand, have usually charged Barber's work not with "investigator-bias" but instead with "experimenter-bias."

Because the charge of "experimenter-bias" is quite serious, one would expect investigators who make it to base their statements on solid evidence. In fact, not a single study attempting to directly relate "experimenter-bias" to Barber's work has ever been carried out. In lieu of direct evidence, some investigators have supported the charge of "experimenter-bias" in Barber's research with two types of indirect evidence. This evidence may be phrased in the following manner: (1) A great deal of psychological research, carried out by Rosenthal and his associates (Rosenthal, 1966) clearly indicates that "experimenter-bias" is a potent variable in psychological research. Although Rosenthal has not investigated the role of "experimenter-bias" in hypnosis research, Barber's failure to find significant differences between hypnotic and task-motivation conditions, and between hypnotic induction procedures presented orally or by tape, smacks of such a bias (Rosenhan, 1967; Wachtel, 1969). (2) Barber obtains results which are different from the results obtained by investigators with theoretical orientations different from his. These findings indicate that Barber is biasing his subjects (Rosenhan, 1967). This "evidence" will now be examined in more detail.

The suggestion that Barber's results may be due to "experimenter-bias" is, of course, based on the supposition that "experimenter-bias" is a demonstrable and potent psychological phenomenon. Barber's critics employ Rosenthal's (1966) work as the major source of empirical support for this supposition. Rosenthal has carried out a great many studies which purport to demonstrate the "experimenter-bias" effect. Recently, Barber and Silver (1968a, 1968b) demonstrated that none of these studies unambiguously demonstrate such an effect. Barber and Silver (1968a, 1968b) showed that over half of these studies contain inadequate statistical analyses which obviate the conclusions concerning "experimenter-bias." Barber and Silver did find several studies which demonstrated significant results in the direction predicted by the "experimenter-bias" hypothesis. They pointed out, however, that these studies do not conclusively demonstrate an "experimenter-bias" effect, that is, they do not demonstrate that the results were due to subtle transmission of the experimenters' biases, because, with one or two exceptions, the possibility was not excluded that the results were due to gross factors such as misjudging, misrecording, or fudging of data by the undergraduate students who served as experimenters.

A series of investigators (Barber, Calverley, Forgione, McPeake, Chaves, & Bowen, 1969; Jacob, 1968; McFall & Saxman, 1968; Strauss, 1968; Wessler, 1968, 1969; Wessler & Strauss, 1968; Zegers, 1968) working in separate laboratories and employing careful statistical techniques have been unable to replicate the "experimenter-bias" effect. Clearly, the failure of investigators to reliably uncover an "experimenter-bias" effect, when such an effect is expressly being investigated, indicates that a great deal of caution should be exercised, and a good deal of direct experimental evidence amassed, before the charge of "experimenter-bias" is blanketly leveled against the work of any investigator.

Rosenhan (1967) supported his charge of "experimenter-bias" by contending that Barber obtained results which are different from those obtained by investigators who hold opposing theoretical orientations. Let us examine this contention in more detail. It is obvious that experimenters in any science may investigate the same general problem in a myriad of different ways. Different experimenters may use different dependent measures, manipulate different antecedent variables, and employ different experimental designs. These procedural differences can lead to differences in results. Furthermore, there is evidence to indicate that the experimental methodologies which investigators choose may be intimately related to the theoretical conceptualizations which guide their research (Kuhn, 1962). None of these facts, however, suggests that serious investigators bias their actual experimentation; that is, none of these facts indicates that experimenters unconsciously bias their subjects' responses by subtly transmitting their expectations to subjects. In order to demonstrate "experimenter-bias" it is necessary to show that experimenters with different expectations obtain different results when ostensibly carrying out the same experimental procedures. Thus, with respect to Barber's experimentation, the relevant question regarding the issue of "experimenter-bias" becomes: Can Barber, and investigators who hold theoretical orientations at variance with that of Barber, replicate each other's experimental results? The answer to this question is clearly affirmative. Let us look closely at one example.

Williamsen, Johnson, and Eriksen (1965), investigators with a theoretical orientation at variance with that of Barber, carried out an experiment dealing with hypnotic amnesia. Before administration of the treatment conditions all subjects learned a list of six common words to a criterion of 100% recall. After successfully meeting this criterion, subjects were administered one of three treatment conditions. The treatment conditions consisted of (a) an hypnotic induction procedure followed by suggestions of amnesia for the six words, (b) a waking condition in which suggestions of amnesia for the six words were not administered, and (c) a waking condition in which subjects asked to simulate hypnosis were administered suggestions of amnesia for the six words. Amnesia was assessed by four different measures. Williamsen, Johnson, and Eriksen (1965) found that simulating subjects displayed the most amnesia on all measures, and that waking subjects not administered amnesia suggestions displayed the least. Hypnotic subjects administered amnesia suggestions fell between these extremes on each experimental measure of amnesia.

Barber and Calverley (1966) replicated Williamsen, Johnson, and Eriksen's (1965) experimental procedure in every important respect. They (Barber & Calverley, 1966) employed the same amnesia suggestions, the same statistical analyses, and the same four dependent measures as did Williamsen, Johnson, and Eriksen (1965). Barber and Calverley's results paralleled those of Williamsen, Johnson, and Eriksen on each of the dependent variables assessed. That is, Barber and Calverley, like Williamsen, Johnson, and Eriksen, found that on each of the four dependent variables, simulating subjects displayed the most amnesia, waking subjects displayed the least, and hypnotic subjects fell between these two extremes. Furthermore, not only were the mean scores for corresponding treatment groups parallel across the two experiments, the absolute mean scores for corresponding groups were quite similar. These findings clearly indicate that Barber and his associates do achieve the same results as hypnotic-state theorists when they carry out the same experimental manipulations.[2]

Other examples in which Barber and his associates have replicated the experimental results of hypnotic-state theorists can also be cited (i.e., Barber & Calverley, 1968; Spanos & Barber, 1968). By the same token, investigators whose theoretical perspective differs widely from that of Barber have obtained results which are congruent with Barber's findings. Let us look at a few examples.

Wachtel (1969) has suggested that Barber and Calverley's (1964b) failure to find significant differences in suggestibility when hypnotic-induction procedures were spoken or presented by tape recording might be due to "experimental-bias." Wachtel (1969) cited no experimental evidence in support of this contention, and he failed to mention that Hoskovec, Svorad, and Lanc (1963) and Shor and Orne (1962) also found that the two methods of presentation produced equivalent results. The theoretical stances of Hoskovec, Svorad, and Lanc (1963) and Shor and Orne (1962) are, however, at variance with Barber's theoretical position.

Barber's finding of equivalent results when comparing hypnotic and various control treatments (usually a task-motivation treatment) has also been replicated by hypnotic state theorists. For instance, Casey (1966) and Edmonston and Erbeck (1967) replicated earlier results of Barber

---

[2] Barber and Calverley pointed out that the antecedent variables in the Williamsen *et al.* experiment were confounded. Thus, along with replicating the Williamsen *et al.* study, Barber and Calverley extended it by adding a number of experimental treatments which Williamsen *et al.* did not include in their experiment. These extensions indicated that Williamsen *et al.* were incorrect concerning the conclusions they had drawn from the data.

and Calverley (1964f) by finding that hypnotic subjects and nonhypnotic subjects responded in the same fashion on a time-distortion task. Kramer and Tucker (1967) obtained similar results on a suggested "deafness" task. London, Ogle, and Unikel (1968) found that subjects administered an hypnotic-induction procedure and subjects administered an equivalent of Barber's task-motivation instructions, performed equally well on a pursuit-rotor task under varying conditions of heat stress. As mentioned earlier, a number of investigators (Hilgard & Tart, 1966; Sarbin & Andersen, 1963; Thorne, 1967a, 1967b) have replicated Barber's findings of high base-line levels of response to suggestions of amnesia, catalepsy, hallucination, and so on.

In summary, there exist no available data to support the contention that Barber's findings are a function of "experimenter-bias." In fact, there are few data to suggest that "experimenter-bias" occurs at all when minimal standards of appropriate scientific procedure are met. The contention that Barber, and investigators who hold theoretical positions at variance with that of Barber, are unable to replicate each others experimental findings, is simply untrue.

## SUMMARY AND CONCLUSIONS

Any theoretical conceptualization which presents an alternative to an established scientific paradigm is bound to meet criticisms from adherents of the established paradigm. These criticisms will often involve (a) the development of *ad hoc* propositions which are congruent with the assumptions of the established paradigm and which can incorporate anomalous findings, and (b) attempts at demonstrating that anomalous findings presented by an alternative conceptualization are, in fact, invalid. This paper has evaluated recent criticisms which have been leveled against Barber's theoretical and empirical reconceptualization of hypnosis.

Four criticisms have been leveled against Barber's interpretations of his data. Three of these criticisms involve direct attempts at reinterpreting Barber's findings within the framework of hypnotic-state theory. These criticisms are based on the assumption that the hypothetical construct "hypnotic trance state" can be unambiguously and nontautologically denoted. As Barber has pointed out, however, such a denotation for this construct has yet to be achieved. The fourth criticism of Barber's theoretical interpretations states that Barber attempts to explain all of the phenomena of hypnosis as resulting from increases in subjects' motivation. This criticism constitutes an oversimplification of Barber's theoretical work. Barber has demonstrated that numerous antecedent variables are important in eliciting hypnotic behavior. He has not attempted to explain this behavior as a function of "motivation" or any other single antecedent factor.

Two criticisms have been leveled against Barber's empirical results. The first suggests that some of Barber's results are due to his use of an insensitive experimental design. The second contends that Barber and his associates inadvertently bias their experiments and thereby achieve results which are in line with their expectations. An examination of the experimentation used in support of the first criticism indicates that it either contains methodological deficits which render its results equivocal or employs methodological procedures which make its relevance to Barber's work difficult to evaluate. In short, the suggestion that some of Barber's research results are a function of an insensitive experimental design receives little direct experimental support. An examination of the suggestion that Barber's results are due to "experimenter bias" indicates that no direct or indirect evidence exists to support this hypothesis, and that the evidence which is available indicates that experimenter bias is not a factor in Barber's experimentation.

Although Barber's theoretical and experimental work capably withstands the criticisms of hypnotic state theorists, the converse is not as true. As pointed out above, Barber's criticisms of the "hypnotic-state" construct have not been adequately answered by hypnotic-state theorists. This has placed some of these theorists (McGlashon, Evans, & Orne, 1969) in the awkward position of agreeing that Barber's criticisms are essentially correct, while continuing to employ the "hypnotic state" construct in a circular fashion. Other theorists have either misunderstood Barber's criticisms (Conn & Conn, 1967) or have chosen to simply ignore them. Two alterna-

tives suggest themselves in light of hypnotic-state theorists' inability to present viable answers to the criticisms leveled against the central construct in their theoretical system. The first step is that hypnotic-state theorists continue in their attempts at delineating and interrelating behavioral indices in hope of achieving scientific respectability for the hypnotic state construct. The second alternative, which has been advocated by Sarbin (1962), suggests that the term "hypnosis" and its "trance state" connotations be stricken from the professional vocabulary of psychology.

### REFERENCES

ANDERSEN, M., & SARBIN, T. R. Base rate expectancies and motoric alterations in hypnosis. *International Journal of Clinical and Experimental Hypnosis*, 1964, **12**, 147–158.

BARBER, T. X. Toward a theory of pain: relief of chronic pain by prefrontal leucotomy, opiates, placebos and hypnosis. *Psychological Bulletin*, 1959, **56**, 430–460.

BARBER, T. X. Experimental controls and the phenomena of "hypnosis": a critique of hypnotic research methodology. *Journal of Nervous and Mental Disease*, 1962, **134**, 493–505. (a)

BARBER, T. X. Hypnotic age-regression: a critical review. *Psychosomatic Medicine*, 1962, **24**, 286–299. (b)

BARBER, T. X. "Hypnosis" as a causal variable in present-day psychology: a critical analysis. *Psychological Reports*, 1964, **14**, 839–842.

BARBER, T. X. Measuring "hypnotic-like" suggestibility with and without "hypnotic induction;" psychometric properties, norms, and variables influencing response to the Barber Suggestibility Scale (BSS). *Psychological Reports*, 1965, **16**, 809–844.

BARBER, T. X. "Hypnotic" phenomena: a critique of experimental methods. In J. Gordon (Ed.), *Handbook of clinical and experimental hynosis*. New York: Macmillan, 1967. Pp. 444–480. (a)

BARBER, T. X. Reply to Conn and Conn's "Discussion of Barber's 'hypnosis' as a causal variable . . . ." *International Journal of Clinical and Experimental Hypnosis*. 1967. **15**, 111–117. (b)

BARBER, T. X. An empirically-based formulation of hypnotism. *American Journal of Clinical Hypnosis*, 1969, **12**, 100–130. (a)

BARBER, T. X. *Hypnosis: a scientific approach*. New York: Van Nostrand–Reinhold, 1969. (b)

BARBER, T. X., & CALVERLEY, D. S. The relative effectiveness of task-motivating instructions and trance induction procedure in the production of "hypnotic-like" behaviors. *Journal of Nervous and Mental Disease*, 1963, **137**, 107–116.

BARBER, T. X., & CALVERLEY, D. S. An experimental study of "hypnotic" (auditory and visual) hallucinations. *Journal of Abnormal and Social Psychology*, 1964, 63, 13–20. (a)

BARBER, T. X., & CALVERLEY, D. S. Comparative effects on "hypnotic-like" suggestibility of recorded and spoken suggestions. *Journal of Consulting Psychology*, 1964, 28, 384. (b)

BARBER, T. X., & CALVERLEY, D. S. Effects of *E's* tone of voice on "hypnotic-like" suggestibility. *Psychological Reports*, 1964, 15, 139–144. (c)

BARBER, T. X., & CALVERLEY, D. S. Empirical evidence for a theory of "hypnotic" behavior: effects of pretest instructions on response to primary suggestions. *Psychological Record*, 1964, 14, 457–467. (d)

BARBER, T. X., & CALVERLEY, D. S. Experimental studies in "hypnotic" behavior: suggested deafness evaluated by delayed auditory feedback. *British Journal of Psychology*, 1964, 55, 439–446. (e)

BARBER, T. X., & CALVERLEY, D. S. Toward a theory of "hypnotic" behavior: an experimental study of "hypnotic time distortion." *Archives of General Psychiatry*, 1964, 10, 209–216. (f)

BARBER, T. X., & CALVERLEY, D. S. Toward a theory of "hypnotic" behavior: effects on suggestibility of defining the situation as hypnosis and defining response to suggestion as easy. *Journal of Abnormal and Social Psychology*, 1964 68, 585–592. (g)

BARBER, T. X., & CALVERLEY, D. S. Empirical evidence for a theory of "hypnotic" behavior: effects on suggestibility of five variables typically induced in hypnotic induction procedures. *Journal of Consulting Psychology*, 1965, 29, 98–107. (a)

BARBER, T. X., & CALVERLEY, D. S. Empirical evidence for a theory of "hypnotic" behavior: the suggestibility-enhancing effects of motivational suggestions, relaxation sleep suggestions, and suggestions that the subject will be effectively "hypnotized." *Journal of Personality*, 1965, 33, 256–270. (b)

BARBER, T. X., & CALVERLEY, D. S. Toward a theory of "hypnotic" behavior: experimental analysis of suggested amnesia. *Journal of Abnormal Psychology*, 1966, 71, 95–107.

BARBER, T. X., & CAVERLEY, D. S. Toward a theory of "hypnotic" behavior: replication and extension of experiments by Barber and co-workers (1962–65) and Hilgard and Tart (1966). *International Journal of Clinical and Experimental Hypnosis*, 1968, 16, 179–195.

BARBER, T. X., & CALVERLEY, D. S. Effects of hypnotic induction, suggestions of anesthesia, and distraction on subjective and physiological response to pain. Paper read at Eastern Psychological Assn. annual meeting, Philadelphia, April 10, 1969. (a)

BARBER, T. X., & CALVERLEY, D. S. Multidimensional analysis of "hypnotic" behavior. *Journal of Abnormal Psychology*, 1969. 74, 209–220. (b)

BARBER, T. X., CALVERLEY, D. S., FORGIONE, A., McPEAKE, J. D., CHAVES, J. F., & BOWEN, B. Five attempts to replicate the experimenter bias effect. *Journal of Consulting and Clinical Psychology*, 1969, 33, 1–6.

BARBER, T. X., DALAL, A. S., & CALVERLEY, D. S. The subjective reports of hypnotic subjects. *American Journal of Clinical Hypnosis*, 1968, 11, 74–88.

BARBER, T. X., & DEELEY, D. C. Experimental evidence for a theory of hypnotic behavior: I. "Hypnotic" color-blindness without hypnosis. *International Journal of Clinical and Experimental Hypnosis*, 1961, 9, 79–86.

BARBER, T. X. & HAHN, K. W., JR. Physiological and subjective responses to pain-producing stimulation under hynotically suggested and waking-imagined "analgesia." *Journal of Abnormal and Social Psychology*, 1962, 65, 411–418.

BARBER, T. X., & SILVER, M. J. Fact, fiction, and the experimental bias effect. *Psychological Bulletin*, 1968, 70, (6, Pt. 2), 1–29. (a)

BARBER, T. X., & SILVER, M. J. Pitfalls in data analysis and interpretation: a reply to Rosenthal. *Psychological Bulletin*, 1968, 70 (6, Pt. 2), 48–62. (b)

BOWERS, K. Hypnotic behavior: the differentiation of trance and demand characteristic variables. *Journal of Abnormal Psychology*, 1966, 71, 42–51.

BOWERS, K. The effects of demands for honesty on reports of visual and auditory hallucinations. *International Journal of Clinical and Experimental Hypnosis*, 1967, 15, 31–36.

BOWERS, K. S., & GILMORE, B. J. Subjective reports and credibility: an inquiry involving hypnotic hallucinations. *Journal of Abnormal Psychology*, 1969, 74, 443–451.

BUT, S. D., & FISKE, D. W. Comparison of strategies in developing scales for dominance. *Psychological Bulletin*, 1968, 70, 505–519.

CAMPBELL, D. T., & FISKE, D. W. Convergent and discriminant validation by the multitrait-multimethod matrix. *Psychological Bulletin*, 1959, 56, 81–105.

CASEY, G. A. Hypnotic time distortion and learning. Unpublished Ph.D. dissertation. Michigan State University, 1966.

CHAVES, J. F. Hypnosis reconceptualized: an overview of Barber's theoretical and empirical work. *Psychological Reports*, 1968, 22, 587–608.

CONN, J. H., & CONN, R. N. Discussion of T. X. Barber's "Hypnosis as a causal variable in present-day psychology: a critical analysis." *International Journal of Clinical and Experimental Hypnosis*, 1967, 15, 106–110.

EDMONSTON, W. E. Hypnosis and electrodermal responses. *American Journal of Clinical Hypnosis*, 1968, 11, 16–25.

EDMONSTON, W. E., & ERBECK, J. R. Hypnotic

time distortion: a note. *American Journal of Clinical Hypnosis*, 1967, **10**, 79–83.

EDMONSTON, W. E., & ROBERTSON, T. G. A comparison of the effects of task motivational and hypnotic induction instructions on responsiveness to hypnotic suggestibility scales. *American Journal of Clinical Hypnosis*, 1967, **9**, 184–187.

ERICKSON, M. H. A study of clinical and experimental findings on hypnotic deafness: I. Clinical experimentation and findings. *Journal of General Psychology*, 1938, **19**, 127–150. (a)

ERICKSON, M. H. A study of clinical and experimental findings on hypnotic deafness: II. Experimental findings with a conditioned response technique. *Journal of General Psychology*, 1938, **19**, 151–167. (b)

ERICKSON, M. H. The induction of color blindness by a technique of hypnotic suggestion. *Journal of General Psychology*, 1939, **20**, 61–89.

EVANS, F. J. Recent trends in experimental hypnosis. *Behavioral Science*, 1968, **13**, 477–487.

GARNER, W. R., HAKE, H. W., & ERIKSEN, C. W. Operationalism and the concept of perception. *Psychological Review*, 1956, **63**, 149–159.

GRAVITZ, M. A., & HOPKINSON, D. Methodological developments in contemporary scientific research in hypnosis. *International Journal of Clinical and Experimental Hypnosis*, 1969, **17**, 167–179.

HILGARD, E. R. Hypnotic susceptibility. New York: Harcourt, Brace, & World, 1965.

HILGARD, E. R. Altered states of awareness. *Journal of Nervous and Mental Diseases*, 1969, **149**, 68–79.

HILGARD, E. R., & TART, C. T. Responsiveness to suggestions following waking and imagination instructions and following induction of hypnosis. *Journal of Abnormal Psychology*, 1966, **71**, 196–208.

HOSKOVEC, J., SVORAD, D., & LANC, O. The comparative effectiveness of spoken and tape-recorded suggestions of body sway. *International Journal of Clinical and Experimental Hypnosis*, 1963, **11**, 163–164.

HULL, C. L. *Hypnosis and suggestibility*, New York: Appleton, 1933.

JACOB, T. The experimenter bias effect: a failure to replicate. *Psychonomic Science*, 1968, **13**, 239–240.

KLINE, M. V., GUZE, H., & HAGGERTY, A. D. An experimental study of the nature of hypnotic deafness: effects of delayed auditory feedback. *Journal of Clinical and Experimental Hypnosis*. 1954, **2**, 145–156.

KRAMER, E., & TUCKER, R. G. Hypnotically suggested deafness and delayed auditory feedback. *International Journal of Clinical and Experimental Hypnosis*, 1967, **15**, 37–43.

KUHN, T. S. *The structure of scientific revolutions*. Chicago: University of Chicago Press, 1962.

LONDON, P., OGLE, M. E., & UNIKEL, I. P. Effects of hypnosis and motivation on resistance to heat stress. *Journal of Abnormal Psychology*, 1968, **73**, 532–541.

LUDWIG, A. M., & LYLE, W. H., JR. Tension induction and the hyperalert trance. *Journal of Abnormal and Social Psychology*, 1964, **69**, 70–76.

McFALL, R. M., & SAXMAN, J. H. Verbal communication as a mediator of expectancy effects. Methodological artifact? *Psychological Reports*, 1968, **23**, 1223–1228.

McGLASHON, T. H., EVANS, F. J., & ORNE, M. T. The nature of hypnotic analgesia and placebo response to experimental pain. *Psychosomatic Medicine*, 1969, **31**, 227–246.

McPEAKE, J. D. Hypnosis, suggestions and psychosomatics. *Diseases of the Nervous System*, 1968, **29**, 536–544.

ORNE, M. T. On the social psychology of the psychological experiment: with particular reference to demand characteristics and their implications. *American Psychologist*, 1962, **17**, 776–783.

ORNE, M. T. Hypnosis, motivation and compliance. *American Journal of Psychiatry*, 1966, **122**, 721–726.

ROSENHAN, D. On the social psychology of hypnosis research. In J. Gordon (Ed.), *Handbook of clinical and experimental hypnosis*. New York: Macmillan, 1967.

ROSENTHAL, R. *Experimenter effects in behavioral research*. New York: Appleton-Century-Crofts. 1966.

SARBIN, T. R. Attempts to understand hypnotic phenomena. In L. Postman (Ed.), *Psychology in the making*. New York: Knopf, 1962. Pp. 745–785.

SARBIN, T. R., & ANDERSEN, M. L. Base-rate expectancies and perceptual alterations in hypnosis. *British Journal of Social and Clinical Psychology*, 1963, **2**, 112–121.

SARBIN, T. R., & JUHASZ, J. B. The historical background of the concept of hallucination. *Journal of the History of the Behavioral Sciences*, 1967, **3**, 339–358.

SCHEIBE, K., GRAY, A. L., & KEIM, C. S. Hypnotically induced deafness and delayed auditory feedback: a comparison of real and simulating subjects. *International Journal of Clinical and Experimental Hypnosis*, 1968, **16**, 158–164.

SCHNECK, J. M. Observations on hypnotic dreams. *Perceptual and Motor Skills*, 1969, **28**, 414.

SHOR, R. E. Three dimensions of hypnotic depth. *International Journal of Clinical and Experimental Hypnosis*, 1962, **10**, 23–38.

SHOR, R. E., & ORNE, E. Harvard group scale of hypnotic susceptibility: Form A. Palo Alto: Consulting Psychologist Press, 1962.

SILVER, M. J. Experimenter modeling: a critique.

*Journal of Experimental Research in Personality,* 1968, **3**, 172–178.

SILVER, M. J., & BARBER, T. X. Controversy in hypnosis research as a function of investigator effects, experimenter effects, and experimenter bias. Harding, Mass.: Medfield Foundation, 1969. (mimeo).

SPANOS, N. P., & BARBER, T. X. "Hypnotic" experiences as inferred from subjective reports: Auditory and visual hallucinations. *Journal of Experimental Research in Personality,* 1968, **3**, 136–150.

SPANOS, N. P., BARBER, T. X., & LANG, G. The effects of an hypnotic induction procedure, analgesia suggestions, and demands for honesty on subjective reports of pain. Dept. of Sociology, Boston University, 1969. (mimeo).

SPANOS, N. P., & CHAVES, J. F. Converging operations and the "hypnotic state" construct. *Proceedings of the American Psychological Association,* 77th annual convention, 1969.

SPANOS, N. P., & CHAVES, J. F. Hypnosis research: a methodological critique of experiments generated by two alternative paradigms. *American Journal of Clinical Hypnosis,* in press.

STOYVA, J., & KAMIYA, J. Electrophysiological studies of dreaming as the prototype of a new strategy in the study of consciousness. *Psychological Review,* 1968, **75**, 192–205.

STRAUSS, M. E. Examiner expectancy: effects on Rorshach experience balance. *Journal of Consulting and Clinical Psychology,* 1968, **32**, 125–129.

SUTCLIFFE, J. P. "Credulous" and "skeptical" views of hypnotic phenomena: a review of certain evidence and methodology. *International Journal of Clinical and Experimental Hypnosis,* 1960, **8**, 73–101.

TART, C. T., & HILGARD, E. R. Responsiveness to suggestions under "hypnosis" and "waking-imagination" conditions, a methodological observation. *International Journal of Clinical and Experimental Hypnosis,* 1966, **14**, 247–256.

THORNE, D. E. Is the hypnotic trance necessary for performance of hypnotic phenomena? *Journal of Abnormal Psychology,* 1967, **72**, 233–239. (a)

THORNE, D. E. Memory as related to hypnotic suggestion, procedure, and susceptibility. Unpublished doctoral dissertation, University of Utah, 1967. (b)

WACHTEL, P. L. Wanting nothing and getting nothing: on negative results in hypnosis research. *American Journal of Clinical Hypnosis,* 1969, **11**, 209–220.

WEITZENHOFFER, A. M., & HILGARD, E. R. *Stanford hypnotic susceptibility scale. Forms A and B.* Palo Alto, Calif.: Consulting Psychologists Press, 1959.

WESSLER, R. L. Experimenter expectancy effects in psychomotor performance. *Perceptual and Motor Skills,* 1968, **26**, 911–917.

WESSLER, R. L. Experimenter expectancy effects in three dissimilar tasks. *Journal of Psychology,* 1969, **71**, 63–67.

WESSLER, R. L., & STRAUSS, M. E. Experimenter expectancy: a failure to replicate. *Psychological Reports,* 1968, **22**, 687–688.

WILLIAMSEN, J. A., JOHNSON, H. J., & ERIKSEN, C. W. Some characteristics of post-hypnotic amnesia. *Journal of Abnormal Psychology,* 1965, **70**, 123–131.

ZEGERS, R. A. Expectancy and the effects of confirmation and disconfirmation. *Journal of Personality and Social Psychology,* 1968, **9**, 67–71.

# Some Comments on Barber's 27
## "Reconceptualization" of Hypnosis

### Auke Tellegen

Barber's assertions concerning the hypnotic-state construct and hypnotic research are critically discussed. Barber's charge that hypnotic-state theories are circular and tautological is found unwarranted. Also, the fallibility of hypnotic indicators and induction techniques stressed by Barber is considered no more reason for rejecting the hypnotic-state concept than for abandoning other well-established constructs. Barber's own "empirically-based" formulation is primarily methodological and appears not to be "motivated." The value of Barber's contributions to a more rigorous and critical empiricism in the area of hypnosis is acknowledged.

Spanos' paper (Spanos, 1970) succinctly and effectively stated Barber's views of hypnotism, augmenting the now familiar arguments with pertinent comments on more recent material. The author has adopted Barber's orientation and his brand of what Hilgard (1969b) has called "contemporary behaviorism" which distinguishes itself, among other things, by a reluctance to adopt "mental state" concepts. Spanos' paper is only the most recent one in a series of exchanges between Barber (and his students) and others. Yet, in this author's opinion, some of Barber's basic assertions have still not received the critical attention they require. In the following an attempt will be made to provide such an evaluation as a supplement to Spanos' discussion. The author hopes that his remarks will contribute to a balanced and not an insipid view of hypnosis.

First, it is necessary to distinguish between different aspects of Barber's work. His critical evaluation of various alleged facts concerning hypnosis is one aspect. Another contribution, also critical in intent, is his conceptual and methodological evaluation of the concept of hypnosis as a "state." Finally, in a more constructive vein, Barber also offers his own "empirically-based" conception of hypnotism as a guide for future research.

Not much will be said about Barber's critical assessment of certain factual claims involving hypnosis. Some claims, attributing to hypnotized individuals a capacity for exhibiting symptoms such as "true" blindness or deafness or analgesia, were undoubtedly overgeneralized and exaggerated. Barber's review of the evidence and his own research have provided a needed, more stringent and sober assessment of the phenomena in question. It is fair to say that Barber has not advocated that we ignore from now on all reported phenomena of a rare and dramatic nature. Rather, he suggested that the antecedents of such phenomena be tied down as specifically as is possible.

**369**

### BARBER'S CRITICISMS OF THE HYPNOTIC-STATE CONSTRUCT

More should be said about Barber's criticisms of formulations invoking a "hypnotic state" or "trance" as an explanatory construct ("state theories" for brevity). A number of different criticisms can be distinguished here.

According to one criticism, state theories are guilty of "circular" reasoning and of being "tautological." One of Barber's assertions is that state theorists consider a subject's response to suggestions the result of his hypnotic trance state, but at the same time "circularly" attribute the trance state to the subject's response to suggestions. This criticism is in this author's opinion based on an incorrect characterization of what state theorists believe. What state theorists can be assumed to assert is that earlier suggestions may affect a hypnotic subject in such a way as to facilitate his response to later suggestions. To present this assertion as circular is to misstate it.

A somewhat different charge of circularity is based on Barber's observation that state theories first infer a trance state on the basis of such observations as the subject's response to test suggestions and his relaxed appearance, and then invoke the trance state to explain in turn these observations. Barber argued that these two steps together constitute circular reasoning. As stated, this conclusion is incorrect and seems to be based on a mistaken conception of circularity. It would be circular reasoning if, for example, one inferred a state of hypnotic trance on the basis of the subject's state of relaxation if the latter itself had been inferred from the subject's trance state, or to use a different example, if one were to infer a bone fracture from a reported X-ray photo if the report itself turned out to be an inference based on the postulated fracture and not an observation. But it is not circular to infer a hypnotic trance state from certain observations in order to explain these observations, just as it is not circular to infer from an actual X-ray photo the existence of a fracture in order to explain certain features of the photo. Both cases are instances of the kind of causal inference that links observations to an inferred state. They are not instances of reasoning that in true circular fashion

bases a proof or inference on what was set out to be proved or inferred.

Even if it is conceded that causal inferences invoking an inferred state are not, in principle, circular, one may still want to raise questions specifically concerning hypnosis as an explanatory construct. Here the term "tautology," sometimes used by Barber in reference to state theories, may be relevant. As I understand his view, the term "hypnotic state" as actually used by state theorists would merely designate certain traditional phenomena, such as response to suggestions and relaxed appearance. Thus the words describing the latter, and the term "hypnotic trance," would, in fact, mean exactly the same thing, even though state theorists themselves are supposedly not aware of this implicit identity. In that case, it would indeed be specious and self-deceptive to invoke a "hypnotic state" as an explanation for hypnotic phenomena, since it would mean to attribute something causally to itself.

The above argument is, unfortunately, also based on misinterpretation. In state theoretical formulations, the hypnotic state, far from being a mere label for certain traditionally included phenomena, clearly functions as a theoretical construct (cf. Cronbach and Meehl, 1955). As such the hypnotic state is endowed with "surplus" meaning and has been embedded in a network of hypothetical relationships that are to link it to various observables which are not exclusively composed of those used to infer its presence. For example, someone like Orne might infer with a certain degree of confidence a hypnotic trance state in one of his subjects on the basis of the latter's response to suggestions and his relaxed appearance. But he could then go on to predict and test his subject for manifestations of "trance logic," since "trance logic" is part of the surplus meaning of the hypnotic state as Orne conceived it (e.g., Orne, 1959). It is not too difficult to draw similar examples from other state theoretical formulations. It is not suggested that empirical confirmations of postulated surplus meanings have at this point put the hypnotic state construct on a firm footing. It is also not denied, instead it is emphasized, that ingenuity along with more precise specifications would often be needed before one could subject some of the propositions of hypnotic-state theory to empirical tests. While questions of explicitness and confirmation are of central importance, they are not the ones at issue here. Here the question is whether one should dismiss the hypnotic-state construct, as advanced by state theorists, as "circular" or "tautological." The answer is that one cannot.

As Spanos pointed out, Barber has also taken critical note of certain problems in the identification and manipulation of the hypnotic state. The implication seems to be again that these difficulties call the hypnotic-state construct itself into question.

In regard to the identification of the hypnotic state, Barber stressed the fact that extraneous factors can affect certain indicators of the hypnotic state. He pointed out, for example, how easily one allegedly prime hypnotic indicator, the individual's own testimony, is influenced by the wording of the questions submitted to him. Thus, Barber, Dalal, and Calverley (1968) found that many more subjects described hypnosis and waking state as similar in response to a positively worded than to a negatively worded question. In response it might be useful to point out first, that the two questions, in spite of appearing to produce inconsistent results, might still be measures of the same subjective dimension, yielding correlated answers and differing only in endorsement frequency ("difficulty level"). Secondly, one should note that state theorists generally consider the hypnotic trance state to be a variable, ranging from "extremely light" to "extremely deep." Questions directed as assessing a distinct hypnotic experience but posed in either–or fashion are presumably difficult to answer and quite sensitive to wording. But a more important and general point is the following: One cannot assume hypnotic-state theorists to be so naive as to assert a direct and simple connection between a person's words and his subjective experiences. Contemporary psychologists don't need to be told that certain questions can produce answers which, appraised in isolation, lead to inconsistent conclusions. Any experienced interviewer knows that the way questions are worded can greatly influence the answers one receives. Yet the interview is considered a very useful tool as long as the interview questions are carefully worded and answers are evaluated in the context both of the particular question asked and of answers given to other questions. All this applies *a fortiori* when the inquiry happens to concern an individual's private experiences. A thoughtful hypnotic state theorist can be assumed to recognize that a systematic reconstruction of someone else's private experiences requires as sensitive and ingenious an inquiry as one is capable of. Barber's questions, referred to above, would not seem to illustrate such an approach. While one may have good reasons for being skeptical about the significance of certain postulated private experiences, skepticism is not justified by the results of unsophisticated inquiries.

Even a carefully developed individual indicator is still not expected to be infallible. But fallibility is not necessarily fatal to an indicator, or to the contruct to which it was linked. If one considers "intelligence" to be a viable construct, then it is in this context helpful to remember that on the item level many indicators of intelligence are highly fallible, and of slight value if used singly, although useful when combined with other indicators. Even multiple indicators could yield unsatisfactory results if all belonged to the same type; for example, if they all measured overt responses to suggestions, or if all measured the subject's reported experiences or aspects of his expressive behavior. Even though these different types of variables can be expected to converge and in general to be positively correlated, one cannot expect any of them to be wholly "pure." The probable presence of "instrument" factors and other special factors militates against the latter expectation. Whether assessing hypnosis or intelligence, the use of multiple indicators belonging to multiple types is the method of choice.

Barber also seemed to question the validity of those indicators whose manifestations can be suppressed even though the indicated state is presumably still present. Thus, he pointed out that "relaxed appearance," often considered an indicator of hypnotic trance, can be removed by appropriate instructions, although the subject is presumably still in a hypnotic trance (Barber, 1969a). Must this type of finding lead one to criticize the use of "relaxed appearance" as a hypnotic indicator? I don't think so. One should recognize that useful indicators besides being fallible are also only conditionally valid. To give one illustration: Scores on a normally valid intelligence-test item would no longer reflect the subject's aptitude, if he had seen and rehearsed the correct answers beforehand, or if he was overly or insufficiently "motivated," or was motivated to do poorly, or even if he was trying to give answers that were cleverly wrong.

In sum, it is true that the hypnotic state may be related to certain phenomena without being either necessary or even sufficient to produce these phenomena. It is also true that this same loose and conditional relationship between inferred constructs and indicators holds in the case of other, better-established constructs such as sleep and arousal. Barber and others would miss the point if it were their intention to "prove" that presumed hypnotic indicators are capable of error, bias, and inconsistency. Such a demonstration is easy and trivial. The real question is whether sustained and skillful efforts will result in improved hypnotic measurement and in the discovery of new and interesting relationships. The failure to make such discoveries in spite of sustained efforts would finally discourage one from further attempts to assess "hypnosis" and ultimately from maintaining the construct itself. In the meantime it is to Barber's credit to have forced the realization that still not enough systematic efforts have been made to improve hypnotic state assessment.

It appears, then, that Barber's critical evaluation of hypnotic state indicators provides in some ways a stimulus for better methodology, but that it is, conceptually speaking, not especially compelling. State-oriented investigators, on the other hand, seem not to have perceived clearly enough the disadvantages of insufficiently developed indicators and of reliance on indicators of a single type. For example, the carefully developed Stanford Hypnotic Susceptibility Scales (which measures susceptibility as a trait by assessing the hypnotic state in a standard induction setting) cover a broad spectrum of observable responses to suggestions, but do not provide

for a systematic assessment of the subject's experiences. This "objective" emphasis contrasts with the conviction generally held by state theorists that the subjective report is a prime (or "privileged") hypnotic indicator. Barber, whose own susceptibility scale consists of both a subjective and objective part, can certainly claim to have stressed the need for considering a variety of hypnotic indicators, even though improved psychometric attainment of a hypothetical hypnotic state seems not to have been his motivating reason. My colleague, Alan Roberts, and I have started using a standard inquiry concerning subjective experiences when administering our modified version of the Harvard Group Scale. We found the experiential and behavioral scores to be highly correlated. Combining the two scores resulted in a substantial increase in reliability.

Barber has also called attention to difficulties involving the manipulation of the hypnotic state. Again, the facts invoked are not disputed here. It has been found in several studies that the performance differences between "hypnotic" subjects, given a formal induction, and "control" subjects, who received "imagination," "task motivation," or "simulation" instructions are small or negligible. As Spanos pointed out, state theorists have offered the partial explanation that subjects receiving a hypnotic induction will not invariably enter a trance state, and conversely, that control subjects, even if told to simulate only, may nevertheless "slip" into a hypnotic state. For state theorists intent on studying hypnosis experimentally these manipulation problems are a nuisance. But Barber and Spanos, in turn, took offense to state-oriented attempts at explaining the occurrence of these difficulties. Spanos labeled these attempts *ad hoc* explanations for "anomalous" findings, "anomalous," since, for instance, "the notion that subjects might spontaneously slip into hypnosis was not a prediction generated by hypnotic state theory." This assertion, however, is not justified.

First, state theoretically oriented researchers are certainly not new to the fact that individuals differ in hypnotic susceptibility, witness the fact that some investigators have made attempts to assess these differences. Consistent with a recognition of differential responsiveness to hypnotic induction is the expectation that a given formal induction method is not invariably a sufficient condition for inducing hypnosis or a certain level of hypnotic trance.

Second, state theorists would have no reason to reject the assumption that "trancelike" phenomena occur outside formal induction situations—this assumption accounts, in fact, for part of the general interest value of the hypnotic state construct. State-oriented researchers have actually studied, in a number of investigations, individual differences in the tendency to have such trancelike experiences. This research interest is not surprising since a state theoretical position does not entail the belief that formal induction is a necessary condition for phenomena of a hypnotic nature.

In other words, it is recognized that formal induction is neither sufficient nor necessary for the occurrence of hypnotic phenomena. These facts are compatible with a state theoretical orientation and do not require ad hoc explanations of a kind straining the original position. State theoretical positions, as far as I can tell, never implied an "operational" definition which designates a phenomenon as hypnotic if and only if it is a response to certain specified induction procedures. It would be regrettable if the perceived purpose of future comparisons of different procedures remained limited to the narrow and mistaken polemical objective of demonstrating the untenability of an operational definition of hypnosis. On the other hand, a continuing search for really effective new methods of induction could be of value to anyone, regardless of whether he hopes to delineate a hypnotic state concept more clearly, or "merely" desires to extend his empirical knowledge.

One regrets, of course, the failure of state theories to specify the exact conditions leading or not leading to a hypnotic trance. It is this looseness of formulation, rather than incorrect predictions, which invites ad hoc explanations for certain findings. However, a comparison with the research area of sleep may put this matter in better perspective. To distinguish real sleep from apparent sleep present-day investigators would not rely on the knowledge of having used a particular "sleep-induction" method. Instead, they rely on certain state indicators such as are provided by the EEG. This comparison underscores the point, made earlier, that the hypothetical hypnotic state is in need of further improved assessment methods. And this improvement does not have to await discovery of, say, some new near-infallible physiological indicator. As a beginning, existing indicators could be more systematically developed for conjoint use.

To summarize the discussion so far, most researchers who are sympathetic to a hypnotic-state construct would concede that hypnosis is a still vague and loosely anchored, rather than a well-defined and highly confirmed construct. But in charging hypnotic-state formulations with circularity and tautology Barber goes too far. Also, the evidence that hypnotic indicators and techniques for manipulating the hypnotic state are fallible is convincing evidence against a hypnotic-state construct only for those who unconditionally require quasi-infallible indicators and precise manipulative techniques. To take such a position nearly amounts to a rejection of any mental state or trait construct, whether it be hypnosis, anxiety, depression, sleep, or intelligence. This is not the place to discuss the merits of a view which is opposed in this general way, to mental-state concepts. The methodological and philosophical issues involved are interesting but are not about to be resolved by Barber or anyone else. Barber's criticisms of the hypnotic-state construct insofar as they are based on a general skepticism regarding state constructs can be considered expressions of a defensible view, to be taken note of, but not really amenable to conclusive discussion. On the other hand, Barber's specific criticisms of the particular construct of hypnosis, while a better subject for debate, are not convincing.

## BARBER'S "RECONCEPTUALIZATION" OF HYPNOSIS

At this point it may be good to turn attention from Barber's criticisms to his own "empirically-based formulation" of hypnotism. Barber essentially advocated an enumeration of low-level empirical behavioral laws stating relationships between various specified antecedent conditions and consequent behaviors in the domain of hypnosis. Barber argued that a large number of such empirical relationships would first have to be established before one could fruitfully formulate higher order theoretical concepts. This position is consistent, of course, with the attitude of skepticism alluded to earlier, regarding the usefulness of "open," mentalistic concepts such as the hypnotic-state construct. While Barber's espousal of behavioristic empiricism combined with considerable theoretical restraint represents a respectable position, it is not the only defensible position. Hilgard's "contemporary functionalism," for example, is one of several alternative approaches which do permit the investigator to develop and evaluate a hypnotic-state theory.

These differences in theoretical outlook should not obscure the fact that there are certain basic standards that contemporary investigators of differing persuasions all seem to subscribe to. It may be helpful to conclude this discussion with a comparison of Barber's position and the state theoretical view in the light of two such criteria.

One shared standard is that one's approach be an empirical one. The demands for empiricism are equally stringent whether one adopts a state-oriented view or Barber's "empirically-based" formulation. It would be simply incorrect to consider a state-oriented position as one that somehow compromises or dilutes one's commitment to confirmation or refutation by facts. To draw a comparison from a different area, Tolman's and Hull's theoretical behaviorisms, or Hebb's neuropsychology of learning, are or were no less committed to empiricism than Skinner's "radical" behaviorism. Barber has done a service exposing unwarranted inferences based on premature or incorrect factual beliefs held by some state oriented investigators. But these mistakes are not inherent to a state theoretical position. They are instances of poor theorizing as well as of inadequate empiricism.

The question as to what function, then, good theorizing serves leads to a consideration of a second criterion. This criterion is, I believe, also subscribed to, at least implicitly, by contemporary investigators, and could be labeled "motivation." There is obviously a great deal that is subjective, arbitrary, or accidental in one's selection of research problems. Nevertheless, any investigator could be expected to formulate as thoughtful and careful a rationale as he is capable of to guide his research effort.

State theories provide this type of motivation. They advance hypnosis as a particular psychological state and prompt investigations of selected and distinct observable consequences of this state. Whether hypnosis is a fruitful state concept remains in my opinion still an undecided question.

Barber, however, has already answered this question in the negative and has advanced what he considers a preferable alternative approach. Proper consideration of Barber's views not only requires an evaluation of his critique of state theories, but also an inquiry into the motivation of his own proposals and his own research insofar as it carries out these proposals.

Much of Barber's own research effort, as reviewed by Spanos, is in my opinion best understood as still motivated by the hypnotic-state construct. To be sure, the motivation is the negative one of raising critical questions concerning the necessity and plausibility of a state construct. But this negative motivation serves the same function as a positive one would have: it provides a focus.

However, in formulating his own "empirically-based" approach Barber has attempted to move beyond a negative position. As seen earlier, this approach is essentially one that stresses the need for systematic empirical methodology. It should now be added that a proposed methodology, no matter how commendable, does not in itself generate a program of motivated substantive research. In answer to the question as to what kind of hypnotic research should be done we find Barber simply suggesting that we study the observable antecedents of "the behaviors that have been historically associated with the word *hypnotism*" (cf. Barber, 1969a). For example, since a "hypnotic" (relaxed) appearance is one of the phenomena historically associated with hypnotism, Barber proposed that we conduct studies "to isolate all of the important antecedent variables" which determine whether or not a subject presents a relaxed appearance. Among the possible antecedents Barber mentioned such factors as wording and tone of suggestions, definition of the situation, experimenter's vocal characteristics, his personality characteristics, age, sex, etc., which are to be studied as main effects as well as in interaction with other variables. My first reaction to these suggestions is to inquire why we want to know these facts. In other words, what motivates these proposals?

It is reported that Tycho Brahe, the 16th century Danish astronomer, was primarily concerned with observation and measurement, and that he left formulation of the grand generalizations concerning planetary motion, for which he helped lay the groundwork, to his one-time assistant Kepler. As may have become apparent, Barber believes that research in hypnosis should proceed in much the same way. We saw that he encourages researchers to begin with a quasi-exhaustive investigation of possible functional relationships between the many antecedent and consequent variables that have been identified in the field of hypnosis as traditionally defined. He believes that after a survey of this kind it will become possible to "subsume the empirically-determined antecedent-consequent relations under a small number of general principles." This expectation seems unrealistic. The Brahe–Kepler case is special in that it involved an important but comparatively simple physical system. According to Kuhn (1962), whom Barber cited, the scientific enterprise depends in general heavily on the formation of so-called paradigms which direct the scientist's thinking, telling him what to look for and how to look for it. I believe that Kuhn's idea, although developed in reference to the physical sciences, is particularly valid in the domain of the social sciences. Here one faces a wealth of complex phenomena and an infinitely large number of initial questions that could be asked and answered empirically. One simply cannot escape the venture and risks of deciding which questions are important. In other words, one cannot function here without some kind of orientation motivating one's research decisions.

What, then, if one were to relinquish hypnosis as a theoretical and research motivating concept? What if one concluded that hypnosis is without "essence" and all "artifact," to use Orne's terms? It would not follow automatically that from then on the artifacts would be the phenomena to be studied. Some researchers might just abandon the area of hypnosis, and some have done so. And even if one of these artifacts would appear worthy of study for its own sake, it would in all likelihood not just motivate research of phenomena "historically associated" with hypnotism. This point is illustrated by Orne's ingenious studies of "demand characteristics" (Orne, 1959; Orne, 1962; Orne & Scheibe, 1964). Demand characteristics is one of the artifacts Orne wishes to distinguish and separate from hypnotism proper, but also one he became interested in for its own sake. Significantly, in pursuing this new problem Orne moved, for good reasons, outside conventional hypnotic situations. His work in this area clearly reflects the redirection which takes place when research is motivated by a new interest.

It is actually not difficult to identify in Barber's own writings certain potentially motivating considerations. For example, Barber has tentatively identified several antecedent variables which might eventually account for a major portion of hypnotic phenomena (e.g., Barber, 1969b). These variables are closely related to Orne's artifacts and include such factors as subjects' expectancies, task motivational instructions, and experimenter role. Insofar as these variables are of intrinsic interest they can certainly motivate focussed research efforts. But this research is unlikely to deal solely with traditional hypnotic phenomena.

On the dependent-variable side, Barber noted that some of the effects linked to hypnotism are beneficial; for example, pain reduction, increased physical endurance, and improved cognitive functioning. He believes that as a result of his approach these effects "will be produced more simply and directly than at present," using only those traditional antecedent variables that are found to be actually effective. The study of pain illustrates the issue at hand.

First, it is easy to see how someone with a state theoretical orientation could develop an interest in hypnotic analgesia. Hilgard's work in this area is a good example of the research that can result from such an interest (cf. Hilgard, 1969a). In spite of its possible practical payoff for the technology of pain control, the motivating focus of this research, explaining its peculiar characteristics, was the hypnotic state and not pain. On the other hand, some one who had given up on hypnosis as a construct might still consider pain reduction by psychological means to be a worthwhile research objective in itself. But a creative pursuit of this new objective would not be helped by the stipulation (now arbitrary because no longer motivated) that the variables under consideration be traditionally associated with hypnotism. A better-motivated problem selection is called for.

It seems then, that neither Barber's formulation, nor his stated substantive interests provide motivation to study hypnotic phenomena in the manner he proposes. The hypnotic-state concept, on the other hand, obviously does provide motivation for investigating some of the phenomena in question.

It has not been argued here that research, to be motivated, must be guided by highly inferential concepts of the kind that Barber would be uncomfortable with. To think so would be a mistake. Skinner's radical behaviorism is perhaps the best known example of a well-motivated but "atheoretical" approach. Skinner's approach derived its focus from a strong and early confirmed belief in the power of reinforcement and a well-reasoned preference for response rate as a dependent variable. A significant part of this selective orientation was to ignore, at least for the time being, a host of variables that were (to paraphrase Barber) "historically associated with the word *learning*," such as T-maze choice behavior, runway latencies, VTE-ing, latent learning, etc.

## CONCLUSIONS

It is time to sum up this rather lengthy discussion. First, it would be a mistake to minimize the contribution of Barber's vigorous empiricism to the cause of sound hypnotic research. Furthermore, one can adopt the view that acquaintance with hypnotic phenomena is likely to stimulate diverse lines of worthwhile research, a view which is in the spirit of Barber's and Orne's approaches alike.

On the other hand, there are no compelling reasons for adopting Barber's negative view of hypnotic-state theory. Rather than as cogent specific criticisms Barber's arguments are more easily understood as reflecting a general methodological and philosophical reluctance to incorporate inferential mentalistic concepts into his thinking. But no matter how well considered Barber's methodological orientation may be, it remains a matter of personal preference, and cannot, in all fairness, be treated as if it were the only defensible stance.

Barber's own "empirically-based" formulation appears primarily to be methodological. Neither this formulation, nor his own tentative substantive generalizations or practical interests justify (motivate) the blanket endorsement of investigations relating antecedents and consequents traditionally associated with hypnotism. Whatever the shortcomings of hypnotic-state concepts may be, new formulations might be expected to generate research efforts that are no less motivated. Innovation and discovery are in part matters of luck, but one assumes that their occurrence is made more likely by research that is motivated and imaginatively implemented than by either nebulous theorizing or too pat an empiricism.

## REFERENCES

BARBER, T. X. An empirically-based formulation of hypnotism. *The American Journal of Clinical Hypnosis*, 1969, **12**, 100-130. (a)

BARBER, T. X. *Hypnosis: A scientific approach.* New York: Van Nostrand–Reinhold, 1969. (b)

BARBER, T. X., DALAL, A. S., & CALVERLEY, D. S. The subjective reports of hypnotic subjects. *The American Journal of Clinical Hypnosis*, 1968, **11**, 74–88.

CRONBACH, L. J., & MEEHL, P. E. Construct validity in psychological tests. *Psychological Bulletin,* 1955, **52,** 281–302.

HILGARD, E. R. Pain as a puzzle for psyc! ology and physiology. *American Psychologist,* 1969, **24,** 103–113. (a)

HILGARD, E. R. Altered states of awareness. *The Journal of Nervous and Mental Disease,* 1969, **149,** 68–79. (b)

KUHN, T. S. *The structure of scientific revolutions.* Chicago: University of Chicago Press, 1962.

ORNE, M. T. The nature of hypnosis: artifact and essence. *Journal of Abnormal and Social Psy-*

*chology,* 1959, **58,** 277–299.

ORNE, M. T. On the social psychology of the psychological experiment: with particular reference to demand characteristics and their implications. *American Psychologist,* 1962, **17,** 776–783.

ORNE, M. T., & SCHEIBE, K. E. The contribution of nondeprivation factors in the production of sensory deprivation effects. *Journal of Abnormal and Social Psychology,* 1964, **68,** 3–12.

SPANOS, N. P. Barber's reconceptualization of hypnosis: an evaluation of criticisms. *Journal of Experimental Research in Personality,* 1970, **4,** 241–258.

# A Reply to Tellegen's 28
## "Comments on 'Barber's Reconceptualization of Hypnosis'"

### Nicholas P. Spanos

Tellegen argues that (*a*) Barber's attribution of circularity to the concept "hypnosis" is incorrect and (*b*) the "hypnotic state" may constitute a useful hypothetical construct for investigating the phenomena traditionally subsumed under the rubric hypnosis. However, an analysis of Tellegen's arguments concerning circularity indicates that they are based on erroneous assertions concerning hypnotic state theory and, therefore, do not constitute a challenge to Barber's contention. Although Tellegen may be correct in suggesting that hypnosis can be employed as a useful hypothetical construct, this remains to be demonstrated.

In commenting on my paper (Spanos, 1970), Tellegen (1970) presented a series of arguments in defense of hypnotic state theory. In the brief space available, I will comment only on some of the more salient issues.

One of the most important issues concerns the purported circularity of the concept "hypnosis." According to Tellegen, Barber is incorrect in asserting that hypnotic state theorists employ the concept "hypnosis" circularly. Tellegen contends that "what state theorists really assert is that earlier (induction) suggestions may affect a hypnotic subject in such a way as to facilitate his response to later suggestion." Tellegen's contention merely states an empirical generalization accepted by *all* investigators regardless of their theoretical persuasions. It does not represent a theoretical point of contention between Barber and hypnotic state theorists. However, hypnotic state theorists (Evans, 1968; Hilgard, 1965; Orne, 1966) clearly go beyond this empirical generalization by asserting that hypnosis refers *not* to a set of induction suggestions but, instead, to an altered state which may be produced by a wide variety of procedures and which is instrumental in facilitating response to suggestion. When the term "hypnosis" is defined in this manner (as it invariably is by hypnotic state theorists) then, as Barber correctly points out, it very often *is* employed circularly.

Tellegen later contends that "it is not circular to infer a hypnotic trance state from certain observations in order to explain these observations, just as it is not circular to infer from an actual X-ray photo the existence of a fracture in order to explain certain features of the photo." One can infer a fracture from an X-ray photo without circularity because the fracture *can be objectively denoted independently of the photo*. Inferring an hypnotic trance state on the basis of subjects' behavior is not analogous to inferring a fracture from an X-ray because an objective denotation for the "trance state," which is independent of the behavior to be explained, is not available. Therefore, inferring hypnosis in order to explain certain observations (unlike inferring a fracture from a photo) usually *is* a circular procedure. In short, it appears that Barber's attribution of circularity to hypnotic state theorists is quite justified and not based on any misunderstanding of their position.

Many of Tellegen's comments were aimed at justifying the utility of employing hypnosis as a hypothetical construct. Tellegen may well be correct in suggesting that the "trance state" concept could be developed into a viable hypothetical construct embedded within a nomological net of empirical and theoretical relationships. However, this remains to be demonstrated. A useful hypothetical construct should meet at least two criteria (Campbell & Fiske, 1959; Garner, Hake, & Eriksen, 1956). First, it should be indexed by at least two empirical operations. Second, these independent operations should "converge" to eliminate alternative explanations of the phenomena under consideration. As yet, there is little convincing evidence to suggest that hypnosis as a construct meets these criteria successfully (Spanos & Chaves, 1969).

Tellegen has also pointed out that the concept "hypnosis" has motivated a great deal of research by providing a focus for study and by guiding the research questions investigators have chosen to ask. He implies that the abandonment of the "hypnosis" concept would lead to a lack of interest in the study of hypnotic phenomena and their interrelationships. While Tellegen is certainly correct in stating that the concept "hypnosis" has guided much of the research in this field, he neglects to mention that hypnotic state theorists have often *failed* to ask pertinent theoretical questions and failed to employ appropriate research methodologies because they have, at times, been effectively blinded by their perspective (Spanos & Chaves, 1970). The fact that the two leading nonstate theorists, Barber and Sarbin, have, for two decades, carried out extensive research on the phenomena traditionally subsumed under the rubric of hypnosis clearly indicates that the abandonment of the "hypnotic state" construct does not lead to a withering of interest in these phenomena.

## REFERENCES

CAMPBELL, D. T., & FISKE, D. W. Convergent and discriminant validation by the multitrait-multimethod matrix. *Psychological Bulletin*, 1959, **56**, 81–105.

EVANS, F. J. Recent trends in experimental hypnosis. *Behavioral Science*, 1968, **13**, 477–487.

GARNER, W. R., HAKE, H. W., & ERIKSEN, C. W. Operationalism and the concept of perception. *Psychological Review*, 1956, **63**, 149–159.

HILGARD, E. R. Hypnotic susceptibility. New York: Harcourt, Brace, & World, 1965.

ORNE, M. T. Hypnosis, motivation and compliance. *American Journal of Psychiatry*, 1966, **122**, 721–726.

SPANOS, N. P. Barber's reconceptualization of hypnosis: an evaluation of criticisms. *Journal of Experimental Research in Personality*, 1970, **4**, 241–258.

SPANOS, N. P., & CHAVES, J. F. Converging operations and the "hypnotic state" construct. *Proceedings of the American Psychological Association 77th Annual Convention*, 1969, 905–906.

SPANOS, N. P., & CHAVES, J. F. Hypnosis research: a methodological critique of experiments generated by two alternative paradigms. *American Journal of Clinical Hypnosis*, 1970 (in press).

TELLEGEN, A. Some comments on "Barber's reconceptualization of hypnosis." *Journal of Experimental Research in Personality*, 1970, **4**, 259–267.

# Effects of Hypnotically $29$

# Suggested Analgesia on Physiological

# and Subjective Responses to Cold Stress

## Michael B. Evans and Gordon L. Paul

Relative effects of suggested analgesia and hypnotic induction were evaluated with regard to reduction of stress responses (self-report, heart rate, pulse volume) to the physical application of ice-water stress. Four groups ($N = 16$ each) of undergraduate female Ss, equated on hypnotic susceptibility, were run individually, receiving (a) hypnotic induction plus analgesic suggestion, (b) hypnotic induction alone, (c) waking self-relaxation plus analgesic suggestion, or (d) waking self-relaxation alone. The major findings were that suggestion, not hypnotic induction procedures, produced reductions in the self-report of distress, and that the degree of reduction was related to hypnotic susceptibility in both "hypnotic" and "waking" conditions. Neither suggestion nor hypnotic induction procedures resulted in reduction of the physiological stress responses monitored in this study. Several methodological issues are discussed. Although findings add to the bulk of evidence supporting the "skeptical" view of hypnotic phenomena, results are related to other literature, suggesting that an adequate evaluation of hypnotic analgesia as used clinically has not yet been undertaken.

Since Esdaile's (1957) dramatic claims of over 1,000 minor and 300 major surgical operations performed in conjunction with hypnotically suggested analgesia, numerous reputable clinical reports have appeared supporting the use of hypnotic analgesia in major and minor surgery, labor and child birth, dentistry, and relief of pain from terminal diseases and physical trauma (see Barber, 1963). However, recent reviews of the experimental literature (Barber, 1963; Shor, 1967; Sutcliffe, 1960) conclude that the clinical claims of effectiveness of hypnotic analgesia have not been supported in the laboratory.

Autonomically mediated physiological responses should provide data regarding the credulity of hypnotic analgesia, since such responses are documented in reaction to the presentation of stressful stimuli either in actuality or in imagination (e.g., Barber, 1964;

Barber & Hahn, 1962, 1964; Paul, 1969a; Shor, 1967). Unfortunately, experimental studies of the effectiveness of hypnotically suggested analgesia in inhibiting the physiological response to physical stress are both few and lacking in control procedures required to establish the presence or absence of cause-effect relationships. Of the 10 reports available in the current literature which even approximate adequate experimental controls (Barber & Hahn, 1962; Brown & Vogel, 1938; Doupe, Miller, & Keller, 1939; Dynes, 1932; Hilgard, 1969; Hilgard, Cooper, Lenox, Morgan, & Voevodsky, 1967; Sears, 1932; Shor, 1962; Sutcliffe, 1961; West, Neill, & Hardy, 1952), all but the reports of Hilgard have been included in recent critical reviews (Barber, 1963; Shor, 1967). Whether results were interpreted as positive or negative, five of the earlier studies (Brown & Vogel, 1938; Doupe et al., 1939; Dynes, 1932; Sears, 1932; West et al., 1952) suffered from small select samples, inadequate statistical analyses, and gross confounding of variables (see Shor, 1967). Additionally, of the latter five studies, only Sears (1932) documented the existence of a physiological stress response to the presumed physical stressor prior to experimental manipulations. The importance of establishing

[1] This study was based on a thesis submitted to the graduate college of the University of Illinois in partial fulfillment of the requirements for the MA degree in psychology by the senior author, under the direction of the junior author. Appreciation is expressed to Frederick S. Fehr for assistance with instrumentation and procedure.

[2] Requests for reprints should be sent to Michael B. Evans, Children's Research Center Building, University of Illinois, Champaign, Illinois 61820.

the occurrence of a physiological stress response is highlighted by the reports of Sutcliffe (1961) and Shor (1962) in which sophisticated experimental designs were employed, but equivocal results obtained because the "stressor" (electric shock) failed to produce sufficient reactivity to be alleviated by any manipulation.

Hilgard et al. (1967) reported promising results with "cold pressor" (immersion of an extremity in ice water), in which both self-report and heart rate yielded consistent stress responses prior to experimental manipulations. While clear reductions in stress were obtained for self-report with hypnotic analgesia as compared to waking conditions without analgesic suggestions, heart rate data appeared variable, and were not systematically analyzed due to the preliminary nature of the report. In two later investigations reported by Hilgard (1969), blood pressure and self-report stress responses were clearly obtained in waking no-suggestion conditions as a result of cold stress and "ischemic pain" (response following cessation of squeezing a dynamometer with a tourniquet just above the elbow). In highly susceptible Ss, self-report of distress in response to cold stress was significantly reduced with hypnotically suggested analgesia as compared to waking and hypnotic conditions without analgesic suggestions; however, the physiological stress response was not. In the second study, with ischemic pain, both self-report and blood-pressure stress responses were reduced with hypnotically suggested analgesia as compared to waking conditions without suggestions. Interpretation of the latter study is restricted due to the prior selection of Ss for their ability to reduce pain, and the absence of either hypnotic no-suggestion or waking suggestion control conditions.

While none of the studies reviewed above possesses sufficient internal validity to document cause-effect relationships, taken as a group they suggest that hypnotically suggested analgesia may be superior to an uninstructed condition in reducing physiological responsiveness to physical stressors for some Ss. However, they do not provide even suggestive evidence that a hypnotic induction or an analgesic suggestion is necessary in order to achieve such an effect. They merely suggest that the combined experimental variables might be more effective than no instructions at all.

In the most adequate study to date, using cold stress with susceptible Ss, Barber and Hahn (1962) found hypnotically suggested analgesia did attenuate self-report of distress and physiological responses amenable to direct voluntary control, but to no greater degree than Ss instructed to imagine a pleasant situation in the waking condition. Neither treatment condition was found to affect the physiological stress response for systems not under direct voluntary control. However, Barber and Hahn did not compare the effects of suggested analgesia in waking versus hypnotic conditions, with the result that little experimental evidence can be brought to bear on the relative contribution of these two variables, alone or in combination. It is also possible that Barber and Hahn failed to detect existing differences between groups as a result of their method of analysis, in which individual response measures were analyzed for all Ss combined. The latter method of analysis fails to take into account individual differences in "relative response stereotypy" of physiological systems which typically occur in stress research (Lacey & Lacey, 1958), that is, given the degrees of physical stress which can be ethically applied in experimental investigations, only the more reactive physiological systems are likely to show a stress response, and these systems will likely differ for different individuals. The most sensitive analysis will therefore include only those systems which have been shown to produce a stress response to the stressor applied for each individual S (see Paul, 1969a). None of the studies of hypnotic analgesia to date have taken response stereotypy into account.

A related difficulty in the analysis of physiological response to a physical stressor is the need to document the existence of a response to stress rather than a simple startle or orienting response to a change in stimulation. Of the previous physiological investigations of hypnotic analgesia, only the Hilgard (1969) study convincingly documents such a response. Additionally, very few studies of hypnotic analgesia have analyzed physiological data in a manner which partials out the influence of prestress basal level on the magnitude of stress response (Lacey, 1956; see Barber & Hahn, 1962, and Hilgard, 1969, for two different means of overcoming this problem).

In summary, the clinical reports of the effectiveness of hypnotic analgesia have not received adequate documentation in the laboratory. However, laboratory investigations of the effects of hypnotic analgesia on the physiological response to physical stressors have either focused on different questions, or suffered from methodological difficulties to the extent that evidence to date is equivocal. In the study reported below, an attempt was made to assess the role of hypnotic induction procedures and suggested analgesia in reducing subjective and physiological response to physical stress ("cold pressor") while more adequately taking into account the methodological problems of previous experimental work.

## METHOD

### Subjects

A total of 64 female *S*s, 17–23 years old, participated in the experiment as part of an introductory psychology research requirement. No prior information was provided about the experiment except that *S*s were scheduled for two one-hour sessions in successive weeks. The *S*s were assigned to one of four groups of 16 *S*s each, equated (*M* and *SD*) on a modified version (10 of the 12 subtests) of the Harvard Group Scale of Hypnotic Susceptibility (Shor & Orne, 1962). The *S*s in each group individually received one of the following treatment or control procedures: (*a*) hypnotic induction plus analgesic suggestion, (*b*) hypnotic induction alone, (*c*) waking self-relaxation plus analgesic suggestion, or (*d*) waking self-relaxation alone.

### Procedure

A single *E* handled all *S* contacts.[3] During the first session, the modified Harvard Group Scale of Hypnotic Susceptibility was administered in groups of approximately 10 *S*s each. After distribution of the latter response booklets, and when all scheduled *S*s had been seated, the following general introduction was presented:

This experiment is being done in order to learn more about the clinical treatment of anxiety. Several of the procedures which we will use are taken directly from the clinical setting. Of special interest in the treatment of anxiety are the specific physiological manifestations of tension, or physiological arousal. We suspect that normal subjects such as yourself will show differing physiological systems involved in stress and anxiety, even of very mild sorts. We hope that this experiment will lead to a technique whereby psychologists can quickly localize the areas where a given person's tension and anxiety are expressed, and whereby we can determine the best way of overcoming

them. So in participating here tonight you are contributing to scientific knowledge of a kind that can be used to help people. One important aspect involved in this localization appears to be suggestibility, or hypnotic susceptibility. The purpose of tonight's session is to provide us with an indication of your level of suggestibility.

Immediately following the general introduction, the modified Harvard scale was administered. At the end of the first session, all *S*s were told that they would be scheduled individually for the second session which would involve polygraph measures of heart rate and pulse volume. Between sessions, the protocols were scored and *S*s assigned to treatments so as to equate all conditions on hypnotic susceptibility scores.

Upon entering the experimental room for the second session, *S* was seated in a semirecumbent position in a recliner chair, while the general introduction from the first session was paraphrased. During the next five minutes, *E* and a polygraph operator [4] attached the electrodes and strain gauge for physiological recording, being careful to explain the function of each and assuring *S* that no shock would be involved. The common introduction then continued to explain that cold stress would be employed, describing the stimulus as one which had been shown to be "quite stressful, but to have absolutely no harmful physical effects." After *S* was given the opportunity to resign from the experiment (none did), the procedure for the remainder of the session was presented:

Specifically then, this session will involve the use of a stressor, cold water, and the measurement of your reactions to it. It will be presented twice, once at the beginning and once at the end of the session. Each time it will be preceded by a dip in water at room temperature—this merely acts as a control for the measures we are taking. This session will also involve the use of a commonly used therapeutic technique known as hypnosis (or self-relaxation depending on the experimental condition).

The polygraph operator then retired to the adjoining control room while *E* proceeded to give introductions specific to hypnotic induction and self-relaxation conditions following procedures previously reported by Paul (1969b). After questions were answered, a 10-minute silent adaptation period began, with *S* instructed to sit quietly with her eyes open while the instruments were calibrated.

The pretreatment stress procedure was then undertaken. The *S* was first asked to close her eyes, and her right hand was gently immersed in water at room temperature for one minute. The latter control dip served to provide a base line for response to nonstressful stimulation. The hand was then removed and gently but immediately immersed in the water at 0° to 2° centigrade for one minute to obtain a pretreatment stress response. Immersion of the hand in water at this temperature has been shown to be

[3] The senior author served as *E* for all procedures, under the general supervision of the junior author. At the time of this investigation, *E* was a graduate student in clinical psychology, with one year's clinical experience, including one semester's training in hypnotic techniques with the junior author.

[4] Appreciation is expressed to Karen Evans for serving as polygraph operator and assisting in data reduction.

highly stressful, reaching "intolerable pain" in approximately 30 seconds and peak stress response in approximately one minute, with little adaptation until at least two minutes after hand immersion (Barber & Hahn, 1962, 1963; Benjamin, 1958; Hertzman & Dillon, 1939; Hilgard, 1969; Wolf & Hardy, 1941). Floating ice cubes were circulated in the ice water immediately prior to each dip; floating wooden blocks were similarly circulated for the control dip.

On completion of the "stress dip," S's hand was withdrawn and wiped dry. The S was then asked to open her eyes and rate how her hand felt while it was in the ice water on the following 7-point scale of subjective distress:

____|____|____|____|____|____|____
Pleasant        Uncomfortable        Very Painful

Treatment or control procedures were conducted for the next 25 minutes. Upon completion of the hypnotic induction or comparable self-relaxation time period, posttreatment control and stress dips were conducted in the same manner as the pretreatment dips. Following the posttreatment stress dip, Ss again rated subjective distress (after "trance" termination for Ss in hypnotic conditions). On completion of the posttreatment rating, S was disengaged from the polygraph, taken into the adjoining control room, and shown the polygraph and her record.

## Treatment

*Hypnotic suggestion.* The Ss assigned to this group received a hypnotic induction procedure devised by Paul [5] for resistant Ss, which has been described elsewhere (Paul, 1969b). In brief, the technique begins with an eye-fixation induction emphasizing direct suggestions of heaviness, drowsiness, sleep, and relaxation, but directed to S's image of herself. Direct suggestions of heaviness, warmth, and relaxation are then focused on S's own specific muscle groups, followed by numerical deepening and a test challenge for arm immobilization from the Stanford Hypnotic Susceptibility Scale (Weitzenhoffer & Hilgard, 1962). The entire procedure is administered in a lulling, soothing, "hypnotic tone," emphasizing focus on E's voice, and direct suggestions of drowsiness, sleep, warmth, comfort, heaviness, relaxation, and slow and regular breathing. The induction itself lasted for 25 minutes. Immediately after the induction and test challenge for arm immobilization, and prior to the posttreatment immersion, the following analgesic suggestion was given:

Now focus your attention on your right arm. This time notice how your right arm is becoming numb. It has less and less feeling. The numbness begins in your shoulder, flows down your upper arm to your elbow, then down your forearm to your wrist, then into your hand—all sense of feeling flowing out of your entire arm and hand —becoming so numb, more and more numb and relaxed with no feeling at all. You don't mind—

---

[5] G. L. Paul. Supplementary notes on the clinical use of hypnosis. Unpublished course supplement, University of Illinois, 1965.

just feeling comfortable and relaxed as all the feeling flows out of your right arm and hand. Completely relaxed, breathing slowly and deeply— your hand becoming more and more numb with each breath, less and less feeling with each exhalation. You feel as if you have no feeling in your right hand and arm, they are completely numb. You *have* no feeling in your right hand, it is completely numb! In fact, it is so numb and without feeling that when I dip your hand into some water in a few moments, you will have no sensation at all, other than a possible feeling of pleasant dampness.

The hypnotic patter, along with suggestions of analgesia like those above, continued while S's hand was immersed in water for both control and stress dips.

*Hypnotic no-suggestion.* The members of this group received the same induction and test challenge for arm immobility as the hypnotic suggestion group. However, no verbalization or suggestion of analgesia was given prior to the posttreatment hand immersion.

*Waking suggestion.* The members of this group were told that the present experiment was a study investigating the effects of self-relaxation, being told, simply, to try to become completely relaxed (see Paul, 1969b). Thus, for the time during which hypnotic groups received induction procedures, these Ss relaxed themselves in the presence of E. At the end of the 25 minutes of self-relaxation, these Ss were given the following suggestion of analgesia:

In a moment I will again dip your hand into some water. Because you have been relaxing yourself for the last 25 minutes, you probably won't feel much of anything at all except perhaps a pleasant dampness. In fact, I'd like you to imagine that your hand has no feeling—you might find this easier if you attend to your breathing. Your hand has no feeling at all, you won't be able to feel anything at all except perhaps a pleasant dampness!

The same "hypnotic" patter and suggestions of analgesia received by the hypnotic suggestion group were continued with the waking suggestion group during the posttreatment hand immersions.

*Waking no-suggestion.* Like the waking suggestion group, this group was told that this was a study investigating the effects of self-relaxation and given identical instructions. Unlike the waking suggestion group, however, these Ss received no suggestion or verbalization prior to posttreatment hand immersions.

## Apparatus

The four treatment and control conditions instituted during the second session were conducted in an air-conditioned shielded room-within-a-room below ground level. The polygraph, with an earth ground, was located in an adjoining room which was separated from E and S by a one-way glass. All electrodes were fed through a junction box within the experimental room (with a common S ground from the right leg) through shielded cable to the control room (see Paul, 1969b, for details).

Physiological measures were continuously recorded during both control and stress dips, and for one minute prior to each control dip, on a Beckman Type RB Dynograph, equipped with 474A amplifiers, on Offner No. V654 chart paper driven at 5 millimeters per second. Grass EC2 electrode cream was used for heart rate and ground connections. The skin area for electrode placements was first cleaned with alcohol, then rubbed vigorously with a gauze pad coated with electrode cream. The electrodes were then filled with cream and taped directly to the skin area. Heart rate electrodes were wrapped lightly with an elastic bandage to prevent movement artifact.

Heart rate was recorded from Grass No. E5G electrodes, placed over the radial artery of the left wrist and on the fleshy lateral surface of the right ankle just above and behind the ankle bone, and fed through a Beckman 9857 Cardiotachometer Coupler. Heart rate was then determined by counting the pulses from the cardiotachometer recording, or the R-wave peaks from the EKG recording, within the last 30 seconds of both control and stress dips, converting to beats per minute for pretreatment and posttreatment assessments.

Pulse volume was obtained from a Parks mercury strain gauge placed around the finger which most nearly approximated 4.5 centimeters (usually the second, or largest finger) halfway between the nail and the first joint. The strain gauge activated a Parks 270 Plethyzmograph which fed directly through a Beckman 9853 Strain Gauge Coupler. Pulse volume was then determined by measuring the vertical displacement of each pulse within the last 30 seconds of the control and stress dips and converting to average deflection in millimeters for both pretreatment and posttreatment assessments.

All data reduction was carried out by $E$ and the polygraph operator, overlapping scoring on 32 occasions for each measure, with interscorer reliability exceeding .999 on both heart rate and pulse volume. Data analyses were performed by the IBM 7094 computer of the University of Illinois Computer Science Laboratory.

### RESULTS

Before presenting results, the adequacy of stress procedures, hypnotic induction, and pretreatment equation of groups needs documentation. The adequacy of equating procedures for the Harvard Group Scale of Hypnotic Susceptibility was clear on the basis of analysis of variance and Bartlett's Test for homogeneity of variance (all $ps > .50$). The mean susceptibility scores for the four groups were 5.88, 5.94, 5.94, and 5.94, respectively, for the hypnotic suggestion, hypnotic no-suggestion, waking suggestion, and waking no-suggestion groups. Since the latter means were based on only 10 of the 12 items, they appear representative of the performance of Shor and Orne's (1962) nonvolunteer standardization group which averaged 6.73 of 12 possible on

the total scale. Additionally, examination of response to the arm immobilization challenge, for the two hypnotic groups during the experimental session, found a positive response for 31 of the 32 $Ss$ as compared to 14% and 36% on standardization samples (Hilgard, 1967), indicating a highly effective induction procedure by usual standards. In order to document the existence of pretreatment stress response to hand immersion in ice water, the pretreatment responses to stress and control dips were examined for all $Ss$ combined via $t$ test for correlated means. The results for heart rate ($t = 6.325$, $p < .001$) and for pulse volume ($t = 8.366$, $p < .001$) indicate that a significant overall stress response was produced on both physiological measures (heart rate increase; pulse volume decrease) and that the physiological measures selected were appropriate for the stressor used. In addition, analysis of variance on change from pretreatment control to stress dips across groups for both heart rate and pulse volume found no differential reactivity between groups to exist before treatments (both $Fs < 1$).

### Physiological Measures

In order to take each $S$'s "relative response stereotypy" into account, a single score for composite stress response was derived for pretreatment stress and for posttreatment stress in the following manner: First, Lacey's (1956) "liability scores" were computed for each $S$ on heart rate and pulse volume separately, thus providing standardized scores reflecting response to the stress dip with the influence of the prestress control dip partialed out. Pulse volume scores were converted so that higher lability scores always reflected greater stress response on both measures; then, the lability scores for *only* those measures (heart rate and/or pulse volume) showing a greater response to the pretreatment stress dip than to the control dip were included, averaging the two for the individual $S$ who responded on both measures. The criteria for including either or both measures were based on blind scoring of the polygraph record. Thus, all $Ss$ received one prescore and one postscore reflecting physiological response to ice-water stress beyond the response to dipping the hand in water at room temperature, based on their own response stereotypy.

A three-way analysis of variance (Hypnosis × Suggestion × Pre–Post) was then performed on the latter composite lability scores, with the result that only the pre–post main effect reached significance ($F = 9.137$, $df = 1/60$, $p < .01$). None of the two-way interactions, nor the three-way interaction, was significant, although the Hypnosis × Suggestion interaction approached significance ($F = 3.14$, $df = 1/60$, $p < .10$). The findings of the analysis of variance combined with inspection of means (see Table 1) show a reduction of physiological stress response upon repeated presentation and a tendency for the differential effects of suggestion–no-suggestion to be greater for the hypnotic groups than for the waking groups. However, there is no evidence that hypnotic induction or suggested analgesia, either alone or in combination, was effective in suppressing the physiological response to the physical stressor. Individual analyses including all Ss on each measure also found no significant main effects or interactions, with the exception of a significant pre–post adaptation main effect for heart rate ($F = 6.437$, $df = 1/60$, $p < .025$).

Since Ss in the present study covered the full range of hypnotic susceptibility scores, it seemed plausible that suppression of the physiological stress response as a result of suggested analgesia and/or hypnotic procedures might be a function of hypnotic susceptibility.

In order to investigate this possibility, a Kruscal-Wallis analysis of variance on ranked composite lability scores was performed, including only those Ss scoring 7 or above on the modified Harvard Group Scale of Hypnotic Susceptibility ($N = 28$, 7 per group), resulting in a nonsignificant $H$ value. Additionally, Spearman rank-order correlational analyses were undertaken between hypnotic susceptibility scores and change in composite lability scores. Reduction in the composite lability score over all groups combined ($N = 64$) was found to be unrelated to susceptibility ($r = .05$, $p > .50$). Similarly, no significant relationships were obtained between hypnotic susceptibility and composite lability score reduction for the combined suggestion groups ($r = .15$, $p > .20$), the combined no-suggestion groups ($r = .08$, $p > .20$), nor within any treatment group (all $r \leq .22$, $p > .20$). Thus, the present study finds no evidence for the effectiveness of hypnotically suggested analgesia, hypnotic induction alone, or suggested analgesia alone in suppressing the physiological response to the physical stressor, whether Ss were high or low on hypnotic susceptibility.

### Subjective Report

The self-report of subjective distress, obtained after the pretreatment and posttreatment stress tests, was similarly subjected to

TABLE 1

Means for Heart, Rate, Pulse Volume, Composite Lability Score, and Self-Ratings of Distress

| Measure | Hypnotic suggestion | | Hypnotic no-suggestion | | Waking suggestion | | Waking no-suggestion | | Total | |
|---|---|---|---|---|---|---|---|---|---|---|
| | M | SD | M | SD | M | SD | M | SD | M | SD |
| Heart rate–lability score | | | | | | | | | | |
| Pre | 54.582 | 8.208 | 51.159 | 7.147 | 50.504 | 10.892 | 49.507 | 9.251 | 51.438 | 8.973 |
| Post | 50.829 | 10.986 | 45.484 | 15.124 | 49.400 | 7.228 | 48.721 | 8.551 | 48.608 | 10.814 |
| Pulse volume–lability score | | | | | | | | | | |
| Pre | 53.598 | 13.058 | 48.870 | 8.279 | 50.114 | 11.058 | 51.743 | 10.571 | 51.081 | 10.763 |
| Post | 51.596 | 5.856 | 50.514 | 6.036 | 48.330 | 13.032 | 45.717 | 9.425 | 49.039 | 9.142 |
| Composite lability score | | | | | | | | | | |
| Pre | 56.669 | 5.924 | 51.308 | 5.088 | 51.651 | 7.689 | 53.071 | 6.868 | 53.175 | 6.664 |
| Post | 52.483 | 7.584 | 49.160 | 10.770 | 47.967 | 12.048 | 49.830 | 5.724 | 49.860 | 9.298 |
| Self report of distress | | | | | | | | | | |
| Pre | 5.938 | .574 | 5.438 | .814 | 5.563 | .629 | 5.625 | .885 | 5.614 | .743 |
| Post | 4.250 | 1.065 | 5.313 | 1.352 | 4.313 | 1.352 | 5.563 | .892 | 4.859 | 1.296 |

Note.—$N = 16$ per group.

a three-way analysis of variance. In contrast to the lack of significant treatment effects found with physiological indexes, self-report data showed significant main effects for both suggestion ($F = 6.825$, $df = 1/60$, $p < .025$) and pre–post reduction ($F = 21.478$, $df = 1/60$, $p < .005$). More importantly, a significant Suggestion × Pre–Post interaction was found ($F = 16.632$, $df = 1/60$, $p < .005$). As with the physiological data, neither the main effect nor interactions involving hypnotic induction approached significance for self-report (all $p$s > .25).

The source of the significant Suggestion × Pre–Post interaction was further analyzed by the Duncan multiple-range test, which revealed a significantly greater reduction of subjective distress for the two suggestion groups combined than for the no-suggestion groups combined, without significant differences obtaining between hypnotic suggestion and waking suggestion groups, or between hypnotic no-suggestion and waking no-suggestion groups ($p < .05$, with a probability of 85% that all statements are correct). Thus, the findings for self-report data indicate that (a) those Ss given analgesic suggestions reported a greater reduction in subjective distress in response to the stressor than those Ss not given such suggestions; (b) hypnotic induction alone did no better than self-relaxation instructions; and further, (c) hypnotic induction did not significantly facilitate the effects of suggested analgesia.

Correlational analyses were also undertaken between hypnotic susceptibility and reduction in rated subjective distress. As for the composite lability scores, the Spearman rank-order correlation between hypnotic susceptibility scores and reduction of subjective distress over all groups combined was not significant ($r = .19$, $p > .10$). However, unlike the composite lability scores, self-report yielded a moderate but significant correlation ($r = .46$, $p < .005$) for the combined suggestion groups, while a zero correlation was found for the combined no-suggestion groups. Further investigation of the same correlations within treatment groups revealed a correlation of .48 ($p < .05$) for both hypnotic suggestion and waking suggestion groups, while the hypnotic no-suggestion and waking no-suggestion groups produced correlations of −.04 and .02, respectively (both $p$s > .80). Comparison of the correlations for the com-

bined suggestion versus combined no-suggestion groups revealed that the difference was significant ($Z = 1.89$, $p < .06$). Thus, results of the correlational analyses indicate that for self-report, the effect of suggestion varied with hypnotic susceptibility as assessed by the modified Harvard Group Scale of Hypnotic Susceptibility, whether or not the suggestion was an accompaniment of hypnotic induction. The usual lack of correspondence between self-report and physiological data also obtained in the present study in which no significant correlations were found between composite lability score reduction and reduction in rated subjective distress (all $p$s > .10).

## DISCUSSION

The results of the present investigation lend support to the clinical claims of the effectiveness of hypnotic analgesia to the extent that self-report of distress in response to a physical stressor was significantly reduced. These results clearly support conclusions of earlier reviews of the effects of hypnotic procedures in general (Barber, 1965; Rosenhan, 1967) and hypnotically suggested analgesia in particular (Barber, 1963; Sutcliffe, 1960) to the effect that (a) hypnotic suggestion did produce significant effects in the response system under direct voluntary control (self-report), but did not produce significant effects in response systems not under direct voluntary control (heart rate and pulse volume); and (b) response to suggestion was not significantly different under hypnotic conditions than under motivated waking conditions.

While these consistent results in controlled experimentation clearly support what Sutcliffe (1960) has termed the "skeptical" view of hypnosis, such support does not shed doubt on the fact that hypnotically suggested analgesia has been used to assist large numbers of individuals to endure extremely stressful physical experiences. However, it does suggest that (a) verbal and motoric performance may frequently differ from the experience of distress, especially under motivated conditions such as those usually obtaining in clinical work; and (b) "hypnotic phenomena" represent nothing discontinuous from other forms of behavioral influence (see Ullmann & Krasner, 1961, pp. 69–91). Indeed, equally dramatic clinical cases exist in which individuals have endured stressful physical experiences without benefit of either anesthetic or hypnotic analgesia, as seen in reports of the "relief of pain" of physical trauma by placebos (Haas, Fink, & Hartfelder, 1963), surgery performed under emergency conditions (Barber, 1963), and the continuation of a population in the absence of widespread use of analgesic agents, that is, labor and childbirth.

Although the majority of the latter cases represent nonhypnotic examples of verbal and motoric performance as if physical stress were reduced, presumably without actual reduction of physiological responsiveness, the placebo literature does provide documented evidence of the reduction of physiological responses, even to the extent of reversing the effects of pharmacologically active drugs (Wolf, 1959). Thus, one likely means of reducing stress responses would be through the presentation of stimuli which elicit responses incompatible with those of physical stress. Reduction in the general level of physiological arousal (anxiety), through removal of ambiguity (Shor, 1967) or production of physiological relaxation (Paul, 1969a), has also been found to reduce the intensity of stress response in given circumstances. A third mechanism which has been shown at least partially effective in reducing stress response is distraction through direction of attention away from the stressful stimulus (Barber & Hahn, 1962; Kanfer & Goldfoot, 1966).

While each of the above procedures (presentation of stimuli eliciting previously acquired incompatible responses, production of relaxation, redirection of attention) might form the basis for specific therapeutic techniques to reduce stress responses, their importance for present purposes is that even within the "skeptical" view of hypnosis, all three factors could be involved in the application of "hypnotic analgesia" (see Paul, 1963, 1966, 1969b). However, experimental evidence, at best, supports the contention that individuals subjected to hypnotically suggested analgesia perform as if they were not experiencing stress, but on the basis of physiological responses appear that they are experiencing stress.

Further examination of the literature suggests that well-controlled investigations of hypnotic analgesia, or waking suggestion, as used clinically, have not yet been performed: namely, those inadequately controlled investigations with positive reports, and suggested analgesia in clinical situations, nearly always

involve two or more training sessions between the operator and *S*. The three experimental investigations to date in which methodological problems were overcome sufficiently to provide relatively unconfounded results all involved *S*s undergoing their first clinical–experimental induction (although preceded by a "test" induction for assessment purposes).

While a single hypnotic session has been found effective in redirection of attention (e.g., Fehr & Stern, 1967), recent studies (Paul, 1969a, 1969b) have found reduction in physiological systems not under direct voluntary control (such as those of the present study), and suppression of physiological response to stressful imagery, to reliably occur only after two induction sessions. The results of the latter studies suggest that one clinical–experimental session is not sufficient for most *S*s to achieve a significant degree of relaxation to reduce physiological stress responses, nor is training in contingent response to the operator sufficient to reliably elicit incompatible responses in that period of time. The investigators in the present study had assumed that the test induction for assessing susceptibility would provide sufficient training that the clinical–experimental induction would be equivalent to the second session in Paul's earlier work. It is clear that this proved to be an unwarranted assumption, since no differences in basal physiological response were obtained from pretraining to posttraining between groups—paralleling the findings for the first, rather than second, session in the earlier work. Since Paul (1969a) did not test for suppression of stress responses after a single session, it is unclear whether the difference in findings of the present study relates to the difference in stressful stimuli (imaginal vs. physical) or to the absence of a sufficient degree of physiological relaxation in the present study.

Note should also be made of the desirability of including methodological controls such as those of the present study in future investigations. The need for multiple-channel measurement, and allowance for individual response stereotypy, is clear from the zero-order correlation between responses of the two channels to the degree of stress employed, and by the fact that 20 of the 64 *S*s showed reactivity on only one of the two physiological channels (either heart rate or pulse volume).

Even more important for stress research in general is the need to distinguish response to stress over and above startle or orienting response. For example, in the present study, 58 of 64 *S*s (or 92%) showed orienting responses on at least one channel from the pretreatment basal level to the *control dip*, without any physical stress being involved. Had the assessment of stress response not been from control dip to stress dip, and had the measurement period not been delayed 30 seconds past introduction of the stimulus, no assurance of the validity of the stress response would have been obtained.[6] Perhaps the best strategy for future research on hypnotic analgesia, or other techniques directed toward reducing responsiveness to physical stressors, would be to focus on controlled studies with measurement in the clinical setting (e.g., oral surgery) where physical stress occurs. In this way, motivation of *S*s would likely insure repeated training, and the greater stress involved should minimize problems of response stereotypy and confounding by orienting responses.

[6] The extent to which confounding of stress response by orienting response can occur is especially evident with measures of skin conductance or galvanic skin response. The point was emphasized most strongly to the investigators when 20 pilot *S*s for the present investigation failed to show increases in skin conductance from the control dip to the stress dip, even though consistent responses were obtained from basal level to control dip, that is, the simple orienting response to the change in stimulation occasioned by the dip in water at room temperature was greater for galvanic skin measures than the actual stress of ice water. For additional discussion of problems of this nature regarding skin conductance, see Paul (1969b).

## REFERENCES

BARBER, T. X. The effects of "hypnosis" on pain: A critical review of experimental and clinical findings. *Psychosomatic Medicine*, 1963, **25**, 303–333.

BARBER, T. X. "Hypnosis" as a causal variable in present day psychology: A critical analysis. *Psychological Reports*, 1964, **14**, 839–842.

BARBER, T. X. Experimental analyses of "hypnotic" behavior: A review of recent empirical findings. *Journal of Abnormal Psychology*, 1965, **70**, 132–154.

BARBER, T. X., & HAHN, K. W. Physiological and subjective responses to pain producing stimulation under hypnotically-suggested and waking-imagined "analgesia." *Journal of Abnormal and Social Psychology*, 1962, **65**, 411–418.

BARBER, T. X., & HAHN, K. W. Hypnotic induction and "relaxation." *Archives of General Psychiatry*, 1963, **8**, 295–300.

BARBER, T. X., & HAHN, K. W. Experimental studies in "hypnotic" behavior: Physiologic and subjective effects of imagined pain. *Journal of Nervous and Mental Disease*, 1964, **139**, 416–425.

BENJAMIN, F. B. Effect of aspirin on suprathreshold pain in man. *Science*, 1958, **128**, 303–304.

BROWN, R. R., & VOGEL, V. H. Psychophysical reactions following painful stimuli under hypnotic analgesia, contrasted with gas anesthesia and Novocain block. *Journal of Applied Psychology*, 1938, **22**, 408–420.

DOUPE, J., MILLER, W. R., & KELLER, W. K. Vasomotor reactions in the hypnotic state. *Journal of Neurology and Psychiatry*, 1939, **2**, 97–106.

DYNES, J. B. An experimental study of hypnotic anesthesia. *Journal of Abnormal and Social Psychology*, 1932, **27**, 79–88.

ESDAILE, J. *Hypnosis in medicine and surgery.* New York: Julian, 1957.

FEHR, F. S., & STERN, J. A. The effect of hypnosis on attention to relevant and irrelevant stimuli. *International Journal of Clinical and Experimental Hypnosis*, 1967, **15**, 134–143.

HAAS, H., FINK, H., & HARTFELDER, G. The placebo problem. *Psychopharmacology Service Center Bulletin*, 1963, **2**, 1–65.

HERTZMAN, A. B., & DILLON, J. B. Selective vascular reaction patterns in the nasal septum and skin of the extremities and hand. *American Journal of Physiology*, 1939, **127**, 671–684.

HILGARD, E. R. Individual differences in hypnotizability. In J. E. Gordon (Ed.), *Handbook of clinical and experimental hypnosis.* New York: Macmillan, 1967.

HILGARD, E. R. Pain as a puzzle for psychology and physiology. *American Psychologist*, 1969, **24**, 103–113.

HILGARD, E. R., COOPER, L. M., LENOX, J., MORGAN, A. H., & VOEVODSKY, J. The use of pain-state reports in the study of hypnotic analgesia: the pain of ice water. *Journal of Nervous and Mental Disease*, 1967, **144**, 506–513.

KANFER, F. H., & GOLDFOOT, D. A. Self-control and tolerance of noxious stimulation. *Psychological Reports*, 1966, **18**, 79–85.

LACEY, J. I. The evaluation of autonomic response: Toward a general solution. *Annals of the New York Academy of Science*, 1956, **67**, 123–164.

LACEY, J. I., & LACEY, B. C. Verification and extension of the principle of autonomic response stereotypy. *American Journal of Psychology*, 1958, **71**, 50–73.

ORNE, M. T. The nature of hypnosis: Artifact and essence. *Journal of Abnormal and Social Psychology*, 1959, **58**, 277–299.

PAUL, G. L. The production of blisters by hypnotic suggestion: Another look. *Psychosomatic Medicine*, 1963, **25**, 233–244.

PAUL, G. L. The specific control of anxiety: "Conditioning and hypnosis." In L. Oseas (Chm.), Innovations in therapeutic interactions. Symposium presented at the meeting of the American Psychological Association, New York, September 1966.

PAUL, G. L. Inhibition of physiological response to stressful imagery by relaxation training and hypnotically suggested relaxation. *Behaviour Research and Therapy*, 1969, **7**, 249–256. (a)

PAUL, G. L. Physiological effects of relaxation training and hypnotic suggestion. *Journal of Abnormal Psychology,* 1969, **74**, 425–437. (b)

ROSENHAN, D. On the social psychology of hypnosis research. In J. E. Gordon (Ed.), *Handbook of clinical and experimental hypnosis.* New York: Macmillan, 1967.

SEARS, R. R. Experimental study of hypnotic anesthesia. *Journal of Experimental Psychology,* 1932, **15**, 1–22.

SHOR, R. E. Physiological effects of painful stimulation during hypnotic analgesia under conditions designed to minimize anxiety. *International Journal of Clinical and Experimental Hypnosis,* 1962, **10**, 183–202.

SHOR, R. E. Physiological effects of painful stimulation during hypnotic analgesia. In J. E. Gordon (Ed.), *Handbook of clinical and experimental hypnosis.* New York: Macmillan, 1967.

SHOR, R. E., & ORNE, E. C. *Harvard Group Scale of Hypnotic Susceptibility: Form A.* Palo Alto, Calif.: Consulting Psychologists Press, 1962.

SUTCLIFFE, J. P. "Credulous" and "skeptical" views of hypnotic phenomena: A review of certain evidence and methodology. *International Journal of Clinical and Experimental Hypnosis,* 1960, **8**, 73–103.

SUTCLIFFE, J. P. "Credulous" and "skeptical" views of hypnotic phenomena: Experiments on esthesia, hallucination, and delusion. *Journal of Abnormal and Social Psychology,* 1961, **62**, 189–200.

ULLMANN, L. P., & KRASNER, L. *A psychological approach to abnormal behavior.* Englewood Cliffs, N. J.: Prentice-Hall, 1969.

WEST, L. J., NEILL, K. C., & HARDY, J. D. Effects of hypnotic suggestion on pain perception and galvanic skin response. *American Medical Association Archives of Neurology and Psychiatry,* 1952, **68**, 549–560.

WOLF, S. The pharmacology of placebos. *Pharmacological Review,* 1959, **11**, 689–704.

WOLF, S., & HARDY, J. D. Studies on pain: Observations on pain due to local cooling and on factors involved in the "cold pressor" effect. *Journal of Clinical Investigation,* 1941, **20**, 521–533.

WEITZENHOFFER, A. M., & HILGARD, E. R. *Stanford Hypnotic Susceptibility Scale, Form C.* Palo Alto, Calif.: Consulting Psychologists Press, 1962.

# Effects of EMG Feedback 30
## Training on Susceptibility to Hypnosis:
## Preliminary Observations

I. Wickramasekera

Relaxation instructions seem to be one of the independent variables that increase suggestibility (Barber, 1969). There is a growing recognition (Bandura, 1969) that verbal instructions and cognitive factors can significantly add to the power of reinforcement variables. It seems likely that a combination of verbal instructions and response-contingent feedback will be more effective in deepening muscular relaxation than verbal instructions alone. A study by Paul and Trimble (1970) appears to attribute the inferiority of verbal relaxation instructions presented by tape, compared to live instructions, to the lack of response-contingent progression in relaxation training. Engstrom, London, and Hart (1970) have reported that EEG alpha-rhythm feedback training increases hypnotic susceptibility.

Electromyographic (EMG) feedback seems useful in the induction of muscular relaxation (Budzynski & Stoyva, 1969; Green, Walters, Green, & Murphy, 1969). The purpose of this study was to determine if taped verbal relaxation instructions and response-contingent EMG feedback training will increase suggestibility or hypnotic susceptibility over that obtained with instructions and false or noncontingent feedback. The specific hypothesis tested was that six sessions of relaxation practice with response-contingent EMG feedback will result in greater increase in hypnotic susceptibility as measured by the Stanford scales than will relaxation and noncontingent feedback.

# METHOD

## Subjects

The *S*s were 12 white undergraduate males between the ages of 18-22, who volunteered for a study of "relaxation training and hypnosis." The *S*s who admitted to a history of psychiatric problems were excluded from the sample.

## Procedure

All *S*s were first tested individually with the Stanford Hypnotic Susceptibility Scale Form A (Weitzenhoffer & Hilgard, 1959). The *S*s were then assigned randomly and equally to either a control or experimental group. All *S*s then listened to a set of taped instructions which stated that they were to be trained to relax deeply and that the EMG auditory feedback would facilitate this training process. The taped instructions followed closely those in the manual that accompanies the portable EMG feedback apparatus. It includes a simple explanation of the feedback system as basically an information system. The sequence of EMG training and the practice of tension-release cycling followed closely the instructions in the manual. Training is started with both auditory and visual feedback at the lowest sensitivity level. As *S* demonstrates progress by keeping the feedback at a low level ($< 4 \mu v.$), the sensitivity is raised successively to the medium and high ranges, and held there until he can reach the previous criteria at these sensitivity levels. A final plateau is reached in forearm training when *S* can maintain a low level ($< 4 \mu v.$) of feedback on high sensitivity. Next, the electrodes are attached to the area of the frontalis muscle of the forehead, and the previous training sequence (e.g., low to high sensitivity) is run. Both experimental and control *S*s were reminded by the same taped instructions at the start of each training session to watch for and become familiar with the proprioceptive cues (heaviness, tingling, numbness) of deep relaxation.

Procedures with controls differed from those with experimental *S*s only with respect to the following conditions: (*a*) Control *S*s received false or noncontingent EMG feedback; (*b*) no changes in the sensitivity levels were made for control *S*s (controls had no knowledge of this); and (*c*) the electrodes were moved from forearm to forehead for all control *S*s at the start of the fourth session of training.

Feedback training consisted of six 45-min. sessions. The *S*s were seated on a large padded recliner during all procedures. After terminating his sixth training session, each *S* was immediately retested with Form B of the Stanford Hypnotic Susceptibility Scale. All procedures were conducted individually and all administered by the same *E*, the writer. The entire study was done in *E*'s office at a mental health clinic, and *E* attempted to restrict his verbal contact with *S*s to the taped instructions. During the orientation period (first 10 min. of first session), all *S*s (control and experimental) were given both visual and auditory "true" or response-contingent EMG feedback. After the orientation, the EMG console and visual feedback were placed on a table behind *S*'s chair. The earphones of control *S*s were disconnected without their knowledge from the EMG console, and connected to a recorder that delivered taped auditory EMG feedback from the actual first six relaxation training sessions of a psychiatric patient bearing "true" or response-contingent auditory EMG feedback.

## RESULTS

Not all experimental *S*s reached the preestablished criterion of relaxation training, but all approximated it at the end of the sixth session of training. None of the control *S*s even approximated the criterion for forehead muscle relaxation. Table 1 presents the pre- and posttest scores and differences on the Stanford Hypnotic Susceptibility Scale of the two groups.

**TABLE 1**

Pre- and Posttest Scores on the Stanford
Hypnotic Susceptibility Scale

| Group | Pretest | Posttest | Difference |
|-------|---------|----------|------------|
| Experimental | 4.83 | 10.16 | 5.33 |
| Control | 5.00 | 5.16 | .16 |

A Mann-Whitney test of the difference between the posttest scores of the experimental and control groups yielded a significant difference ($p = .001$); a similar analysis yielded a nonsignificant difference between pretest scores.

## CONCLUSION

The very small size and select nature of this sample necessitates caution in drawing conclusions and generalizing from these data. A study with a larger sample of outpatients is in progress. The possibility of experimental bias in the use of the Stanford Hypnotic Susceptibility Scale Forms A and B must be considered.

If the above results are replicable, EMG training could be used to increase the efficacy of automated relaxation training procedures within systematic desensitization and to avoid the problem (Paul & Trimble, 1970) which seems to arise because of the lack of response-contingent progress when tape-recorded relaxation instructions are used.

### REFERENCES

Bandura, A. *Principles of behavior modification.* New York: Holt, Rinehart & Winston, 1969.

Barber, T. X. *Hypnosis: A scientific approach.* New York: Van Nostrand Reinhold, 1969.

Budzynski, T. H., & Stoyva, J. M. An instrument for producing deep muscle relaxation by means of analog information feedback. *Journal of Applied Behavior Analysis,* 1969, **2,** 231-237.

Engstrom, D. R., London, P., & Hart, J. T. EEG alpha feedback training and hypnotic susceptibility. *Proceedings of the 78th Annual Convention of the American Psychological Association,* 1970, **5,** 837-838. (Summary)

Green, E. E., Walters, E. D., Green, A. M., & Murphy, G. Feedback technique for deep relaxation. *Psychophysiology,* 1969, **6,** 372-377.

Paul, G. L., & Trimble, R. W. Recorded vs. "live" relaxation training and hypnotic suggestion: Comparative effectiveness for reducing physiological arousal and inhibiting stress response. *Behavior Therapy,* 1970, **1,** 285-302.

Weitzenhoffer, A. M., & Hilgard, E. R. *Stanford Hypnotic Susceptibility Scale, Forms A and B.* Palo Alto: Consulting Psychologists Press, 1959.

[1] The author would like to express his appreciation to C. H. Patterson for his critical reactions to this paper.

Requests for reprints should be sent to I. Wickramasekera, 320 East Armstrong Avenue, Peoria, Illinois 61603.

# Toward an Explanation
# 31
## of Stage Hypnosis

## William B. Meeker and Theodore X. Barber

Stage hypnosis can be explained by eight principles which do not utilize the concept of "hypnotic state" or "trance." To produce an "amazing" performance, stage hypnotists rely *primarily* on (a) the high base rate of "waking" suggestibility, (b) a highly selective procedure for screening Ss, (c) the heightened suggestibility that is produced when the situation is defined to Ss as "hypnosis," and (d) important social-psychological variables that are present in the stage situation. In addition, *some* stage hypnotists *at times* use (e) the "stage whispers" technique (in which Ss are told privately, in whispers, to help make the demonstration a success), (f) the "failure to challenge" technique, (g) trained Ss to carry out the difficult stunts, and (h) one or more "tricks" such as pressure on the carotid baroreceptors which produces stupor.

How does the stage hypnotist so quickly induce his S to behave in very unusual ways— to be unable to move a limb, to support a very heavy weight on his chest while he is suspended between two chairs, to sing like Frank Sinatra, or to crow like a rooster? Although stage hypnosis is one of the most powerful social influence phenomena known to man, no one has as yet formulated a theory to explain it. In this paper, we shall move toward a preliminary theory of stage hypnosis.

This paper is based on (a) data derived from recent experimental research in hypnosis, (b) our own personal experience or training in stage hypnosis, (c) our observations of the performance of professional stage hypnotists, and (d) a survey of publications on stage hypnosis. The publications include manuals, books of instructions, and mimeographed manuscripts from which stage hypnotists learn the essentials of their craft. Some of these manuals (e.g., Tracy, 1952) are readily

[1] Work on this paper was supported by Research Grant MH-11521 from the National Institute of Mental Health, United States Public Health Service.

[2] Requests for reprints should be sent to Theodore X. Barber, Medfield Foundation, Harding, Massachusetts 02042.

available. However, most of the publications on stage hypnosis (e.g., Calostro, 1949; Lonk, 1947; Lustig, 1956; McGill, 1947; Nelson, 1965; North, 1954) are not easily obtained by individuals outside the circle of professional stage performers. In fact, the latter publications can be purchased only from companies which supply equipment to magicians and stage hypnotists or from private instructors who print and publish their own courses.

Although stage hypnotists differ widely in their methods and techniques, there are, nonetheless, four basic principles and four secondary principles which underlie stage hypnosis. The four basic or major principles are as follows:

1. Base level or "waking" responsiveness to suggestions is much higher than is commonly assumed.

2. Very responsive Ss can be easily and quickly selected.

3. When the situation is defined as "hypnosis," it is clear to Ss that a high level of responsiveness to suggestions and commands is desired and expected.

4. The stage setting has unique expectancy characteristics which are very helpful in

**395**

eliciting apparent hypnotic behaviors.

The four secondary principles are as follows:

5. Some stage hypnotists at times use the technique of "stage whispers," that is, they whisper private instructions to their Ss that help make the demonstration a success.

6. Some stage hypnotists at times use the "failure to challenge" technique which misleads the audience to believe that Ss are having highly unusual experiences.

7. Some stage hypnotists at times use either stooges or pretrained Ss to insure the success of the show.

8. Some stage hypnotists at times use one or more "tricks" to elicit ostensibly unusual behaviors.

We will discuss each of these principles in turn.

### Principle 1

Stage hypnotists have long been aware that the induction of "hypnotic trance" is not necessary to elicit a high level of responsiveness to suggestions from a substantial number of unselected Ss and from a very large number of volunteers. Lonk (1947) emphasized that

In fact, the subject need not be in any stage of sleep. Sleep is not always necessary for the production of the suggestible state [p. 34].

Similarly, Tracy (1952) pointed out that

A good hypnotic subject will respond to many suggestions just as quickly in the waking state as in a hypnotic trance. Your confidence and your commanding tone of voice are all that is necessary [p. 152].

Along related lines, Arons (1961) delineated the use of "waking hypnosis" in stage performances and noted that "This phase of the demonstration illustrates forcibly that the hypnotic 'trance' is not needed to perform a hypnotic demonstration [p. 10]." The *Encyclopedia of Stage Hypnotism* states unequivocally that "it is possible to produce very striking hypnotic effects in the waking state, entirely independent of the trance [McGill, 1947, p. 28]" and discusses in detail the effectiveness of waking suggestions in eliciting behaviors such as the following: inability to close mouth, inability to separate fingers, inability to stop stuttering, forgetting of one's own name, getting drunk on a glass of water, and hallucination of a mouse. With respect to the last-mentioned behavior, the *Encyclopedia* bluntly reminds the reader that

You have observed in this experiment a very interest-

ing type of hypnotic phenomenon, for you have produced a hallucination in the waking state [McGill, 1947, p. 173].

In brief, most manuals of stage hypnosis assert that a high level of responsiveness to suggestions can be elicited from a substantial proportion of Ss without "sleep" or the induction of hypnosis. This assertion is supported by experimental studies. Surprisingly high levels of response have been demonstrated in a series of experiments in which standardized test suggestions were administered to unselected college students without any special preliminaries, that is, under a base-level waking condition (Anderson & Sarbin, 1964; Barber, 1969; Weitzenhoffer & Sjoberg, 1961). For instance, three studies with the Barber Suggestibility Scale (Barber, 1965) showed the following: When unselected "awake" Ss were tested without any special preliminaries (base-level condition), about *half* were unable to unclasp their hands when told they could not do so (Hand Lock), about *one-fourth* could not get up from the chair (Body Immobility) and could not say their name (Verbal Inhibition) when told they could not do so, and about *one-eighth* passed the "Posthypnotic-like" Response and the Selective Amnesia items. Supplementary experiments, summarized elsewhere (Barber, 1969, 1970), similarly found that unselected Ss show a surprisingly high base-level waking response to various types of suggestions including suggestions of visual and auditory hallucination, analgesia, age regression, and heightened strength and endurance.

### Principle 2

The high base-level suggestibility that is found among members of the audience is almost sufficient by itself to conduct a successful stage demonstration. However, the stage hypnotist does not recruit members of the audience in a haphazard manner. On the contrary, he easily and quickly selects the most responsive Ss. For example, Tracy (1952, pp. 108–109) noted that excellent Ss can be readily selected by the following method: (a) The members of the audience are told that they will be shown how easy it is to relax through the power of suggestion alone. (b) The performer administers repeated suggestions of relaxation and eye-closure and then suggests an inability to open the eyes. (c) Next, the performer goes up to each member of the audience who has not opened his eyes, tells him that he can now open them, and then instructs him to go up to the stage. Tracy pointed out that this method is preferable to asking for volunteers because many good Ss are too timid to volunteer and some who volunteer do so only to prove to their friends that they can resist the hypnotist.

Although many stage hypnotists ask for volunteers, they only use those who are the most responsive. For instance, the *Encyclopedia of Stage Hypnotism* recommends the following:

*Look over your subjects carefully now* [after they have been exposed to one or more tests of suggestibility], *for here is your chance to diplomatically get rid of those persons you do not wish to keep on the stage . . .* quietly approach them, and whisper, "Thank you very much for volunteering, but will you quietly leave the stage now" *. . . Be firm about this and rid yourself of all of your undesirable material at this time . . . This spotting and judging of good and bad subjects is one of the first things the Stage Hypnotist must learn for the smooth staging of his show* [McGill, 1947, pp. 181–182 and p. 252].

### Principle 3

The stage hypnotist inevitably defines the situation to his Ss as hypnosis. Simply labeling the situation as hypnosis is sufficient by itself to raise response to suggestions above the already high base level. In recent experiments (Barber & Calverley, 1964, 1965), Ss were randomly assigned to experimental groups. One group was told that it was participating in a hypnosis experiment and another group was told that it was to be tested for ability to imagine. The Ss in both groups were then treated *identically*; that is, they were tested individually on response to the standardized test suggestions of the Barber Suggestibility Scale. The Ss told they were participating in a hypnosis experiment were significantly more responsive to the test suggestions than those told they were participating in an imagination experiment.

Why are Ss more responsive to suggestions when they are told that they are participating in a hypnosis experiment rather than in an "imagination" experiment? Postexperimental interviews with Ss suggest the following tentative answer: When Ss are told that they are participating in a hypnosis experiment, they typically construe this as implying that (*a*) they are in an unusual situation in which high response to suggestions and commands is desired and expected, and (*b*) if they actively resist or try *not* to carry out those things suggested, they will be considered as poor or uncooperative Ss, the hypnotist will be disappointed, and the purpose of the experiment will be negated. On the other hand, when Ss are told that they are to be tested for imaginative ability, they are being told by implication that they are not necessarily expected to show a high level of response to suggestions of the type traditionally associated with the word hypnosis.

Since the introduction of one word, hypnosis, into the experimental situation raises Ss responsiveness to suggestions, we can expect a high level of suggestibility in the stage situation which is inevitably defined as hypnosis and which includes a performer who has been widely advertised as a highly effective hypnotist.

### Principle 4

The stage performer also utilizes several social-psychological factors that are unique to the stage setting. The *Encyclopedia of Stage Hypnotism* conceptualizes these factors as follows:

[There] is a sort of bond that unites the performer and the mass attention of the audience. You, as the performer, are in the situation as a leader, and as such it spurs you along. Your subjects, on the other hand, are in the situation in submissive roles, and every last one of them feels it . . . there is a certain atmosphere about the stage that is extremely conducive to the successful demonstrating of Hypnotism. The lights, the music, the curtains, the tenseness of being on the stage, and above all the expectancy centered on each subject by the audience—expectancy that he will be hypnotized, are factors working . . . powerfully in the performer's favor [McGill, 1947, pp. 137 and 248].

The *Encyclopedia* also points out that

Considerable number of subjects, especially in the extravert enterprise of performing on the stage, tend to simulate . . . . This simulation is not necessarily voluntary deception, for it is frequently born of an extreme desire to cooperate with the performer and help out the show . . . [McGill, 1947, p. 257).

Nelson (1965) utilized a different set of concepts to describe the unique factors in the stage setting:

To revolt or rebel, is to place the subject "on a spot," and stand out among the others as a "hold out." With the eyes closed, the subject does not know how the other subjects are reacting, but definitely senses the audience's reactions. The subject subconsciously gets the idea and *gets into the act.* It's *fun*—the ham in them exhibits itself and they are *actors* (acting the part of a hypnotized subject). They realize they have a perfect shield to hide behind if they engage in any odd or silly tactics (they are *hypnotized*, which is the excuse), and begin competing among each other for the best performance—like a real *actor*. There are always one or two of the subjects out of a group that will out-do the others and give an outstanding performance. They sense the audience re-actions and applause, and love it and are impelled on in their efforts like a hungry actor. Many times they will react in a slightly exaggerated manner, which the hypnotist must anticipate and capitalize on. Once the ball has started to roll, they all fall into the fun idea and play the role of an actor, the hypnotist merely being the *director* in the ensuing entertainment [p. 30].

Orne (1962) presented the special factors in the stage situation from another perspective:

the entertainer-volunteer relationship legitimizes an extremely wide range of social control with relatively diffuse boundaries. One need only observe such programs as Truth or Consequences, Double or Nothing, and People are Funny to be struck by the remarkably broad range of control which the entertainer may successfully exert over the volunteer-participant. When watching such a performance, the observer somehow does not believe that he could be induced to behave in this manner, while volunteers on the stage very rarely refuse to play their roles. Indeed, it is probably the discrepancy between the amount of control which we would expect an entertainer to have over the volunteer and the amount of control which he actually does have which is responsible for the dramatic appeal of such programs [p. 145].

Let us summarize the material up to this point. To produce an "amazing" show, stage hypnotists rely *primarily* on (a) the high base rate of waking suggestibility, (b) a highly selective procedure for screening Ss, (c) the heightened suggestibility that is produced when the situation is defined as "hypnosis," and (d) important social-psychological variables that are present in the stage situation. These factors appear to be sufficient to produce many, if not most, of the performances observed during stage hypnosis. However, stage hypnotists usually have at least four additional techniques in their repertoire which they *at times* utilize. These four supplementary techniques include stage whispers, failure to challenge, use of stooges or pretrained Ss, and tricks such as pressure on the carotid baroreceptors. These four techniques, which are used *at times* by *some* stage hypnotists, will now be discussed in turn.

*Principle 5*

Marcuse (1959) stated that

The procedure when performing in a theatre is somewhat as follows: the "hypnotist" obtains six or seven volunteers from the audience and—here the crux of the

act is involved—obtains their cooperation in "fooling the audience." This is usually done by whispering instructions to the volunteers, which the audience, unable to hear, thinks is part of inducing hypnosis [p. 180].

The *Encyclopedia of Stage Hypnotism* presents further specifications. It instructs the stage hypnotist to make "gentle pass-like gestures in the air" while whispering to the Ss,

We are going to have some good laughs on the audience and fool them . . . so when I tell you to do some funny things, do exactly as I secretly tell you. O.K? Swell! [McGill, 1947, p. 236].

The *Encyclopedia* also instructs the stage hypnotist to wink at the volunteer in a friendly fashion and then adds that

your words to him are in the nature of a "whispered confidence" of producing laughs on the rest of the spectators in the audience. The volunteer thus begins to feel important that he is in on a secret, and is to become "part of the show." Your bold "O.K? Swell!" . . . implies his automatic acceptance of willingness to follow your instructions, and your parting *wink* cinches the spirit of "good fellowship" between you. Handled thus, any spectator who happens to come up on the stage quickly becomes "a perfect hypnotic subject" for your demonstrations [McGill, 1947, pp. 236–237].

The *Encyclopedia* also adds that, even when the volunteers are first told to "help fool the audience," there soon arises a point where it is almost impossible to tell which responses are deliberate on the part of the Ss and which are involuntary (McGill, 1947, p. 247).

Nelson (1965) presented a brazen justification for this technique:

To the serious minded student of hypnotism, who wishes to produce a hypnotic show for entertainment purposes, it is recommended that he forget all about trying to be a legitimate hypnotist, and turn to the little known secrets of the profession. Modern show business demands rapid and sensational routine, comedy relief, and of course, audience participation . . . experience has shown down thru the years that the hypnotic show must be faked, at least partially so, to hold audience interest, and be successful as an entertainment feature [p. 3].

Although the direct request to Ss to "help fool the audience" was widely used by stage hypnotists in former years, it appears to us that present-day performers rarely use this technique. However, there is evidence to indicate that some if not many modern stage performers use a modified version of the technique. Instead of directly asking the Ss to fool the audience, special instructions are whispered to the Ss which help to elicit the desired phenomena. For instance, the *Encyclo-*

*pedia of Stage Hypnotism* points out that, when the volunteer *S* is receiving suggestions of body sway, the hypnotist should whisper, "Let yourself go and don't resist. Let yourself come right back towards me . . . [McGill, 1947, p. 150]." The *Encyclopedia* also adds that

*These little intimate asides to the subject are most important.* The audience only hears the major portions of your comments that describe and explain the experiment, but the subject receives full benefit of your confidence that tend to make him feel very much obligated to properly perform his portion of the experiment [McGill, 1947, p. 150].

Along similar lines, Nelson (1965) pointed out that

Ninety-nine times out of a hundred—if the performer has any ability whatsoever, he can "stage whisper" his instructions to the subject, and receive full cooperation. With his back to the audience, the hypnotist is in a perfect position to whisper instructions and requests to the subject in a low voice [p. 14].

For instance, if the stage performer wants an *S* to sing like Frank Sinatra (or to crow like a rooster), he may whisper to his most extroverted *S*, "Please give the audience a good act of singing like Sinatra (or crowing like a rooster)."

### Principle 6

Schneck (1958) carefully observed the performance of "a world renowned hypnotist," and documented his use of the failure to challenge technique as follows:

1. After a hypnotic induction procedure had been administered, the volunteer *S*s sat quietly with eyes closed. The stage hypnotist then implied that each *S* was hypnotized, but he made no attempt to question *S*s about their experiences or to test their responsiveness to suggestions.

2. Each *S* was told to clasp his hands together and then told that the hands were stuck and he could not take them apart. No *S* was challenged to try to take his hands apart. Instead, after a few seconds, each *S* was told he could now unclasp his hands. According to Schneck, the audience apparently assumed that all of the *S*s were unable to unclasp their hands.

3. The stage performer placed each *S*'s arm at an angle with the body, and told each *S* that the arm was stiff and he could not bend it. He never challenged any of the *S*s to attempt to bend the arm. Instead, he simply told each *S*, after a few seconds, that he could

now relax or bend the arm. Schneck (1958) commented that

The point to be noted is the play on the suggestibility of the audience rather than the examination of the subject response. The implication was to the effect that when the subject retained, even for a few seconds, the arm in an outstretched position, it followed that he would in fact be unable to bend it. This was clearly a non-sequitur. No verbal or other response at this point was requested of the subject [p. 175].

4. Next, the stage performer suggested to a female *S* that her right arm was insensitive. He then asked her to touch her right arm with her left hand in order to note the lack of sensation. However, he did not ask her if the arm actually felt insensitive. Schneck (1958) commented that

Undoubtedly many in the audience accepted the implication that having gone through the motions, this girl actually did experience anesthesia . . . no one in the audience was bold enough or possessed the interest or intention to challenge the hypnotist directly in connection with any of his claims [pp. 175–176].

Although we cannot state with certainty how often the failure to challenge technique is used in stage hypnosis, it is our impression, from observing various performances, that most present-day performers are aware of the technique and use it at times in their show.

### Principle 7

Nelson (1965) pointed out that

Most of the old time hypnotists carried their own *stooges*—planted them in the audience, and they promptly responded as "legitimate spectator volunteers," and were, of course, accepted as such by the other members of the audience [p. 3].

Although practically all manuals of stage hypnosis state that stooges or plants were commonly used in earlier stage performances (Calostro, 1949; Gibson, 1956; Lonk, 1947; Lustig, 1956), this practice has markedly declined since the days of vaudeville.

A few modern stage performers at times use stooges only as "starters" for the other *S*s. As McGill (1947) pointed out,

With two or three plants . . . you can always feel certain that your critical "example tests" are going to work, which is an important factor in getting the rest of the [volunteer *S*s] to properly respond. A few hypnotic plants in various parts of the theatre also will assist in acting as "starters" in getting subjects to come forward to the stage so you can start the show without delay [p. 253].

A few modern stage performers, who do not use stooges in the strict sense of the term, at times use a trained S in order to demonstrate the more difficult feats, such as the cataleptic feat in which two or more men stand on the rigid S who is suspended between two chairs. However, it appears that the great majority of present-day stage performers do not attempt to deceive their audience when they use a trained S. They typically tell the audience that the next task is especially difficult, and, to demonstrate it successfully, they will use an S who has previously shown that he can carry it out.

Although a small number of present-day performers may use stooges as "starters" or may use a trained S to demonstrate the more difficult feats, it appears that most modern performers do not use either stooges or trained Ss. It is often impossible to use stooges when performing at private clubs where only members are present. Furthermore, it is very difficult for the modern stage hypnotist to use stooges when he appears at the same nightclub, day after day, for many months. In fact, it appears that the use of plants in the audience and trained Ss has markedly declined in the last two or three decades in the same way as the use of "hypnotic passes" and the "hypnotic gaze." Most present-day performers do not need either stooges or trained Ss to carry out a dramatic show (Nelson, 1965). Instead, they rely on the high base rate of waking suggestibility, a highly selective procedure for screening Ss, the suggestibility-enhancing effect of defining the situation as hypnosis, important social-psychological variables present in the stage situation and, at times, the stage whispers technique, the failure to challenge technique, and one or more tricks which are discussed next.

### Principle 8

Two or three decades ago, stage hypnotists used a wide variety of tricks to elicit apparent hypnotic behaviors from their Ss. Since these tricks are presented in most of the recent manuals of stage hypnosis, modern performers are well aware of their existence. However, it is our impression that most present-day performers use only one or two of the following tricks in their show.

*The human plank feat.* The stage performer may suggest to his selected S, who has ostensibly been placed in hypnosis, that his body is stiff and rigid. After S appears rigid, he is suspended between two chairs, one chair below

his head and the other at his ankles. The S remains suspended between the two chairs for several minutes while the orchestra plays a crescendo and the audience gapes in astonishment.

Although laymen believe that S must be in "trance" in order to perform the human plank feat, it can be easily performed by unselected Ss without any kind of hypnotic procedure. Barber (1969) found that at least 80% of unselected "awake" Ss are able to remain suspended between two chairs when they are simply told to keep their body rigid. Collins (1961) obtained similar results in an earlier study: When given suggestions to become rigid and to stay rigid, Ss in a waking control group (and also Ss in a hypnotic group) remained suspended for 2–4 min. In postexperimental interviews, most of the waking control Ss (and also most of the hypnotic Ss) stated that they were amazed at their own performance since they did not believe initially that they had the ability to become human planks.

*The cataleptic feat.* Some stage hypnotists do not simply demonstrate the human plank suspended between two chairs. Instead, they demonstrate the more difficult cataleptic feat in which one or more individuals stand on the human plank. However, when the cataleptic feat is to be performed: (a) a trained S is often used and (b) S is given additional support by placing one chair underneath his *shoulders* and the other chair underneath *the calves of his legs*. In fact, all manuals of stage hypnosis that describe this stunt emphasize that, when a person is to stand on the rigid S, the shoulders and the lower part of the legs must be supported (Lonk, 1947, p. 46; McGill, 1947, p. 217; North, 1954, p. 26; Tracy, 1952, p. 156). Usually one, but at times, two or more men are invited to stand upon S's rigid body for a few seconds. After they step down, S is lifted from the chairs (still rigid), placed on his feet, and "awakened" by the performer (McGill, 1947; Nelson, 1965).

Although most members of the audience accept the cataleptic feat as a valid demonstration of "deep hypnotic trance," there are usually a few individuals who believe that it involves some form of trickery, for instance, the use of a mechanical brace for the body. After noting the slight stature of the S used in the performance he witnessed, Wells (1946) concluded that "by some Houdini-like trick a plank [must have] been slipped under the subject [p. 149]." How could such a small person support the weight of several men? However, it is the use of a small-framed person that not only creates the desired sensational effect but, in fact, helps to make it possible (Nelson, 1965, pp. 19–20). Nelson explained that the shorter the *S*, the easier the stunt is to perform since the distance between the supporting bases is less. In addition, large cushions affixed to the chairs "increase the supporting surface, and lessen the distance between the two inner edges of the support [Nelson, 1965, p. 20]."

The secret in preparing *S* is as follows:

Have the subject stand straight with his heels together. Now, have the subject grasp the back of his trouser leg with each hand, and pull the trousers backward (not upward). Place the shoulders in such a position that the arms will be behind the back and run straight down the back, where the hands grasp the trousers at their own length . . . tell [the] subject to try and bend forward. If the position is held, this is readily found impossible. The body is so braced that it cannot bend so long as the arms are in position and clenched to the trousers . . . suspend the weight of your body on the subject's body, while suspended on two chairs. Do so easily, and observe the results. It will prove somewhat of a strain to the subject at first, and it will be necessary to experiment several times to ascertain the best distribution of weight over the subject's body [Nelson, 1965, pp. 19–20].

The weight applied to the rigid *S* should be distributed evenly over his body. This is typically accomplished by (*a*) placing a heavy, stiff pad over the rigid *S*'s midsection to offer a large supporting surface and (*b*) distributing the weight of the standing person over the human plank's chest and over the lower part of his legs which are almost directly above the supporting chairs. If three men are to stand on the human plank, (*a*) two of the men are placed almost directly above the supporting pads on the chair (one man above the chest and the other above the ankles or calves), and the third man is placed on the lower chest area with feet about a foot apart; and (*b*) the thinnest man is placed in the center and the two heavier men at the ends so that most of the weight falls on that part of the *S*'s body that is best supported by the chairs (Lonk, 1947, p. 46).

Nelson (1965) stated that, although a stooge or a trained *S* is used when more than one man is to stand on the human plank, practically all *normally awake* male *S*s are able to support the weight of *one* man on their chest if they are given task-motivational in-

structions, for example,

Keep up your running line of talk and continually say, "rigid, now rigid, steady boy!" Place confidence in the subject that he can hold the weight and that he must not let down [p. 22].

Sometimes the cataleptic feat involves placing a felt pad and then a large rock about 3 ft. square and a foot in thickness on the human-plank's chest. The performer then breaks the rock by striking a blow with a large, heavy sledge hammer. Although this feat is quite dramatic, it is much easier to perform than the one described above in which two or more men stand on the rigid *S*. McGill (1947) writes that the rock-breaking stunt

can hardly be called hypnotic, but it is so spectacular that it is very much worthwhile using. The rock is of sandstone and hence breaks quite readily. The felt pad over the chest of the subject takes some of the blow, and the inertia in the rock itself absorbs the large majority of it. Actually the subject experiences little more than a slight jar . . . [p. 219].

Nelson (1965) added that although this stunt is much simpler than it appears, nevertheless the stage performer should experiment considerably before attempting it in public.

*Eyeball fastening.* The stage performer directs *S* to close his eyes and to roll his eyeballs upward as far as possible, as if he were looking through the top of his forehead. After *S* is told repeatedly to keep his eyelids closed tight while looking higher and higher, he is challenged to open his eyes. The *S* finds it impossible to do so until told that he can now relax his eyes.

If the reader tries this stunt, he will see that it is physically impossible to keep the eyeballs rolled upward and at the same time open the eyelids (Lonk, 1947; Lustig, 1956; McGill, 1947, p. 139; Nelson, 1965, p. 8; Tracy, 1952, p. 131).

*Anesthesia test.* The *S* is asked to extend one arm out horizontally with the palm facing downward. The stage performer then suggests numbness and absence of feeling in *S*'s hand. As these suggestions are continued, the performer takes out a cigarette lighter and runs the flame slowly back and forth under the outstretched hand from the palm to the tips of the fingers and back again. The *S* typically shows no reaction to the flame, apparently under the influence of "hypnotic anesthesia."

Tracy (1952) admonished the stage hypnotist not to hold the flame too close to the skin or too long in one spot and herein lies the secret. In photographic illustrations of this stunt (Lonk, 1947, p. 35; Tracy, 1952, p. 133), the flame is held at least 1 in. away from $S$'s palm. If the reader tries it, he will find that anyone can easily withstand the heat of a flame, provided that the flame is kept moving at a steady pace and at a distance of about 1 in. The precise distance, of course, depends on the speed at which the flame is moved, and both can be found with a little practice.

In rare instances, stage hypnotists may place a lit match *directly upon* $S$'s palm or finger and move it back and forth. If the reader tries it on himself, he will find that the fire from a match can be easily withstood and no burning will result, provided that the match is placed rather quickly upon the palm or finger and is rather quickly moved back and forth. The only possibility of burning occurs if the lit match is brought toward the hand too slowly or is moved back and forth too slowly.

*The pin through the flesh test.* The pin through the flesh test was commonly used 20 or 30 yr. ago to demonstrate "hypnotic anesthesia." Although the test is not often used at present, competent stage hypnotists know how to perform the test and may decide to use it in order to convince a skeptical audience.

The test is usually performed with a stooge or a trained $S$. With the sleeve rolled back, $S$'s arm is held up horizontally and passes are made along the arm while suggestions of numbness and loss of feeling are given. At the climax, the stage hypnotist picks up a long sterilized needle or hatpin and, taking hold of the fleshy part of the $S$'s arm, slowly thrusts one or more pins through the flesh.

Nelson (1965) revealed that the secret of this stunt is that

The subject suffers very little pain. Just as the needle pierces the skin, the performer *pinches* the flesh, which practically deadens the pain, with the exception of the needle point piercing the outer skin. Just as soon as the first layer of skin is broken, the pain ceases . . . . To those who have never tried this experience, they may doubt this assertion, but it is nevertheless true [p. 9].

McGill (1947) gives additional tips that are helpful in performing this test:

Never mention to the subject that you are going to pass a needle through his flesh, merely suggest that the arm feels all dead-like, and then perform the test without comment. Use a sharp needle . . . . Pinch the flesh sharply between your thumb and forefinger just before you pass the needle through . . . . The

experiment, you will find, is a very easy one to perform . . . [pp. 213–214].

Lonk (1947) presented a cogent argument that the pin through the flesh test should be performed by pushing a sterile needle through the lower lobe of the ear because "There are not many nerves in this part of the body and it produces very little pain." He also noted that, after the needle has been withdrawn, "Pressure of your sterilized thumb on the wound will prevent any bleeding [Lonk, 1947, p. 45]."

*"Stopping the blood flow."* This stunt, which is in the repertoire of some stage performers, is conducted as follows: the performer apparently induces the blood to stop flowing in an $S$'s arm by suggesting stiffness and rigidity in the arm and by making mysterious passes over it. The $S$'s arm appears white and lifeless until the performer subsequently suggests that the arm is relaxing, whereupon the blood appears to flow back into the arm and its natural coloring returns. In some cases, a member of the audience, perhaps a physician, may be invited to test $S$'s pulse, which may prove to be imperceptible (Lonk, 1947; Lustig, 1956; McGill, 1947). There are at least three different methods for producing these effects:

1. The first method requires the use of a stooge. The stooge seats himself sideways on a high-backed chair and holds one arm horizontally across the top of the chair while the stage hypnotist makes passes and gives suggestions as if he is controlling the circulation of the blood in the arm. With his fist clenched and his arm rigid, the stooge presses his upper arm down hard on the back of the chair, thus effectively stopping the circulation in the arm so that no pulse can be detected and the hand shows a pale appearance (Lonk, 1947, pp. 57–58; Stein, undated, p. 20). Stein added that

Naturally the hypnotist must do a lot of talking along scientific lines during the entire trick so as to keep the audience keyed up to the right pitch where they are willing to believe most anything [p. 20].

2. A second method achieves the same effect, but without the suspicious presence of the chair. Prior to the performance, a golf ball is placed in the armpit of a stooge and fastened there by an elastic. When the hypnotist suggests that the blood is leaving the arm, the stooge presses his arm against the golf ball and the circulation and pulse are obliterated (Lonk, 1947, p. 58; Lustig, 1956, p. 15).

3. A third method does not require a stooge

or a trained *S*. After a volunteer *S* has clenched his fist with his arm at his side, the stage performer suggests rigidity and stiffness and directs the blood to flow out of the arm. Next, the performer suddenly swings *S*'s arm upward to a horizontal position and gives forceful suggestions of rigidity in the arm and shoulder. McGill (1947) stated that "The effect of these suggestions is to cramp the muscles of the arm and shoulder, driving the blood from the arm." He also advised that "a fleshy pink-skinned type of subject" should be used for this test since "plump persons have a transparency to their skins that emphasize the effect greatly [pp. 211–212]."

*Pressure on the carotid sinus*. When using this technique, the stage performer exerts pressure on the baroreceptors at the carotid sinus. This produces a vagus-induced bradycardia and vasodilation which leads to sudden hypotension and fainting [Ganong, 1967, pp. 508–509].

Nelson (1965) described the carotid technique as follows:

Here is a sure-fire method of instantly inducing hypnotic sleep to most any subject. It will be welcomed by the fraternity at large as being *one* method whereby the performer can hypnotize the most skeptical, the *Let's see you do it kind* and others . . . . The method . . . was long ago in use, and has been a closely guarded secret for years. It is well-known among a small group of stage hypnotists, who use it daily in their performance. It is the *one* legitimate test they can and do employ to combat the skeptic [p. 15].

The *Encyclopedia of Stage Hypnotism* presents gruesome details on how to use this technique:

Standing directly in front of the subject, push his head well back with your left hand on the front of his forehead. Then place the thumb and first finger of your right hand directly on his exposed throat, just above the Adam's apple. You can quickly find the exact spot by the feel of the blood pounding through the veins [sic, actually arteries] in his throat beneath your fingers. Push firmly in upon these veins, at the same time requesting the man to breathe deeply. (Even if he doesn't wish to comply, he'll be largely compelled to do so in order to get air in such a position.) Maintain this pressure upon the veins in his throat for a moment, and at the same time push his head further backward . . . and carefully watch your subject.

You will find that he will suddenly *go limp*. Catch this moment and shout loudly, "*Sleep,*" *and let him drop to the floor in a heap.*

Step aside to give the audience a chance to see the 'hypnotized' man on the floor. Then quickly bend over the subject and hit him gently on the back of the neck while saying in a loud voice, "All right now, wake up now . . . wide awake!"

After that demonstration you will find the subject will be most docile and willing to follow whatever whispered instructions you care to give. It also serves to impress the other subjects on the stage to the end that they'd better co-operate along with you—*or else* [McGill, 1947, pp. 243–244].

After presenting a somewhat different description of the carotid technique, Lonk (1947) urged stage hypnotists to "Master this instantaneous method so you can put one over on the 'wise guy' that insists that you go ahead and hypnotize him [p. 32]." However, practically all manuals of stage hypnosis caution the performer to use the carotid technique with caution. For example, Lonk (1947) stated that this drastic method should not be used with individuals who are suffering from high blood pressure or heart disease, or who are past 50, or who are not in the best of health. There is little doubt that the carotid technique is potentially dangerous because

Brain damage from lack of blood and even death may result if the pressure is maintained too long on the vagi and carotids, and 15 seconds of such pressure is the very maximum which is safe [Whitlow, 1948, p. 62].

LeCron (1948) has noted that, "It is rather remarkable that [the carotid technique] should have been used so often without bad results [p. 56]."

### DISCUSSION

Many laymen who observe a demonstration of stage hypnosis seem to believe the following: (*a*) the stage performer places his *S*s in a "hypnotic state" or "trance"; (*b*) "hypnotic trance" is an altered state of consciousness which resembles the state of the sleep-walker or somnambulist; and (*c*) *S*s on the stage behave in unusual ways *because* they are in hypnotic trance. These notions are misleading. Notions that are closer to the truth include the following: The suggestions given by the stage hypnotist are effective in eliciting ostensibly unusual performances *primarily* because of the following: (*a*) Base-level "waking" responsiveness to suggestions is much higher than is commonly believed. (*b*) Very responsive *S*s can be rather easily selected. (*c*) Since the situation is inevitably defined as hypnosis, it is clear to all *S*s that a high level of responsiveness to suggestions and commands is desired and expected. (*d*) The stage setting, which places *S* at the center of attention and expectancy, is conducive to eliciting unusual behaviors. Furthermore, *some* stage performers also *at times* use (*e*) the technique of "stage whispers" or "intimate asides to subjects," (*f*) the "failure to challenge" technique, (*g*) pretrained *S*s to demonstrate the more difficult stunts, and (*h*) one or more "tricks" which make it appear that unusual phenomena are being produced.

Although laymen seem to believe that the stage performer is a highly effective hypnotist who places his *S*s in a hypnotic trance, a more valid conception is that the stage performer is an actor playing the part of a hypnotist. As Nelson (1965) bluntly pointed out:

The successful hypnotic entertainer of today is actually not interested whether or not the subjects are really hypnotized—his basic function is to *entertain*. He is interested in his ability to *con* his subjects into a pseudo performance that appears as hypnotism—to get laughs and entertain his audience . . . . [The subjects] enjoy their part and react as they are *told* to do. Hypnotism, as done today for entertainment, is as simple as all this [pp. 29–31].

## REFERENCES

ANDERSEN, M. L., & SARBIN, T. R. Base rate expectancies and motoric alterations in hypnosis. *International Journal of Clinical and Experimental Hypnosis*, 1964, 12, 147–158.

ARONS, H. *How to routine an ethical hypnotic lecture-demonstration*. Irvington, N. J.: Power Publishers, 1961.

BARBER, T. X. Measuring "hypnotic-like" suggestibility with and without "hypnotic induction"; psychometric properties, norms, and variables influencing response to the Barber Suggestibility Scale (BSS). *Psychological Reports*, 1965, 16, 809–844.

BARBER, T. X. *Hypnosis: A scientific approach*. New York: Van Nostrand Reinhold, 1969.

BARBER, T. X. *LSD, marihuana, yoga, and hypnosis*. Chicago: Aldine, 1970.

BARBER, T. X., & CALVERLEY, D. S. Toward a theory of hypnotic behavior: Effects on suggestibility of defining the situation as hypnosis and defining response to suggestions as easy. *Journal of Abnormal and Social Psychology*, 1964, 68, 585–592.

BARBER, T. X., & CALVERLEY, D. S. Empirical evidence for a theory of "hypnotic" behavior: Effects on suggestibility of five variables typically included in hypnotic induction procedures. *Journal of Consulting Psychology*, 1965, 29, 98–107.

CALOSTRO. *Entertaining with hypnotism*. New York: Robbins, 1949.

COLLINS, J. K. Muscular endurance in normal and hypnotic states: A study of suggested catalepsy. Honors thesis, University of Sydney, Department of Psychology, 1961.

GANONG, W. F. *Review of medical physiology*. (3d Ed.) Los Altos, Calif.: Lange Medical Publications, 1967.

GIBSON, W. B. *The key to hypnotism*. New York: Key Publishing Co., 1956.

LECRON, L. M. Editor's note. In L. M. LeCron (Ed.). *Experimental hypnosis*. New York: Macmillan, 1948.

LONK, A. F. *A manual of hypnotism and psychotherapeutics*. (Rev. 3rd ed.) Palatine, Ill.: Author, 1947.

LUSTIG, D. J. *You, too, can be a hypnotist*. Philadelphia: Kanter's Magic Shop, 1956.

MARCUSE, F. L. *Hypnosis: Fact and fiction*. Baltimore: Penguin Books, 1959.

McGILL, O. *The encyclopedia of stage hypnotism*. Colon, Mich.: Abbott's Magic Novelty Co., 1947.

NELSON, R. A. *A complete course in stage hypnotism*. Columbus, Ohio: Nelson Enterprises, 1965.

NORTH, R. L. *Ultra-modern hypnotism*. Boston, Mass.: Author, 1954.

ORNE, M. T. Antisocial behavior and hypnosis: Problems of control and validation in empirical studies. In G. H. Estabrooks (Ed.), *Hypnosis: Current problems*. New York: Harper & Row, 1962.

SCHNECK, J. M. Relationship between hypnotist-audience and hypnotist-subject interaction. *Journal of Clinical and Experimental Hypnosis*, 1958, 6, 171–181.

STEIN, M. *Magic for home and stage*. Chicago, Ill.: Max Stein Publishing Co., undated.

TRACY, D. F. *Hypnosis*. New York: Sterling Publishing Co., 1952.

WEITZENHOFFER, A. M., & SJOBERG, B. M., JR. Suggestibility with and without "induction of hypnosis." *Journal of Nervous and Mental Disease*, 1961, 132, 204–220.

WELLS, W. R. A basic deception in exhibitions of hypnosis. *Journal of Abnormal and Social Psychology*, 1946, 41, 145–153.

WHITLOW, J. A rapid method for the induction of hypnosis. In L. M. LeCron (Ed.), *Experimental hypnosis*. New York: Macmillan, 1948.

(March 18, 1970)

# Imagery and "Hallucinations": 32
## Effects of LSD Contrasted with
## The Effects of "Hypnotic" Suggestions

Theodore X. Barber

Vivid imagery, "hallucinations," and other alterations in visual perception are said to be produced by lysergic acid diethylamide (LSD) and also by suggestions given under hypnosis. Do similar processes or mechanisms underlie the imagery or hallucinations found in an LSD situation and those that are elicited by suggestions in a hypnotic situation?

The visual phenomena associated with LSD include changes in color perception, distortions, illusions, and vivid imagery or hallucinations; these can be related to physiologically based alterations that have occurred in the pupil, the lens, the intraocular fluid, the retina, and in other structures within the visual system. The hallucinations that are said to be produced by hypnotic suggestions are somewhat different, as will be explained more fully in this chapter.

I will look closely at the reports of vivid imagery or hallucinations which are proffered by some hypnotic subjects, and also by some control subjects, who have received suggestions to hallucinate. Two major questions will underlie this part of

[1] Work on this paper was supported by a research grant (MH-11521) from the National Institute of Mental Health, U.S. Public Health Service.

the discussion: Do suggestions to see an object that is not actually present produce reports of visual hallucinations when honest reports are explicitly demanded? Do these suggested hallucinations give rise to any observable or objective effects which are independent of the subjects' verbal reports?

In addition, I will try to determine whether the visual phenomena associated with LSD are functionally related to subjects' expectancies, or to explicit or implicit suggestions made to the subjects. Finally, I will consider what areas of fruitful research are suggested by the data that we have at present.

## LSD, PSILOCYBIN, AND MESCALINE[2]

Before we focus on the effects of LSD, we should note that psilocybin and mescaline also produce similar effects.

LSD is usually given orally at doses of about 100 to 300 micrograms whereas psilocybin is usually given at a much larger dose (30,000 to 60,000 micrograms) and mescaline at a still larger dose (350,000 to 600,000 micrograms). At these common doses, subjects generally report that the subjective effects of LSD, psilocybin, and mescaline are very similar (Abramson, 1960; Hollister and Hartman, 1962; Isbell, 1959; Unger, 1963; Wolbach, Miner, and Isbell, 1962). Furthermore, when a subject becomes tolerant to one of these drugs, that is, when he requires larger and larger doses to experience the characteristic effects of the drug, he also becomes tolerant to the others (Balestrieri and Fontanari, 1959; Isbell, Wolbach, Wikler, and Miner, 1961). Although LSD, psilocybin, and mescaline produce very similar *subjective* effects, there are some objective differences in their mode of action. For example, at commonly administered doses, LSD and mescaline exert noticeable psychological and physiological effects over a period of 8 to 12 hours, whereas the action of psilocybin lasts only 3 to 4 hours. However, the important point that requires emphasis is that the similarities in the subjectively reported effects of LSD, psilocybin, and mescaline far outweigh the differences.[3]

[2] The first half of this paper, which pertains to LSD and related drugs, is based on material presented in more detail elsewhere (Barber, 1970).

[3] There are many other drugs that appear to produce at least some of the effects that are characteristic of LSD, psilocybin and mescaline. These include dimethyltryptamine (DMT), diethyltryptamine (DET), tetrahydrocannabinol (THC), and dimethoxymethylamphetamine (DOM, also known popularly as "STP") (Hollister, Macnicol, and Gillespie, 1969; Isbell, 1967; Isbell, Gorodetzsky, Jasinski, Claussen, Spulak, and Korte, 1967; Rosenberg, Isbell, Miner, and Logan, 1964; Snyder, Faillace, and Hollister, 1967; Snyder, Faillace, and Weingartner, 1968; Szara, Rockland, Rosenthal, and Handlon, 1966). Other drugs that may also produce some LSD-type effects have been reviewed by Farnsworth (1968), Hoffer and Osmond (1967), Hollister (1968), and Schultes (1969).

# GENERAL EFFECTS OF LSD

Although the effects of LSD are often discussed as if they constituted an undifferentiated conglomerate, they can actually be differentiated into a series of distinguishable effects (Barber, 1970). These isolable effects of LSD include the following:

1. *Somatic–sympathetic effects.* These effects which are usually found within the first hour after ingestion of the drug and which are related to changes occurring in the autonomic nervous system include subjective reports of physical weakness, dizziness, restlessness, or difficulties in breathing, and objectively observable phenomena such as pupillary dilation and elevation in body temperature and blood pressure.

2. *Changes in "body image."* Subjects report that the body (or parts of the body, especially the limbs) feel strange—heavier or lighter, or changed in size, shape, or in relative proportions.

3. *Dreamy, detached feelings.* Subjects report that things are strange or distant, and they feel that they are observing the world in a dreamlike way. To an objective observer the subjects may appear to be in a state of reverie, fantasy, or introspection.

4. *Changes in perception of time.* Subjects almost always report a change in their perception of the passage of time and they typically judge a short period as a longer period.

5. *Changes in tactile sensitivity.* Subjects typically report that their fingers or extremities are numb or rubbery, and that objects feel different when they are touched.

6. *Changes in visual perception.* These visual effects, which will be discussed in detail below, include changes in color perception, illusions, distortions, and vivid imagery or hallucinations.

7. *Changes in audition, gustation, and olfaction.* Subjects characteristically report that music or other sounds have changed in quality, food tastes different (better or worse), and odors are more pronounced.

8. *Synesthesia.* Some subjects report that one sense modality affects another sense modality. For example, the visual forms which the subject perceives with eyes closed are altered whenever the music which is being played changes in tempo.

9. *Changes in moods, emotions, and cognitions.* Some individuals who have taken LSD do not show marked changes in moods, emotions, or cognitions.

However, most subjects who have taken this drug do show emotional and cognitive reactions. Some subjects become euphoric (and may move on to joy, bliss, or a "psychedelic" reaction), whereas others become anxious (and may move on to a panic reaction).

Although each of these nine effects of LSD is important in understanding the effects of this drug, in this chapter I will focus only on the changes in visual perception.

## EFFECTS OF LSD ON VISUAL PERCEPTION

When subjects ingest LSD at usual doses (100–300 micrograms), almost all report some changes in the perception of colors, or in the size or form of objects, persons, or their own body (Fiddleman, 1961). These visual phenomena are among the most characteristic effects of LSD and have given this drug the name of "hallucinogen."

### VISUAL EFFECTS WITH EYES CLOSED

When the eyes are closed, normal individuals perceive phosphenes (starlike objects and colors) in their visual field. When subjects who have received LSD (or psilocybin or mescaline) close their eyes in a dark room, they typically report that the phosphenes are more vivid than those perceived normally; in fact, some subjects report that the luminescent lights, colors, and patterns change into formed structures such as gemlike or architectural-like objects (Cohen, 1968, pp. 22-24; Ditman, Moss, Forgy, Zunin, Lynch, and Funk, 1969; Huxley, 1954). In most instances, the subjects continue to see these colorful patterns or structures when they open their eyes in a dark room. However, when the lights are turned on in the room, almost all subjects report that the visual phenomena have become very faint or have disappeared (Pahnke and Richards, 1966).

Experiments by Knoll and his associates seem to corroborate the reports that LSD (and psilocybin and mescaline) augment the phosphene phenomenon. First, these investigators showed that complexly patterned phosphenes can be evoked by electrical stimulation of the brain with pulses ranging in frequency from 1 to 30 cps (Knoll and Kugler, 1959). Then, in a second experiment (Knoll, Kugler, Hofer, and Lawder, 1963), they showed that under LSD (and psilocybin and mescaline) a greater number of complexly patterned phosphenes are elicited by the electrical stimulation and there is an increase in the vividness of these phosphenes.

VISUAL EFFECTS WITH EYES OPEN

Within an hour or two after taking LSD, and usually continuing in a wavelike manner for several hours, many subjects report that colors seem brighter or more intense or vivid. Also, subjects typically report that they can see rainbowlike colors, colored patterns, or halos at the edges of objects or on the wall and that colored afterimages persist longer than usual (Bercel, Travis, Olinger, and Dreikurs, 1956; Masters and Huston, 1966, pp. 152–153).

Perception of depth and perspective are also altered. A change in depth relations is indicated by subjects' reports that two-dimensional objects at times seem to be three-dimensional (Kieffer and Moritz, 1968). The outlines or contours of objects, especially the edges, appear to become sharper (Kluver, 1966). Corridors often appear longer than usual and objects at times seem to fluctuate in distance (Andersen and Rawnsley, 1954; Hoffer and Osmond, 1967, p. 112). Also common is a magnification of detail, which may be related to the changes in contours, perspective, or simultaneous contrast (Rodin and Luby, 1966). The constancies of perception are no longer constant—a typical report is, "As I moved my hand toward me, it increased in size." These changes in depth perception and in the constancies of perception are clearly noted when the subject looks in a mirror; practically all subjects who have taken LSD report that their own image in a mirror or the image of another person appears distorted in some way (Masters and Huston, 1966, p. 83).

Other common visual phenomena associated with LSD include alterations in the size or shapes of objects. Parts of one's own body, or the features of another person, or objects in the room may be perceived as changed in some way if not markedly distorted. Also, at higher doses of LSD (above 350 micrograms), subjects often report apparent undulations or movements of surfaces; a piece of paper may seem to be making wavelike motions and the wall may seem to ripple in and out (Ditman *et al.*, 1969; Hoffer and Osmond, 1967, pp. 113–114).

Experimental studies tend to corroborate the subjects' reports that the visual world has changed. Hartman and Hollister (1963) demonstrated that colored afterimages and also the subjective colors elicited by flicker were increased by LSD (and also by psilocybin and mescaline). The same investigators also showed that the duration of afterimages was prolonged by psilocybin, although the effect was not significant for LSD and mescaline. Along similar lines, Keeler (1965) demonstrated, under double-blind conditions, that psilocybin significantly changed an objective measure of afterimage perception.

LSD augments the variability in judging the size of test objects (Weckowicz, 1959) and increases the degree of displacement of the vertical that is produced by tilting the body (Liebert, Wapner, and Werner, 1957). Edwards and Cohen (1961) found that the Mueller-Lyer illusion was slightly enhanced under LSD and the same investigators showed that constancy decreased when the standard object was nearby (30 centimeters away) but not when it was further away (180 centimeters).

## VISUAL EFFECTS AS A FUNCTION OF SUBJECTS' NORMAL VISUAL IMAGERY

Practically all subjects who have received a moderate dose of LSD (100–300 micrograms) report some changes in visual perception. However, as compared to individuals with ordinary visual imagery, individuals with exceptionally strong visual imagery (who normally project visual images in front of their eyes) report a greater number of more intense visual effects with LSD (Brown, 1968; Shryne and Brown, 1965). The subjects' visual imagery abilities interact with the drug dose to affect the visual manifestations; that is, subjects with weak imagery require a higher dose of LSD to report as many or as intense visual effects as those with strong imagery.

## VISUAL EFFECTS AS A FUNCTION OF DOSE

A relationship between the drug dose and the number and intensity of the visual effects is difficult to demonstrate when comparisons are made among subjects (interindividual comparisons) (Klee, Bertino, Weintraub, and Callaway, 1961). Subjects differ in response to the same dose. Also, two subjects may report very similar visual effects even though one receives a high dose and the other a low dose. Different responses to the same dose may be due to differences among subjects in ability to detoxify and excrete the drug. Different responses to the same dose may also be related to differences among subjects in normal visual imagery abilities, in personality characteristics, and in motivations, expectancies, and attitudes toward the situation.

Although a dose-response relationship is difficult to demonstrate when interindividual comparisons are made, such a relationship can be clearly demonstrated when the *same* subject receives various doses of LSD (intraindividual comparisons). Any one subject will tend to report a greater number of more intense visual effects with increasingly higher doses of LSD (Abramson, Kornetsky, Jarvik, Kaufman, and Ferguson, 1955; Isbell, Belleville, Fraser, Wikler, and Logan, 1956; Klee *et al.*, 1961).

This important relationship, between the dose of LSD and the number and intensity of the visual effects, was clearly demonstrated in an experiment by Klee *et al.* (1961). In this experiment, 12 subjects, seen together as a group, were given LSD in 3 sessions at doses around 70, 140, and 280 micrograms, and then were given LSD again in 3 additional sessions at doses around 280, 560, and 1120 micrograms. A latin square design was used to counterbalance the doses and the experiment was double-blind (neither the subjects nor three medical observers knew which dose of LSD was being used). There was perfect agreement among the three observers as to the dose received by any one subject over three sessions; that is, the medical observers were able to tell which of the three doses each subject had received. For any one subject, the number and intensity of the visual effects clearly increased with increasingly higher doses of LSD up to the highest dose (around 1120 micrograms). (At the highest dose, confusion and disorientation were common.)

## VISUAL EFFECTS, EXPECTANCY, AND SUGGESTIONS

As can be surmised from the study by Klee *et al.* described above, the visual effects of LSD appear to be more closely related to the drug dose than to the subjects' expectancies or to suggestions which are explicit or implicit in the experimental situation. Supporting data for this supposition, that expectancies and suggestions, at best, play only a minor role in producing the visual effects, have been presented by Ditman *et al.* (1969), Levis and Mehlman (1964), Fogel and Hoffer (1962), and Johnson (1968).

In the investigation by Ditman *et al.* (1969), 1 of the following 3 drugs were administered in randomized order and under double-blind conditions to 99 alcoholics: 75 milligrams of methylphenidate (Ritalin), which is usually categorized as a mild stimulant; 75 milligrams of chlordiazepoxide (Librium), which acts as a tranquilizer; or 200 micrograms of LSD. All subjects were told that they were receiving LSD and were treated as if they had received LSD. A major question that the study was designed to answer was: Would drugs, thought by the subjects to be LSD, produce the visual effects that have been associated with LSD, when the situation and the subjects' expectancies remain constant, although the actual drug administered varied? Following the drug session, all subjects checked a series of items which pertained to drug experiences. LSD far outranked the other two drugs in enhancing the phosphene phenomenon ("With my eyes closed I saw multicolored moving designs"), in affecting color perception ("Colors seemed brighter"), and in producing visual distortions, illusions, or hallucinations ("Solid objects changed their shapes and even disappeared," "Objects seemed to glow around the edges," and "Other people's faces seemed to become changing masks").

In a double-blind experiment (Levis and Mehlman, 1964), 15 subjects were given a placebo and another 15 subjects were given mescaline (350,000 micrograms). The subjects were divided into 3 groups, each group containing 5 placebo subjects and 5 mescaline subjects. One of the 3 groups was not given suggestions as to what to expect. The other 2 groups received a list of written statements suggesting what to expect from the drug. For instance, subjects in one group were told that they would experience visual illusions, and subjects in the other group were told that they would not experience visual illusions. The suggestions did *not* exert a significant effect on the visual phenomena produced by mescaline. Regardless of the suggestions, subjects receiving mescaline, but not those receiving the placebo, reported visual hallucinations (with eyes closed) and visual illusions and distortions (with eyes open).

Fogel and Hoffer (1962) attempted to reverse the visual effects of LSD by suggestions given under hypnosis. The subject in this study had taken 100 micrograms of LSD and was reporting visual phenomena; for instance, she stated that the face of the experimenter was altered in appearance. At this point, a hypnotic induction procedure was administered and the subject was given the suggestion that on opening her eyes everything would look normal. The subject stated that although the experimenter's face now looked more normal it still remained somewhat distorted. Although Fogel and Hoffer concluded that hypnotic suggestions negated the visual effects of LSD, a more justifiable conclusion is that hypnotic suggestions, at best, reduced but did not eliminate the visual changes produced by LSD.

Johnson (1968) showed that the visual effects of LSD are elicited when expectancies and suggestions are minimized, that is, when the subjects do not know that they have received LSD. Johnson administered 500 or more micrograms of LSD to one group of alcoholics and a combination of sodium amytal with methamphetamine to another group. The patients did not know that they were receiving LSD. The patients receiving LSD, but not those receiving sodium amytal with methamphetamine, reported the characteristic distortions and illusions which have been associated with LSD.

## VISUAL EFFECTS AND HALLUCINATIONS

The discussion up to this point can be summarized as follows. When LSD (or mescaline or psilocybin) is taken at the doses which are commonly used in experimental studies, and the subject's eyes are closed, subjects typically report that they perceive vivid colors, patterns, and, at times, formed objects. Also, when the subjects' eyes are open, they report some alteration in visual perception such as changes in the color and form of objects. These visual phenomena which increase in number and in intensity in any one subject as the drug dose is increased and which are affected only to a minor degree by expectancies and suggestions have been commonly subsumed under the term "visual hallucination," and the drugs have been labeled as "hallucinogens." Is the term "hallucination" applicable?

The term visual hallucination, as used by different investigators, subsumes at least 4 dimensions: (a) the complexity of the phenomena which the subject reports (the visual phenomena can vary in complexity from simple lights or colors to completely formed persons or objects); (b) whether the subject's eyes are closed or open when he reports that he perceives the phenomena; (c) whether the subject reports that he perceives the phenomena "out there" or in his imagination or "mind's eye"; (d) the degree to which the subject believes that the things he perceives actually have an independent existence, are actually out there.

If the term hallucination is used strictly to refer to the extreme end of each of the four dimensions, it is clear that LSD (and psilocybin and mescaline) rarely produce hallucinations. That is, subjects who have ingested one of these drugs very rarely report, when their eyes are open, that they perceive formed persons or objects which they believe are actually out there (Cohen, 1967). Although complex, formed objects are at times reported, this almost always occurs only when the subjects' eyes are closed. Also, whenever formed objects are reported (either with eyes opened or closed), the subjects are practically always aware that the visual effects are due to the drug and are not actually out there. Very few subjects who have taken LSD report perceiving formed objects which they believe are actually out there. In these rare cases the subjects have almost always taken a high, toxic dose of the drug, and are confused and disoriented (Cohen, 1967, p. 52).

On the other hand, hallucinations can be said to be quite common with LSD provided that the term hallucination is used to refer either to (a) the subject's report (when his eyes are open) that he perceives lines, patterns, or colors out there (which he knows are not actually out there), or to (b) the subject's report (when his eyes are closed) that he perceives complex, formed objects in his visual field.

## PHYSIOLOGICAL BASIS OF THE LSD VISUAL PHENOMENA

LSD becomes highly concentrated in the visual system. For instance, as compared to its concentration in the cortex, cerebellum, and midbrain, the concentration of LSD in the iris is 18 times as high and its concentration in the optic chiasma and lateral geniculate nucleus of the visual system is 2 to 6 times as high (Snyder and Reivich, 1966).

The visual phenomena that follow ingestion of LSD appear to be correlated with physiological changes that occur throughout the entire visual system, extending from the pupil, lens, and retina, on through the lateral geniculates and the occipital cortex. I will now trace the physiological changes that occur in various structures within the eyeball (pupil, lens, intraocular fluid, and retina), the possible relations between the LSD visual phenomena and entoptic phenomena, and the relation of the visual phenomena to physiological changes that have occurred at higher levels of the visual system.

PUPIL

LSD, psilocybin, and mescaline produce an enlarged pupil (mydriasis). Since dilation of the pupil allows more light to stimulate the retina, reduces the depth of focus, and maximizes the effects of spherical, chromatic, and other aberrations, it may play a role in producing some of the visual effects that are associated with these drugs. For instance, it may be related to the reports, proffered by some subjects who have taken LSD, that their vision is blurred, they find it difficult to focus their eyes, and they feel as if there is too much light. Furthermore, since the pupillary dilation maximizes chromatic aberrations, it may give rise to the "rainbow effect" (the perception of a series of rainbowlike colors at the edges of objects) which is reported by some subjects who have taken LSD.

Although the mydriasis produced by LSD, psilocybin, and mescaline may give rise to blurring, difficulties in focusing, and possibly the rainbow effect, it is not important in producing the other visual effects such as the illusions and distortions, that are commonly associated with these drugs. In a relevant experiment (Bertino, Klee, Collier, and Weintraub, 1960), subjects first received a sympathetic blocking agent (dibenzyline) and then ingested LSD. Although dibenzyline blocked the pupillary dilation produced by LSD, the subjects still manifested most of the visual distortions and illusions which are characteristically found with LSD.

CILIARY MUSCLE AND LENS

LSD affects the ciliary muscle, producing partial paralysis of the accommodation mechanism (Payne, 1965). Since the adjustment of the lens for various distances (accommodation) is due to contraction of the ciliary muscle (resulting in relaxation of the lens zonules and an increase in the lens thickness), the physiological effect of LSD on the ciliary muscle may play a role in producing the distortions of spatial perception. For example, these changes in the functioning of the lens may give rise to the LSD subjects' reports that objects appear larger or smaller than normal (Heaton, 1968, pp. 138–139).

PRESSURE OF THE INTRAOCULAR FLUID

By exerting pressure on the closed eyeballs, normal individuals (who have not taken a drug) can increase the vividness of the phosphenes. In fact, continuous pressure on the eyeballs at times transforms the starlike objects and luminescent colors into gemlike objects or architectural-like structures.

LSD tends to produce a significant rise in intraocular pressure (Holliday and Sigurdson, 1965). Since phosphenes may be due, in part, to pressure on the retina by the fluids of the eyeball (Ladd-Franklin, 1927), the elevated intraocular pressure may be functionally related to the LSD subject's report that the luminescent dots and colored patterns which he perceives with closed eyes are more vivid than normal or are transformed into gemlike objects or architectural-like structures.

The elevated intraocular pressure may also be related to the rainbow effect that is reported by some subjects who have ingested LSD. This possibility is suggested by the fact that whenever a patient reports that he perceives colored halos around lights the trained ophthalmologist immediately suspects that the pressure in the patient's eyeball may be abnormally high (Adler, 1962, p. 8).

## ENTOPTIC PHENOMENA

Every normal individual is able to see some structures within his own eyeball. These entoptic phenomena (visual phenomena that have their seat within the eyeball) include, for example, the small hazy spots, specks, and hairlike objects that drift across the field of vision with movements of the eyes. These "spots before the eyes" are due to floating impurities in the vitreous humor, such as red blood cells, which cast shadows on the retina and are seen as hovering in space (White and Levatin, 1962).

Marshall (1937) hypothesized that mescaline (and presumably LSD and psilocybin) reduce "the threshold of the visual centres for the perception of low intensities of light-energy so that, with closed eyes or in the dark such almost infinitesimal [entoptic] stimuli . . . are in some measure perceived." Kluver (1966) pointed out that subjects who have taken mescaline typically perceive 3 types of forms when their eyes are closed: spiral-like forms; tunnel- or funnel-like forms; and grating- or lattice-type forms. Kluver hypothesized that mescaline gives rise to these 3 types of forms by enhancing the subject's sensitivity to entoptic phenomena; for instance, the spiral-like forms could be due to entoptic observation of the superficial retinal blood vessels, and the grating- or lattice-type forms could be due to entoptic observation of the regular arrangement of the rods and cones.

Further studies are needed to test the hypothesis that LSD (and psilocybin and mescaline) lower the threshold for the perception of entoptic phenomena. If the hypothesis is valid, we would have an explanation of the mechanisms which underlie some of the visual effects that are associated with these drugs.

## RETINA

It appears that LSD may exert a direct effect on the retina which is independent of its effects on higher levels of the visual system.

Burian, Fleming, and Featherstone (1958) presented subthreshold light flashes to rabbits that were immobilized in a light-tight box. The subliminal stimuli were presented to one group of animals under a control condition and to another group under LSD. The voltage on the electroretinogram produced by the subthreshold stimuli was significantly greater under LSD as compared to the control condition.

Working with humans, Krill, Wieland, and Ostfeld (1960) and Rodin and Luby (1966) found that the beta wave of the electroretinogram increased in amplitude with LSD. Krill, Alpert, and Ostfeld (1963) also showed that the effect on the beta wave is most likely due to a direct action of LSD on the retina (not due to centrifugal influences on the retina from higher centers). These investigators gave LSD to two subjects with total optic nerve atrophy but with functioning retina. Since the beta wave amplitude increased in these subjects in the same way as in normal subjects, it appears that LSD exerts a direct effect on the retina.

Edwards and Cohen (1966) attempted to determine whether the locus of misperception of size with LSD is peripheral or at higher levels of the visual system. They compared subjects' misperception of size when two stimuli are presented simultaneously to both eyes and also independently to the two eyes. Edwards and Cohen reasoned that if the misperception occurs at the retinal level, the two situations should produce the same degree of misperception, that is, higher levels of the visual system should receive information from the retina which was already distorted. Since the two situations produced an equal degree of misperception of size, Edwards and Cohen concluded that the locus of the LSD effect on perception was peripheral, presumably retinal, rather than at higher levels of the visual system.

Studies by Apter and Pfeiffer (1957), Short (1958), and Jacobson and Gestring (1959), which attempted to demonstrate a direct effect of LSD on the retina, led to equivocal results.

Apter and Pfeiffer (1957) observed spontaneous retinal potentials in anesthetized cats 10 minutes after intraperitoneal injection of 100 micrograms of LSD. Two sets of data indicated that the potentials originated in the retina and were not due to centrifugal fibers. (a) The spontaneous potentials were first picked up in the retina and then in the optic nerve. (b) When the optic nerve was cut while the spontaneous potentials were being recorded, the spikes in the occipital cortex and those in the proximal stump of the optic nerve disappeared, while those in the distal stump of the optic nerve and those in the retina persisted. However, Short (1958) failed to confirm these results. In a brief note, Short reported that no significant increase in spontaneous potentials was found in the cat electroretinogram following injections of LSD over a wide range of doses.

Jacobson and Gestring (1959) reported that large doses of LSD (more than 50 micrograms per kilogram of body weight) produced spontaneous retinal potentials in 40% of their animals (cats). However, in contradistinction to the results presented by Apter and Pfeiffer (1957), the spontaneous retinal potentials were no longer observed when the optic nerve was cut. To explain their results, Jacobson and Gestring (1959) hypothesized the existence of an inhibitory center at a higher level of the nervous system which affects the electrical activity of the retina through centrifugal fibers.

In brief, it appears that LSD may effect the retina directly, and also indirectly through an effect on obscure centrifugal pathways.

## HIGHER LEVELS OF THE VISUAL SYSTEM

The visual phenomena associated with LSD (and with psilocybin and mescaline) are not solely due to physiological effects produced by these drugs on structures within the eyeball (the pupil, the lens, the intraocular fluid, and the retina). Higher levels of the visual system are also involved. Reciprocal interactions and feedback mechanisms appear to integrate all levels of the visual system. Activity in the retina and in other structures within the eyeball appears to be integrated with activity at higher levels of the visual system. Consequently, the visual phenomena associated with LSD (and with psilocybin and mescaline) are probably related to the effects of these drugs on the total visual system and are not simply due to their effects on localized anatomical areas such as the retina.

Jacobson and Gestring (1959) could explain their results concerning retinal activity with LSD only by positing a higher center that exerts an inhibitory effect on retinal functions. Krill *et al.* (1963) also presented data which indicated that higher centers are involved. These investigators administered LSD to individuals who were blind, but who still perceived spots, flickers of light, or colors in their visual field. LSD increased the frequency and intensity of the spots, lights, and colors in these blind individuals. Since the retina was not functioning in these subjects, it appears that a normal retina is not necessary for the occurrence of at least some of the visual effects associated with LSD, and that higher levels of the visual system must also play a role in producing these phenomena. In fact, some of the visual phenomena associated with these drugs may be related to the simple noncolored forms that are commonly obtained by stimulation of Area 17 of the occipital lobe, to the complex and colored visual phenomena that are at times elicited by stimulation of the temporal lobe, and to the simple and complex visual phenomena that can be produced by stimulation of other areas of the visual system such as the optic radiations, optic tract, optic chiasma, or optic nerve (Penfield, 1958; Weinberger and Grant, 1940).

From the study of the effects of LSD on blind individuals, Krill *et al.* (1963) concluded that the concept of "localization" may be misleading in attempting to comprehend the visual phenomena associated with LSD. This cogent conclusion is in line with that of Purpura (1967, pp. 158–185) who stated that, "Perceptual disturbances produced by LSD obviously involve more than the neural machinery comprising the classical visual pathways. Insofar as activation of a considerable proportion of the neuraxis from mesencephalon to forebrain occurs as a consequence of a particular visual stimulus, it is well to keep in mind the involvement of diffusely organized nonspecific projection systems in the overt manifestations of the drug."

We will look at the effects of LSD on vision once again at the end of this paper after we have discussed the visual hallucinations that are said to be produced by suggestions.

## SUGGESTIONS, HYPNOTIC INDUCTION, AND VISUAL HALLUCINATION

It has been claimed that suggestions to hallucinate are effective in producing visual hallucinations in many subjects who have been exposed to a hypnotic induction procedure and in some control subjects who have not been exposed to a hypnotic induction (Barber, 1969a; Estabrooks, 1943; Hilgard, 1965; Weitzenhoffer, 1953). Let us first denote the three critical terms in this assertion, namely "suggestions to hallucinate," "hypnotic induction procedure," and "visual hallucination."

Statements such as, "In a moment you will see a [specified object] in the room," are labeled as suggestions to hallucinate when they are given in a situation in which the object is not actually present.

The term hypnotic induction refers to various procedures. For example, the subject may be instructed to keep his gaze on a swinging pendulum or a blinking light, he may be told that he is becoming progressively more and more relaxed, or he may be told repeatedly that he is becoming drowsy, sleepy, and is entering a hypnotic state. These and other procedures are termed hypnotic inductions because they include one common element: they explicitly or implicitly suggest to the subject that he is now entering a unique or different state (a hypnotic or trance state) in which he will be able to have unique or different experiences.

The term visual hallucination commonly refers to the subject's report that he clearly saw the suggested object out there. A few subjects who report that they clearly see the suggested object also report that they believe it is actually out there, and a few behave overtly as if it is actually out there. For example, they "pet" a suggested cat. I will henceforth use the term visual hallucination as is commonly done when referring to the subject's report that he clearly sees the suggested object out there, regardless of whether or not he believes or acts as if what he sees has an independent existence.

In discussing the suggested visual hallucination we can easily fall into a quagmire. Subjects participating in any experiment, and especially subjects participating in an experiment which involves suggestions, may proffer verbal reports which are not in line with their private experiences in order to fulfill the desires of the experimenter or to be "good" subjects (Barber, 1962, 1967 pp. 444–480; Barber and Silver, 1968a, 1968b; Rosenthal, 1968). Specifically, when subjects are instructed to see an object (which is not actually present) they may state that they see it in order to meet the explicit experimental demands. This important consideration must be kept in mind while examining the relevant data.

Four recent studies (Barber and Calverley, 1964; Barber, Spanos, and Merritt, 1970; Bowers, 1967; Spanos and Barber, 1968) attempted to specify the parameters of the suggested visual hallucination. In each of these studies subjects were given suggestions worded as follows: "I want you to look at your lap and to see a cat sitting there. Keep looking at the cat until I tell you to stop." Afterwards the subject checked a rating scale pertaining to the vividness of the suggested hallucination; for example, on the rating scale they checked, "Saw the cat clearly," "Saw a vague impression of the cat," and "Did not see the cat." Some of the subjects in these experiments received the suggestion to hallucinate under a control condition (without any special preliminaries), others received the same suggestion after they had received a hypnotic induction procedure, and still others were given the suggestion after they had received special instructions designed to elicit maximal performance (task-motivational instructions). Also, prior to completing the rating scale pertaining to the vividness of the suggested hallucination, some of the subjects were and others were not exposed to explicit demands for honesty. The results of these experiments can be briefly summarized as follows:

1. *Quite a few subjects reported a visual hallucination when it was suggested under the control condition.* In three of the experiments cited above (Barber and Calverley, 1964; Bowers, 1967; Spanos and Barber, 1968) unselected subjects (college students and nursing students) were given the suggestion to see the cat without any special preliminaries (control condition). From 20% to 33% of the subjects in these control groups reported that they clearly saw the suggested object.

In one of these experiments (Spanos and Barber, 1968) subjects in the control group were told by a co-experimenter that honest reports were desired and that they should not state they saw the object simply because they thought it would please the experimenter. This demand for honesty was made toward the end of the experiment and immediately before the subject rated the vividness of the suggested hallucination. The demand for honesty did not significantly affect the reports of visual hallucinations. Regardless of whether or not honesty was demanded, from 20% to 33% of the control subjects reported that they clearly saw the suggested object.

2. *When honesty was not demanded, more "task-motivated" subjects than control subjects reported visual hallucinations. However, when honesty was demanded once at the end of the experiment, task-motivational instructions did not raise reports of visual hallucinations above the control level.* In 3 of the experiments cited above (Barber and Calverley, 1964; Bowers, 1967; Spanos and

Barber, 1968), some of the subjects were given task-motivational instructions before they received the suggestions to hallucinate. In these task-motivational instructions, the subjects were told that they could perform well on the hallucination task if they tried to "control their mind" and if they took the attitude that it was easy to perform. About 50% of these task-motivated subjects reported that they clearly saw the suggested object. However, when honesty was explicitly demanded of these task-motivated subjects, reports of visual hallucinations were no greater than under the control condition (Barber, 1969b; Bowers, 1967; Spanos and Barber, 1968).

3. *When honesty was not demanded, and also when honesty was demanded only once toward the end of the experiment, more hypnotic subjects than control subjects reported visual hallucinations. However, when honesty was demanded at the beginning of the experiment and several times during the experiment, a hypnotic induction procedure did not raise reports of visual hallucinations above the control level.* When honesty was not demanded, from 53% to 65% of the subjects who had been exposed to a hypnotic induction procedure reported that they clearly saw the suggested object (Barber and Calverley, 1964; Spanos and Barber, 1968). When honesty was demanded once toward the end of the experiment, immediately before the subjects completed the rating scale, 40% of the hypnotic subjects reported a visual hallucination (Spanos and Barber, 1968). However, when subjects were told at the very beginning of the experiment, and several times during the experiment, that complete honesty was desired, the percentage of subjects (18%) under the hypnotic induction condition reporting a visual hallucination was no greater than under the control condition (Barber, *et al.*, 1970).

These results can be compressed as follows: When honesty is demanded once toward the end of the experiment, at least 20% of subjects in a control group and in a task-motivated group report that they clearly saw a suggested object. When honesty is demanded at the beginning of the experiment and several times during the experiment, about 20% of the subjects who have received a hypnotic induction procedure report that they clearly saw a suggested object.

How would we interpret these results? Unfortunately, none of the studies cited above attempted to determine what the subjects meant when they reported that they clearly saw the suggested object. Did some subjects mean that they saw it in the same way that they see an actual object? Did other subjects mean to say that they saw it in the same way they see an afterimage? Did other subjects mean that they clearly saw it in their "mind's eye"? Until such questions are answered, the results cannot be clearly interpreted.

Further studies in this area may find that at least some subjects who state that they clearly see the suggested object are saying that they see it clearly or vividly imagine it in their mind's eye. A neglected study by Sidis (1906) is relevant here. Sidis found that when subjects participated in hypnotic training sessions they reported that the suggested object became increasingly more vivid. However, Sidis also presented data indicating that the trained hypnotic subjects had not learned to hallucinate more proficiently; on the contrary, it appeared that the trained subjects had learned to give the type of verbal reports that were desired and expected. Sidis observed that the subjects gave more emphatic reports concerning the clarity and reality of the suggested object as they participated in more and more hypnotic sessions even though they showed as many signs of deep trance in the first session as in the later sessions. He interpreted these data as indicating that the subjects vividly imagined in the same way in all sessions but had learned, after participating in a number of hypnotic training sessions, that emphatic verbal reports concerning the clarity and lifelike qualities of the suggested object were desired and expected.

Goldiamond and Malpass (1961) also presented data indicating that the reports of hypnotic subjects with respect to visual hallucinations can be rather easily manipulated experimentally. Working with nonhypnotic subjects, Dobie (1959) demonstrated that nonverbal reinforcement procedures are effective in inducing a substantial proportion of normal individuals to testify that they see objects that are not present. Along related lines, Murphy and Myers (1962) found that reports of visual hallucinations in a pseudosensory-deprivation situation (remaining in the dark for only 10 minutes) can be augmented and also inhibited by simple preexperimental instructions to the effect that such hallucinations are normal and desirable or abnormal and undesirable.

Fisher (1962, pp. 109–126) hypothesized that subjects participating in hypnotic experiments "learn the intended thoroughness of hallucinations just as they learn other behavioral consistencies—from reinforcements, approvals, and disapprovals in the context of the situation." Careful research is needed to confirm Sidis' results and to test Fisher's related hypothesis. It may be that 3 factors are involved in the suggested hallucination: (a) the subject's normal ability to image or to imagine; (b) the removal of inhibiting factors so that the subject can utilize his normal abilities maximally; (c) the reinforcement given to the subject for reporting that the suggested object is clear and realistic. The reinforcement may produce more and more emphatic *reports* while the subject's imagery, or imagining, or hallucinating remains constant.


## OBJECTIVE CONCOMITANTS OF SUGGESTED HALLUCINATIONS


A series of investigators have looked at the suggested visual hallucination to try to determine whether there are any objectively measurable effects that are correlated with the subject's report that he clearly sees the suggested object. Objective concomitants of suggested visual hallucinations have been assessed by

measuring pupil dilation and contraction, negative afterimages, distortions produced by optical illusions, and nystagmus. Let us look at the studies pertaining to
each of these measures.

## PUPIL DILATION AND CONTRACTION

The pupil of the eye contracts when stimulated by light and dilates in
darkness. When subjects are given suggestions to visualize vividly or to hallucinate a
bright light, do they show pupillary contraction? Also, when subjects are given
suggestions to visualize vividly or to hallucinate total darkness, do they show
pupillary dilation?

Lundholm (1932) administered a hypnotic induction procedure to selected
hypnotizable subjects and suggested that they were being stimulated by a very
bright light. Although the subjects testified that they clearly saw the suggested
light, none showed observable contraction of the pupil.

In a recent experiment, which is not yet published, Nicholas Spanos and I
used a modern, automatic pupillometer[4] to measure pupil size accurately in two
groups of subjects—a group exposed to a hypnotic induction procedure and a
control group. Subjects in both groups were instructed individually to visualize
vividly that the room was totally dark. Also, the room was made totally dark and
subjects in both groups were instructed to visualize vividly a bright light in the
room. Although some of the subjects in both groups testified that they could
vividly visualize both the totally dark room and the bright light in the room, none
showed clear-cut pupillary dilation when visualizing total darkness or unambiguous
pupillary contraction when visualizing the bright light. The size of the pupils varied
continuously during the experiment and it appeared that pupillary dilation and
contraction were closely related to such factors as "trying to carry out instructions," "mental effort," or "concentration" rather than to "visualizing" per se.

## NEGATIVE AFTERIMAGES

Introductory texts in psychology and physiology characteristically describe
the negative afterimage phenomenon as follows. If a person with normal color
vision fixates on a yellow surface for about 30 seconds and then looks at a neutral
(gray or white) surface, he will see a blue afterimage; and if he fixates on a green
surface and then looks at a neutral surface, he will see a red afterimage. Also, vice
versa, fixation on a blue surface yields a yellow afterimage and fixation on a red
surface gives rise to a green afterimage.

[4] We are indebted to the Polymetric Company of Hoboken, New Jersey, for the loan of
the Pupillometer System, Model V-1165-IR.

Do suggested or hallucinated colors give rise to negative afterimages in the same way as actual colors? Working with selected "good" hypnotic subjects, Erickson and Erickson (1938) and Rosenthal and Mele (1952) reported that "hallucinated colors" gave rise to appropriate negative afterimages in a substantial proportion of subjects. An experiment by Barber (1959) included a group of selected good hypnotic subjects who were exposed to a hypnotic induction procedure and a group of unselected control subjects. Both groups were given suggestions to hallucinate the primary colors. Some subjects in both the hypnotic group and the control group reported that the hallucinated colors gave rise to negative afterimages. When interviewed postexperimentally, almost all of the subjects participating in the experiments of Erickson and Erickson, Rosenthal and Mele, and Barber denied that they had prior knowledge of the negative afterimage phenomenon.[5]

The conclusion indicated by the three studies described above, namely, that suggested or hallucinated colors give rise to negative afterimages, cannot be viewed as firmly established (Barber, 1964). Dorcus (1937), Naruse (1962, pp. 37–55), Elsea (1961), and other investigators failed to find any hypnotic subjects who reported negative afterimages to hallucinated colors. Sidis (1906) found that hypnotic subjects never claimed that hallucinated colors gave rise to negative afterimages when they were unacquainted with the negative afterimage phenomenon; however, they always reported such afterimages after this phenomenon had been carefully explained to them. Hibler (1935, 1940) found that the afterimages reported by hypnotic subjects varied with their preconceptions concerning the afterimage phenomenon. For instance, prior to the formal experiment, Hibler's subjects A, B, and C believed that the afterimage of blue was blue, orange, and yellow, respectively. When exposed to a hypnotic induction procedure and to suggestions to hallucinate blue, subjects A, B, and C testified, in harmony with their preconceptions, that the hallucinated blue gave rise to blue, orange, and yellow afterimages, respectively.

It appears possible that the subjects participating in the experiments that yielded positive results, namely, the experiments of Erickson and Erickson (1938), Rosenthal and Mele (1952), and Barber (1959), also had prior knowledge of the negative afterimage phenomenon. The subjects participating in these experiments almost always described the afterimage of hallucinated blue as yellow, of hallucinated green as red, and vice versa. Although introductory texts give the

[5] Many of these issues were discussed by Segal in the previous chapter. In many instances, the same articles were cited. However, Segal's conclusions are quite notably different from Barber's. Close reading of the relevant sections in the two papers will reveal that there is no real difference of opinion concerning the content of the papers cited, but rather in the relative emphases and the interpretation. Since the interpretations could not be reconciled without seriously violating the viewpoint of at least one of the two authors, the controversy is retained, and the reader can arrive at his own conclusions. (Editorial note.)

impression that blue produces a yellow afterimage, green a red afterimage, and vice versa, there are two reasons why these are misleading statements:

1. When individuals actually look at primary colors, they do *not* describe the negative afterimages in the simplified manner that is stated in introductory texts or in the manner of subjects giving a "correct" performance in the experiments of Erickson and Erickson, Rosenthal and Mele, and Barber. On the contrary, many subjects describe the afterimage of red as various shades of blue (not as green), many subjects describe the afterimage of green as pink, purplish pink, or violet (not as red), and many subjects describe the afterimage of yellow as violet or purple (not as blue) (Elsea, 1961).

2. Not only are there wide interindividual differences in the descriptions of the colors of afterimages, but as Downey (1901) observed, "even under the most unvarying conditions variations in the results obtained from any one individual will occur."

The above considerations suggest that, in the experiments of Erickson and Erickson, Rosenthal and Mele, and Barber, the subjects (college students) who reported red as the afterimage of hallucinated green, blue as the afterimage of hallucinated yellow, and vice versa, may have previously read about the negative afterimage phenomenon. As Sutcliffe (1960) has cogently noted, carefully controlled studies are needed to determine whether individuals who do not have prior knowledge of the afterimage phenomenon experience negative afterimages to vividly imagined or hallucinated colors. Further studies along these lines will have an important bearing in understanding the ramifications of processes labeled as "vivid imagining" or hallucinating.[6]

OPTICAL ILLUSIONS

To determine whether suggested hallucinations produce objective consequences which resemble those produced by actual visual stimulation, Underwood (1960) and Sarbin and Andersen (1963) used two optical illusions in which a series of lines distort a geometric figure. The subjects were shown the geometric figures *without* the distorting lines and were given suggestions to imagine vividly or to hallucinate the lines. If vivid imagining or hallucinating produces objective consequences similar to those produced by visual perception or visual stimulation, then the hallucination of the lines should produce an optical illusion, that is, should

---

[6] Several investigators have reported that some subjects with eidetic imagery perceive negative afterimages when they visualize colors (Kluver, 1928). The considerations mentioned above with respect to hallucinated colors also apply to the earlier studies on eidetic imagery. That is, it appears possible that the eidetic subjects had prior knowledge of the negative afterimage phenomenon, and it remains to be determined whether eidetic subjects who do not have such prior knowledge report negative afterimages when they visualize colors.

produce distortions in the appearance of the geometric figure. (Since the optical illusions were culled from obscure research reports, the investigators could be practically certain that the subjects were not previously acquainted with them.)

Underwood (1960) selected 6 subjects (from an original group of 195) as the most hypnotizable and as having the greatest ability to hallucinate. The 6 subjects were exposed to a hypnotic induction procedure and, when they were judged to be in "deep trance," were shown the geometric figures and given suggestions to hallucinate the lines superimposed upon them. Each of the 6 hypnotic subjects testified that he could clearly see the (suggested) lines. A control group, comprised of 6 unselected subjects, was asked to guess in what way the geometric figures would be distorted if the lines were superimposed. As compared to the control group, there was a nonsignificant tendency for the hypnotic subjects to report more distortions in the geometric figures. However, the distortions in the geometric figures produced by the hallucinated lines differed in several important respects from the distortions produced by the actual lines.

Sarbin and Andersen (1963) conducted a related study with 120 unselected college students. Under normal (nonhypnotic) conditions, the subjects were shown the same geometric figures that had been used by Underwood and were asked to imagine vividly that the lines were superimposed. Nine percent of the subjects reported some distortions in the geometric figures which tended to resemble those normally produced by the optical illusion but were not identical with them. Unfortunately, Sarbin and Andersen did not use a control group of subjects asked to try to figure out how the geometric figures would be distorted if the lines were superimposed.

In brief, the experiments of Underwood and of Sarbin and Andersen failed to demonstrate that hallucinating or vivid imagining produces effects which are similar to those produced by actual visual stimulation by an optical illusion figure. However, these experiments offer some tentative support for the hypothesis that hallucinating or vivid imagining may give rise to *some* objective effects. Further studies with the optical illusions which are designed to test the hypothesis should, of course, compare a group of hallucinating subjects with a group told simply to try to figure out the effect.

## NYSTAGMUS

When an individual gazes steadily at a rotating kymograph drum which is painted with vertical black and white stripes, he manifests nystagmus, that is, his eyes move rhythmically from side to side, quickly to one side and then slowly to the other. Brady and Levitt (1966) reasoned that if visual hallucinations induced in hypnotic subjects produce objective effects similar to those produced by visual stimulation, then the hypnotic subjects should show nystagmus when they hallucinate the rotating black and white drum. To test this hypothesis, 9 hypnotic subjects were carefully selected from an original group of 48 individuals as meeting criteria for vivid visual hallucinations. During the experiment, eye movements were monitored electrically on a polygraph. The selected subjects first watched the black and white stripes rotating on the drum. The drum was removed and, after a hypnotic induction procedure was administered, suggestions were given to induce a hallucination of the rotating drum. When hallucinating the rotating drum, 1 of the 9 hypnotic subjects showed nystagmus 70% of the time, 3 showed nystagmus about 10% of the time, and the remaining 5 subjects did not manifest nystagmus.

Hahn and Barber (1966) conducted a similar experiment but they did not use hypnotic induction procedures. The technique for measuring nystagmus was the same as that used by Brady and Levitt (1966). Nine unselected subjects were tested individually under normal (nonhypnotic) conditions. Each subject first watched the black and white stripes rotating on the drum. After the drum was removed each subject was instructed to imagine vividly and to visualize the rotating black and white drum. When vividly imagining the rotating drum, 1 of the 9 subjects showed clear-cut nystagmus. Rhythmical side-to-side movements of the eyes (quickly to one side and then slowly to the other) were present more than 90% of the time when the subject was vividly imagining the rotating drum regardless of whether her eyes were open or closed. Of the remaining 8 subjects, 3 showed nystagmus at least 35% of the time when they were imagining the rotating drum and the remaining 5 did not show nystagmus.

In both the Brady and Levitt and the Hahn and Barber experiments, the subjects failed to manifest nystagmus when they were asked to try to produce it voluntarily. However, Reich (1970) recently presented data indicating that some subjects are able to produce nystagmus "through conscious, voluntary efforts while awake."

In brief, the studies of Brady and Levitt (1966) and of Hahn and Barber (1966) appeared to indicate that when vividly imagining or hallucinating a black and white rotating drum some individuals show eye movements (nystagmus) which resemble those found when they actually look at the rotating drum. However, since a recent study (Reich, 1970) indicates that some subjects can produce nystagmus voluntarily, extreme caution is needed in interpreting these results. Further studies are needed before we can unequivocally reject or accept the hypothesis that vivid imagining or hallucinating per se gives rise to an objective effect (nystagmus) which resembles that produced by actual visual stimulation.

## SUMMARY AND CONCLUSIONS

Although LSD produces a wide variety of effects, including alterations in body-image, in tactile sensitivity, and in perception of time, I have focused in this paper on the effect of LSD on visual perception. When an individual closes his eyes after he has taken a moderate dose of LSD, he typically perceives vividly colored forms. Also, when his eyes are open, he reports a change in his perception of colors and in the size and shape of objects, persons, and his own body. Speaking more generally, LSD affects the constancies of perception and tends to produce distortions, illusions, vivid imagery, and hallucinations.

The subject's attitudes, expectancies, and personality characteristics may affect the contents of the LSD visual phenomena. As compared to individuals with ordinary imagery, individuals with strong imagery (who normally project their visual images in front of their eyes) report more intense visual phenomena with LSD. Also, the characteristics of the visual phenomena may be affected to some extent by explicit or implicit suggestions. However, these kinds of variables, suggestions, expectancies, personality characteristics, etc., have been overemphasized in previous discussions of this topic. Although the characteristics of the subject and suggestions imbedded in the situation may play a role, they are *not* the most important factors either in eliciting the LSD visual phenomena or in determining their contents or intensity. What needs to be emphasized now is that the visual phenomena associated with LSD are closely correlated with the *dose* of the drug. The number and intensity of the visual phenomena are strongly associated with the dose of LSD and weakly associated with the subject's expectancies and with suggestions that are present in the situation.[7]

It appears that LSD gives rise to changes in visual perception by producing physiological changes in the visual system. Some of the visual phenomena associated with LSD appear to be closely related to alterations produced by this drug on structures within the eyeball (the pupil, the lens, the intraocular fluid, and the retina). This includes the blurring of vision, difficulties in focusing, and the rainbow-effect. The distortions in spatial perception and the alterations in the constancies of perception which are associated with LSD may be due to the partial paralysis of the ciliary muscle (and the concomitant deficiency in the accommodating power of the lens). The vivid patterns that are perceived with eyes closed may be related both to the increased intraocular pressure which is produced by LSD and also to a direct effect of this drug on the retina.

Some, but not all, of the visual phenomena associated with LSD appear to be due to a physiological effect of this drug on structures within the eyeball. However, to understand all of the LSD visual phenomena we need to delineate more precisely the effects of LSD on the entire visual system. The data at present suggest that LSD does not simply affect the functioning of structures within the eyeball; it appears that LSD also affects the lateral geniculates and the occipital cortex and, more generally, exerts an effect on the functioning of the total visual system.

[7] Although the *dose* of LSD accounts for most of the variance with respect to the *visual phenomena,* suggestions, expectancies, attitudes, personality characteristics and other non-drug variables are the critical factors in determining the subject's moods, emotions, and cognitions in the drug situation (Barber, 1970).

It has been stated that the vivid imagery or hallucinations that are produced by LSD can also be produced by suggestions given under hypnosis. However, it seems that the hypnotic or suggested phenomena differ in several important respects from the LSD phenomena.

When unselected subjects (college students or nursing students) are exposed to a hypnotic induction procedure and are given suggestions to see an object that is not actually present, more than half report that they clearly see the object. However, when the subjects are told at the beginning of the experiment and several times during the experiment that honest reports are wanted, less than 20% of the hypnotic subjects report that they clearly see the suggested object. Also, when an honest report is demanded once at the end of the experiment, about 20% of unselected subjects who have *not* been exposed to a hypnotic induction procedure (controls) state that they clearly see the suggested object.

It is by no means clear, at the present time, what these subjects (around 20% in a hypnotic group and also in a control group) mean when they report that they clearly see a suggested object. Unfortunately, no empirical studies have as yet ascertained whether subjects mean that they see the suggested object in the same way they see an actual object or in the same way they see a negative or positive afterimage, or whether they simply mean that they see it clearly in their mind's eye.

Regardless of whether or not some subjects see a suggested object out there and others see it in their mind's eye, it has not as yet been shown that these suggested hallucinations give rise to objective effects which are independent of the subjects' verbal reports. There is no clear evidence that suggested hallucinations give rise to pupillary dilations or contractions, or to negative afterimages. Also, a suggested hallucination of an optical illusion does not have the same effects as an actual illusion. And, even though vivid imagery of revolving stripes may produce objective nystagmus, this is not a conclusive demonstration, as nystagmus can be produced voluntarily.

In brief, it appears that subjects who have taken LSD experience alterations in visual perception which are based on physiological changes that have occurred throughout the visual system. The effects of suggestions to hallucinate (given under either hypnotic or nonhypnotic conditions) appear to differ qualitatively from the visual effects of LSD. There is no evidence that suggestions to hallucinate produce physiological changes in the visual system which affect visual perception. In fact, the hypothesis that needs to be tested in further research is that suggestions to hallucinate simply induce the subject to imagine or to image to the best of his ability.

## REFERENCES

Abramson, H. A. Lysergic acid diethylamide (LSD-25): XXX. The questionnaire technique with notes on its use. *Journal of Psychology*, 1960, **49**, 57-65.

Abramson, H. A., Kornetsky, C., Jarvik, M. E., Kaufman, M. R., & Ferguson, M. W. Lysergic acid diethylamide (LSD-25): XI. Content analysis of clinical reactions. *Journal of Psychology*, 1955, **40**, 53-60.

Adler, F. H. *Textbook of ophthalmology.* (7th ed.) Philadelphia: W. B. Saunders, 1962.

Anderson, E. W., & Rawnsley, K. Clinical studies of lysergic acid diethylamide. *Monatsschrift für Psychiatrie und Neurologie*, 1954, **128**, 38-55.

Apter, J. T., & Pfeiffer, C. C. The effects of the hallucinogenic drugs LSD-25 and mescaline on the electroretinogram. *Annals of the New York Academy Sciences*, 1957, **66** (Art. 3) 508-514.

Balestrieri, A., & Fontanari, D. Acquired and crossed tolerance to mescaline, LSD-25, and BOL-148. *Archives of General Psychiatry*, 1959, **1**, 279-282.

Barber, T. X. The after-images of "imagined" and "hallucinated" colors. *Journal of Abnormal and Social Psychology*, 1959, **59**, 136-139.

Barber, T. X. Experimental controls and the phenomena of "hypnosis": A critique of hypnotic research methodology. *Journal of Nervous and Mental Diseases*, 1962, **134**, 493-505.

Barber, T. X. Hypnotically hallucinated colors and their negative after-images. *American Journal of Psychology*, 1964, **77**, 313-318.

Barber, T. X. "Hypnotic" phenomena: A critique of experimental methods. In J. E. Gordon (Ed.) *Handbook of clinical and experimental hypnosis.* New York: Macmillan, 1967.

Barber, T. X. *Hypnosis: A scientific approach.* New York: Van Nostrand Reinhold, 1969. (a)

Barber, T. X. "Hypnosis," suggestions, and auditory-visual "hallucinations": A critical analysis. Paper presented at Eastern Psychiatric Research Association, New York, November 14, 1969. (b)

Barber, T. X. *LSD, marihuana, yoga, and hypnosis.* Chicago: Aldine, 1970.

Barber, T. X., & Calverley, D. S. An experimental study of "hypnotic" (auditory and visual) hallucinations. *Journal of Abnormal and Social Psychology*, 1964, **68**, 13-20.

Barber, T. X. & Silver, M. J. Fact, fiction, and the experimenter bias effect. *Psychological Bulletin*, 1968, **70**, No. 6, Part 2 (Monograph Supplement), 1-29. (a)

Barber, T. X., & Silver, M. J. Pitfalls in data analysis and interpretation: A reply to Rosenthal. *Psychological Bulletin*, 1968, **70**, No. 6, Part 2 (Monograph Supplement), 48-62. (b)

Barber, T. X., Spanos, N., & Merritt, J. The effect of strong demands for honesty on the suggested ("hypnotic") hallucination. Harding, Mass.: Medfield Foundation, 1970.

Bercel, N. A., Travis, L. E., Olinger, L. B., & Dreikurs, E. Model psychoses induced by LSD-25 in normals: I. Psychophysiological investigations with special reference to the mechanism of the paranoid reaction. *Archives of Neurology and Psychiatry*, 1956, **75**, 588-611.

Bertino, J. R., Klee, G. D., Collier, D., & Weintraub, W. Clinical studies with dibenzyline and lysergic acid diethylamide. *Journal of Clinical and Experimental Psychopathology*, 1960, **21**, 293-299.

Bowers, K. S. The effects of demands for honesty on reports of visual and auditory hallucinations. *International Journal of Clinical and Experimental Hypnosis*, 1967, **15**, 31-36.

Brady, J. P., & Levitt, E. E. Hypnotically induced visual hallucinations. *Psychosomatic Medicine*, 1966, **28**, 351-363.

Brown, B. B. Subjective and EEG responses to LSD in visualizer and nonvisualizer subjects. *EEG Clinical Neurophysiology*, 1968, **25**, 372-379.

Burian, H. M., Fleming, W. J., & Featherstone, R. M. Electroretinographic effects of LSD-25, Brom-LSD, and LSM (lysergic acid morpholide). *Federation Proceedings*, 1958, **17**, 355.

Cohen, S. *The beyond within: The LSD story.* (2nd ed.) New York: Atheneum, 1967.

Cohen, S. A quarter century of research with LSD. In J. T. Ungerleider (Ed.), *The problem and prospects of LSD.* Springfield, Ill.: C. C. Thomas, 1968.

Ditman, K. S., Moss, T., Forgy, E. W., Zunin, L. M., Lynch, R. D., & Funk, W. A. Dimensions of the LSD, methylphenidate, and chlordiazepoxide experiences. *Psychopharmacologia,* 1969, **14,** 1-11.

Dobie, S. Operant conditioning of verbal and hallucinatory responses with nonverbal reinforcement. Paper presented at Midwestern Psychological Association, Chicago, May, 1959.

Dorcus, R. M. Modification by suggestion of some vestibular and visual responses. *American Journal of Psychology,* 1937, **49,** 82-87.

Downey, J. E. An experiment on getting an after-image from a mental image. *Psychological Review,* 1901, 8, 42- 55.

Edwards, A. E., & Cohen, S. Visual illusion, tactile sensibility and reaction time under LSD-25. *Psychopharmacologia,* 1961, **2,** 297-303.

Edwards, A. E., & Cohen, S. Interaction of LSD and quantity of encoded visual data upon size estimation. *Journal of Psychopharmacology,* 1966, **1,** 96-100.

Elsea, O. C., Jr. A study of the effect of hypnotic suggestion on color perception. Unpublished doctoral dissertation, University of Oklahoma, 1961.

Erickson, M. H., & Erickson, E. M. The hypnotic induction of hallucinatory color vision followed by pseudo negative after images. *Journal of Experimental Psychology,* 1938, **22,** 581-588.

Estabrooks, G. H. *Hypnotism.* New York: E. P. Dutton, 1943.

Farnsworth, N. R. Hallucinogenic plants. *Science,* 1968, **162,** 1086-1092.

Fiddleman, P. B. The prediction of behavior under lysergic acid diethylamide (LSD). Unpublished doctoral dissertation, University of North Carolina, 1961.

Fisher, S. Problems of interpretation and controls in hypnotic research. In G. H. Estabrooks (Ed.) *Hypnosis: Current problems.* New York: Harper & Row, 1962.

Fogel, S., & Hoffer, A. The use of hypnosis to interrupt and to reproduce an LSD-25 experience. *Journal of Clinical and Experimental Psychopathology,* 1962, **23,** 11-16.

Goldiamond, I., & Malpass, L. F. Locus of hypnotically induced changes in color vision responses. *Journal of the Optical Society of America,* 1961, **51,** 1117-1121.

Hahn, K. W., Jr., & Barber, T. X. Hallucinations with and without hypnotic induction: An extension of the Brady and Levitt study. Harding, Mass.: Medfield Foundation, 1966.

Hartman, A. M., & Hollister, L. E. Effect of mescaline, lysergic acid diethylamide and psilocybin on color perception. *Psychopharmacologia,* 1963, **4,** 441-451.

Heaton, J. M. *The eye: Phenomenology and psychology of function and disorder.* Philadelphia: J. B. Lippincott, 1968.

Hibler, F. W. An experimental study of positive visual hallucinations in hypnosis. Unpublished doctoral dissertation, Ohio State University, 1935.

Hibler, F. W. An experimental investigation of negative after-images of hallucinated colors in hypnosis. *Journal of Experimental Psychology,* 1940, **27,** 45-57.

Hilgard, E. R. *Hypnotic susceptibility.* New York: Harcourt, Brace & World, 1965.

Hoffer, A., & Osmond, H. *The hallucinogens.* New York: Academic Press, 1967.

Holliday, A. R., & Sigurdson, T. The effects of lysergic acid diethylamide II: Intraocular pressure. *Proceedings of the Western Pharmacological Society,* 1965, **8,** 51-54.

Hollister, L. E. *Chemical psychoses: LSD and related drugs.* Springfield, Ill.: C. C. Thomas, 1968.

Hollister, L. E., & Hartman, A. M. Mescaline, lysergic acid diethylamide and psilocybin: Comparison of clinical syndromes, effects on color perception, and biochemical measures. *Comprehensive Psychiatry,* 1962, **3,** 235-241.

Hollister, L. E., Macnicol, M. F., & Gillespie, H. K. An hallucinogenic amphetamine analog (DOM) in man. *Psychopharmacologia,* 1969, **14,** 62-73.

Huxley, A. *The doors of perception.* New York: Harper, 1954.

Isbell, H. Comparison of the reactions induced by psilocybin and LSD-25 in man. *Psychopharmacologia,* 1959, **1**, 29-38.

Isbell, H. *Studies on tetrahydrocannabinol. I. Method of assay in human subjects and results with crude extracts, purified tetrahydrocannabinols and synthetic compounds.* Lexington, Kentucky: University of Kentucky Medical Center, 1967.

Isbell, H., Belleville, R. E., Fraser, H. F., Wikler, A., & Logan, C. R. Studies on lysergic acid diethylamide (LSD-25): I. Effects in former morphine addicts and development of tolerance during chronic intoxication. *Archives of Neurology and Psychiatry,* 1956, **76**, 468-478.

Isbell, H., Gorodetzsky, C. W. Jasinski, D., Claussen, U., Spulak, F. V., & Korte, F. Effects of $(-)$-$\Delta^9$*trans*-tetrahydrocannabinol in man. *Psychopharmacologia,* 1967, **11**, 184-188.

Isbell, H., Wolbach, A. B., Wikler, A., & Miner, E. J. Cross-tolerance between LSD and psilocybin. *Psychopharmacologia,* 1961, **2**, 147-151.

Jacobson, J. H., & Gestring, G. F. Spontaneous retinal electrical potentials. *Archives of Ophthalmology,* 1959, **62**, 599-603.

Johnson, F. G. LSD in the treatment of alcoholism. Paper presented at American Psychiatric Association, Boston, June, 1968.

Keeler, M. H. The effects of psilocybin on a test of after-image perception. *Psychopharmacologia,* 1965, **8**, 131-139.

Kieffer, S. N., & Moritz, T. B. Psychedelic drugs. *Pennsylvania Medicine,* 1968, **71**, 57-67.

Klee, G. D., Bertino, J., Weintraub, W., & Callaway, E. The influence of varying dosage on the effects of lysergic acid diethylamide (LSD-25) in humans. *Journal of Nervous and Mental Disease,* 1961, **132**, 404-409.

Kluver, H. Studies on the eidetic type and on eidetic imagery. *Psychological Bulletin,* 1928, **25**, 69-104.

Kluver, H. *Mescal and mechanisms of hallucination.* Chicago: University of Chicago Press, 1966.

Knoll, M., & Kugler, J. Subjective light-pattern spectroscopy in the electroencephalographic frequency range. *Nature,* 1959, **184**, 1823.

Knoll, M., Kugler, J., Hofer, O., & Lawder, S. D. Effects of chemical stimulation of electrically induced phosphenes on their bandwidth, shape, number and intensity. *Confinia Neurologica,* 1963, **23**, 201-226.

Krill, A. E., Alpert, H. J., & Ostfeld, A. M. Effects of a hallucinogenic agent in totally blind subjects. *Archives of Ophthalmology,* 1963, **69**, 180-185.

Krill, A. E., Wieland, A. M., & Ostfeld, A. M. The effects of two hallucinogenic agents on human retinal function. *Archives of Ophthalmology,* 1960, **64**, 724-733.

Ladd-Franklin, C. Visible radiation from excited nerve fiber: The reddish blue arcs and the reddish blue glow of the retina. *Science,* 1927, **66**, 239-241.

Levis, D. J., & Mehlman, B. Suggestion and mescaline sulphate. *Journal of Neuropsychiatry,* 1964, **5**, 197-200.

Liebert, R. S., Wapner, S., & Werner, H. Studies in the effects of lysergic acid diethylamide (LSD-25). Visual perception of verticality in schizophrenic and normal adults. *Archives of Neurology and Psychiatry,* 1957, **77**, 193-201.

Lundholm, H. A hormic theory of hallucinations. *British Journal of Medical Psychology,* 1932, **11**, 269-282.

Marshall, C. R. An enquiry into the causes of mescal vision. *Journal of Neuropathology and Psychopathology,* 1937, **17**, 289-304.

Masters, R. E. L., & Houston, J. *The varieties of psychedelic experience.* New York: Holt, 1966.

Murphy, D. B., & Meyers, T. I. Occurrence, measurement, and experimental manipulation of visual "hallucinations." *Perceptual and Motor Skills*, 1962, **15**, 47-54.

Naruse, G. Hypnosis as a state of meditative concentration and its relationship to the perceptual process. In M. V. Kline (Ed.), *The nature of hypnosis*. New York: Institute for Research in Hypnosis, 1962.

Pahnke, W. N., & Richards, W. A. Implications of LSD and experimental mysticism. *Journal of Religion and Health*, 1966, **5**, 175-208.

Payne, J. W. LSD-25 and accommodative convergence ratios. *Archives of Ophthalmology*, 1965, **74**, 81-85.

Penfield, W. *The excitable cortex in conscious man*. Springfield, Ill.: C. C. Thomas, 1958.

Purpura, D. P. Neurophysiological actions of LSD. In R. C. Debold and R. C. Leaf (Eds.) *LSD, man and society*. Middletown, Conn.: Wesleyan University Press, 1967.

Reich, L. H. Optokinetic nystagmus during hypnotic hallucinations. Paper presented at Eastern Psychological Association, Atlantic City, April 4, 1970.

Rodin, E., & Luby, E. Effects of LSD-25 on the EEG and photic evoked responses. *Archives of General Psychiatry*, 1966, **14**, 435-441.

Rosenberg, D. E., Isbell, H., Miner, E. J., & Logan, C. R. The effects of *N,N*-dimethyltryptamine in human subjects tolerant to lysergic acid diethylamide. *Psychopharmacologia*, 1964, **5**, 217-227.

Rosenthal, B. G., & Mele, H. The validity of hypnotically induced color hallucinations. *Journal of Abnormal and Social Psychology*, 1952, **47**, 700-704.

Rosenthal, R. Experimenter expectancy and the reassuring nature of the null hypothesis decision procedure. *Psychological Bulletin*, 1968, **70**, No. 6, Part 2 (Monograph Supplement), 30-47.

Sarbin, T. R., & Andersen, M. L. Base-rate expectancies and perceptual alterations in hypnosis. *British Journal of Clinical Psychology*, 1963, **2**, 112-121.

Schultes, R. E. Hallucinogens of plant origin. *Science*, 1969, **163**, 245-254.

Short, W. B., Jr. The effects of drugs on the electroretinogram of the cat. *Journal of Pharmacology and Experimental Therapeutics*, 1958, **122**, 68A.

Shryne, J. E., Jr., & Brown, B. B. Effect of LSD on responses to colored photic stimuli as related to visual imagery ability in man. *Proceedings of the Western Pharmacological Society*, 1965, **8**, 42-46.

Sidis, B. Are there hypnotic hallucinations? *Psychological Review*, 1906, **13**, 239-257.

Snyder, S. H., Faillace, L., & Hollister, L. 2,5-Dimethoxy-4-methylamphetamine (STP): A new hallucinogenic drug. *Science*, 1967, **158**, 669-670.

Snyder, S. H., Faillace, L. A., & Weingartner, H. DOM (STP) a new hallucinogenic drug, and DOET: Effects in normal subjects. *American Journal of Psychiatry*, 1968, **125**, 357-364.

Snyder, S. H., & Reivich, M. Regional localization of lysergic acid diethylamide in monkey brain. *Nature*, 1966, **209**, 1093-1095.

Spanos, N. P., & Barber, T. X. "Hypnotic" experiences as inferred from subjective reports: Auditory and visual hallucinations. *Journal of Experimental Research in Personality*, 1968, **3**, 136-150.

Sutcliffe, J. P. "Credulous" and "sceptical" views of hypnotic phenomena: A review of certain evidence and methodology. *International Journal of Clinical and Experimental Hypnosis*, 1960, **8**, 73-101.

Szara, S., Rockland, L. H., Rosenthal, D., & Handlon, J. H. Psychological effects and metabolism of *N,N*-diethyltryptamine in man. *Archives of General Psychiatry*, 1966, **15**, 320-329.

Underwood, H. W. The validity of hypnotically induced visual hallucinations. *Journal of Abnormal and Social Psychology,* 1960, **61,** 39-46.

Unger, S. M. Mescaline, LSD, psilocybin, and personality change. *Psychiatry,* 1963, **26,** 111-125.

Weckowicz, T. E. The effect of lysergic acid diethylamide (LSD) on size constancy. *Canadian Psychiatric Association Journal,* 1959, 4, 255-259.

Weinberger, L. M., & Grant, F. C. Visual hallucinations and their neuro-optical correlates. *Ophthalmologic Reviews,* 1940, **23,** 166-199.

Weitzenhoffer, A. M. *Hypnotism: An objective study in suggestibility.* New York: Wiley, 1953.

White, H. E., & Levatin, P. "Floaters" in the eyes. *Scientific American,* 1962, **206,** No. 6, 119-127.

Wolbach, A. B., Miner, E. J., & Isbell, H. Comparison of psilocin with psilocybin, mescaline, and LSD-25 *Psychopharmacologia,* 1962, 3, 219-223.

# VIII

## APPLICATIONS

# Autogenic Therapy: Excerpts 33 on Applications to Cardiovascular Disorders and Hypercholesteremia

W. Luthe

The method of autogenic training, developed many years ago in Germany, is a series of six exercises. These are practiced several times a day until eventually the individual becomes readily able to shift to a low arousal (trophotropic) condition whenever he wishes to do so. This low arousal (trophotropic) condition is conceived as having effects opposite to those produced by stress.

The Standard Exercises are preferably carried out in quiet surroundings. Exercise 1 focuses on the cultivation of heaviness in the limbs, Exercise 2 on the cultivation of warmth in the limbs. Both heaviness and warmth sensations, it may be noted, are physiologically linked with muscular relaxation and increased peripheral blood flow.

There are four additional exercises. Cardiac regulation is the focus of Exercise 3, while Exercise 4 consists of passive concentration on breathing. In Exercise 5, the trainee cultivates feelings of warmth in his upper abdomen. Finally, Exercise 6 involves the cultivation of agreeable sensations of coolness in the forehead.

Learning the Standard Exercises can take anywhere from several weeks to many months, depending on the patient's ability. An important feature of the training is that the progression and sequencing of the exercises is tailored to the requirements of the individual. In order for the therapist to guide his progress, the patient regularly reports on the sensations he experienced during the exercises—so there is actually a type of feedback built into the system.

Also of great importance is the use of frequent home practice—a minimum of three five-minute sessions per day is recommended. For every exercise a "verbal formula" is employed. For example, in the heaviness exercise, the trainee repeats "my arms and legs are heavy" during the course of the exercise. This procedure helps the subject to pay attention to the appropriate bodily part or function—e.g., heaviness in right arm, or warmth in arms and legs.

As he carries out a given exercise, the trainee's attention to a particular body part must *not* be of the intense, striving kind. Rather, his attitude must be of the quiet, "letting it happen" variety. This is referred to as "passive concentration" and is absolutely essential to progress in the exercises.

The basic autogenic exercises—along with certain additional techniques which are adapted to fit the needs of the individual patient—have been applied to a formidable array of disorders, many of them stress-related. Included in the following excerpts from Luthe's recent five-volume work on *Autogenic Therapy* (1969, 1970; Grune and Stratton) are a short history of the technique and a discussion of its application to angina pectoris, essential hypertension and hypercholesteremia.

# 1. Introduction

Autogenic training is the basic therapeutic method of a group of psychophysiologically oriented autogenic approaches which constitute "Autogenic Therapy." In contrast to other medically or psychologically oriented forms of treatment, the methods of autogenic therapy approach and involve mental and bodily functions simultaneously.

The term "autogenic" (self-generating) refers to two therapeutic aspects which distinguish this therapy from other methods. From a psychophysiologic point of view, the term "autogenic" characterizes the therapeutic implications resulting from a self-induced psychophysiologic shift to a specific state (autogenic state) which facilitates autogenic (brain-directed, self-generating, self-regulatory) processes of self-normalizing nature. In other words, autogenic training and related autogenic approaches are designed to promote and to give specifically adapted support to those brain-directed self-regulatory (autogenic) mechanisms which normally participate in homeostatic, recuperative and self-normalizing processes. From a clinically very general point of view, the physiological and psychophysiologically oriented effects of autogenic approaches may be considered as being diametrically opposed to changes elicited by stress.

In a larger methodologically oriented sense, the term "autogenic" also encompasses the favorable therapeutic implications related to the fact that the patient is largely responsible for carrying out his own treatment by performing certain mental exercises regularly ("training"), thus promoting in himself certain self-normalizing functions which are directed and coordinated by his brain.

From a technical point of view, the autogenic approach hinges initially on bringing about a psychophysiologic shift (*Umschaltung*) from a normal state to the autogenic state which facilitates and mobilizes the otherwise inhibited activity of recuperative and self-normalizing brain mechanisms. The shift to the autogenic state is facilitated by conditions involving a significant reduction of afferent and efferent impulses, and the regular practice of short periods of *passive concentration* upon psychophysiologically adapted stimuli (i.e., autogenic standard formulae).

During the autogenic state, which is not identical with apparently similar phases of sleep or hypnosis, combinations of various physiologically or psychologically oriented approaches specifically adapted to given therapeutic requirements can be applied. Essentially six categories of autogenic approaches may be distinguished (see Fig. 1):

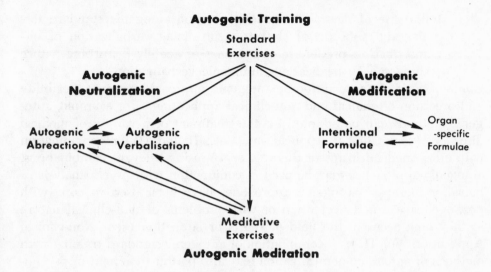

FIG. 1. Schematic presentation of various combinations of autogenic approaches. The arrows indicate therapeutic possibilities of treatment programs using case-adapted combinations of specific autogenic methods, which may be indicated after the patient has learned the six standard exercises of autogenic training.

(a) Use of *passive concentration* on autogenic standard formulae aiming mainly at multidimensional psychophysiologic relaxation and facilitation of certain self-normalizing brain functions during the autogenic state (Autogenic Training: six standard exercises).

(b) Use of *passive concentration* for the purpose of promoting additional physiologic changes of a more specific nature (Autogenic Modifications: organ-specific exercises).

(c) Use of *passive concentration* on additional case-adapted formulas which are more specifically designed to support or neutralize psychologically oriented functions (Autogenic Modifications: intentional formulae).

(d) Initial use of *passive concentration* upon autogenic standard formulas (see a) with subsequent engagement in advanced exercises of the Meditative Series (Autogenic Meditation: seven meditative exercises).

(e) Initial use of *passive concentration* upon autogenic standard formulas (see a) and subsequent shift to *passive acceptance* ("*carte blanche*") for further facilitation of brain-directed processes of psychophysiologic neutralization (Autogenic Neutralization: autogenic abreaction).

(f) Initial use of *passive concentration* upon autogenic standard formulas and subsequent shift to neutralizing verbalization of circumscribed or predetermined themes of acutely disturbing nature (Autogenic Neutralization: autogenic verbalization).

Combinations of these different autogenic approaches permit flexibility and precision of clinical and non-clinical application. For example, autogenic methods can be adapted for the treatment of a variety of medical disorders (see: Clinical Applications, Vols. II and III) in combination with other medical forms of therapy, or, by using relevant combinations, autogenic approaches may be used in conjunction with psychoanalysis or behavior therapy. Autogenic approaches have been used to cope with post-operative urinary retention or with problems of non-clinical nature as they may occur in the field of sports or education (see: Non-clinical Application, Vol. III). A combination of autogenic standard training with methods of autogenic neutralization may also permit treatment of psychodynamic disturbances which are beyond the limits of psychoanalysis.

For purposes of quick orientation, a number of points concerning applicability, predictability and control of autogenic therapy may be presented:

Clinical results demonstrate that many patients suffering from a variety of long-standing psychosomatic disorders like chronic constipation, bronchial asthma, cardiospasm, and sleep disorders have been cured or have improved considerably in periods ranging from two to eight months.

It has been observed that behavior disorders and motor disturbances like stuttering, writer's cramp, nocturnal enuresis, certain states of anxiety and phobia and other neurotic disorders can be treated effectively. Over periods ranging from a few weeks to several months, depending on the particular case, patients have reported that their anxiety, insecurity and neurotic reactions have smoothed out or have gradually lost their significance. Generally, an increase in emotional and physiologic tolerance, with a considerable decrease in the previous need for reactive affective discharge, is reported. Social contact becomes less inhibited and more natural. Interpersonal relations are reported as warmer and more intimate with certain persons and less emotionally involved with others.

It has been noted that autogenic therapy improves self-regulatory functions and thus not only enhances a person's overall capacity for psychophysiologic adaptation but also increases bodily resistance to all kinds of stress.

Furthermore, it has been observed that with the help of autogenic training, unconscious material becomes more readily available. Dream material and memories can be more easily reproduced by trainees than by other patients, and free association also appears to be enhanced.

In contrast to other psychotherapeutic approaches, relatively little time is required for this type of therapy. When each step of a series of mental exercises has been introduced to the patient, only periodic control sessions for guiding the patient are required. The patient carries out his own therapy by performing a number of mental exercises for about ten minutes three times a day.

Group therapy is possible.

The effectiveness and the progress of the therapy can be controlled by physiologic and psychologic tests. In most cases it can be predicted, after only a few sessions, whether or not the patient will respond to the therapy.

Autogenic training can be applied to about eighty to ninety per cent of adults of all ages. Treatment of persons with severe mental deficiencies is usually regarded as impossible.

The method has been applied successfully to adolescents and children, although below the age of ten difficulties may be frequent and no success has been reported with children below the age of six.

Clinical observations and experimental data indicate that autogenic therapy consists of systematic mental manipulation of psychophysiologic functions involving functional changes of highly differentiated mechanisms in the diencephalic area. Since the verbal content of the autogenic formulae, as well as the duration and sequence of the exercises, must be carefully adapted to the patient's functional state, a careful and critical control of the patient's training symptoms is required. For these reasons the application of autogenic training must remain in the hands of physicians, who are able to evaluate the patient's condition and the symptoms he notices during the therapy.

The following chapters concentrate on various aspects of (a) autogenic standard training, (b) therapeutic combinations involving organ-specific and intentional formulae, and (c) the practice of meditative exercises. A discussion of the vast clinical area covered by methods of autogenic neutralization will be undertaken in Volumes V and VI. However, for purposes of general orientation, and in order to establish cross-references, the methods of autogenic neutralization have been mentioned occasionally in connection with relevant areas of clinical application, research or theoretically oriented considerations.

## BACKGROUND OF AUTOGENIC METHODS

Autogenic training originated from research on sleep and hypnosis carried out during the years 1894-1903 by the renowned psychophysiologically oriented neuropathologist Oskar Vogt[1750,1751] and his disciple and close collaborator Korbinian Brodmann* of the Berlin Neuro-Biological

---

* Brodmann, K.: Zur Methodik der hypnotischen Behandlung. *Ztsch. f. Hypnotismus, Psychotherap., Psychophysiolog. u. Psychopatholog. Forschg.,* 1902, X, 314-375 (236, 356, 357).

Brodmann, K.: Zur Methodik der hypnotischen Behandlung. *Ztsch. f. Hypnotismus,*

Institute.[1444,1549] O. Vogt† observed that intelligent patients who had undergone a series of heterohypnotic sessions under his guidance were able to put themselves, for a self-determined period of time, into a state which appeared to be very similar to a hypnotic state. During the induction of these "autohypnotic" exercises associations of feelings of heaviness and warmth‡ appeared to be of some functional significance. O. Vogt's patients reported that these "autohypnotic rest" exercises had a remarkable recuperative effect.

At the time, Oskar Vogt observed that these short-term mental exercises, when practiced several times during the day, reduced such stressor effects as fatigue and tension. Other disturbing symptoms (e.g., headaches) could be avoided, and it seemed that one's overall efficiency could be enhanced. On the basis of these observations O. Vogt and K. Brodmann considered such self-directed mental exercises, which were called "prophylactic rest-autohypnoses" (*prophylaktische Ruhe-Autohypnosen*), to be of therapeutic value.

Stimulated by Oskar Vogt's work, J. H. Schultz, psychiatrist and neurologist in Berlin, started in 1905[1499] to explore the therapeutic potentialities of hypnosis and various forms of suggestions. His aim was to find a therapeutic approach which would reduce or eliminate the unfavorable aspects of contemporary hypnotherapy, such as the passivity of the patient and his dependence on the therapist.

During subsequent years,[1470,1482,1516,1534] while investigating hallucinations in normal persons, J. H. Schultz[1245,1246,1247] made observations which appeared to link up with O. Vogt's prophylactic mental exercises. Many of J. H. Schultz's hypnotized subjects reported experiencing two types of sensations during the initial phases of hypnosis: feelings of relaxation and heaviness in the extremities, often involving the whole body, and feelings of agreeable warmth which were usually noted soon afterwards.

Basing his initial approach on these observations, J. H. Schultz attempted to induce a hypnotic state by asking his patients first to think of heaviness in the limbs, then to imagine a feeling of warmth in the extrem-

---

*Psychotherap., Psychophysiolog. u. Psychopatholog. Forschg.*, 1898, VII, 5, 266-284 (273, 274, 275).

Marcinowski, Dr.: Selbstbeobachtungen in der Hypnose. II. Zur Technik der hypnotischen Suggestionen. *Ztsch. f. Hypnotismus, Psychotherap., Psychophysiolog. u. Psychopatholog. Forschg.*, 1899-1900, IX, 177-190 (184, 187).

† Ref.: 1750, p. 333, 334. See Glossary.

‡ Vogt, O.: Die Zielvorstellung der Suggestion. *Ztsch. f. Hypnotismus, Psychotherap., Psychophysiolog. u. Psychopatholog. Forschg.*, 1897, 5, 332-342 (334).

ities. When corresponding effects were reported by a patient, concentration on the activity of the heart and subsequently on respiration was added. Because of the tranquillizing and agreeable effects of warm baths and cool compresses on excited patients, Schultz then asked his subjects to think of warmth in the abdominal region and finally to imagine, "My forehead is cool."

These six physiologically oriented steps—heaviness and warmth in the extremities, regulation of cardiac activity and respiration, abdominal warmth and cooling of the forehead—became the core of autogenic training.[1248] During his initial studies, J. H. Schultz very soon observed that the best results were reported by those subjects who assumed a casual and passive attitude during concentration on, for example, heaviness and warmth in the limbs. Gradually, the technique was refined. A number of approaches, verbal formulae and training postures were tried out, and from this evolved what are today called the "autogenic standard exercises." For advanced trainees another series of exercises, focussing on certain mental activities, was added. In distinction to the physiologically oriented standard exercises, the latter are called "meditative exercises." Later clinical observations led to the development of a number of physiologically oriented, "organ-specific exercises" which were designed to meet the pathophysiologic requirements of certain disorders (e.g., bronchial asthma)—more specifically. Similar to the organ-specific exercises, another category of complementary approaches, the "intentional formulae," were designed to influence more specifically certain mental functions and behavior deviations. Both the organ-specific exercises and the intentional formulae are always applied in addition to or in combination with the standard exercises.

The development of (brain-directed) autogenic abreaction followed later as it became evident that the autogenic state facilitates the self-normalizing activity of unknown brain mechanisms which select, coordinate, adapt and terminate the release of a variety of neuronal impulses which are related to accumulated brain-disturbing material. Further studies of self-curative brain-directed (autogenic) dynamics led to the development of a complementary technique of neutralization called autogenic verbalization (see Fig. 1).

• • • • • • • • • • • •

## Ischemic Heart Disease

The application of autogenic training to patients suffering from various consequences of inadequate blood supply for the heart (e.g., angina pectoris, myocardial infarction, cardiac failure, arrhythmias) must be evaluated on clinical grounds in each case.

The clinical usefulness of autogenic training centers around two major areas: (a) non-specific psychophysiologic relaxation, and (b) promotion of desirable physiologic changes involving cardio-circulatory variables (e.g., decrease of vascular constriction, increase of coronary blood flow, peripheral vasodilatation, decrease of hypertension).[2181] Numerous clinical observations (see references of following sections, and p. 68) and a few experimentally oriented studies (see p. 119; Vol. IV) have contributed to our understanding of the clinically very favorable potentialities of autogenic approaches. In this connection it is, for example, of specific interest, that P. Polzien, in a group of 35 patients with repeatedly confirmed ST segment depression and lowering of the T wave (without any other cardiocirculatory disorder) observed an elevation of the ST segment and increase of the T wave by 0.05 mV or more in 28 patients during passive concentration limited to heaviness formulas of the First Standard Exercise (see Vol. IV).[1073,1083] Of clinical interest, as far as the prophylactic value of autogenic training is concerned, are studies by W. Luthe[885,892,2070] and Y. Aya[1910] showing significant lowering of elevated serum cholesterol levels in patients who practiced autogenic training (see Figs. 10, 24-28; and Vol. IV). In good correspondence with these findings are clinical observations by J. A. Laberke[760,761,2042] indicating that patients with angina pectoris are significantly less prone to develop myocardial infarction when they practice autogenic standard exercises (see p. 56).

It is understood that patients with evidence of ischemic heart disease require careful differential diagnostic evaluation, close medical supervision and, in cases where autogenic training is adopted as part of the treatment program, a case-adapted, well-controlled application of autogenic formulae.

## ANGINA PECTORIS

Since attacks of various forms and degrees of ischemic pain do not permit a clear distinction between angina pectoris and myocardial infarction, the application of autogenic training to patients with angina should be undertaken with the same care and respect as in cases with infarction.

Clinical and experimental observations indicate that autogenic training is useful during the following three treatment phases of ischemic heart disease:

1. During the prophylactic phase, in order to forestall early development of ischemic heart disease in "coronary prone individuals."

2. After appearance of angina (as a valuable adjunct in combination with other forms of conventional treatment) during early stages of oncoming attacks.

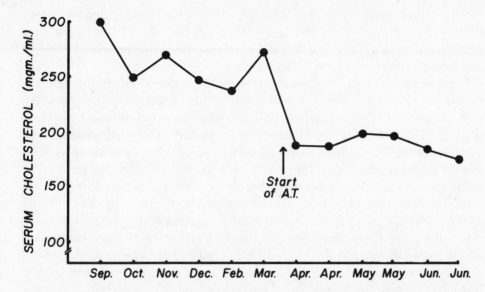

FIG. 10. Lowering of serum cholesterol after a patient with myocardial infarction started practicing autogenic standard exercises regularly. (Courtesy of Y. Aya, Oskar Vogt Institute, Kyushu University, Fukuoka.)[1910]

3. During long-term therapy, in combination with other conventional means of therapeutic management.

*Prophylactic application.* Ideally, the regular practice of autogenic standard exercises should be started as early as possible and become a routine means of self-protection in "coronary prone persons." This view is based on the multidimensional psychodynamically and physiologically oriented stress-neutralizing effects of autogenic training, as they are presented in the various sections of this book. Better adjustment of blood pressure, of cardiac activity, of coronary and peripheral circulation, buffering and reduction of psychologic stress, as well as lowering of serum cholesterol (see Subject Index, p. 117, 121) are some of the factors which are considered helpful in delaying or preventing undue acceleration of progressive atheromatosis, the onset of angina pectoris and the possibility of myocardial infarction.[479] Apart from the daily benefits resulting from a regular practice of standard exercises, a well trained person has better possibilities of adjusting favorably to ischemic conditions in case they should develop.*

---

* The American Heart Association and other organizations interested in the prevention of heart disease appear to be blissfully unaware of one of the most effective approaches in their own field.

*After appearance of angina pectoris.* When occlusive coronary artery disease has advanced to the point of producing a relative imbalance between oxygen supply and oxygen needs of the myocardium, the use of autogenic training may be considered.

Since a patient's first episodes of anginal pain are conventionally followed by a thorough clinical evaluation of his condition (e.g., participation of anemia, thyrotoxicosis, valvular disease, arrhythmias) there is little possibility that autogenic training is applied to anginal patients who are not yet under medical care. However, even when new patients with angina pectoris claim that they have been investigated in the past, autogenic training should not be started without carrying out another reassuring clinical evaluation. Participation of psychodynamic disorders (e.g., anxiety reaction, depression, accumulated aggression, infarctophobia) require adequate therapeutic management. Furthermore, since unpredictable massive autogenic discharges (e.g., anxiety, motor, sensory, palpitations, difficulty of respiration, dizziness) may occur in trainees with a history of severe accidents (e.g., car crash, sports), a careful screening of the patient's history is required in this direction (see Case: 19/I, p. 83; Case 20/I, p. 84; Case 13, p. 45).

In simple cases of angina pectoris, when reliable collaboration of the patient is ascertained and regular medical supervision and control is possible, autogenic training may be started.[1952] The emphasis is on a slow step-by-step progress through the heaviness formulae of the First Standard Exercise. Training protocols require periodic discussion, about once a week. The use of case-specific medication (e.g., nitroglycerin, tranquilizers) should not be discouraged. Since anginal attacks are more likely to occur in a recumbent than in a sitting posture, preference must be given to practice of autogenic exercises in the reclining chair posture and the simple sitting posture (see Vol. I). The use of passive concentration on a peaceful background image is considered helpful for many patients. However, patients with obsessive manifestations (e.g., chronic sexual deprivation), anxiety states, grief reactions and post-traumatic psychodynamic disorders may experience difficulties in finding or holding a peaceful background image. When such difficulties are noted, the use of a peaceful image should be immediately stopped, and passive concentration strictly limited to the autogenic formulae. In cases where this rule is not observed, the therapist may unexpectedly find himself confronted with complicated tension and anxiety-producing dynamics of spontaneously developing processes of autogenic abreactions. In such instances tranquilizing medication is useful. When trainees with angina pectoris have difficulty in finding or maintaining a peaceful image, or when passive concentration on standard formulae is frequently disturbed by powerful interferences of disagreeable thoughts, it is advisable to practice series of very brief (15–30 sec.) exercises until it becomes easier for the patient to maintain passive concentration for longer periods.

Problems requiring careful differential diagnostic evaluation may arise from autogenic discharges involving the heart or chest (e.g., pain, pressure, constriction, palpitation, shortness of breath, dizziness, epigastric discomfort, nausea). After clinically significant changes have been excluded and the nature and pattern of such discharge modalities has been determined, it is important to explain in detail the harmless and rather beneficial nature of such training symptoms.

Periodic control of heart rate and blood pressure reactivity before, during and after autogenic exercises is recommended. Unwanted circulatory reactions (e.g., sharp drop of blood pressure, bradycardia, tachycardia, flushing of face) require prompt attention. Individual adaptation of formulae, duration of passive concentration, number of exercises per set (e.g., two instead of three) help to avoid unfavorable reactions.

The warmth formulae of the Second Standard Exercise are not introduced as long as a trainee shows undue vasomotor reactions or other undesirable training symptoms (e.g., paradox reactions, increase of heart rate, increase of blood pressure, feelings of anxiety, strong motor discharges, dizziness, onset of headaches).

When the trainee's progress is uneventful, the warmth formulas (starting out with the right arm) are introduced one by one at weekly intervals. When unduly strong circulatory reactions are observed, slower progress with reduced warmth formulas (see Vol. I) is indicated. Reflectory connections between the left arm (proximal portion) and coronary blood flow are of particular importance for anginal patients. During advanced phases of warmth training, a step-by-step (l. hand, l. wrist, l. forearm, l. elbow, l. upper arm, l. shoulder) procedure of passive concentration on warmth in the left arm has been recommended.[639,662,1182] According to H. Kleinsorge[639] and G. Klumbies[662] electrocardiographic evidence (e.g., elevation of ST segment) supported the assumption that an increase of coronary blood flow can be achieved indirectly by passive concentration on warmth in the left arm (with emphasis on the proximal arm and shoulder portions).

The Third Standard Formula ("Heartbeat calm and regular") is usually postponed until the end of the standard series of autogenic exercises.[756, 864,1002,1003,1424] Depending on the psychophysiologic reactivity of each case, modified heart formulae are used (e.g., "Heartbeat calm and easy"). [574,755,757,758,760] The relieving effect of the heart formula may be reinforced by passive concentration on "flowing warmth to the heart"[987,994] or, "My heart is agreeably warm." Trainees who use these organ-specific approaches usually note an agreeable sensation of warmth in the cardiac area.[896] This effect supports the hypothesis that passive concentration on warmth in the cardiac area improves coronary circulation and contributes to widening of inter-coronary collateral channels in patients with coronary artery disease.

The Fourth Standard Formula ("It breathes me") usually follows after satisfactory progress with the warmth formulae of the Second Standard Exercise has been made. This formula is generally appreciated by the trainee because of its calming and relieving effects. In certain patients, favorable training effects can be enhanced by reducing passive concentration on warmth in the limbs (with exception of the left arm) to very short periods, and by remaining for longer periods with the Fourth Standard Formula.

The Fifth Standard Formula ("My solar plexus is warm" has occasionally caused some undesirable reactions.[1175,1424] Sometimes these are related to disagreeable modalities of autogenic discharges (see Tables 4-6; Cases 10, 24, 25), sometimes there is indication that changes of the gastrointestinal motor pattern or hemodynamic changes (see Case 48), are involved. When, during or after the introduction of "My solar plexus is warm," undesirable training reactions are noted, it is preferable to practice this formula only for very brief (e.g., 10-20 sec.) periods. In anginal patients with a history of gastritis, peptic ulcer, or association of anginal attacks with epigastric pain,[1175] it is preferable not to use the Fifth Standard Exercise. Furthermore, it is suggested that passive concentration on abdominal areas be avoided, when these have been involved in accidents or relevant traumatisms (e.g., "hit into the abdomen with brief loss of consciousness at age 13").

The Sixth Standard Formula ("My forehead is cool") may activate disturbing autogenic discharges (e.g., headaches, throbbing, pressure, anxiety, dizziness) in patients with a history of accidents involving the cranial region. However, a modified standard formula: "My forehead is *agreeably* cool," may be tried.

Although it can not be expected that significant organic changes can be reversed, clinically encouraging and sometimes surprisingly good results in patients with advanced coronary sclerosis have been observed.[141,156,160, 161,302,410,574,581,620,639,646,649,658,659,662,669,755,757,758,760,761,771,773,883,885,888,930,935, 994,1001,1003,1072,1163,1171,1175,1182,1433,1528,1927,1952,1979,1986,2042]

With regular and frequent practice of case-adapted autogenic exercises, most patients note definite improvement after four to eight weeks. Associated disorders as, for example, headaches and sleep disturbances subside; various other disorders (e.g., constipation, shortness of breath, belching, "gas pains") tend to disappear; apprehension, tenseness and anxiety decrease; anginal attacks occur less frequently and are less severe.[160,302,410,581,658,757,760,1163,1433,1927,2155] During more advanced phases of autogenic standard training, patients are able to control tachycardia and many learn to intercept oncoming attacks without the help of nitroglycerin.[620,760,935] For example, H. Kenter[620] reported on a group of 42 stenocardiac patients, who were treated only with autogenic training (no medication). In 34 cases the anginal symptoms disappeared. H. Kenter also noted that small groups of four to five outdoor patients did better than small groups of hospitalized patients.[620] J. H. Schultz,[1377] who treated 80 anginal cases (27 of predominantly organic and 53 of predominantly vasomotor nature) reported no success in 27 cases, very good results in 38, and moderate but significant improvements in 15 patients. Similar results were observed by J. A. Laberke,[757] A. Jouve and M. Dongier,[581] and J. Bobon, M. Breulet, M. Degossely and M. Dongier.[160,1927]

*Long-term therapy.* Together with other conventional measures (e.g., weight reduction, dietary adaptation, elimination of smoking, moderate physical exercise, avoidance of stressors, drugs) the regular practice of case-adapted daily programs of autogenic exercises is considered a valuable adjunct in long-term therapy. Apart from multidimensional psychophysiologic relaxation, the emphasis is on case-adapted passive concentration on warmth in the cardiac area. Regular promotion of favorable hemodynamic and metabolic functions (e.g., lowering of elevated levels of serum cholesterol[885,892,1910,2070]) are essential elements of an efficient long-term treatment program (see Figs. 24-27). In this connection J. A. Laberke's observations of two groups of clinically comparable anginal patients are of clinical interest. Thirty-one practiced autogenic training, while the other group of 30 patients relied on medication only. In the control group of untrained patients there were four infarctions within one to four years of observation. No infarctions occurred during the same period in the patients who practiced autogenic training.[760,761]

The long-term use of autogenic training by patients with ischemic heart disease is, however, associated with certain problems. Firstly, certain patients feel so well that they are prone to forget about their organically determined limits of permissible activities.[574,1175,1433] J. H. Schultz[1433,1528] observed a few cases who died at later points without forewarning. The same category of patients also tends to reject periodic medical controls, and they also tend to stop practicing autogenic training because they think the time-consuming exercises are not needed anymore. Secondly, a number of patients give up autogenic training because friends, nurses,[620] dentists or other physicians with inadequate, outdated, or incomplete knowledge of autogenic training discredit the method.

Thirdly, and this is a conclusion from more recent observations,[896] there is a reasonable probability that spontaneous and abortive brain dynamics of autogenic neutralization are triggered by certain events, and that the usually disagreeable psychophysiologic consequences of this motivate the patient to stop autogenic training and resort to drugs.

Considering the pathologic implications of ischemic heart disease, and the known problems associated with long-term practice of autogenic training, it is a medical responsibility to impress the anginal patient with the need for periodic medical control and guidance. The patient should feel invited to call any time when unusual training symptoms or other phenomena are noticed. Particular attention is indicated when anginal patients have been involved in recent traffic accidents or mortality of persons close to the patient has occurred.

● ● ● ● ● ● ● ● ● ● ● ●

## Alterations in Blood Pressure

With due consideration of non-functional pathologic variables (e.g., renal disorders, coarctation of the aorta, toxaemia of pregnancy, Cushing's syndrome, pheochromocytoma, thyrotoxicosis, atheroma of the aorta, aortic incompetence, arotic stenosis) it has been emphasized that the regular practice of autogenic standard exercises over prolonged periods has beneficial effects on a variety of physiologically and psychodynamically oriented functional variables which may participate in causing or amplifying certain hyper- and hypotensive[244,1787,2065] conditions. It is in this sense that autogenic training has been applied either as an adjunctive measure in the treatment program of certain organically determined forms of hypertension (e.g., atheroma of the aorta, thyrotoxicosis), as a prophylactic approach (e.g., evidence of hereditary predisposition, arteriosclerotic factors), and as a therapeutic mainstay when, after exclusion of other causes, unusual instability of blood pressure and hypertension is assumed to be due to psychophysiologically oriented functional variables (e.g., emotional stress, accumulated aggression, resentment, feeling menaced or trapped).

Although many etiologic and pathophysiologic aspects of various forms of alterations in blood pressure remain to be clarified, clinical and experimental studies of patients practicing autogenic training have indicated a number of physiologic and psychologic changes which appear to be of particular value in the treatment of hypertensive patients. Physiologically, the vasodilatory and circulatory effects (see Fig. 15; Fig. 5/I, 7/I), associated with passive concentration on the different standard formulae and certain organ-specific formulae, appear to include a number of desirable variables, which are known to participate in lowering elevated blood pressure readings. Furthermore, of perhaps even more clinical importance is the multidimensional psychophysiologic shift towards a pattern of reactivity and relevant functional changes the direction of which is diametrically opposed to the pattern of changes elicited by stress.

In the treatment of hypertensive conditions, clinical observers have reported variable results. Depending on participation of known and unknown etiologic variables, the clinical results vary between excellent and an apparently complete failure of response.[115,323,678,1800] However, it is generally agreed that the effectiveness of autogenic standard exercises increases as the hypertensive condition is due to functional factors of psychophysiologic nature.[56,96,269,339,418,823,852,1494,1495,1668,1951,2079] In many cases of essential hypertension (primary hypertension, hypertensive vascular disease) marked improvement has been noted after four to eight weeks of regular standard training.[115,160,247,323,481,678,758,760,870,872,873,877,878,879,880,935,987,1377,1625,1787,2122,2178] Readings taken before and after one set of standard exercises usually show a 5–12 per cent reduction of diastolic values, and a 5–25 per cent decrease of systolic blood pressure (see Fig. 14). In some cases, the systolic blood pressure may even drop 30 to 50 mm.Hg within a few minutes, during one exercise.[870,987,1377,1452] Studies involving larger groups of patients suffering from essential and other forms of hypertension have shown failure rates between 10 and 50 per cent.[160,323,678,1377,1927] The incidence of early dropouts in hypertensive trainees is known to be unusually high (25 to 70 per cent) and constitutes a particular problem for the therapeutic management of this category of patients.

While investigating various aspects of hypertension, G. Klumbies and G. Eberhardt[323,678] applied autogenic training to a group of 83 male hypertensive patients. Fifty-seven patients discontinued their treatment during initial phases of autogenic training. This unusually high rate (69 per cent) of early dropouts was viewed as being related to (a) the fact that the hypertensive disorder did not cause any subjective complaints, (b) that most of the dropouts were rather young (below age 26), and (c) that the treatment program was intentionally limited to the learning, practice and control of autogenic exercises (excluding individual discussions of a psychotherapeutic nature). The remaining 26 (17 below age 26) learned all standard exercises and participated in periodic control sessions over a period of 5–15 months. In this group, blood pressure readings were taken repeatedly before starting autogenic training and during subsequent control periods (see Fig. 12). The most significant decrease

of systolic and diastolic readings occurred during the first month of autogenic training (see Fig. 13). Further decrease continued during the
second, third and fourth month, with little or no change occurring during subsequent periods. In correspondence with other observations,[56,160,
407,409,418,535,873,878,879,935,1538,1927,2122] G. Klumbies and G. Eberhardt noted
considerable variations of the individual treatment response (see Fig.
12) with more marked decreases of the systolic component (average decrease 35 mm. Hg, single cases up to 55 mm. Hg): The decrease of the
diastolic values was 18 mm. Hg on the average, with some cases reaching
a reduction of 30 mm. Hg.[678] Normalization of blood pressure deviations
was noted in 22 of the group of 26 patients. The authors emphasize that
the treatment with antihypertensive drugs is less time consuming for both
the therapist and the patient. However, group training (up to 10) is time-
saving, and in view of the beneficial short- and long-range effects of the
regular practice of autogenic standard exercises and the elimination of
unfavorable side-effects caused by antihypertensive drugs (e.g., impotence, gastric distress, diarrhea, psychic disturbances), autogenic train-

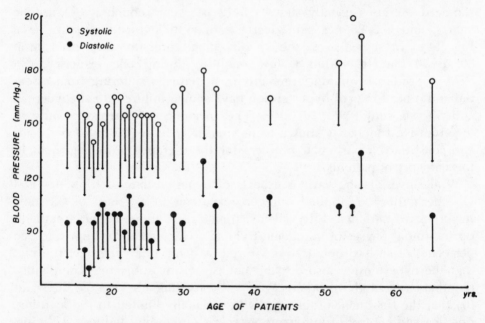

FIG. 12. Changes of systolic and diastolic blood pressure in a group of 26
hypertensive patients. The graphic representation of changes in each patient
is based on arithmetical means of repeated readings carried out under comparable conditions on different days, before and towards the end of a four-
month treatment period with autogenic training. (Courtesy of G. Klumbies
and G. Eberhardt, University of Jena.[323,678])

ing appears to be the method of choice for many patients suffering from forms of essential hypertension.

A more detailed study of the effects of the different standard exercises on blood pressure and cardiac activity has revealed that there are persons in whom a set of three heaviness exercises induces a gradual and significant increase in diastolic and systolic blood pressure (see Fig. 14). In a number of subjects, it has been observed that disturbances in passive concentration (intruding thoughts, sleep, snoring, minor movements) tend to coincide with a slight increase in diastolic and systolic blood pressure.[535] These observations indicate that the effect of the exercises on the trainee's blood pressure should be determined at regular intervals. Until

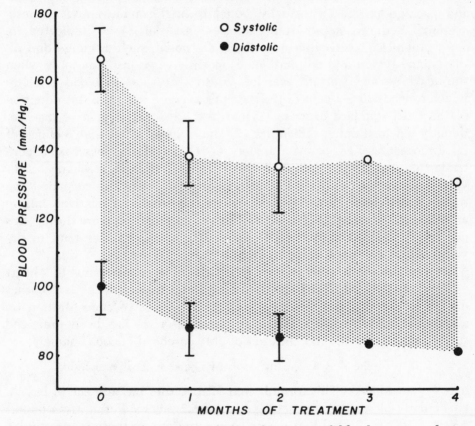

Fig. 13. Changes of systolic and diastolic range of blood pressure during a four-month period in a group of 26 hypertensive patients practicing autogenic standard exercises (based on arithmetical means of repeated reading in each case, taken before the beginning of A.T. and towards the end of each subsequent month; standard deviations as indicated). (Courtesy of G. Klumbies and G. Eberhardt, University of Jena.[323,678])

further information is available, it is advisable to discontinue autogenic therapy in cases in which correct and undisturbed exercises cause a significant increase in the blood pressure. In this respect, it must be kept in mind that there is experimental evidence that any minor voluntary motor activity (e.g., moving a hand, talking, etc.) as well as various modalities of autogenic discharges (e.g. intruding thoughts) and transitory states of sleep occurring during the exercises may reduce the beneficial effect of the autogenic exercises and may even provoke unwanted physiologic changes.[535] Clinical observations also indicate that the duration and sequence of the standard exercises should be adapted to the patient's functional state. Regular control of training symptoms is required.

In most patients suffering from hypertension, normal training symptoms and average progress is usually noted during heaviness and warmth training. Reduced step-by-step exercises (see Vol. I) are indicated in cases in which disagreeable side-effects are noted, such as congestion of the cranial region and palpitation. Slow progress is also advisable when the heaviness and warmth exercises cause a decrease in blood pressure which exceeds 15 per cent of the patient's average readings. Introduction of the third standard exercise ("Heartbeat calm and regular") has frequently led to training difficulties. Trainees have noted that feelings of uneasiness, tenseness or even anxiety developed during passive concentration on the heart. Although the psychophysiologic mechanisms involved are not yet entirely understood, there is some evidence that the trainee's feeling of uneasiness and anxiety is related to a relatively strong and sudden decrease (20 per cent or more) in blood pressure during this exercise.[987] As a consequence of such experiences, trainees tend to develop resistance to autogenic therapy.

Because of these observations it is advisable to postpone the heart exercise till the end of the standard series and to introduce "It breathes me" in its place. This exercise is followed by passive concentration on abdominal warmth. After the solar plexus exercise has been practiced successfully, a specific modification of "My forehead is cool," namely:

"My forehead is agreeably cool. My head is clear and light."

may be introduced. This formula and "It breathes me" appear to have a particularly pleasant and relieving effect on trainees suffering from hypertension. It is suggested that passive concentration on these two formulae be emphasized and prolonged during each set of exercises. Finally, passive concentration on the heart may be introduced by using a modified heart formula:

"Heartbeat calm and easy."

At this period of autogenic therapy, after the other five exercises have

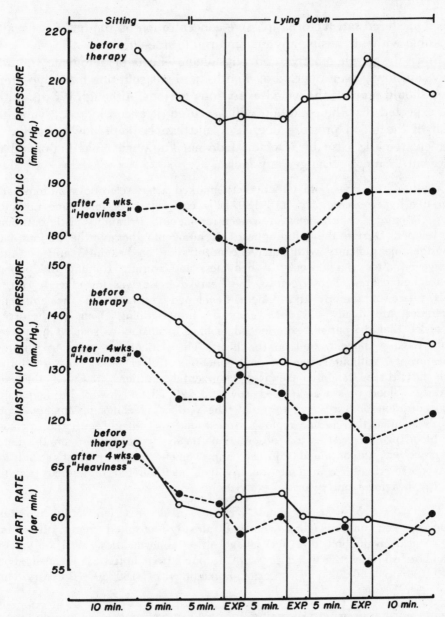

Fig. 14. The effects of heaviness exercises upon the blood pressure and heart rate of a 57-year-old teacher with hypertension of about 15 years' duration. Mean values of readings taken on three different days before (solid lines) and three different days after (broken lines) four weeks of heaviness training. The decrease in systolic blood pressure is about 12% (P <.01). The response of the diastolic blood pressure is less marked and about 5.5% (P <.01). The response of the heart rate is typical but not statistically significant.

been mastered satisfactorily, passive concentration on the heart is usually possible without causing any uncomfortable side-effects.

Since the psychoreactive and physiologic effects of autogenic training develop slowly over a period of months, patients suffering from hypertension should practice the exercises for long periods. Although it can hardly be expected that the condition will be cured, it is considered a valuable gain if the blood pressure decreases and can be kept down, so that a patient remarks casually "Doctor, I do not know what has happened to me, but I cannot get angry any more."

*Case 24:* A 55-year-old patient with marked arteriosclerotic symptoms and variable hypertension (155/110–180/120) complained of increasing nervousness, insomnia, disturbances in concentration, and irritability with outbursts of temper. During the initial phases of autogenic therapy the patient had considerable difficulty with passive concentration on heaviness and warmth. However, after a few weeks of heaviness and warmth training the patient felt much calmer. Subsequently, the heart exercise was introduced. During this phase of therapy the patient developed resistance to the autogenic exercises and finally did not want to continue doing them. A discussion revealed that the patient experienced feelings of anxiety as soon as he started with passive concentration on the heart. The patient had tried to suppress the anxiety, without success. A subsequent control of blood pressure during the first three standard exercises (horizontal position) revealed that the trainee's blood pressure dropped down to 120/70 and lower during passive concentration on the heart formula. The patient's feelings of anxiety (with localization in the cardiac region) were found to coincide with the decrease in blood pressure. After this observation, passive concentration on the heart formula was discontinued. Marked improvement in the patient's condition was observed after autogenic therapy had been limited to regular practice of the heaviness and warmth exercises.[987]

*Case 25:* A 56-year-old female patient (anxiety reaction, labile hypertension, marked underweight) who had already consulted many physicians. A clinical evaluation did not reveal other abnormalities. With autogenic standard exercises the blood pressure dropped from initial readings of about 240/130 to 150/70 and occasional readings of 180/80 (2 years control).[1163,1171]

Since norepinephrine-producing pheochromocytomas are much more frequent than previously suspected, a more systematic screening of hypertensive trainees who do not show satisfactory responses to autogenic training, is suggested (see Case 23/I, p. 97; Case 54, p. 139). This precaution is particularly indicated in presence of paroxysmal hypertension, which may or may not be triggered by autogenic discharges.

In hypertensive patients who do not show a satisfactory response to autogenic training,[115,1175,1800,2122] case-specific combinations of antihypertensive and tranquilizing drugs can be added after involvement of a pheochromocytoma has been excluded. Although systematic research is lacking, there are isolated clinical observations[935,2065] indicating that autogenic training appears to enhance the antihypertensive action of certain drugs in certain patients, thus permitting a desirable low dosage treatment over more prolonged periods. It is in this connection that the experimental studies carried out by D. Langen, J. M. Hohn, W. Vogel and G. Schwarz,[527,528,814,1558,1747] and especially the summation of vasodilatory and circulatory effects resulting from combinations of autogenic training with relevant drugs, are of particular clinical interest (see Vol. I).

Repeated observations of a significant increase of diuresis in trainees practicing autogenic exercises for prolonged periods, undergoing autogenic abreaction or practicing autogenic verbalization[418,895,897,898,901,1927] provided indication that circulatory and other renal functions appear to undergo certain changes, which may be of special value in the treatment of hypertensive patients. Considering relevant experimental findings which indicated that passive concentration on organ-specific formulae (e.g., "My stomach is warm"; "My lower abdomen is warm") produce an increase of blood flow (e.g., fingers, gastric mucosa, colon wall), trials with passive concentration on "My right kidney is heavy,"* "My left kidney is heavy,"* and "My kidneys are heavy"* were started.[2065] It is hypothesized that this organ-specific approach may amplify desirable circulatory effects (e.g., decrease of resistance of blood flow) already produced by the standard formulas by enhancing disturbed conditions of blood flow in renal vessels.

*References:* 56, 96, 115, 156, *160*, 244, 247, 269, 302, *323*, 339, 407, 409, 410, 418, 482, 535, 581, 602, 639, 658, 662, *678*, 758, 760, 771, 823, 852, 870, 872, 873, 876, 877, 878, 879, 880, *883*, 887, 888, 896, 935, 987, 994, 1163, 1175, *1182*, 1314, 1377, 1433, 1452, 1494, 1495, 1528, *1537*, 1538, 1541, 1625, 1668, 1784, 1787, 1800, *1927*, 1951, 1979, 2065, 2079, 2122, 2178.

● ● ● ● ● ● ● ● ● ● ●

## DISORDERS IN LIPID METABOLISM

Disturbances of lipid metabolism as associated with increased or normal serum lipids may involve hereditary factors (e.g., familial pre-beta lipo-proteinemia, familial fat-induced hyperlipemia, hypercholesterolemia with hyperglyceridemia), or may be related to other pathologic processes

---

* These organ-specific formulas should not be used until further information is available.

(e.g., biliary cirrhosis, hypothyroidism, diabetes, pancreatitis, nephrotic syndrome). Furthermore it is known that the complexity of physiologic variables (e.g., endocrine) which participate in lipid metabolism are also influenced by unknown regulatory mechanisms responding to psychologic stress. It is in this connection, and with specific reference to the literature, which suggests a statistical relationship between serum cholesterol levels and the incidence of arteriosclerotic heart disease, that clinically and experimentally (see Vol. IV) oriented studies of the psychophysiological effects of autogenic training are of practical therapeutic interest.[892,1910,2070]

Stimulated by clinical observations indicating that the regular practice of autogenic training has a normalizing effect on certain hyperthyroid conditions, W. Luthe began a study of serum cholesterol. In a first report on a group of 20 psychosomatic and neurotic patients who were tested under standard conditions (e.g., 8:30 a.m., after 14 hr. fasting, routine tests, research project unknown to the laboratory personnel) before starting autogenic training, and after variable periods (e.g., 2–50 months), W. Luthe[892] summarized the findings as follows:

1. Statistically, there was no significant difference between a group of ten patients who had received medication (e.g., imipramine, meprobamate, chlordiazepoxide) for transitory periods and the group of ten patients who did not receive supportive medication.

2. In both groups there was a significant difference ($P < .01$) between the first and the second determination of serum cholesterol ($F = 9.04$).

3. There was no apparent correlation between the time interval (between the two determinations), and relevant changes of the serum cholesterol values.

4. There was no correlation between the changes of serum cholesterol values and the age or sex of the patients.

5. There was some indication that patients whose condition requires transitory support by imipramine, meprobamate or chlordiazepoxide are liable to show a tendency towards higher and more fluctuating levels of serum cholesterol.

6. The results indicated that initially high serum cholesterol levels decrease more markedly than initially low values.

These findings were confirmed as the investigation was continued with a larger group of patients (see Fig. 24-25).[2070]

The changes of serum cholesterol values seen in Fig. 24-26 indicate that there appears to be a biologically determined "adjustment zone" located between 150–200 mg./ml., towards which initially elevated serum cholesterol levels adjust (see Fig. 24 and Fig. 25). Values which initially

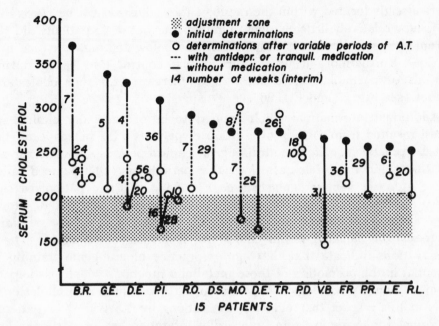

FIG. 24. Lowering of serum cholesterol in patients suffering from hyper-cholesteremia (normal range: 150–250 mg./ml.).

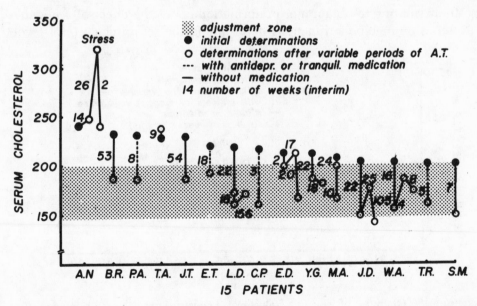

FIG. 25. Lowering of serum cholesterol in patients with "high normal" values (normal range: 150–250 mg./ml.) before starting autogenic training.

were already located within the range of the "adjustment zone" (see Fig. 26) show relatively little changes. Only in four out of 45 patients did the serum cholesterol readings drop transitorily below 150 mg./ml. (see Fig. 24-26). Furthermore it was observed that control tests taken during periods of particular stress showed an increase of serum cholesterol values (see Fig. 25 and Fig. 26).

Additional information which appears to be of particular clinical interest resulted from a study of a group of patients who (a) gave up the regular practice of autogenic training for certain periods, (b) interrupted treatment and came back after variable periods, or (c) practiced autogenic exercises very irregularly (see Fig. 25). In these patients a significant increase (P < .01) of serum cholesterol levels was noted. However, as these patients resumed the regular practice of autogenic standard exercises, the elevated serum cholesterol levels decreased again. These observations indicate that the *regular* practice of autogenic training is essential in the promotion of those metabolic functions which participate in maintaining physiologically well-adjusted levels of serum cholesterol. It is in this respect that clinical observations by Y. Aya[1910] in patients suffering, for example, from myocardial infarction are of particular interest for therapeutic programs aiming at the prevention, the delay of onset and the slowing down of coronary heart disease (see Fig. 10, p. 52) and atherosclerosis obliterans.

In attempting to obtain more information about the effect of autogenic exercises on metabolic functions determining the serum cholesterol level,

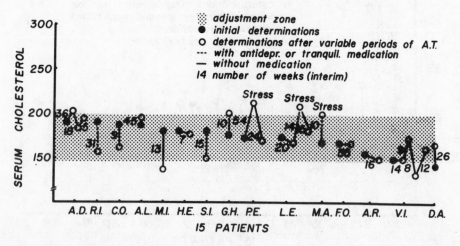

FIG. 26. Changes of serum cholesterol levels in patients with normal or "low normal" values (normal range: 150–250 mg./ml.) before starting autogenic training.

Y. Aya[1910] carried out a pilot study with ten psychosomatic patients (e.g., same food program, same experimental procedure) who had practiced autogenic training (heaviness, warmth) for only three weeks (see Fig. 28). Determinations of serum cholesterol values from samples taken directly after termination of a 20-minute period of autogenic training did not show a consistent pattern of changes. In contrast with these findings are values from blood specimens obtained thirty minutes after termination of autogenic training which showed a reactive lowering in 9 cases and no change in one trainee (see Fig. 28). Y. Aya's data seem to indicate that relevant metabolic adjustment reactions due to autogenic training involve a latency period. Further studies of this nature, however, including carefully matched control groups of non-trainees practicing simulated exercises, and others who apply active concentration, would be of clinical interest (see also Vol. IV).

Considering the known correlations between the rate of incidence of coronary disease and the level of serum cholesterol (or related lipids) it is hypothesized that the regular practice of autogenic standard exercises may play a valuable role in the prevention of early onset and undue acceleration of arteriosclerosis and associated forms of heart disease.

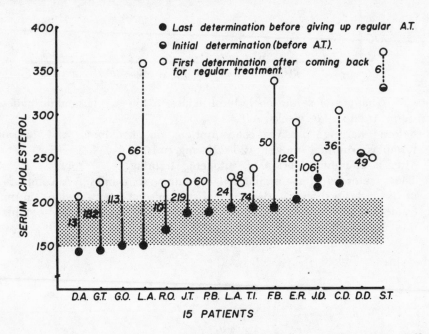

Fig. 27. Increase of serum cholesterol levels (normal range: 150–250 mg./ml.) in patients who (a) interrupted treatment, (b) stopped practicing autogenic training for other reasons, or (c) practiced autogenic training very irregularly.

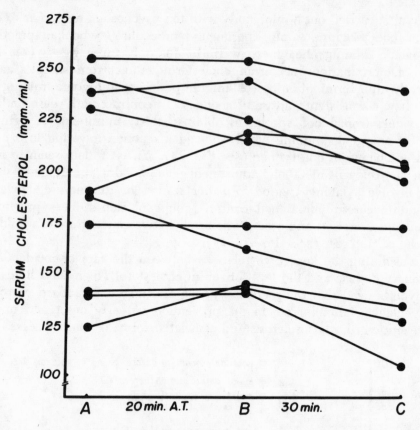

FIG. 28. Changes of serum cholesterol values in ten psychosomatic patients (short-term trainees, 3 weeks A.T.).

A. Before starting passive concentration on heaviness and warmth formulas (normal range: 120–220 mg./ml.).

B. After a 20-minute period of autogenic training.

C. Thirty minutes after termination of autogenic training. A comparison of B and C shows a decrease of serum cholesterol values in nine trainees, and no change in one. (Courtesy of Y. Aya, Oskar Vogt Institute, Kyushu University, Fukuoka.[1910])

# The Two Methods of Tension Control and Certain Basic Techniques in Anxiety Tension Control

34

Edmund Jacobson

## THE TWO METHODS OF TENSION CONTROL

METHODS of tension control are considered basic to psychosomatic medicine and to psychotherapy because they take into account not only anatomical considerations but also electrophysiological, chemical, mechanical, caloric and psychological factors in emotion and other types of mental activities. A visiting psychiatrist from the United States Navy stated emphatically, "If you say this quite clearly and illustrate it so that it is well understood, you will have all psychiatrists with you!" I shall try here to do so.

### Neuromuscular Practises Have Physical Aspects

"Please bend your left hand back at the wrist," I said to him. He did so. "It is certain," I said, "that muscle fibers are shortened in the upper muscles of your left forearm, namely, the extensor muscles of the hand. To this extent, then, your act is mechanical. However, we can look upon this act of yours also as a chemical activity; for it is a process of combustion, requiring oxygen and other elements, in which rich phosphate bonds, possibly including those of adenosinetriphosphate, are broken down to furnish the energy for muscular contraction. At the same time waste products of combustion are formed, including carbon dioxide, lactic acid, pyruvic acid, creatinine, mineral ash and others. This leads us to look upon your act of bending back your left hand from a third point of view, namely, that of the circulatory system. For the oxygen supply is brought to the muscle by the bloodstream, particularly through the medium of sustained or increased blood pressure, and the avenue is likewise employed for the removal of

**463**

waste products of combustion. Fourth, your act of bending back your left hand can be considered electrophysiologically. Concomitant with the chemical processes and doubtless as a sign of their occurrence electrical pressures accompany shifts of charge and these pressures can be measured in terms of what are commonly called 'action-potentials.' In this laboratory and clinic we record the active muscular contractions, the neuromuscular activities, by extremely delicate forms of electroneuromyometry. Fifth, your act of bending back your left hand can be looked upon as thermodynamic. It is heat productive not only in its contractile stage but also in the relaxation which follows.

### But Also Purpose Which Is mental

"Sixth, your act has at least one more than all the five characters already mentioned. We ask, 'What is the purpose of your bending back your left hand?' You will answer that your purpose is to do as I say, to cooperate, possibly to learn something. Often you bend your hand back similarly in daily pursuits such as brushing your hair or lifting some object. Then also you have purposes. From the standpoint of these purposes, your act obviously cannot be classed as solely mechanical, chemical, circulatory, electrophysiological or caloric. Your purposes obviously are psychological and your act is more than would fit into any of the five categories mentioned previously. Therefore when the doctor employs methods of tension control, it is untrue that he is using a 'physical' method to accomplish a psychological purpose. Instead, from the very first day, he is using a method which has all of the six characters mentioned above. He can be expected, therefore, to produce effects on emotions and on the 'mind' precisely because from the very outset he is employing mental as well as physical measures."

### Importance of Eye and Speech Activities—"Cause" of Emotions

These considerations apply to every muscle in the body. However, our clinical and laboratory findings have indicated that certain neuromuscular regions play a most significant role in the guidance and determination of our mental activities and their order. Particularly significant are the muscles of the eyes, controlling vision but also controlling visual imagination. Of similar importance are the muscles of speech, controlling not only what is said but what is spoken in imagination as well. These two regions, I have found, incite or trigger the reactions of the total organism more than do any other system of voluntary muscles. To be sure, in the case of the eyes we must not assume that the inciting or triggering is wholly neuromuscular tension; we must take into account in addition the visual images as well as the eye-region tension patterns.

## Importance For Sleep

To illustrate the dominant role of the two regions mentioned above, we can cite our clinical and laboratory experience that if the action potential values both from the eye and speech regions are at approximately zero level for a relatively brief period of time such as about thirty seconds, the individual is asleep. The relationships between these findings and those which have followed the discovery of Magoun on the activating function of the reticular network lie close at hand. From the standpoint of energy expenditure, it is clear that while the muscles of the eyes and of speech are relatively small in volume as compared with the larger muscles of the limbs, nevertheless for the direction of mental activity the expenditure of a given quantum of energy can be expected to be far more important in the region of the trigger tension than in the large response muscle of the limbs. Nevertheless in emotional conditions we should not devote our teaching mostly to the eyes and speech. We should be making the same mistake as would be made in any army if attention were devoted chiefly to the excellence of operation of the commanding generals to the neglect of the soldiers. The whole army needs drill, not just the leaders. Likewise the whole musculature of the patient stands in need of drill.

Bearing these points in mind, we can proceed first to distinguish very briefly between the original method, progressive relaxation, and the offshoot method of self-operations control and then to outline in figures and cuts with appropriate directions features common to both methods.

## Progressive Relaxation

Progressive relaxation or, if desired, abbreviated relaxation methods can be applied to any class of people, whether primitive or cultivated, provided that they understand the language employed and that they will practise. Occasionally, understanding patients do well without practising at all, but like any other skill, tension control skill develops particularly with practise. Progressive relaxation has been previously described (1). (This is the method which will be illustrated in the relatively unabridged case reports appearing in Chapters 7 to 16 inclusive.)

## Daily Efficiency

The individual is shown how to recognize tensions in serial order in his various muscle groups and how to relax these muscles to an extent not previously achieved, guided by electrical measurements. This instruction is given in the lying posture at first, as a rule, and then the serial education is repeated in the sitting posture. Finally he is given instruction during activities that are of his everyday habit, such as reading or writing. He is encouraged to observe his tension patterns and to diminish these so far as is compatible with his job productivity in each and every task of his daily activities. Such tasks include not only reading and writing but talking, walking, driving a car, and various pursuits of leisure and sport.

## Primary and Secondary Tensions

The individual learns to observe tension patterns requisite to each act that he performs, called primary tensions, but attended by other tensions not at all necessary, which are not only wasteful of energy but also distract him. He is trained to relax differentially which means that he uses those tensions that are primary for every task but avoids excess in them, while he attempts to relax toward the zero level tensions that are distracting or of a secondary character. It is a common misimpression that relaxation techniques are devoted solely to showing the individual how to sleep and how to rest. On the contrary, general relaxation, which means lying down to rest more completely, and differential relaxation, the term for efficient conduct of daily affairs, both aim at increased accomplishment through economy of energy.

## Two Methods of Tension Control

Tension control is a common term which I apply to the various educational methods of energy conservation which we employ. It covers both (1) progressive relaxation methods in (a) prolonged courses and (b) abbreviated forms and (2) the method of self-operations control.

Each patient is trained (1) in a method of relaxation or (2) of self-operations control, but not in both. The latter method is a product of this industrial, "push-button" age.

When the doctor employs progressive relaxation methodology, he proceeds on the commonly accepted view of human life as a pursuit for goals, however, variable from person to person, from race to race, from epoch to epoch, and even from moment to moment. The aim is to render man more efficient in achieving goals, in eliminating wasteful and less desired goals and thus to achieve integration of efforts.

## Self-Operations Control

However, when the doctor practises or teaches self-operations control, he proceeds from a view of human life different from that which prevails in our culture, It is the new but obviously sound and practical view that man can be regarded as the most complicated yet integrated instrument known to us. Among the quickest to learn to apply controls are those individuals who habitually run cars, planes and other instruments. This class includes particularly farmers, laborers, mechanics and engineers who actually run the instruments with which their lives are associated. Since many others of our present population are accustomed to motor cars as well as to planes, the method of self-operations control can be taught them with favorable results. In my experience with selected individuals, the method of self-operations control can be learned faster and eventually proves more effective than do any of our other relaxation methods. In teaching progressive relaxation, the muscular sensation of Bell is called the "sensation of tenseness" or "tension." In teaching the method of self-operations control, the muscular sensation of Bell is called the "control sensation."

Self-operations control has been described previously(2). This is the method which will be illustrated in the relatively unabridged case reports appearing in Chapters 17 to 19, inclusive.

### Summary of Self-Operations Control

In brief, the patient is to learn to operate his organism as he would learn to run any other complicated apparatus, namely, efficiently. Just as he learns to run a motor car, so he is to learn to run himself. This is no merely verbal analogy, but pedagogy is used to proceed from the familiar to the unfamilar. The motor car has wheels, whereby it is able to move forward and backward and when these wheels are turned it can move in an arc. Locomotion is the only function in which the motor car engages. However, locomotion is only one of very many functions in which the human organism engages. Accordingly, when we ask the patient what are the wheel substitutes in mankind, the appropriate answer, we need to explain, is not his legs. What we are really inquiring is what, like wheels in a motor car, enable man to engage in whatever motion occurs in his parts or in his whole organism? He learns that since his brain and other sections of nervous system do not move when they operate, the nervous system is not equivalent to the wheels of the motor car. Just as wheels engage in every performance of a motor car (which involves motion), so the only tissue which analogously engages in man is muscle. Just as wheels can be called the performers or effectors in the car, so muscles can be called the performers or effectors in human activity. He learns that the nervous system, including the brain, is really the equivalent of what "lies under the hood." The nervous system, including the brain, is necessary for motion but is not sufficient. Only the shortening and lengthening of muscle fibers effect motion in man. Thus he is enabled not only to walk but also to move his eyes, his head, to speak and to listen and to perform all the diverse functions of his daily living. It is explained to the patient that in this laboratory and clinic, it has been shown that mental activity is no exception to the rule that striated muscular action is essential in every effort, including so-called "mental" as well as so-called "physical" activity.

## Initial Instructions

Initial teaching in self-operations control is to impress the individual that just as there are controls in the motor car, so there are controls which he can learn to operate in himself. In the motor car the controls are on the dashboard conveniently arranged for the driver. In the human organism, however, the controls are in the muscle fibers themselves, namely, in the muscle spindles. Obviously, if the controls in the motor car were located in the wheels, the driving would be impossible from the front seat. We need to understand, then, that since the controls of muscle are in the muscles themselves, the only reason that the patient can master them is because he is both the driver and the driven. He can learn to perceive his controls through the muscle sense.

## Indicator of Effort-Energy Expenditure

In instruction, we begin by having the patient bend his hand back to learn to distinguish the control signal which enables him to perceive the controls in the muscle from the strain signal which has to do with joints. There is no direct control of joint sensations, but only indirect control. All direct controls depend upon the afferent end-organs in the muscle spindles. As in the method of progressive relaxation instruction, he learns that the control sensation affords him a gross indication of energy expenditure. His task will be to learn to run his organism most expeditiously, namely, with an optimum output of energy to accomplish his purposes. He is taught to recognize the control sensation in each of his principal muscle groups in succession, just as is done in the method of progressive relaxation. He is taught that going on with the power involves energy expenditure, while going off with the power involves no such expenditure. If he expends energy to go off with the power, namely to relax, he fails to relax. At all points he is given drill. He is taught that his neuromuscular mechanisms are not like the electric light switch controls on the wall. When power is switched on, movement of the switch is performed by force over distance, which is work. Once this work is performed the light performer continues in action. However, when he bends back his hand, this is performed without such a switch. Continual work is required if the muscle fibers are to remain shortened over any period of time. This is continual work performance in the controls, whereas in the wall switch the work ceases in the switch and goes on only in the performer, the light. To discontinue this performance, he is requested to turn off the light. This he does and it is pointed out to him that he has done work on the switch, namely, he has moved it by force a certain distance.

## Going Negative Requires No Effort

However, muscular performance is different. To go off with the muscular power, no work performance on the part of a switch is required, nor is it possible, since there is no such switch. Upon bending back his hand continuously there is continuing work in the controls. To discontinue requires no work but only to cease to expend energy. To avert misunderstanding, he is shown a device in which pressure of his finger gently is accompanied by lighting of a bulb, but dimly. To go with this lighting power, he fails if he performs more work, namely by pressing the spring switch more strongly. The only way to discontinue the light is to cease pressing the switch with his finger. This is ceasing to work. The purpose is to show him that the difference between the mechanism of the light switch and the mechanism of his bending back his hand is not because the light switch is constructed by man, whereas the muscular on-and-off arrangement is constructed by nature, but that man often constructs a controlling device similar to that which occurs in his muscle spindles. He can be shown the water faucets in the surgeon's office, which, controlled by a foot pedal, operate approximately on the same general principle as do his muscle controls.

Learning self-operations control generally proves fascinating. The doctor may begin, if he chooses, in the sitting posture. As stated previously, children take to it eagerly. It is helpful to tell the patient to remind himself briefly many times a day that he is to run his organism.

We must outline the physiology of the control of muscular contraction on which the method of self-operations control is based. This has been brilliantly worked out on laboratory animals by various investigators as follows:

## Control Mechanisms

Striated muscle contraction has been shown to depend largely or completely on impulses flowing out from spindles located within the muscle(3). Each spindle consists of two contractile muscular poles, the intrafusal muscles, jointed by a non-contractile sensory portion. Upon stretch of this middle portion, the sensory end-organs within it are stimulated. This mechanism alone is believed to determine the outflow of impulses from the muscle spindle.

The intrafusal fibers contract, stretching the sensory middle portion of the spindle, upon receiving discharges from small calibre motor fibers, called "gamma efferents" by Leksell. By causing contraction of the intrafusal fibers, excitation of the gamma efferents adjusts the bias on the sensory endings in the central portion of the muscle spindle(4).

## " Cerebral Control" of Muscle Spindle Action

Direct evidence of the action of gamma efferents has been published(5). Cerebral control of the muscle spindle action was established by Granit and Kaada. They found that the 'tonic' background discharge could be selectively augmented or suppressed upon stimulation of several different localities in the central nervous system(6).

According to Merton, a servo-control of movement thus is provided by action of the muscle spindle(7). The supraspinal control of the muscle spindles was further illuminated by Elfred, Granit and Merton(8).

In the cat the gamma efferent fibers (which control the spindle and thus the action of the striated muscle) are 3-8 microns in diameter and conduct at rates between 15 and 50 m/sec. They compose about one third of the lumbosacral ventral root nerve supply(9), according to Kuffler, Hunt and Quilliam (1951).

Supraspinal control of the spindles has been shown not to be dependent on afferent support, as to a large extent is the main muscle (Eldred, Granit and Merton). Proprioceptive influence of the gamma motoneurones is chiefly inhibition during stretch, confirming Hunt(10). The three authors mentioned conclude that during cerebral stimulation the whole physiological range of movement is adequately covered by the range of bias that the gamma efferents apply to the spindle and which is at the command of the supraspinal centers. In the types of contraction which they studied, activity of the gamma efferents keeps in advance of muscular contraction. They conclude that this indicates that a decisive fraction of the excitation of muscular contraction reaches the larger (alpha) motoneurones of the muscles via the gamma efferent system and the monosynaptic spindle afferents.

Active contraction has been found to slow the spindle (Matthews). Eldred, Granit and Merton conclude that gamma efferent activity reflexly controls contraction of the main muscle. They see the gamma system "at the behest of the higher centers regardlessly switching the spindle up and down even to the extremes of its range" (11).

## Tension Control Is Voluntary and Spontaneous

Every step in the teaching of tension control is taken from the standpoint and viewpoint of the patient himself. Nothing is to be forced upon him, nothing is to be done to him, as occurs when surgery is applied, medicines are prescribed, hypnosis is induced, suggestion or autosuggestion is introduced, or shock treatment is given. It is the volition of the individual which we approach; he is to learn according to the interests of his own organism or being as he interprets them. We modify his outlook and his daily mode of living but only insofar as he effects this modification in and by himself. Our procedures are teaching methods only.

## It Evolves Freedom from Undesired Inhibitions

We produce no catharsis, no transference, no new and different person, but only one who, in the larger sense, is more himself than when neurotic. If he follows directions based upon scientific experience, with proper controls, we find that he gains what may be called a new freedom within himself.

## It Cultivates Independence

We can not wish this on him. He must learn for himself. In my experience, anxiety control can not be accomplished by indoctrination. The patient needs to observe what he really does at the moment of anxiety tension. He needs to learn to recognize his effort energy expenditures through the muscle sense and to make this habitual. Thereupon he readily recognizes when he becomes unduly tense. When he has learned to recognize excessive tension as in undue anxiety and to relax it, he will have taken a step toward increased personal efficiency. A further step is taken when with increasing skill he learns to relax such tension for optimum accomplishment. Obviously this is the reverse of sloth. Effort tensions required for his tasks are not to be relaxed toward zero but only insofar as they prove excessive. The objective is the golden mean which in any form of conduct is known as 'skill." Often it proves best to retain a moderated but protective degree of anxiety tension. Complete freedom from anxiety would be as dangerous as complete freedom from pain sense.

Illustrations will follow in the case histories.

Various brain controls are recognized, but in treatment we focus on peripheral controls.

# NOTES

(1) Jacobson, Edmund: PROGRESSIVE RELAXATION, 2nd ed. Chicago, U. of Chicago, 1938.

(2) Jacobson, Edmund: ANXIETY AND TENSION CONTROL, loc. cit., Chapters 5, 6, pp. 48-115.

(3) Leksell, L.: THE ACTION POTENTIAL AND EXCITATORY EFFECTS OF THE small ventral root fibers to skeletal muscle. Acta Physiol Scand, 10(Suppl. 31), 1945. G. Rossi advanced the theory earlier: Asimmetrie tonische posturate, ed. asimmetrie motorie. Arch Fisiol, 25:145-157, 1927.

(4) Knowledge of this mechanism derives from the experiments of B.H. Matthews, Nerve endings in mammalian muscle. J Physiol, 78:1-53; S.W. Kuffler and C.C. Hunt: The mammalian small-nerve fibers: A system for efferent nervous regulation of muscle spindle discharge. In Patterns of organization in the central nervous system. Res Publ Ass Nerv Ment Dis, 30, 1952.

(5) Hunt, C.C.: The reflex activity of mammalian small nerve fibers. J Physiol 115:456-459, 1951. Kobayashi, Y., K., Dshima, and Tasake, J.: Analysis of afferent and efferent systems in the muscle nerve of the toad and cat. J Physiol 117:152-171.

(6) Granit, R., and Kaada, B.R.: Influence of stimulation of central nervous structures on muscle spindles in cat. Acta Physiol Scand, 27:130-160, 1952.

(7) Merton, P.A.: Significance of the 'silent period' of muscles. Nature, (London), 166:733-734, 1940. Speculations on the servo-control of movement. In THE SPINAL CORD, p. 247. Ciba Foundation Symposium. London, Churchill, 1953.

(8) Eldred, E., Granit R., and Merton, P.A.: Supraspinal control of the muscle spindles and its significance. J Physiol, 122:498-523, 1953.

(9) The remaining portion consists of large nerve fibers, 8-18 microns in diameter, conducting at the rate of 50-110 m/sec. and setting up the motor unit switch response. Hunt, C.C. and Kuffler, S.W.: Further study of efferent small-nerve fibers to mammalian muscle spindles: Multiple spindle innervation and activity during contraction. J Physiol, 113:283-297, 1951. Kuffler, S.W., Hunt, C.C., and Quilliam, J.P.: Function of medullated small-nerve fibers in mammalian ventral roots: efferent muscle spindle innervation. J Neurophysiol, 14:29-54, (Jan.) 1951.

(10) Hunt, C.C.: The reflex activity of mammalian small nerve fibers. J Physiol 115:456-469, 1951.

(11) Loc. Cit., p. 519.

# CERTAIN BASIC TECHNIQUES IN ANXIETY TENSION CONTROL

OUR techniques of tension control have been under continual scrutiny with a view to further improvement. They result from the application of underlying branches of knowledge, including physiology, psychology and clinical psychiatry, but the approach at all times has been experimental rather than final. As in aviation, the hypothesis has been that at any stage of development further improvement is possible.

Experience with anxiety states supports the view that each case is highly individuated. Just as individuals differ from one another in their thumbprints, their blood pictures, their electrocardiograms and various other functions, so likewise we find that in their anxiety patterns they are never completely alike. Indeed, in each individual every anxiety tension pattern varies with each moment and thus is a time function. Even in one and the same person, anxiety and other neuromuscular-image patterns do not recur quite identically, but generally change much from instant to instant, minute to minute, hour to hour, day to day and month to month. In later chapters of this volume case histories will illustrate how unique and how changing are the tension patterns. Their continually changing variety can be dramatically presented on the oscilloscope screen. There the patient can see his tension patterns directly before him. To prove really effective any form of treatment must provide for individuation plus variability.

Some new but basic techniques presently developed will be outlined in the following paragraphs. Presumably these methods can be usefully adapted and applied in every case of chronic anxiety tension. As in all cases of clinical pedagogy, however, the skill, experience and discrimination of the doctor will be required to fit the pedagogy to the individual case. Because of individual variations, the doctor may select his timing of instructive procedures. Thus the unique features and the variations of anxiety patterns which every individual presents can be met effectively.

What position does tension control methodology take with respect to "unconscious" motivation in persistent anxiety patterns? During my internship many doctors indicated their belief that the "neuro" does not fully want to get well but is motivated to continue in his symptoms. Psychoanalysts attribute this to "the unconscious" and through dream and other analysis try to redeem the patient to emotional health. Unfortunately, although they often perform such analysis almost every day for years, there have been no convincing statistics showing success of analysts in overcoming anxiety.

Admittedly, many anxious patients often behave as if they did not fully seek freedom from emotional disturbance. However, the results secured by others and by myself through psychoanalytic methods have failed to equal those following use of methods of tension control(1). Recently after a year of instruction in our newer methods, one experienced analyst has joined me in this comparison. He has found that phobias and anxieties which had proved unyielding to analysis over the years nevertheless, have yielded to tension control instruction with relative promptness. He has been amazed at the improvement shown even in several months.

Whatever the motivation, we evidently get best results in therapy upon following the hypothesis that the patient really wants to get well although at times he may behave as if he does not.

By way of illustration of recent addenda to basic methods, we turn to some particulars in the case of an attorney, white, male, 41 years old. The diagnosis was essential hypertension, early coronary sclerosis, anxiety tension. For six years he had been under daily medication of sedatives and tranquilizers but had continued in legal practise. After about ten months of instructive treatment in progressive relaxation (later changed to self-operations control), his blood pressure values became stabilized within normal range, affording values usually on the order of 136/80. This result was achieved without the use of any hypotensive drug whatsoever.

Later on, after he had broken the habit of taking tranquilizer and hypnotic medication (by his own choice), the pressure values none the less continued within this normal range.

Accordingly he was informed that in my experience with moderate hypertension in patients who persistently practise daily at tension control, the blood pressure values generally continue within normal range. Previously he had been informed, however, that we do not rely on reassurance. It was added that if our findings become favorable, we recognize them as such, just as in driving a plane the pilot takes into account favorable weather and the plane's responses or the reverse. He received the favorable information with a satisfaction which did not persist, for from time to time later he stated that he did not accept the view that his blood pressure had become normalized(2).

Anxiety had been chronic, he stated, since early youth. It had become aggravated and directed toward his heart and blood pressure since the death of his father following coronary infarction about six years prior to his entering my clinic. During these six years, as indicated above, he had been taking daily doses of tranquilizer and of hypnotic. He had long believed that his emotional state was due to external pressures or to internal pathology, rather than to his own subjective habits. Most people, like him, naively believe that the difficulties they meet really are the cause of their anxieties. They will say, for example, "These matters have made me nervous!"

Following the reduction of his blood pressure in my clinic, he began to be greatly concerned about pains in the chest which might point to severe coronary heart disease. One evening in Chicago he notified me by phone that for the first time severe cardiac irregularity had set in. Upon examining him in his hotel room, no marked irregularity appeared. Upon being informed that the symptoms in his chest apparently were associated with esophageal spasm, he soon wondered whether this might be the first sign of diabetes or of carcinoma. His anxiety also took other turns. At times his concern turned to his competence as an attorney. He emphasized that this really was his "basic anxiety."

I related to him frankly that about one half of American males are said to show early coronary sclerosis beginning in the age range of thirty-five to forty years. I added that in his case the electrocardiograms were approximately negative, yet I ventured the tentative diagnosis of early coronary sclerosis along with early essential hypertension and anxiety state, so as not to conceal anything from him.

From the standpoint of tension control, I pointed out, we would not assume that his emotional difficulties could be traced to one "basic matter" of anxiety. I reminded him that when he no longer engaged in anxiety about one matter, he habitually turned to another. Doubtless it seemed to him and to most people that the cause of anxiety is one or another difficulty in life. Developments in his responses, however, soon afforded me the opportunity to cast doubt on this view. He was ignoring the part played by his own tendencies to be anxious. Like others who share his view of causation of anxiety, he was overlooking his own habits of response.

Proceeding to learn self-operations control, his task would be to relax the neuromuscular controls of anxiety if excessive whether or not he really had something to fear. We proceed now to outline six cardinal points of instruction applied in this case. Evidently these points apply to most cases of chronic anxiety.

1. While bending his right hand back at the wrist, he was instructed, "This is an example of independent action. In fact, contraction of the skeletal muscles is the basis of all independence, of all freedom of action. This is your doing. In order to emphasize this point to you we can dramatize it. We can say that a discovery of this clinic is that action and inaction of the striated muscles is the basis of all freedom and independence. If you please, since it is your doing, you may cease to do it. We can say that contraction of this sort is independent action and that ceasing to contract is independent inaction. It would be false to aver, 'I can't do it!' "

2. "When you engage in anxious reflection, you are making efforts for your welfare. Behind them is your purpose to meet the difficulty. Such efforts engage skeletal muscles and to this extent are of your own doing. As a layman untrained in the

tension states, you have not known this. Since you have begun your course here, you have learned to identify skeletal muscle tensions and have become aware that anxieties which formerly appeared to be forced on you really are in part your own doing and can be decreased if you identify the anxiety tension patterns and relax them.

Even so, the past habits of ignorance of this point tend to persist in you. In your past life you have lived largely in terms of goals. We call this 'goal living.' However, here and now you are to begin to take into account clearly and scientifically the self-operations control which can be employed in your every contraction for a purpose.

3. "We can define the words, 'hard' and 'easy.' We can agree to use the word, 'hard,' as meaning work performance, and 'easy.' as involving no work whatsoever. Then, insofar as bending the hand back includes work performance, it is by definition 'hard.' Conversely, insofar as going negative (or relaxing) requires no work performance, it is easy.

4. "As you have been able to observe during your training, the efforts of anxious reflection always include signals which you receive from tension patterns in the eyes as in visualizing the matter of your concern, or in the speech apparatus, as in saying something about it, or in skeletal muscle tensions elsewhere in the body as if to do something about the problem. Accordingly we can say that all these anxiety tensions are just as much your doing as is your act of bending back the hand. With know-how and skill, it is correct to say "It is easy to relax anxiety-tensions."

5. "Your hesitation, indecision, and lack of confidence that you can exercise control really arises from ignorance. This ignorance has been habitual from past lack of knowledge that during anxiety there is always the same kind of muscular tension pattern as there is in bending the hand back. Accordingly this ignorance needs now to give way to fact and to know-how. You can drive a motor car only if you employ

the controls set before you in the driver's seat.

6. Your task is to understand these principles, to learn to observe your controls and to apply yourself until you have made self-operations control a daily habit."

In teaching anxiety control, the doctor should remind himself and the patient constantly that we all tend to neglect the neuromuscular aspects of our mental activities, including our emotions. Prior to present training, we have never really had firsthand acquaintance much less familiarity therewith. Instead, we have always focussed our attention and interest on the issues of the moment. Even when we worry about our own health, although we note our subjective distressful and other sensations, before training we fail to observe the neuromuscular and image procedures by which we engage in the act of worry.

Observation of our effort energy expenditures belongs in general education, I believe, possibly as basically as "reading, writing and arithmetic." Children can learn this readily and even eagerly, as we have been finding in investigations at the University of Montreal. We have too long neglected personal efficiency not only in ourselves and in our patients: It is time I believe to take steps forward in prophylaxis against tension disorders and in the interests of saving our energies for useful job productivity.

The reason for bringing up matters of general education into our present discussion can be stated simply. It can prove of useful interest to the overemotional patient that we are teaching him controls which belong not only in medical treatment but have a widespread place in the public welfare.

With these points in view, we proceed to a summary of rules for educating the anxiety-prone patient, which for practise we doctors should first apply in our own daily lives.

STEP 1. Distinguish between the issue or problem or difficulty which you need to meet and your subjective response or representation thereof.

This is a method which improves our clarity of thinking objectively. The patient needs to be reminded repeatedly that while he engages in Step 1, he is not to relax. Notwithstanding this reminder, many patients try to relax extremely and to think more or less simultaneously during Step 1. According to our experience, this mixed procedure does not cultivate anxiety control, as becomes evident from the patient's continuing complaining.

Accordingly the rule for Step 1 can be stated thus: Sit down for a period of time, whether minutes or a half hour as seems suitable, and WITHOUT RELAXING determine what is the problem or issue or difficulty which you need to meet successfully. The doctor may illustrate to the patient what such matters have been in the case of others; examples follow: "My job is in jeopardy. My boss has been unfavorable!" "My wife has carcinoma!" "My child is doing badly in school." "My health is not good!" "I have pains in the chest which may be angina pectoris."

The doctor will need to leave the room while the patient takes Step 1. Upon his return the patient tries to state the issue stripped from his feelings and other reactions. Most patients require drill in this because they confuse their personal evaluations with objective facts. Many experience a feeling of relief when first they become able to state their difficulties more clearly. Not until success is achieved in clear objective statement does the doctor proceed to Step 2.

Step 2 is for patients who have had preliminary training in observation covering the entire neuromusculature, including that of the ocular and speech apparatus.

In STEP 2 the instruction is, Without relaxing, think of the difficulties which you delineated in Step 1. Observe your tension and image patterns as you do so.

Again the doctor steps out of the room to give the patient time by himself. In this step, however, the patient is to observe his effort tensions and other experiences at the moment he now engages in thinking over his difficulties. He is to think thus without relaxing as if he never had anxiety control. When the doctor returns, he is to report what he has observed himself doing in this interval. He is to report what he did just now. Here the doctor needs to be on the alert lest the patient generalize, telling how he has pictured difficulties in recent days and other times. This is wrong. What he is to report is precisely how he represented subjectively the objective matters which he delineates at the end of Step 1. In other words, in Step 2 he employs his trained powers of autosensory observation. This will not be done by persons who have not previously been trained in observation. The preliminary training that he has received is best offered in terms of non-anxious experiences. Only the skilled observer becomes able to experience trying emotions while observing simultaneously.

Step 3 follows Steps 1 and 2 successively. The patient has now delineated the difficulty objectively and has reported technically to the doctor how he has represented his difficulty in tension and image patterns during the intervals of Step 2.

In STEP 3 he is to RELAX SPECIFICALLY THE TENSION PATTERNS REPORTED at the end of Step 2.

Drill is to be given until taking Steps 1, 2 and 3 in succession has become a habit in daily living. Since the patient is to gain independence, this is stated to him as often as proves necessary. He is to be his own boss—he is to learn to run himself efficiently. This means without undue anxiety in his daily living.

## NOTES

(1) CF. BIOLOGY OF EMOTIONS, Table, pp. 166-169.

(2) His response is still another instance of evidence that our methods are not based on therapeutic suggestion. He explained his persistent doubts on habitual lack of self-confidence in overcoming difficulties and on his legal argumentativeness but also on his hesitation to accept an outcome favorably for fear of disappointment.

# Meditation as Meta-Therapy: 35
## Hypotheses Toward a Proposed
## Fifth State of Consciousness

### Daniel Goleman

Our normal waking consciousness . . . is but one special type of consciousness, whilst all about it, parted from it by the filmiest of screens, there lie potential forms of consciousness entirely different. We may go through life without suspecting their existence; but apply the requisite stimulus, and at a touch they are all there in all their completeness, definite types of mentality which somewhere have their field of application and adaptation. No account of the universe in its totality can be final which leaves these other forms of consciousness quite disregarded. How to regard them is the question—for they are so discontinuous with ordinary consciousness. . . . At any rate, they forbid a premature closing of our accounts with reality.

—William James, *The Varieties of the Religious Experience*

One year after I began my graduate training in clinical psychology, I started meditating regularly. As my training continued and as the effects of meditation started to be felt, I was struck by the similarity between changes I felt in myself, also observed in friends who were meditating, and those changes in personality and behavior that are the treatment goals of psychotherapy. My own experience concurs with a report by Herbert Benson (1969) at Harvard Medical School, who was using practitioners of transcendental meditation as subjects in a study of blood-pressure changes. Nineteen of the twenty volunteer subjects had previously used drugs ranging from marijuana and LSD to heroin: "All reported that they no longer took these drugs because drug-induced feelings became extremely distasteful as compared to those experienced during the practice of transcendental meditation."

*similarities in changes*

A more formal survey of the results of transcendental meditation reported in the *Hospital Times*, May 1, 1970, found:

> Increased energy and efficiency in performing any kind of work; increased calmness and decreased physical and mental tensions; increases in creativity, productivity, inventiveness, discrimination, intuitiveness and concentration; loss of a desire for or complete elimination of hallucinogenic or depressant drugs such as LSD, marijuana, amphetamines, tobacco, alcohol or coffee; attenuation of such symptoms as bad body posture, insomnia, high blood pressure; and better mobilization of body resources to combat various strenuous circumstances such as in accidents, sensory monotony, confined places, and cases of injury.

In the last three years I've had experience with a wide range of meditation techniques; transcendental meditation as taught by Maharishi Mahesh Yogi is the one I've practiced longest, am most thoroughly familiar with theoretically, and about which I hypothesize here. Transcendental meditation, or TM, like most yoga systems taught in the US, traces its roots back to the tradition of which Patanjali's *Yoga Sutras* is the classic statement. TM is a departure from the main body of contemporary Yogic practices. Maharishi (1969, p. 470) defines the technique as

*brief description of TM technique*

> . . . turning the attention inward towards the subtler levels of a thought until the mind transcends the experience of the subtlest state of the thought and arrives at the source of thought. . . . A thought-impulse starts from the silent creative centre within, as a bubble starts from the bottom of the sea. As it rises, it becomes larger; arriving at the conscious level of the mind, it becomes large enough to be appreciated as a thought, and from there it turns into speech and action. Turning the attention inwards takes the mind from the experience of a thought at the conscious level to the finer states of the thought until the mind arrives at the source of thought.

The vehicle for transcending the level of conscious thought is a *mantra*, a key word or sound taken from Sanskrit and given to the practitioner of TM by a trained teacher who instructs him in its use at an initiation. TM is practiced twice a day for 15 to 20 minutes sitting in a comfortable position with the eyes closed. Unlike some other meditation systems with which I'm familiar, TM does not use concentration but rather "passive volition," as is used in Autogenic Feedback Training (Green et al., 1970) for control of the autonomic nervous system. Maharishi (p. 471) emphasizes that TM "is neither a matter of contemplation nor of concentration. The process of contemplation and concentration each hold the mind on the conscious thinking level, whereas transcendental meditation systematically takes the mind to the source of thought, the pure field of creative intelligence." Some, though not all, meditation systems emphasize the active and effortful control of the mind. In sharp contrast in technique with TM, for instance, is Satipatthana, "mindfulness" meditation; instructions to the meditator in Buddhaghosa's fifth-century treatise on dealing with thoughts include (Conze, 1969, p. 83):

> . . . with teeth clenched and tongue pressed against the gums, he should by means of sheer mental effort hold back, crush and burn out the (offending) thought; in doing so, these evil and unwholesome ideas, bound up with greed, hate or delusion, will be forsaken and disappear; from their forsaking thought will become inwardly settled and calm, composed and concentrated.

The extent to which my analysis fits other meditation systems is an empirical question. There are systematic differences among meditation systems, but the consequences of these differences are unexplored. Charles Tart (1969) points out that the findings that Zen monks do not habituate to external stimuli during meditation, while practitioners of *raj yoga* do not even notice external stimuli, are behavioral reflections of the essence of the two philosophies—Zen mindfulness of, and yogic renunciation of, the sensory world. Different philosophical doctrines may well give rise to distinctive meditation techniques, which result in disparate psychological and behavioral outcomes. Or, they may all be pathways to the same ultimate destination. One necessary area of investigation is the comparative study of meditation techniques; the prime question is whether differences in technique are "real"—i.e., are psychophysiologically consequential—or whether structurally different meditation techniques are functionally equivalent. My hypotheses are generated from experience with TM,[1] but are framed in terms of meditation in general in the hope that they will be tested on a variety of different systems.

*consequences of differences in meditation systems unexplored*

*hypotheses framed for testing on a variety of systems*

[1] I recommend TM to those interested in doing experimental studies of meditation. Though Zen is probably more commonly known, TM is the most widely practiced technique in the US, having upward of 40,000 initiates. Any city or town with a large university or college is likely to have a Students' International Meditation Society, thus making samples readily available. Transcendental meditators are given uniform instruction, and practice on their own the same procedure no matter where they may be. SIMS is quite receptive to research proposals, and is establishing an institute to facilitate research much like the Zen Institutes in Japan (SIMS Institute for Advanced Study, 1015 Gayley Ave., Los Angeles, California 92024).

I conceptualize meditation as a "meta-therapy": a procedure that accomplishes the major goals of conventional therapy and yet has as its end-state a change far beyond the scope of therapies, therapists, and most personality theorists—an altered state of consciousness. Just as behavior therapy and psychoanalysis proved to embody the visions of the first and second forces in psychology, and as the encounter group is the main vehicle for the third force, so may meditation be the main route for the newly emergent fourth force. In his introduction to the section on meditation in *Altered States of Consciousness*, Charles Tart notes the mental-health implications of the dramatic effects obtained with ordinary subjects practicing meditation, but notes that despite these results, systematic investigation has been nil. This theoretical ground-breaking expedition in mapping the mechanisms of meditation, a *terra incognita* in relationship to more familiar psychological terrain, is meant as an invitation and spur to thoroughgoing empirical studies.

*meditation, meta-therapy and the fourth force*

*Hypothesis 1: Meditation can accomplish the same type of behavior change as does systematic desensitization, and (A) change will be less immediate with meditation than with desensitization (B) change will be more global with meditation than with desensitization.*

In 1934 Edmund Jacobson, a Chicago physician, proposed "a practical method of reducing the strains of modern living" in a best-selling book called *You Must Relax*. Jacobson later documented a number of cases (1964), covering the range of psychosomatic diseases, cured with his relaxation technique. This list is virtually duplicated by the survey of results of practicing transcendental meditation, and includes ulcers, asthma, insomnia, epilepsy, allergies, high blood pressure, migraine headaches, etc. Basing his technique on physiological studies of muscular tension, Dr. Jacobson propounded the principle—that relaxation is the direct physiological opposite of tension—on which is founded the behavior therapy technique most closely resembling meditation. The technique is "systematic desensitization" as practiced by Joseph Wolpe and Arnold Lazarus (1966).

*brief description of "systematic desensitization"*

Systematic desensitization involves three principle operations: (1) Training in deep muscle relaxation. The method is taught as Jacobson designed it, and requires training the patient to relax in sequence the various muscle groups throughout the body. The training takes about six interviews, and the patient practices at home for two fifteen-minute periods a day. (2) The construction of an anxiety hierarchy

—a graded list of anxiety-eliciting stimuli. The hierarchy systematically orders the situations, events, thoughts, or feelings in any way distressing to the patient according to the degree of anxiety elicited by each. The patient is taught to visualize as vivid an image as possible for the items in the hierarchy. (3) Graduated pairing, through mental imagery, of anxiety-eliciting stimuli with the state of relaxation. Each item is presented in order, starting with the least anxiety-eliciting, and is repeated until all anxiety is eliminated, and the next item presented. The hierarchy is thus ascended from weakest to strongest stimuli until there is no anxiety elicited by any item.

Many investigators have found that Yoga and Zen meditation markedly reduce basal metabolism rates (see, for example, Anand et al., 1961; Kasamatsu and Hirai, 1966; Akishige, 1968). In studying the physiological effects of transcendental meditation, Wallace (1970) found a decrease in the volume of oxygen consumed to 20 percent below base rate; Allison (1965) found a reduction to 4-6 breaths/minute from a base rate of 12-14, rises in skin resistance up to 500 percent, reduced blood pressure (20 percent and more according to Datey et al., 1969), with cardiac output reduced 25 percent and muscle activity reduced to zero. All these measures taken together indicate a relaxation more profound than that of deep sleep.

With the inward turning of attention in meditation, the meditator becomes keenly aware of the random chaos characteristic of thoughts in the waking state. The train of thought is endless, stops nowhere, and has no destination. The meditator witnesses the flow of psychic events, plannings, paranoias, hopes, fantasies, memories, yearnings, decisions, indecisions, observations, fears, scheming, guilt, calculations, exaltations and on and on and on. The whole contents of the mind compose the meditator's "desensitization hierarchy." The contents of this hierarchy are organic to the life concerns of the meditator; they are drawn from the stored pool of his total experience. This hierarchy is inherently self-regulating: the organizing principle for item presentation is literally "what's on one's mind," and so optimal salience is guaranteed.

*whole content of mind as meditators "desensitization hierarchy"*

As in the desensitization paradigm, the "hierarchy" is presented coupled with the deep relaxation of deep meditation. Unlike the therapy, desensitization is not limited to those items which therapist and patient have identified as problematic, though those are certainly included, but extends to

*mental stance of meditator toward his thoughts*

all phases of experience. Apart from the element of physiological relaxation, the mental stance of the meditator toward his thoughts can be one of three sorts: (1) totally immersed in one's thoughts; (2) wholly oblivious to thought, having transcended it through use of mantra or by other means. This state is "pure consciousness" as Lesh (1970, p. 46) describes it: "There is no cognition, no dreaming, no hallucinations, no data input (via normal sensory modalities), no information processing, no conscious activity at all, just full waking attention." On the basis of physiological evidence, Wallace (1970a) proposes this transcendental state as "a fourth major state of consciousness." (3) The third is to be in this transcendental "fourth state" and simultaneously witness thought.

There are two ways in which meditation "desensitizes." In the first state the meditator is deeply relaxed while exposed to a hierarchy, much as in conventional behavior therapy. In the third mental stance one is in the position which Maslow (1969, p. 57) discusses as the sense in which one "transcends" in psychotherapy: "This parallels the process in psychotherapy of simultaneously experiencing and of self-observing one's own experience in a kind of critical or editorial or detached and removed way so that one can criticize it, approve or disapprove of it and assume control, and therefore, the possibility of changing it exists." Maupin (1965, p. 144) in a study of Zen meditation, notes "subjectively felt benefits similar to those resulting from relaxation therapies were reported by several subjects." In meditation, relaxation is deep, the hierarchy of thoughts is innately experience-encompassing, self-observation conditions are such that inner feedback for behavior change is optimal. It is natural, global self-desensitization.

*Hypothesis 2: Meditation will reduce symptoms arising from anxiety in psychiatric disorders, especially "anxiety neurosis."*

*Hypothesis 3: Post-meditation performance in learning tasks will be significantly improved over pre-meditation performance.*

*Hypothesis 4: Post-meditation performance in perceptual tasks will be significantly improved over pre-meditation performance.*

*Hypothesis 5: Persons who have meditated extensively, compared to non-meditating controls, should be more accurate in perception of others.*

*Hypothesis 6: Persons who have meditated extensively, compared to non-meditating controls, should have less discrepancy between real and ideal self.*

The role of anxiety in psychological disorder is universally acknowledged by therapists. Angyal (1965, p. 72), for example, sees anxiety as "the crucial issue, the basic phenomenon in psychopathology. It is anxiety that creates, or marks, the parting of the ways between health and neurosis." Indeed, Cattell (1961) has based his system of diagnosis, prognosis, and therapy on the central variable of anxiety. Sullivan (1953) saw anxiety as the basis of the development of the self-system and severe anxiety as precluding clear comprehension of the immediate situation. Anxiety and consequent security operations, insofar as they are adaptive, are "of indispensable utility to each and every one of us," says Sullivan (p. 374), but are "a powerful brake on personal and human progress." He gives as an illustration the process of "selective inattention": *anxiety and selective inattention*

> By selective inattention we fail to recognize the actual import of a good many things we see, hear, think, do, and say. . . . Good observation and analysis of a mass of incidents selectively overlooked would expand the self-system, which usually controls the contents of awareness and the scope of the referential processes that are fully useful in communicating with others . . . selective inattention explains the faith we have in unnumbered prejudicial verbalisms, "rationalizations," about ourselves and others . . .

Recent research into the biochemistry of anxiety by Pitts (1969) at Washington University has shown that anxiety symptoms and attacks can be induced by infusions of lactate. Lactate is a normal product of cell metabolism, the end-product of the process by which cells break down glucose and extract energy from it. As muscles work, they convert glycogen to lactic acid, which diffuses into the bloodstream until eventually resynthesized into glucose in the liver. One property of the lactate ion is that it forms a chemical bond with calcium, which plays an important role in the transmission of nerve impulses. When calcium is injected along with lactate, there is a significant reduction in anxiety symptoms produced. Pitts theorizes that it is through interference with normal functioning of nerve impulses that excess lactate can cause anxiety symptoms. *biochemistry and anxiety*

As part of his study of physiological effects of TM, Wallace (1970a) took a timed series of blood samples before, during, and up to thirty minutes after meditation. He found that lactate decreases markedly at the beginning of meditation and continues to decrease during meditation; after meditation it remains at a low concentration. One subject showed a drop to 50 percent of his pre-meditation level, the other dropped 25-30 percent; both subjects maintained a reduced level to the end of the sampling period.

Should further testing bear out these initial lab findings, the implications for control of anxiety are striking. TM would be a beneficial addition not only in the lives of "anxiety neurotics" or in other disorders where anxiety plays a role, but for "normals" as well. In the case of the former, anxiety attacks would abate. For the latter, insofar as selective in-attention would be reduced, to that degree would we *not* "fail to recognize the actual import of a good many things we see, hear, think, do and say." As a consequence, perception of and communications with others should be improved, and self-perception should likewise become more realistic.

*meditation and perception of self and others*

Some preliminary findings support the idea that meditation improves self-perception; one study of long-time Zen meditators reported by Akishige (1968) found no difference between their self-estimate of ideal self and actual self. Maupin (1965) failed to find any relationship between attention functions among the college students he trained in zazen, but felt that this failure was due to their inexperience and discomfort in the face of "strange inner experience."

*meditation and empathy*

Lesh (1970) trained counseling students in zazen and found their performance on an empathy measure significantly better than students who did not meditate; he suggests that a therapist who could achieve the level of detached awareness attained in zazen during a counseling session would "more fully understand and appreciate what the client is saying and feeling." Lesh interprets his results in the regression-in-the-service-of-the-ego model, and attributes his findings to the effects of experiencing the primary process mode during zazen. He notes, however, that all subjects, including controls, were students in a class where the instructor caused them to get increasingly tense and angry as the term progressed. The zazen sessions were held once daily; as it happened, this was immediately after the tension-provoking class. In view of the possible efficacy of meditation in reducing anxiety, the improved empathy finding could alternatively be interpreted as the result of anxiety-reduction. No measures of anxiety were administered.

Another area in which meditation-reduced anxiety would
be significant is learning. It is axiomatic that high anxiety
levels inhibit learning ability. Brown (1970) of the Stanford
Research Institute reports that while working in biofeedback
control of autonomic functions—an extremely subtle learning
situation—he found the task strenuous. During this period he
began the regular practice of transcendental meditation. Experimenting with the relationship between TM and control
of autonomic functions, he discovered that the learning task,
such as emitting and maintaining any EEG brain-wave
rhythm he chose, was significantly facilitated by practicing
TM immediately prior to the training sessions. There is the
possibility that apart from facilitation effects due to reduced
anxiety, simply the practice gained with meditation in working at the subtler levels of the mind aids mastery in the
specific learning task of brain-wave control—but that is an
empirical question.

*meditation and learning*

*Hypothesis 7: Meditators Will Have More Energy and Need
Less Sleep Compared to Their Energy and Sleep Levels
Before Beginning to Meditate.*

*Hypothesis 8: Several Years of Meditation Will Produce
Deep Level Personality Changes in the Direction of "Mental
Health."*

*Hypothesis 9: Several Years of Meditation Will Produce
Changes in Musculature and Posture in the Direction of
"Improvement."*

*Hypothesis 10: Meditators Will Tend to Be More Resistant
to Stress-Induced Fatigue than Will Non-Meditators.*

Freud believed in the "mysterious leap from mind to body,"
and based his early theory of anxiety on the transformation
of physical into mental. But though he saw the brain and
nervous system as "the bodily organ and scene of action" of
mental life he saw no means of connecting acts of consciousness with their physiological substrata. He despaired of finding systematic connections between consciousness and the
nervous system (1938, p. 44): "Everything that lies between
these two terminal points is unknown to us and, so far as
we are aware, there is no direct relation between them."
From Freud on, mainline psychoanalytic practice if not
thinking, has focused on the intra-psychic to the exclusion
of the body.

Beginning with Wilhelm Reich (1948), refocusing attention on the patient's "character armor" as revealed in his posture, movements, facial expressions, etc., a growing therapeutic school has begun to chart and use the direct relations between mind and body. With the contributions of Lowen's (1958) bioenergetic analysis, Perls' (1969) gestalt therapy, Pesso's psychomotor therapy, and others, that leap has become increasingly less mysterious. The theoretical underpinning and key to the mind-body leap of these approaches is summarized in the "psychophysiological principle" (Green et al., 1970):

*"psycho-*
*physiological*
*principle"*

> Every change in the physiological state is accompanied by an appropriate change in the mental-emotional state, and conversely, every change in the mental-emotional state, conscious or unconscious, is accompanied by an appropriate change in the physiological state.

*significance of*
*"unstressing"*

In meditation, the psychophysiological principle can be used to understand the significance of "unstressing," a term used by practitioners of TM. Unstressing takes the form during meditation of completely involuntary, unintended, and spontaneous muscular-skeletal movements and proprioceptive sensations: momentary or repeated twitches, spasms, gasps, tingling, tics, jerking, swaying, pains, shaking, aches, internal pressures, headaches, weeping, laughter, etc. The experience covers the range from extreme pleasure to acute distress.[2] In TM, unstressing is gradual during regular daily meditation, so that it is not always discernible. During

*discussion of*
*"unstressing"*

special extended meditation sessions where one meditates throughout much of the day, more extreme forms of unstressing can occur. When Maupin taught zazen to a group of college students as part of an experiment, they mentioned to him the emergence of "hallucinoid feelings, muscle tension, sexual excitement, and intense sadness" (1965, p. 145). Because of the unpredictable nature of unstressing, meditators who are unprepared for it, or who are in the midst of others who do not understand the process, can become agitated when it occurs in disturbing forms. For this reason teachers of TM and other systems recommend day-long meditation only in supervised and secluded situations. Psychiatric clinics are beginning to get new patients who have been meditating on their own all day for many days, and are brought in by others who can't understand and are disturbed by behavior

---

[2]Vivid and detailed first-person accounts of unstressing are reported in *Guruvani* magazine by students of the ashtanga yoga system of Swami Muktananda. An elaborate and detailed description of these involuntary movements in Taoist meditation is given in Charles Luk's *Secrets of Chinese Meditation* (Luk, 1966)

changes they see; the dynamics of this influx are parallel to the continuing wave of "bad trips" due to drugs. As with acute drug cases, the psychiatric intervention may worsen and prolong distress rather than alleviate it, while someone familiar with meditation can reassure the person and alleviate the crisis without recourse to the paraphernalia of psychiatry.

The fundamental assumption in understanding the function of unstressing is, as in psychoanalytic thought, that all past experience leaves its mark on present behavior. In accord with the psychophysiological principle, mental-emotional events are parallelled by physiological changes, and so the organism is shaped by the events of a lifetime. The nervous system is the repository of all experiences of emotional strain, pleasure, fatigue, tensions, stresses, etc., whether of "physical" or "mental" origin. It is through reading extensions of the nervous system such as musculature that the gestalt or bioenergetic or psychomotor therapist gets to the major issues in a person's life—literally, to what has shaped him—and begins the work of freeing the person from the grip of the past events that have left that particular mark.

In meditation this same process of liberating the nervous system from past stresses is undergone without effort, volition, or intention. As the meditator reaches a level of profound relaxation and pure awareness with no thoughts, a wide range of kinesthetic sensations, vague feelings, or any of the array of psychic events can be triggered at random. Autokinesthesia may be accompanied by thoughts or may occur alone; or one may notice only thoughts but no movement, as is the case in the following passage, in which Herrigel (1953, p. 56) describes this process in zazen:

> This exquisite state of unconcerned immersion in oneself is not, unfortunately, of long duration. It is liable to be disturbed from the inside. As though sprung from nowhere, moods, feelings, desires, worries and even thoughts incontingently rise up, in a meaningless jumble . . .

If attention is turned to scanning the body when thoughts alone are experienced, underlying proprioceptive kinesthetic sensations invariably will be noticed.

Lerner (1967) has proposed that kinesthetic sensations of this sort are, in fact, the stuff dreams are made of. In one of Dement and Kleitman's (1957) first REM-EEG studies, they noticed very fine digital movements in sleeping subjects.

*"the stuff dreams are made of"*

Wolpert (1960), following up on this lead, compared dream reports with muscle-potential activity and found that the fine movements executed, described as "slight, abortive muscular stirrings," were appropriate to the content of the dreams. Conceptualizing dreams as "kinesthetic fantasy" (i.e., fantasy in the kinesthetic modality, as opposed, say, to the visual or auditory), Lerner points out that in sleep, gross body movements build up to a peak just before the onset of the dream state, terminate abruptly with the onset of dreaming, and reappear when the dream REMs cease. This pattern is just the reverse of fine muscular stirrings, which occur primarily during dreaming but are negligible other times (or which may fade into the background when gross movements are present). Dement and Wolpert (1958) report that gross body movements indicate an absence of dreams. On this basis, Lerner suggests that gross, overt motor activity is antithetical to kinesthetic fantasy, and that the key factor in the facilitation of kinesthetic fantasy is physical immobility.

*kinesthetic fantasy and physical immobility*

Dement (1960) has shown that persons deprived of dreamtime in sleep exhibit symptoms of personality disorganization, including heightened levels of tension, anxiety, and irritability, difficulty in concentrating, impaired motor coordination, and so on. They also make increasingly frequent efforts to dream; when allowed to do so their total dream time rose significantly and stayed high until the time lost was made up. Thus dreaming is in some way a vital function for the maintenance of personality organization. Lerner suggests that "one may sleep in order to dream," and proposes (p. 98)

> that body image forms the basis of ego and that in order to maintain the coherence of body image and thus of personality organization, kinesthetic activity must be supplemented by the sort of kinesthetic fantasy which takes place in and is facilitated by the dreaming state.

Lerner assumes that the crucial restorative effects of dreaming can occur only in sleep because only then is the normal person in a "relatively profound, sustained, and pervasive state of physio-logical immobilization." This affords the opportunity to engage in kinesthetic fantasy that is fully elaborated, as opposed to the truncated kinesthetic fantasy that fleetingly may occur in the waking state. Wallace (1970b) in his study of TM found evidence that the decrease in metabolic rate during meditation is in some ways *more* profound a physiological immobilization than that of sleep. In their EEG study of zazen, Kasamatsu and Hirai (1966) found the cerebral excitatory level gradually lowered as it is in sleep, but in a way fundamentally distinct from the sleep pattern. Thus meditation would also qualify as a time when kinesthetic fantasy, with all its beneficial effects, could occur: the basic pre-condition of physiological immobilization prevails. But because the meditator maintains awareness during the process, his experience can encompass the kinesthetic byplay as well as any accompanying thoughts or fantasies; and so he reports "unstressing." The dreamer, in part because of a Western cultural tendency to ignore kinesthetic experience, recalls mainly visual and auditory elements of the same process. Another factor distinguishing the experience of dreaming from unstressing is that rapid eye movements—an indicator of dreaming—while themselves kinesthetic, provide an unstructured visual stimulus which the dreamer shapes into meaningful configurations in dream construction; in meditation there are no REMs (Wallace, 1970b).

*similarities and differences between dreaming and meditation*

I propose that unstressing serves the same psychological function for the meditator as do dreams for the dreamer. In keeping with the psychophysiological principle, each movement in unstressing signals the release of a stored mental-emotional state, event, or impression, and each such psychic event indicates the release of stress on the level of nerve-and-muscle. That is, each kinesthetic event is parallelled by a psychic one, and each psychic event by a kinesthetic one. Just as Wolpert (1960) found that muscle movements in dreaming are systematically related to the content of dreams, and as Freud (1956) noted that the content of dreams may derive from a residue of that day's events or from events in the dreamer's remote past, so with unstressing: movements and thoughts are related to each other and to past events.

*psychological function of dreams and of "unstressing" in meditation*

Lowen (1957, p. 14) analyzes the psychic and somatic functions in terms of a unitary system and notes that "the sum total of the muscular tensions seen as a gestalt . . . is seen on the psychic level as character." Lowen's bioenergetic therapy assumes that every emotional disturbance involves a block in the flow of energy to the organs of discharge. When the therapist facilitates the discharge of blocked energy on the bodily level, the patient relives the situation that induced the block. As Reich (1942, p. 267) put it, "dissolution of a muscular rigidity not only liberates vegetative energy, but, in addition, also brings back into memory the very infantile situation in which the repression had taken effect." According to Lowen (p. 103), every bioenergetic change acts on two levels simultaneously: "on the somatic level there is an increase in motility, coordination and control; on the psychic level there is a reorganization of thinking and attitudes."

The same relationship between psyche and soma obtains with unstressing in meditation, and the same results. The following self-report from a woman in her late forties who practices TM will illustrate:

> Last night I started to meditate . . . and all of a sudden I felt small, like my head only reached the tabletop. My mother came down and took my hand and I had feelings of intense pleasure. And then I had an overwhelming sadness and I tried to see my mother's face and couldn't, it was all foggy. And then I realized this total sadness and started weeping profusely and an overwhelming sense of panic came, and I repeatedly wanted to see her face and couldn't, and I started to shake and my bladder started to empty as it does in a little girl, and that brought me out of meditation. I remembered violently that my mother was dead and felt this sadness and then it lessened and ever since then I've been having vivid memories of things I hadn't been able to remember since her death. I wasn't seeing that child—I *was* that child. I've been living every emotion of it. Since back then it's the first time I've felt that happy feeling I had with my mother. Since then I felt this terrible sense of loss and cried several times. I didn't when my mother died. I feel undone inside. I'm geared to sad memories of my childhood and all these happy ones are flooding in now. Today when I saw my daughters' faces I really saw them like I hadn't ever before, and they knew, they responded. I'm seeing every person as though for the first time they're 3-dimensional instead of 2-dimensional. I've always been very controlled, I don't think I've given myself permission to react before. Now I don't feel these are people, but playmates. It's a good feeling. I didn't know I wasn't feeling anything before, but I know from now I didn't. It's like all the grey cardboard figures came to life. Had you asked yesterday I would have felt my perception was excellent, but I've been perceiving people through learned responses, like a nurse, registering skin tone, calcium deposits on teeth, but not *seeing* them. All that is different now.

*body image and tension release*

Lerner proposes that the positive benefits of dreams are due to their role in maintaining coherence of body image. I suggest that their function on another level is in the release of tensions accruing from the past life events in which they originated. The tensions may be unnoticed in their occurrence —as when the auditory system registers the noise of a city to which one has become habituated—or they may be barely noticed and soon forgotten—as in the case of a flinch response to a flying object—or they may be of major import as part of an emotional crisis—as when one restrains oneself from hitting an opponent in an argument. It is this last variety of tension-inducers that therapists like Reich and Lowen traditionally deal with; the body expels the whole range in dreams during sleep and in unstressing during meditation, as in the case above.

Abreaction in unstressing can occur wholly on the body level. A twenty-two-year-old girl reports:

> I had very crooked teeth when I was a child. My teeth are so big for my jaw they had to pull eight teeth. When my second teeth came in I started to notice my jaws didn't match. For several months when I meditated I would feel my jaw move around, always pulling toward the right. It got more and more intense and then the other day there was a very strong and painful pull, a large "Crack!" and my jaw moved over. When it happened I was so amazed, it was so intense, but I didn't stop meditating. I knew what was happening. When I looked in the mirror, my teeth were aligned. Now my mouth muscles are more relaxed; when I smile now it feels different.

Body image "exists" on the level of mind; kinesthesia on the level of body. But body and mind are a duality, not opposites. When the organism is impinged upon by tension-inducing events during the day, the work it must do to maintain its functional integrity is to "cast out" those tensions. This is what is happening in dreaming and unstressing: the organism is maintaining itself as an integrated unit by readjusting to a state of normality parts that have become misshapen and dysfunctional during waking activities. The psychological meaning of this process is that coherent body image is maintained or restored and thus ego-wholeness preserved.

*body and mind a duality, not opposites*

What Luthe (1969) says of autogenic training applies equally to meditation: that it can enable natural mechanisms in the body to regain their "otherwise restricted capacity for self-regulatory normalization." Stress release is one of these mechanisms. Luthe (p. 318) says

> the long-range effects resulting from the practice of Autogenic Training are manifold and depend largely on the psychophysiological constellation of the individual. . . . Briefly one could say that a gradual process of multidimensional optimazation develops. This process is reflected in psychodynamic changes which can be verified by physiologic measurements and [psychological] tests.

*verifiable psychodynamic changes*

The same is true for meditation.

*Hypothesis 11: A fifth major state of consciousness exists which is a fusion of the fourth state with the waking, sleeping, and dreaming states but has properties distinct from the first four states.*

*Hypothesis 12: People in the fifth state do not tend to habituate in daily experience during the waking state.*

*Hypothesis 13: People in the fifth state will experience in meditation minimal unstressing and preponderant pure awareness: unstressing will be derivative of "day-residue" from activities prior to the meditation session.*

*EEG patterns and meditation*

In reporting on operant control of the EEG alpha rhythm, Kamiya (1966) mentions that the state of consciousness associated with alpha is one of "a general calming down of the mind" in which thoughts interfere with maintenance of the state. He also reports that his best subjects tend to be people that have practiced meditation in one form or another. An EEG study of Zen meditation (Kasamatsu and Hirai, 1969) found that production of alpha was associated with proficiency at meditation and with number of years practicing. Some very proficient subjects, who had been practicing zazen for more than twenty years, showed heavy alpha production which gave way to theta trains. Yogis practicing *raj yoga* who were tested in India (Anand et al., 1961) also showed the alpha rhythm. Wallace's (1970a) study of TM found that during meditation alpha-wave activity predominates; some subjects showed EEG patterns similar to those found in twenty-year practitioners of zazen. Taking this finding in conjunction with those of lowered basal metabolism, lowered lactate level, etc., Wallace (1970b) proposes the existence of a "fourth major state of consciousness"—that special psychophysiological state of rest and pure awareness one can reach in meditation. Tart (1970, p. 37) refers to the phenomenological experience of this state as "the Void," where the person's "identity is potentiality, he's aware of everything and nothing, his mind is absolutely quiet, he's out of time, out of space. . . ." A Tibetan description of the same state is given by Evans-Wentz (1969, p. 211):

In its true state, mind is naked, immaculate; not made of anything, being of the Voidness; clear, vacuous, without duality, transparent; timeless, uncompounded, unimpeded, colourless; not realizable as a separate thing, but as the unity of all things, yet not composed of them; of one taste, and transcendent over differentiation.

Kasamatsu and Hirai (1966) describe this state of restful awareness as a "special state of consciousness in which the cortical excitatory level becomes lower than in ordinary wakefulness but is not lowered as in sleep"; they add, "and yet outer and inner stimulus is precisely perceived with steady responsiveness." This "steady responsiveness" among the Zen meditators means that alpha blocking during meditation is less susceptible to habituation to sensory stimuli than in the ordinary waking state. Wallace (1970b) also found no habituation with TM. Kasamatsu and Hirai report (1969, p. 449):

*responsiveness without disturbance*

> In this state of mind one cannot be affected by either external or internal stimulus, nevertheless he is able to respond to it. He perceives the object, responds to it, and yet is never disturbed by it. Each stimulus is accepted as stimulus itself and treated as such. One Zen master described such a state of mind as that of noticing every person one sees on the street but of not looking back with emotional curiosity.

In commenting on these findings, Tart (1969) points out that ordinarily, people "substitute abstract cognitive patterns for the raw sensory experience." That is, people "habituate" to their surroundings—one doesn't notice the places passed by daily on the way to work save in a stereotyped manner. Schachtel (1966) describes this natural tendency of people to habituate, i.e., not to see or attend to the world surrounding them—including other people—except in terms of set perceptual patterns; the rationale for the Rorschach test is in large part built upon the twin assumptions of habituation in everyday life and of the power to break up these perceptual sets inherent in the uniqueness of the blots as stimuli. Fromm (1960) sees this phenomenon of habituation to self and to others as essentially opposite to a psychological definition of "enlightenment":

*discussion of habituation*

> . . . it is a state in which the person is completely tuned to the reality outside and inside of him, a state in which he is fully aware of it and fully grasps it. *He* is aware of it—that is, not his brain nor any other part of his organism, but he, the whole man. He is aware of *it*; not as an object over there which he grasps with his thought, but *it*, the flower, the dog, the man, in its or his full reality. He who awakes is open and responsive to the world, and he can be open and responsive because he has given up holding on to himself as a thing, and

*a psychological definition of "enlightenment"*

thus has become empty and ready to receive. To be enlightened means "full awakening of the total personality to reality."

*meditative exercises and "autonomic" body functions*

A number of alpha studies report the occurrence of prominent alpha activity in subjects' normal waking state: Anand et al. found it in four practitioners of *raj yoga*; Kasamatsu and Hirai noticed persistent alpha even after the end of Zen meditation; Wallace (1970b) reports that with TM, after meditation ended, regular alpha activity continued while eyes were closed, and irregular alpha continued after eyes were open. The more one produces alpha, the easier it becomes; Kamiya (1970) observes that every subject who produced a high percentage of alpha rhythm in a training session with eyes open was a natural high producer with eyes closed. Wallace (1970a) presents evidence that other types of "autonomic" body functions apart from alpha production can be controlled or changed through TM, and that the effects of these changes persist after meditation has ended and into the waking state. This has been demonstrated, for example, for lowering lactate level and blood pressure (Wallace, 1970a), and may be the psychophysiologic ground for reports of an "afterglow" effect in the waking state after meditation is over. Citing a range of psychophysiological evidence, Luthe (1969) concludes that the regular practice of autogenic meditative exercises brings about "certain functional changes in the trainee's brain" of a lasting nature.

It seems that the more meditation is practiced, the easier it becomes to produce and maintain the alpha rhythm and concomitant physiological changes that Wallace calls the "fourth major state of consciousness." These psychophysiological changes observed in meditation—the fourth state—

*prototypic experience of fifth state of consciousness*

can become infused into the waking activities of the meditator to produce a "fifth state" of consciousness which is on the psychophysiological level a function of waking-state and fourth-state psychophysiology but identical to neither, and which is on the psychological level what Fromm describes as "enlightenment." The prototypic experience of the fifth state, and the ground from which it grows, is the presence in meditation of fourth state pure awareness coexistent with thought processes. The process whereby this occurs involves a "purification" or "culturing" of the nervous system, through processes such as unstressing and experiencing subtler and subtler levels of thought, which are prerequisite to and necessary for the sustained maintenance of fourth-state effects in waking-state activities. Maharishi (1969, p. 173) describes the effects on consequent waking activity of TM:

When the mind transcends during transcendental meditation, the metabolism reaches its lowest point; so does the process of breathing, and the nervous system gains a state of restful alertness which, on the physical level, corresponds to the state of bliss-consciousness, or transcendent Being. . . . activity after meditation brings an infusion of transcendental Being into the nature of the mind and through it into all aspects of one's life in the relative field. With the constant practice of meditation, this infusion continues to grow and when it is full-grown cosmic consciousness will have been attained.

There is at present only circumstantial and anecdotal evidence to support these propositions. Green et al. (1970), for example, trained subjects via autogenic feedback to lower muscle tension levels, raise skin temperature, and increase percentage of alpha—all effects Wallace found as naturally occurring in TM. They report that their most proficient subjects were practitioners of Yoga. To my knowledge there have been no studies of fourth-state psychophysiologic effects on subjects in the waking state performing normal activities. The fifth state seems to occur naturally, but its occurrence, like the birth of quadruplets or a large meteor striking the earth, is a statistically rare event and so not easily studied. But there are reports of people who seem to be experiencing the fifth state. Bucke's *Cosmic Consciousness* is one such. Yogananda (1946) describes the transition from fourth state to fifth, which he calls *sabikalpa samadhi* and *nirbikalpa samadhi*, respectively:

*transition from fourth state to fifth state*

In *sabikalpa samadhi* the devotee attains temporary realization of his oneness with Spirit but cannot maintain his cosmic consciousness except in the immobile trance state. By continuous meditation he reaches the higher state of *nirbikalpa samadhi*, in which he moves freely in the world and performs his outward duties without any loss of God-perception.

This transition can occur rapidly or may take many years, as a function of the state of the nervous system of the individual. During this process the composition of meditation sessions changes from an initial stage of preponderant unstressing (thoughts, sensations, autokinesthesia, etc.) and momentary or extended pure awareness, to a final stage of momentary unstressing and preponderant or even unbroken fourth state pure restful awareness. This transition marks the purification necessary to maintain the fifth state. Over the next few years a large enough sample may emerge from among those practicing TM and other techniques to allow experimental studies of the fifth state of consciousness.

*Hypothesis 14: People in the fifth state have "lucid" dreams as a regular occurrence.*

*description of "lucid" dream*

One attribute of the fifth state, according to Maharishi (1969), is that pure awareness infuses not only the waking state but also the dreaming and sleep states. With all the first three states of consciousness infused with the fourth, one can witness himself going through the sleeping and even the dreaming processes, just as one can witness thought process in meditation. This aspect of the mind is called "the Witness" in the Gurdjieffian system (see Ouspensky, 1938). Witnessing of the dream state has been reported by Ouspensky using a method of holding in mind a definite image or thought while falling asleep. Other writers have described the same phenomenon when naturally occurring and called it the "lucid" dream. Tart (1970, p. 170) has had lucid dreams about three times in his life, and characterizes them this way: "The dreamer 'wakes' from an ordinary dream in that he feels he is suddenly in possession of his normal waking consciousness and knows that he is actually lying in bed asleep *but*, the dream he is in remains perfectly real." This aptly describes the fifth-state experience of dreaming save that the person would not have to "wake" but rather would go into a dream while already fully aware, observing the whole process from beginning to end while experiencing the "reality" of the dream. This dual process also characterizes the fifth-state experience of both the sleep and waking states: both realities are fully experienced simultaneously with pure awareness.

*Hypothesis 15: People in the fifth state will tend to have an absence of psychopathology and of "metapathology."*

*Hypothesis 16: People in the fifth state will function on the level of "metaneeds" and "B-cognition."*

Because of the beneficial side-effects of meditation already discussed, a person who had achieved the fifth state via this path would be a fully integrated personality by the time he arrived. In undergoing the process of deep relaxation, unstressing, and consequent purification of the nervous system, he would undergo on a profound, nonverbal level those major changes that psychotherapies aim for. Harman (1969, p. 131) proposes as the central concept for a unified view of the processes of personal change that "personality and behavior patterns change consequent upon a change in self-image, a modification of the person's emotionally felt perception of himself and his relationship to his environment." Meditation provides this in the form of what Harman calls "the subjective experiencing of a 'higher self' and the development of a self-image congruent with this experience."

The fifth-state meditator should be gratified in basic needs and have become "self-actualized" and "metamotivated" by "B-values" in Maslow's (1967) terms. Maharishi (1969, p. 164) says of the level of integration of a fifth-state man, "He is established in the Self, and by virtue of this, even when he acts in the field of the senses and experiences their objects, he is not lost in them; maintaining his status in Being, he quite naturally maintains evenness of mind." After only four weeks experimental zazen, Lesh's (1970) subjects showed significantly more openness to experience and empathic ability, and Lesh was ready to conclude, "Meditation appears to be an effective means of assisting people in self-actualization." Moyer (1965) calls meditation the "doorway to wholeness," and notes the similarities between Maslow's self, the being life, and meditation's dictum of "total attentiveness" to immediate reality.

The dangers of falling into what Maslow (1967) calls a "metapathology," such as cynicism, nihilism, hatred, bleakness, black-and-white thinking, disintegration, boredom, hopelessness, insecurity, selfishness, confusion, conflict, depression, uneasiness, and so on, would be minimal for the fifth-state meditator, because the experience of the "spirit" requisite for escaping them is built into meditation. Maslow describes techniques for re-education and realization of "the Real Self" (1967, p. 117):

> exercises which help to develop (or teach) our sensory awareness, our body awareness, our sensitivities to the inner signals (given off by our needs, capacities, constitution, temperament, body, etc.)—all these apply also . . . to our inner metaneeds, i.e., to the education of our yearning for beauty, law, truth, perfection, etc.

Meditation, the essence of (though not the same as) introspection, certainly qualifies. Just as dream-deprivation produces symptoms of psychological disorder, loss of motor coordination, and the like, it may be that the metapathologies are all symptomatic of "meditation-deprivation."

In the fifth state the "peak" of experience has become a

plateau, what Maslow (1970) describes as "serene and contemplative B-cognitions rather than climactic ones." The
fifth state corresponds to what Maslow describes as "transcending self-actualizers" in his Theory Z (p. 38):

> They perceive unitively or sacrally (that is, the sacred within
> the secular), or they see the sacredness of all things *at the
> same time* that they also see them at the practical, everyday
> D-level. They can sacralize everything at will, i.e., perceive
> it under the aspect of eternity. This ability is in *addition* to
> —not mutually exclusive with—good reality testing.

*various
attributes of
fifth state*

Among other attributes Maslow postulates for this fifth-state
type are: the role of innovator, Taoistic objectivity, "people
who know who they are, where they are going, what they
want, what they are good for, in a word strong Selves, using
themselves well and authentically and in accordance with
their own true nature," profoundly "religious" or "spiritual"
in either the theistic or non-theistic sense. The fifth-state
person is at the level of "supernormal Man" in Assagioli's
(1965) sense, is "liberated" as Watts (1961) uses the term
and "non-mechanical" as Ouspensky (1969) means it, and
has attained "true sanity" as Laing (1967) describes it:

> true sanity entails in one way or another the dissolution of
> the normal ego, that false self completely adjusted to our
> alienated social reality . . . and the eventual re-establishment
> of a new kind of ego functioning, the ego now being the
> servant of the divine, and no longer the betrayer.

And yet the fifth-state person continues to function as though
completely adjusted to social reality, for he has readjusted
at a higher level of integration.

A man in the fifth state has undergone profound psychological changes, but there are no necessary concommitant external manifestations of these changes on the level of social
role. Maharishi (1969, p. 174) explains that "when the men
of the world, actively engaged in many phases of life, reach
the state of cosmic consciousness through Yoga, they continue to act, mainly from force of habit." As the Zen maxim
puts it: Before enlightenment, chop wood and carry water;
after enlightenment, chop wood and carry water.

With Maslow, I caution those who might do research in this
area that fifth-state people will be distributed as heavily
among businessmen, workers, managers, educators, and
political people as among "the professionally 'religious,' the
poets, intellectuals, musicians and others who are *supposed*

to be transcenders and are officially labeled so." And I must state that this paper is the bare beginning of the delineation of the process whereby meditation changes the meditator into the fifth-state being, nor does it do justice to describing what that state is like—in Maslow's words, "They are certainly this; but they are also more than this."

## REFERENCES

AKISHIGE, Y. (ED.) Psychological studies in Zen, *Bull. Fac. Lit. Kyushu U.*, No. 5 and No. 11, Fukuoka, Japan, 1968.

ALLISON, J. Respiratory changes during the practice of the technique of transcendental meditation, *Lancet*, April, 1970.

ANAND, B., CHHINA, G., SINGH, B. Some aspects of EEG studies in Yogis, *EEG Clin. Neurophysiol.*, 1961, *13*, 452-56. Also in C. Tart (Ed.), *Altered states of consciousness*. New York: Wiley, 1969.

ANGYAL, A. *Neurosis and treatment*: *A holistic theory*, E. Haufman and R. M. Jones, Eds. New York: Wiley, 1965.

ASSAGIOLI, R. *Psychosynthesis*: *A manual of principles and techniques*. New York: Hobbs, Dorman, 1965.

BENSON, H. Yoga for drug abuse, *New Eng. J. Med.*, Nov. 13, 1969, vol. 381, no. 20.

BROWN, D. Lecture, Teacher Training Course, Humboldt State College, Arcata, California, Aug. 23, 1970.

BUCKE, R. *Cosmic consciousness*: *A study in the evolution of the human mind*. New Hyde Park, N.Y.: University Books, 1961.

CATTELL, R. B., SCHEIER, I. H. *The meaning and measurement of neuroticism and anxiety*. New York: Ronald Press, 1961.

CONZE, E. *Buddhist meditation*. New York: Harper & Row, 1969.

DATEY, K., DESHMUKH, S., DALVI, C., VINEKAR, S. Shavasan: a Yogic exercise in the management of hypertension, *Angiology*, 1969, *20*, 325-33.

DEMENT, W. The effects of dream deprivation, *Science*, 1960, *131*, 1705-7.

DEMENT, W., KLEITMAN, N. Cyclic variations in the EEG during sleep and their relation to eye movements, body motility and dreaming, *Electroencephalogr. Clin. Neurophysiol.*, 1957, *9*, 673-90.

DEMENT, W., WOLPERT, E. The relation of eye movements, body motility, and external stimuli to dream content, *J. Exp. Psychol.* 1958, *55*, 543-53.

EVANS-WENTZ, W. Y. *The Tibetan book of the great liberation.* London: Oxford University Press, 1969.

FISHER, C., DEMENT, W. Studies on the psychopathology of sleep and dreams, *Amer. J. Psychiat.*, 1963, *119*, 1160-68.

FREUD, S. *An outline of psychoanalysis.* Vol. 23, *Complete works.* London: Hogarth Press, 1938.

FREUD, S. *The interpretation of dreams.* New York: Basic Books, 1956.

FROMM, E., ET AL. *Zen Buddhism and psycho-analysis.* London: Allen & Unwin, 1960.

GREEN, E. E., GREEN, A. M., WALTERS, E. D. Voluntary control of internal states: psychological and physiological, *J. Transpersonal Psychol.*, 1970, *2*, 1, 1-26.

*Guruvani Magazine.* Ganeshpuri, India: Shree Gurudev Ashram, publishers.

HARMAN, W. W. The New Copernican Revolution, *J. Humanistic Psychol.*, 1969, *9*, 2, 127-34.

HERRIGEL, E. *Zen in the art of archery.* New York: McGraw-Hill, 1953.

*Hospital Times,* Towards pinning down meditation, London, May 1, 1970.

JACOBSON, E. *You must relax.* New York: McGraw-Hill, 1957.

JACOBSON, E. *Anxiety and tension control.* Philadelphia: Lippincott, 1964.

KAMIYA, J. Operant control of the EEG alpha rhythm and some of its reported effects in consciousness, in C. Tart (Ed.), *Altered states of consciousness.* New York: Wiley, 1969, 507-17.

KASAMATSU, A., HIRAI, T. An EEG study of Zen meditation, *Folia Psychiat. Neurol. Jap.*, 1966, *20*, 315-36. Also in C. Tart (Ed.), *Altered states of consciousness.* New York: Wiley, 1969.

LERNER, B. Dream function reconsidered, *J. Abnorm. Psychol.*, 1967, 72, 2, 85-100.

LESH, T. V. Zen meditation and the development of empathy in counselors, *J. Humanistic Psychol.*, 1970, *10*, 1, 39-74.

LOWEN, A. *Physical dynamics of character structure.* New York: Grune & Stratton, 1958.

LUK, C. *Secrets of chinese meditation.* London: Rider & Co., 1966.

LUTHE, W. Autogenic training: Method, research and application in medicine, in C. Tart (Ed.), *Altered states of consciousness*. New York: Wiley, 1969, 309-19.

MAHARISHI MAHESH YOGI. *The science of being and the art of living*. Los Angeles: SRM Publications, 1966.

MAHARISHI MAHESH YOGI. *The Bhagavad-Gita: A new translation and commentary*. Baltimore: Penguin, 1969.

MASLOW, A. *Toward a psychology of being*. Princeton: Van Nostrand, 1962.

MASLOW, A. A theory of metamotivation: The biological rooting of the value life, *J. Humanistic Psychol.*, 1967, 7, 2, 93-127.

MASLOW, A. Various meanings of transcendence, *J. Transpersonal Psychol.*, 1969, 1, 1, 57-66.

MASLOW, A. Theory Z, *J. Transpersonal Psychol.*, 1970, 2, 1, 31-47.

MAUPIN, E. W. Responses to a Zen meditation exercise, *J. Consulting Psychol.*, 1965, 29, 2, 139-145.

MOYER, H. F. Meditation: the doorway to wholeness, *Main Currents in Modern Thought*, 1965, 22, 2, 35-40.

OUSPENSKY, P. D. *A new model of the universe*, London: Kegan Paul, 1938.

OUSPENSKY, P. D. *The psychology of man's possible evolution*. New York: Ballantine, 1969.

PERLS, F. S. *Ego, hunger, and aggression*. New York: Random House, 1969.

PITTS, F. The biochemistry of anxiety, *Sci. Amer.*, Feb., 1969.

REICH, W. *The function of the orgasm*. New York: Orgone Institute Press, 1942.

REICH, W. *Character analysis*. London: Vision Press, 1948.

SCHACTEL, E. G. *Experiential foundations of Rorschach's test*. New York: Basic Books, 1960.

SULLIVAN, H. S. *The interpersonal theory of psychiatry*. New York: W. W. Norton, 1953.

TART, C. *Altered states of consciousness*. New York: Wiley, 1969.

TART, C. Transpersonal potentialities of deep hypnosis, *J. Transpersonal Psychol.*, 1970, 2, 1, 27-40.

WALLACE, R. K. Physiological effects of transcendental meditation: A proposed fourth major state of consciousness, PhD thesis, Dept. of Physiology, UCLA, 1970a.

WALLACE, R. K. Physiological effects of transcendental meditation, *Science*, 1970b, 166, 1751-54.

WATTS, A. *Psychotherapy east and west*. New York: Ballantine, 1961.

WOLPE, J., LAZARUS, A. *Behavior therapy techniques.* New York: Pergamon, 1966.

WOLPERT, E. Studies in the psychophysiology of dreams: II, *Arch. Gen. Psychiat.*, 1960, 2, 231-41.

YOGANANDA, P. *Autobiography of a yogi.* Los Angeles: SRF Publishers, 1946.

# Operant Conditioning of Heart 36
## Rate in Patients with Premature
## Ventricular Contractions

## Theodore Weiss and Bernard T. Engel

Operant conditioning of heart rate (HR) was carried out in 8 patients with premature ventricular contractions (PVCs). All of the patients showed some degree of HR control. Five of these patients showed a decrease in PVCs in association with the learning of HR control. Four patients have shown persistence of a low PVC frequency after study, the longest followup being 21 months. Pharmacologic studies suggested that decreased PVC frequency was mediated by diminished sympathetic tone in 1 patient and increased vagal tone in another.

These findings suggest that some aspects of cardiac ventricular function can be brought under voluntary control. Once such control has been acquired, it can mediate clinically significant changes in cardiac function.

For many years, and in a multiplicity of experimental situations, the technics of operant conditioning have been employed to modify and control somatic behavior—ie, actions involving the use of skeletal muscle (1). In the last decade, a large volume of additional research has accumulated, indicating that visceral and other involuntary responses also are amenable to operant control (2, 3). Response systems studied have included heart rate (4–7), blood pressure (8, 9), rate of urine formation (10), regional blood flow (11), vasoconstriction (12), and galvanic skin potential (13–15).

In addition to reports of operant conditioning of visceral responses in normal man and in animals, there are three studies in which patients with pathologic visceral responses showed improvement after operant training. Engel and Melmon (16) conditioned more regular cardiac rhythms in patients with several kinds of cardiac arrhythmias, and White and Taylor (17) and Lang (18) each conditioned patients to stop or decrease ruminative vomiting.

Several studies have shown the effects of neural impulses on premature ventricular contractions (PVCs) (19). Hypothalamic lesions and stimulation (20–22), afferent vagal stimulation (20, 23), efferent cardiac sympathetic nerve impulses (20, 24), and cardiac sympathectomy (25) all have been shown to produce dramatic changes in PVC frequency. Also, both increases and

From the Section of Physiological Psychology, Laboratory of Behavioral Sciences, Gerontology Research Center, National Institute of Child Health and Human Development and Baltimore City Hospitals.

The authors would like to thank Drs. Gustav C. Voigt and Kenneth M. Lewis for permitting them to draw patients from the Clinic, and for regular consultation on the patients; Drs. Lewis A. Kolodny and Jay J. Platt for referring Patients 6 and 7, respectively; Mr. Reginald E. Quilter for assisting in the development and maintenance of various instruments used in this study; and Mr. Richard H. Mathias for assisting in the analysis of the ward telemetry data.

Received for publication Aug 6, 1970; revision received Nov 23, 1970.

Address for reprint requests: Bernard T. Engel, PhD, Baltimore City Hospitals, Baltimore, Md 21224.

*Dr. Weiss is now at the Department of Psychiatry, University of Pennsylvania.

decreases in PVC frequency have been reported using classic conditioning technics (26, 27).

Because of these considerations, we undertook a study of patients with PVCs to see if operant conditioning could produce clinically significant control of this arrhythmia.

## MATERIALS AND METHODS

### Patients

*Selection.* Eight patients with PVCs were obtained from Baltimore City Hospitals, and from referrals by private physicians.

*Hospitalization procedure.* Patients were hospitalized for the duration of the study and given passes each weekend. After admission, they were given a complete physical examination and a standard battery of laboratory tests including a 12 lead EKG and PA and lateral chest X-rays.

### Experimental Design

*Laboratory.* All formal cardiac training took place in the laboratory although each patient was encouraged to practice his technics outside the laboratory as well.

While in the laboratory, the patient lay in a hospital bed in a sound-deadened room. At the foot of the bed was a vertical display of three differently colored light bulbs, an intercom and a meter.

The three lights provided the patient with feedback information about his cardiac function. The top light (green) and the bottom light (red) were cue lights. The middle light (yellow) was the reinforcer; it was on when the patient was producing the correct heart rate (HR) response. Our system enabled us to feed back this information to the patient on a beat-to-beat basis.

When the fast (green) cue light was on, a relative increase in HR would turn on the reinforcer light. When the slow (red) cue light was on, a relative decrease in HR would turn on the reinforcer light.

The meter accumulated time. Whenever the patient was performing correctly, the meter arm moved, and when he performed incorrectly, it stopped.

One to three 80-minute conditioning sessions were carried out daily. A typical session began with about 10 minutes for the attaching of EKG leads, and of a strain gauge around the lower chest to monitor breathing. Then, the patient lay quietly for 20 minutes more. During the last 10 minutes of this period, a baseline HR was obtained. The feedback lights were off throughout the baseline period. Two to three minutes were allowed for setting the trigger level for heart rate (HR) conditioning. The trigger level was the HR (eg, in a speeding session) at or above which the reinforcer light would go on. Then the patient had either one 34-minute period during which the feedback lights were on, or two such periods of 17 minutes each, separated by a 10-minute rest period.

Because this was primarily a clinical study, the patient's reponses at any stage of the study always dictated the procedure. In general, however, we followed a standard sequence for conditioning. During the initial or control session, the patient simply lay in bed in the laboratory for the prescribed time period. The feedback lights were never turned on. Next, HR speeding was taught for about 10 sessions, followed by HR slowing for about 10 sessions. For about 10 further sessions, a differential contingency was taught, in which the patient alternately had to increase and decrease his HR during periods of 1–4 minutes throughout the session. During these sessions, the green and red cue lights would come on alternately so that the patient would know whether to speed or to slow.

The last training contingency usually was a range situation in which the patient had to maintain his HR between preset upper and lower limits. Only the yellow light would be on when the HR was within this range. When the rate was too fast, the yellow light would go off and the red light would go on, cueing the patient to slow down. When the rate was too slow, the green light would come on, cueing the patient to speed up. Because a premature beat caused the HR to go above range, and the compensatory pause caused the HR to go below range, this contingency also gave the patient prompt feedback every time he had a PVC.

In the range contingency, feedback was phased out gradually. Initially, the feedback was available for 1 minute and unavailable for the next. In later sessions, it was available for 1 minute and unavailable for 3; in the final sessions, it was on for 1 minute and off for 7. By this procedure, the patient was weaned from the light feedback and made to become aware of his PVCs through his own sensations.

Each patient was told in detail about the nature of the experiment, and he was allowed to inspect all his data throughout the study.

*Ward.* The patient's EKG was monitored three nights per week for 10 minutes out of every hour, using a telemetry apparatus.

*Pharmacologic studies.* In 3 patients, studies were carried out with the use of some or all of the following autonomically active drugs—isoproterenol, propranolol, atropine, edrophonium, phenylephrine and phentolamine—administered intravenously. This was done in the laboratory after conditioning had been completed in order to elucidate the mechanism underlying HR and rhythm changes.

*Followup.* Clinical follow-up was done in the Baltimore City Hospitals Cardiac Clinic by Dr. Weiss, and by the referring physicians. The visits usually included an EKG with a 1–2 minute rhythm strip.

## Apparatus

*Laboratory.* Variations in interbeat intervals were detected by a Beckman-Offner cardiotachometer and converted into electrical signals whose magnitudes were proportional to HR. The cardiotachometer output was also fed into a BRS Electronics Schmitt trigger, which was used to control the patient's feedback. The input to the Schmitt trigger was regulated by a zero suppression circuit on the amplifier to permit adjustment of the trigger point. In order to reduce the hysteresis in the Schmitt triggers, we grounded the emitters. An EKG from a precordial lead was recorded on a Beckman-Offner dynograph, and on magnetic tape using an Ampex SP 300 tape recorder.

*Ward.* The EKG signal from two chest electrodes was transmitted to a Parks model 220-1 converter and a telemetry receiver in an adjacent room, where the EKG was recorded on a tape recorder for subsequent analysis.

## Analytic Procedures

*Laboratory.* All heart beats were counted automatically, and mean HRs were calculated from these data. PVCs were counted manually, all being counted when they were less frequent (under 10/min) ; and two to four 1-minute samples per 10 minutes being counted when they were more frequent.

*Ward.* Mean HR was determined by counting five to six 10-beat samples or five 30-second samples distributed across each 10-minute epoch. All PVCs were counted.

*Pharmacologic studies.* Heart rate was counted either automatically or manually from a continuous EKG record. All PVCs were counted manually from the same record.

*Clinical history and followup.* Heart rate and PVC frequency generally were determined from EKGs. Some data were derived from physical examinations.

## RESULTS

The results will be presented on a patient-by-patient basis. However, since the findings do suggest some general principles, these will be presented as well. Each of the tables summarizes some of the major findings for each patient; however, specific references to these data will be made in the individual patient presentations.

*Patient 1.* LR, a 52-year-old Caucasian female, had a history of five myocardial infarctions (MI) in the 13 years prior to study. In association with the last two, 8 months and 5 months prior to study, she had PVCs. Maintenance quinidine therapy was required to suppress them after the last MI. She had been on digoxin for 1 year. Because of persistent diarrhea, the quinidine was discontinued 2 weeks prior to study, and PVCs increased in frequency from about one to two per minute to ten per minute.

*Laboratory.* Table 1 reports the proportion of sessions during which this patient performed successfully as measured by changes in heart rate or (during the range sessions) by percentage of time heart rate was within the correct range. Figure 1 shows the absolute heart rates and the frequencies of occurrence of PVCs during the training periods of each session.

During speeding training, the patient was able consistently to increase her HR from baseline in the afternoons but not in the mornings (when she also had few PVCs). In association with these successful performances, her PVCs increased to over 23/min (Fig p). The patient said that she thought about relaxing to speed her heart. During the slowing sessions, the patient was able consistently to decrease her HR from baseline, and PVCs were consistently less frequent—1–4/min (Fig 2). She said that she concentrated on breathing maneuvers.

The patient differentiated consistently although she did not increase her HR with respect to her baseline rate during the speeding phases of the sessions. PVC incidence was quite low, under 1/min. At this time, the patient reported that her heart was functioning in a dysrhythmic fashion, when actually it was beating quite regularly. Her cardiograms were shown to her, and the differences between her rhythm strips during the speeding sessions and the

**Table 1.** Ratios of Sessions During Which Each Patient Performed Successfully To Total
Number of Sessions for Each Contingency

| | | | | | Range | | | | | |
| | | | | | 1:1 | | 1:3 | | 1:7 | |
| Patient | Speed | Slow | Differ-ential | CRF | On | Off | On | Off | On | Off |
|---|---|---|---|---|---|---|---|---|---|---|
| 1 (Study 1) | 4/9 | 4/6 | 7/9 | 5/6 | — | — | — | — | — | — |
| 1 (Study 2) | — | — | — | 8/10 | 3/5 | 4/5 | 2/4 | 3/4 | 2/4 | 2/4 |
| 2 | 11/14 | 5/7 | 9/9 | 10/10 | 2/2 | 2/2 | 2/2 | 2/2 | 3/3 | 3/3 |
| 3 | 5/11 | 9/10 | 8/10 | 2/3* | 4/4* | 4/4* | 3/4* | 3/4* | 5/5* | 5/5* |
| 4 | 6/10 | 5/10 | 10/10 | 5/5 | 11/11 | 11/11 | 7/7 | 7/7 | — | — |
| 5 | 1/10 | 9/9 | 12/14 | 15/15 | — | — | — | — | — | — |
| 6 | 1/6 | 5/11 | — | 13/16 | — | — | — | — | — | — |
| 7 | 2/8 | 7/10 | — | 2/4 | — | — | — | — | — | — |
| 8 | — | 16/18 | — | 15/15 | — | — | — | — | — | — |

During the range sessions, successful performance was defined as maintenance of HR within the
correct range for more than 50% of the time.
* Slow.

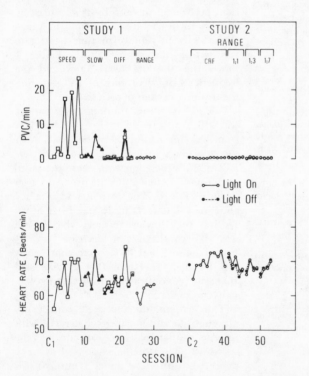

**Fig 1.** Patient 1. PVC and HR
levels during training; C1 and C2
are initial sessions during Studies 1
and 2, respectively, when no feedback was provided. Diff, differential
conditioning; CRF, continuous feedback; 1:1 feedback on 1 minute, off
1 minute; 1:3 feedback on 1 minute,
off 3 minutes, etc; □, speeding;
▲, slowing; ○, range.

present sessions were explained to her in
detail. After her misconceptions had been
clarified, she subsequently learned to recognize correctly the presence of PVCs.

During the range sessions, the patient
consistently maintained her HR within the

predetermined, 10-beat range (usually
60–70 beats/min) and PVCs were very infrequent, generally about 0.2/min.

After a 3-week recess, the patient's digoxin was stopped. The only discernible effect
was an increase in baseline HR of about 5

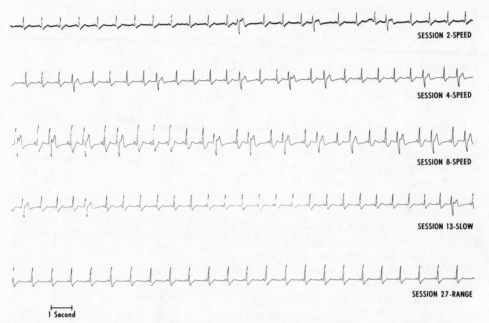

SESSION 2-SPEED

SESSION 4-SPEED

SESSION 8-SPEED

SESSION 13-SLOW

SESSION 27-RANGE

|——————|
1 Second

**Fig 2.** Patient 1. EKG rhythm strips during conditioning. These tracings show increase in PVCs during speeding conditioning, and decrease in PVCs during slowing and range conditioning.

beats/min to about 68. Twenty-three further range sessions were carried out. Gradually, the patient's feedback was decreased until it was present only 1 minute out of 8 by the last four sessions. PVCs remained very rare, about 0.1/min. She was discharged off all medications.

**Ward.** Cardiac activity on the ward (Tables 2 and 3) paralleled events in the laboratory—ie, her PVC incidence was highest during the period when she was speeding, and lower during the period when she was slowing.

**Pharmacologic studies.** After the study, we tested the patient with pharmacologic agents. Atropine (1.0 mg) speeded her HR to 98 but did not produce PVCs. Isoproterenol (0.5–1.5 $\mu$g/min) speeded her

**Table 2. Premature Ventricular Contraction Frequencies (PVCs/min) on Ward During Different Phases of Study**

| Patient | Speed-ing | Slowing | Differ-ential | Range or PVC avoidance |
|---------|-----------|---------|---------------|------------------------|
| 1 | 10.7 | 7.6 | 2.0 | 0.8 |
| 2 | 1.4 | 2.3 | 1.1 | 0.5 |
| 3 | 34.4 | 30.0 | 12.4 | — |
| 4 | 6.6 | 5.7 | 5.0 | 2.1 |
| 5 | 10.2 | 6.6 | 4.9 | 3.8 |
| 6 | 3.1 | 7.1 | — | 6.5 |
| 7 | 16.6 | 4.7 | — | 9.4 |
| 8 | — | 15.2 | — | 10.2 |

**Table 3. Heart Rates (beats/min) on Ward During Different Phases of Study**

| Patient | Speed | Slow | Differ-ential | Range or PVC avoidance |
|---------|-------|------|---------------|------------------------|
| 1 | 66.9 | 67.5 | 66.8 | 67.0 |
| 2 | 51.7 | 50.9 | 50.7 | 50.4 |
| 3 | 82.9 | 83.4 | 69.7 | — |
| 4 | 61.0 | 57.1 | 56.0 | 53.2 |
| 5 | 77.3 | 75.0 | 71.5 | 74.0 |
| 6 | 62.5 | 79.2 | — | 66.8 |
| 7 | 74.4 | 76.1 | — | 72.7 |
| 8 | — | 83.4 | — | 88.7 |

heart rate and produced PVCs when the HR was above 90. The PVC configuration was the same as those she had spontaneously and during conditioning to speed her heart rate. This suggests that decreased sympathetic tone accounts for her diminished PVC incidence.

**Followup.** Twenty-one months of follow-up data have been obtained. PVCs remained quite low for 4 months, none being seen on five EKGs. Subsequently, they became more variable—commonly about 1/min, but as high as 6/min. The patient continues to be able accurately to identify PVCs. She says she rarely has significant numbers of them at home. When she does, she sits down and rests, and they stop within 20 minutes and do not return.

**Patient 2.** IW was a 62-year-old Caucasian male with a history of one MI 7 years prior to study. Thereafter, he had intermittent angina on exertion. PVCs were noted first in 1965; they were present on four of six EKGs taken thereafter, at times in a bigeminal rhythm. The average frequency was 14/min on EKG, and 3–5/min clinically. Two months prior to study, his angina worsened. An exercise tolerance test, performed to clarify the relationship between his angina and his PVCs produced bigeminy and multifocal PVCs in association with a heart rate of 95–100 beats/min. Modest exercise, raising HR from the usual level of about 55–80 beats/min, was associated with a temporary cessation of PVCs. When the HR slowed below 60, the PVCs returned. A subsequent therapeutic trial on diphenylhydantoin produced no significant change in the PVC frequency or in the patient's angina.

**Laboratory.** The patient performed successfully in all phases of the study as measured by changes in heart rate (Table 1). Figure 3 reports his absolute heart rates and PVC incidences during each training session.

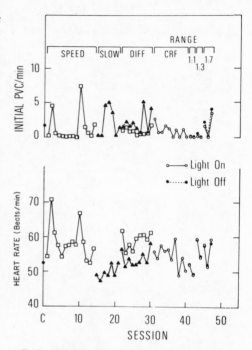

**Fig 3.** Patient 2. PVC and HR levels during training.

In order to speed his heart, the patient said that he thought about "pushing or forcing" his heart to the left, and about its beating rapidly. In several of the speeding sessions, he had long periods of bigeminal rhythm, the PVCs having two configurations. One configuration was like that of the patient's usual PVCs, with the major vector in the same direction as that of the regular QRS. It will be referred to as the *usual type PVC.* The other configuration was seen in the laboratory only in association with HR speeding. Its major vector was in the opposite direction from that of the normal QRS. It will be referred to as the *speeding type PVC.* Apart from the bigeminy, the patient's PVCs were infrequent during speeding, usually less than 1/min. The patient also had several prolonged episodes of bigeminy on the ward recordings of the night after speeding session 11, and on the following night. Both times, these occurred during waking hours when he said he would practice HR control. Many of the bigeminal PVCs on telemetry were of the speeding type. This type of PVC had not been seen on telemetry prior to then.

PVCs were more frequent during slowing, usually 1.5–5/min. They were of the usual type. No bigeminy was seen. He said that he concentrated on the "heart slowing down and stopping."

During the differentiation sessions, PVCs occurred more and more frequently in the slowing periods and less frequently in the speeding periods (Fig 4). The PVCs were of the usual type. The patient said that he used the same technics for HR speeding and slowing described above. At comparable heart rates, PVCs were most frequent during HR slowing, least frequent during HR speeding and of intermediate frequency during the baseline periods. These findings suggest that the active processes involved in slowing and speeding the heart were more important in modulating PVC frequency than was the heart rate per se.

During range conditioning sessions, PVCs generally were infrequent, usually less than 1/min.

**Ward.** Telemetry data showed little variation in HR (Table 3). Apart from periods of bigeminy during the waking hours, PVCs were infrequent (Table 2). As in the laboratory, they were most frequent during the slowing contingency.

**Pharmacologic studies.** Studies with autonomically active drugs were done in this patient. Isoproterenol (0.5–1.0 $\mu$g/min) led to a HR increase from the resting level of 52 beats/min to 93 beats/min, and to bigeminy and ventricular tachycardia. The PVCs were of the speeding type. The ventricular tachycardia stopped after the isoproterenol infusion was stopped. No antiarrhythmic agents were required. Atropine (1.0 mg) also speeded the HR to 86 beats/min and increased PVC frequency from zero to 8/min. These PVCs were of the usual type. Both edrophonium (1–10 mg) and propranolol (0.5 mg every 3 minutes for six times) separately slowed the heart to

about 48 beats/min, but neither affected the frequency of PVCs. They generally remained below the baseline frequency of 2.5/min. When isoproterenol was readministered (same dosages) after propranolol administration, PVCs increased in frequency to about 10/min although HR did not increase. Their configuration was of the usual type. These results suggest that PVCs of the speeding type were related to increased sympathetic tone. They do not clarify the mechanism underlying the usual type of PVCs.

**Followup.** The patient has been followed for 10 months since the study. Initially, he continued to have very rare PVCs, averaging 0.4/min on three EKGs. When they were more frequent at home, he said he could decrease them by concentrating on a steady heart beat. His angina continued to worsen, and 4 months after discharge, he had another MI. After recovery from this, the patient's PVCs were somewhat more frequent, averaging 2.2/min in the clinic and, according to him, more at home. He said that it took 15–20 minutes to stop them with HR speeding at home. We therefore readmitted him 9 months after the first study. At that time, PVCs were rare, less than 1/min in the laboratory and on the ward. Because they originated consistently from two foci, quinidine was added to the patient's regimen. This reduced them even further, to one every 4–5 minutes.

**Patient 3.** MK was an obese 36-year-old Caucasian female with an 8-year history of documented PVCs. They were present on four of six EKGs taken during the 8 years prior to study. The average frequency was 12.8/min. During the last several months before the study, she had had three to four syncopal episodes. An EKG taken by her private physician shortly after one of these revealed unifocal PVCs at a frequency of 21/min. The syncopal episodes had occurred when she was angry or excited. She also reported "a big thumping feeling"

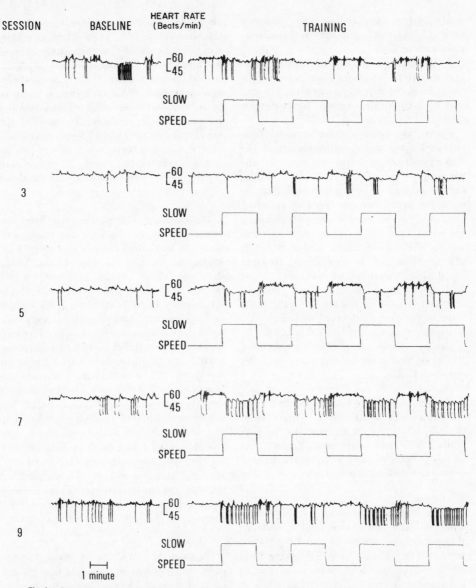

**Fig 4.** Patient 2. Differential HR conditioning. Tracings are cardiotachometer records. PVCs are shown by long vertical lines. As differentiation proceeds, patient speeds and slows appropriately, and PVCs are progressively more concentrated in slowing periods.

in her chest in association with strong emotions and moderate physical exertion such as walking half a mile. To stop this, she said that she sat down and relaxed for half an hour or more.

***Laboratory.*** The patient did not speed consistently from baseline (Table 1); however, she did perform successfully in all other phases of the study. During the speeding sessions. PVC frequency was high—up to 40/min (Fig 5)—and at times, coupling of PVCs occurred (Fig 6). The patient said that she thought about arguments with her children and about running through a dark street during the speeding sessions.

During the slowing sessions, PVC frequency fell to about 20/min (Fig 5). The patient said she thought about swinging back and forth in a swing during these sessions.

The patient differentiated well although she speeded from baseline during the

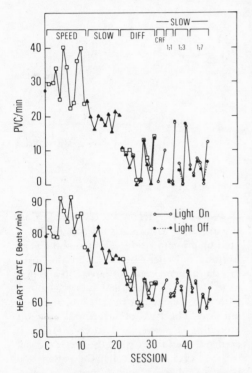

**Fig 5.** Patient 3. PVC and HR levels during training. Slow$_1$ refers to first block of slowing sessions; Slow$_2$ to second block.

speeding blocks in only one session. She slowed during the slowing blocks in all ten sessions. PVCs became much less frequent, usually under 10/min, and at times there were none for periods ranging up to 8 minutes. She said that she concentrated on the same things described above during the conditioning periods.

Because PVC's were least frequent at the lower HRs, slowing of the HR under 65

beats/min rather than range control was taught next. The patient's HR was under 65 beats/min during twelve of the sixteen sessions. She said that she thought about swinging on a see-saw and about relaxing during these sessions. PVC frequency was usually under 10/min; it was at zero for periods as long as 17 minutes (Fig 6).

The patient frequently decreased her PVCs when the training portion of the session began and the feedback lights were turned on (Fig 7). Also, the PVCs often returned promptly when the training portion of the session ended and the lights were turned off (Fig 7). During the training sessions in which the light was off part of the time, PVC frequency was as low or lower when the light was off as when it was on (Fig 5).

**Ward.** Cardiac activity on the ward generally paralleled events in the laboratory. Heart rate (Table 3) was highest during speeding and slowing, intermediate during the second slowing block (not shown in Tables 2 or 3), and lowest during the differential conditioning sessions. The PVC pattern was the same as that for HR (Table 2). Their lowest average frequency was about 12/min during the differential contingency. At the end of the study, they averaged about 19/min.

**Pharmacologic studies.** Both edrophonium (1–10 mg) and propranolol (0.5 mg every 3 minutes for eight times) separately slowed the heart from about 80 to about 73 beats/min. Neither had any effect on PVC frequency which remained at about 20/min. When administered together (edrophonium, 10 mg at the end of the above administration of propranolol), they slowed the heart from 75 to 60 beats/min and abolished PVCs from a prior level of 20/min. Phenylephrine (7–28 μg/min) increased the blood pressure from 104/70 to 138/76, slowed the HR from 77 to 54 beats/min, and abolished PVCs from a prior level of 12/min. Isoproterenol (0.5–1.0 μg/min) speeded the HR from 78 to 95 beats/min and stopped PVCs, the prior level being

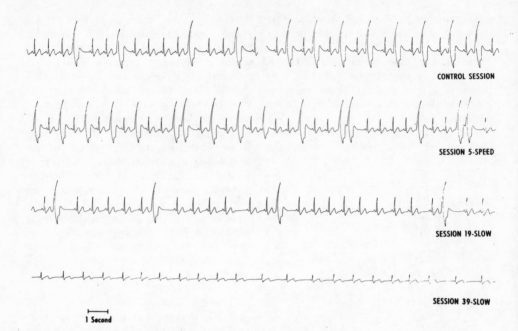

CONTROL SESSION

SESSION 5-SPEED

SESSION 19-SLOW

SESSION 39-SLOW

1 Second

**Fig 6.**    Patient 3. EKG rhythm strips during conditioning.

25/min. Atropine (1.5 mg) speeded the HR from 75 to 97 beats/min and PVCs increased from 19/min to a bigeminal rhythm with 48/min. Phentolamine (5 mg), given at a time when PVC frequency was low (1/min), had no obvious effect on PVCs. It decreased the blood pressure from 108/68 to 90/62, and increased the HR from 75 to 82 beats/min.

These findings suggest that in this patient strong vagal tone inhibits PVCs, regardless of sympathetic input. Weaker vagal tone associated with β-sympathetic inhibition also inhibits PVCs. Vagal blockade leads to frequent PVCs.

**Followup.**    The patient has been followed for 3 months since the study. PVCs have continued to be frequent on EKG during clinic visits, averaging 17.1/min on three EKGs. However, the patient says that she is able to stop them at home using the HR slowing technic learned in the laboratory. She has not been able to do so in the clinic. She has had no dizziness or syncope since the study.

**Patient 4.**    RL was a 68-year-old Caucasian male with a history of an MI 4 months prior to study. Three months prior to study and after discharge from the hospital, the patient began to have PVCs. These were typically bigeminal or trigeminal, with a frequency of over 20/min, and were unifocal. The PVC occurred well after the preceding T wave, and after exercise, it occurred even later. Also, the PVCs did not increase with exercise; and the patient was unaware of their occurrence. For these reasons, no medications were given to control them.

**Laboratory.**    The patient did not perform reliably during the slowing and speeding training sessions (Fig 8 and Table 1), and his PVC frequency was highly variable throughout these sessions. He did differentiate consistently, however. Furthermore, he speeded from baseline during the speeding blocks in six of the sessions, and slowed from baseline in seven of them. He said that he moved his shoulders to increase his HR, and lay still and stared at

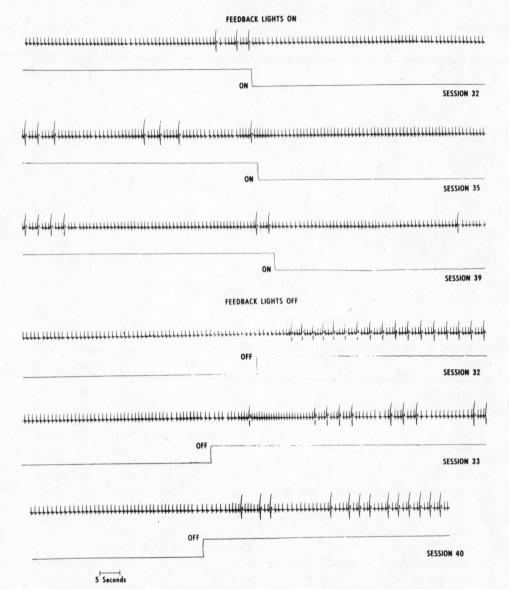

**Fig 7.** Patient 3. EKG rhythm strips at onset and offset of feedback during HR slowing. These tracings show that patient was able to stop having PVCs when feedback began, and PVCs returned at end of sessions.

the light to slow his HR. PVC frequency was variable, but was under 10/min in seven of the ten sessions. The PVCs were more frequent in the speeding blocks in seven of the ten sessions.

During the range sessions, the patient said that he generally just watched the light to keep PVCs infrequent. He said that sometimes he also moved his shoulders. PVC frequency was low, under 8/min throughout. During the first five sessions of the range contingency, when the feedback was on during the entire training period, the patient had 2.1 PVCs/min or less (Fig

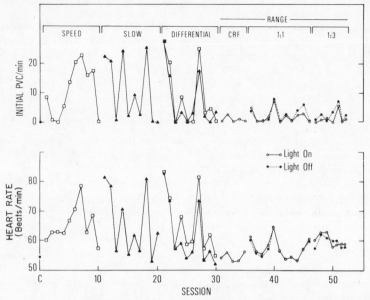

**Fig 8.**   Patient 4. PVC and HR levels during training.

8). As the feedback was phased out, PVCs became somewhat more frequent. It is of note that the patient could not tell when he was having PVCs except when the feedback lights were on or when he took his pulse.

***Ward.***   Ward data paralleled the laboratory data. Heart rates (Table 3) were highest during speeding and slowing and lowest during the range training. Similarly, PVCs (Table 2) were most frequent during speeding and slowing and least frequent during the range contingency.

***Pharmacologic studies.***   No drug studied were performed on this patient.

***Followup.***   Because PVCs were noted to come from two foci (Fig 9), the patient was started on quinidine at the time of discharge. PVC frequency has been low on followup visits, averaging 3.2/min on 5 EKGs. Because the patient was unable to detect PVCs except by taking his pulse, he was given twenty-four further training sessions to learn PVC detection. This was done 1 month after the first study. Whereas

the patient initially was unable to detect any of his PVCs except by taking his pulse, by the end of the second study, he was able to detect them accurately 35–40% of the time without the light feedback. He said that he felt a sensation of warmth across the precordium when PVCs were occurring. When PVCs were frequent—eg, 15/min— he also noted diaphoresis.

In one additional followup visit after the second study, there were no PVCs on EKG. During the clinic visit, the patient was able to sense that he was having infrequent PVCs (6/min). He reported that at home he also could sense his PVCs by the precordial warmth—verified by taking his pulse—and by sitting quietly, he could abolish them in half an hour. They stayed away for variable periods of time thereafter, usually for about an hour.

***Patient 5.***   CA was a 73-year-old Caucasian male with a 19-month history of documented PVCs.

On thirteen visits to his private physician during the 19 months prior to our study, the patient was described as having no ectopic beats on five occasions, few to moderate ectopic beats ("few," "occasional," "slight irregularity of pulse," "irregularity of heart rate") on six occasions, and many ectopic beats on two occasions. The patient said that he could not sense the PVCs.

**Laboratory.** The patient was unable to speed his heart during the speeding sessions; however, he was consistently successful at slowing his heart (Table 1). The patient differentiated well (Fig 10). He slowed from baseline during all sessions, and he speeded from baseline in five of the sessions, including four of the last seven. In order to speed his heart, the patient said that he thought about bouncing a rubber ball. To slow his heart, the patient said that he counted the amount of time the reinforcement light was on.

PVC frequency was highly variable during the speeding sessions (Fig 10). During slowing, PVC frequency declined to about 5/min, and during the differentiation sessions, they fell still further so that there were fewer than three PVCs/min during the last six of these sessions. During the range sessions, PVC frequency remained low, averaging 4/min.

PACs increased slightly during the study, from about 14/min during speeding to about 18/min during the range condition (Fig 10). The patient said that he still could not tell when the PVCs occurred.

**Ward.** There was little fluctuation in HR on the ward (Table 3). As in the laboratory, PVCs (Table 2) were most frequent during speeding and were fewest during the later range and differential contingencies. PACs on telemetry also paralleled their behavior in the laboratory, being least frequent early (9.5/min during speeding) and more frequent later (17.1/min during the range contingency).

**Pharmacologic studies.** Drug studies were not done in this patient.

**Followup.** During 5 months of followup, the patient has been seen three times by his private physician. He was described as having no ectopic beats on two occasions, few to moderate ectopic beats on one occasion, and many ectopic beats on no occasions. An EKG taken 5 months after the study revealed 0.3 PVC/min and 22 PACs/min.

Patients 6, 7 and 8 all failed to learn to control their PVCs. Brief summaries of their cases are included in this report because they highlight important aspects about the limitations of operant training in the control of PVCs.

**Patient 6.** LS was a 60-year-old Negro male with a 5-year history of cardiac disease, including five hospitalizations for congestive heart failure.

His activities were severely limited by exertional dyspnea and palpitations, and less frequently by angina. He has paroxysmal nocturnal dyspnea about two nights per week. Chest X-ray revealed massive cardiomegaly, with a cardiac/thoracic ratio of 20/27.5. For almost 4 years prior to study, he had had premature atrial and ventricular contractions. Either or both of these were present on eight of nine EKGs during the 4 years prior to study. PVCs averaged 3.7/min and PAC, 1.6/min.

**Laboratory.** This patient was unable consistently to slow or speed his heart rate; however, he was quite successful at maintaining his rate within a ten-beat range (Table 1). His absolute heart rate declined from about 90 beats/min in the early sessions to about 65 beats/min by the end of speeding (slow training was given first in his case). The most likely explanations for this decline in HR are that during his period of hospitalization, he took his medications more regularly, and he reduced his alcohol consumption substantially.

During all training conditions, the frequency of his premature beats was highly variable, ranging from 1/min to 15/min. EKG tracings in the laboratory and on the ward were such that PVCs could not be differentiated from PACs; thus, all are listed together as premature beats.

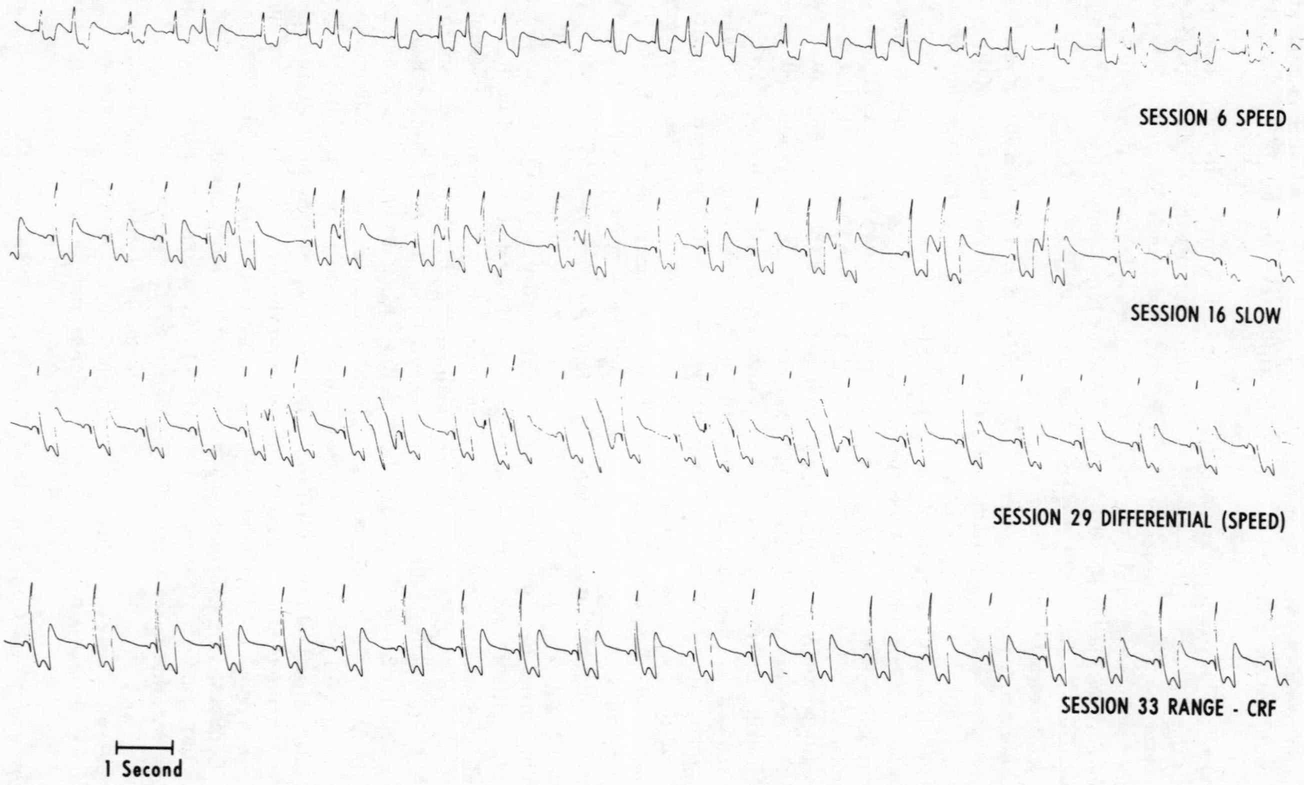

SESSION 6 SPEED

SESSION 16 SLOW

SESSION 29 DIFFERENTIAL (SPEED)

SESSION 33 RANGE - CRF

1 Second

Fig 9.    Patient 4.  EKG rhythm strips during conditioning.

It should also be noted that the patient drank heavily while on weekend passes so that he was too inebriated to return on Sunday evening as requested, and had to be fetched the next morning.

**Followup.** In 4 months of clinic followup, the patient continued to have many premature beats. On two EKGs, PVCs averaged 5.9/min and PACs, 9.7/min. His clinical status was unchanged. Thereafter, he was lost to followup. It was learned later

that he died at home 10 months after the study.

**Patient 7.** EC was a 48-year-old Negro male with a history of hypertension for 27 years and cardiomegaly for 5 years, with hospitalization for congestive heart failure 4 years prior to study. After discharge from the hospital, the patient returned to work (manual labor) but he was so limited by dyspnea on exertion, that he was forced to quit. He proved to be little motivated to

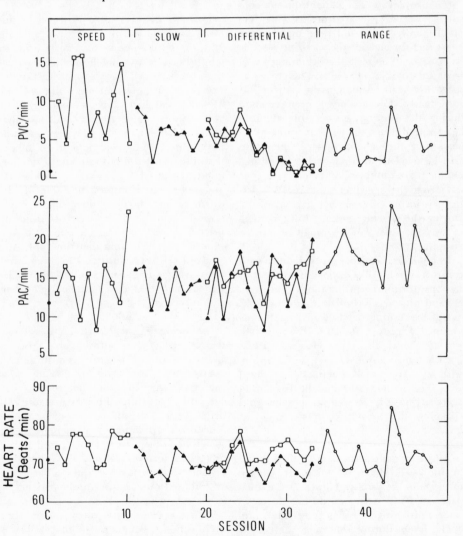

**Fig 10.** Patient 5. PVC and HR levels during training.

take a less strenuous job, and despite several professional attempts at rehabilitation, he has not worked since. At the time of study, he was functional Class II-B. The patient had had PVCs for 18 months prior to study, these being consistently present on physical examinations and on EKGs during that time. Their average frequency on three EKGs during that period was 9.0/min. The patient was an active Baptist, attending services twice a week.

**Laboratory.** The patient did not consistently speed his heart from baseline (Table 1); however, he did raise his absolute heart rate throughout the speeding sessions from 61 beats/min at the beginning to 78 beats/min by the end. He said he prayed to speed his heart. Although the patient did consistently slow his heart from baseline during the slowing sessions, his absolute heart rate did not change, remaining at 75 beats/min throughout these sessions. He said he tried to manipulate his breathing, and he prayed to slow his heart.

During the speeding sessions, PVC frequency increased from 6/min to 24/min. During the slowing sessions, PVC frequency was variable, ranging from 10/min to 20/min.

In an effort to enable this patient to gain control over his PVCs, he was given four sessions of training in the range contingency, and nine sessions of training in a PVC avoidance contingency in which a soft tone sounded whenever he had a PVC; his task was to silence the tone. However, PVCs persisted generally between 7 and 20/min, with an average of 12.4/min. HR averaged 76.2. The patient said that he tried mild exercise in bed, as well as praying and changing his breathing to decrease his PVCs.

**Ward.** Telemetry data (Tables 2 and 3) indicated that HR did not change throughout the study. However, the incidence of PVCs decreased during the slowing conditioning and then returned to prestudy levels during the range and PVC avoidance training.

**Pharmacologic studies.** No drug studies were done in this patient.

**Followup.** During 17 months of follow-up, he has continued consistently to have PVCs, averaging 6.1/min. His clinical status is unchanged. The patient subsequently revealed that he was afraid that if his PVCs improved, he might lose his disability benefits and have to return to work. It is possible that this concern affected his performance during the study.

**Patient 8.** JF was a 77-year-old Caucasian male with a history of two probable MIs, the second one being 3 years prior to admission. He was not hospitalized on either occasion, and subsequent EKGs did not reveal definite evidence of an old MI. He also had had diabetes mellitus for 7 years. Shortly after the second probable MI, the patient developed CHF, and was hospitalized. PVCs were noted then for the first time. They did not respond to amelioration of the CHF (digoxin, chlorothiasize and potassium chloride), procaine amide, dilantin, or discontinuing digoxin for several months. They were consistently present thereafter, being seen on all of the nine EKGs taken from that time until the study. They were multifocal in origin, and their average frequency was 12.4/min. The patient said that he could not tell when they occurred.

**Laboratory.** Although there was evidence of heart rate control (Table 1) and a fall in absolute HR from an initial 90 beats/min to 76/min during slowing training, PVC frequency did not decrease. It should be noted that this patient had PVCs of at least four different configurations. Sometimes certain ones were more frequent; sometimes others were. This posed severe difficulties for our HR and PVC detection system. It also made it quite difficult to provide accurate feedback to the patient.

**Ward.** Telemetry data paralleled events in the laboratory in that HR was lower during the slowing periods (Table 3), and PVCs remained frequent (Table 2).

**Pharmacologic studies.** No drug studies were performed in this patient.

**Followup.** Followup for 8 months revealed no significant changes in the patient's cardiovascular status. PVCs were present on all of four EKGs taken during these visits, with an average frequency of 10.0/min. The patient died suddenly at home 2 weeks after his last clinic visit.

## DISCUSSION

This study shows that patients can be taught to control the prevalence of their PVCs. Patients 1–4 showed clear evidence of PVC control in the laboratory, and evidence of transfer of the learned effect to the ward. Patient 1 has sustained her low PVC rate for 21 months, and each of these other 3 patients who have been followed for shorter periods of time reports that he is able to detect and modify his PVCs while at home. Also, Patient 5 has maintained a low PVC frequency for 5 months after the study.

The presence of PVCs is associated with an increased probability of sudden death (28). Corday et al have demonstrated experimentally that PVCs can diminish coronary artery blood flow (29) and cerebral blood flow (30). The fact that Patient 1 has had no further myocardial infarctions in the 21 months of followup, as contrasted with three in the 11 months preceding the study, may be related to her decreased PVC frequency.

In the patients in this study, at least two different mechanisms of PVC control appear to have been involved. The drug studies in Patient 1 suggested that reduced sympathetic tone to the heart was responsible for the decreased incidence of PVCs. As the cardiac sympathetic nerves are known to influence the ventricle strongly (31, 32), this effect probably occurred directly at the ventricular level. In Patient 3, the drug studies suggested that increased vagal tone decreased her PVC frequency. This may

have represented a direct vagal effect on the ventricle, as there is anatomic evidence for vagal innervation of the ventricle in mammals (33, 34), and physiologic evidence for vagal effects on the mammalian ventricle (35, 36).

The flexibility of operant conditioning is demonstrated by the fact that PVCs were reduced whether they were mediated primarily by the sympathetic or by the parasympathetic nervous system. This underscores the fact that operant conditioning can be used to alter pathologic conditions mediated by different mechanisms.

Heart rate per se does not determine the presence or absence of PVCs. Similar HRs in Patient 2 were associated with different PVC frequencies depending on the experimental contingency under which they occurred. Also, in Patient 1, HRs between 90 and 100 beats/min induced by isoproterenol were associated with PVCs, whereas similar HRs induced by atropine were not. In Patient 3, the opposite occurred. Atropine-induced HRs above 90 beats/min were associated with PVCs, while similar HRs induced by isoproterenol were not. This also suggests that extensive, short-term, experimental drug studies—of the type carried out in Patient 3—might be useful in clarifying the mechanisms of PVCs in different patients.

The imagery which patients reported while controlling their heart rates has been presented. However, the reports are highly idiosyncratic, and no consistent pattern is apparent.

There seem to be six elements that are important for successful learning of PVC control. These are:(a) peripheral receptors which are stimulated by the PVC; (b) afferents which carry the information to the CNS; (c) CNS processing to enable the patient to recognize the PVC and to provide the motivation and flexibility necessary to enable learning to occur; (d) efferents to an effector organ which can bring about the desired change in the pathologically functioning heart; (e) a heart which is not too diseased to beat more regularly; (f) a homeostatic system in the patient which will tolerate the more normal functioning of the heart.

Patient 4 illustrates the role of the afferent system. He did well at controlling his PVCs when he had continuous feedback in the range portion of Study 1, but did more poorly as the feedback was phased out. After Study 2, he was able to detect his PVCs, and then to reduce their frequency.

Patient 1 illustrates the importance of CNS processing. She had to learn to be comfortable with infrequent PVCs, whereas early in the study, she had been interpreting frequent PVCs as comfortable. This underscores the fact that physicians cannot always rely on the naive patient's interpretation of his physiologic state. The concern which Patient 7 expressed regarding his disability benefits suggests that motivation is also an important, CNS-mediated factor.

The grossly enlarged heart of Patient 6 and the electrically very unstable one of Patient 8 illustrate the importance of the heart itself. These hearts may have been too diseased to beat regularly for prolonged periods of time.

Early intervention may facilitate the learning of PVC control—eg, during convalescence from an infarction as in Patient 4. (The severity of the arrhythmias which the patients were able to generate in the course of conditioning was striking. Therefore, it would seem advisable not to attempt to condition patients during the acute, postinfarction period.)

This study was not concerned with optimization of technics. It should be possible to accomplish comparable results in much shorter periods of time, as more nearly optimal conditioning technics are employed. For example, studies should be feasible on an outpatient basis; and pretesting with autonomically active drugs such as those used in this study should suggest whether the patient will benefit more from being taught to slow or to speed.

## REFERENCES

1. Skinner BF: The Behavior of Organisms. New York, Appleton-Century-Crofts, 1938
2. Kimmel HD: Instrumental conditioning of autonomically mediated behavior. Psychol Bull 67:337–345, 1967
3. Miller NE: Learning of visceral and glandular responses. Science 163:434–445, 1969
4. Shearn DW: Operant conditioning of heart rate. Science 137:530–531, 1962
5. Hnatiow M, Lang PJ: Learned stabilization of heart rate. Psychophysiol 1:330–336, 1965
6. Engel BT, Hansen SP: Operant conditioning of heart rate slowing. Psychophysiol 3: 176–187, 1966
7. Levene HI, Engel BT, Pearson JA: Differential operant conditioning of heart rate. Psychosom Med 30:837–845, 1968
8. DiCara LV, Miller NE: Instrumental learning of systolic blood pressure responses by curarized rats: dissociation of cardiac and vascular changes. Psychosom Med 30:489–494, 1968
9. Shapiro D, Turksy B, Gershon E, et al: Effects of feedback and reinforcement on the control of human systolic blood pressure. Science 163:588–590, 1969
10. Miller NE, DiCara LV: Instrumental learning of urine formation by rats: Changes in renal blood flow. Amer J Physiol 215:677–683, 1968
11. DiCara LV, Miller NE: Instrumental learning of vasomotor responses by rats: learning to respond differentially in the two ears. Science 159:1485–1486, 1968
12. Snyder C, Noble M: Operant conditioning of vasoconstriction. J Exp Psychol 77:263–268, 1968
13. Fowler RL, Kimmel HD: Operant conditioning of the GSR. Psychol Rep 7:555–562, 1960
14. Kimmel HD, Baxter R: Avoidance conditioning of the GSR. J Exp Psychol 65:212–213, 1964
15. Shapiro D, Crider A: Operant electrodermal conditioning under multiple schedules of reinforcement. Psychophysiol 4:168–175, 1967
16. Engel BT, Melmon KL: Operant conditioning of heart rate in patients with cardiac arrhythmias. Conditional Reflex 3:130, 1968
17. White JD, Taylor D: Noxious conditioning as a treatment for rumination. Ment Retard 5:30–33, 1967
18. Lang PJ, Melamed BG: Case report: avoidance conditioning therapy of an infant with chronic ruminative vomiting. J Abn Psychol 74:1–8, 1969
19. Scherf D, Schott A: Extrasystoles and allied

arrhythmias. New York, Grune and Stratton, Inc, 1953, pp 253–274

20. Korth C: The production of extrasystoles by means of the central nervous system. Ann Intern Med 11:492–498, 1937

21. Weinberg SJ, Fuster JM: Electrocardiographic changes produced by localized hypothalamic stimulations. Ann Intern Med 53:332–341, 1960

22. Attar HJ, Gutierrex MT, Bellet S, et al: Effect of stimulation of hypothalamus and reticular activating system on production of cardiac arrhythmia. Circ Res 12:14–21, 1963

23. Scherf D, Blumenfeld S, Yildiz M: Experimental study on ventricular extrasystoles provoked by vagal stimulation. Amer Heart J 62:670–675, 1961

24. Gillis RA: Cardiac sympathetic nerve activity: changes induced by ouabain and propranolol. Science 166:508–510, 1969

25. Estes EH Jr, Izlar HL Jr: Recurrent ventricular tachycardia: a case successfully treated by bilateral sympathectomy. Amer J Med 31:493–497, 1961

26. Peimer IA: Conditioned reflex extrasystole in man. Fiziol Zh SSSR Sechenov 39:286–292, 1953

27. Perez-Cruet J: Conditioning of extrasystoles in humans with respiratory maneuvers as unconditional stimulus. Science 137:1060–1061, 1962

28. Chiang BN, Perlman LV, Ostander LD Jr, et al: Relationship of premature systoles to coronary heart disease and sudden death in the Tecumseh epidemiologic study. Ann Intern Med 70:1159–1166, 1969

29. Corday E, Gold H, DeVera LB, et al: Effect of the cardiac arrhythmias on the coronary circulation. Ann Intern Med 50:535–553, 1959

30. Corday E, Irving DW: Effect of cardiac arrhythmias on the cerebral circulation. Amer J Cardiol 6:803–807, 1960

31. Rushmer RF: Autonomic balance in cardiac control. Amer J Physiol 192:631–634, 1958

32. Sarnoff SJ, Brockman SK, Gilmore JP, et al: Regulation of ventricular contraction: influence of cardiac sympathetic and vagal nerve stimulation on atrial and ventricular dynamics. Circ Res 8:1108–1122, 1960

33. Mitchell GAG: Cardiovascular Innervation. Edinburgh and London, Livingstone, Ltd, 1956

34. Hirsch EF, Kaiser GC, Cooper T: Experimental heart block in the dog. III. Distribution of the vagus and sympathetic nerves in the septum. Arch Path 79:441–451, 1965

35. Wildenthal K, Mierzwiak DS, Wyatt HL, et al: Influence of efferent vagal stimulation on left ventricular function in dogs. Amer J Physiol 215:577–581, 1969

36. Daggett WM, Nugent GC, Carr PW, et al: Influence of vagal stimulation on ventricular contractibility, $O_2$ consumption and coronary flow. Amer J Physiol 212:8–18, 1967

# Decreased Systolic Blood Pressure Through Operant Conditioning Techniques in Patients with Essential Hypertension

## 37

Herbert Benson, David Shapiro, Bernard Tursky, and Gary E. Schwartz

Abstract. *Operant conditioning–feedback techniques were employed to lower systolic blood pressure in seven patients with essential hypertension. In five of the patients, meaningful decreases of systolic blood pressure were obtained in the laboratory, ranging from 16 to 34 millimeters of mercury. The therapeutic value of such techniques remains to be established.*

Arterial blood pressure in animals can be made to rise and fall predictably when environmental stimuli are scheduled according to variations in blood pressure (*1, 2*). Further, unanesthetized squirrel monkeys with behaviorally induced hypertension can be trained by operant conditioning techniques to lower their mean arterial blood pressure to control levels (*2*). Normotensive human subjects can also be trained to raise and lower arterial systolic and diastolic blood pressure by the use of similar procedures (*3*). The present report describes the lowering of systolic arterial blood pressure through operant conditioning–feedback techniques in seven patients with essential hypertension.

The diagnosis of essential hypertension was established by exclusion of the known causes of hypertension. The patients had moderate or severe hypertension. All had complete medical eval-ulations, including renal arteriography in patients Nos. 2 and 6. The patients were ambulatory and were attending the Hypertension Clinic of the Boston City Hospital. The average age of the patients was 47.9 years (Table 1). There were five males and two females. Six of the seven were taking antihypertensive medications. Medications were not altered during the experimental sessions, and all patients had maintained constant medication regimens for at least 2 weeks prior to any laboratory sessions. Informed consent was obtained from each patient. They were told they would be paid $5.00 per session to come to the behavioral laboratory and have their blood pressure measured automatically for approximately 1 hour while they sat quietly. They were also informed that no other medications or invasive techniques would be employed and that the procedures might be of value in lowering

528

Table 1. Patient characteristics and effects of operant conditioning on systolic blood pressure.

| Patient No. | Age (yr) | Sex | Antihypertensive medications administered throughout the study | | No. of control sessions | No. of conditioning sessions | Median systolic blood pressure (mm-Hg) | | |
|---|---|---|---|---|---|---|---|---|---|
| | | | Medication | Amount (mg/day) | | | Last five control sessions | Last five conditioning sessions | Conditioning minus control |
| 1 | 30 | M | None | | 5 | 8 | 139.6 | 136.1 | − 3.5 |
| 2 | 49 | F | Spironolactone<br>Methyl dopa<br>Guanethidine | 100<br>1500<br>30 | 5 | 33 | 213.3 | 179.5 | −33.8 |
| 3 | 52 | M | Methyl dopa | 500 | 5 | 22 | 162.3 | 133.1 | −29.2 |
| 4 | 54 | M | Chlorothiazide<br>Spironolactone<br>Methyl dopa | 1000<br>100<br>1500 | 16 | 34 | 166.9 | 150.4 | −16.5 |
| 5 | 44 | M | Chlorothiazide | 1000 | 15 | 31 | 157.8 | 141.7 | −16.1 |
| 6 | 53 | F | Chlorothiazide<br>Spironolactone<br>Methyl dopa | 1000<br>100<br>1000 | 15 | 12 | 165.7 | 166.6 | + 0.9 |
| 7 | 53 | M | Hydrochloro-<br>thiazide<br>Spironolactone<br>Methyl dopa | 100<br>100<br>1000 | 15 | 12 | 149.0 | 131.7 | −17.3 |
| Mean | 47.9 | | | | 10.9 | 21.7 | 164.9 | 148.4 | −16.5 |

their blood pressure.

Median systolic blood pressure was recorded by use of an automated constant cuff-pressure system (3). A standard, 13-cm wide blood pressure cuff was wrapped around the left arm and inflated to a given pressure by a regulated, low-pressure, compressed-air source. The cuff was connected by plastic tubing to the air-filled chamber of a Statham P23Db strain gauge pressure transducer. The electrical output of the strain gauge was recorded on one channel of a Beckman type RM polygraph. The output of a crystal microphone, placed under the cuff and over the brachial artery, recorded Korotkoff sounds on a second channel of the polygraph. The electrocardiogram was recorded on a third channel. By setting the cuff at a constant pressure, close to systolic blood pressure, increases or decreases in systolic pressure with each heart beat relative to the cuff pressure could be ascertained. When cuff pressure exceeded brachial artery systolic pressure, no Korotkoff sound was produced; when cuff pressure was less than brachial artery systolic pressure, a Korotkoff sound was present. During each trial, the cuff was inflated for 50 consecutive heart beats (recorded automatically from the electrocardiogram) and then deflated. The presence or absence of a Korotkoff sound was noted within 300 msec after the R-wave of the electrocardiogram. Median systolic blood pressure during the trial was equal to cuff pressure when 14 to 36 Korotkoff sounds per cycle of 50 heart beats were present (3, 4). If less than 14 Korotkoff sounds were present, indicating cuff pressure exceeded systolic arterial pressure for most of the trial, the cuff pressure was decreased by 4 mm-Hg for the next cycle. If more than 36 Korotkoff sounds were present, indicating cuff pressure was lower than arterial pressure for most of the trial, the cuff pressure was increased by 4 mm-Hg. Thus, median systolic pressure was tracked throughout each session.

The patients were studied on consecutive weekdays. During all sessions, median systolic blood pressure was measured for 30 trials. Between trials, the cuff was deflated for 30 to 45 seconds. There were 5 to 16 control sessions for each patient during which median systolic blood pressure was recorded with no feedback or reinforcement of lowered systolic pressure. Thus, the control pressures represented median systolic blood pressure of between 7,500 and 22,500 heart beats.

In each of the following conditioning sessions, the first five trials had no reinforcement presented. However, in the subsequent 25 conditioning trials, relatively lowered systolic pressure, indicated by the absence of a Korotkoff sound, was fed back to the patient by presentation of a 100-msec flash of light and a simultaneous 100-msec tone of moderate intensity. The patients were told that the tone and light were desirable and they should try to make them appear. As a reward, after each 20 presentations of tones and lights, a photographic slide, equivalent to $0.05, was shown for 5 seconds. The slides consisted of scenic pictures and reminders of the amount of money earned. The conditioning sessions continued until no reductions in blood pressure occurred in five consecutive sessions.

Blood pressures did not change within the first five control sessions. In the four patients with 15 or 16 control sessions, no decreases in blood pressure were noted after the initial five control sessions (5). Average median systolic blood pressure during the last five control sessions in the seven patients was 164.9 mm-Hg (Table 1). Pressures in the last five conditioning sessions were used as an index of the effectiveness of training. During these sessions, average median systolic blood pressure was 148.4 mm-Hg ($P < .02$) (6). In the individual patients, systolic blood pressure decreased 3.5, 33.8, 29.2, 16.5, 16.1, 0, and 17.3 mm-Hg.

Systolic blood pressure did not change significantly within each control session. However, it decreased an average of 4.8 mm-Hg ($P < .001$) (6) within each conditioning session. This within-session decrease is equivalent to that observed in normotensive subjects with similar training (3). In the two patients with little or no decrease in systolic blood presure, patient No. 1 did not have elevated systolic blood pressure, while patient No. 6 had renal artery stenosis. No consistent changes in heart rate were present in any of the patients during the blood pressure changes.

Elevated arterial blood pressure increases the risk of coronary artery disease and cerebrovascular accidents (7). This increased risk is lessened by lowering blood pressure (8). At the present time, the means of lowering blood pressure are pharmacological or surgical or both. In the present experiments, systolic blood pressure could be decreased by operant conditioning techniques in six of seven patients with essential hypertension. Since the decrease in systolic pressure was measured only in the laboratory and no consistent measurements were made outside the laboratory, the usefulness of such methods in the therapeutic management of hypertension remains to be evaluated (9–12).

HERBERT BENSON
*Harvard Medical Unit, Boston City Hospital, Boston, Massachusetts 02118*
and *Department of Medicine,*
*Harvard Medical School, Boston 02115*
DAVID SHAPIRO
BERNARD TURSKY
GARY E. SCHWARTZ
*Massachusetts Mental Health Center,*
*Harvard Medical School*

# Alpha Enhancement 38

## as a Treatment for Pain: A Case Study

### Linda Gannon and Richard A. Sternbach

**Summary**—Drawing on past reports of raised pain thresholds of yogis in a meditative state, the high alpha content during meditation, and reports of operant alpha wave conditioning, a hypothesis was formulated that a high alpha state and pain are incompatible behaviors, and thus the production of alpha could be used for symptomatic treatment of pain. A patient, who suffered from severe headaches resulting from head injuries, went through 67 alpha conditioning sessions and increased his alpha activity from 20 per cent time alpha with eyes closed to 92 per cent time alpha with eyes closed and 50 per cent with eyes open. Although the patient was not able to rid himself of pain by achieving a high alpha state, he was in some instances able to prevent pain by going into a high alpha state before the headache began.

ANAND, CHHINA and SINGH (1961) observed that in some instances yoga meditators were able to raise their pain thresholds. In their study, 2 yogis, while in meditation, were able to keep their hands in water at 4°C for up to 55 minutes without subjective pain sensation and without alpha blocking. EEG recordings were taken before and during meditation. Before meditation, the subjects showed prominent alpha activity and alpha blocking when stimulated. However, when the yogis were meditating, their EEG records showed no blocking during stimulation.

In our laboratory, we have conducted some pilot research on alpha feedback training. The subjects' description of the high alpha state was similar to that reported by Kamiya (1969). Our results in alpha conditioning were not as dramatic as those reported by Kamiya, but they were in the same direction. The procedure for alpha conditioning that we developed in the pilot research was used in the present study.

The yoga study implies that the meditative state and pain are incompatible behaviors and that one component of the meditative state is a high alpha content. In light of this research and our own observations, we decided to investigate the possibility of utilizing the ability to achieve a high alpha state as symptomatic treatment for intractable pain. To test this hypothesis, we used a patient who was suffering from recurrent pain for which orthodox medicine had given little or no relief.

## MEDICAL HISTORY OF THE PATIENT

The patient's problem began in the fall of 1964 when he suffered a head injury. Six weeks after the injury, he began having headaches. The diagnosis was that he had had a concussion resulting from the head injury. Pain medication was prescribed and the headache disappeared in 3–4 weeks. In January, 1965, the patient suffered a second head injury and 4 weeks later the headache returned. The diagnosis was that he had had a relapse of the concussion and the patient took pain medication for 6–7 weeks. In May, 1965, the headache returned, possibly caused by a third slight head injury 3 weeks previous. This time the patient required pain medication for 6 months. In June, 1966, the patient hit his head a fourth time and 2 weeks later the headaches recurred. This time he took medication to control the dilation of blood

*Requests for reprints to: Linda Gannon, Department of Psychology, University of Wisconsin, Madison, Wisconsin 53706.

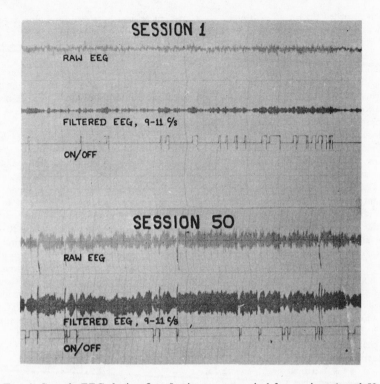

FIG. 1. Sample EEG during first 5-minute rest period for sessions 1 and 50.

vessels. This enabled him to function better, but the pain persisted for almost 2 years. In May of 1968, the patient suffered a fifth head injury, and 6 weeks later the headaches reappeared. In January, 1970, he still had headaches and at that time, we began our treatment. Usually, each series of headaches was most intense and of longest duration when it started, gradually decreasing in intensity and duration and finally disappearing. From 1966 to 1969, the patient had three neurological examinations and a psychiatric evaluation—the results of which were essentially negative. The final diagnosis was inadequate control of dilation and constriction of blood vessels as a result of the head injuries.

At the time the patient started treatment in our laboratory, his headaches had abated somewhat, but were still fairly constant and prevented him from exerting himself physically or mentally. Usually after about 15 minutes of exertion, a headache would either begin or, if he already had one, would become more intense to the point of being incapacitating.

## PROCEDURE

EEG recordings were taken from two occipital leads on the right side of the head with a ground electrode on the ear. We used Grass Type E–1A Durable Disc Silver electrodes which were filled with Redux Electrode Paste, and after Redux had been rubbed into the scalp, they were applied with Collodion. The brain waves were amplified by a Grass EEG preamplifier, model 5P5B, calibrated at 30 $\mu$V equal to 0·5 cm and recorded on a Grass polygraph, model 5A running at 5 mm/sec. At the same time, the signals were passed through a Krohn-Hite electronic band pass filter, model 330BR set at 9–11 cycles/sec, and this filtered output was recorded on a separate channel of the polygraph. From the band pass filter the data went to a Schmitt trigger which was set at 0·5 cm (later at 0·6 cm). When the alpha amplitude reached 30 $\mu$V, the Schmitt trigger set off a timer to record the seconds of alpha, a Magnecord tape recorder to supply feedback to the patient in the form of a tone or music, a counter to record the number of alpha bursts, and a third channel on the polygraph which recorded the *on–off* of alpha.

The patient was in a dimly-lighted room seated in a comfortable chair. Instructions were given through a speaker situated behind him. He was told to keep the tone or music on as much as possible during the learning periods, and simply to rest during the rest periods.

Each session lasted 29 minutes and consisted of five 2-minute learning periods (later changed to four 3-minute learning periods) with one minute of rest between learning periods and a 5-minute rest period at the beginning and end. During the rest periods the patient received no feedback. During the learning periods, he received instant feedback consisting of either tones or music, and at the end of each learning period was told the number of seconds he had had alpha. The amount of alpha was recorded for both the learning and rest periods.

We started with five 2-minute learning periods with the triggering amplitude at 30 $\mu$V. When the patient's EEG showed the specified frequency (9–11 cycles/sec) and amplitude, he heard a low tone; at other times he heard a high tone. This procedure was used for four sessions. We then changed to four 3-minute learning periods at the patient's request. After three more sessions, we substituted organ music for the low tone and eliminated any sound for the non-alpha state. This was done because the patient reported that he often used organ music as a background for studying—he enjoyed it, but it did not distract him. He also reported that the high tone irritated him.

We continued in this manner for 30 sessions. At this point we changed the procedure so that during part of the session, the patient would have his eyes open. We felt it necessary for him to be able to achieve a high alpha state with his eyes open, so that it might be possible for him to get rid of his pain and, at the same time, function normally.

After 4 sessions, the patient increased eyes closed alpha time to the point where it was no longer challenging; so we raised the required amplitude to 36 $\mu$V and conducted 19 more sessions in this way. In the last 4 sessions we eliminated the music and the patient's only feedback was a report to him on the amount of alpha during each learning period. We did this to encourage him to attempt a high alpha state outside the laboratory where he would not have instant feedback. This concluded the conditioning procedure. In the next few months, the

patient returned 3 times for follow-up sessions.

In Fig. 1, the obvious change in the patient's resting EEG can be seen. In the upper portion is a sample of the patient's EEG record during the first 5-minute rest period of session 1. In the lower portion is a sample of the patient's EEG record during the first 5-minute rest period of session 50. There a marked increase in alpha time and amplitude.

Fig. 2 summarizes the procedures used and the results obtained over all sessions. For the first 41 sessions, alpha was defined as a frequency of 9–11 cycles/sec and a minimum amplitude of 30 $\mu$V. For the remaining sessions, the minimum amplitude was raised to 36 $\mu$V. As can be seen in the graph, the introduction of music in place of the tones seemed to help the patient increase his per cent alpha time.* Also, when we changed to eyes open during part of the session, the eyes closed alpha time showed a very large increase—during one session as high as 92 per cent.† After we increased the amplitude requirement, there was a sharp drop after which eyes open and eyes closed per cent alpha time tended to converge.

## DISCUSSION

Our original hypothesis was that pain and a high alpha state are incompatible behaviors. Therefore, if a person suffering from pain were able to achieve a high alpha state, he would have no pain, or at least report feeling no pain. We found this not to be true with our patient. He often reported having a headache when he came to the laboratory, and although he never had much alpha when he had a headache, he always had some alpha. When he had a headache, he was not able to concentrate enough to achieve a high alpha state. But when he did not have a headache, and was able to achieve a high alpha state, he always reported that he felt much better after the session. So it seemed that all we were able to do was to make him feel better when he felt normal, but that we had no effect when he was already experiencing pain.

The intensity and duration of the patient's headaches did decrease gradually during the course of treatment but this result was confounded with spontaneous improvement. Because of the patient's previous experience, one would expect the headaches to improve without any treatment. We therefore cannot determine to what extent improvement occurred spontane-

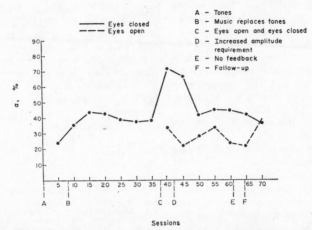

A — Tones
B — Music replaces tones
C — Eyes open and eyes closed
D — Increased amplitude requirement
E — No feedback
F — Follow-up

FIG. 2. Percentage time alpha averaged over successive series of 5 sessions. The letters A, B, etc., mark the points at which changes of procedure were introduced.

*The rest periods and learning periods were combined to form these percentages because, as his ability to produce alpha increased, his resting alpha increased also. Since our purpose was not only to provide the patient with a means of treating his pain, but also to raise his pain threshold by increasing the amount of alpha in his resting EEG, we thought it best to represent his progress by total per cent alpha.
†It should be noted that there was a great deal of variability in the total per cent alpha. Some days, usually when the patient had a headache or was tired, he had very little alpha—as little as 12 per cent.

ously and to what extent it occurred as a result of our treatment. The patient, however, did benefit from our treatment in two ways.

1. After 20 sessions, he reported that his attention span had lengthened, and that he was able to read without getting a headache for about 30 minutes—as opposed to 15 minutes before treatment. There are, as far as we can determine, two possible explanations for this. The first is that his pain threshold was actually raised. The alpha conditioning sessions were 29 minutes long, and he may have trained himself to achieve a high alpha state for that period of time, consequently being able to avoid a headache for 30 minutes. The fact that in the first few sessions his per cent alpha was much higher during the first 15 minutes than during the last 15 minutes tends to substantiate this explanation. He gradually learned to extend his high alpha state to include all 29 minutes.

The other explanation is that we trained him to increase his attention span by putting him in a situation in which it was necessary to concentrate for 30 minutes. It is possible that we could have asked him to read for 30 minutes every day, and he would have gradually learned to do the task without a headache. In other words, his increased attention span may have

been due to concentration training rather than alpha training.

2. The other beneficial result of our treatment was noticed by the patient after about 50 sessions. He reported that when he participated in certain activities, such as swimming or attending a rock concert, he always had a headache afterward. Generally, he would avoid these activities but when he did engage in them, he expected the resulting headache. After about 50 treatment sessions, the patient attended a rock concert. When the concert was over, he realized that he had been in a sort of trance during the concert. He described this state of mind as being very similar to a high alpha state during a treatment session with the added dimension of a condensed time perception. When the concert was over he had no headache. He had a similar experience when he was swimming a few days later. He had no headache afterward and felt that he had been in a sort of trance similar to a high alpha state. Neither of these experiences was planned by the patient beforehand, but when he reported them to us, we encouraged him to try to achieve a high alpha state whenever he was in a potentially headache-producing situation. He tried this and was quite often, though not always, successful. He may

have been more successful after fewer sessions had we begun with this goal in mind. As it was, we only discovered it because of the perceptiveness of our patient.

Although we had not expected the phenomenon discussed above, it is compatible with the yogi's raised pain threshold. The yoga meditators were not in pain when they began meditation, but were exposed to a painful stimulus after they were in a meditative state. Our subject's experience was similar in that he could prevent the onset of pain, although he could not get rid of pain already present.

There is obviously much more research to do in this area before arriving at even tentative conclusions. Not only do we need a larger sample and adequate controls, but also a procedure requiring fewer sessions. One hypothesis in this area which merits future research is the possibility that psychophysiological variables other than EEG exhibit marked changes during the yoga meditative state. If this is so, simulation of the meditative state might be achieved more completely and in a shorter period of time by conditioning more of the relevant physiological functions. With all its limitations, however, this single case study does provide some evidence that it is possible for a patient to learn to prevent the onset of pain by means of operant alpha conditioning techniques.

### REFERENCES

ANAND B. K., CHHINA G. S. and SINGH B. (1961) Some aspects of electroencephalographic studies in Yogis, *Electroenceph. clin. neurophysiol.* 13, 452–456.

KAMIYA J. (1969) Operant control of the EEG alpha rhythm and some of its reported effects on consciousness. In *Altered States of Consciousness* (Edited by C. T. TART) John Wiley, New York.

*Acknowledgements*—The authors wish to thank Jan Martinson for designing the equipment, and Burt Kaplan and David Rice for their helpful comments. The study was supported in part by USPHS Grant No. MH12858–01, NIMH, and by University of Wisconsin Medical School Research Committee Grant No. M–321–24 to David Rice.

# Voluntary Control of Eroticism 39

## Donald E. Henson and H. B. Rubin

A recent study reported that motivated human male subjects were able voluntarily to inhibit penile erection in the presence of effective erotic stimulation (Laws and Rubin, 1969). However, because this study required attendance only to the display area of erotic stimuli, there was a possibility that inhibition resulted from their subjects not attending to the content of the stimuli. The present study utilized a procedure that guaranteed subjects' attendance to the content of the erotic stimulation, i.e., a description of the behavioral content of the erotic stimulus film. Nevertheless, every subject was able to inhibit penile erection almost as effectively as when no film description was required. Furthermore, the verbal description prevented the production of competing asexual stimuli; a technique that all subjects, in both the Laws and Rubin study (1969) and the present study, reported using to inhibit penile erection when no description was required. This suggests that although concentration on asexual stimuli may be the preferred method of reducing sexual arousal to erotic stimulation, penile erection can be inhibited by other methods.

There is an extensive literature demonstrating that human subjects can exert voluntary control over such autonomic responses as the galvanic skin response (Birk, Crider, Shapiro, and Tursky, 1966; Crider, Shapiro, and Tursky, 1966; Gavalas, 1957; Johnson and Schwartz, 1967; Senter and Hummel, 1965) and heart rate (Engel and Chism, 1967; Engel and Hansen, 1966; Hnatiow and Lang, 1965). Since most visceral responses can be affected by voluntary skeletal behaviors, e.g., changing muscle tension and respiratory pattern (Miller and Carmona, 1967), there is a

possibility that the voluntary modification of GSR and heart rate resulted from mediational skeletal responses and not direct instrumental learning. However, when the possibility of emission of voluntary skeletal behaviors was eliminated by utilizing curarized animals as subjects, heart rate (DiCara and Miller, 1968a; Miller and DiCara, 1967; Trowill, 1967), intestinal contractions (Banuazizi, 1967; Miller and Banuazizi, 1968), blood-vessel diameter (DiCara and Miller, 1968b), and rate of urine formation (DiCara and Miller, 1967) were nevertheless modified by operant conditioning techniques, indicating that autonomic visceral responses can be subject to direct voluntary control.

Laws and Rubin (1969) reported that penile erection, an autonomic visceral response (Kelly, 1961) that is generally considered involuntary (Houssay, 1955), could be voluntarily controlled by normal human male subjects. Their subjects were able both to produce erections in the absence of erotic stimuli and inhibit erections in the presence of effective erotic stimulation. Each subject reported that

[1]This investigation is based in part on a thesis submitted by the senior author to Southern Illinois University in partial fulfillment of the requirements for the M.S. degree. The research was supported by grants from the Mental Health Fund of the Illinois Department of Mental Health and the National Institute of Mental Health Grant 04926. We wish to thank Drs. R. Campbell and R. Sanders and the late Dr. E. Sulzer for their helpful suggestions, and Dr. P. Gebhard and the Institute of Sex Research, Indiana University for providing access to their collection of films. Reprints may be obtained from H. B. Rubin, Behavior Research Laboratory, Anna State Hospital, Anna, Illinois 62906.

**537**

tumescence was achieved by "fantasizing" about erotic events, and that inhibition was accomplished by producing competing stimuli, *i.e.*, concentrating on asexual stimuli (Laws and Rubin, 1969).

Since the attending indicator of the Laws and Rubin study (1969) ensured attendance only to the display area of the erotic stimulation, the contention can be made that their subjects were not attending to the content of the stimuli when voluntary inhibition occurred. However, if penile inhibition is possible when attendance to the content of erotic stimulation is guaranteed, then it must be assumed that the autonomic visceral response of penile erection can be at least partially modified by voluntary controls.

## METHOD

### Subjects

Eight adult males (age 21 to 30 yr) volunteered to serve as subjects. Two (S-1 and S-2) were employees of Anna State Hospital, had participated in an earlier study (Laws and Rubin, 1969), and received no remuneration. Three subjects (S-3, S-4, and S-5) were experimentally naive, were students at Southern Illinois University, and were remunerated for their transportation and time at the rate of $2.50 per hour.

The remaining three subjects did not complete the study, two because during their baseline test session, sample stimulus films were ineffective in eliciting full penile erection, and the third because he attempted to control his penile erection by manipulating his penis. All subjects were fully informed of the nature of the experiment.

### Apparatus

The apparatus was similar to that of Bancroft, Jones, and Pullan (1966) as modified by Laws and Rubin (1969). Basically, this apparatus was a mecury strain gauge transducer constructed of a 12-in. (30.5-cm) length of silicone rubber tubing filled with mercury and plugged at both ends with platinum wire. The tubing was attached to a small plastic holder to form a loop of 3-in. (7.6-cm) circumference that when in position, encircled the penis. This loop functioned as one leg of a bridge circuit that was powered by four 1.35-v mercury batteries. The resistance in the circuit was balanced by a variable resistor on another leg.

Any changes in the circumference of the penis changed the length of the loop, resulting in a change in the diameter of the enclosed mercury, and this changed the electrical resistance of the mercury. These resistance changes resulted in changes in current flow through the mercury that were amplified and recorded by a polygraph (Grass, Model 7). The transducer was calibrated before and after each session by placing the loop around two standard cylinders and recording the resultant current flow.

An intercom located in the sound-proof, private chamber permitted communication between the subject and the experimenter, but the subject could be heard only if he depressed the "transmit" lever on the unit.

### Stimuli

Stimuli were erotic motion pictures of approximately 10 min duration presented on a rear-projection screen in the experimental chamber. The onset and termination of the films were automatically recorded by a multi-pen event recorder.

### Recording Apparatus

A microphone in the experimental chamber permitted non-audible recording of the subjects' verbal descriptions of the stimulus film on a tape recorder located in the adjacent control room. Before the experiment, each subject was fully informed of the presence and function of the tape recording equipment. The tape recorder was manually synchronized with the film projector to allow later comparisons of verbal descriptions and film content.

### Detection Signals

To ensure that subjects were attending to the area of the film presentation, each subject was instructed to depress a button located on the arm of his chair whenever a brief (200 msec) flash of light appeared upon the projection screen. The lights could appear at either the top or the bottom of the projected image, and each was controlled by an independent VI 30-sec schedule; thus, a flash appeared on the average of once every 15 sec. Both signals and responses were recorded by a multi-pen event recorder.

### Procedure

The procedure was similar to that employed by Laws and Rubin (1969). Each subject participated in a baseline test session in order to determine penile circumference of the flaccid state and full erection and the ability of the test stimulus film to elicit a full erection. The subject was instructed to place the transducer loop around the center of his penile shaft with the plastic holder on the underside of the penis; he was cautioned not to touch his penis or the transducer for the duration of the experiment, and was informed that such behaviors could be identified from the polygraph recording. The flaccid state was individually defined as the penile circumference recorded when penile size stabilized (less than 1% of full scale variability for at least 30 sec) after emplacement of the transducer. Full erection was individually defined as the maximum penile circumference recorded from subjects who reported having a full erection while viewing the test stimulus film. These maximums were never exceeded in any subsequent recordings from the subjects. A second test stimulus film was shown to subjects who reported that they did not experience a full erection during the first test film; if the second film did not elicit a full erection from a subject, he was not allowed to complete the study. Partial erections were defined as any penile circumference that resulted in a current flow greater than the flaccid state and less than full erection. Full erections were reported as 100%, flaccidity as 0%, and partial erections as a percentage of full erection. The test session and experimental session for each subject were separated by a minimum of 24 hr, and films presented during the test session were never presented during the experimental sessions.

Every subject viewed the same stimulus film during their experimental sessions; a session consisted of showing a subject the same film five times in succession. The criterion for the onset of the first film presentation of a session was at least 30 sec of penile stability (flaccid state). Subsequent presentations of the film during a session were dependent upon penile circumference returning to within 5% of the flaccid state and remaining stable for at least 30 sec.

For the first presentation of the film the instructions to each subject were: ·

"During this presentation of the film, do nothing to inhibit your sexual response to the film. Remember you must depress the button on the arm of your chair whenever

a detection signal appears on the projection screen."

For the second film presentation the instructions to each subject were:

"During this presentation of the film, avoid getting an erection by any means possible except not looking at the film. Remember you must depress the button on the arm of the chair whenever a detection signal appears on the screen."

For the third film presentation the instructions to each subject were:

"During this presentation of the film, avoid getting an erection by any means except not looking at the film. Also, you are to describe what is going on in the film as it occurs, that is, give a running description of the action. There will be no detection signals during this presentation."

For the fourth film presentation the instructions to each subject were:

"During this presentation of the film, do nothing to inhibit your sexual response to the film. Also, you are to describe what is going on in the film as it occurs, that is, give a running description of the action. There will be no detection signals during this film presentation."

For the fifth film presentation the instructions to each subject again were:

"During this presentation of the film, do nothing to inhibit your sexual response to the film. There will again be detection signals during this presentation of the film."

When verbal descriptions were required, detection signals were not presented; detection signals were presented during film presentations 1, 2, and 5, verbal descriptions were made during film presentations 3 and 4. Table 1 gives a summary of the experimental procedure. The subjects did not remove the transducer or leave the chamber for the duration of the session. Each session was of approximately 90-min duration.

A paired-comparison discrimination procedure was used to determine if naive observers could detect a qualitative difference in the verbal descriptions made under the two instructional conditions by each of the five subjects. The standard stimulus for each subject

Table 1

| Film Presentation | Instructions | Attending Indicator |
|---|---|---|
| 1 | Do Not Inhibit | Detection Signal |
| 2 | Inhibit | Detection Signal |
| 3 | Inhibit | Verbal Description |
| 4 | Do Not Inhibit | Verbal Description |
| 5 | Do Not Inhibit | Detection Signal |

was always the same 30-sec segment of one of his descriptions and was randomly selected from either his inhibit description or his do not inhibit description. Three 30-sec segments from each of the two film descriptions made by a subject served as comparison stimuli. The standard stimulus and comparison stimuli were never descriptions of the same sections of the film. Each comparison stimulus was paired with the standard stimulus three times; thus, there were 18 pairs of descriptions for each subject. The total of 90 pairs of descriptions (18 pairs from each of five subjects) were tape recorded in random order and subsequently played to the observers. The instructions to each of three observers were:

You will listen to several pairs of descriptions of film content made under different instructional conditions. Each pair will be numbered and will correspond to a number on your score sheet. Each pair will consist of a standard description and a comparison description made by the same subject at two different times. However, both the standard and the comparison will be from descriptions of the same film. The standard description will always be the first of each pair and may differ in content from the comparison. Some of the comparison descriptions were made under different instructional conditions than the standard, while others were made under the same instructional conditions as the standard. Your task will be to determine if the comparison description was made under the same or under different instructional conditions. The text of the description will *not* give a clue to aid in this discrimination. If you judge the second description of a pair to have been made under the same instructional conditions as the first, circle the "S" under the appropriate pair number on the score sheet. If

you judge the second description of a pair to have been made under different instructional conditions than the first, circle the "D" after the pair number on the score sheet. You will have 10 sec to make your decision.

The entire procedure required approximately 2 hr to complete. Transcriptions were made of all six of the 30-sec segments of the verbal descriptions of each subject. A word count from these transcripts provided a measure of rate of speech under the two instructional conditions.

Finally, the entire recording of each verbal description was played through a voice-operated relay (Grason-Stadler Model E7300A-1) and the number and total duration of all pauses of at least 0.5 sec were automatically recorded on a counter and running time meter.

## RESULTS

The calibration of the transducer never differed by more than 2% of full scale, within or between sessions.

Eighty-seven per cent of all detection signals were accurately detected; each subject accurately detected between 74% and 100% of the signal lights that appeared during any one film presentation. During the first presentation of the film, when the instructions were to not inhibit sexual responding, the accurate detection of signal lights averaged 84% for all subjects and ranged from 76% to 93% for individual subjects. During the second presentation, when instructions were to inhibit penile erection, signal detections were made with a mean accuracy of 91% for all subjects; with a range of from 86% to 97%. During the fifth film presentation, when the instructions not to inhibit penile erection were repeated, the average percentage of accurately detected signal lights was 87%, with a range from 74% to 100%. In the entire experiment (651 signal presentations), there were 14 false postive responses, *i.e.*, responses made without the appearance of a signal light.

Analysis of the subject's descriptions of the film, made while simultaneously listening to the tape recordings and viewing the film, indicated that all subjects accurately depicted the behavior in the film. Although there were numerous individual differences with respect to the vocabularies utilized, the two descriptions made by each subject contained both scientific or medical terminology and the sexual vernacular. The descriptions of four of the five subjects were generally fluent and continuous, and at no time did a pause of more than 10 sec occur in their descriptions. However, both reports made by S-1 were interrupted by several pauses ranging from 10 sec to 25 sec in duration.

discrimination test did not support the judgment of the experimenters; a chi square analysis of the data indicated that none of the three observers was able to detect a difference, at the 5% level significance, between the two descriptions of any subject. In addition, as can be seen in Table 3, there was no consistent change in either the rate of words spoken or pausing between the instructional conditions.

Table 2

Observer Accuracy in Paired-Comparison Discriminations of the Two Verbal Descriptions

| | Subject | | | | | | | | | |
|---|---|---|---|---|---|---|---|---|---|---|
| | 1 | | 2 | | 3 | | 4 | | 5 | |
| Observer | % Correct | $\chi^{2*}$ | % Correct | $\chi^{2*}$ | % Correct | $\chi^{2*}$ | % Correct | $\chi^{2*}$ | % Correct | $\chi^{2*}$ |
| 1 | 56 | 0.22 | 72 | 3.56 | 67 | 2.00 | 56 | 0.22 | 67 | 2.00 |
| 2 | 50 | 0.00 | 67 | 2.00 | 39 | 0.89 | 39 | 0.89 | 50 | 0.00 |
| 3 | 44 | 0.22 | 56 | 0.22 | 39 | 0.89 | 72 | 3.56 | 56 | 0.22 |

$*\chi^2 \geq 3.84$ necessary for 0.05 level of significance

A comparison of the two descriptions made by each subject resulted in the experimenters judging that S-3 attempted to alter his "emotional" involvement with the content of the film under the two different instructional conditions. It was judged that when the instructions were to inhibit penile erection and describe the film, S-3 spoke at a faster rate, similar to a radio sportscaster, than during the do not inhibit-verbal description condition when he engaged in a slower, more relaxed report of the film. However, as can be seen in Table 2 the results of the paired-comparison

Three subjects (S-2, S-3, and S-4) spoke faster during the inhibit instructions; the remaining two subjects spoke slower. One subject (S-1) had a longer mean pause duration during the inhibit-instructions, while two subjects (S-3 and S-4) had shorter pause durations, and two (S-2 and S-5) were unchanged.

Figure 1 shows the amount of penile erection produced by each of the five subjects during the five successive film presentations. During the first presentation, when the instructions were for subjects to do nothing to inhibit penile erection, every subject exhibited

Table 3

Analysis of Verbal Descriptions of the Stimulus Film

| Subject | Instructions | Mean Words per Minute[a] | Total Pause Time (Minutes)[b, c] | Number of Pauses[b] | Mean Pause Duration (Seconds)[b, c] |
|---|---|---|---|---|---|
| 1 | Inhibit | 41 | 8.28 | 68 | 7.31 |
| | Do Not Inhibit | 73 | 6.49 | 72 | 5.41 |
| 2 | Inhibit | 144 | 2.81 | 128 | 1.32 |
| | Do Not Inhibit | 123 | 1.56 | 70 | 1.34 |
| 3 | Inhibit | 167 | 0.58 | 86 | 0.47 |
| | Do Not Inhibit | 91 | 3.01 | 114 | 1.58 |
| 4 | Inhibit | 167 | 4.13 | 138 | 1.80 |
| | Do Not Inhibit | 109 | 6.35 | 117 | 3.26 |
| 5 | Inhibit | 105 | 5.19 | 140 | 2.22 |
| | Do Not Inhibit | 134 | 4.24 | 118 | 2.16 |

[a]Computed from transcripts of three, 30-sec segments of each description. The same segments were used for each subject.
[b]Determined for entire description duration (10.6 min). Only pauses of 0.5 sec or longer included.
[c]Not including first 0.5 sec of each pause.

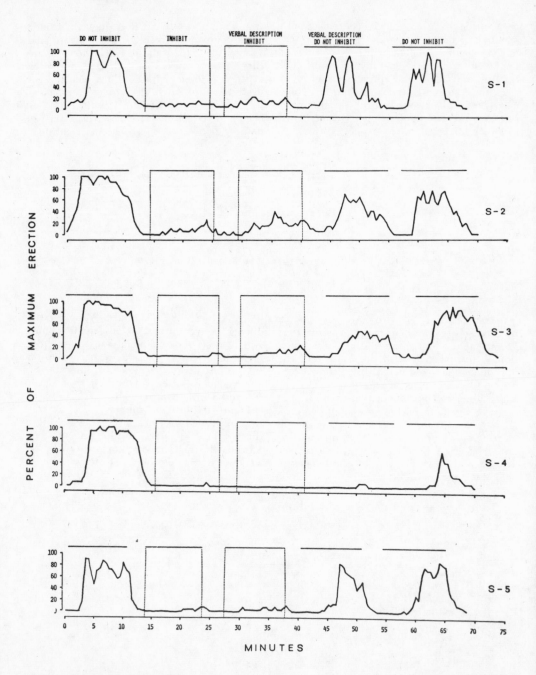

Fig. 1. Per cent of maximum penile erection elicited from five subjects during five successive presentations of an erotic film. The horizontal lines above each graph indicate those periods of time that the film was projected. Subjects were instructed to inhibit during presentations enclosed by dotted lines, and not to inhibit during all other presentations. Subjects were required to give a continuous account of the behavioral content of the film during those presentations labelled verbal description, and were required to make a detection response to the appearance of signal lights on the projection screen during all other presentations.

a full erection during some portion of the film presentation. Each subject's maintenance of full erection ranged from less than 30 sec (S-5) to almost the entire duration of the film (S-2). Average erection for all subjects during this condition was 65% of maximum.

No subject produced a full erection during the second presentation of the film, when each subject was instructed to inhibit sexual responding. At no time during this condition did the penile circumference of any subject exceed 25% of maximum, and only S-2 exhibited an erection that was greater than 15% of maximum. The average erection for all subjects during this condition was 5% of maximum.

During the third film presentation, when the instructions were to inhibit penile erection and to describe orally the behavioral content of the film, again no subject produced a full erection. Only S-2 displayed an erection that exceeded 25% of maximum. Three subjects exhibited slightly more tumescence and one subject slightly less tumescence during this condition than during the inhibit without verbal description condition. The remaining subject (S-5) developed identical peak erections during both inhibit conditions, but his average erection during the inhibit-description condition exceeded by a small amount that exhibited during the condition when instructions were to inhibit and no description was required. The average erection for all subjects during this condition was 9% of maximum.

During the fourth presentation, when the subject was instructed not to inhibit sexual responding and to describe the film, four of the five subjects exhibited a greater degree of tumescence than during any inhibit condition; although the peak erection (6% of maximum) attained by S-4 during this condition was identical to that reached during the inhibit-without description condition, the average erection was greater than that during any inhibit condition. Every subject exhibited substantially less tumescence during this condition (do not inhibit-description) than during the first presentation when the only instructions were not to inhibit penile erection. The average for all subjects during this condition was 28% of maximum.

During this final film presentation, when the instructions to do nothing to inhibit penile erection were repeated, every subject displayed more tumescence than during any condition but the first, when the instructions were also not to inhibit penile erection. The film was effective in eliciting a full erection from only S-1 during this final presentation, as compared to every subject during the first do not inhibit condition. The average erection for all subjects during this condition was 38% of maximum.

## DISCUSSION

Laws and Rubin (1969) reported that motivated males were able to inhibit penile erection while attending to the display area of erotic stimuli. All of their subjects reported that they accomplished inhibition of penile erection by thinking about asexual stimuli that required some concentration, e.g., lyrics to popular songs, multiplication tables, verses to poetry, or the immediate detection of stimulus lights (Laws and Rubin, 1969). All subjects in the present study reported using the same methods of intellectual asexual stimulation to inhibit tumescence when their attention to the erotic stimuli was monitored by the detection signal response. The substitution of the verbal description for the detection signal response, as an attending indicator, served two functions. The description guaranteed that the subjects were attending to the content of the erotic stimuli and afforded the subjects little or no opportunity to concentrate on a competing asexual stimuli; yet all subjects were able to inhibit their penile erections to about the same degree as when they were able to produce competing stimuli. Thus, the present study not only confirms the results of Laws and Rubin (1969), but also suggests that the self-generation of such competing asexual stimuli is not essential for successful inhibition of penile erection.

All subjects reported that they were motivated for their penile responding to conform to the instructions to inhibit penile erection; however, none could identify the mechanism by which inhibition was achieved when they were required to describe the stimulus film. The only behavior that subjects reported engaging in was the description of the film itself. A comparison of the penile responding during the final two conditions, in which instructions not to inhibit were in effect, indicated a reduction in tumescence when a description was required as compared to when none was required. Therefore, the verbal description might have functioned as a competing behavior that resulted in reduction of penile erection. The inhibitory effect of the description was most dramatic for S-4, penile erection was almost totally eliminated when he was required to describe the film. For the other four subjects, the decrease in penile tumescence generated by the description was small compared to the marked reduction in penile circumference when the instructions were to inhibit, regardless of whether a description was required.

Since the act of describing the film was the only behavior that subjects reported engaging in when they effectively inhibited penile erection, perhaps the control over penile tumescence resulted from subjects differentially describing the film under the two instructional conditions. However, analysis of the two descriptions made by each subject did not confirm this hypothesis. Although the experimenters judged that S-3 gave qualitatively different descriptions under the different instructional conditions, three observers were not able to detect a difference between the two descriptions made by each subject and, an analysis of the speech patterns of all subjects indicated no consistent change in either the rate of words spoken or in the pattern of pausing. Each subject was able to exert voluntary control over penile erection while attending to the content of erotic stimuli, but at this time the method of such control is not known by either the subjects or the experimenters.

## REFERENCES

Bancroft, J. H. J., Jones, H. G., and Pullan, B. R. A simple transducer for measuring penile erection, with comments on its use in the treatment of sexual disorders. *Behavior Research and Therapy*, 1966, **4**, 239-242.

Banuazizi, A. Modification of an autonomic response by instrumental learning. *Psychonomic Bulletin*, 1967, 1, 30.

Birk, L., Crider, A., Shapiro, D., and Tursky, B. Operant electrodermal conditioning under partial curarization. *Journal of Comparative and Physiological Psychology*, 1966, **62**, 165-166.

Crider, A., Shapiro, D., and Tursky, B. Reinforcement of spontaneous electrodermal activity. *Journal of Comparative and Physiological Psychology*, 1966, **61**, 20-27.

DiCara, L. V. and Miller, N. E. Instrumental learning of urine formation by curarized rats. *Psychonomic Bulletin*, 1967, **1**, 23-24.

DiCara, L. V. and Miller, N. E. Changes in heart rate instrumentally learned by curarized rats as avoidance responses. *Journal of Comparative and Physiological Psychology*, 1968, **65**, 8-12. (a)

DiCara, L. V. and Miller, N. E. Instrumental learning of vasomotor responses by rats: Learning to respond differentially in the two ears. *Science*, 1968, **159**, 1485-1486. (b)

Engel, B. T. and Chism, R. A. Operant conditioning of heart rate speeding. *Psychophysiology*, 1967, **3**, 418-426.

Engel, B. T. and Hansen, S. P. Operant conditioning of heart rate slowing. *Psychophysiology*, 1966, **3**, 176-187.

Gavalas, R. J. Operant reinforcement of an autonomic response: two studies. *Journal of the Experimental Analysis of Behavior*, 1967, **10**, 119-130.

Hnatiow, M. and Lang, P. J. Learned stabilization of heart rate. *Psychophysiology*, 1965, **1**, 330-336.

Houssay, B. S. *Human physiology*. New York: McGraw-Hill, 1955.

Johnson, H. J. and Schwartz, G. E. Suppression of GSR activity through operant reinforcement. *Journal of Experimental Psychology*, 1967, **75**, 307-312.

Kelly, G. L. Impotence. In A. Ellis and A. Arbarbanel (Eds.), *Encyclopedia of sexual behavior*. New York: Hawthorne Books, 1961. Pp. 515-518.

Laws, D. R. and Rubin, H. B. Instructional control of an autonomic sexual response. *Journal of Applied Behavior Analysis*, 1969, **2**, 93-99.

Miller, N. E. and Banuazizi, A. Instrumental learning by curarized rats of a specific visceral response, intestinal or cardiac. *Journal of Comparative and Physiological Psychology*, 1968, **65**, 1-7.

Miller, N. E. and Carmona, A. Modification of a visceral response, salivation in thirsty dogs, by instrumental training with water reward. *Journal of Comparative and Physiological Psychology*, 1967, **63**, 1-6.

Miller, N. E. and Dicara, L. V. Instrumental learning of heart rate changes in curarized rats: shaping and specificity to discriminative stimulus. *Journal of Comparative and Physiological Psychology*, 1967, **63**, 12-19.

Senter, R. J. and Hummel, W. F. Suppression of an autonomic response through operant conditioning. *The Psychological Record*, 1965, **15**, 1-5.

Trowill, J. A. Instrumental conditioning of the heart rate in the curarized rat. *Journal of Comparative and Physiological Psychology*, 1967, **63**, 7-11.

*Received 29 June 1970.*
*(Revised 20 November 1970.)*

# Discriminated Aversive Control 40
## in the Moderation of Alcholics'
## Drinking Behavior

### S. H. Lovibond and G. Caddy

A treatment procedure designed to train the alcoholic to become a moderate, controlled drinker, is described. The subject is first trained to discriminate his own blood alcohol concentration (BAC) from zero to 0.08%. In the next phase, drinking is followed by strong electric shock if the BAC is above 0.065%, and is allowed to occur with impunity below this level. The co-operation of a family member is sought, and considerable emphasis is placed on the part played by the subject's self-control. To date, 31 subjects have entered the experimental treatment program. Three have dropped out: 21 are regarded tentatively as complete successes in that they have been drinking in a moderate fashion for 16–60 weeks. Success in the remaining seven cases has been partial only.

The post-treatment alcohol intake of experimental subjects is significantly less than that of control subjects, who are given noncontingent shocks during conditioning sessions, but are otherwise treated identically. The dropout rate of experimental subjects is also significantly lower than that of the control group.

An incidental finding is that, rather than developing a marked aversive reaction to alcohol, many successfully treated subjects appear to lose the desire to drink after the first few glasses.

In the field of treatment of alcoholism, it is assumed almost universally that the alcoholic can never become a controlled or social drinker. Consequently, the usual goal of treatment is total abstinence. In the treatment to be described, however, the therapeutic goal is to train the alcoholic to drink in moderation.

The treatment procedure consists essentially of two phases. In the first phase, the subject is trained to discriminate his own blood alcohol concentration (BAC) within the range zero to 0.08%. In the second, or aversive conditioning phase, the consumption of alcohol is follwed by strong elec-

[1] This investigation was supported by Research Grant 65/15863 from the Australian Research Grants Committee. The authors wish to express their gratitude to Tooheys Ltd. who supplied a Breathalyzer unit and alcoholic beverages, and Penfold Wines Pty. Ltd. who also supplied alcoholic beverages. Requests for reprints should be sent to S. H. Lovibond, School of Applied Psychology, University of New South Wales P. O. Box No. 1, Kensington, N. S. W. 2033. Australia.

**545**

tric shock if the subject's BAC is above 0.065%,[2] but is allowed to occur with impunity if the BAC is below this value.

## METHOD

### Discrimination Training

At the beginning of discrimination training, the subject is provided with a very general scale of the behavioral effects which typically accompany different BACs. For example, he is told that at a BAC of about 0.04–.05%, drinkers usually experience the first feelings of warmth and relaxation, and that between 0.05 and 0.08% they become aware of a progressive loss of social inhibitions. The subject is then asked to consume pure alcohol in fruit juice, and to examine his subjective experience and behavior as a basis for estimating his BAC. Every 15–20 min a Breathalyzer reading is taken, and the subject is required to make an estimate of his BAC. Immediately an estimate is given, the subject's actual BAC is fed back to him in the form of an adjustment to the reading of a large meter in front of him. Each time a BAC is presented to the subject, he is encouraged to associate his present subjective state with the meter reading and to construct his own BAC symptom scale.

During discrimination training a personal history is obtained, and the subject is given a detailed account of the nature and aims of the treatment procedure to follow. A training session lasts 1½–2 hr, during which time the subject's BAC rises to about 0.08% and then declines. One training session only is given prior to conditioning.

### Conditioning Procedure

During the conditioning or treatment phase, a ½-in. square stainless-steel shock electrode is attached by adhesive tape to a point approximately 1 in. below chin level, and a similar electrode is positioned on various areas of the face and neck. The subject is required to drink his preferred alcoholic beverage at a steady rate designed to raise his BAC to 0.065% in approximately 1½ hr. As in the first phase, estimates of BAC are required every 15–20 min, followed by feedback of actual BAC on the meter. The subject is told that he may drink with impunity as long as his BAC remains below 0.065%, the "red-line" on the meter. As soon as his BAC rises above this value, however, he must expect to be shocked when he drinks. The subject is required to continue drinking after the BAC reaches 0.065%, and shocks are administered according to a prearranged schedule. The shock schedule is designed to maximize uncertainty (Lovibond, 1968, 1970(a)). First, drinking is shocked on only 80% of occasions, and, on nonshock trials, the subject is allowed to swallow a small quantity of alcohol. Second, the duration of the shock is varied from 1–6 sec. Third, shock intensity is varied from intense to very intense (4–7 mA). Fourth, the point in the drinking sequence when the shock occurs is varied from trial to trial. Occasionally, the shock occurs when the subject picks up his glass, but on most trials the shock is delayed until the subject is in the act of swallowing the alcohol.

The treatment is conducted on an outpatient basis, and the subject is encouraged to pursue his normal occupation and social activities.

The first three sessions are spaced approximately 5–7 days apart, and some 8–10 shocks are administered if the subject can tolerate this number. The duration of the conditioning sessions is approximately 2 hr. Later sessions are spaced more widely, and the number of shocks per session is reduced to 3–4. After some 6–12 sessions and 30–70 shocks, depending on the progress of the subject, treatment is discontinued.

---

[2] A BAC of 0.065% represents a concentration of ethanol in the blood of 65 mg/100 ml of blood volume, and is the approximate level typically reached when 2–3 double martinis are consumed within an hour at a cocktail party.

When possible, a member of the subject's family attends at least some of the treatment sessions, and the importance of the supporting role of the family member is stressed. The involvement of a family member also enables a check to be made on the subject's reports concerning his drinking behavior.

Throughout the program, the subject is treated as a person with a particular problem, and a set of associated problems, to be overcome. It is pointed out to the subject that the treatment alone cannot ensure control of his drinking behavior. He is told that the purpose of the treatment is to provide him with an inbuilt stop mechanism which will assist his own efforts at self-control. His self-control, however, is ultimately decisive. In short, the general therapeutic goal is to assist the subject to regain self-respect by exerting the self-control necessary to maintain a pattern of moderate social drinking.

### Control Procedure

As a control procedure, a group of subjects has been given a period of treatment identical to that of the experimental subjects, except for the removal of the contingencies between the shock and BAC and drinking behavior. Control subjects receive initial training in BAC discrimination, the support of a family member, and self-control instructions. In the conditioning sessions they drink the same amount of alcohol as experimental subjects, and receive equivalent shocks. The shocks begin, however, before the BAC reaches 0.065%, and thereafter occur at random intervals, with the restriction that no shock is given during the 2-min period prior to drinking, or the 3-min period after drinking. The control subjects receive random shocks during the first three conditioning sessions only. In the remaining sessions, shocks are made contingent on BAC and drinking as in the case of experimental subjects.

### Apparatus

Blood alcohol concentration is measured by a Breathalyzer Model 900. (It is unlikely that the high degree of precision of this instrument is essential to the treatment process, and the possibility of developing a cheaper instrument of sufficient precision deserves investigation.)

A modified milliammeter with an 8-in. dial is used to feed back actual BACs to the subject. The milliammeter scale is replaced by a BAC scale reading from zero to 0.10%, with a red band extending from 0.065–0.10%. The meter is in circuit with dry cells and a potentiometer under the manual control of the experimenter.

The stimulator in current use is a Grason Stadler Model E1064 modified to give an output of 7 mA. (As there is no evidence to suggest that type of shock is an important variable in the present type of therapy, any AC stimulator with the necessary output should be equally satisfactory.)

### Subjects

The only criteria used for selection of subjects have been willingness to accept the electric shocks and absence of obvious psychoticism. Only one volunteer has so far been refused entry into the program. To date 44 subjects, with an age range of 22–56 years, have been accepted. Of this number, 31 (25 males and six females) have been allocated to the treatment group, and 13 (10 males and three females) have been selected at random for control treatment.

Some subjects were referred by general medical practitioners or psychiatric hospitals, but most were self-referred after publicity given the project by the news media. On the average, subjects were found to have had a history of alcoholism extending over a period of 10 years prior to acceptance, and most had been hospitalized for alcoholism on numerous occasions. Many subjects were found to have additional psychological problems, such as depression and character disorder.

Twenty-eight of the 31 treatment subjects have completed the full treatment course. Three subjects failed to return after the first or second session. Five of the 13 control subjects have completed the three sessions of the control treatment procedure. Three control subjects dropped out after the first session, and a further five did not return after the second session.

Follow-up information has been obtained from all subjects at regular intervals since treatment. Contact has been maintained by telephone and occasional interviews. In all cases, subjects' reports have been corroborated by a member of the family or other informant, e.g., foreman or employer. The follow-up period has extended over 16–60 weeks.

### RESULTS AND DISCUSSION

It has been found that most nonalcoholics and alcoholics can learn to estimate their BACs with a high degree of accuracy. After a single training session, errors in excess of $\pm0.01\%$ rarely occur (Lovibond, 1970(b)). Most subjects are able to find symptoms corresponding to different BACs, particularly when the BAC is rising. For example, a subject may note that, at about the 0.03% concentration, the skin on his cheeks tightens slightly, and at 0.06% his ears seem to pop.

Table 1 presents a summary of treatment outcome derived from follow-up data obtained from the 28 experimental subjects who have completed treatment. Twenty-one of the 28 subjects are regarded tentatively as complete successes in that they are drinking in a controlled fashion, and exceeding the 0.07% BAC only rarely. Three subjects have been categorized as considerably improved. These subjects are drinking considerably less, but are still exceeding a BAC of 0.07% once or twice per week. Four subjects are considered to be only slightly improved. They are not getting drunk as often as before, but they are drinking only a little less than previously, and they are not at all satisfied with their progress.

Figure 1 shows the mean weekly alcohol intake of experimental and control subjects before treatment, during treatment, and at follow-up. It can be seen that in the experimental group there is a marked drop in alcohol intake after the first treatment session. There is a suggestion of a slow recovery in alcohol intake subsequent to treatment, but the intake

TABLE 1
Outcome of Completed Treatment of 28 Experimental Subjects

| Category | Definition | No. of cases |
|---|---|---|
| Complete success | Drinking in controlled fashion, exceeding 0.07 only rarely | 21 |
| Considerably improved | Drinking less but exceeding 0.07 once or twice per week | 3 |
| Slightly improved | Drinking only slightly less | 4 |

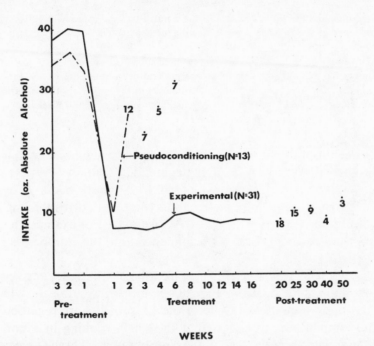

FIG. 1. Mean weekly alcohol intake, expressed in ounces of pure alcohol, of experimental and control subjects before, during, and after treatment. (Numbers by data points indicate reduced number of subjects at those points.)

means in the later stages of follow-up are based on very small numbers. It should be noted also that the mean intake of the three subjects who have been followed for 50 weeks is not in excess of the weekly alcohol consumption of the average Australian drinker (Rankin, 1970; Sargent, 1968). The alcohol consumption of the control subjects also drops sharply during the initial period of control treatment. Unlike the experimental subjects, however, the controls rapidly return to intakes approaching their pretreatment levels. The divergence between the two groups is such that by the end of the third week of treatment, the intake of control subjects is significantly higher than that of the experimentals (Mann–Whitney $U = 192.5$, $z = 3.169$, $p < .008$). (Subjects who dropped out during the first 3 weeks of treatment were followed whenever possible, and the data from these subjects are included in the graph).

The dropout rates of the experimentals (10%) and controls (61%) after the second session also differ significantly ($\chi^2 = 13.14$, $df = 1$, $p < .001$).

It seems likely that the control group's initial reduction in alcohol intake is largely a function of commitment to treatment, but some generalized effect of the shock might also be present. It seems probable also, that a substantial dropout rate will continue to be observed in the control subjects, because these subjects fail to detect any substantial benefits from

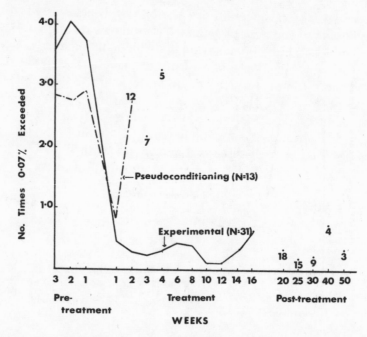

FIG. 2. Mean number of times per week subject's blood alcohol concentration has exceeded 0.07% before, during, and after treatment. (Numbers by data points indicate reduced numbers of subjects at those points.)

the treatment. By contrast, the treatment subjects are positively reinforced by observing the therapeutic effects of the first treatment session, and this feedback seems to be sufficient to sustain most subjects through the highly unpleasant treatment procedure. It is in order to maximize the subject's perception of immediate therapeutic benefit that as many shocks as the subject can tolerate are administered in the first treatment session.

Figure 2 shows the estimated mean number of times subjects' BACs have exceeded 0.07%, before, during, and after treatment. In general, the changes occurring in this measure are similar to those observed in the measure of weekly intake of alcohol, with a significant difference between the two groups emerging by the end of the third week of the program (Mann-Whitney $U = 163.5$, $z = 3,70$, $p < .0001$).

It should be noted that in the experimental group there is typically a sharp difference between the pre- and post-treatment episodes of drinking in excess of 0.07%. Unlike those prior to treatment, post-treatment episodes rarely involve levels much higher than 0.07%, and, in addition, they are of short duration.

In addition to the reduction in alcohol intake, there has been a dramatic improvement in the general health, well-being, and self-respect of most subjects in the experimental group. Perhaps the most interesting change observed, however, has been in the desire to drink. It is usually believed that conditioning treatment of alcoholsim produces its effect by developing in the subject a conditioned aversion to alcohol, and indeed, when the present work was begun, the aim was to produce a discriminated conditioned aversion. In other words, an attempt was made to render drinking aversive, if, and only if, the BAC was above 0.065%. It has been found, however, that a marked conditioned aversion develops in only about 20% of the subjects. The more common outcome is simply a loss of desire to continue drinking beyond three or four glasses, with little evidence of a conditioned aversive reaction. In other words, the treatment typically produces a motivational change rather than merely a conditioned fear reaction. Although the control subjects report some loss of desire to drink, the change in the treatment subjects is much more dramatic.

It is clear that a much longer follow-up period is required to evaluate fully the therapeutic procedure outlined. It can be argued, however, that there are good reasons for optimism regarding the outcome of long-term follow-up. First, in other areas of behavior therapy it has been found that the majority of relapses occur rather early, so that it is possible to estimate the ultimate relapse rate from the number of early relapses. Second, the emphasis placed throughout on self-control means that the subject is not passively relying on a conditioning mechanism, but has an active participatory role in limiting his consumption of alcohol. Consequently, his ability to maintain a pattern of controlled drinking is inherently reinforcing. Third, it is emphasized to the subject during treatment, that it is quite normal to exceed a BAC of 0.06% occasionally. Consequently, the patient does not experience a sense of complete therapeutic failure if he occasionally drinks in excess of the 0.06% level. It seems not unreasonable to believe that under these conditions the probability of relapse is reduced.

On the other hand, it is possible to question the validity of the follow-up data obtained. Despite the insistence on corroborative reports from a family member or a close associate, it is conceivable that, in some cases, optimistic reports have been received.

The adequacy of the control procedure used in the present study might also be questioned on the grounds that a therapist with a psychological investment in the outcome treated both experimental subjects and controls. It is difficult to believe, however, that unintentional interpersonal influences could produce outcome differences between experimental and control subjects as marked as those observed. In any case, replication by other workers must be the final arbiter. If replication affirms the effectiveness of the therapeutic program, the obvious next step is to carry out an experimental analysis of the treatment procedure.

In choosing 0.065% as the BAC to be discriminated in training, it was assumed that this concentration would not significantly impair learning capacity, and would not unduly restrict the subsequent use of alcohol as a social relaxant. It is now believed that 0.065% is an unnecessarily liberal training concentration, and in current work the concentration has been lowered to 0.05%.

One of the possible fields of application of the present method is the treatment of problem drinkers who have been convicted of driving under the influence of liquor. It is now well documented that problem drinkers are responsible for a disproportionate share of serious road accidents. Hence, any procedure which reduces the excessive use of alcohol by such persons, particularly the younger ones, will help to reduce the severity of two problems simultaneously—alcoholism and road accidents. It is unlikely that young incipient alcoholics who are convicted of drinking–driving offenses will be willing to undergo treatment aimed at making them total abstainers. On the other hand, treatment designed to moderate the drinking habits of such persons might be an acceptable alternative to the usual statutory punishments for drinking–driving offenses.

Finally, the method would appear to merit a trial in the treatment of other types of positively motivated behavior disorder, providing a reduction in the frequency of the behavior in question is an acceptable therapeutic goal.

## REFERENCES

LOVIBOND, S. H. The aversiveness of uncertainty: an analysis in terms of activation and information theory. *Australian Journal of Psychology*, 1968, **20**, 85–91.

LOVIBOND, S. H. Aversive control of behavior. *Behavior Therapy*, 1970, **1**, 80–91. (a)

LOVIBOND, S. H. Pure and applied psychology: towards a significant interaction. *Australian Psychologist*, 1970 **5**, 120–140. (b)

RANKIN, J. G. The size and nature of the use and misuse of alcohol and drugs in Australia. Paper presented at the 29th International Congress on Alcoholism and Drug Dependence, Sydney, Australia, 1970.

SARGENT, M. J. Heavy drinking and its relation to alcoholism—with special reference to Australia. *Australian and New Zealand Journal of Sociology*, 1968, **4**, 146–157.

INDEX

# NAME INDEX